PAUL I OF RUSSIA

The Academy of Sciences portrait of Paul I. By permission of the British Library.

PAUL I OF RUSSIA
1754–1801

RODERICK E. McGREW

CLARENDON PRESS · OXFORD
1992

Oxford University Press, Walton Street, Oxford OX2 6DP
Oxford New York Toronto
Delhi Bombay Calcutta Madras Karachi
Petaling Jaya Singapore Hong Kong Tokyo
Nairobi Dar es Salaam Cape Town
Melbourne Auckland
and associated companies in
Berlin Ibadan

Oxford is a trade mark of Oxford University Press

Published in the United States
by Oxford University Press, New York

© Roderick E. McGrew 1992

All rights reserved. No part of this publication may be reproduced,
stored in a retrieval system, or transmitted, in any form or by any means,
electronic, mechanical, photocopying, recording, or otherwise, without
the prior permission of Oxford University Press

British Library Cataloguing in Publication Data
Data available

Library of Congress Cataloging in Publication Data
McGrew, Roderick E. (Roderick Erle)
Paul I of Russia, 1754–1801 / Roderick E. McGrew.
p. cm.
Includes bibliographical references and index.
1. Paul I, Emperor of Russia, 1754–1801. 2. Soviet Union—Kings and
rulers—Biography. 3. Soviet Union—History—Paul I,
1796–1801. I. Title. II. Title: Paul the First of Russia, 1754–1801.
DK186.M39 1992   947'.07'092–dc20   [B] 91-39188
ISBN 0-19-822567-9

Set by Hope Services (Abingdon) Ltd.
Printed and bound in
Great Britain by Bookcraft Ltd.
Midsomer Norton, Bath

For Peg

PREFACE

Tsar Paul first attracted my attention nearly forty years ago when I was completing my dissertation on his younger son, Nicholas I. I did not begin to collect material on him systematically, however, until the early 1960s, and the present book was not conceived until 1979. Unless one has a taste for authoritarian militarists with more than a touch of megalomania, Paul does not greatly charm. On the other hand, to study imperial Russian political history in the first half of the nineteenth century, and especially from the context of a radically changing European world, without considering Paul seemed unfinished and incomplete. The marks of his thinking appeared again and again in the political culture of the pre-Reform era, and it became clear to me that he deserved more than a passing thought. A heightened awareness of Paul's significance brought the further conclusion that his image in the historical literature was distorted while the available interpretations of his work, including those of writers who wanted to rescue him from obloquy or oblivion, were missing the mark. Chapter 1 treats the historiographical question in some detail and identifies the problems which, in my opinion, suggested the value of doing a new book.

A biography of Paul was the furthest idea from my mind when I began to organize myself to write about him. My interests were in his reign, in what he had done, and in particular in his sometimes primitive, sometimes inspired efforts at social engineering. But the more closely I looked at his attempts to use discipline as a social instrument, or his adventures in teaching his servitors the values he believed to be fundamental to good order and a virtuous polity, the more questions arose to vex me. These concerned the shaping of his ideals, his education, and his actual role at court, to say nothing of his relationship with his mother, one of the most dominant and vital women in modern history. Though what I finally wrote comes closer to being a biographical essay than a full biography, it reflects my conviction that Paul evolved into the person he was in 1796, and that it was important to trace that evolution while seeking to identify core ideas that connected his earlier and later public personae. Paul was a different person in 1773 than he was in 1796; the reasons behind the shift were obviously important. But formative influences were significant as well, and in the end, I have given as much weight to the years 1754 to 1796 as I have to the years in power. If nothing else, I have satisfied myself that I can follow the formation of his personality and his ideology to the point that they became critical to Russia's history.

Paul was a conservative before the doctrine was really named. In the lurid glare of 1789, he was a fanatic on the issue, but his focus was always on values rather than institutional forms as such. His great western tour, to which I devote most of Chapter 5, exposed him to a wide range of experiences. There is little evidence to suggest, however, that these did much more than reinforce his already powerful inclination for the symbols of the old regime. Certainly his vision of what the Russian nobility ought to become gained colour from his exposure to the French court, while Joseph II's eleemosynary projects, his enlightened support for the economy, and his involvement in the day-to-day life of his empire chimed exactly with Paul's predispositions. Similarly, the backwardness and poverty in Italy underlined the importance of strong government for prosperity. But Joseph II, enlightened though he may have been, was never Paul's ideal, nor did Austria offer an example he was willing to follow. His heart was always in Berlin, and it was Frederick the Great whom he chose to emulate. The *ancien régime*, organized according to Prussian military principles, became the essence of Paul's vision for Russia. And it was something of this sort that he saw as the ultimate barrier against the oozing spread of modernity and especially democratism.

Such conservatism plainly had psychological as well as philosophic and historical roots. Here the approach I have followed recognizes that phenomenon, describes aspects of Paul's personality which undoubtedly influenced his planning and thinking, and identifies elements in his environment to which he reacted. But here I also feel the need for caution. The record as we have it is far too uncertain and much too far removed from the person himself to permit an excursion into psychoanalysis, while attempts to formulate quasi-medical diagnoses of what Paul's emotional structures may have been are, at best, informed speculation. It is certain that Paul was an explosive personality, that he carried a mighty burden of grievances in his later years, that he was often depressed and unhappy, and that he suffered from an outrageous temper. All this and more is part of the record, and I have tried to weave these elements into the fabric of Paul's story. Moreover, where his emotional state becomes a central issue, as it does in the run-up to his assassination which I cover in Chapter 10, these phenomena are given weight as an integral part of the events described. What I have not attempted to do is to provide a psychoanalytical, that is, as Freud might have put it, a 'causal' analysis of the behaviours described. This would go beyond what I think we have the information to judge, and while I am quite comfortable with my conviction that Paul was in no wise clinically insane, I am not prepared to explain the dynamics of his personality.

Writing in this same vein, it is also important to emphasize that this book is basically a reworking and rethinking of an established body of data. I have found no unpublished diaries, no unexpected correspondence, and no treasure troves of material hidden away in secret archives. Nor have I had access to Soviet archival collections. At the time I was collecting material for the book, the kind of creative archival exploration necessary to produce 'a new word' was quite impossible owing to Soviet policies toward foreign researchers. I greatly admire the work that some of my younger colleagues, John Alexander for example, have been able to do in Soviet archives. And certainly the time will come when a scholar or scholars will be able to study systematically and definitively the unpublished record of Paul's life and reign. Suzanne Massie's use of the grand ducal correspondence in her study of Pavlovsk, which unfortunately came too late to hand to be incorporated into my account, suggests some of the treasures waiting to be found. Such a newly comprehensive study would undoubtedly enrich and deepen our appreciation for Paul's role at a critical juncture in Russian history. Whether it would significantly alter what I have written here is another matter entirely.

The one exception to what I have said concerning new material is the use that I have made of diplomatic reports, including unpublished data from the English, Austrian, Swedish, and papal archives. As I suggested in a brief essay a number of years ago, foreign office archives contain much of value for Russian domestic history, and when there is a long period of reporting by experienced and knowledgeable persons, the diplomatic reports become a connected and hence especially valuable historical record, a chronicle, a contemporary diary of events with all the freshness of daily observation and the immediacy of a participant's reactions. The most valuable material for this purpose which I found were Count Cobenzl's reports to his superiors in Vienna, supplemented by special consular dispatches and Count Dietrichstein's separate (though official) correspondence. Charles Whitworth's reports to London were the second most valuable connected record, though certain of Curt von Stedingk's individual letters were noteworthy. Other European archives would undoubtedly have added further insights, and I especially regret not having studied the Sardinian, Prussian, and Danish reports systematically. But these, together with the Bavarian and especially the French, are well represented in the secondary literature. Moreover no one enjoyed so long a tenure at the Russian court as Louis de Cobenzl, nor combined such extraordinarily good contacts with a positive compulsion to record and pass on what he knew. Whitworth, who was second only to Cobenzl in time of service, wrote much less on domestic issues and that in a laconic often summary style which glossed more interesting details.

In general, I have preferred the diplomats' reporting to contemporaries' memoirs and diaries which generally appeared long after the events described and commonly were written or rationalized in later life. Indeed, they are different kinds of sources with the diplomatic reports enjoying superior immediacy and contemporaneity. Where policies are concerned, published official papers provide a check on the diplomats who are, after all, only informed observers and commentators. But for those purposes, they are valuable, and I have used them extensively.

A number of people and institutions have assisted me in bringing this project to completion. I am particularly indebted to the Joint Committee on Slavic Studies of the American Council of Learned Societies and the Social Science Research Council, to the American Philosophical Society, to the graduate research councils of the University of Missouri (Columbia) and Temple University, and to the sabbatical programmes of both institutions for financial help. Further, Temple University's Voluntary Early Retirement Program provided a non-teaching stipend which has permitted me to spend the last six years on my research, this project included. So far as the book itself is concerned, my most serious intellectual obligations, and they are considerable, are discharged in the text and footnotes. There are, however, special debts. The first is to Mr Mark Hamilton of A. M. Heath, Ltd., who not only handled the placement of the book but read it in various stages of its development and gave me frank opinions. Our talks together were among the really happy times in bringing this book foward, and since his financial reward has been virtually non-existent and promises at most to be modest, I can only believe that these talks were generated in his love of history and books about it. Such generosity of spirit changes fundamentally the author–agent relationship and contributed in the best way possible to the book's progress. I am grateful as well for the assistance of the people at Oxford University Press, most notably Tony Morris, the editor, assistant editor Anne Gelling, and Jane Robson, who did the copy editing. Their unfailing warmth and courtesy combined with a notable professionalism is an amalgam greatly to be appreciated. Among my academic friends, the person from whom I have received the most is Professor Hugh Ragsdale. His generosity in showing me his work as it evolved was very helpful, and his contributions go beyond what can be cited in notes and text. Professor A. G. Cross of Cambridge, and the Society for the Study of Eighteenth-Century Russia which he founded, have been important in a special way. In the summer of 1980, they listened to an extended preliminary report on this book; in 1989, Professor Cross invited me back for a lecture to the society summarizing the completed work. The opportunity to talk to thoroughly knowledgeable people on those two widely separated occasions was invaluable for assisting me in drawing the material together. I also wish to make special mention of Mr Robert Dimsdale who has been both generous and hospitable in making Baron Thomas Dimsdale's papers relating to his Russian visits and the contents of the Dimsdale archive available to me. Finally, and most important of all, I want to thank my wife, Margaret P. McGrew, for her very major contributions. The book is dedicated to her, but it is also quite literally true that her work as my researcher was essential to the book's completion. Her moral support throughout the long and difficult process of putting the book together never flagged, while her labours in archives and libraries as well as her opinions, criticism, and insights are all integral to what the book has become. Whatever weaknesses or errors the book contains are, of course, my responsibility alone.

R. M.

London
29 August 1991

CONTENTS

ABBREVIATIONS — xiv

1. A Beginning in the End: The Problem of Paul I — 1
2. Background and Family Origins — 19
3. Formative Years: 1762–1773 — 44
4. Politics and Marriage — 70
5. On being Grand Duke at Home and Abroad: 1776–1783 — 105
6. The Long Wait: 1783–1796 — 143
7. Tsar Reformer — 192
8. The Bank, the Court, and the Knights of Malta: 1797–1798 — 244
9. Peace and War: 1797–1801 — 282
10. The End of the Beginning — 322

BIBLIOGRAPHY — 358

INDEX — 381

ABBREVIATIONS

HHSA   Haus- Hof und Staatsarchiv
PRO   Public Record Office
PSZ   *Polnoe sobranie zakonov rossiiskoi imperii*
SIRIO *Sbornik imperatorskago russkago istorischeskago obschestva*

I

A BEGINNING IN THE END: THE PROBLEM OF PAUL I

Shortly after midnight on 12/24 March 1801, Paul I, then ruling tsar of all the Russias, was murdered in his bedroom in the newly finished Michael Palace in St Petersburg. His death was violent, brutal, and probably premeditated, though subsequent accounts created an illusion of passionate spontaneity. Paul was the victim of a conspiracy which was first organized in 1799 and reorganized in 1800. Its purpose was to replace him as tsar with his eldest son, the grand duke Alexander. Paul was to be given the opportunity to abdicate. If he refused, he was to be arrested and declared deposed, presumably on the ground that he was no longer competent to govern. The acquiescence of his son was essential to the plan, and after months of vacillation, Alexander was finally brought to agree on the understanding that his father would be unharmed. This was ingenuous. Just minutes before the conspirators set out on their fateful march, someone asked Count Peter von der Pahlen, the leader of the conspiracy, what would happen if the tsar resisted. Pahlen replied with that chilling cliché that to make an omelette one must be prepared to break eggs. Within two hours the eggs were broken; Paul was dead, and Alexander, the first of that name to rule in modern times, was tsar.[1]

The announcement of Paul's death laid it to an apoplectic stroke. That explanation was never rescinded. The fact that he was murdered, however, was soon common knowledge, as was the identity of his murderers. The latter called themselves tyrannicides and were received as liberators. As the word that Paul was dead spread outward from the palace through St Petersburg, people left their homes to test what they were hearing, and as certainty replaced caution and incredulity, they began to celebrate. Broad smiles were everywhere. Neighbour greeted neighbour with the warmth of feeling usually reserved for Easter. The day became a holiday, and in the evening, to cap it off, there was a spontaneous illumination of the city with lights glowing in every window. Only the Winter Palace

[1] For materials on the conspiracy and Paul's death, see below: Ch. 10 n. 1.

remained dark. People acted as if an invisible weight had been lifted from their shoulders, and there was a surge of love, even adoration, for the golden successor, the angelic Alexander, who was said to embody all the virtues the dead tsar lacked. In the meantime, Paul's strangled, bruised, and battered body was prepared to receive the people's last respects; the formal mourning period was set to last for one full year.

The new tsar gave every sign of being overwhelmed by what had happened. He wept bitterly when told that his father was dead, nor did the memory of that moment fade with time. Alexander carried the weight of Paul's death for the rest of his life, a burden of guilt which never left him. He flatly denied any responsibility for what had happened when his distracted mother demanded publicly, just hours after the event, if he had known, though later he talked at length with her, presumably explaining and qualifying what he had said. Subsequently Alexander's relations with his mother cooled, though she never showed the fiercely vengeful face towards him that she turned against the conspirators. Mariia Fedorovna, Paul's widow and now the dowager empress, became the tsar's most prominent mourner. Of all the adult members of the imperial entourage, she knew the least about the intrigue, if she knew anything at all, and when Madame, later Countess, Charlotte von Lieven woke her with news of a disaster, she thought first of her daughter who was in childbed (and in fact had died on 4/16 March), and then of her youngest son, Michael, who had been ill. Madame von Lieven had to tell her that the terrible news concerned her husband, and that he was dead. Mariia Fedorovna gave way to an extravagant grief which eventually settled into a lifelong vigil of remembrance. She kept mementoes from the room in which Paul died, particularly his camp-bed with its blood-flecked linens, and his uniform, and she spent a part of nearly every day contemplating them. She also declared a personal vendetta against the conspirators. She hounded von der Pahlen into exile, making it impossible for him ever to return to Petersburg, and she was instrumental in driving Count Nikita Petrovich Panin, who was involved in the original plot but was away from Petersburg when the *coup* occurred, out of her son's service. She apparently never fully understood the role played by General Leo Bennigsen, and he escaped her vengeance. Yet it was he who led the conspirators who entered Paul's bedchamber, and it was he whom Alexander blamed for his father's death, though other men delivered the blows and twisted the scarf which finally extinguished his life. Mariia Fedorovna divided the world into those who had conspired against her husband and those who had not. With the former she was implacable and spared no effort to do them injury. Her search for revenge underlined the fact that no official action was ever taken against the conspirators, and none was contemplated. The fiction that Paul died of natural causes was necessary to the new regime's legitimacy. There could never be a formal investigation, and for more than a century the censorship forbade any published discussion of the conspiracy or its outcome.

Reflecting on Paul's reign, the historian and conservative ideologue, Nikolai Mikhailovich Karamzin, declared that Paul was a tyrant, the second such in Russia's history (Ivan the Terrible was the first), and that his death was a deliverance.[2] This echoed the conspirators' song; the moment after Paul was dead, one of them seized his former emperor by the hair, banged his head on the floor, and shouted, 'There is the tyrant!' And this was also society's verdict. Paul had few supporters and in the months before his death he had dismissed or exiled most of those. During his brief tenure, there had been an unprecedented flight from service, civil as well as military, while the numbers he personally expelled into various exiles were literally in the thousands. For those who chose to go, intensified discipline, increasingly severe punishments, and Paul's own violent and uncertain temperament had been primary reasons, while reforms which impinged on long-established interests aroused fear and discontent throughout the military, landed, and government élites. Paul's impact was felt most sharply by the educated, the influential, and the affluent. It was this group which formed the clientele for which the conspirators spoke when they declared their tsar a tyrant, and which breathed a collective sigh of relief when he was replaced. Karamzin's judgement was in fact that of educated society in general; virtually no one contradicted it.

Very little is known certainly about reactions to Tsar Paul's death outside the circle of privilege, though it appears that they were very different. Paul was always popular with common people and seemed far more successful and comfortable in dealing with them than he was with the nobility. Kotzebue, the German dramatist whose memoirs on his experiences in Paul's Russia were published in 1802, remarked that when Paul died everything went back to normal, since there was no longer anyone to restrain the arrogance and wilfulness of the great. In his opinion, out of a population of thirty-six million, at least thirty-three million had every reason to bless Paul's name.[3] It

[2] Nikolai Mikhailovich Karamzin, *Memoir on Ancient and Modern Russia*, ed. and trans. Richard E. Pipes (Cambridge, Mass., 1959), 135–7.
[3] Valentin graf Zubow, *Paul der Erste: Mensch und Schicksal* (Stuttgart, 1963), 212–13.

is said that a popular tradition arose, which lasted through the century, that Paul was martyred by the great because of his love for the people, and that a prayer at his grave was particularly effective for the victims of injustice. In this connection, more candles were lit before his tomb than any other ruler's, and nearly every day there were several privately ordered masses for his soul. Common soldiers were thought to be particularly devoted to him. One anecdote records how, at the first parade after Paul's death, the officers exhorted their glum-faced ranks to 'Cheer up, little brothers, the tyrant is dead!' To which came back the answer, 'For us he was no tyrant but a father.' The soldiers' appreciation of Paul was real. He took a personal interest in their problems, paid close attention to their physical needs, and rewarded them, when he was pleased, with vodka. His willingness to punish officers rather than ordinary soldiers made a strong impression and reinforced the idea that he was their father tsar. Although there was resentment over excessively long hours of drill and manœuvre as well as a brutal disciplinary code and finicky uniform details, Paul stood well with the troops, so much so that this became a factor which the conspirators had to consider in their planning.[4]

Nevertheless, the relief which greeted the news of Paul's death reflected widespread public sentiment. No one could consider the four years and three months that he was tsar a distinguished or brilliant period, and for anyone who lived in the capital or belonged to official society, it was a dangerously unpleasant time as well. Indeed, it was worse. Privileged persons found they had no protection against this tsar's anger; it was as if time had turned back to the sixteenth century. Even the recent charter codifying nobiliary rights offered no certain shield. Traditional usages up to and including the special position of the guards were considered abuses to be legislated away, and in time a horrified nobility, which had seen its members publicly humiliated or summarily dispatched into exile, watched in disbelief as a cashiered officer was brutally flogged. Such treatment was common for the rank and file—military discipline throughout Europe was notoriously harsh—but to batter officers was a shocking violation of everything considered normal. The symbols of those bad few years were the kibitkas, the two-wheeled

---

[4] 'Neizdannoe sochinenie Avgusta Kotsebu', *Tsareubiistvo 11 Marta 1801 goda: Zapiski uchastnikov i sovremennikov* (St Petersburg, 1907), 360, 363; Anon., *Anekdoten aus dem Privatleben der Kaiserin Catherina, Paul der Ersten, und seiner Familie* (Hamburg, 1797), for Paul's character as a thoughtful general officer; John L. H. Keep, 'The Russian Army's Response to the French Revolution', *Jahrbücher für Geschichte Osteuropas*, NS 28/4 (1980), 500–23, qualifies this view.

horse-drawn carts in which condemned officers or officials were whisked away to Siberia, and the spontoon, the long, round-headed cane taken over from the Prussian army, which the drill-master tsar wielded as he counted out the cadences at the daily *Wachtparade*, another institution imported from Berlin.

As Paul's seemingly inexhaustible animus against the nobles found its sharpest focus in the officer corps, it was hardly surprising that officers with a grudge formed the conspiracy's inner circle, or that its leaders were generals while the guards provided cover. What is surprising, and a measure of the profound dislike which Paul inspired, was the failure of anyone to betray the plot. In the days immediately before the *coup*, there were hints that Paul was beginning to suspect danger, and that he was becoming uncertain of von der Pahlen, the official who currently had his greatest trust. But apart from trying to recall Generals Lindener and Arakcheev, who were temporarily in exile, Paul took no steps that would indicate that he knew how serious the threat was, or how imminent. Even men who were loyal to the tsar kept what they knew to themselves.[5] In the end, apart from two hussars who tried to defend Paul's door against the conspirators' charge, there was no one who had a word, much less a life, to give for this tsar.

The events of 11/23 March 1801 raise a series of questions. Were the conspirators, as their leader proudly announced, 'Romans' who knew their duty and set out to do it, were they *frondeurs* determined to defend their class against a powerful and too active ruler, or were they merely violent and self-interested men who were furious at the affronts they had had to bear and were determined to put up with them no longer? It was said openly that Paul was out of his mind; the implication was that he should be stopped before he totally wrecked an already dismasted ship of state. Was there, in fact, a case for forcing an abdication (the murder is another matter, a question of tactics rather than strategy), or was this essentially constitutional issue raised by the tsar's success in shaping Russian institutions to a new mould which severely cramped those accustomed to power and influence? What, in fact, was Paul attempting to do, and was it of any significance? Was he simply a prisoner of his hatred against his

---

[5] General N. A. Sablukov, 'Reminiscences of the Court and Times of the Emperor Paul I of Russia up to the Period of His Death', from the papers of a deceased Russian general officer, 2 pts., *Fraser's Magazine for Town and Country*, 72 (July–Dec. 1865), 222–41, 302–27. *Zapiski N. A. Sablukova obremenakh Imperatora Pavla i konchina etogo gosudaria*, ed. K. Voenskii (St Petersburg, 1911). Sablukov, though loyal to Paul, and not lacking in sympathy for him, on advice closed his eyes and ears to what was happening.

mother and all her works, or did he have a plan with which to challenge the old in favour of the new? Since he did not become tsar until he was 42 years old, he had already had one career as grand duke, living in his mother's shadow. The influence of so protracted an apprenticeship is obviously integral to understanding Paul and his fate, as are those remoter circumstances under which he was raised from infancy to maturity. How precisely do they fit together? A brief review of how some of the questions raised here have been treated by others who have passed this way will be useful for establishing the place Paul already occupies in history, to look at the contradictory ideas that have grown up around him, and to explain why it is worthwhile to look again at so apparently unpromising a man.

For many years, the standard work on Paul I was General N. K. Shil'der's massive biography published in 1901.[6] Based on materials from the imperial archives as well as exhaustive coverage of contemporaries' published letters and memoirs, Shil'der's book concentrates on the court and diplomacy. Paul is portrayed as a difficult and resentful man who on becoming tsar set out to obliterate his mother's memory. In the process, he created a personal despotism. The best and brightest of that time, Grand Duke Alexander and his circle, were appalled, committing themselves to good works in the cause of enlightened, constitutional government for that indefinite future when Paul's nightmare reign would end. Shil'der leaves no doubt that he considers Paul a tyrant—he quotes Karamzin at length on the subject—and, without ever facing the issue squarely, makes it abundantly clear that he believes that Paul's deteriorated mental state, his incompetence in fact, left no alternative to his removal. Shil'der's status as an official or at least approved historian for the court shows clearly in how much he is able to say that is pointedly critical of Paul, and that describes, and by implication approves, the formation first of an opposition, and then of a conspiracy against him. The treatment of Alexander's role in events ranges from the sketchy to the explicit depending on whether one consults the first two volumes of Shil'der's Alexander biography,

[6] Nikolai Karlovich Shil'der, *Imperator Pavel I: Istorikobiograficheskii ocherk* (St Petersburg, 1901). Shil'der's *Imperator Aleksandr Pervyi*, 4 vols. (St Petersburg, 1897–8; 2nd edn. 1905–6), contains a history of Paul's reign as the 2nd pt. of vol. i. Dmitri de Benckendorff took from this an *Histoire anecdotique de Paul Ier* (Paris, 1899) which he published under the name of 'N. Schilder' with the notation 'taken from the Russian'. This book contains more detailed and different material than *Aleksandr I*, vol. i, and differs as well from *Pavel I*. Greater publishing freedom on the subject of Paul I outside Russia may have allowed Shil'der to convey more of the story in his French version than he could in the Russian; it is also possible that Benckendorff added material with or without Shil'der's permission.

the *Histoire anecdotique de Paul I*ᵉʳ, or the Paul biography itself. The last two leave no doubts at all that Alexander was informed and had agreed to the *coup* on 11/23–12/24 March. There is no description of the murder (even Shil'der could not entirely ignore the long-time prohibition on discussing Paul's fate) and, if one reads quickly, the impression is that the tsar died of an apoplectic stroke suffered in the course of a confrontation with his enemies.[7] The underlying point is that Paul was responsible for what happened to him; that he created an intolerable situation which only his removal could resolve. Neither Karamzin at the century's beginning, nor Shil'der at its end, was prepared to advocate overthrowing a tsar, though Shil'der had no serious difficulty accepting the idea of an abdication in favour of the legitimate heir. A regency for a demented ruler, particularly in Russia, would be more difficult. As we read Shil'der, however, there can be no doubt that he considered Paul a disaster which had already happened; his removal, risky as it may have been, was essential and, though it was Paul's misfortune to have died, the new tsar was precisely what Russia needed and wanted.

E. S. Shumigorskii, who published six years after Shil'der, and who wrote biographies of the two main women in Paul's life, took a rather different tack to arrive at the same destination.[8] His Paul was an able, intelligent person who came to the throne with a developed concept of what the state should be, but who carried some dangerously explosive emotional baggage which had been acquired in the course of the long and frustrating years his mother reigned. Without specifying Paul's world outlook, Shumigorskii emphasized his administrative and social reforms, which aggrandized the central authority at the expense of the established classes, and the tsar's attempt to personalize control over all important areas of decision. Though Shumigorskii portrayed Paul's policies sympathetically, he also chronicled the tsar's disintegration as he tried to do more than it was possible for him to do, as his suspicious nature led him to hoard decisions while driving potential helpmates away, and as the various élites, disturbed by what Paul seemed to want to do with them, withdrew their support and left his service. Shumigorskii suggested

---

[7] This would appear to be the way Grand Duchess Elizabeth, Alexander's wife, understood what happened. Shil'der publishes her letters to her mother, dated 13/25 March 1801, in full.

[8] E. S. Shumigorskii, *Imperator Pavel I: Zhizn i tsarstvovanie* (St Petersburg, 1907); id., 'Pavel I', *Russkii biograficheskii slovar* (St Petersburg, 1902), xiii. 4–64; id., *Imperatritsa Mariia Fedorovna*, 2 vols. (St Petersburg, 1892); id., *Ekaterina Ivanovna Nelidova: Ocherk iz istorii imperatora Pavla* (St Petersburg, 1898). Dmitri de Benckendorff, *La Favorite d'un tzar: Catherine Ivanowna Nelidow, 1758–1839* (Paris, 1902), is 'after E. S. Schoumigorskii'.

that, in the later stages of this disintegrative process, Paul's mental balance, never entirely secure, was unhinged by the extraordinary burdens which he had to bear. In the end, though more sympathetic and altogether more insightful that Shil'der, Shumigorskii arrived at much the same place his more critical colleague did. Paul was a tragic figure whose excesses, largely self-generated, turned him into a victim.

On the eve of the First World War, the prolific and eminently readable Kasimir Waliszewski produced a political-biographical analysis of Paul in French which was translated into English, Polish, and Russian.[9] It is this book in which most western readers have found what they know about Paul I. Waliszewski followed the line established by Shil'der and Shumigorskii, though leaning towards the former. He relied heavily on the anecdotal literature, interspersed with some interesting documents culled from French and English archives, and he presented a lively if strongly coloured narrative. The primary emphasis fell on Paul's character, which he painted in progressively darker tones, on court affairs, foreign policy, and the events which ended Paul's reign. Waliszewski left the impression that Paul was a megalomaniac who, by the end of reign, was for all practical purposes, insane; that he saw himself as Europe's saviour from Jacobinism; that he became as extreme a monarchist as the Jacobins were democrats; that his distorted views of himself, his associates, and his world owed much to the psychological manipulation he suffered as Catherine's son; and that he was altogether an emotional and political misfit whose foolishly cruel and unpredictable behaviour generated the conspiracy which destroyed him. In this last connection, it should be remembered that, until after the revolution of 1905, public discusson of Paul's murder was forbidden, and it is, as we have noted, cause for wonder that Shil'der was able to print so much material from contemporary sources that was scurrilous and, under the terms of the regulation, disrespectful of a monarch. Waliszewski was under no such restraint. On the contrary, since the prohibition on publishing material about the conspiracy was formally lifted in 1907 (the first important collection appeared two years earlier during the revolution), he was able to provide a much more comprehensive account than any that appeared before. To that degree, Waliszewski's entertaining, sometimes eccentric, and largely derivative biography marked a step beyond what had been possible; it also was important in fixing Paul's historical reputation.

[9] Kasimir Waliszewski, *Le Fils de la grande Catherine: Paul Ier empereur de Russie: Sa vie, sa règne et sa mort: 1754–1801*, 3rd edn. (Paris, 1912). Id., *Paul I of Russia* (London, 1913). The English edn. lacks notes.

Two other books which described Paul's life from his birth to his accession have contributed to the consensual view.[10] The first, by Dmitri Kobeko, was published in 1883 with an excellent German translation three years later. The account—substantial, straightforward, and impressive for its clarity—was intended to explain the foundations for Paul's behaviour when he became tsar. Kobeko saw Paul as a man with ability and good intentions who was betrayed by his own disorderly emotions and the terrible stresses under which he lived. His mature character, in Kobeko's opinion, was formed between 1782 and 1796, his years in the wilderness, so to speak, when he became the darkly suspicious, angry, and unhappy man who ascended the throne. Though oriented to a psychological point, Kobeko's book deals basically in ideas and their implications, political issues, and personal relationships. He is sympathetic, though like Shumigorskii who used the book, it is sympathy for one of history's tragedies.

Pierre Morane, who published twenty-four years later, had the advantage of Shil'der's and Shumigorskii's work as well as Kobeko, and he also read extensively in unpublished French and Prussian diplomatic records. The book should be better than it is. Though there is much that is useful, Morane's treatment is highly charged, sometimes careless, and the medical and psychological conclusions are unconvincing, Nevertheless, it does emphasize two themes which are important to the conventional interpretation: that Paul was physically weak and emotionally unstable from his earliest days, and that the rivalry with Catherine created a traumatic, conflict-ridden relationship from early childhood. Morane, even more dramatically than Kobeko, portrayed Paul as a psychological disaster at the time of Catherine's death.

Relatively little interest attached to Paul from the end of the First World War through the Second World War. It was born again in the 1950s and 1960s, and first took the form of recycling available information to tell once more the tragic story of Catherine's ugly and unpleasant son.[11] One author, however, Valentin graf Zubow, chose

[10] Dmitri Kobeko, *Tsesarevich Pavel Petrovich, 1754–1796*, 2nd edn. (St Petersburg, 1883); German trans. (Berlin, 1886). The trans. is accurate, but the Berlin edn. lacks notes. Dmitrii de Benckendorff, *La Jeunesse d'un tzar* (Paris, 1896), is based on Kobeko but leaves out substantial sections while adding material not in the original. Pierre Morane, *Paul Ier de Russie: avant l'avènement: 1754–1796* (Paris, 1907).

[11] See Marivic Charpentier, 'Le Tsar implacable: Paul Ier', *Les Œuvres libres* (Paris, 1952), 203–30; E. M. Almedingen, *So Dark a Stream: A Study of the Emperor Paul I of Russia, 1754–1801* (London, 1959); Constantine de Grunwald, *L'Assassinat de Paul Ier tsar de Russie* (Paris, 1960); Zubow, *Paul der Erste*.

to stress an aspect different from the others. Zubow portrayed Paul as an early romantic with a well-developed religious sensibility, a deep feeling for the medieval past, and a utopian vision of the future for Russia and Europe. He also wanted to see him as a liberator for the peasant classes, a defender of the people, and an enemy of the special privileges and powers which the nobility had acquired. Beginning from V. O. Kliuchevskii's suggestion that Paul was the first anti-gentry (*dvorianstvo*) tsar, Zubow compared Paul's programme with the famous 4 August 1789 resolutions abolishing feudalism in France. This comparison is extreme and an exaggeration, as was the importance Zubow attached to Paul as the progenitor of a new Christian community in Europe and the reunifier of the eastern and western churches. But it also served to challenge the consensual view of Paul's minor and destructive place in Russia's history. In Zubow's view, Paul was a man whose story would repay further attention.

Over the next decade, a new generation of historians began to look more closely at what Paul had done, though their inspiration came less from Zubow and his shifting of the biographical perspective than from two substantial early studies on Paul as a diplomat and a legislator. In the middle of the nineteenth century, General Mikhailovskii-Danilevskii started and Colonel (later Count) D. M. Miliutin developed and completed a monumental history of the second coalition and the war with France in 1799.[12] Paul created the alliance and put Russia at the centre of a complex series of military manœuvres which ranged from the eastern Mediterranean through Italy, Switzerland, and the Rhine to the Low Countries and the North Sea. This vast enterprise failed, in Miliutin's portrayal, owing to a fundamental incompatibility of goals between Russia and Austria, exacerbated by Austrian duplicity, arrogance, inefficiency, and bad faith. Paul, on the other hand, comes off extremely well. Under enormous provocation, he remained controlled and exhibited a statesmanlike far-sightedness, forbearance, and understanding. The book is particularly valuable for its extensive publication of Paul's correspondence with his advisers, his allies, and his generals, as well as for its step-by-step narrative describing the campaigns and the diplomacy. Miliutin argues that Paul had no territorial ambitions of his own. He went to war in the face of a new wave of French aggression in order to secure order in Europe, a goal which required

[12] Aleksandr Mikhailovskii-Danilevskii and Dmitri Ivanovich Miliutin, *Istoriia voiny Rossii s Frantsieiu v 1799 gody*, 5 vols. 8 pts. (St Petersburg, 1852). Pt. 1, A. Mikhailovskii-Danilevskii; pts. 2–8, D. Miliutin German trans., C. Schmitt, *Geschichte des Krieges Russlands mit Frankreich unter der Regierung Kaiser Pauls I im Jahre 1799*, 5 vols. (Munich, 1856–8).

that the French be forced to disgorge their conquests as the preliminary to reconstituting former principalities under the control of their dispossessed owners. It was here that one fundamental problem with Austria arose. Paul's goal was to re-establish a European community in which security, equilibrium, order, and acknowledged rights of possession were the governing principles. Ironically, it was just such an approach which Austria's Metternich invoked during his long tenure from the end of the Napoleonic wars to the revolutions of 1848.

Miliutin's very positive treatment of Paul was largely ignored by later writers. Its substance hardly fitted the developing consensus, and it has remained to the revisionists of our time to see its significance. More important, and more influential altogether as a challenge to the conventional interpretations of Paul I, was M. V. Klochkov's lengthy monograph on administrative affairs published in 1916.[13] All previous writing on Paul, according to Klochkov, had been preoccupied with his personality problems, with diplomacy, the army, and the court. Concentrating on these subjects not only failed to reveal Paul's historical significance, but actually obscured historical realities by overemphasis on unimportant (if titillating) details, and by building cases on contemporary memoirs and correspondence which were fundamentally unreliable. In a long introductory chapter, Klochkov impeached the entire previous literature by demonstrating how little there was in the memoir tradition which could be verified, and how extensively the major works on Paul relied upon those slender and unreliable data. To correct the inevitable errors, and to provide insight into Paul's actual position in Russia's history, Klochkov turned to primary legal sources (basically the collected laws) to reconstruct Paul's social, economic, military, and administrative policies. The result was a radically different picture. Paul emerged as an enlightened absolutist in the modernizing tradition, who came to the throne with a worked-out plan for rationalizing political and military structures, disciplining the gentry, promoting economic growth, and protecting the peasantry against the landlords' abuses. The combination of this innovative programme, which threatened traditional interests, with an abrasive and irascible personality made Paul vulnerable to those he pushed too hard. Hence the origins for his downfall lay as much in what he tried to do as in the kind of person that he was. Finally, though the brevity of Paul's reign left much that he began unfinished, the changes he did introduce proved to be an important legacy. From

---

[13] M. V. Klochkov, *Ocherki pravitel'stvennoi deiatel'nosti vremeni Pavla I* (Petrograd, 1916).

that point of view alone, Paul was a more significant figure than he had been accounted, while his reign was notable for new and ultimately progressive initiatives.

A mounting interest in what the autocracy actually achieved, followed by new sensitivity to the historical importance of enlightened absolutism and the critical role of 'the well ordered police state', the intensive study of bureaucracies, and the need to understand the dynamics of modern developing societies, have provided an historiographical context which has been congenial to Klochkov's theses and to a new look at Paul I. The new revisionists, if that is the proper term to describe recent scholars working on Paul, have accepted the idea that his life and work were important without becoming his historical partisans. The new scholarship has followed Klochkov's lead in seeking better evidence for its conclusions than the memoir tradition. It has given personal factors less significance in interpreting events, and it has been, on balance, more sympathetic to Paul than the conventional literature. In effect, the recent revisionist tradition has begun to ask more serious questions about Paul and his age, about what actually happened as opposed to what interested people said had happened.[14] The result has been a clear gain in new information and a more substantial base for interpretation. David Ransel's important monograph on factional politics and the Panin party under Catherine establishes the moral and philosophical tradition in which Paul was raised, while significantly moderating some of the more exaggerated claims made concerning Paul's presumed political rivalry with Catherine up to his majority.[15] John

---

[14] Hugh Ragsdale (ed.), *Paul I: A Reassessment of His Life and Reign* (Pittsburgh, 1979), provides a collection of articles including historiographical and bibliographical comment. See also: Keep, 'Russian Army's Response'; James J. Kenney, jun., 'Lord Whitworth and the Conspiracy against Paul I: The New Evidence of the Kent Archive', *Slavic Review*, 36 (June 1977), 205–19; Roderick E. McGrew, 'A Political Portrait of Paul I from the Austrian and English Diplomatic Archives', *Jahrbücher für Geschichte Osteuropas*, NS 18/4 (1970), 503–29; Claus Scharf, 'Staatsauffassung und Regierungsprogramm eines aufgeklärten Selbstherrschers', in E. Schulin (ed.), *Gedenkschrift Martin Göhring: Studien zur Europäische Geschichte* (Wiesbaden, 1968), 91–106.

[15] David L. Ransel, *The Politics of Catherinian Russia: The Panin Party* (New Haven, Conn., 1975). See also: Walter S. Gleason, *Moral Idealists, Bureaucracy, and Catherine the Great* (New Brunswick, 1981); G. Makogonenko, *Denis Fonvizin: Tvorcheskiy put* (Moscow, 1961); N. Ia. Eidel'man, *Gran' vekov: Politicheskaia borba v Rossii konets XVIII–nachale XIX stoletiia* (Moscow, 1982), is particularly appropriate, important, and valuable. Isabel de Madariaga's magisterial *Russia in the Age of Catherine the Great* (New Haven, Conn., 1981) clarifies the political environment for Paul's development; its detailed discussion of Catherine's reforms establishes the basis for contrast with what Paul did. See also

L. H. Keep's essays on the militarization of bureaucratic modes in Paul's time and the bases for political protests in the army between 1796 and 1825 give both data and insights important for analysing Paul's reforms and the reaction to them. There has been useful work on the fiscal reforms and the ideological traditions to which Paul responded, while the greatest volume of work has been on the conduct of foreign policy. In that area, Norman Saul, Muriel Atkin, and especially Hugh Ragsdale, invest Paul's diplomacy with a high degree of reasonableness, practicality, and concern for peace.[16] As the breakdown of Paul's diplomacy in 1800 was the immediate background to his overthrow, and the cause for contemporaries' belief that the tsar had lost all hold on reality, these contributions pose the revisionists' position in its starkest form.

Efforts to probe the underpinnngs of the conspiracy have produced little of consequence in the way of new information, but a Soviet writer, N. Ia. Eidel'man, has connected the opposition to Paul to a constitutional orientation among the educated, the product of two generations of Enlightenment influence, combined with the nobility's fears for its newly codified privileges. Eidel'man links the events of 1801 restrospectively to the revolt against Peter III which brought Catherine to the throne in 1762, and to the failed Decembrist revolt of 1825 which demanded the constitution which Alexander I had failed to provide. With access to archival material, he is able to correct some of the exaggerated charges against Paul, though one of the themes in his treatment is Paul's evolution from enlightened autocrat to tyrant. At base, however, the author is rather less

John T. Alexander, *Catherine the Great: Life and Legend* (New York, 1989). This sympathetic and richly detailed biography, which is equally successful in showing what Catherine was and what she was not, appeared too late to be used systematically in preparing this study of Paul.

[16] Hugh Ragsdale, 'Was Paul Bonaparte's Fool?', in Ragsdale (ed.), *Paul I: A Reassessment of His Life and His Reign* (Pittsburgh, 1979), 76–90; id., 'Russia, Prussia, and Europe in the Policy of Paul I', *Jahrbücher für Geschichte Osteuropas*, NS 31/1 (1983), 81–118; id., *Détente in the Napoleonic Era: Bonaparte and the Russians* (Lawrence, Kan., 1980); Norman E. Saul, 'The Objectives of Paul's Italian Policy', *Reassessment*, 31–43; id., *Russia and the Mediterranean* (Chicago, 1970); Ole Feldback, 'The Foreign Policy of Tsar Paul I, 1800–1801: An Interpretation', *Jahrbücher für Geschichte Osteuropas*, NS 30/1 (1982), 16–36; id., *Denmark and the Armed Neutrality, 1800–1801: Small Power Policy in a World War* (Copenhagen, 1980). Feldback 'answers' the revisionists. Muriel Atkin, 'The Pragmatic Diplomacy of Paul I', *Slavic Review*, 38/1 (1979), 60–74. For the rather different Soviet position on Paul's diplomacy, see e.g. A. M. Stanislavskaia, *Russko-angliiskie otnosheniia i problemy Sredizemnormor'ia, 1798–1807* (Moscow, 1962); id., *Rossiia i Gretsii v kontse XVIII–nachale XIX veke: Politika Rossii v Ionicheskoi respublike, 1798–1807* (Moscow, 1976).

interested in Paul than in the nature of his opposition and its relationship to the emergence of the anti-autocratic intelligentsia.[17]

The work which has been done on the vexed problem of Paul's psychological state has reaffirmed the judgement offered as long ago as 1907 that he was not clinically insane. Beyond that, the effort to extract significant symptoms from his behaviour and to build a diagnosis from them remains inconclusive, though Hugh Ragsdale has gone a considerable distance in that direction, and a recent essay by Richard Wortman hints at the possibilities for a psychoanalytic interpretation. Clearly, what Paul felt reinforced what he believed, and connecting his thought, his experiences, and his behaviour takes us a long step towards understanding his subjective world. It is here that Ragsdale makes his most important contribution, and it is that approach which underlies the present work.[18]

Paul's role in Russia's development as a modern society is more accessible. To the extent that he has been identified as a reformer or an enlightened absolutist, it is implicit that his reign had a modernizing potential which the conspiracy aborted, and that Russia, in fact, lost something of value when he was overthrown. Whether the Russian version of an enlightened, absolutist monarchy could, in fact, have been midwife to an open, pluralistic system under law was a major argument throughout the nineteenth century which growing numbers of Russians answered in the negative. That it remains a theme in Klochkov's interpretation of Paul as late as 1916 only suggests how tenacious the doctrine was. But modern historians have also tended to accept the idea that all societies must pass through a consolidating (i.e. centralizing) phase in which freedom will be less important than order, security, and economic growth. A centralized state system, even a despotic one, can, if it will, create the circumstances under which growth will occur, and at first glance Paul appears to fit this mode. In fact, however, taking this position not only ignores most of what contemporaries believed about Paul, but more significantly it overlooks what Paul himself said and did. Such terms as 'reformer' or 'enlightened', carry connotations which are at

---

[17] For the conventional Soviet view of Paul, see S. B. Okun, *Ocherki istorii SSSR: Konets XVIII–pervaia chetvert XIX veka* (Leningrad, 1956), 26–7, 32–45, and esp. 49–68. Cf. Eidel'man, *Gran'vekov*.

[18] V. F. Chizh, 'Imperator Pavel I: Psikologicheskii analiz', *Voprosy filosofii i psikologii*, 8 (1907), 221–90, 391–468, 585–678. Cf. Hugh Ragsdale, 'The Mental Condition of Paul', *Reassessment*, 17–30, and, most importantly, *Tsar Paul and the Question of Madness: An Essay in History and Psychology* (Westport, Conn., 1988). See also Richard Wortman, 'Images of Rule and Problems of Gender in the Upbringing of Paul I and Alexander I'. I am indebted to Professor Wortman for a copy of this paper which he prepared for the Festschrift for Professor Marc Raeff.

odds with 'despot' or 'tyrant' and suggest a long-range significance which may, in fact, have little to do with the person concerned. That appears to be the case here. Paul was a reformer who was educated in an enlightened mode, but the principles to which he was committed were the reverse of the innovative or progressive. This, however, brings us back to the problem of the historical Paul and how to read his record.

There is little doubt, to return to one of Klochkov's most influential arguments, that many of the stories told about Paul, especially the more outrageous ones, cannot be verified, and it is likely that some of the best publicized among them, particularly those in the last years of his life, were actually contrived. What this means is that Paul's advisers, and specifically von der Pahlen, may have encouraged his tendency to extreme or dramatic solutions in order to impugn his credibility. Even granting this, however, it does not follow that Paul was really very different from the way the anecdotes described him, or even that the 'rational' or 'progressive' policies embodied in his governing reforms were, in fact, either rational or progressive. Nor does it follow that because Paul's education was excellent, and because he studied Montesquieu, Voltaire, or Rousseau, Tacitus, Pufendorff, or Molière, that he understood what they were saying, or held views congruent with theirs, or with the generation raised on them. There is a great deal to suggest that he did not. What the revisionist writing as a whole has demonstrated is that Paul accomplished far more than his detractors claimed, and that in this respect he was a much more substantial historical figure than he has been portrayed. But the implication that history has maligned him, that he was not only more substantial but different from the way he had been portrayed, is another matter entirely. The evidence is massive that Paul was, in fact, irrational, unpredictable, and temperamental; that he used his powers as he saw fit to punish and reward, and this without reference to law or regular procedures; and that in just over four years, despite a favourable beginning, he not only failed to win support for what he was doing, but alienated large segments of the population, some of which should have supported him. Not unnaturally, he made numerous powerful enemies, some of whom hated him profoundly. And the tone of their reaction is significant. There is rancour, bitterness, and a strong element of contempt in what contemporaries wrote about Paul. There is no grandeur in the evil they portrayed, but rather an arbitrary pettiness which made the punishments he meted out more personal and harder to bear. And this leads to the further conclusion that the suggestion that personal issues have been overemphasized in the early works on Paul I is simply wrong. Paul as a political actor, an active participant, is fundamental to understanding what actually happened between 1796 and 1801, and what the revolt against him meant. Here biography becomes integral to history.

The personal dimension is also important for placing Paul's reign in the larger patterns of Russian history. As a convinced autocrat, Paul belongs in the mainstream of Russia's political development. He belongs as well in the broad traditions of European absolutism. But it is our view that Paul had his own version of these abstractions, a version which was highly personalized, even idiosyncratic, and in its purest form, nearly solipsistic. Yet it was Paul rather than Catherine who struck the keynote for Russia's nineteenth century; who pointed society, with the state in the vanguard, towards a severely hierarchical and essentially militarized mode of organization; and who reoriented political values toward a primary emphasis on discipline, order, and stability. Paul's values found their most complete realization in the reign of his younger son, Nicholas I (1825–55), while the influence of that essentially conservative ideology remained central in Russian governing institutions into the revolutionary era.

It would be fatuous to argue that Paul I created nineteenth-century Russia and, as we will see later, some of his most inventive legislative efforts scarcely outlived him. But in his febrile, furious way, Paul identified and reacted to what was eventually believed to be the fundamental issue of the time: how to maintain conventional, long-established social and political values in a world turned upside down. For reasons that were personal, subjective, quintessentially psychological, Paul exploded on the Russian scene not just as a conservative, but as a radical, activist, and total conservative (though he would hardly have labelled himself as such) who believed he knew what had to be done to preserve his world against the moral destruction threatened by rationalism, scepticism, and materialism, by cynical self-serving, and what he considered to be a pervasive disregard for loyalty, sacrifice, and commitment to God and the crown in defence of society's welfare.

Lest we again are carried away by the rhetoric, Paul's reactions were those of *émigré* aristocrats and other apologists for the old regime. But his diagnosis of the crisis, and the prescriptions he formulated to meet it, were peculiar to him and were rooted in his personal interpretation or adaptation of monarchical ideology. Paul was a moralist rather than a politician; it was this which gave a utopian cast to those projects which were nearest to his heart, and a totalitarian tone to the ensemble of his policies. The nature of his vision carried him beyond specific military or administrative reforms, though they were clearly influenced by it, and in fact no particular aspect of his reign should be emphasized over any other. Paul is most interesting as a product of the rip-tides of the revolutionary era, as a forerunner of the nineteenth century's dominant military style, and above all as a counter-modernizer, a Russian Canute willing the winds of change to cease. Within the smallish world which he could dominate, Paul insisted on the perfection of his vision. Almost no one met his standards, and eventually those who failed, and who were punished for their failure, proved stronger than he was. The conspiracy incubated in resistance to Paul's measures for enforcing his special perception of society. It succeeded as he failed to protect himself. His enemies killed him and wrote his epitaph. That they were able to do so, and to escape any official retribution, is a dramatic measure of how far Paul had removed himself from the realities of the world in which he lived.

To understand how all this came about, it is necessary to reconstruct the kind of person Paul was, the influences which shaped his life and outlook, the political culture within which he was raised, and the way these circumstances brought him to see the crisis of the revolutionary era. This reconstruction will draw on both the conventional and revisionist literatures, though trying to avoid the excesses of both, to arrive at a new perception of Paul and the importance of his reign. We will look at him as a ruler whose programme stands as Europe's first systematic effort to assert traditional values against the insidious effects of social and economic innovation, a moral absolutist in the style of Robespierre whose vision for the future built on Montesquieu and the Prussian manual of arms, Stoic ethics, Christian faith, the ruler as God's instrument, and the spirit of chivalry. Some of this was reduced to statutes, though Paul's limitations as a legislator and a politician seriously flawed some of his most interesting ideas. But the core of what he did, especially with the state administration and the army, carried forward, while the pointedly militaristic code and style which he introduced into court and governmental life remained to shape Russia's official world through the entire coming century.

Paul's brutal death, our beginning in the end, was a personal failure. It was Paul who was rejected. But his principles, in foreign as well as domestic policy, marked out the Russian future. Undoubtedly the deadly challenges which the Napoleonic era set for Russia helped to consolidate the authoritarian, militarized, and hierarchical system towards which Paul turned at the end of 1796. It is probably also true that what Paul did confirmed the failure of Catherine's legislative efforts to promote local initiative and participation in governing processes. Certainly what Catherine had created was incapable of serving the functions Paul believed to be essential for the defence of the fatherland. He changed the system to accord with his own activitist, chain-of-command philosophy. His successor cleared away his father's excesses, but left the system's basic character undisturbed. The state, powerful as always, turned from innovation towards a conserving, protective stance. Paul's spirit lived on.

2
BACKGROUND AND FAMILY ORIGINS

Paul I was born in St Petersburg on 20 September/1 October, 1754, but his story actually began thirteen years earlier when Elizabeth, Peter the Great's youngest daughter, captured the throne in a *coup d'état*.[1] There had been no law of hereditary succession in Russia since 1722 when Peter legislated the tsar's right to choose his own successor. Peter then died without making a choice, but a court faction headed by his close lieutenant, Alexander Menshikov, placed his widow, Catherine, on the throne. Until Paul himself re-established the hereditary succession in 1797, the Russian crown became a prize which was contested among various parties seeking to protect their several interests. Foreign diplomats were often involved, the élite guards regiments provided conspirators with military support, and the *coup d'état* became a political art form. The candidates were not wholly without credentials. In one way or another, at least until 1762, they were linked with Peter the Great, the last unequivocally legitimate tsar, who had already become a Russian legend. In Elizabeth's case, this connection was both close and very important to her success. As great Peter's daughter, she could present herself as Russia's defender against the foreign adventurers who had gained control over the Russian state, a posture that was particularly attractive to discontented officers, to the guards who were imbued with the Petrine heritage, and to that segment of the privileged class which had been displaced by the ruling clique.

Elizabeth was lively, large, and very handsome. Until 1741, she showed no notable political interests and lived apart from the court. In her early days, her father considered her a candidate for a dynastic marriage which would have linked Russia with France, but those plans failed, and a further effort to marry her to Charles Augustus of

---

[1] For Elizabeth's reign, S. M. Solov'ev, *Istoriia Rossii s drevneishikh vremen* (Moscow, 1963), bks. 11, 12, 13 (vols. xxi–xxvi). Bk. 11, pp. 7–129, covers background and the *coup*, pp. 129–31 for the succession. V. O. Kliuchevskii, *Kurs russkoi istorii: Sochineniia v vosmi tomakh* (Moscow, 1956–9), iv. 302–47, and esp. 338–42 on Elizabeth. Valentin Gitermann, *Geschichte Russlands*, 3 vols. (Hamburg, 1949), ii. 164–89; M. Florinsky, *Russia: A History and Interpretation* (New York, 1955), i. 449–58 (diplomacy), 481–95 (internal affairs).

Holstein, bishop of Lübeck, was frustrated when the bishop died in 1727. But Elizabeth had no need for status. Like her father, she had a taste for ordinary people, and she found friends, confidants, and lovers in the regiments of guards. Entirely uninhibited, extremely attractive to men, and with great physical vigour, Elizabeth won a gaudy reputation as a libertine, forming a succession of liaisons capped by a long-term love affair with Alexis Razumovskii, an illiterate but physically powerful and wonderfully handsome Cossack with a fine singing voice. Razumovskii was her mainstay, and after she became empress, a leading figure at her court.

It was probably inevitable that Elizabeth would be drawn into politics, though she avoided that fate until 1740. Then, however, she became important to the French ambassador, le marquis de La Chétardie, and to Count Nolcken, the minister of Sweden. Armand Lestocq, her personal physician, played pander in this political cabal, supporting the Franco-Swedish conspiracy, and urging Elizabeth to join it. The position was a complicated one. When the empress Anne died in 1740, her nephew, the son of Princess Anne of Brunswick, had been designated heir and titled Ivan VI. Ivan, however, was less than a year old, so a regency had been established under Empress Anne's favourite and long-time lover, Count Biron (Bühren). In November 1740, Anne of Brunswick, who claimed the right to act for her son, successfully overthrew Biron. It was her group, the so-called Brunswick faction, which La Chétardie and Nolcken hoped to replace with Elizabeth. When this intention came to the regent's attention, Elizabeth faced arrest, imprisonment, and possibly execution. Only when the danger of her situation was brought fully home to her did she give over vacillating and agree to a *coup*. With the guards' support, the Brunswick faction fell; there was no serious resistance.

One of Elizabeth's first acts was to arrange for her own successor. Her choice was the duke of Holstein, Charles Peter Ulrich, who was also her nephew. The Brunswick faction had its connection with the Romanov ruling house through the descendants of Ivan V, Peter the Great's brother and co-tsar until his death in 1696. The Holstein branch, however, descended directly from Peter. Anne of Holstein-Gottorp, Peter Ulrich's mother, was Elizabeth's older sister. This dynastic connection was reinforced by political considerations. The Holstein branch was viewed favourably by France, Prussia, and Sweden, and thus the choice of Peter Ulrich supported the interests of those diplomats who organized the coup against the Brunswick regency. There is also a tradition that Elizabeth was sentimentally predisposed to the Holsteiners because her heart had been captured by Charles Augustus, her lost fiancé. Peter Ulrich was brought to

Russia in 1742, confirmed in the Orthodox church as Peter Fedorovich, and proclaimed the official heir to his aunt's throne. The court which was established for him became a centre for political intrigues in support of Franco-Prussian interests, and it was this orientation which influenced the selection of Grand Duke Peter's bride.

The leadership of the ousted Brunswick faction was first promised amnesties, but the new government felt insecure, and while the family was imprisoned, its main supporters were condemned to death. The sentence was finally commuted to exile in Siberia. The Brunswick faction and Ivan VI were still considered threatening, however, and in 1743 were accused of conspiring with the Austrian ambassador to overthrow Elizabeth and return Ivan VI to the throne. No evidence that the conspiracy was any more real than the manœuvrings of Elizabeth's profoundly anti-Austrian physician, Lestocq, have come to light, but the accused principals in the affair were savagely tortured, and presumed participants, including the sister-in-law of the vice-chancellor Bestuzhev, were flogged and had their tongues branded. A marriage for the grand duke Peter followed by the birth of an heir would give further security to the ruling empress and her supporters. In a near crisis atmosphere, the search for a bride for Peter was rushed ahead. The choice fell on Princess Sophia Augusta Frederica of Anhalt-Zerbst, a minor principality connected with the kingdom of Prussia. The princess arrived in Russia in 1744, received instruction in the Russian church, was confirmed as Catherine Alexievna, and married Grand Duke Peter on 21 August/1 September 1745.

Charles Peter was a stunningly bad choice for Elizabeth's successor. This was not immediately apparent on his arrival, but it soon became so. As grand duke, Peter revealed himself to be ill-educated and backward, undisciplined, childish, and, worst of all, virtually unteachable. A programme was hastily drawn up to remedy his worst deficiencies, but the effort was a failure. Peter found little in it that was to his taste, and as concentration on any subject was exceedingly difficult for him, his tutor was finally forced to admit defeat. The grand duke was noisy, excitable, militantly unintellectual, and lacking in any mature sense of responsibility. He loved games and make-believe, dolls and toy soldiers; he disliked Russia and hated being there. Peter never did identify himself in any way with the country he was eventually to govern. He considered himself German. He never gained adequate command of the Russian language, he was contemptuous of the Russian church and paraded his Lutheran preferences publicly. As he grew older, he affected the style of a German squire, maintained a regiment of Holsteiners for his household troop, and learned to carouse, smoke, and swear like one of his own non-commissioned officers. His manners could be unspeakable. When drunk, his voice ran up to a whinny-like scream, and as he grew older he was often drunk. He also fiddled, one of his few accomplishments, and he kept a pack of dogs in his antechamber which he tormented in the name of training. Loud, coarse, uncontrolled, and seemingly insensitive, Peter Fedorovich became an object of nearly universal dislike. His aunt seriously considered removing him as heir, while his bride had to learn how best to tolerate his ways.[2]

The obvious purpose of the marriage between Peter and Catherine was to produce an heir which would stabilize and guarantee the succession. That purpose was frustrated for nine long years. Elizabeth herself, who generally remained aloof from governmental affairs, was deeply interested in this aspect of her plans and, as the barren months passed by, sent increasingly pointed messages about Catherine's responsibility for producing a child. There was, however, very little hope. In 1745, both Catherine and Peter were extremely young, and the bonds which linked them seemed to be more an alliance against the adult world than a sexually productive relationship. Peter, according to Catherine, was not unattractive when she first saw him, and they found many things in common. But illness, Peter's increasingly eccentric personal habits, and her own rapid physical and emotional maturation, created a virtually unbridgeable gulf. Although they shared the same room and the same bed for over eight years, there is no suggestion that they ever established a satisfactory sexual relationship, and there is some evidence to the contrary. The Herzen edition of Catherine's memoirs contains an incoherent note which Peter is supposed to have written to Catherine in December 1746 but which probably never reached her. It leaves

---

[2] The main source for describing Peter is Catherine's memoirs. There are several versions. See Catherine II, *Sochineniia*, ed. A. N. Pypin, 12 vols. (St Petersburg, 1901), xii *passim*. The most complete version is the one designated IVa. See also *Mémoires de l'impératrice Catherine II écrits par elle-même*, ed. A. Herzen, 2nd edn. (London, 1859). The comments, plans, and reminiscences of Jakob von Stählin, Peter's tutor in Russia, are helpful. See Karl Stählin, *Aus dem Papieren Jakob von Stählins* (Königsberg, 1926). Catherine's bias against Peter, and the enlightened character of certain of his reforms, have raised the possibility that he was both less objectionable and more able than he is commonly portrayed. See e.g. Hedwig Fleischhacker, 'Porträt Peters III', *Jahrbücher für Geschichte Osteuropas*, NS 5/1–2 (1957), 127–89. Marc Raeff, 'The Domestic Policies of Peter III and His Overthrow', *American Historical Review*, 75/5 (1970) 1289–1310, rejects the revisionist view while reviewing what Peter actually did.

little doubt that their relationship was highly unsatisfactory, and can be read to mean that the marriage was never consummated. Peter signed himself, 'Your very unfortunate husband who[m] you never condescend [to call by] this name—', while addressing his wife in tones of pain and some bitterness: 'I pray you not to inconvenience yourself by sleeping with me tonight for it is no longer time [necessary?] to deceive me. [T]he bed has been too narrow after two weeks of separation from you [counting from] today after noon.'[3]

Catherine complained bitterly about her husband's noisy, uncouth, later drunken behaviour, yet for all that there was a kind of bond between them which persisted for nearly thirteen years. Peter allowed her to administer his Holstein territories until 1758, when a major crisis in her relations with Elizabeth occurred. Until then, she seemed to find pleasure and a degree of personal satisfaction in helping her husband order his personal affairs, in protecting him against the consequences of his often clumsy and sometimes childish machinations, and altogether acting as a slightly scornful, always superior, big sister to her bumptious spouse. Peter seemed to have had little sense of Catherine being his wife. He ran to her with tales of women who caught his eye, he made no effort to hide his attempts at dalliance, and he was curiously immune to suspicion, jealousy, or even wounded pride when his wife became involved with other men. He was not, however, without feelings, and his eventual attachment to the ill-favoured but loving ('nurturing' would be more accurate) Elizabeth Vorontsova was probably rooted in needs which he could never satisfy with Catherine. Eventually, the relationship between Peter and Catherine entirely deteriorated, and after Peter became tsar, his determination to divorce her and marry his mistress was a precipitating cause in Catherine's decision to overthrow him.[4]

---

[3] In French: 'Madame, Je vous prie de ne point vous incommodes cette nuis de dormir avec moi car il n'est plus tems de me trompes, le let a étè trop étroit, apres deux semaines de separation de vous aujourd'hui apres mide. Votre tres infortuné mari qui vous ne daignez jamais de ce nom Peter'. The note indicates that the letter retains the original orthography and that it was intercepted before it could be delivered. *Mémoires de l'impératrice Catherine II*, ed. Herzen, 353. Catherine's recollections of her wedding night were that she waited patiently until all hours for her new husband to leave his cronies and come to her. *Sochineniia*, xii, *Mémoires* (I), 69. In another version she describes Peter's childishness, remarks that she might have loved him, but that the way he was led her to reject him. *Mémoires* (II), 74–5. Daria Oliver, *Elisabeth de Russie* (Paris, 1962), 243–4, believes the marriage was not consummated on the wedding night, and probably never was. See also Alexander, *Catherine the Great*, 32–43.

[4] Alexandre Ivanovich Turgenev (ed.), *La Cour de Russie il y a cents ans, 1725– 1783: Extraits des dépêches des ambassadeurs anglais et français*, 3rd edn. (Leipzig, 1860), 185–7, 191; Fleishhacker, 'Porträt', 152–4.

The young court was kept under constant surveillance. Catherine complained about the spies and tattlers with whom she was surrounded, but while she complained, she was careful to avoid actions which would turn Elizabeth against her. She found outlets for her burgeoning energies in outdoor sports and concentrated study, and she gathered lively young people around her who came to form a personal cabal. In 1752, Catherine established a liaison with a handsome, dissolute, and entirely attractive young officer of distinguished family, Sergei Saltykov, who became her first lover. Catherine believed that she was pregnant in December, but the symptoms ended after violent cramps, and she wondered if she had suffered a false pregnancy. She was definitely pregnant the following summer, aborted in the fall, and then recognized the signs of a third pregnancy in February 1754. This time she carried to term, and Paul was born on 20 September/1 October.[5]

There is, of course, no definitive evidence concerning Paul's paternity. But the presumptive evidence is very strong indeed that Paul's father was Sergei Saltykov. For the more than eight years before her affair with him, Catherine was barren. Once Saltykov became her lover, she was pregnant twice, and may have been a third time. So far as is known, however, Peter failed ever to father a child, while Catherine had at least two more children, a daughter whose father was Stanislaus Poniatowski, and a son with Grigorii Orlov. Peter probably knew that Paul was not his son. He paid virtually no attention to him, and when Catherine was pregnant later with her daughter, he was heard to remark that God alone knew where his wife found her pregnancies, and while he supposed that this one too would be laid to his account, he knew nothing of the matter. Catherine found this disavowal threatening and challenged Peter through her intimate friend and court jester, Lev Naryshkin, to take an oath that he had not slept with her, and then present the evidence to Alexander Shuvalov, the imperial grand inquisitor, for action. Peter reacted to this suggestion with an angry 'Go to the devil, and say nothing more about it!' He also made no more remarks. Later, when he had become tsar and was considering divorcing Catherine and disinheriting Paul, Peter became interested in Ivan VI and is supposed to have secretly interviewed him. It is possible that he was simply interested in the old scandal, but it seems more likely that he was disturbed by the possibility that he could not father an heir, and came to consider Ivan as a possible alternative to Paul. How far he

---

[5] Catherine II, *Sochineniia*, xii, *Mémoires* (IV^2), 314–15, 320, 324–5, 336, 345, 347–8.

was prepared to go in this direction, or whether he actually intended to take any steps at all, is impossible to say.[6]

One curious tale bearing directly on Paul's paternity was reported by J. H. Castera at the end of the eighteenth century, reappeared in Bil'basov's work on Catherine the Great, and was fully developed on the basis of the original document by Kasimir Waliszewski. A memorandum prepared for the French cabinet by de Champeaux in 1758 not only identified Peter's problem as impotency, but recorded what supposedly was done about it. De Champeaux reported that Grand Duke Peter was 'incapable of having children by reason of an obstacle which circumcision corrects among the oriental peoples, but which he believed was without remedy'. Since Catherine had no taste for Peter's attentions, and did not feel the necessity for securing the succession with a child, she regarded this impediment as an advantage. Peter was said to be so ashamed of his condition that he would not mention it. When, however, Saltykov realized that Catherine could be seduced, Peter's deficiency became a threat, and the would-be lover intrigued to get the empress's approval for an operation which would correct Peter's problem. He succeeded. A crowd of jolly friends convinced the grand duke that he had nothing to fear and everything to gain, and at the critical moment Boerhaave, the court physician together with a surgeon, made their entrance, and the operation was successfully carried out. Saltkykov received a fine diamond from the empress for his trouble, and it seemed that the way was clear for him to enjoy Catherine's favours without fear. His enemies, however, influenced the empress with stories of how Saltykov was bent on seducing Peter's wife. Elizabeth demanded that when Peter was well enough to sleep with Catherine and consummate the marriage, the proofs of the grand duchess's virginity were to be delivered directly to her. The delivery was made in a casket which Peter himself sealed and sent to the empress, and 'the liaison between the grand duchess and Saltikov was not interrupted and lasted another eight years [sic] in all its vigour'.[7]

[6] Turgenev, *La Cour de Russie*, 167, states as blunt fact that Saltykov was Paul's father. Breteuil, the French representative, wrote on 5 Jan. (NS) 1762 that Peter believed Paul was a bastard and intended to disinherit him. Ibid. 191. He also believed that Saltykov was a source of information for Peter. Ibid. 191–2. Fleischhacker, 'Porträt', 143 and nn., for the confrontation over Catherine's pregnancies. After becoming tsar, Peter visited Ivan VI in the Schlüsselburg and was reported to intend freeing Ivan, arranging his marriage, and making him his heir. See Morane, *Paul Ier*, 17, 28–9. Fleischhacker, 'Porträt', 168–70, confirms Peter's interest but argues that it is impossible to know what he intended.

[7] Kasimir Waliszewski, *Le Roman d'une impératrice: Catherine II de Russie d'après ses mémoires, sa correspondance et les documents inédits des archives d'état,*

De Champeaux's story is interesting because it reflects the widespread conviction that Peter's impotence was the reason he and Catherine had had no children. It also explains how it might have been possible for Peter actually to have been Paul's father. However, the anecdote does not claim to prove this, asserting only that Catherine's relationship with Saltykov could continue without fear of interruption. In fact, as Catherine herself made clear, her relations with Saltykov were cooling even before Paul's birth, while her subsequent affair with Poniatowski pushed Saltykov entirely out of the picture. More seriously, the idea that circumcision could correct any significant impediment to sexual performance is hard to credit and, as we saw above, there is no evidence at all that Peter's sexual powers changed in any important respect throughout the whole period of his marriage.

The de Champeaux story, however, contradicts another for which there is some support in Catherine's memoirs. If we believe de Champeaux, Elizabeth was concerned over both Catherine's failure to conceive and her personal morals. It was also said, however, that Elizabeth's primary interest was that an heir be born, and when Peter and Catherine failed to give her one, she finally accepted the idea that the fault was with Peter rather than his wife and (supposedly on biblical precedent) agreed that Catherine should take a lover who could father a child. The long-time advocate for this solution, according to Catherine, was Madame Choglokova, wife of the marshal of the young court and her own personal overseer. The choice offered was Lev Naryshkin or Sergei Saltykov, and Catherine chose the latter.[8] Another story, current at the time Paul was born, claimed that Elizabeth herself had a baby which was then substituted for Catherine's offspring. This story, far-fetched though it sounds, may have reflected contemporaries' surprise at Elizabeth's fiercely possessive and strongly maternal attitudes towards Paul and Catherine's remoteness. And it may have given voice to an underlying wish for an heir of Russian descent by rejecting the 'foreigners', Peter and Catherine, as the parents for an heir to the throne.[9]

3rd edn. (Paris, 1897), 59–60, 83–5. Waliszewski records that the version of de Champeaux's memo printed in the appendices to Bil'basov's history of Catherine the Great is incomplete. He cites the full document from vol. 57 (Russie) of the archives of the ministry of foreign affairs. The portions omitted in Bil'basov appear in italics. Cf. V. A. Bilbassov [Bil'basov], *Geschichte Katharina II*, trans. M. V. Pezold, 2 vols. (Berlin, 1891), ii. 62–74 and esp. 64–5 and 67–70.

[8] Catherine II, *Mémoires* (Herzen), 179–180, 186–7.
[9] Bil'basov, *Katharina II*, i n. 1, pp. 347–8.

Too little is known about Saltykov to contribute much to understanding Paul. Portraits of the young Paul were said to resemble Saltykov's brother, while Paul's quick and clever mind as a child was reminiscent of 'le beau Serge'. On the other hand, Saltykov was tall and well-formed which Paul most emphatically was not. It also has to be said that many of Paul's traits—his enthusiasm and engagement, his quickness, his impatience and need for movement—resembled Catherine, with whom, in fact, he had many points in common. Whether Paul gave much thought to the problem of his paternity is unknown. It is difficult to believe that he was unaware of the common opinion, and at least one memoirist records a scene, unconfirmed in other sources, in which Paul's governor, Count N. I. Panin, told the grand duke with brutal frankness that he was not Peter III's son, that he was, in fact, nothing but a bastard who owed his position to his mother's sufferance.[10] The alleged reason for the revelation, and for Panin's uncharacteristic harshness, was the fear that Paul's complaints, which he had begun to voice as his majority approached, about his mother's having usurped his rights would lead the empress to take steps against him. Even so, whatever Paul may have been told, he never showed the slightest indication that he considered his paternity doubtful. He always referred to Peter as 'my father', and he took particular pride in being a direct descendant of Peter the Great. If he had doubts, they were deeply buried.

Paul's birth was a major event. It was celebrated at the court with balls, masques, receptions, and illuminations, while vast spreads of food and drink were laid before the common people. The festival lasted a year. Among the highlights was a masked ball given by Count Shuvalov, Elizabeth's favourite, that went on without interruption for two days and two nights.[11] Throughout his life, Paul's birthday and name day were important court occasions marked by a reception, a dinner, and a ball or theatrical presentation. And this points up an important fact. From the beginning, he enjoyed an accepted and honoured position at court and with the public. He was the object of that ritual adulation

[10] Fedor Golovkine, *La Cour et le règne de Paul Ier* (Paris, 1905), 102–3.
[11] Semon Andreevich Poroshin, 'Zapiski, sluzhashchiia k istorii ego imperatorskago vysochestva blagovernago gosudaria tsesarevicha i velikago kniazi Pavla Petrovicha', *Russkaia starina*, 32 (St Petersburg, 1881), 597–601; see also vols. 30, 31. Diplomats reported Paul's birth and the celebrations. See e.g. M. Guy Dickens's reports to Whitehall, Public Records Office (PRO) [Great Britain], SP/91/60; 61, St Petersburg, 20 Sept./1 Oct. 1754; 27 Sept./8 Oct. 1754; 15/26 Oct. 1754; 25 Mar./5 Apr. 1755; Sir Charles Hanbury Williams, 14 Oct. (NS) 1755. See also: Kobeko, *Pavel Petrovich*, 3–5; Shil'der, *Pavel I*, 3–4; Morane, *Paul Ier*, 11–12.

reserved for a future ruler, and he received the special care, training, and education which his position demanded. Far from neglected, Paul was surrounded by nurses, governors, and tutors who formed his personal society until he reached maturity. These people made him aware from his first moments of consciousness of his essential importance and the special status he enjoyed. Paul was born to be a monarch; this was the foundation for his identity as a person.

Paradoxically, there was no legal basis for Paul's favoured status, nor would there be for nearly eight more years. Elizabeth had declared Peter Fedorovich her successor; it was Peter who had to choose Paul to be his heir. In fact, he never did so. Paul's status as heir to the throne was not established until after Catherine had overthrown her husband in 1762 and was herself proclaimed empress. It was she (just as Panin allegedly told Paul) who formally designated him heir to the throne. Yet from the moment of his birth, Paul was treated as if he were to be the tsar. So he learnt to see himself, and so he was considered by the public. It was this rather than the legal position which created problems for Catherine after 1762 and gave Paul his grievance against her.

Elizabeth treated Paul as her own child. The umbilical had scarcely been cut when the empress swept into the room where Catherine lay, ordered the midwife to take up the new-born babe, and bring him to the nursery in her apartments. The empress's confessor named the child, a wet-nurse was provided, and Paul was put down in a cradle beside the empress's bed. At first, Elizabeth abandoned everything else to devote her entire attention to this surrogate son. The novelty soon passed, however, and when Elizabeth lost interest, Paul was taken over by nurses who close-swaddled him in the Russian manner, and wrapped him in quilts. So his mother saw him, weeks later, asleep in a cradle decked with black fox fur, red-faced and sweating in the heat. Such treatment was bound, in Catherine's opinion, to undermine his health, and she held that it was responsible for his life-long susceptibility to chills and colds. All this strengthened her conviction that the women caring for Paul were incompetent and ignorant. Their ministrations, in her view, 'did him infinitely more physical and moral harm than good', and she was not surprised to learn that in the first week of Paul's life he suffered so severely from gumboils that it was feared he would not survive. Catherine was certain that she knew how children should be cared for, but she had no opportunity to practise her ideas until she took over Paul's first-born sons, Alexander and Constantine, in 1777 and 1779.[12]

[12] Catherine II, *Mémoires* (IV²), 216, 221; Kobeko, *Pavel Petrovich*, 5–6; Morane, *Paul Ier*, 14–15.

Background and Family Origins

Paul's birth gave Catherine no satisfaction. She began her labour around 2 in the morning, and the midwife finally delivered her at noon. The birth was normal, but she was exhausted and in need of care when it had finished. She did not receive it. When the baby was taken from her, she was left lying on a bed which was sweat-soaked and soiled with the recent birthing. Elizabeth had neglected to give orders concerning her, and Catherine, as she relates the story, was unable to get fresh linens, a cover against the chilling drafts from two adjacent windows and a door, or even a drink of water. It was hours before anyone paid the least attention to her, and she was brought forcibly to realize that she was entirely isolated and on her own. She had expected little from the empress and less from her husband, but the loneliness, physical discomfort, and frustration of those hours after Paul's birth left a mark. She could be excused for feeling persecuted. She was not permitted to see her friends, and when she did begin to learn what was happening in the world outside, the first news was that Saltykov had been sent abroad to carry the news of Paul's birth to Stockholm and Copenhagen. Later, her favourite among the women serving her was also sent away. Almost it seemed as if she was being punished.[13]

Catherine remained in isolation for the mandatory six weeks of recovery. The empress sent her a gift of 100,000 rubles and a selection of jewels, but when her husband heard of the reward, he demanded the same amount for himself. The cash was not available, and Catherine was urgently requested to loan back her gift to permit the empress to compensate the grand duke. The money was returned in January 1755, but the whole affair made a very bad impression which the jewels did nothing to relieve. These, Catherine sniffed, were mere baubles of no account whatsoever and set in the worst possible taste; she had no intention of ever wearing them. Peter, apart from one brief sortie into Catherine's room, went on with his usual occupations. He showed no interest in Catherine's situation, or in Paul. Catherine herself only heard rumours about her son's progress. She did not see him until he was six weeks old when he was brought to her rooms for prayers. On that occasion, she claimed to find him handsome and took some joy in his appearance, but her pleasure was short-lived, for he was removed as soon as prayers were finished. She was permitted to look in on him after Easter the following year, when she was able to confirm what she had been told about the way he was wrapped and swaddled, but there was nothing

---

[13] Catherine II, *Mémoires* (IV²), 216; *Mémoires* (Herzen), 215–18, 221–4.

to be done, and Catherine's interests were already turning elsewhere. Her memoirs tell us nothing further about her son.[14]

Bitter though Catherine was towards Elizabeth, her resentment did not extend to Paul. But there was little to support any strong maternal feelings. Four years later, when Catherine bore her daughter, mother and child were treated just as at Paul's birth. Elizabeth looked on Catherine as a sort of biological machine which produced a valuable product, but which could be ignored when not in use. So long as Peter was complaisant, paternity was no problem, and the empress raised Catherine's progeny as if they were her own. None of this encouraged a maternal attitude on Catherine's part. Her third child, the son fathered by Grigorii Orlov, posed a different problem. That pregnancy had to be concealed from the empress, who was dying, and even more from Grand Duke Peter, who then was seriously considering divorce. An illegitimate child would have given him the excuse he needed. Catherine bore the child in secret and, with Orlov's help, spirited it away to be cared for by foster parents. Though she apparently considered killing the infant, once she decided to run the risks of permitting it to survive, she provided money for its raising and kept in contact with its foster family. The child was named Alexei Bobrinskoi, and Catherine eventually identified herself to him, and provided for his career. She never, however, officially acknowledged him.[15]

Paul appears to have been a difficult and sickly babe, fussy, colicky, highly strung, and easily upset. He suffered digestive problems, was prone to constipation, and cried a great deal. The care which he received was inconsistent and may well have contributed to his problems. Elizabeth was undisciplined and disorderly in her personal life. She had no fixed time for rising, retiring, or eating, and this lack of order in her household affected Paul. Meals were haphazard, there was no regular bedtime, and it was possible for the child to be forgotten entirely. On one occasion he fell out of his crib and slept the night away unnoticed on the floor. In later years, Paul was compulsive about ordering every aspect of his personal life. He suffered from profound insecurities which he dealt with by rigid controls over those aspects of daily living which fell within his grasp. Certainly, for a child so obviously nervous, and in need of

---

[14] Catherine II, *Mémoires* (Herzen), 221–5, 223; in *Mémoires* (v), 466, Catherine expressed joy at the birth of her son.

[15] On the birth of Catherine's daughter, *Mémoires* (Herzen), 303–5; Madariaga, *Catherine the Great*, 27 and n. 25, 599–600 (for Bobrinskoi); Alexander, *Catherine the Great*, 56–7, 60, 234–5.

comforting regularity, the environment in which Elizabeth first raised him was unsatisfactory and potentially harmful.

There is, of course, another side. Throughout Paul's nursery years, he was an object of concern and love. Though his nurses may have been careless and ignorant, they were also warm-hearted and demonstrative. It may even be true that it was they who introduced him at an early age to Russia's rich folk culture and created an emotional bond with the common people which lasted throughout his life. We can imagine him listening wide-eyed to tales of wizards and sorcerers, bogatyry and boyari, sly merchants, clever peasants, and magic fowl. Perhaps it was here that Paul's later interest in the supernatural and his evident religiosity were rooted. It was reported that he half believed that the empress, whom he seldom saw as he grew older, was a witch, and that his future tutor was a sorcerer. And there may have been some malice in all this. Apart from the nurses' anxiety and fear of displacement, Paul's nervousness and fearfulness made him a delight to tease. That, too, belonged to the culture of the village.[16]

In another sense, the nursery years were empty ones for Catherine's child. He was isolated and shut away, he had no family as such, and there were no other children. This was unfortunate. It was also a function of his special status, combined with the empress's secretive and suspicious nature. Instead of rolling around the hearth in a noisy crowd of urchins of every age, size, and disposition, Paul's relationships were always with adults. Not until he was 4 and his half-sister was born did his world include another child. She, however, lived only nine months, and her brief appearance did little more than underscore how lonely his life actually was. The problem, however, was more than loneliness. Paul never learnt to deal with people of his own age. As he grew older, he desperately wanted company and would eagerly seek to have one boy or another brought to play with him. Yet when they came his patience was short, and when they offended him, as inevitably they did, he would send them away, often not to see them again.[17] Paul became intensely self-centred at a very early age, and with no necessity for developing the skills of living with people, he fell back on a kind of imperiousness

[16] Kobeko, *Pavel Petrovich*, 5–6; Morane, *Paul Ier*, 23; Constantine de Grunwald, *L'Assassinat*, 23; Zubow, *Paul der Erste*, 16–17. For Paul's memories of his early years, 'Vospominaniia Velikago Kniazia Pavla Petrovicha o zhizni ego s 1755 po 1761 god', zapisanniya s ego selov S. A. Poroshinym v 1764–65', *Russkaia starina*, 32 (1881), 602–14.

[17] Poroshin, *Russkaia starina*, 32 (1881), 605, and *Zapiski, passim*. As Poroshin described him, Paul spent virtually all his waking hours with adults. See also Kobeko, *Pavel Petrovich*, 33.

which, of course, his special status strongly reinforced. In the end, though his nurses teased him and catered to him, he was never anything but the tsar-to-be. He could rely on adults for what made him comfortable, and he was never forced into the competitive give and take of the child's world. In effect, he was never forced to learn the arts of human relationships. In this sense his childhood was not only lonely but impoverished.

In 1758, the year Paul's sister died, General Fedor Dmitrievich Bekhteev was recalled from his diplomatic post in Paris to become court master of ceremonies and to direct the grand duke's formal schooling. He joined Aleksei Grigorevich Zubtsov and Count Martin Karlovich Skavronskii as Paul's first teachers. None of the three was particularly distinguished. The curriculum they taught was strongly laced with social graces—politesse or etiquette, dancing, and French—but it also included religious instruction and a sniff of the natural sciences. Bekhteev was responsible for commissioning Paul's first textbook, a book on natural history, though it is questionable that he was ever taught from it since it only became available at the time Bekhteev was replaced. More importantly, Paul now found himself in a very different atmosphere. The indulgent life of the nursery disappeared. Bekhteev was a hard taskmaster who believed in discipline. It was he who devised a gazette which purported to relate everything the grand duke did. Paul was told that this paper was read throughout Europe, that he was the cynosure of every eye, and that when he failed or refused to do what he was supposed to, the whole world could point a finger at him. This extraordinary ploy had the potential both to enhance Paul's already developed sense of his own importance, and to feed his insecurities. A more destructive disciplinary instrument can hardly be imagined. Fortunately, Bekhteev's tenure was short, and the reports, which Paul learned to dread, were relatively few.[18]

Bekhteev's charge was to prepare Paul to enter adult society. He succeeded admirably. The grand duke made his first public appearance in July 1760, when he dined with the empress. The English ambassador noted that he behaved 'well and gravely', that they conversed in French, and that Paul could turn a nice phrase. On 25 September/6 October, he attended the court theatre to watch a French farce. On this occasion Ambassador Keith commented that Paul was 'very handsome and seems to have a great deal of life'. The

---

[18] Kobeko, *Pavel Petrovich*, 6–7. The title of the commissioned science text was *Kratkoe poniatie o fizke delia o upotrebleniia Ego Imperatorskago Vysochestva Gosudaria Velikago Kniazia Pavla Petrovicha* (St Petersburg, 1760). See also Morane, *Paul Ier*, 23–4.

following year, he appeared for the first time in the drawing-room and it was reported that 'he dances wonderfully well for one of his age', and on 3/14 July, attended by his parents, he received compliments on his name day from the court for the first time.[19] Early in 1763, Buckingham, Keith's replacement in St Petersburg, had his first audience with Paul who then was just 8. Buckingham reported that 'His address and manner are agreeable and engaging, and his Deportment very extraordinary considering how very young he is'. Their conversation was carried on in French. The reports on Paul's formal appearances continued to be most favourable. He was praised for his command of etiquette and for his skill as a horseman; he was known to dance well and to fence passably, and when he appeared in a court ballet at the age of 6, he performed well and seemed to take pleasure in what he was doing.[20]

In 1759, Count Nikita Ivanovich Panin was brought to Petersburg to become Paul's personal governor, to oversee his household, and to establish the educational programme which the grand duke would follow over the next thirteen years. The decision was a momentous one, for it introduced into Paul's life an individual who was to be closer to him for a longer period of time than anyone except his second wife. Panin created the environment in which Paul spent his boyhood and adolescent years, and he remained a friend and adviser when Paul's education was finished.[21]

Count Panin belonged to a family which had won distinction in the service of Peter the Great. His father reached the rank of colonel in 1712, married a niece of the powerful prince Alexander Menshikov, and entered the fifth rank in the service hierarchy in 1722. He was named senator by Empress Anne, and at the time of his death in 1736 he held the rank of lieutenant-general. His daughters, Anna and Alexandra, married well, the former to Prince Alexander Borisovich Kurakin, a leading diplomat and senator of the Petrine era, and the latter to I. I. Nepliuev, who was also a senator and responsible for building the Orenburg frontier province. Though the Panins were not wealthy—Ivan Vasil'evich left a mere 400 serfs to his children—they were extremely well connected, and their father apparently spared nothing in promoting their education. Nikita Ivanovich gained an

[19] Robert Keith to Whitehall, PRO, SP 91/68, no. 68, St Petersburg, 13/24 July 1760; no. 98, St Petersburg, 25 Sept./7 October 1760; no. 205, St Petersburg, 26 April/7 May 1761; no. 224, St Petersburg, 3/14 July 1761.

[20] Buckingham to Whitehall, PRO, SP 91/71, no. 18, Moscow, 10 Jan. (NS) 1763; no. 39, 13 Jan. (NS) 1763. Kobeko, *Pavel Petrovich*, 35-6 on theatre in Paul's life.

[21] The best as well as the most recent work on Panin and his role in raising Paul is David Ransel, *The Politics of Catherinian Russia: The Panin Party* (New Haven, Conn., 1975). The following section on Panin is based on Ransel.

enviable reputation for his intellectual attainments, for his knowledge of politics, science, and literature; he was well informed on contemporary medicine, and he was known as a lively conversationalist with a special interest in history, manners, and mores. Curiously enough, little is known about the way he acquired his knowledge.

The post of governor or *oberhofmeister* for the heir to the Russian throne was extremely important in the configurations of Russian court politics. It involved a substantial budget, overseeing a numerous household, and responsibility for educating the heir apparent. It was also a position of some security since changes in the grand duke's circle were considered undesirable. They might give rise to rumours concerning the succession itself. Panin made the position of *oberhofmeister* a power base from which he wielded major influence in Catherine's court. The importance he attached to the office appears in the fact that he regularly rejected all other titles and appointments, even when he came to be recognized as one of the most powerful persons in St Petersburg.

The man ultimately responsible for choosing Panin was Chancellor M. L. Vorontsov. His reasons were quintessentially political.[22] Vorontsov considered Panin sympathetic to his faction's aristocratic constitutionalism (the Shuvalovs, their principal rivals, favoured advancing middle-class interests at the expense of the traditional nobility) and hence a potential ally. Panin was also an adroit courtier who stood well with both Catherine and Elizabeth. There would be no problem in gaining their approval. It is also likely that his considerable intellectual attainments recommended him, and he was interested in educational ideas. He had observed the way the heir apparent was educated in Sweden, and he studied other countries' methods while expanding on his own knowledge of contemporary educational theory. And, as matters turned out, he proved to be a sympathetic person who could exercise his powers with concern, humanity, and grace. Paul was approaching 6 when Panin appeared on the scene. He was frightened and unsure on meeting his new governor, but Panin was soon able to gain his confidence and eventually his affection. Contemporaries were impressed with the way Panin organized the grand duke's household, while Catherine found herself in touch with a man who responded to, and could advance, her own intellectual interests. This choice, though rooted in politics, proved highly satisfactory on every count.

All the while, other events were gathering which played a determining role in Paul's life. Before his birth, Catherine had been

---

[22] Ransel, *Panin Party*, 33–7.

quiescent politically. Afterwards, she became increasingly involved, and not least as the result of a new love affair. Sir Charles Hanbury Williams arrived as the British representative in 1755, bringing a young Pole, Stanislaus Poniatowski, with him as one of his secretaries. Poniatowski fell in love with Catherine and she with him, while Williams became her confidant, adviser, and correspondent.[23] This happened at a time when political relationships were shifting radically. The traditional alignments among the European states which found France joined with Prussia, and England with Austria, were breaking down, while at the Russian court, Chancellor Bestuzhev was being pressed by his enemies, the Vorontsovs and the Shuvalovs. Bestuzhev was pro-English, and in 1755 he worked out an agreement with the British government to protect Hanover against Prussia. This understanding was intended to serve as the cornerstone of an Anglo-Russian alliance against France and Prussia. Early in 1756, however, Prussia and Britain signed an undertaking at Westminster which gave mutual guarantees of their respective territories and rendered the 1755 Anglo-Russian agreement nugatory. Bestuzhev's policies, which were both anti-French and anti-Prussian, had become irrelevant, the chancellor was openly criticized, and a special council was formed to oversee his decisions. In the event, Bestuzhev drew closer to the English minister and, through him, to Catherine. Old enmities were put aside as Bestuzhev and Catherine became allies and eventually friends.[24]

When Frederick the Great invaded Silesia in 1756, Russia supported Austria against Prussia and England. This put Catherine in a potentially compromising situation. Her connections with Hanbury Williams, her affair with Poniatowski, and her close bond and extensive correspondence with Bestuzhev all made her vulnerable. England was the ally of Russia's enemy; Catherine was perilously close to committing treason. Moreover, her relations with her husband were deteriorating. Though Peter seemed unconcerned about Catherine's infidelities, he had established his own liaison with Elizabeth Vorontsova, and he was already considering the possibility of a divorce so that he could marry his mistress. He was also outspoken in support of Prussia, a particularly irritating posture in

[23] Catherine II, *Mémoires* (Herzen), 238–40, 245–6; Madariaga, *Catherine the Great*, 11–13. See also *Correspondence of Catherine the Great with Sir Charles Hanbury Williams*, ed. the earl of Ilchester (London, 1928).

[24] For diplomacy, S. M. Solov'ev, *Istoriia Rossii*, xii. 305–444; L. Jay Oliva, *Misalliance: A Study of French Policy in Russia during the Seven Years War* (Berkeley, Calif., 1968); Waliszewski, *Roman d'une impératrice*, ch. 1, bk. 2, pp. 95–137. Catherine's *Mémoires* (Herzen), 246–352, summarize events to spring 1759.

view of Russia's policies, while his behaviour had become obnoxious enough to disenchant the empress who pondered removing him from the succession in favour of Paul. This possibility was also discussed between Bestuzhev, who formulated a plan to that effect, and Catherine, though Catherine was cool to the idea and avowed that it was impractical.[25]

Affairs reached a crisis in September 1758, when Elizabeth suffered what appeared to be a stroke outside the imperial chapel at Tsarskoe Selo. General Apraksin, who had fought a difficult and successful action against the Prussians at Gross Jägersdorf, failed to follow up his advantage. His decision not to press ahead was laid to his fears that Elizabeth might die, and Peter would change the direction of Russian policy. But the empress recovered and, angered as she was at the idea that policies had been shifted in anticipation of her death, began to listen seriously to the insinuations of the Shuvalovs who controlled the secret police. They spoke of a conspiracy with Bestuzhev and Catherine at its core, and Catherine soon became aware that she was in very serious danger. Bestuzhev was arrested, but he was able to destroy whatever might have been incriminating in his correspondence with Catherine, while a search of Apraksin's papers revealed only three letters from Catherine in which she urged him to support the empress's policies. There was also evidence that Apraksin had made his recommendations for a withdrawal to his command council before news of Elizabeth's illness reached him.

Despite this temporary respite, Catherine remained convinced that she was in danger and that only the boldest action could save her. She therefore wrote Elizabeth requesting that she be sent back to Germany since she was no longer welcome in Russia. Elizabeth granted an interview on the basis of that note. The interview was held, however, after six weeks of intensive investigation. Nor was it held in camera. Grand Duke Peter was present, as was Alexander Shuvalov, head of the secret chancellory. I. I. Shuvalov, Elizabeth's new favourite, was hidden behind a curtain. The meeting was extremely tense. Peter wanted a hearing on his complaints that Catherine mistreated him, but Elizabeth silenced him. Those matters were of no moment. The charge the empress laid against Catherine was treason in her relationship with Bestuzhev. Catherine denied the charge and, refusing to be moved even by threats that Bestuzhev would be tortured, maintained her innocence and loyalty. Eventually, with neither documents nor denunciations to support her suspicions,

[25] Fleischhacker, 'Porträt', 136–43, 151.

Elizabeth grudgingly accepted Catherine's protestations, and the danger was past, though its threatening memory lingered on. Having escaped once, however, Catherine was forced into an uncharacteristically circumspect life, and she avoided any further clash with the ageing empress.[26]

The immediate consequence of Catherine's confrontation with authority was that she found herself entirely isolated. Poniatowski and Hanbury Williams were gone; Bestuzhev was under arrest; her husband was openly at odds with her; and there seemed to be nowhere else to turn. It was under these circumstances that she formed another liaison, this time with a much-decorated guards officer and hero of the Prussian campaign named Grigorii Orlov. There is no doubt that Orlov was handsome and vital, and that he had immense appeal for Catherine. It is also true that he and his four brothers formed a link to the regiments of guards and therefore were potentially significant politically. For the rest, and in the wake of the great crisis of 1758–9, Catherine went into semi-retirement. She appears to have understood that her husband's mounting animosity threatened both her future and that of Paul, yet she also appears to have harboured the conviction that, once Elizabeth was gone, she, Catherine, would play a major role in affairs.

Paul's part in the events described was minor. It did seem that Elizabeth favoured him, and it was widely believed (or hoped) that she would replace Peter Fedorovich with Paul as her successor. Shortly before she died she took him into public with her for supper and a command performance at the court theatre. She also presented him to the guards assigned to protect her, singling out those who were with her in 1741. But nothing came of this display. Elizabeth was too tired, sick, and old to change the succession. When she died at Christmas 1761, her Holstein nephew took control of the government as Peter III. Catherine was his empress while Paul supposedly was grand duke and heir. There was no mention of either in the accession manifesto, however, and this dramatized the dangerous position in which both, but especially Catherine, were placed. Catherine's personal relations with her husband had degenerated into a continuing and acrimonious row. Peter, it was said, was ready to divorce her, disinherit his son, and marry Elizabeth Vorontsova. The rights of succession would be conferred on his first child with her. Whether Peter actually intended to do these things is by no means certain. And the suggestion that he might yet father a

[26] Catherine II, *Mémoires* (Herzen), 298–345, esp. 338–45; Madariaga, *Catherine the Great*, 12–17; Fleischhacker, 'Portät', 144–52; Solov'ev, *Istoriia Rossii*, bk. 12, pp. 444–9.

child was wholly unrealistic, though there was also the possibility that the deposed Ivan VI might be brought back. However the succession was decided, Catherine considered her danger real and organized her friends to assist her.[27]

During the first months of Peter's reign, Catherine was pregnant with Orlov's child. She concealed the pregnancy, aided by the voluminous skirts dictated by contemporary fashion, and she stayed away from court whenever possible. Peter gave her every reason to absent herself by shouting at her publicly, insulting her, and eventually threatening her. These public outbursts brought Catherine sympathy and support which she exploited as, once her child was born and spirited away, she planned in earnest to overthrow her husband. Panin was her councillor and played a leading part in the conspiracy, while the Orlovs provided the essential link to the guards. The intrigue gained a wide circle of supporters which included Princess Dashkova, herself a Vorontsov and sister to the tsar's mistress. Panin advised caution, pointing out to Catherine that both Ivan VI, imprisoned twenty-one years earlier, and Paul had stronger claims than any she could muster. Ivan, in fact, had briefly reigned. It was Panin's advice that, when Peter was overthrown, she should restrict herself to acting as Paul's regent. Claiming the throne in her own right would set a dangerous precedent. Neither Catherine nor the Orlovs ever accepted this argument. If Peter could be brought down, then Catherine should rule. She did, however, at least honour Panin's scruples with an excuse. When the event actually occurred, there was, as she later explained it, no time for legal niceties. Swift and certain action was essential to survival.[28]

Peter's legislative programme should have won him wide support. He emancipated the nobility from compulsory service, though stopping short of guaranteeing noble rights; he reduced the tax on salt to lighten the living costs of the lower classes; and he abolished the dread secret chancery, an institution with literally unlimited powers to investigate and punish suspected threats to the sovereign and the state. But Peter was so cordially disliked that even enlightened and humanitarian reforms brought grumbling, while his entering on an intensive programme of secularizing church lands,

---

[27] For background on the 1762 *coup*, Madariaga, *Catherine the Great*, 21–9; Fleischhacker, 'Porträt', 152–7.

[28] For Panin's role, Ransel, *Panin Party*, 59, 65–7. See also Madariaga, *Catherine the Great*, 27–9; Fleischhacker, 'Porträt', 151. For the French and English diplomatic reports, Turgenev, *La Cour de Russie*, 176–200. The diplomats were well informed. Keith was favourably disposed to Peter; the French were anti-Peter and brutally critical.

reorganizing the state administration, and reforming the army along Prussian lines created a furore. Peter approached his reforms from the position that Russia was a barbarous society living under institutions that more enlightened states had long since abandoned. He was dismissive of the victories Russian armies had won against Prussia, and as soon as he was tsar he ended Russia's alliance with Austria to join Frederick and to embark on a campaign against Denmark over Holstein. He was openly disrespectful at Elizabeth's funeral, laughing and talking during the service, and this was taken as further evidence of both his shallow character and his anti-Russian bias. But his most serious error was to challenge entrenched court and administrative interests, the army, especially the guards, and the church, without having created a viable power base of his own. Peter played directly into the hands of Catherine and her supporters who saw the problem in the clear light of political survival and struck hard. Whether Peter's policies would have ignited a rebellion had Catherine not been an issue is difficult to say. Since she was, and since she was prepared to seize the initiative, early confrontation was inevitable.[29]

The coup was precipitated when a member of the conspiracy, a certain Captain Passek, was arrested, and it was feared that he would reveal what he knew.[30] The tsar was at Oranienbaum and Catherine was at Peterhof when Alexis Orlov brought the message, at 5.00 a.m. on 28 June/9 July 1762, that it was time to move. Catherine went directly to St Petersburg. The Orlovs had done their work well. The Semenovskii and Izmailovskii regiments of guards declared for Catherine, and by the time she reached Kazan cathedral to receive the church's benediction, the military was entirely on her side. Paul was at the Summer Palace while these events were taking place. He was forgotten until just before the ceremony of induction when he was rushed to the cathedral in his night clothes to stand behind his mother while she was proclaimed empress and autocrat (*samoderzhavitsa*). Paul was named her heir.

Peter III was ignorant of the events in Petersburg. He was engrossed in preparations for his name day fête which was planned

[29] Raeff, 'Domestic Policies of Peter III'; Fleischhacker, 'Porträt', 157–63, 165–7, 171–2; Madariaga, *Catherine the Great*, 22–7; Turgenev, *La Cour de Russie*, 181–5, for diplomats' appraisals of Peter's reforms.

[30] For Catherine's version of the *coup*, *Mémoires* (Herzen), 359–70 (to Poniatowski); Robert Keith's account is PRO, SP 91/70, St Petersburg, 1/12 July 1762; cf. Turgenev, *La Cour de Russie*, 202–12; Princess E. R. Dashkova, *Mémoires de la princesse Dashkaw d'après le manuscrit revu et corrigé par l'auteur*, Arkhiv kniazia Vorontsova, xxi, ed. P. Bartenev (Moscow, 1881), 67–83; Madariaga, *Catherine the Great*, 29–32; Alexander, *Catherine the Great*, 3–16.

for Peterhof. Later on the same morning that Catherine went to Petersburg, Peter arrived at Peterhof to find his wife gone. After searching through her apartments and gardens, he waited irresolutely until he learnt that Catherine had left for the capital. He then sent emissaries to discover what was happening, and returned to Oranienbaum. The aged count Münnich, one of several German servitors he had recalled from exile, urged immediate action, so the tsar attempted to reach Kronstadt by boat. But the fortress was already held by Catherine's partisans, and he was forced to turn back. He did nothing further. On the following morning, Catherine, dressed in a guards uniform and accompanied by Princess Dashkova, led a column of troops in a triumphant rush to arrest the tsar whose deposition had been announced the previous day. There was no resistance. Peter signed an act of abdication and agreed to his own incarceration. He did request that Elizabeth Vorontsova be allowed to accompany him, and that he be permitted to take his dog, his Negro servant, his pipes, and his fiddle with him to prison. The request for his mistress and his servant was denied, the rest was granted, and he was carried away to the nearby estate of Ropsha where he was to be held until he could be transferred to the Schlüsselburg fortress. The Orlovs were made his gaolers; five days later he was dead.

Though what happened at Ropsha is hardly mysterious, the circumstances remain cloudy. More precisely, it is impossible to state with any certainty whether Catherine ordered her husband's murder, though there is no doubt that she played a leading part in concealing it once it had been committed.[31] Perhaps Peter III deposed and alive would have been a serious problem for Catherine. It is quite possible that she and her closest supporters, particularly the Orlovs, saw the issue in that light. Peter would have been a major impediment to Grigorii Orlov's ambition to marry Catherine, though what he wanted and what she was willing to do were by no means the same thing. But if Catherine did actually consider Peter more a threat than an inconvenience, her fears would have had to outrun what she knew. The ease with which she took control, and the support which she enjoyed once she had declared herself, were eloquent testimony to the gulf which yawned between Peter and the influential members of the society he governed. Though individuals were loyal to him, he had no solid basis of support, no strong foundation for his position in society. There was, of course, always the possibility that an opposition faction might use him as a stalking horse in some

[31] Turgenev, *La Cour de Russie*, 216–19 for contemporary speculation on this point.

indefinite future. Whether Catherine considered such a danger to be a sufficient cause for ordering him killed is unknown; it is also difficult to credit.

Alexis Orlov announced Peter's death in a note delivered personally to Catherine. Visibly shaken and distrait, Orlov avowed that the former tsar died in a brawl which started between him and Fedor Bariatinskii and which turned into a free-for-all. Orlov left no doubt that it was Peter's gaolers—himself, his brothers, and their helpers—who were responsible. He also claimed that it was an accident and begged abjectly for forgiveness.[32] Whether Catherine felt relief, joy, annoyance, or despair, she moved quickly to cover up the crime. The former tsar, it was announced, had died unexpectedly of a severe colic following a haemorrhoidal haemorrhage. The body was opened to see if there were signs of poisoning. There were none. To allay any doubts that Peter was dead, the body was displayed before it was interred at the Nevskii monastery. Observers reported that the face was blackened and distorted, an appearance consistent with a violent death, probably by strangling. The official explanation stood, however. In the next year, when Catherine invited the famed mathematician and *philosophe*, Jean Le Rond d'Alembert, to come to Russia to assist in educating Paul, d'Alembert politely refused, but when he commented on the invitation in a letter to Voltaire, he remarked that he would hardly have dared go since he was himself prone to haemorrhoids, and this was obviously a very dangerous disease in Russia.[33]

Peter's death was quickly absorbed into popular folk myth and produced some curious consequences. Though German in his cultural style, and a man who never identified with the Russian

---

[32] *Arkhiv kniazia Vorontsova*, xxi. 430 for the note. Count Rostopchin reported that when Paul saw the note he thanked God that she (Catherine) was not involved. Ibid. 431-2. See also Dashkova's memoirs, *Arkhiv kniazia Vorontsova*, xviii. 94 and n.

[33] Turgenev, *La Cour de Russie*, 317, for an abridged version of the circular with comments. To Poniatowski, Catherine added some flourishes: 'La colique hémorroïdale lui reprit avec le transport au cerveau; il fut deux jours dans cet état, d'où s'ensuivit une grande faiblesse, et, malgré les secours des médecins, il rendit l'âme en demandant un prétre luthérien.' She also confessed to a fear that the officers guarding him might have given him poison, 'so much was he hated'. *Mémoires* (Herzen), 365-6. Keith wrote: 'On Sunday last, about ten at night, a secretary from the College of Foreign Affairs brought me a paper to read. It was in French and to the following purpose. The Imperial Ministry of Russia think themselves obliged to inform the Foreign Ministers that the late Emperor, *le cy-devant Empereur*, having had a violent cholick occasioned by the Piles with which he was frequently incommoded, dyed yesterday.' PRO, SP/90/70, no. 83, St Petersburg, 9/20 July 1762. For d'Alembert's sly remark, Morane, *Paul Ier*, 57-8.

people, Peter became a kind of populist symbol. Where peasant anger against the landlords rose, 'good tsar Peter' was invoked to rally the rebels against the gentry and the evil woman who supported them. At least two false Peters were declared before the most dangerous of them all, the cossack Emelion Pugachev, announced in 1773 that he was Peter III come back to rescue Russia and her people from the thieves despoiling her. He also declared his firm intention to establish his son, Paul, on the throne. Paul's portrait was prominently displayed in Pugachev's headquarters. Undoubtedly the Pugachev uprising would have happened whether Peter III had lived or not, but his name on the rebel's proclamations served as a bitter reminder of how and why he died. Moreover, Pugachev's advocacy of Paul's rights, coming at the very time that Paul reached his majority and, according to some, should have replaced Catherine, was even more disturbing.[34]

Looking at Paul's life from the end rather than the beginning, it would be difficult to exaggerate the importance of Catherine's *coup*. In political terms, though Catherine confirmed him as her successor, she also took over all the powers Paul thought belonged to him. For thirty-four years, Catherine's success left her son languishing far from the centre of Russian political life, a man with an indefinite future and a wholly truncated present. Even as a boy, Paul resented his loss and feared the woman who had seized his inheritance. As he pondered on what had happened to him, he came to the mature conviction that it was his purpose in life to undo the evil Catherine and her cohorts had done to Russia when they took what was rightfully his. If Catherine had to consider Paul a kind of rival in the decade after her revolution, he learnt to see her and her nearest supporters as his enemies. Had she been willing to admit him to her confidence as he grew older, or to give him some status in her government, he might well have responded differently; as we shall see, however, she could not, and their basic relationship remained one in which the empress dominated and the grand duke observed all her requirements while hating his subordination.

The *coup* could only have been a major trauma for an insecure and sensitive child. Paul must have been terrified. Panin protected him the first night, taking him into his own bed, but in the morning Panin had to be elsewhere. Paul was forgotten, virtually abandoned, until someone, possibly Catherine herself, noticed his absence. It was said that on that day, Paul fainted or had a seizure when someone remarked in his hearing that Peter had intended he should die. The

---

[34] Fleischhacker, 'Porträt', 188 and n.

story was interpreted to mean that he was epileptic, though nothing in his medical history supports that allegation.[35] In the aftermath of the *coup*, however, Paul's health, never strong, deteriorated markedly. He was repeatedly ill, twice very seriously, and it was widely believed that he would never survive his childhood. How much of this was due to the traumas he suffered on 29–30 June 1762 cannot be more than guessed at; it is not unreasonable, however, to suppose that there was a connection.

Personally and politically, Catherine's *coup* was the most important event to have occurred in Paul's young life. And its shadow hung over the rest of his days. His life-long preoccupation with legitimacy and loyalty can be traced to the events of 1762 which he could neither forgive nor forget. His father's death, the long-held suspicion that Catherine was responsible for the deed done by Alexis Orlov and his colleagues, helped to convince him that his own life could well be forfeit to those who stood nearest to him. Paul not only developed a fixation about revolutions and the conspiracies which he believed produced them, but he looked for them first among the members of his family, particularly his eldest sons and his second wife, whose intention to betray him he seemed almost to take for granted. And in his last days, he appeared to be reliving the earlier *coup* with himself in Peter's role.[36] The revolt of 1762 became an obsession with Paul, a mirror in which he saw his world, and a kind of prophecy of his own fate. His belief in this became, in fact, the first long stride on the path which led him to the Michael Palace thirty-nine years later.

---

[35] Sabathier de Cabre, 19 Aug. (NS) 1770, Turgenev, *La Cour de Russie*, 252. On Paul's health, see below, Ch. 3. There is no independent evidence to support de Cabre's allegation.

[36] 'Iz zapisok grafa Lanzherona', *Tsareubiistvo 11 Marta 1801* (1907), 138–40. See below, Ch. 10.

3
FORMATIVE YEARS: 1762–1773

Paul's formal education was Count Panin's responsibility. On the whole, he discharged it very well. He created a comfortable environment in which Paul lived, for the most part happily, for thirteen years, while studying a rich and varied curriculum under a surprisingly good group of teachers. Panin's success with Paul owed to his own broad cultural background, his sympathetic and kindly ways, his personal commitment to Paul's welfare, and to the educational philosophy on which he built his programme. When chosen *oberhofmeister* for the heir, Panin knew little or nothing about his future charge. But he was familiar with several European courts, and he was interested in contemporary educational theories. Muscovy's princes had traditionally received a narrow training based on theology. The cultural climate, however, had changed radically since the seventeenth century, and no one seriously considered a traditional Russian education for Paul. The problem was to choose among contemporary European alternatives.[1]

While on diplomatic service at the Swedish court, Panin was favourably impressed with a plan Count Tessin devised for educating Sweden's crown prince Gustave Adolph. He was also interested in Leibnitz's educational ideas which were in vogue at several German courts and which Jakob von Stählin had brought to Russia in the course of his own ill-starred efforts to repair Grand Duke Peter Fedorovich's educational deficiencies.[2] Panin followed none of these examples slavishly, but rather formulated a plan of his own in which these influences, together with progressive ideas from such as Comenius, Fénélon, and Locke, joined with Panin's own moral and political convictions to compound an approach he thought appropriate for one who someday would govern Russia. The progressive

---

[1] Ransel, *Panin Party*, esp. ch. 8, pp. 201 ff.; Kobeko, *Pavel Petrovich*, 8–29; Petr Lebedev, *Grafy Nikita i Petr Paniny* (St Petersburg, 1863), 37–83, for a critical appraisal. See also Morane, *Paul Ier*, 59–62. Poroshin's *Zapiski*, the only intimate source for Paul's life under Panin, has been read to show the frivolity of Paul's education (Lebedev) and its high quality (Ransel). Our judgement follows Ransel.

[2] *Aus dem Papieren Jakob von Stählins*, ed. K. Stählin, 103 ff.; Fleischhacker, 'Porträt', 128–9.

elements in Panin's plan make it a landmark of sorts in the history of Russian educational thinking, though its primary significance for our purpose is for what it tells us about the intentions behind the education Paul received.[3]

The new philosophy as Panin applied it combined a natural, unforced approach to learning with orderliness, regularity, and structure. There was a daily schedule which was to be followed closely, and the moral tone was severe and puritanical. Paul's court was to be maintained in a style 'appropriate to his rank', but it was also to be 'decorated only by decency and good behaviour'. This did not mean that life was to be grim or unpleasant. On the contrary, in addition to such formal studies as mathematics and the sciences, religion, history, literature, and language, there was provision for sports and entertainment, including fencing, horseback-riding, and theatricals. Panin defined his own role as one of guide and protector. The routines and regulations he proposed were to be enforced without harsh punishments or threats; there was to be a substantial measure of personal freedom, but always within well-defined limits.

Rote learning was considered inferior to education through experience and Paul was to be led to see and formulate for himself the principles which governed both the natural world and the social order. To this end, teaching aids, including maps, charts, and globes, observational instruments and specimen collections, were essential. But Panin went further. Paul's household was to be a learning environment dedicated to his instruction with the dinner table as a kind of centrepiece. Dinner became a forum for discussing virtually anything, but especially such important subjects as history and politics, philosophy, literature, and science. There were always guests drawn from the court, the army, the diplomatic service, and the arts and sciences, and as the conversations flowed, Paul was there to listen, absorb, and occasionally participate. (He also complained and begged tearfully to be excused; high-mindedness could be burdensome for a lively and self-centred boy.)[4] Instructors, in Panin's system, were supposed to be friends and counsellors, not just walking books, who were prepared to turn any circumstance into something worth knowing or understanding. In this respect, Simon Poroshin, the mathematics tutor, seems to have come closest to realizing

---

[3] See N. I. Panin, 'Vse poddaneishee pred'iavlenie slabogo poniatia i mneniia o vospitanii ego imperatorskogo vysochestva, gosudaria velikogo kniazia Pavla Petrovicha', ed. T. A. Sosnovskii, *Russkaia starina*, 36 (Nov. 1882), 315–30; Ransel, *Panin Party*, 204–11, for summary and analysis.

[4] Poroshin, *Zapiski*, pp. 166, 240–1, 246, and *passim*. Ragsdale, *Tsar Paul*, 10, emphasizes impatience and thoughtless arrogance.

Panin's ideal. Sympathetic, warm, knowledgeable, a friend to be trusted with confidences, yet withal a teacher who translated everyday experience into a lesson, Poroshin could have been invented to fit Panin's plan.[5]

The intellectual atmosphere Panin proposed was to reflect both contemporary enlightened values and a strong religious emphasis. There was no room for materialism or agnosticism, to say nothing of atheism; equally, sectarianism and bigotry were to have no place. Panin hoped to have Paul led towards 'an appreciative knowledge of the Creator, His holy purpose in creating us, and our consequent devoted duty to Him', and he believed that these ideas were best approached through the principles of Orthodox Christianity and instruction in the scriptures. Here again Panin was fortunate to find an unusually well-qualified person to instruct his charge. Father Platon Levshin, later metropolitan of Moscow, was a cosmopolitan and enlightened priest who was also pious and deeply committed to his religious vocation. His teachings reinforced Paul's disposition to believe and so consolidated a lifelong religious commitment. They also became a central feature in his political evolution.[6]

The empress Elizabeth, who was deeply religious, was favourably impressed with the central role Panin gave spiritual matters. This was just as well since Elizabeth's approval for the plan was necessary. But Panin's programme also showed his belief in science and the arts as foundations for an educated person's culture. Mathematics occupied a particularly important place since Panin believed that it fostered clear thinking, while humanistic studies including history, literature, and languages were prominent. In the teaching strategies, writing played an important part. Paul was to be set essays in which he was encouraged to express what he thought or felt. The purpose was to engage him in the subject, to make him want to know or understand more while helping him to develop logical organization, elements of

[5] On Poroshin, see Konstantin Nikolaevich, 'Semen Andreevich Poroshin', *Russkii vestnik*, 8 (1866), 421–55.

[6] On Platon Levshin, see K. A. Papmehl, *Metropolitan Platon of Moscow (Petr Levshin, 1737–1812): The Enlightened Prelate, Scholar, and Educator* (Newtonville, Mass., 1983). The author does not discuss Platon's theology but is thorough on his ecclesiastical administrative career. There is no attempt to assess the substance of his teachings to Paul; his teaching role is described from material in Poroshin. Platon's catechism for Paul was *Pravoslavnoe uchenie ili sokrashchennaia khristianskaia gosloviia dlia upotrebleniia ego imperatorskago vysochestva presvetleishago vserossiiskago naslednika, belago vernago gosudaria tsesarevicha i velikago kniazia Pavla Petrovicha* (St Petersburg, 1765: hereafter, *Pravoslavnoe uchenie*). This work subsequently appeared in French, English, and German translations.

Formative Years: 1762–1773

style, and control over the written language. In somewhat the same vein, French and German were taught through conversations. Learning the grammatical rules could wait until Paul's mind was sufficiently mature to grasp and apply them.[7]

Poroshin's diaries confirm the considerable degree to which Panin's progressive principles were implemented. The structure and orderliness in Paul's life were unmistakeable. He rose around 7, dined at 1, and had supper at 8.30. Lessons were done through the morning and in the afternoon after dinner. Religious instruction was given three times a week, while on Sundays and religious holidays there were special readings appropriate to the day or the season before and in addition to the regular church service. Paul participated actively in the social and recreational life of the court. He was at the theatre at least three times a week, appeared occasionally in ballets or spectacles, gave audiences, and assisted at court functions. Only illness and special events—when Catherine visited Moscow, for example—were permitted to interfere with the schedule, or to intrude on the privacy of the household.[8]

No effort was spared to provide Paul with everything his governor claimed he needed. When Panin took over from Bekhteev, an educational fund in excess of 100,000 rubles was already available. Elizabeth added to it. Peter III distrusted and disliked Panin, but he was unwilling to attack him directly, and continued the funds for Paul's household. After Catherine seized the throne, she settled 120,000 rubles a year on her son, made provision for him and his suite to have apartments in the Winter and Summer Palaces, at Tsarskoe Selo (Catherine's favourite), in the Moscow Kremlin, and in 1766 built a residence for him at Kamennyi Ostrov. In addition to Panin, Paul's establishment included a regular teaching staff of six, two personal physicians, and special instructors for dance, fencing, declamation, music, and design. There was also a librarian. The library was particularly impressive. The holdings, which eventually were in excess of 35,000 volumes, built solidly on European classics in history, political philosophy, and literature. Writers of current reputation were well represented, and Russian publications were included as they appeared, though inevitably they comprised only a fraction of the total. It was this library which later became the core

---

[7] For a catalogue of miscellaneous materials useful for appraising Paul's education, see Grand Duke Konstantin Nikolaevich, 'Tsesarevich Pavel Petrovich: Istoricheskie materialy v biblioteke dvortsa goroda Pavlovska'. *Russkaia starina*, 8 (1873), 649–90, 853–84; 9 (1874), 37–56, 277–300, 473–512, and esp. 667–84.

[8] Kobeko, *Pavel Petrovich*, 25–9.

collection for the imperial library of the grand duchy of Finland in Helsinki, and it was one of Paul's most prized possessions.[9] Language training was an important part of Paul's early education. Russian was his native and preferred language, and he continued to study it throughout his schooling years. As we have seen, he spoke French fluently by the time he was 6. He was reading serious literature by the age of 10. French, of course, was the language of high culture, and Paul's reading, at least through his early years, was either in major French authors—Voltaire, Diderot, d'Alembert, Fénélon, Bossuet, Montesquieu, and many more—or in French translations. So it was that he read the histories of Hume and Robertson, Bielfeld's cameralist work, or the classic Roman authors. Paul studied Latin, though not intensively, and he had some exposure to Italian. He never learnt the language well enough to use it, a fact which, according to his second wife, Mariia Fedorovna, he very much regretted while travelling in Italy in 1781–2. He studied and read German, though he seems to have known it less well than either Russian or French, and German literature (except in translation) does not appear in the catalogues of his work. Paul did meet Russian writers, and Poroshin's reports on table conversations indicate that a great deal was said about what Russians were writing and the creative potential in Russian culture. But the high culture Paul absorbed was that of contemporary France, hence the conceptual vocabulary he knew best was, broadly speaking, that of the French Enlightenment.[10]

Though there is no way to measure its effects, the theatre was a persistent, pervasive, and immediate presence in Paul's life. He memorized and declaimed the classic French authors, and hardly a day went by when he did not attend the court theatre where the usual bill was a farce or comedy, a ballet, and a comic opera or some set piece. Possibly one third of the offerings, both drama and dance, were by Russians, though the style was always French. Nor was the substance particularly heavy. Catherine, as Panin was said to have remarked, was not fond of tragedies, and the result was a virtually unrelieved diet of froth and fluff. Paul appeared in some of these productions, and from childhood until well into maturity (the change came after his first wife's death in 1776), he gave a substantial part of his time and attention to theatricals. Even as he came to

[9] Kobeko, *Pavel Petrovich*, 7–16; M. V. Klochkov, *Pravitel'stvennoi deiatel'nosti*, 587 ff.

[10] On Paul and the Enlightenment, Claus Scharf, 'Staatsauffassung und Regierungsprogramm'; Ragsdale, *Tsar Paul*, chs. 2 and 5, for a particularly effective summary of Paul's cultural environment.

Formative Years: 1762–1773

participate less, he continued to attend, while the theatrical style became integral to his public life. Paul thrilled to spectacle and dramatic moments; he loved costumes and playing roles, and when he became tsar, he gave close attention to rituals and ceremonial occasions. His public appearances were carefully orchestrated. Contemporaries complained that the master of ceremonies was the most important official in Paul's court, and in at least one sense they were right: pageant was a necessary adjunct to majesty; the court was theatre.[11]

By the time Paul reached 14, he was an accomplished courtier. He commanded most of the social graces, had a passing familiarity with the classics of his time, and had achieved a firmly grounded religious faith. He showed skill in both mathematics and drawing, was a good if cautious horseman, a passable fencer, and an acceptable dancer. He had little interest in science. His greatest pleasures came from drama and history, a not unlikely combination, though the history which interested him most was moral and European. He was drawn to the stories of such royal martyrs as Henry IV and Charles I, or the faithful Buckingham who was slaughtered in the Stuart service. He also pondered the life of Marie de Medici and the fate of Julius Caesar, and he immersed himself in the unremitting struggle of the knights of St John of Jerusalem, the very model of aristocratic chivalry and Christian caring, against the infidel. Underlying all of this, as well as the way he saw the history of his own times, was the confrontation between self-interested and criminally ambitious men and women who forgot the loyalty they owed to those who trusted them, and faithful, dedicated, yet modest heroes who knew what their responsibilities were and if necessary gave their lives to discharge them. Russia's distant past piqued the curiosity of his circle, but Paul showed little interest in it and was taught relatively little about it. In contrast, Peter the Great was a regular topic for discussion, and the Petrine era formed a major segment of Paul's historical studies.[12]

If only because it was planned and systematically carried out, Paul's early education was probably better than that of most

---

[11] Poroshin, *Zapiski, passim* shows the frequency of Paul's theatre attendance. See also Kobeko, *Pavel Petrovich*, 35–8. On the importance of ceremonial for Paul as tsar, McGrew, 'Political Portrait', 515–16; Wortman, 'Images of Rule'.

[12] Ransel, *Panin Party*, esp. 287 ff., stresses Peter the Great's importance in Paul's education. Paul's historical interests appear in Konstantin Nikolaevich, 'Tsesarevich Pavel Petrovich', *Russkaia starina*, 9 (1874), 679–84. McGrew, 'Paul I and the Knights', 45 and n. 3, 67. Paul's interest was rooted in l'abbé Vertot's monumental history of the order.

contemporary princes and Paul was a good student, quick to learn, with a retentive memory. He was also a complex and difficult person who needed special attention. The child Panin met in 1758 was nervous, highly strung, and sensitive. Panin's plan permitted, even encouraged, a natural and unforced development through childhood and into adolescence under conditions which were secure and in the company of people who showed concern and affection. The style of Paul's early education thus fitted closely with his deepest emotional needs. He was never challenged beyond his capacities; his daily routines were orderly and stable; and the discipline he lived with was unobtrusive and benign. Crises occurred outside this protected world; within, there was authority, order, and peace. If this was a poor preparation for dealing with the contentious and violent society which lay just beyond Paul's door, it also meant that he suffered little provocation, and the umbrageous, defensive, sometimes paranoid, and potentially explosive side to his personality was seldom seen. It was, however, there.

Before his adolescent years, Paul was small and wiry, winsome, graceful, and compact. The broad forehead, large eyes, and tipped-up nose which appear in his later portraits were already plainly visible, though the face itself was full and rounded. A picture in the possession of the Stroganov family, which showed him at the age of 7, in later years was confused by people unfamiliar with the gallery with a portrait of Paul's eldest son, Alexander, at the same age. Alexander was a notably attractive child, and so, it would appear, was Paul.[13] By the age of 17, however, his childish bloom was long past. He was described as small of stature, and meagre in muscle, bulk, and bone. He showed early signs of baldness, and his skin had a yellowish tinge. His best feature was thought to be his eyes which were large and luminous. He had strong teeth which seemed oversized and out of proportion to his mouth and jaw, while his bony face with its tight-stretched skin reminded some observers of a death's head. The comparison was extreme, though not entirely inaccurate. As he grew older, Paul developed a rather affected stance and gait together with an ironic twist to his lips. He also put on weight, his trunk thickening and becoming less agile. As an adult, Paul was physically unattractive, and even as a young man, his manner could be more pleasing than his appearance. As a child, however, he had been both appealing and attractive.[14]

[13] Golovkine, *La Cour de Paul Ier*, 100.
[14] Ibid. Thomas Dimsdale's physical description of Paul tallied with Golovkin's. See *Tracts on Inoculation Written and Published at St. Petersburg in the Year 1768 by Command of Her Imperial Majesty, The Empress of All the Russias, with*

Fedor Golovkin laid Paul's physical transformation to a severe illness which he was supposed to have suffered in 1764 or 1765. Since the condition involved operations, it may have been diphtheria, though Paul's personal physician referred only to suppurating glands.[15] Other explanations for his appearance were that he suffered from a dangerous nervous disorder, or that he had inherited a debilitating condition which sapped his vitality and engendered a premature ageing. Catherine reported that Paul's nearly fatal illness in 1771 radically altered his appearance, though what she was describing was maturation rather than degeneration.[16] In his early years, he learnt to exhibit a certain grave formality of manner which suited the ritual functions he was expected to perform. Behind that façade, however, was an energetic, possibly hyperkinetic boy who could never be still. His excessive energy bubbled over in irrepressible enthusiasms and exploded in excitment. Poroshin recorded how Paul was always moving and always ahead of everybody else. He bounded out of bed, rushed to table before meals were ready, finished before others were barely started, and then complained about how slow they all were. And he kept the same pace going until night when he was impatient to go to bed in anticipation of the new day coming. He talked incessantly, argued interminably, and when angered or frustrated, grumbled and complained long after the occasion had passed. His explosive vitality was married to a compulsive stubbornness which made him difficult and wearying as well as quick, frank, naïve, and occasionally winning.

Poroshin was devoted to Paul, and poured all his energies into guiding, counselling, and teaching him. In turn, Paul gave Poroshin his confidence, talking freely with him about his most intimate feelings. It is not surprising, then, that Poroshin's diary contains the most detailed record available of what Paul said and did, or that it presents the most favourable assessment of Paul's abilities and character that we have. Poroshin believed that Paul was an extraordinary child, a boy who, as he remarked, had he been born to a less

---

Additional Observations on Epidemic Small-Pox, on the Nature of that Disease, and on the different Success of the various Makes of Inoculation (London, 1781), 46–52. Mme Vigée-Lebrun thought Paul's appearance lent itself to caricature. Waliszewski, *Paul Ier*, 50–1.

[15] 'Extrait des maladies survenus à Son Altesse impériale depuis Sa Naissance jusqu'à ce jour', St Petersburg, 23 Sept. (os) 1768, by G. Foussadier, Dimsdale Family Papers, A–38. I am most grateful to Mr Robert Dimsdale for showing me this and other materials relating to Baron Dimsdale's visits to Russia in 1768 and 1781.

[16] Catherine II to Mme Bielke, 12 Aug. (os) 1771; 29 Aug. (os) 1771; 3 Oct. (os) 1771, SIRIO, 13, pp. 144–5, 148–9, 172–4.

exalted station might well have become a Russian Pascal.[17] This was a child of strong imagination and intuitive intelligence, a child of feeling who needed careful training to channel his energies into an enlightened, humanitarian, and spiritually rich maturity. Poroshin's hopes were probably exaggerated, and they were certainly coloured by his own sensibilities, but even allowing for such a bias, Paul, as Poroshin portrayed him, promised exceedingly well.

This is not to say that Poroshin was blind to Paul's weaknesses, or that he was unaware that there were difficulties in dealing with him. Poroshin believed that Paul suffered from having things too much his own way, and while he was affectionate and could be loving, he was also swift to resent any interference with what he wanted. Disciplining Paul, especially in the permissive atmosphere Panin created (and with which Poroshin was entirely in accord) was extremely difficult, and there was always the temptation to let him have his head. But that way led to chaos, for Paul was uncompromising, unaccommodating, and giving in to his demands only weakened an adult's position. Since his outbursts tended to be as short as they were violent, Poroshin believed that it was best to be firm and to resist him, though always explaining the necessity for doing so. How well this tactic worked is hard to tell. Paul accepted authority, defended the way his teachers taught him, and revealed an underlying dependence on them which made their task easier. But this exposed a contradiction in his character which appeared again and again. Though headstrong, demanding, and even arrogant, Paul relied on others for direction, apparently needing the security of some authority he could accept. Despite temperament and tantrums, he was essentially submissive. He was also fickle, changing his affections according to the influence of the last person who talked with him. It was not at all unusual for someone to be on good, even intimate terms with him one day, and to be treated with cold disdain the next. It usually meant that someone else had whispered in his ear. Such versatility, lack of consistency, and willingness to believe the worst he heard made Paul vulnerable to manipulation as well as an object for dislike. It also led Poroshin to warn him that, unless he was very careful, he would end by making himself hated. The warning was, in fact, a prophecy.[18]

Beyond his changeable disposition, Paul showed a violent temper. Poroshin seemed to believe that Paul's temper flared when he was frustrated, and that with patience it would soon be over. But others

[17] Poroshin, *Zapiski* (1844), 22.
[18] Ibid. 89 ff.; Kobeko, *Pavel Petrovich*, 29–32. De Grunwald, *L'Assassinat*, 30, notes negative aspects in Poroshin's description of Paul. Cf. Zubow, *Paul der Erste*, 23–5.

thought the problem more serious. Aepinus, a distinguished scientist, and another of Paul's instructors, remarked that while the grand duke normally was rational and capable of cool, connected thought, there appeared to be a sort of mechanism in his mind which, when triggered, took over entirely, and then cool reason disappeared until the storm had run its course.[19] Nearly four decades later, Paul's daughter-in-law, Tsar Alexander's wife, remembered the terrifying speed with which Paul would change from a pleasant if rather mannered demeanour to one of total fury, with his neck corded and swollen, his face red, and his eyes blazing. Though worse when he was older, Paul's temper was a problem for him throughout his life. In the aftermath of his explosions, he sometimes showed guilt, even apologized, and as a young man he came to recognize that his penchant for furious rage was something which he had to control. Control, however, also generated further tensions, and when the Aepinus mechanism was set in motion, Paul's efforts to restrain it only seemed to make the final outburst worse.[20]

Volatile and temperamental, Paul was also thought to be physically delicate, so much so that there was more than ordinary concern over whether he would survive to maturity. The diplomatic correspondence from 1754 to 1771 is peppered with references to his illnesses. These matters were reported regularly since Count Panin conducted Russia's diplomatic business, and when Paul was sick, Panin was invariably unavailable.[21] Panin was, if anything, overly solicitous of Paul's health. This was an obvious way to show his devotion and commitment to duty. He also knew that it was dangerous to give the impression that Paul was too sickly to be able to survive. That issue became important during the court's stay in Moscow at the time of Catherine's coronation when Paul's ill health was used to support the argument that Catherine should marry and

[19] Kobeko, *Pavel Petrovich*, 32.
[20] At the time of Paul's accession, Count Cobenzl, the Austrian ambassador, remarked that 'at base he [Paul] has a feeling heart, though the first movement [of his rage] is terrible'. Haus-Hof und Staatsarchiv (hereafter HHSA), Russland II Berichte, Carton 84, no. 79, apostille 2, Cobenzl to Thugut, 15/26 Dec. (NS) 1796. Paul's temper was an important element in his poor reputation as grand duke. McGrew, 'Political Portrait', 504–11.
[21] The English correspondence is typical. References to Paul's poor health or instances of illness appear in PRO, SP/19/70, no. 193, Moscow, 21 Oct. (NS) 1762; no. 233, Moscow, 4 Nov. (NS) 1762; SP/91/71, no. 67, Moscow, 27 Jan. (NS) 1763 (a new condition) identified in no. 75, 31 Jan. (NS) 1763 as measles; no. 102, Moscow, 21 Feb. (NS) 1763 (smallpox feared); no. 96, St Petersburg, 22 Aug. (NS) 1763 (a weak constitution and expectation of an early and inevitable death); no. 38, 23 Dec. (NS) 1763; no. 50, St Petersburg, 10 Jan. (NS) 1764; no. 80, St Petersburg, 31 Jan. (NS) 1764; etc.

secure the succession. In this case, Panin took Paul out for a long ride in inclement weather, and then showed him off in public, mud-spattered and rosy with exertion, the very picture of rude health.[22] It was Panin's duty to protect Paul, so far as he could, from the illnesses to which he was susceptible. Such susceptibilities, however, did not mean, as contemporaries were inclined to say, that Paul was congenitally weak, or that his health was such as to arouse concern for the succession.

The particular problems from which Paul suffered are difficult to identify. This would be true even if there were extensive contemporary medical records, which there are not. What do exist are various comments in contemporaries' correspondence, and the brief medical history which Paul's physicians compiled for Dr (later Baron) Thomas Dimsdale in 1768 to assist him in preparing Paul for his smallpox inoculation. When Dimsdale examined Paul, he described him as being 'of a susceptible but sound constitution'. He thought him rather underdeveloped, but perfectly healthy with no signs of nervous or physical disorders. He was inclined to agree with Paul's physicians (and with Catherine) that the sickliness all noted probably owed to the inadequate, even incompetent, treatment he had received as a baby.[23]

The medical history itself, though not detailed, is helpful in confirming the picture of a child prone to repeated superficial illnesses. Paul had both measles and chicken pox, the latter shortly before he was inoculated. He began life, as we have seen, with a severe attack of gumboils, became colicky, suffered repeated gastric upsets and diarrhoeas, severe constipation and haemorrhoids, and proved to be extremely susceptible to respiratory infections, colds, swollen glands, and what was probably influenza. Colds and flu were endemic to Petersburg, which had the reputation of being one of the most unhealthy spots in Europe. This, given Paul's propensity for respiratory illness, justified concern and rigorous preventive measures. Beyond that, his digestive system troubled him throughout his life. He had to be careful about what and how much he ate, and he was always abstemious with alcohol. His most serious illness was in 1771 when he suffered a violent influenza or possibly an attack of typhus. It was weeks before he was pronounced out of danger, and longer still before he finally recovered.[24] That was also, however, the last time that he was dangerously ill. His health stabilized with maturity.

[22] Morane, *Paul Ier*, 40, cites Bérenger, 30 May (NS) 1763.
[23] Foussadier, 'Extrait des maladies'; Dimsdale, *Tracts on Inoculation*, 45–51.
[24] Kobeko, *Pavel Petrovich*, 64–5; see below, Ch. 4, on Paul's illness with flu (or typhus).

There are no credible data to support the idea that Paul was syphilitic, a theory put forward to explain his alleged madness in the last years of his life, nor does his medical history sustain the idea that he suffered from severe neurological disorders. On the other hand, chronic digestive problems, repeated sickness vaguely defined, and tendencies toward insomnia and nightmares all suggest tension, nervousness, and stress.[25] Once Paul matured, he was seldom physically sick, but he was always compulsive about his body's needs. In the instruction he prepared for his second wife, he called attention to the special consideration his state of health required. He emphasized that leading a carefully regulated life was the key to keeping himself well. He needed a fixed early bedtime and punctual meals. Sleep was especially important. To be certain that he would sleep well, his bed had to occupy a particular place in the room; the room temperature had to be rigidly controlled; and he had to lie in the bed in a certain place and posture. If these conditions were not met, he would be condemned to a sleepless night and suffer in consequence the dangers of a diminished constitution and vitality.[26]

Paul's constitution, in fact, was better than its reputation. He survived the most serious of his illnesses to grow into a healthy, strong maturity. He was a good horseman, capable of long hours in the saddle; he spared himself no more than he did his officers or men on the drill field and in manœuvres; and he lived a hard, active, spartan life to the day he died. Nevertheless, what we learn from the medical record complements the sources describing his behaviour, and fills out the picture of a tense, driven, even compulsive personality whose ultimate refuge, physical as well as psychological, was in discipline and an ordered scheme of life.

Paul's sexual awakening was gradual and unforced. Poroshin claimed that at 11 Paul was unaware of the difference between males and females, and when he asked about them, Poroshin put him off. He did not consider the topic worthy of pursuit. Yet there was sex all around. The court theatre dealt with love in all its mannered forms, and this seems to have impressed Paul, setting off undefined longings which he found difficult to express. Talk of marriage embarrassed him. When queried about it at the age of 12, he told a group of adults that he knew he would marry, and that he would undoubtedly love

---

[25] There are repeated references to a 'degenerative disease' and to epilepsy in the literature on Paul. There is no evidence beyond speculation. Such concepts play no part in either Chizh's or Ragsdale's analyses, though both are profoundly concerned with Paul's mental-emotional and neurological make-up.

[26] Paul Petrovich, 'Instruktsiia velikago kniazia Pavla Petrovicha velikoi kniagine Marii Fedorovne (1776)', ed. Shumigorskii, *Russkaia starina*, 93 (1893), 247–61.

his wife very much. He also knew that he would be jealous, and that it would be hateful to him to be made 'to wear horns'. He confided that what troubled him was that those who wore horns neither saw nor felt them, so how would he know when he was wearing them? His perplexity won a general laugh.[27]

Sexual teasing was common currency in the court, though Panin did not much approve and tried to deflect it from Paul. Catherine, after visiting the Smol'nyi institute for girls which she had founded, asked Paul if that wasn't really where he wanted to live, while at the theatre she would whisper in his ear, calling his attention to the charms of different actresses or ballerinas, and asking which of them attracted him the most. Or she would cross-question him as though he had a secret love among her maids of honour. These sallies usually reduced Paul to embarrassed confusion, but on one occasion, Count Grigorii Orlov, Catherine's long-time favourite, delighted Paul with the proposal that they visit his mother's maids of honour in their quarters. Paul wanted to go, but held back for fear of offending Catherine. When she approved, however, he went off in high glee with Orlov and Panin in attendance. When he came back, he was full of his adventure, buttonholing all and sundry with an excited, 'Can you guess where I went?' Finally he settled down to moon and daydream before gathering himself up to go to Poroshin to whom he related the whole adventure. He and his tutor then sat down with the encyclopaedia to read the article on 'l'Amour' all the way through.[28]

These titillations soon gave way to a severe case of first love. Paul became entranced with young Vera Choglokova, an orphan raised at court to become one of Catherine's maids of honour. Her parents, who had died ten years earlier, had been responsible for overseeing Catherine and Peter when they were grand duke and duchess, and played a part in Catherine's affair with Saltykov. This gives a certain symmetry to Paul's infatuation. When Panin asked Paul in September 1765, how long he had been in love, Paul told him that it had been since the previous December, while Poroshin's entries through the fall of 1765 and up to January 1766, catalogue the progress of this first awakening. Paul was all innocence as he worked up his courage to approach Vera. Eventually he danced with her, talked with her, became jealous of another's interest in her, and so fell more and more deeply in love. Catherine encouraged him, Panin chaffed him, and Poroshin sympathized with him, while Paul suffered happily through these delicious miseries.

[27] Kobeko, *Pavel Petrovich*, 39. [28] Ibid. 40.

What happened to end this tale is obscure. Poroshin's diary breaks off abruptly in January 1766, while Paul was still in the grip of his gentle passion. It must, however, have faded rapidly as Baron Osten-Sacken wrote to Prince Alexander Kurakin in May that the 'amorous intrigues' connected with Mademoiselle Choglokov had ended with the masquerade season. Whether Paul lost interest or the affair was interrupted is not known; it appears to have been an innocent infatuation which simply faded away.[29] Two years later, when Catherine was seriously considering finding a bride for Paul, she met the objection that his poor health might prevent his being sexually active and fathering a child. That objection was removed in the most direct way possible. A young widow, the daughter of a former governor of Novgorod, was engaged to sleep with Paul. This Sophie Chartorizhkaia, who was described as 'elegant' and a 'petite-maitresse', shared Paul's bed, became pregnant, and bore a son. Paul was captivated by his mistress, but he was made to understand that he had to give her up. There is no indication that he ever looked back.[30]

According to Panin's original plan, when Paul reached 14 his training was to change its focus from general studies to the specialized work necessary to prepare him to govern. Unfortunately, that aspect to his education never developed. At the time Panin drew up his prospectus, he may have thought it would be indiscreet or even dangerous to say much that was specific about the day when Paul would reign. The empress Elizabeth hated any reference to her own mortality, while Grand Duke Peter Fedorovich was at odds with Catherine. Paul's future, at that time, was better not discussed. The situation did not improve after the *coup*. Paul was the hope of Catherine's opposition. Were Panin, powerful as he was in his own right, to have pressed the issue of Paul's practical training (which carried the implication of a governmental role) he would have

---

[29] For the course of Paul's infatuation, Poroshin, *Zapiski*, for 1765: (all dates OS): 15 Sept.; 7, 10, 13, 14, 18, 20, 21, 28, 29 Oct.; 1, 4, 24 Nov.; 11 Dec.; 3 Jan. 1766. Panin asked Paul if he were in love, and if so, for how long on 2 Sept. Paul confessed that it was since the previous Dec. Poroshin, *Zapiski, Russkaia starina*, 32 (1881), 412–13. This exchange does not appear in the 1st (1844) edn. See p. 394. On the affair's end, Osten-Sacken to Prince Alexandre Kurakin, 9 May (OS) 1766, *Arkhiv kniazia F. A. Kurakina*, ed. M. I. Semevskii and V. N. Smolianinov (Saratov, 1894), v, no. 901, p. 278. For a summary, Kobeko, *Pavel Petrovich*, 40–5.

[30] Kobeko, *Pavel Petrovich*, 67–9. Paul's son was named Simon Velikii. He was raised in Catherine's apartments to the age of 8 when he was sent to the Peter Paul School to be educated. He was not told who he was nor why he was cared for; his friends were to be the children of obscure persons. He entered the navy, became lieutenant, and was sent to England for additional training. Seconded to the English service, he died in the Antilles in 1794.

appeared to align himself with that opposition. This was by no means his intention, nor could he have wanted even inadvertently to encourage the idea that Paul was being readied to challenge his mother. Less dramatically, during the period from the *coup* to the outbreak of the Turkish war, that is, from 1762 to 1768, Panin was the most important figure in Catherine's government, and he remained a major actor through the end of his service as Paul's governor in 1773. Preparing an advanced curriculum for Paul and overseeing it, especially as it would have been politically sensitive, was a task for which he had neither the time nor the will.

Paul never had the intensive work in statecraft for which his general education supposedly prepared him, nor was he ever pushed intellectually to the point where he had to master a discipline. Some projects started, but none survived. Paul himself ended a series of lessons based on current senate cases which Teplov, one of Catherine's state secretaries, set for him. The work was so excruciatingly boring that it was said that Teplov's secret assignment was to disenchant Paul with further administrative studies. If this was so, he succeeded admirably. A further experiment which had Paul attend state council meetings foundered on his own abrasive and hectoring manner, and when Catherine tried personally to take his political education in hand, she found she had neither the time nor the patience for the exercise.[31]

Whereas regularity and systematic organization marked Paul's early education, his last four years of formal studies were essentially extemporized. Some interesting people joined his circle, including H. L. Nicolay, the historian, Levesque, and François Lafermière. Nicolay and Lafermière became permanent members of Paul's household, remaining with him into, and in Nicolay's case through, his reign as tsar. Lafermière worked with Paul's theatre, Leveque was librarian for a time, while Nicolay initially taught poetics. All had literary reputations, all were in the swim of contemporary philosophical discourse, and all reinforced prevailing French literary influences and a modishly enlightened view of politics.[32]

---

[31] The charge that Paul's education was neglected referred to the later stages. There is also less known about this period. See: Ransel, *Panin Party*, 209–12; Kobeko, *Pavel Petrovich*, 53–8; Sabathier de Cabres, *Catherine II; Sa cour et la Russie en 1772* (Berlin, 1862), 36 (on Panin) and esp. 47–9. De Corberon, who came to Russia in 1775, remarked on how undeveloped, even childish, Paul was. Marie Daniel Bourée, baron de Corberon, *Un diplomat français à la cour de Catherine II*, 2 vols. (Paris, 1901), i. 82, 93. Gunning called the neglect of Paul's education shameful. Turgenev, *La Cour de Russie*, 4 Aug. (NS) 1772, p. 253.

[32] Kobeko, *Pavel Petrovich*, 53–4. Nicolay was interested in political economy and was an important member of the empress's party in 1797–8.

Paul also maintained close personal friendships with Count A. G. Razumovskii and Prince A. B. Kurakin. Both had been educated in Europe, Razumovskii at Strasburg (where Nicolay originated) and Kurakin at Leiden. Kurakin became one of Paul's most assiduous correspondents. During his long years abroad, he provided detailed descriptions and commentary on his own university education as well as political and social institutions in the Netherlands, England, and France.[33] These letters are remarkable for the breadth and depth of coverage, for the insights offered, and for the enlightened character of the judgements. Kurakin was favourably impressed with much that he saw, particularly the evidence of freedom and material progress, though he was always careful to emphasize what was superior in Russia (the stability and order associated with autocracy) and how fortunate he was to be a Russian citizen. Paul's side to the correspondence is meagre, amounting to no more than warm thanks and appreciation, so we have no idea how he may have reacted to specific points. It is worth noting, however, that Kurakin became 'chancellor' for Paul's grand ducal court until Catherine exiled him to Saratov in 1782. He returned as vice-chancellor in Paul's first government. Another correspondence which began in 1774, the year after Paul's first marriage, and continued sporadically for more than a decade, brought news of the Parisian cultural and social scene. These letters were written by the critic and author, Jean la Harpe, and are notable primarily for their superficiality and arrogance. They help to explain, however, Paul's familiarity with what was passing in literary circles abroad.[34]

In later years paradomania, a consuming interest in the minutiae of military life, dominated Paul. This had almost nothing to do with his early education. Panin was a man of peace who did not consider army training a desirable preparation for ruling. Such attention as military affairs received from him was in the context of diplomacy or finance. He deplored too lively an interest in war or its accoutrements. Paul gave him reason to be concerned. He enjoyed playing at soldiers or war games. He loved muskets and cannons, uniforms and

---

[33] See *Arkhiv F. A. Kurakina*, v–vii, May 1767–Mar. 1773. There are 18 letters, totalling 115 pp. Paul followed this correspondence closely, but his few and formulaic letters in reply are not included. Morane, *Paul Ier*, 64–73, summarizes some of Kurakin's views.

[34] Jean-François La Harpe, *Correspondance littéraire adressée á Son Altesse Impériale Mgr. le Grand Duc* [Paul] *Aujourd'hui Empereur de Russie, et à M. le comte Schowalow, chambellan de l'Impératrice Catherine II, depuis 1774 jusqu'à 1789*, 4 vols. (Paris, 1801). This was not the La Harpe who tutored Paul's son, Alexander, whose name was Frédéric Caesar, though the two are sometimes confused.

fortresses, drums, bugles, and parades. When at the age of 11 he was allowed to attend manœuvres at Krasnoe Selo, he became so overexcited he fell ill. He treasured Colonel (later Field-Marshal) Kamenskii's description of Frederick the Great's manœuvres at Breslau which the author, despite Panin's disapproval, gave him personally, and he took great satisfaction in discharging his ceremonial duties as grand admiral of the fleet. Later, he was pleased when the director of the naval cadet school, Ivan Golenishchev-Kutuzov, consulted him, invited him to attend classes, and encouraged him to study naval tactics and marine architecture. In this same vein, Panin's brother, Peter, a distinguished general, also actively encouraged Paul's military interests. Yet Nikita Panin's efforts to protect Paul against exposure to the army, and especially its most glamorous side, never wavered. Even when Paul went off to Berlin in 1776 to meet his second wife, Panin wrote to Frederick urging him not to show Paul much of military pomp. Frederick agreed and, as might have been expected, did as he wished. Paul was delighted with the parades and manœuvres.[35]

If Paul never learnt to write a budget, draft a law, or conduct a military campaign, he came from the long years under Panin's tutelage with a strong sense of what he believed a monarch ought to be, and what his obligations were. These convictions, which remained with him to the end of his life, represented the nearest approach to a political philosophy that he possessed. Evidence about them is fragmentary, but there are some revealing items. In 1763, for example, before he was 9 years old, he set down a number of aphorisms, the first of which was dated 8 April: 'So to master both tongue and face that they never betray the heart's secrets is an art which cannot be ignored.' On 18 September, and in a warmer spirit entirely, he recorded the opinion that 'the king's glory is his people's prosperity; his power and his glory reside in the hearts of his subjects'. A week later he abjured himself, 'Be just and impartial and act with [all] men as you would have them do with you.' And he concluded, 'The Prince's best defence is his goodness and virtue.' Finally, on 20 October, he asserted that 'He who neglects his reputation is inclined to give small weight to virtue.' And as if to remind himself, 'It is never necessary to provoke anyone.'[36]

[35] Kobeko, *Pavel Petrovich*, 56–8. Poroshin's diary shows that military subjects often were discussed in Paul's presence (Poroshin was himself an officer), and Paul was interested in all aspects.

[36] 'Slovesny uprazhneniia velikago kniazia Pavla Petrovicha', *Russkaia starina*, 32 (1881), 626–7.

Henry IV of France, who was Paul's hero and a model he sought to emulate, embodied the virtues which were essential to the ruling monarch. Some eight years after the aphorisms, Paul eulogized Henry for his commitment to his people's welfare, for his frankness, his simplicity of style and manner, for his courage, and for his love of humanity. Henry exiled the self-interested, curtailed superfluous luxuries, and found his greatest fulfilment, or so Paul saw it, in serving the people. If such a ruler, Paul mused, were to appear in Russia, correcting false policies, softening harsh spirits, and civilizing unsociable manners, the Russian people would be the envy of their neighbours. This was a man who 'never sought to be great, but only wished to be useful' to the people who were in his charge.[37]

Paul's formal religious instruction under Father Platon, which began in 1763, had a political side which was complementary with the spirit of the aphorisms and the values Paul identified in Henry IV. At the time he was selected to be Paul's catechizer, confessor, spiritual father, and religious mentor, Platon was already known for his powerful sermons and his enlightened outlook. He became as distinguished and as widely known in ecclesiastical and theological matters as Panin was in politics. The catechism which he prepared for Paul was translated and published throughout Europe. Travellers who knew nothing else about Russia knew who Platon was and sought him out, while within the Russian church he contributed in important ways to seminary education and ecclesiastical administration. In the later years of Catherine's reign, Platon's career suffered from his close association with Paul and his family. Ironically, when Paul became tsar, Platon almost immediately lost favour with him and never recovered. There was no personal contact between the two men after 1798.[38] In the early years, however, Platon, whom Paul liked and respected, was so placed as to be able to influence him strongly, so much so that Paul's later political behaviour virtually mirrored the principles Platon taught him.

Platon's message for Paul was that God had chosen him to rule Russia, that no law which man might make could call him to account, that the ruler's statutes had the force of divine decree, and that observing God's law was the best, indeed the only way, for rulers to avoid abusing the powers they wielded. The sovereign was a living manifestation of God's will, an example for all men of the spirit of religion in action, 'a veritable mirror in which his subjects can always see the spirit of the faith to imitate it'. And he emphasized

[37] Konstantin Nikolaevich, 'Tsesarevich Pavel Petrovich', *Russkaia starina*, 9 (1874), 681–3.
[38] See Papmehl, *Metropolitan Platon*, *passim*, on which this paragraph is based.

that the 'good or bad example of the chief leads [his subjects] to good or evil'. It was the sovereign's duty to promote peace and the well being of his subjects, to preserve justice, to punish transgressors, to ensure that both the civil and the spiritual powers perform their tasks, 'and in everything to show himself a father who diligently cares for the good of his children'. All subjects owe absolute obedience to the sovereign 'who is the supreme magistrate and the first governor under God'. And society should love the sovereign, render him high honours, obey his every command willingly and without complaint, pay taxes cheerfully, pray for his good health and prosperity, and defend his honour with their very lives against enemies, rebels, or traitors. In support of these propositions, Platon quoted Romans 12: 1–2: 'For there is no power but of God. Whosoever, therefore, resisteth the power, resisteth God.' Platon recommended Paul to contemplate the example of his 'illustrious ancestors', and principally that of Peter the Great for guidance, but the challenge he put was unequivocal: 'You, who are the whole hope of Russia, when the hand of the Almighty places the crown upon YOUR head, fulfill our desires, augment our glory, prolong the happiness of YOUR EMPIRE, and do honour to the nobility of the blood of the illustrious house of all the Russias.'[39]

In 1772, Paul produced a fragmentary essay entitled 'Reflections which have occurred to me on the subject of an expression which has often rung in my ears: the principle of government.'[40] The piece is muddled, disorderly, and probably incomplete. It also marks a departure from the doctrines Platon taught, revealing the rather different emphases Paul heard from his secular mentors, and particularly Count Panin. Though not formally a teacher, Panin spent hours talking with Paul, explaining the past, commenting on the present, and returning again and again to the obligations which every ruler bears. Panin was a firm supporter of the Petrine heritage, a commitment he passed on to Paul, but he was also an embryonic constitutionalist. He favoured the idea that law limited what the ruler could do, and he believed that a society governed by law was more advanced than one ruled by the monarch's will alone. He was certain as well that the logic of Peter's reforms pointed towards the establishing of a rule of law, though he praised Peter as an autocratic

---

[39] *Pravoslavnoe uchenie*, introduction. The introduction is unpaginated and is addressed to Paul. In the text proper, part III treats God's law and the sovereign. See esp. 130–2.

[40] 'Réflections, qui me sont venus au sujet d'une expression qu'on m'a fait se souvent sonner aux oreilles, qui est: *les principes du Gouvernement*', Konstantin Nikolaevich, 'Tsesarevich Pavel Petrovich', 678–9.

ruler who used his enormous powers to reform and civilize, and saw no contradiction with the constitutional principle. The Petrine reforms, or so Panin tended to see them, created a rational, orderly, and objective approach to government which could promote uniformity and predictability in the execution of the law. He also seems to have believed, however, that established law would act to limit what the monarch might do in any given situation. It was this last point, which stood in obvious contradiction with Platon's teachings, that Paul attempted to address in his 'reflections'.[41]

The fragment begins with an attempt to explain the phrase, 'the principle of government'. 'Principle', Paul decided, must mean the beginning, the foundation, that on which everything depends, while 'government' is the authority or power established to direct the state. In this case state means society politically organized as differentiated from government which is the instrument of rule. The 'principle of government', then, is the beginning, the foundation, or origin of power, and it derived first of all from physical force. Here Paul appealed to the state of nature in which 'the strongest, after having vanquished the weaker, give them the law, and it [the law] is then the source of power'. This conquest marked the beginnings of political society and laid the foundations for civilization to develop. As civilization progressed, the members of society learnt to aspire to a greater degree of order, and as they did so they came to choose chiefs to rule over them. But there was no restraint on those chosen (any more than there was over the conquerors), and 'growing powerful and seeing nothing to limit their [own] passions, they ruled for themselves and gave themselves up to excess'. Their subjects then dreamt of moderating this power by setting limits to it, and this marked a new stage of political society: the beginning of the rule of law.

There was, however, no prescriptive force in what Paul described. Abuses of authority led men to conceive of a system in which law would curb abuse, but Paul stopped well short of explaining how, in fact, that was to be done. He did say it was society which chose rulers, though he made no claim that this gave society the right to overturn a prince who abused his powers. He went no further than to assert that 'accumulated laws . . . serve as a guide to the directing power'. What Paul's essay does suggest is that he accepted the idea of a body of law which provided precedents and an orderly, rational medium for the conduct of affairs. It was not a means to check or control a ruler. No earthly law, to paraphrase Platon, was superior to

[41] On Panin, Ransel, *Panin Party*, 201–22, 282–9. Ransel discusses the 'Réflections', 222–3.

the monarch's will. On the other hand, the monarch himself bore the obligation to act in accordance with a higher moral imperative, God's law, in effect. Nor was this idea missing from the ideology Panin taught. Paul was steeped in the neo-Stoic belief that it was the ruler's duty to serve society honestly and honourably, together with its corollary that despots, selfish and unrestrained rulers who used their powers to serve themselves, created situations as dangerous as anarchy, and invited their own and society's destruction. A legitimate ruler, that is, a ruler committed to society's welfare, could also expect society's support, while the laws he would promulgate, codified and justly administered, would become the state's constitution, framing and channelling the sovereign power towards its correct ends. Here abuses might indeed exist, but the more important question was whether the ruler understood the moral imperative and acted according to it. Despots ignored the laws' spirit and served themselves; the legitimate ruler accepted the law and followed it. Such a ruler could be 'constitutional', that is, he would rule in accordance with established laws and in the interest of society.

Paul did not make this argument specifically, but it is much closer to the realities of his situation, and it suggests a ground on which he met Count Panin without accepting all the implications of Panin's political philosophy. Moreover, it was a way of looking at politics which was not only consistent with Panin's teachings, but which was ubiquitous in mid-eighteenth-century political philosophy. The concept of a controlling morality and a polity of laws resonated through Fénélon, Voltaire, and Montesquieu, and in the idea of the *Rechtstaat* formed the foundation for the German cameralist tradition which influenced Panin and corresponded closely with Paul's mature vision of the state.[42] The importance of the doctrine was that it was equally relevant for parliamentary or absolutist systems. Its emphasis on high standards of personal morality and a sense of duty in state servants, on a defined body of law administered

---

[42] Ransel, *Panin Party*, 213, argues that the natural-law theorists of the 17th cent. projected reason, order, and moderation against medieval primitivism which was to be replaced with 'a more ordered, psychologically repressed polity governed by functionally differentiated institutions'. In the public arena, changes towards an improved morality were accompanied by the growth of absolutism which was 'enlightened' and followed principles of 'Christian morality and positive law' as they were integrated by 'the growing corps of skilled jurists and administrators in service to the crown'. Ransel sees Panin and Catherine as 'the most prominent representatives of this outlook'. For a comprehensive analysis of the tradition represented here as it appeared in Germany and Russia see Marc Raeff, *The Well-Ordered Police State: Social and Institutional Change through Law in the Germanies and Russia, 1600–1800* (New Haven, Conn., 1983).

even-handedly and efficiently, and on expertise and honesty, was congenial with an enlightened approach to Russia's autocratic heritage. It could encompass Panin's views, and it was probably the idea towards which Paul was groping in 1772.

Panin's influence on Paul was particularly strong where international politics were concerned. As Catherine's first minister for more than a decade, and as a successful diplomat and courtier before that, he was particularly well placed to enlighten his charge. Panin also, of course, was an active politician with a major stake in what was happening. His views comprised a political programme in which he sought to indoctrinate Paul, for the most part successfully. In the summer of 1774, a year after his marriage and the end of his formal education, Paul drafted a memorandum on current politics which was intended as a contribution to policy formation.[43] Though couched in respectful language, it was pointedly critical of the direction and consequences of Catherine's policies. As a result, in place of opening doors to the government, the memo identified Paul with the Panin opposition, thus further alienating him from Catherine's inner circle, and deepening the isolation from affairs in which he already found himself.

The memo was written at a crucial juncture in Russian politics. Catherine's first war with Turkey, whose outbreak had effectively finished the deliberations of her legislative commission working on domestic reforms, was dragging to an end. The war had been a costly and difficult one. The country had lived through an epidemic of bubonic plague which devastated Moscow in 1771, and this was followed two years later by the bloody peasant uprising in the southeastern provinces led by Emelion Pugachev. Far more dangerous than the Turks, the so-called *Pugachevshchina* claimed tens of thousands of lives, visited ghastly retribution on gentry families, and threatened to roll into the heart of European Russia before it was finally halted.[44] On the basis of these events, Paul built a case for reviewing

---

[43] The memorandum's full title is: 'Razsuzhdenie o gosudarstve voobschchee, otnositel'no chisla voisk, potrebnago dlia zashchity onago, i kasatel'no oborony vsiekh predielov.' See: Lebedev, *Grafy Nikita i Petr Paniny*, 184–99; Ransel, *Panin Party*, 224–6. Ransel has seen the complete text in the Lenin Library. Points from the memo are repeated in Paul's correspondence on military reforms in 1778–9 with Count Peter Panin and Prince Repnin. See Velikii kniaz Pavel Petrovich, 'Perepiska v.k. Pavla Petrovicha s gr. Petrom Paninym v 1778 g.', *Russkaia starina*, 33 (1882), 403–18, 739–64. See also Kobeko, *Pavel Petrovich*, 102–4, 167–77.

[44] V. V. Mavrodin, *Krestianskaia voina v Rossie*, 3 vols. (Leningrad, 1961, 1966, 1970), i. 503 ff. See also: John T. Alexander, *Autocratic Politics in a National Crisis: The Imperial Russian Government and Pugachev's Revolt: 1773–1775* (Bloomington,

foreign policy in the light of domestic needs, and in the process he provided the first close insight that we have into the way he had come to think about international affairs. This is important, for the arguments he mustered in 1774 were precisely those which he used in 1796 when he assumed the throne and reordered Russian foreign policy while redefining Russia's national interest.[45]

Paul's basic argument related disorders in the domestic world to foreign policy. He noted in a conciliatory way that the Turkish war had been a notable success, but the price it exacted had been heavy, and the implication was that it was exorbitant. Paul blamed the war for the plague outbreak in Moscow (a position which modern authority supports), and he pointed out that the forced drafts of 'recruitments' with which the army filled its cadres were socially disruptive. A long peace was essential, in his opinion, 'to restore calm', to 'bring affairs into order', and to re-establish public tranquillity. This was not, in Paul's opinion, just a consequence of the Turkish war. He held that war, by its very nature, was disruptive and a social burden, forcing the reallocation of resources from peaceful development to military preparedness. To make his point more graphic, he compared the state to an organism, a body, in which there was a necessary balance among all the components. In this body, the ruler was the head, laws were its soul, its morality was its heart, while its arms, feet, and hands were the military and were necessary for its defence. Religion codified the moral rules under which this Leviathan functioned, while its wealth was the measure of its health and well being. The organic metaphor made the point obvious that the overdevelopment of any one part only could take place at the expense of the rest. Hence overcommitment to the military would inevitably jeopardize the health of the entire organism. And this, Paul concluded, was precisely the effect which the Turkish war had had on Russia.

There was more to the problem. War under the best of circumstances could be expected to unsettle a society, but the effects of Catherine's war had been multiplied many times over by the mistakes of those persons responsible for waging it. Everything necessary to the war effort was used up, nothing was held in reserve, and needed resources had to be withdrawn from other sectors to meet the new conditions. What Paul called 'the Orenburg events', that is, Pugachev's revolt, was the most serious consequence which

Ind., 1969); id., *The Bubonic Plague in Early Modern Russia* (Baltimore, 1980); Madariaga, *Catherine the Great*, 239–55.
[45] See below, Ch. 7.

followed the attempt to satisfy the war's demands. By overburdening the people in wartime, the state, in place of promoting society's welfare, had led people to abandon their settlements, to leave the land uncultivated, and finally to rebel. Miscalculation and mismanagement raised the price of territorial ambitions, and society paid dearly for it.

The idea of balance, which was the centre-piece in Paul's argument, made military expenditures for anything but maintaining internal order and protecting the frontiers questionable. Even a well administered war would be likely to disrupt the organic balance, while a long-term programme of imperial conquests would be dangerous in the extreme.[46] The policy implications were obvious. The Turkish war and what followed it were a warning; the government would be wise to return to more conservative, peace-oriented policies. Paul's strictures on failures in leadership spoke to a different point. Incompetent or corrupt officials would only subvert the state's real interests and pervert its purposes. People were responsible for what happened to societies; individuals had to be held to account. And implicit in this argument was the further idea that the evils which plagued contemporary Russia were less the consequences of a flawed system than the result of individuals abusing, misdirecting, or perverting the existing order to serve their personal ambitions.

Whatever difficulties Russia faced, whether the bloody class war set off by Pugachev or the dangerous instability of the state's finances, could be traced to the frailties and foibles of persons who, while wielding the powers which the ruler settled on them, forgot that their first obligation was to serve society. It was only later in his life that Paul identified his mother as the *fons et origo* of Russia's troubles and turned violently against everything which bore her mark. But even in his early years, he had learnt to believe that favouritism and immorality endangered the social order, that they were in fact a root cause for malfunctions in society's life. The corollary to this conviction was that since the basic order of society was sound (and was, in fact, the product of a natural development), the ruler, supported by his committed friends, should concentrate

---

[46] Prince Alexander Kurakin offered a similar view of war and the need for peace if society was to progress in his letters on Holland. See *Arkhiv Kurakina*, xvi, no. 1041, 20 Sept. (OS) 1771, pp. 288–96 and esp. p. 294. See also his comments on the disastrous effects of Louis XIV's war policies, no. 1085, 5 Sept. (OS) 1772, pp. 403–21 and esp. p. 408. Robert E. Jones, 'Opposition to War and Expansion in Late Eighteenth Century Russia', *Jahrbücher für Geschichte Osteuropas*, NS 32/1 (1984), 34–51, demonstrates that the anti-war view was widespread and deep.

on eliminating particular abuses, educate people to avoid such destructive behaviour in the future, and improve existing institutions to make them more effective. The beginning point was in morality and discipline.

The memorandum of 1774 spoke to issues which were to concern Paul for the rest of his life: the true nature of a nation's interest, the best means for organizing its defences, the necessity for central control over, and orderly deployment of, the military, and the consequences which follow when undisciplined, incompetent, or self-interested individuals exercise power. In the testament he drew up thirteen years later, and then more fully in the legislative programme which he advanced during the first months of his reign, the issues which appear in the 1774 memo are addressed again and again. What must be remembered is that the memo (unlike the 1772 essay) was not an academic exercise. It was a position paper expressing the ideas of a man who saw himself as an integral part of the ruling caste, who was claiming a position in the government. Married the previous year, and finally emancipated from a pupil's status, Paul's memorandum distills essential elements of what he had come to believe. The opinions of Count Panin were obviously influential, especially in the paper's main themes, while the influence of General Peter Panin (with whom Paul later attempted to develop a dialogue on his ideas concerning military organization) was significant as well. In sum, the memorandum was Paul's first step beyond the general or theoretical issues which he contemplated as a student. Government was his vocation; this was his first serious venture into its complexities.

Contemporaries were inclined to fault Paul's education, or to damn it with faint praise. Some of what they said was undoubtedly true. Yet the memorandum shows no serious intellectual deficiencies, but rather is well organized and effectively argued. On the other hand, it shows neither deep scholarship, nor conceptual brilliance. Even so, it is a thoughtful work, and one which promised well. Its most serious failing was that it had nothing to say to Catherine. In this respect, its presentation was probably a significant error in political judgement. Paul regularly made errors of this sort, in part because he firmly believed that his position made him immune to the need to accommodate what others might think or feel. Whether that was the case here, or whether Panin misjudged the political situation, is difficult to say. Certainly Paul's inexperience and newly aggressive enthusiasm played their parts, and we should also consider the fact that in 1774 Paul was still on relatively good terms with his mother, and might have actually believed that his ideas would receive a sympathetic hearing. This brings up a different sort of problem, i.e. Paul's position, perceived and actual, in Catherine's court, and the way relations stood between him and her.

Before leaving Paul's education, it is important to emphasize that by the time his schooling had ended, the main outlines of his political value system were in place. The ruler was the centre of his political composition and bore primary responsibility for all governmental functions. The different orders of society all owed him obedience and support. Law resided in the orderly administration of the state and in the moral imperatives which guided the prince. Later on, he decorated these ideas with various specific proposals. The main ideas, however, changed almost not at all. In fact, Paul developed relatively little intellectually once his education ended. His evolution as a personality was more dramatic, and it was this, together with the ideas he had imbibed, which shaped the kind of ruler he became. In this process, his relations with his mother were critical, as Catherine became the dominant fact in his adult life. For twenty-three years, from 1773 to 1796, Paul was part of an intense, sometimes confrontational, and eventually alienating relationship with her, which had the most serious personal and political consequences. The shape of this relationship began to emerge with Paul's passage from pupil to adult; it was firmly fixed by the time of his second marriage in 1776, and the birth of his first child a year later.

4.
POLITICS AND MARRIAGE

Paul's relations with his mother were ambiguous. In his first six years, he almost never saw her, and it was not until he was nearly 18 that he shared any degree of intimacy with her. Contemporaries thought that Catherine disliked her son. They described her as treating him coolly and with reserve, showing none of the spontaneous warmth which marked her relations with people she liked. Privately, she was more relaxed, teasing or chaffing him, and occasionally quarrelling with him. At most what she offered him, however, was a sort of amused objectivity with no display of spontaneous affection. On his side, Paul was uneasy in her presence. He was reported to have complained that nothing so frightened him as going before his mother, and observers in the court commented that he approached her as if he were guilty of something and expected to be punished. This behaviour contrasted sharply with the ebullience which was his usual style.[1]

Though no direct evidence exists, there can be little doubt that Paul hoped for more from his mother than she could give him. He was an emotional child who craved recognition and affection. While he found both in the household created for him, and especially with Count Panin, he met with neither from his remote yet dominating mother. Nor did that situation change until he was nearly grown, and Catherine, for reasons of her own, undertook to win him over. His reactions then, and the really very good relations which followed and lasted for nearly three years, are an indication of what Paul probably hoped for earlier. The intensity of his few friendships,

---

[1] See e.g. PRO, SP/91/74, Buckingham to Sandwich, 28 Sept. (NS) 1764. Buckingham believed it to be obvious that Catherine 'had no affection for Paul and occasionally neglects him', and that he, young though he was, felt this. Cf. Turgenev, *La Cour de Russie*, 249–52; Kobeko, *Pavel Petrovich*, 63–4. Sabathier de Cabres told how Catherine made no concessions to Paul, treating him 'coolly, majestically, and never as a mother', while Paul appeared before her as 'a respectful and submissive subject', or even 'as an accused before his judge': 2 Apr. (NS) 1770, *SIRIO* 143, pp. 129–32. Kobeko, *Pavel Petrovich*, 39, describes Catherine chaffing Paul, in this case about girls. Kobeko follows Poroshin who shows the more relaxed private world.

Politics and Marriage

and his deeply romantic love for his first wife, also hint at what Paul wanted from his mother and missed.

Why Catherine treated Paul as she did was matter for speculation. Some considered her incapable of maternal affection; others suggested that seeing him was a constant reminder of her own unloved husband and her responsibility for his fate.[2] The most common belief, however, was that Paul was Catherine's rival and a positive threat to her ability to govern. This idea deserves elaboration. Certainly in the days immediately following the *coup* there was evidence of dissatisfaction with the new regime and an apparent interest in legitimacy that seemed especially threatening. The guards who made the revolution were reported to regret what they had done, muttering darkly about having traded 'the last drop of [great] Peter's blood for a barrel of beer', and taking a dangerously warm interest in Paul.[3] Over the next two years, a variety of intrigues or conspiracies aimed at reversing the *coup d'état*. There were also public demonstrations. None of these, including a conspiracy within the Preobrazhenskii regiment, and the desperately foolish attempt to liberate Ivan VI from the Schlüsselburg which resulted in his violent death, approached success, nor did they seriously affect Catherine's ability to govern. And by 1765 they were finished. Worrisome and troubling though they surely were, it is difficult to see them as significant, or as a basis for anything more than caution where Paul was concerned.[4]

So much attention falls on these matters because foreign governments who were anxious to make the most of any political change encouraged their representatives in Petersburg to report as extensively as possible on all evidences of conflict and disorder. They were particularly interested in signs of disaffection, and they feasted on reports of the antagonism between Catherine and her son. The hope that Paul was, in fact, a rival was never far beneath the surface, and there was real disappointment when it became clear first that Panin was Catherine's loyal supporter, and then that Paul himself would never lead a revolt against his mother.[5] There were high hopes of a

---

[2] Masson believed that Catherine's hatred for 'the very sight of Paul' was the sole (and perhaps best) proof that Paul was Peter's son. *Mémoires secrètes sur la Russie . . .*, 2 vols. (Amsterdam, 1800), i. 179–81.

[3] Morane, *Paul Ier*, 37. Quoted from Bérenger's dispatch, 17 Aug. (NS) 1762, Affaires étrangères, LXX, fo. 163.

[4] Morane, *Paul Ier*, 36–93, strongly emphasizes the rivals thesis. Cf. Ransel, *Panin Party*, chs. 8, 9. Madariaga, *Catherine the Great*, 163–7 for post-*coup* political reactions and conspiracies.

[5] See Breteuil's instructions, 10 Sept. (NS) 1762, Affaires étrangères, LXXI, fo. 99, in Morane, *Paul Ier*, 38. See also Choiseul to Sabathier de Cabres, 30 May (NS) 1769, *SIRIO* 143, pp. 8–13.

confrontation when Paul reached his majority in 1773, and there were repeated references to his great popularity with the people (contrasted with an alleged lack of popular enthusiasm for Catherine). In the light of Panin's rock solid loyalty, and Paul's own persistent refusal to play the rebel, this popularity proved to be no more than an interesting fact to be observed.[6] There was, in fact, a crisis during the period 1771 to 1774, but it had to do with court politics and specifically with the decline of the Orlov and Panin factions. It ended with Grigorii Potemkin's emergence as Catherine's favourite and primary adviser. These events were immensely important for Paul's life, though not in the sense of a challenge to Catherine. Indeed, the idea of Paul as Catherine's rival, and the use of that idea to explain her attitudes towards him, seems fanciful. The truth is rather more prosaic.

Whether Catherine ever felt affection for Paul, or even liked him, she accepted him as her successor and treated him accordingly. He was a political reality and a significant aspect of her responsibility for governing Russia. As her successor, he had to be trained and educated. It was also essential for him to have an established place at court, that he be married and have his own family and estates, and that he perform whatever functions the empress required of him. He was in no sense free. Catherine retained control over his household through Count Panin, and then through General Nikolai Saltykov.[7] Paul was wholly dependent on Catherine and responsible to her; only she could alter the conditions of his existence. Her ultimate weapon was her right to continue him as her heir or to replace him with someone else. Whatever life Paul had was on his mother's sufferance. This was the reality in which he lived; this was normality.

Throughout his childhood and youth, Paul accepted his position almost without question. There were reports that he asked about what happened to his father and why his mother rather than he was ruling now. He was quoted as remarking that had the empress Elizabeth lived two weeks longer, he would have been the tsar (in the

[6] For Paul's 'popularity' and the reception in Moscow, Morane, *Paul Ier*, 37–40; Rossignol to de Choiseul, St Petersburg, 19 May (NS) 1768, *SIRIO* 141, pp. 410–11. The French contrasted Paul's popularity with widespread popular dislike for Catherine and believed that, should Paul try, he could overthrow her. Sabathier de Cabres, *Catherine II*, 24–6. The English reports conveyed a similar impression. See PRO, SP/91/72, Buckingham to Sandwich, no. 96, 22 Aug. (NS) 1763 for the guards' loyalty to Paul, and SP/91/88, Cathcart to Suffolk, 26 July/6 Aug. and 2/13 Aug. 1771, for the worried crowd outside the palace when Paul was ill.

[7] Catherine instructed Saltykov to guide and assist the grand duke, and if Paul resisted Saltykov should make it clear that he spoke with Catherine's voice. See *Russkii arkhiv*, 9 (1864), 932; Kobeko, *Pavel Petrovich*, 99–100.

belief that she was prepared to remove the grand duke Peter from the succession). And it was also said that he was fully aware that a conspiracy had stolen his crown, and that he knew who was responsible.[8] Undoubtedly the facts behind these reported words were true. Paul's awareness of 1762 and what it meant began early. Its signficance, however, was more psychological than political. The most it can tell us is that Paul may have felt betrayed very early, but it does not follow from this that he was prepared in his turn to betray the empress or seek to overturn her government. This was not the sort of person he was. We know from Poroshin's diaries just how troubling and tiresome a child Paul could be, yet despite his tantrums and stubbornness, he was always submissive, and gladly so, to the authorities over him. The acceptance of authority was the cardinal principle which Paul affirmed in all his writings, but he lived by it first. He gave obedience without question; later, when he embodied authority, he expected a similar absolute and unquestioning submission. Catherine could worry about what others might do in Paul's name; with him, however, she needed to have no doubts: he was, and was to remain, an obedient and loyal subject.[9]

It was generally agreed that Paul's continued good health was essential to the stability of Catherine's reign. In a curious way, though perceived as his mother's rival, Paul was also seen as conferring a kind of legitimacy on her position, and it was believed that his death, from whatever cause, would have disastrous consequences. One way, it was thought, to ease this problem would have been for Catherine to marry again, and as it was widely believed that the empress Elizabeth had been secretly wedded to her long-time favourite, Alexei Grigorovich Razumovskii, there was a precedent for Catherine to choose her favourite, Grigorii Orlov.[10] Rumours that this might actually happen set off an anti-Orlov demonstration by the Preobrazhenskii, his own regiment, who saw him as no more than a go-between in the recent revolution and feared that his marrying Catherine would endanger Paul's rights. Panin shared

---

[8] Morane, *Paul Ier*, 43, citing Bérenger, 15 July (NS) 1763, Affaires étrangères, LXXIII; Bérenger to the duc de Preslin, 31 July (NS) 1764, SIRIO 140, p. 391; Bérenger to the duc de Preslin, 21 Oct. (NS) 1765, SIRIO, 140, p. 553; Rossignol to the duc de Choiseul, 19 March (NS) 1768, SIRIO 141, p. 410. See also PRO, SP/91/73, 3 Jan. (NS) 1764, and SP/91/74, 28 Sept. (NS) 1764.

[9] Golovkin reported that whenever it was hinted to Paul that his grievances against his mother would justify his acting against her, he would remark: 'A prince is a subject before he is a son and religion has taught me that anything I could undertake against my mother would only serve to sanction what my sons might someday try against me.' *La Cour de Paul Ier*, 103–4.

[10] A. Wassiltchikov, *Les Razoumowski*, i. 23–4 and 179–86.

this view and worked hard to deflect the empress from such an ill-considered action. The marriage issue continued to generate controversy into 1763 when Catherine dropped the matter entirely. Unenthusiastic about it herself, she came to agree that marriage would reduce her own political mobility, and that it could multiply her problems by arousing popular concern over Paul.[11]

Worries over Paul's health and future fed on the thick residues of suspicion towards Catherine and her associates laid down in the period of the *coup* which the sudden death of Ivan Antonovich in 1764 stirred up again. Though the Brunswick faction had been broken up and scattered in the twenty-three years since Elizabeth seized the throne, there was still substantial support for Ivan as tsar, particularly in Moscow, and Catherine gave Count Panin the responsibility for seeing that nothing came of it. Elaborate precautions were taken to guard against any attempt to liberate Ivan, capped by Panin's explicit instructions to the prince's guards to kill him at the first sign of an attack. When Catherine was travelling in the Baltic provinces in the spring of 1764, a young Ukrainian officer named A. Ia. Mirovich mounted a quixotic assault on the Schlüsselburg intending to release Ivan and restore him to the throne. At the first sign of trouble, the gaolers stabbed their ward to death. Mirovich arrived to find a corpse and was taken into custody.[12] It was rumoured that Catherine inspired the attack to rid herself of a threatening competitor. When Bérenger, the French representative in Petersburg, reported Ivan's death, he portrayed Catherine as a murderess whose unbridled ambition had already claimed the lives of Peter III and Ivan VI, and whose next victim would undoubtedly be her own son, the grand duke Paul 'who is showing tendencies which age and [maturing] reason render day by day more dangerous'.[13] Small wonder that, with such suspicions abroad, when Paul fell ill,

---

[11] On the marriage issue, Ransel, *Panin Party*, 124–5; Morane, *Paul Ier*, 38–43; Madariaga, *Catherine the Great*, 33–4; Turgenev, *La Cour de Russie*, 241–51; Shil'der, *Pavel I*, 75–7; Alexander, *Catherine the Great*, 73–6.

[12] For the Mirovich affair, see *Osmnadtsatyi vek: Istoricheskii sbornik*, ed. P. Bartenev, 4 bks. (in 2 vols.) (Moscow, 1868–9), i. 357–87. The material includes Catherine's correspondence with Panin, the manifesto on Ivan Antonovich's death, letters on the trial and the ukaz sentencing Mirovich, excerpts from Mirovich's notebook, and materials on 'cleansing' the gaolers of their 'crime' of killing Ivan. For summaries, Madariaga, *Catherine the Great*, 35–6; Alexander, *Catherine the Great*, 89–92.

[13] Bérenger, 31 July and 1 Sept. (NS) 1764; Affaires étrangères, LXXVI, (quoted) Morane, *Paul Ier*, 46. Buckingham's account is surprisingly favourable to Mirovich. PRO, SP/91/73, Buckingham to Sandwich, St Petersburg, 20 July (NS) 1764.

his life was feared for, and nothing less than his appearance in person would suffice.

One major threat to the lives of all Europeans, princes and peasants alike, was smallpox.[14] Bernouilli, the famed French mathematician and an early student of medical statistics, estimated aggregate mortality from the disease in Europe alone at twenty-five million people. Virtually every royal house had had to cope with the consequences of deaths in the ruling family from smallpox. In Russia, the disease had claimed the life of Peter II, precipitating a constitutional crisis when Anne of Courland was chosen to be empress in 1730. Paul's repeated illnesses and supposedly delicate constitution made smallpox appear to be a particularly pressing problem. Inoculation for him was first proposed in 1764, but the dangers of the operation and the feared consequences of a failure led Catherine to put the idea aside.[15] Four years later smallpox struck the periphery of Paul's own household when the countess Sheremeteva, Count Panin's fiancée, sickened with it and died. Catherine discussed the question of inoculation with the senate, presumably to counter any charge that she had heedlessly endangered Paul's life, and she brought Thomas Dimsdale, an English physician, to Petersburg to perform the operation.[16]

Catherine's medical advisers were unenthusiastic about the inoculation project and gave Dimsdale only grudging co-operation. Jealousies apart, there seemed to be good reason to distance themselves from an undertaking which had an excellent chance of turning out badly. Folk medicine in Europe and Asia had long since discovered that a fleck of infective material from a pox pustule inserted in the nostril, at the hair-line, or even in the arm, would produce a light infection which conferred a lifelong immunity. Regular practitioners (that is, trained medical men) learnt from the folk methods and 'improved' on them. They added severe purges and bleeding to cleanse the system while turning the inoculation itself into a surgical procedure. A large incision was made, usually in the arm, into which the infective material was inserted and the wound was tightly bound. The result was often a full-blown case of smallpox complicated by severe wound infection. Either result could be

[14] For background and bibliography see: 'Smallpox', in Roderick E. McGrew, *Encyclopedia of Medical History* (New York, 1985), 313–17.

[15] The proposal and decision came when Paul's health was believed to be very poor. Inoculation was considered in connection with the succession and Catherine's marriage plans. See PRO, SP/91/74, Buckingham to Sandwich, St Petersburg, 14 Sept. (NS) 1764.

[16] Kobeko, *Pavel Petrovich*, 52; Morane, *Paul Ier*, 67; 'Zapiska Barona Dimsdelia o prebyvannii ego v Rossii', *SIRIO* 2, pp. 295–322.

fatal and the combination was lethal. Anyone would have to be sceptical of inoculation in this form, but there was an alternative. Untrained practitioners (health care entrepreneurs, in fact) appeared to meet the mounting demand for inoculations. They used the basic folk method to 'sell the pox' to good effect. Among the best known of these medical merchants was the Sutton family, father and son, and it was to them that Catherine was first directed. But the Suttons had no interest in travelling so far when business at home was good, and they were comfortable. Thomas Dimsdale, though a regularly trained physician, had developed a method similar to, if not derived from, the Sutton technique. He was available and he set off enthusiastically for Petersburg.[17]

Dimsdale's visit was a resounding success. The operation he performed, first on Catherine (done secretly and without fanfare while Paul was recovering from chicken pox), and then on Paul, produced a minor flare of infection with a light fever which quickly passed off. Everyone was pleased. Dimsdale and his son assisted in introducing Catherine's mass inoculation project which eventually reached some two million of her subjects. Throughout his stay in Petersburg, Dimsdale had an open invitation to dine at Paul's table, he discussed his work tête-à-tête with the empress, and Paul wrote him a graceful note of thanks for his services. In addition to his expenses, he was paid the enormous fee of £10,000, and was granted a Russian title of baron which is still in the family. And when Paul's sons, Alexander and Constantine, were to be inoculated in 1781, Thomas Dimsdale was recalled to Russia to perform the operations.[18]

Though the successful inoculation removed one danger, Paul's health continued to cause worry, and in 1771, with bubonic plague raging in Moscow, he suffered his most prolonged and threatening illness. Whether the disease was typhus or a particularly resistant

---

[17] See Thomas Dimsdale, *Thoughts on General and Partial Inoculations, Containing a Translation of the Two Treatises Written when the Author Was at Petersburg, and Published there, by Command of Her Imperial Majesty, in the Russian Language* (London, 1776).

[18] For Dimsdale's public account of the incoulations, see his *Tracts on Inoculation* . . . (London, 1781). Dimsdale also spoke of his experiences in a personal letter to Nicols, St Petersburg, 8 Sept. (OS) 1768, no. B1, Dimsdale Family Papers. Paul wrote to Dimsdale on 2 Sept. (OS) 1769, thanking him for his marvellous treatment and telling the doctor that he should know that since the inoculation 'my entire constitution has changed . . . I have more appetite, I sleep better, I can withstand greater fatigue, and what is of the greatest consequence to me, I no longer have such frequent indispositions': no. A-3, Dimsdale Papers. Dimsdale requested permission to publish some of the details of his treatment, and Paul wrote on 8/19 May 1776, with grace, respect, and approval: no. A-4, Dimsdale Papers. Dimsdale returned in 1781. See below, Ch. 5.

influenza, it laid Paul low for more than five weeks. His convalescence was very slow as each apparent recovery gave way to an even more severe attack. The disease was first reported in June; Paul was not fully restored to health until the autumn. When he failed to appear in public for days on end, and it became known that he was seriously ill, the inevitable rumours had him poisoned and lying at death's door. Disorders followed, and a mob of unruly people in a menacing mood appeared before the palace demanding to be shown that he was alive. Once satisfied, the crowd dispersed, though the atmosphere remained tense. Catherine behaved in public as if nothing were amiss, but in private, as the days turned into weeks, she became increasingly disturbed, spending hours watching by Paul's bed. Her relief, when the crisis passed and he began to mend, was palpable. This experience brought her closer to Paul than she had been at any time before. It also presented her to him far differently than she had ever appeared before. It may well have been this experience which laid the emotional footings for their improved relations through the next two years.[19]

Paul's illness coincided with the beginning of an era of major changes in court power alignments. Grigorii Orlov, the empress's long-time paramour, was losing his hold on her affections. Panin's influence was increasing, and with Orlov away, first to deal with the Moscow plague and then in 1772 negotiating with the Turks, Catherine accepted a new lover, A. S. Vasil'chikov. When Orlov rushed back to Petersburg, Catherine ordered him into quarantine, and early in the winter of 1773, he departed for the Baltic provinces and Europe. Orlov's fall was not final; he returned later in 1773 to resume his offices, though not his position as favourite. During the time he was gone, however, that is, through much of 1772 and 1773, there was a surprising *rapprochement* between Catherine and Paul which lasted, with certain interruptions, until 1776. Catherine initiated the new relationship. Paul responded, opening like a flower in the warmth of his mother's favour. And she, much to her surprise, found in him a lively, witty, feeling person with whom it was a delight to be. They spent hours together, laughing, talking, and strolling arm in arm. So enraptured was Paul, or so his mother

[19] Kobeko, *Pavel Petrovich*, 64–5. The illness and its political consequences, including the public reaction, were widely remarked. For the French reports, SIRIO 143, pp. 306, 308–9, 312, 321. For the Prussian reports, SIRIO 37, pp. 287–496 (nos. 523–6). For the English reporting, PRO, SP/91/88, nos. 44–51 (24 June/5 July 1771–19/30 July 1771). Catherine confessed to Mme Bielke that in the midst of fires, plague, and war, it was Paul's 'catarrhal fever' that caused her the greatest concern. See SIRIO 13, pp. 141–3 and 148–9 for letters dated 30 July and 29 Aug. (OS) 1771.

reported, that he refused even at dinner to be separated from her, and was caught shifting the place cards so that she would be his table partner.[20]

The effects of this continued into the following year which meant that Paul's majority, which was expected to bring a political crisis, saw mother and son on as good a personal footing as they were to know at any time in their lives together. Paul was a practised dissembler who could hide his true feelings behind façades acceptable to those around him. Yet the strength of his reactions to his mother's advances, the obvious pleasure he took in being her cavalier, in basking in the warmth of her approval, suggest that at base he felt a deep need for her affection and support which had been frustrated all his life. Had Catherine been able to satisfy this need in Paul, his life could have been vastly different. But she was not. Her motives in pursuing him were basically political. The break with Orlov had freed her, and with Paul's marriage as well as his majority pending she needed to know him better. She also undoubtedly hoped to establish ties which would be helpful in case of future troubles. His response was stronger than she expected, though it must be emphasized that, from her side, it changed nothing. Catherine's political needs dominated; in that realm, Paul was expected to be submissive and co-operative. The pleasure she found in him was an unexpected dividend.[21]

Despite all this, the issue of the grand duke as Catherine's rival took on new life as 1773 approached. The problem was less serious than ten years earlier because Catherine had had the opportunity

[20] Catherine described this interlude in two letters to Mme Bielke, *SIRIO* 13, pp. 258–61 (25 June (OS) 1772) and 265–6 (24 Aug. (OS) 1772). Kobeko, *Pavel Petrovich*, 65–7, credited improved relations to Orlov's absence and Catherine's need to know Paul better at a critical juncture. Morane, *Paul Ier*, 86–8, considers Catherine's warmth pure hypocrisy and hints that Paul understood. The *rapprochement* between Catherine and Paul was widely reported. See Sabathier to the duc d'Aiguillon, 15 Sept. (NS) 1772, *SIRIO* 143, p. 489; Solms to the king of Prussia, no. 660, 3/14 Aug. 1772; no. 672, 4/15 Sept. 1772; no. 673, 11/22 Sept. 1772; no. 683, 6/17 Nov. 1772; no. 701, 29 Jan./9 Feb. 1773, *SIRIO* 72, pp. 228, 254–6, 257–60, 274, 315. Solms thought Catherine was reacting to Orlov's absence and the acquisition of a new favourite, Vasil'chikov. He also suggested that Paul was not 'too much persuaded himself by the excess of friendship from Madame his mother'. (p. 315). Gunning reported the 'new' relationship without attaching much importance to it. PRO, SP/91/90, Gunning to Suffolk, no. 9, 3/14 July 1772, and no. 16, 28 July/8 Aug. 1772. See also *SIRIO* 19, no. 130, p. 283.

[21] Gunning noted that both Paul and Catherine were effective dissemblers, that their true feelings were hard to discern, and that Catherine was most concerned over political advantage and Paul's (putative) ambitions. PRO, SP/91/90, no. 16, Gunning to Suffolk, 28 July/8 Aug. 1772.

Politics and Marriage

fully to establish herself. Nevertheless, there were oppositions, and Paul offered a vehicle of sorts for their varied hopes. The most open criticism Catherine took came from what has been called her 'literary opposition', which included two of Russia's brightest intellectual lights, Nikolai Novikov and Denis Fonvizin. These men and their circle were disappointed with Catherine's failure to implement the reform programme they anticipated, and they sharply criticized the persistence of favouritism, corruption, and the exploitation of the common people. Paul's household was hospitable to such critics—the constitutional issue was particularly important—and there was a strong tendency for the critics to see Paul as the beginning point for an enlightened solution to Russia's problems.[22]

Catherine attempted to engage her critics in a political dialogue, but she failed entirely to blunt their persistent attacks. She also noted where the criticism was based. Whether he would or no, Paul became the symbol for a critical opposition committed to high standards of political morality, constitutionalism, and social reform. Eventually his name, together with those of both Nikita and Peter Panin, Princess Dashkova, and even Paul's first wife, the grand duchess Nathalia Alexievna, was to be linked to an alleged conspiracy to overthrow Catherine and to establish a constitutional regime. The author of the constitutional project, first rumoured to be Panin himself, was his secretary, Denis Fonvizin. It is virtually certain that no such plot existed, though Fonvizin's constitutional ideas remain as a testimonial both to his powers as an enlightened political theorist and to the very sophisticated political thinking that percolated through Paul's household. The tradition that a constitutional *coup* was planned remained alive in the Fonvizin family, to surface in connection with the grandson's part in the Decembrist revolt in 1825. It also stands as evidence that commitment to liberalizing political values formed a critical aspect of Russian thought as early as the second half of the eighteenth century.[23]

It was not only intellectuals who saw Paul as an alternative to his mother. Youthful members of the Preobrazhenskii guards organized

[22] Ransel, *Panin Party*, 219–21. Soviet writers stress the political character of the literary opposition. See esp. Eidel'man, *Gran'vekov*, 42–8. Madariaga rejects this position. See *Catherine the Great*, 329–35.

[23] Kobeko, *Pavel Petrovich*, 101–3, relates the story but does not vouch for its truth. Ransel, *Panin Party*, 222, affirms Panin's support for Catherine and his efforts to influence Paul towards understanding and accommodating his mother. For Denis Fonvizin's constitutional project, 'Rassuzhdenie o nepremennykh gosudarstvennykh zakonakh', *Sobranie sochinenii Fonvizina*, ii. 254–67. Ronald Hingley has trans. this work as 'A Discourse on Permanent Laws of State', in Marc Raeff (ed.), *Russian Intellectual History: An Anthology* (New York, 1966), 96–105.

a conspiracy in 1771 similar to the one that failed eight years earlier. The plan was to seize Catherine and proclaim Paul emperor. If he refused, one of their own number would be elevated. The plot remained a secret until, at the last moment, it was broached in confidence to Prince Bariatinskii who had played an important part in the 1762 *coup d'état* and who was believed to support Paul. The plotters thought they could rely on Bariatinskii's discretion while tapping his experience. The prince listened to their plan, and then betrayed them to Catherine. There were no executions, though the conspirators were beaten and exiled.[24]

The most serious threat that Catherine faced at any time in her long reign was the Pugachev rebellion which broke out in the southeastern provinces in 1773 and was not suppressed until the following year. Paul, as we saw earlier, blamed Catherine's war against Turkey for Pugachev's uprising, and the rebellion coincided as well with his achieving his majority. Pugachev's claim that he was Peter III and that Paul was his legitimate successor indicted Catherine as a usurper and could be read to justify a popular revolution to purify the existing order. It also expressed something that was commonly believed: that Peter III had been a true tsar; that Paul was his son and heir; and that Catherine, and those who supported her, were the enemy. In fact, of course, Paul neither could nor would identify himself with a rebel such as Pugachev, while Catherine treated the rebellion as an incipient civil war. She was willing to use whatever force was necessary to suppress it, and she agreed that Pugachev's punishment had to be public and awful. Whether she gave serious thought to what Pugachev's advocacy of Paul's rights meant is obscure. There is no sign that the rebellion influenced their relations in any significant way, though it is difficult to believe that she did not consider the matter.[25]

---

[24] On the Preobrazhenskii uprising, compare Morane, *Paul Ier*, 75–6, with Madariaga, *Catherine the Great*, 258–9. Sabathier reported the rising on 3 July (NS) 1772; the duc d'Aiguillon thought his description suggested a true conspiracy. *SIRIO* 143, pp. 415–16. Solms's reports were more comprehensive. See Solms to the king of Prussia, no. 642, 7 July (NS) 1772, *SIRIO* 72, pp. 164–5. Gunning considered the rising a minor insurrection involving no more than a few sergeants and common soldiers who were whipped and sent to Siberia. PRO, SP/91/90, Gunning to Suffolk, 4/15 Sept. 1772.

[25] See above, Ch. 2 and n. 32. Turgenev considered 'the detestable administration of the government' as the real basis for Pugachev's strength, and while he could be defeated, he had no difficulty, according to Robert Gunning, in replacing his losses from the discontented. Even the clergy and nobility complained that they suffered as much from imperial troops as from the rebels. See *La Cour de Russie*, 279–80, 286–7.

While the *Pugachevshchina* was a major event in Russia's history, it had relatively little resonance for Paul's story. What came to be called the Saldern affair, on the other hand, a court intrigue with roots in Paul's own household, had surprisingly wide repercussions and was minutely analysed and reported. The affair was unusual in that it was an intrigue in which Paul not only became personally involved, but showed to some advantage. Certainly it raised his stock, at least temporarily, with his mother. But its significance goes beyond this. If Pugachev dramatized widespread popular discontent and called attention to Paul as an alternative solution, the Saldern affair helps us to understand how there was no succession crisis in 1773, as well as the extent to which Paul was maturing as a courtier.

Casper von Saldern was a Holsteiner who had made his way as a kind of political agent or expediter.[26] Originally employed by Prussia, he was recruited into the Russian diplomatic service and was posted first to Copenhagen and then to Poland. Finally he was brought to Petersburg. Count Panin was his sponsor and protector. Saldern found a place in Paul's household, ate regularly at Paul's table, and this put him in a position to win Paul's confidence. This he set out to do and was successful. Judging from one of Paul's letters to his friend, Andrei Razumovskii in 1773, Saldern became an older trusted intimate who, like Razumovskii was helping him to understand himself, his need to control his unruly temperament, and how best to do it.[27] But there was more. Saldern appears to have been successful in convincing Paul that Count Panin could not adequately protect his interests, that he had rights Panin was incapable of promoting because he was tied so closely to the empress, and that Paul's enemies were numerous and threatening. Finally, Saldern brought Paul to acknowledge that he needed a political agent and offered himself to act in that capacity. Paul then signed an agreement authorizing Saldern to represent him. It was reported later that what Saldern was promoting was an expanded share in the government for Paul which amounted to a co-regency for him with Catherine. Paul then had serious second thoughts about what he had done and took the story to Panin who recovered the incriminating paper and destroyed it. He said nothing to the empress, however, for fear of

[26] A. F. Asseburg, *Denkwürdigkeiten* (Berlin, 1842), 415–22 on Saldern. Asseburg is hostile. Solms, the Prussian minister in St Petersburg, reviews Saldern's machinations in a letter of 31 Aug./11 Sept. 1773. Ibid. appendix iv, pp. 430–2.

[27] Wassiltchikow, *Razoumowski*, ii/1 9–15, for the letters. Nos. 3, 5, 13, and 15 refer to Saldern and show he attended Paul; no. 10 contains Paul's avowal that his improved state of mind owes to 'the firmness which you together with m. de Saldern begin to inspire in me' (p. 12).

compromising Paul, and perhaps raising questions about the efficacy of his own stewardship.

Saldern was able to retain his trusted position with the empress, and shortly after the confrontation with Count Panin, left Petersburg for Copenhagen where he was to carry through ratification of the agreements concerning Paul's inheritance. With the principal figure out of the country, it was possible that the whole affair would fade away. But Catherine showed her continuing good opinion of Saldern in a letter to her Hamburg friend, Madame Bielke, and this became known in Petersburg. When Paul learnt that Saldern was planning to return, and that he would be well received, he decided it was time to tell the empress everything. In addition to his own bad judgement, he was able to tell her several stories showing Saldern to be greedy, unreliable, and essentially dishonest. Catherine had known none of this and was outraged. She ordered Saldern stripped of his Russian appointments and pension, and threatened his arrest if he ever set foot again on Russian soil. But she praised Paul for reporting to her, and showed herself to be well satisfied with him. In the end, the Saldern affair suggested a growing self-confidence on Paul's part, and he showed some deftness in turning a potentially difficult situation to his own advantage as he improved his standing with his mother.[28]

On Paul's eighteenth birthday, there had been a reception and dinner for the foreign ministers at court to celebrate his coming of age. In a private ceremony which only Paul, Panin, and Saldern attended, Catherine delivered a homily on rulers and their obligations while reconfirming Count Panin's appointment as Paul's governor. This was actually Paul's 'German majority'. He could be recognized as a prince of the empire and receive his German inheritance.[29] When

---

[28] The Saldern affair is extremely tangled. Solms and Gunning give the best contemporary accounts. For Solms's dispatches to Frederick, SIRIO 72. See no. 706, 19 Feb./2 Mar. 1773, p. 345; no. 715, 21 May/1 June 1773, pp. 358–9; no. 721, 14/25 July 1773, pp. 372–4; no. 724, 30 July/10 Aug. 1773, pp. 384–9; no. 725, 27 Aug./7 Sept. 1773, pp. 390–5; no. 744, 14/25 Jan. 1774, pp. 433–4; no. 768, 7/18 Feb. 1774, pp. 490–2. Solms claims the authority of all three principals, Paul, Panin, and Saldern, for his information. Gunning begins to discuss Saldern on 5/16 Apr. 1773. His last report on the subject was 14/25 Feb. 1774. Gunning reported that what Saldern proposed and Paul agreed to approve was a 'co-regency' for Paul and Catherine. He had this on 'indisputable authority'. The more general grant of powers to act which Solms reports seems more realistic. For Gunning's reports: PRO, SP/91/92, 5/16 Apr. 1773; SP/91/93, 31 July/10 Aug. 1773; SP/91/94, 24 September/5 Oct. 1773; 27 Sept./8 Oct. 1773; SP/91/95, 24 December 1773/24 Jan. 1774; 28 January/8 Feb. 1774; 11/22 Feb. 1774; 14/25 Feb. 1774. See also Ransel, *Panin Party*, 241–6; Kobeko, *Pavel Petrovich*, 73–76.

[29] For the ceremony, PRO, SP/91/91, Gunning to Suffolk, no. 35, 21 Sept./2 Oct. 1772; Solms to the king of Prussia, no. 696, 7/18 Dec. 1772, SIRIO 72, p. 294.

he reached his Russian majority the following year, the event passed without remark. People who had looked forward to a crisis between the empress and her son when he reached the age at which he should begin to rule were disappointed. Literally nothing happened. As the Saldern affair showed, neither Paul nor Panin had the least intention of pressing any claim Paul may have thought he had on Catherine. Though Paul weakened briefly, his recovery was unquestionable. He accepted as, for the most part he had done throughout his life, his position as heir and successor. He undoubtedly expected to participate in his country's political life, but even if that were denied, as in fact was to happen, he would remain passive. Certainly he woud never condone, much less promote, a revolution. When Paul was given a particularly enthusiastic reception by the crowd in Moscow, Andrei Razumovskii is supposed to have whispered in his ear, 'Oh, Sire! did you but dare!' which Paul answered with a crooked smile and a flat disclaimer. Catherine had nothing to fear from him, nor, in fact, had she ever. Her son was her most loyal subject.[30]

Paul's marriage provided a diversion from court politics and the succession question. Probably Catherine intended that it would. The story began in 1768 when she entrusted Baron von Asseburg, the Danish minister to her court, with the task of finding an appropriate consort for her son. The search was not completed until five years later when the three unmarried daughters of the Landgrave of Hesse-Darmstadt were invited to St Petersburg. Catherine's first choice would probably have been Sophia Dorothea of Württemberg, but at the age of 12 in 1771 she was much too young. So far as Paul was concerned, Catherine was willing to wait until he was 19, though in fact the arrangements could have been completed sooner. That she waited as long as she did may have reflected the common belief that he was underdeveloped, both physically and emotionally; it is more likely, however, that the marriage was timed to correspond with his majority.

Both Hesse-Darmstadt and Württemberg were connected with Prussia. Frederick was more than happy to expedite arrangements, and when the Landgrafin brought her three daughters to Petersburg, they came by way of Berlin. Loyalties aside, there was some concern for protecting the family if the negotiations fell through. The ostensible purpose for the visit to the Prussian capital was to see

[30] Kobeko, *Pavel Petrovich*, 116; Morane, *Paul Ier*, 79–80. Sabathier to the duc de Choiseul, no. 54, 16 Feb. (NS) 1770, *SIRIO* 143, pp. 103–4, claimed that Paul concealed a determination to act against Catherine but recognized that he would need to mature.

another daughter who was married and living there. The party then slipped away from Berlin to Lübeck where three Russian naval vessels met them and carried them to Reval. Count Orlov escorted the party to Gatchina where Catherine, who had travelled there incognito, was waiting for them. After dinner, the group left for Tsarskoe Selo, meeting Paul on the road.[31]

Though there were three daughters, Catherine from the beginning had leaned towards Wilhelmina, the middle one, and personal acquaintance confirmed her in her choice. Paul, however, approached his intended with what can only be called controlled trepidation. In his letters on the eve of meeting the Darmstadt princesses, he reminded Razumovskii of the fear and embarrassment he was sure he would feel on seeing them, though he also avowed that, after having practised the self-control his good friend had so strongly recommended, he was able to await their arrival 'with the greatest impatience'. Later he confessed that when the first meeting was only a few hours off, he felt 'a secret little movement of embarrassment mixed with shame', but he was also worrying that court intriguers might influence the Landgrafin, the princesses' mother, against him. He worked out an elaborate plan (which Panin duly approved) to protect his interests, though when he met the party everything went extremely well.[32] Count Solms predicted that this would be the case, writing to Baron Asseburg that 'any girl could easily be smitten with Paul, for while small in stature, he has a well formed figure and a charming face'. His excellent manners and fine language made him agreeable in company, while his usual behaviour was 'moderate, very polite, and naturally lively'.[33]

Paul made an excellent impression on both Wilhelmina and her mother. It improved as the wedding drew near. The young couple, as Catherine told Madame Bielke shortly before the wedding, seemed perfectly content with one another, and Paul, at least, was falling in love. Eight days after the wedding, Catherine reported that her son would not stir so much as a step away from his bride, that he affected to live with her in the bourgeois manner, i.e. intimately and without ceremony, and that all this made the prettiest sight imaginable. Nor did his feelings change. Six months later Sir Robert Gunning commented on Paul's devotion to his wife, in what intimacy he lived with her, and how private their life had become. Though married for

[31] Asseburg, *Denkwürdigkeiten*, 144–286, and esp. 250–66; Kobeko, *Pavel Petrovich*, 75–93; Morane, *Paul Ier*, 101–3.
[32] Wassiltchikow, *Razoumowski*, ii/1, no. 2, 27 May (OS) 1773, pp. 19–20; Kobeko, *Pavel Petrovich*, 84.
[33] Solms to Asseburg, 31 Aug. (NS) 1773, Asseburg, *Denkwürdigkeiten*, 166–7.

reasons of state, marriage opened a whole new world for Paul in which he found happiness and personal satisfaction such as he had never known before.[34]

The marriage ceremony was performed on 29 September/10 October 1773. Wilhelmina had taken instruction in preparation for admission to the Russian church from Metropolitan Platon Levshin, Paul's former tutor for religion, and she was admitted to the church with the baptismal name of Nathalia Alexievna. Initially, the marriage reinforced the good relations between Paul and his mother. Catherine had instructed Wilhelmina about the dangers for her lurking in the court as well as what her responsibilities were. She made it plain that the grand duchess was not merely obligated to avoid calumniators who hoped to disturb the family's harmony, but she was expected positively to strengthen the family's bonds while never failing to denounce anyone who tried to influence her against the empress or her husband. Discretion was essential. There would be temptations of all sorts and the grand duchess would be expected to keep her primary obligations in mind at all times while remembering that it was only a short step from familiarity to disrespect and ultimately betrayal. Nathalia was particularly to beware of having private or unofficial contacts with representatives of foreign courts. She was also warned against spending too freely (debt meant dependence), though she should avoid appearing to be mean.[35] Catherine's advice was both counsel and command; however Nathalia chose to take it, it would have been well had she chosen to follow it. In fact, however, Nathalia ignored virtually everything Catherine told her, with the result that her relations with her mother-in-law gradually but certainly deteriorated, while Paul followed loyally after his new wife.

In the early days, Catherine praised her new daughter-in-law enthusiastically. She was 'this woman of gold', this princess endowed with all the best qualities, whose husband adores her, whom all the world loves, and 'with whom I am deeply satisfied'. She went so far as to avow that Nathalia had 'given her back her son', something for which she would be eternally grateful, and that this was a debt she would gladly spend her life discharging.[36] This enthusiasm soon

---

[34] Catherine to Mme Bielke, 18 Aug. and 6 Oct. (os) 1773, *SIRIO* 13, pp. 353–6, 361–3; PRO, SP/91/96, Gunning to Suffolk, 18/29 Apr. 1774; Turgenev, *La Cour de Russie*, 282.

[35] Kobeko, *Pavel Petrovich*, 85–6. These instructions were similar to, though less detailed than, Paul's instructions to his second wife. See below.

[36] Catherine to Mme Bielke, *SIRIO* 13, pp. 387–8; PRO, SP/91/96, Gunning to Suffolk, 18/29 Apr. 1774.

ended, and Catherine began to complain. Eight months after Robert Gunning reported the empress's gratitude to Nathalia, Catherine was writing to Baron Grimm about the vast differences between herself and her daughter-in-law, how difficult the younger woman had become, and how independent the young court was. She absolved Paul from any blame, and noted, somewhat gratuitously, that while he certainly had weaknesses, he was neither wicked nor arrogant. He did, however, want to go his own way, and he had just informed her that he would prefer to remain in Moscow (the court had only recently removed there for the trial and execution of Pugachev; it would remain until the following autumn), and she would not attempt to dissuade him.

Nathalia, however, was a problem. She was sickly, headstrong, spoilt, and lacked any sense of moderation. With her, everything was to excess. If she went for a walk, she was likely to go twenty versts; if she danced, there would be twenty contredanses and as many minuets, to say nothing of the allemands; to avoid overheating a room, there would be no fire at all, and so on, and so on. She refused to take advice (particularly, it would appear, Catherine's) and, up to the point of writing, she showed 'neither grace, nor prudence, nor wisdom'. Worse still, though Nathalia had learnt the responses necessary for the Russian confirmation service, she had totally neglected her studies in the Russian language and after a year and more could not speak a word. She claims she wants to learn, Catherine noted disgustedly, but 'does not give a moment's application to the work ... Everything is spinning about; we cannot stand this or that; we are indebted beyond twice what we have, and what we have is twice more than anyone else [of comparable status] in Europe'. Catherine certainly exaggerated for effect, and she concluded on a somewhat more philosophical note, urging her correspondent (or herself) not to despair of young people, though it was obvious that Nathalia was no longer her golden girl.[37]

That Paul might claim some independence, and that his wife should so openly disregard what Catherine expected of her, was bound to worry and irritate. In fact, there was more of irritation than of worry in what Catherine wrote, though the political situation within the court was changing rapidly, and Catherine recognized the dangers. The Panin party, Paul included, continued to favour Vasil'chikov as Catherine's favourite. There was great consternation when Orlov returned, followed by relief when he did not resume his former role. His presence, however, remained threatening, though it

[37] Catherine to Grimm, 26 Dec. (OS) 1774, *SIRIO* 23, p. 12.

was beginning to appear that Catherine needed and wanted something more than either he or Vasil'chikov could offer. That suspicion became reality when Vasil'chikov was dismissed in favour of General Grigorii Potemkin. This was the man who was to stand as Catherine's primary adviser and expediter from 1774 until his death in 1791. It was his shadow that darkened and chilled Paul's life.[38]

Paul had learnt to hate Orlov as a man who had usurped the powers (and very possibly the attention) he believed his mother should have offered him. Vasil'chikov had posed no such problem. Innocuous in every sense, Paul could accept him as a lesser evil who was no political threat at all. Potemkin was a very different matter. Though in the beginning he had support from Count Panin in consolidating his position against Orlov, Paul resisted him from the start. But Paul was no match for Potemkin in any respect, and he only angered Catherine when he challenged the favourite. Diplomats recorded the dismissive way the empress treated her son and heir (so recently her intimate and cavalier) and his impotence when he attempted to challenge the new favourite directly. Ultimately, Potemkin came to show Paul a kind of contemptuous condescension, though as we shall see, he could be magnanimous when it suited him. Of Catherine's three great favourites, Grigorii Orlov, Grigorii Potemkin, and Platon Zubov, Potemkin was Paul's *bête noire*. It was Potemkin who drove Paul into the political wilderness and kept him there during the critical years between 1775 and 1790. Potemkin's antagonism reinforced Catherine's determination to keep Paul on the fringes of political life. This determination, though not its consequences, was already apparent to observers in 1774–5. It coincided exactly with Panin's decline, and more especially with Potemkin's emergence as the dominant influence in Catherine's court.[39]

In the context of these changing political relationships, Paul's uxoriousness took on further importance. Catherine, after long and troubled deliberations, had decided that Panin should be removed as

---

[38] Given Potemkin's importance, little has been done with his life and career. The basic biography is Aleksandr Brikner, *Potemkin* (St Petersburg, 1891). See also George Soloveytchik, *Potemkin: Soldier, Statesman, Lover and Consort of Catherine of Russia* (New York, 1947); Theresia Adamczyk, *Fürst G. A. Potemkin: Untersuchungen zu seiner Lebensgeschichte* (from the Einstelten, 1936 edn.; Osnabrück, 1966). Ch. 1 surveys work on Potemkin; ch. 2 is a brief biography. Madariaga, *Catherine the Great*, 343–73, summarizes Potemkin's relations with Catherine, emphasizing the political aspect.

[39] Kobeko, *Pavel Petrovich*, 111, 116; PRO, SP/91/95, Gunning to Suffolk, 4/15 Mar. and 7/18 Mar. 1774; 96, 20/31 May 1774; 97, 5/16 Aug. 1774, and 16/27 Mar. 1775. See also Turgenev, *La Cour de Russie*, 280–93; Ransel, *Panin Party*, 248–55.

Paul's governor when Paul married. To ease the break she poured rich gifts over the former master of Paul's household, and made room for his continued participation in state affairs at the highest level.[40] But Panin's day, in fact, was nearly done. During much of Paul's brief marriage to Nathalia, he was separated from his former charge, so much so that by 1775 he could claim that he neither knew nor understood what was happening in Paul's household, and had not the slightest influence over it.[41] General Nikolai Saltykov replaced him as Paul's governor, while Nathalia and young Razumovskii monopolized Paul's time and attention. In fact, with Panin's removal, the central support for Paul's political activities was gone. Saltykov had no comparable standing and no claim on Paul's loyalties (he considered his new governor essentially a spy), and consequently no personal influence whatsoever.[42] Paul and his intimates drifted off in new directions which included developing close ties with the French—Paul affected a trenchant pro-French political stance and paraded his cultural francophilia—through Count Andrei Razumovskii, who appears to have been in the pay of the French embassy.

Moreover the tone of Paul's circle changed. Gone was the stringent asceticism which Panin favoured as Paul gave rein to a taste for indolence and luxury. Paul and his gilded circle became careless of appearances, to such an extent that during the court's stay in Moscow during 1774 and 1775, they deeply offended the local nobility by what was taken as openly expressed distaste for the ancient capital.[43] And Paul became increasingly assertive, quick to take umbrage, and quicker still to demand satisfaction. Gunning reported his anger and immediate protest to Catherine when he found bits of glass in a dish of sausages served him at supper—he charged that someone was trying to poison him—and he attempted to assert his rights against Potemkin. It was in this period that he prepared and submitted his critique of Catherine's policies which we discussed earlier, and he made a point of playing to his popularity with the crowd. On this he temporarily desisted when warned, then returned to making public appearances and encouraging the crowds to come to him. This created great concern while his behaviour in

[40] Ransel, *Panin Party*, 254–5; Alexander, *Catherine the Great*, 138–9.
[41] PRO, SP/91/98, Gunning to Suffolk, 16/27 Mar. 1775; Turgenev, *La Cour de Russie*, 293–4; Wassiltchikow, *Razoumowski*, ii/1. 32.
[42] Paul wanted no governor at all (he was now an adult), and when told Saltykov was, in fact, his mother's spy, he protested to her 'with his accustomed warmth'. And he remained suspicious. PRO, SP/91/94, Gunning to Suffolk, 6/17 Dec. 1773; Kobeko, *Pavel Petrovich*, 98–9.
[43] Wassiltchikow, *Razoumowski*, 34–5. In n. 2 he quotes Durand, the French minister, reporting on 13 Mar. (NS) 1775.

general called up comparison with Peter III. There was no one who set limits on what Paul did, as Panin had done, and it was thought his wife encouraged him in what he did.[44]

From Catherine's perspective, all these tendencies, which she linked to Nathalia's independent and uncooperative ways, were highly undesirable. More, they led her to consider Nathalia a political threat, a woman who, in time, could challenge her directly, and who, so far, had the advantage of her husband's unquestioning support. Indeed, though Paul's wife appeared to be uncaring, careless, and lacking in serious purpose, she also was placed to put effective pressure on her husband to advance his claims against his mother. Paul by himself was not a problem. But Paul, motivated by a determined and unscrupulous wife, would be quite a different matter. Had the situation remained unchanged, a clash between Catherine and Nathalia was almost inevitable. The situation did change, however, and while it gave Catherine an opportunity to warn Paul against his wife, it also showed that Nathalia was, in fact, too light-headed for serious politics. While Paul lived contentedly, some said blindly, with his beloved spouse, Nathalia was busily fixing the cuckold's horns he had worried about years before firmly on his forehead. She did so with Andrei Razumovskii.

While Paul was growing up, Andrei Razumovskii and his brothers belonged to a small group of noble children who were permitted occasionally to see and play with him. These were never easy relationships, but Paul favoured the Razumovskiis, and particularly Count Andrei who was nearly the same age. In 1765, Andrei was sent abroad to study at Strasburg. Three years later he entered the English naval service where he reached lieutenant's rank. A financial crisis brought him back to Russia where he was sent to join the Russian fleet campaigning against the Turks under Admiral Spiridov. He returned to St Petersburg in September 1772, when he was named a gentleman of the chamber, retained his position in the galley fleet, and was promoted to captain-lieutenant on 31 December.[45] His naval connections, Paul's position as grand admiral of the fleet, and Count Andrei's friendship with him from seven years earlier, brought the two together. They became fast friends. Paul opened his innermost

---

[44] PRO, SP/91/94, Gunning to Suffolk, 22 Nov./3 Dec. 1773, for the sausage tale. This and other 'childish and unguarded Expressions of his have, of late, given the Empress much uneasiness', and she took Paul and Nathalia with her to Tsarskoe Selo to sound him further and to get to know his wife better. Gunning reported extensively on Paul's popularity and his exploitation of it, first in Petersburg, later in Moscow. Ibid., 23 Nov./4 Dec. 1773; 96, 18/29 Apr. 1774; 98, 16/27 Mar. 1775.

[45] Wassiltchikow, *Razoumowski*, ii/1. 1–7; Kobeko, *Pavel Petrovich*, 81–2.

feelings to Razumovskii, asked for his advice, and came to believe that Razumvoskii was guiding him into a new and more healthy emotional life.[46]

Paul's private letters to his friend from those months in 1773 before his marriage say a great deal about the loneliness, anxiety, and uncertainties which troubled his adolescent years. We also see the unlimited trust he gave his friend. On 6 March (os) for example, he invited Count Andrei to dine with him the next day. It was time for a long and serious talk. His heart, he told his friend, was sore and empty, but 'your presence will sustain me'. And he closed with, 'Farewell, my dear friend, I love you with all my heart.' Two days later he wrote again, speaking of his deep need to talk with Razumovskii, deploring the circumstances preventing it, and assuring him that 'You have already worked a miracle of friendship on me since I begin to defy my old defiances...'. But, he goes on, 'you must persevere with me, for you are going against the habit of ten years, and you are fighting what fear and habitual torment have engrained in me'. Another letter speaks of waiting impatiently 'for the moment I can see you', the more so as 'three days have passed without you, and therefore in boredom'. Later, in a confident as well as thankful mood, Paul declared that

As for me, I get better from day to day; I don't know to what to attribute it: I think, however, that the firmness which you together with M. Saldern begin to inspire in me gives me more security and more assurance in respect of everything, leaves me more tranquil, and improves both my digestion and my sleep...

And just as Count Andrei was setting sail for Reval, Paul reported how much healthier and less suspicious he was feeling, and vowed that he and his friend would always be together 'in everything we do, whether public or private'.[47]

Razumovskii commanded one of the three ships which brought the Hesse-Darmstadt party to Kronstadt. Lively, presentable, and thoroughly sophisticated, he made a strong impression on the Landgrafin's daughters, and particularly on Wilhelmina. Once in the capital, in consequence of his close association with Paul, Razumovskii became a fixture in the grand ducal household, and after Paul and Nathalia were married, he remained on the most intimate terms with them. That intimacy, and Razumovskii's well-deserved reputation as a rake, gave court gossips all they needed to conclude that an affair was in progress. And Nathalia seemed to encourage such talk. She

---

[46] Wassiltchikow, *Razoumowski*, ii/1. 8–26.
[47] The letters cited are, respectively, ibid. 8–9, 12, 16–17.

Politics and Marriage

saw Razumovskii whenever she pleased, including times when she was entirely alone, always claiming that nothing more than friendship was involved, and that only the most mean-spirited could accuse her of anything else. And Paul supported her on every count: he would hear no criticism of his wife or his friend. Inevitably his reputation suffered, but when his mother protested to him about the damage being done, he refused to believe that there was a problem. It should be added that, beyond the gossip, there is no firm evidence that Nathalia and Andrei ever became lovers, though she was obviously greatly attracted to him.[48]

The court was still in Moscow in the summer of 1775 when Catherine learnt that her daughter-in-law was pregnant. She decreed an immediate return to Petersburg before the heavy frosts began. It had been feared that Nathalia might not conceive. Her health seemed poor; she was tired, wasted, and pale. It was thought possible that she was suffering from phthisis, what the next century would call consumption, and that she faced a long decline into invalidism. All this made the news of her pregnancy doubly welcome. The return to Petersburg was accomplished without incident, and the pregnancy progressed without any recognized complications. Her first birthing pains began on 10/21 April 1776. A midwife was in attendance, and everything seemed normal. The birth, however, was never accomplished. For two days Nathalia writhed in mounting agony punctuated by convulsions. Nothing seemed to help. The court physicians were consulted; other opinions were solicited; the consensus was that there was nothing to be done. The unborn child, a very large boy, was dead, though just when he died is uncertain. Nathalia struggled on for three more days growing weaker by the hour, and finally died on 15/26 April.[49]

---

[48] Kobeko, *Pavel Petrovich*, 82–3; Morane, *Paul Ier*, 138–42. Wassiltchikow, *Razoumowski*, ii/1. 30–1, quotes a letter from Solms calling Razumovskii Paul's nearest and most intimate friend. Gunning made the same point. PRO, SP/91/96, 18/29 Apr. 1774. Sir James Harris portrayed Nathalia as acting under the influence of 'her paramour', Andrei Razumovskii: James Harris, 1st earl of Malmesbury, *Diaries and Correspondence*, 4 vols. (London, 1844), i. 182. Catherine warned Paul about Razumovskii, and Nathalia was questioned. Wassiltchikow, *Razoumovskii*, 37; Harris, *Diaries*, i. 182. Fedor Golovkin reported on the authority of Baron Nicolay and Lafermière, intimates of Paul's household, that Paul allowed Razumovskii limitless freedom. He would arrive while Paul and Nathalia were still in bed and wrestle with Paul while Nathalia giggled and laughed. *La Cour de Paul Ier*, 108. This typified the gossip that circulated.

[49] Kobeko, *Pavel Petrovich*, 120–1; Catherine to Grimm, 27 Aug. (os) 1775, on the pregnancy; 17 Apr. (os) 1776, for Nathalia's death. *SIRIO* 23, pp. 33, 44–5. See also Catherine to Mme Bielke, 28 Apr. (os) 1776, *SIRIO* 27, pp. 79–80.

There were some charges that not everything that could have been done was done, and that the medical handling of the birth showed a lamentable lack of competence. De Corberon remarked that the grand duchess died a victim of the ignorance and barbarism of the country. The judgement was harsh but not entirely false. The midwife in attendance was a woman from Strasburg who had been in Russia for only eighteen months. She had been recommended by Paul's physician Dr Krause, and was thoroughly intimidated by the empress. Krause was a nephew of Boerhaave, who was portrayed as knowing little more than what he read in his uncle's papers. He and the midwife waited two days before calling for help. Only then did a surgeon appear on the scene to wield the obstetrical forceps. As the autopsy later revealed, the birth canal was virtually blocked by a deformation of the spine which made it literally impossible for a normal birth to occur, nor were the forceps successful. There seems to have been no thought given to attempting a caesarean section, a procedure which, while considered radical and very dangerous, was performed successfully in the eighteenth century and was even recommended. It is not clear whether crotchets, sharpened hooks used to dismember and remove a dead child in hope of saving the mother's life, were tried. By the fourth day the inevitable infection had set in and Nathalia knew that she was dying. Moreau, a French physician and de Corberon's informant, did not invite him to the autopsy. He gave it as his opinion, however, that the grand duchess need not have died had she had the proper care; he did not question that Nathalia was deformed and never should have become pregnant. It was the latter point the autopsy proved; the question of what might have been done was never raised.[50]

Whether Nathalia could have been saved or not, the immediate problem to be faced was Paul. Nathalia's death threatened to overwhelm him. For three days he was inconsolable; then, as if he had gathered strength, he repressed his grief and showed signs of a return to normal life. Catherine claimed to fear that he was poised for a long slide into melancholia. She attacked the problem energetically, bundling him off to Tsarskoe Selo in the company of Prince Henry, Frederick II's brother who had arrived in Petersburg just as Nathalia entered on her final days, and she immediately set to

[50] There is no medical account of Nathalia's death. The most detailed descriptions are Catherine to Grimm, 17 Apr. (OS) 1776, *SIRIO* 23, pp. 44–5, and de Corberon, *Un diplomat français*, 226–34. De Corberon criticizes Catherine for not doing more to save Nathalia's life. See also: Morane, *Paul Ier*, 143–7 and n. 1, 147. For relevant background on midwifery, gynecology, obstetrics, the obstetrical forceps, and caesarean section, McGrew, *Encyclopedia*, 122 ff., 203 ff., 227 ff., 323.

work eradicating all vestiges of Nathalia's presence from the apartments the couple had occupied. After the autopsy, the funeral was held and while Catherine attended, Paul did not. An official mourning period of three months was announced, but in fact it was generally ignored. Nathalia was hustled off the scene as quickly as possible.[51]

Catherine had also taken steps to separate Paul and Razumovskii.[52] When the latter tried to see Paul, he was intercepted and sent to the other side of Petersburg carrying a packet of papers to Count Golitsyn. The papers, which were sealed, were actually orders for his detention in preparation for his going into domestic exile. Paul showed no animus towards his friend at their last fleeting encounter outside Nathalia's apartments. But he never answered Razumovskii's subsequent letters, and until he met his former friend in Naples six years later, he made no recorded comment. Then he was reported to have heaped furious reproaches on Razumovskii and even threatened him with his sword.[53] It would appear that while Catherine satisfied herself that there was no political conspiracy involving Razumovskii and Nathalia, she gave Paul to understand that his friend had seduced his wife and besmirched his honour. Nathalia's death and Razumovskii's exile ended the matter.[54] Had Catherine believed Razumovskii to have been guilty of a political conspiracy, she would have punished him more severely. As it was, though he was forbidden the capital for sixteen years, he was permitted to travel internally and abroad, and was given diplomatic appointments. By the time Paul became tsar, Razumovskii was Russian ambassador in Vienna, remaining there until Paul finally replaced him in 1799 for political reasons.

What Catherine actually knew, how she knew it, and what she told Paul are all alike matters for speculation. The one person who

[51] Kobeko, *Pavel Petrovich*, 121–2; Catherine to Grimm, 17 and 18 Apr., 29 June (all OS) 1776, *SIRIO* 23, pp. 45–6, 49–50; Chester V. Easum, *Prince Henry of Prussia, Brother of Frederick the Great* (Madison, Wis., 1942), 281–91, and esp. 284–5. Paul was 'half-hysterical', while Henry was ready to help, day or night. See also Robert Stupperich, 'Die zweite Reise des Prinzen Heinrich von Preussen nach Petersburg', *Jahrbücher für Geschichte Osteuropas*, 3 (1938), 580–600, esp. 588–9.
[52] Wassiltchikow, *Razoumowski*, 11/1, 37–57.
[53] Ibid. 71–3; Morane, *Paul Ier*, 234. See below, Ch. 5.
[54] Fedor Golovkin, on the authority of Lafermière and Baron Nicolay, claimed it was Prince Henry, not Catherine, who informed Paul of his wife's infidelity, and that his information in turn had come from Platon. *La Cour de Paul Ier*, 106–8. The editor's note, p. 108, reports that Golovkin despised Henry and this led him to believe and report this story. De Corberon also accused Prince Henry of blackening Razumovskii's reputation. *Un diplomat français*, i. 230–1.

may have known the full extent of Nathalia's involvement with Razumovskii was her confessor, Father Platon, and it was rumoured that he had told Catherine enough of what Nathalia confessed to him on her deathbed to convince the empress that there had been a liaison. Platon set down hints in his autobiography that he knew things that would have made the empress unhappy, but he gave no indication what they were, and he denied that he had told any part of what he knew to anyone.[55] Nevertheless it would appear that Paul was convinced Razumovskii had betrayed him, though there is no reason to think that he also believed his friend had fathered the child responsible for Nathalia's death. Catherine probably was responsible for Paul's conviction, and it is easy to see how she might have thought that disillusioning him about his wife's virtue would assist him in shaking off the effects of the tragedy. Outwardly, he seemed to recover quickly. When asked how he would feel about marrying again, he made light of the question, enquiring only whether his new bride would be blonde or brunette.[56] This light-hearted response, however, was hardly the measure of his feelings. In a letter to Osten-Sacken, then Russian minister to Denmark and a friend as well as former teacher, Paul wrote that he considered 'this unexpected blow', that is, Nathalia's death, to be a 'test which God has set me, and this consoles me and eases my pain'. And in a fatalistic vein, he asserted that 'It is He who made me; He must know for what He has destined me and recognizes the purpose of everything that happens here.' With this certainty in mind, Paul concluded that it was imperative not to forget 'our principal duties, what we owe to God, to others, and to ourselves'.[57] His religious convictions provided Paul with an inner support which helped him to maintain his emotional footing in deeply traumatic times. But even religion could hardly console him for his most painful loss. What was said to Paul may have routed his despair but it also caused him to turn wholly away

[55] Platon's mourning for Nathalia undermined his status with Catherine. Kobeko, *Pavel Petrovich*, 123. See Papmehl, *Metropolitan Platon*, 32–3, where Platon is quoted: 'But the Empress perceiving something adverse to her own interests (about which my lips shall be sealed) in his [Platon's] continuous attendance on . . . the dying Duchess . . . [reached] conclusions unfavorable for Platon . . . and this was the cause for many unpleasant events for Platon in the future.' There is no 'external evidence' to elucidate these cryptic remarks; it is difficult, however, to credit that Platon would betray Nathalia's confession whatever it contained.

[56] Catherine repeated the remark in her letter to Grimm, 29 June (OS) 1776, *SIRIO* 23, pp. 49–50, and said that Paul brightened at the thought of a new wife. Cf. Kobeko, *Pavel Petrovich*, 127–8.

[57] Paul's letter to Osten-Sacken, Tsarskoe Selo, 7/18 June 1776, *SIRIO* 20, p. 408.

Politics and Marriage 95

from what had been his first deep emotional relationship. Moreover, and potentially more serious, he had suffered a severe blow to his self-esteem, his sense of personal security, and his trust in others. Some hint of how strongly he felt appeared in the way he briefed his new bride-to-be on how to conduct herself in the beargarden that was Catherine's court.[58]

The search for Paul's second mate was not protracted. Most of the women available in the eligible German principalities had already been canvassed, and Catherine was inclined to return to the candidate in whom she had been most interested earlier, Sophia Dorothea of Württemberg. Prince Henry supported this choice, and in one sense laid the groundwork for it. When Nathalia was still living, as he reported to Frederick, he had urged her to tell Paul that he must marry again, that it was his obligation as Russia's future ruler, and that his second bride, like herself, should be chosen from a family with Prussian connections.[59] Württemberg was such a house, and Frederick and Henry between them were able to clear away such obstacles as existed. Sophia Dorothea was Lutheran, but religion would not be permitted to stand in the way. She was also affianced to Louis, the hereditary prince of Hesse-Darmstadt who was Nathalia's brother. Louis, under pressure, hastily renounced his engagement in the name of friendship for Sophia and Paul. To fill the void, he was promised Sophia's younger sister while Catherine granted him a pension of 10,000 rubles both to solace him for his loss and to guarantee, as she wrote to Grimm, that 'I never see or hear him spoken of again'.[60]

Sophia Dorothea was only 17 when she was introduced to Paul. Born in 1759, she spent the whole of her adult life in Russia. By the time she died in 1828, she had created a remarkable legacy. As Paul's wife, she was the mother of two ruling tsars, Alexander I and Nicholas I, who together governed Russia for over half a century. Another son, Constantine, who should have ruled, abdicated his claim. Her society in the years following Paul's death in 1801 became a centre for conservative influences in Alexander's more liberal court, and by the time his reign ended in 1825, it would not be too much to say that the ideology which his mother had jealously guarded, and which she had carried forward from Paul's reign, had become a central theme in Russian autocratic governance. Though she never ruled, Mariia Fedorovna, as Sophia Dorothea was baptized in Russia, played a leading part in the Russian court world and

[58] See below. [59] Easum, *Prince Henry*, 285.
[60] Morane, *Paul Ier*, 153–5; Catherine to Grimm, 29 June (os) 1776, *SIRIO* 23, pp. 49–50.

contributed directly to the autocracy's conservative turn in the early nineteenth century.[61]

However important Sophia Dorothea's life was to be, at the time she married Paul she was hardly out of the egg. Unlike Nathalia, she brought a childlike enthusiasm and trust to her marriage; she was prepared not only to honour but to adore the young prince who became her husband.[62] High coloured and rather plump, Sophia Dorothea was an enthusiast, a sentimental romantic, and an undeveloped if soft and sweet person. She was inclined to a gently mystical outlook, loved her family, was skilled in minor arts, and had already developed a voracious appetite for culture. She communicated some of these interests to her husband. In later years, she showed a strain of toughness and determination which made her formidable, and during her long period as dowager empress, she became a fearsome *grande dame*. She read widely, developed interests in political economy as well as popular literature and philosophy, and for nearly fifteen years was able to maintain an intimate relationship with Paul. Mariia Fedorovna became the single most important person in his adult life, playing a role somewhat comparable to that of Count Panin in the formative years. Though she was not to shape her husband in any particular way, she adorned and decorated his life, and most important of all, provided him with a secure emotional refuge and a personal bond on which he could depend. That they eventually drew apart owed more to Paul's restless and suspicious nature than to anything Mariia Fedorovna was or did. And in the beginning, they were admirably suited to one another.

With the preliminaries out of the way, it was decided that Paul should go to Berlin to meet his intended. The trip turned out to be a triumphal progress. Every town in the Prussian kingdom through which Paul with Prince Henry in attendance passed organized a

[61] During Paul's reign, the 'empress's party' was a central force in domestic affairs. Paul destroyed it in 1798. See below: Ch. 8. Later, Mariia Fedorovna's circle became a centre for conservative critics of Alexander's liberal policies. See Marc Raeff, *Michael Speransky, Statesman of Imperial Russia* (The Hague, 1957), 178–9. Mariia welcomed political economists who were modernizing liberals in their economic views but conservative on processes of social change. See Roderick E. McGrew, 'Dilemmas of Development: Baron Heinrich Friedrich Storch (1766–1835) on the Growth of Imperial Russia', *Jahrbücher für Geschichte Osteuropas*, NS 24/1 (1976), 40–1 and nn. 29, 30, 31.

[62] Kobeko, *Pavel Petrovich*, 133–4. Before leaving for Russia, Sophia Dorothea told Mme Oberkirch that Catherine terrified her, though she was sure she could please her and the grand duke. After her marriage she wrote (16/27 Dec. 1776) that her grand duke was the most adorable of husbands, 'an angel', and 'I love him madly'. *Mémoires de la baronne d'Oberkirch sur la cour de Louis XVI et la société française avant 1789*, ed. Suzanne Burkard (Mercure de France; Paris, 1970), 86.

celebration of greeting which emphasized over and over again how important Paul was, and how much he and his royal host were loved. Local celebrities drawn up in ranks and splendid in their special dress or uniforms joined soldiers, police, governing officials, and the ubiquitous military bands in a crashing welcome to travelling royalty. Hours were spent in these parades and ceremonials with the most fulsome reserved for the entry into Berlin itself and the emotionally charged meeting with Prussia's king.[63] Once arrived, Paul was whirled through a succession of court functions, manœuvres, and parades. Frederick exulted to Catherine over her son's superior qualities, though privately, as he confided in his *Mémoires*, he thought his guest 'arrogant, haughty, and violent', and speculated on whether such a person could rule effectively in Russia. Indeed, he saw a danger that such a man as Paul seemed to be 'would suffer a fate like that of his unfortunate father'. Others found Paul more gauche than threatening, 'a young man, not yet formed, who tries to maintain an appearance of control on those occasions when he feels he has the leading role, yet doesn't know how, and tries to hide his embarrassment behind an affected air of ease'.[64]

Paul himself was excited and stimulated by the scenes he saw. He particularly admired Frederick's style of rule, how he kept everything under his personal control and extended his energetic leadership from the centre outwards to the very boundaries of his estates. Paul was impressed by the fact that, while Prussia had recently passed through a period of severe conflict, people worked and the land prospered. (Undoubtedly he compared this with the disorder in Russia which came in the wake of the Turkish war, and on which he had commented two years earlier.) What Paul found most astonishing, however, were the townsmen, the urban classes, whom he described as well organized, protected by legal institutions, disciplined, and hard-working. He was certain that no such class yet

---

[63] See *Ausführliche Beschreibung der Reise Sr. Kaiserlichen Hoheit des Grossfürsten von Russland Paul Petrowitz von St. Petersburg an den Königl. Preuss. Hof nach Berlin, nebst den dabei vorgefallenen Feyerlichkeiten Freundenbezeigungen, wie auch der Reise Ihre Kaiserl. Hoheit der Prinzessen Sophia Dorothea Augusta Louisa von Würtemberg-Stuttgard verlobten Braut des Grossfürsten von Berlin nach St. Petersburg* (Berlin, 1776). This provides detail on all aspects of the ceremonial receptions. K. K. Reckert, *Wintergemählde* (Berlin, 1777), is dedicated to Prince Henry and is more 'literary', including poems of welcome and other formal greetings, as well as descriptions of what the participants did.

[64] Frederick's fulsome letters to Catherine describing how Paul 'won all hearts' and ravished the heart of the king himself by 'his manner, his sentiments, his virtues' appear in *SIRIO* 20, pp. 357–9, 361. Cf. Frederick II, *Mémoires*, ii. 437. Le marquis de Pons described Paul; quoted, Morane, *Paul Ier*, 177. Morane's account of the Berlin visit is good. See pp. 173–8.

existed in Russia, and he drew the conclusion that 'it is obvious this country of Prussia has two more centuries of civilization than we do'.[65]

The Berlin experience spoke directly to Paul's predispositions. Frederick, like Paul's idealized Henry IV, was a man in control who governed in a military style. That, certainly, was appealing. Moreover, everywhere Paul looked, he found evidence to support his growing conviction that the Prussian model was the one for him to follow. The prosperity, orderliness, and discipline which he observed there were precisely the conditions he wanted to promote in Russia. If Russia lacked the civilizing development which made Prussian society so productive, an active monarch, ruling from the centre, and wielding the state's powers personally, could go far towards overcoming that deficiency and could force the pace of civilizing growth. This, after all, was what Peter the Great had thought, or so Paul's teachers taught him. Prussia was the future or, perhaps better, the way to the future, that Paul was coming to envision for Russia.

If Paul was excited about the prospects Prussia opened, he was pleased with the young woman who was offered as his bride. Nevertheless he disciplined his enthusiasm, though there was no doubt, once they met, that he would accept her. Physically he thought her 'not bad: large and well shaped', but he was particularly taken with her personal qualities, by the warmth, kindness, and benevolence which showed in her animated, smiling face. And he pleased her. She was ready to ignore his small size and features as well as his pug nose. Sophia believed that this was a fine marriage, and she was prepared to find everything that was good and attractive about the man she had been chosen to wed. With no outstanding issues to resolve, the engagement was announced, and the parties concerned set out for Petersburg.[66]

Catherine, on meeting her prospective daughter-in-law, was relieved. This girl was wholly unlike Nathalia. Moreover, Paul was satisfied with her and was approaching his second marriage far more maturely than he had done his first.[67] Catherine applauded her son's

[65] 'Sobstvennoruchnoe chernovoe pismo imp. Ekateriny II k velikomu kniaziu Pavlu Petrovichu v otvet na prieme ego v Berline (11/22 iulia 1776 g.)', *SIRIO* 27, p. 99 n. 1. Paul's letter was dated 9/20 July, the day before he entered Berlin and presented his formal address to Frederick. His description of that event, written on 11/22 July, is in n. 1, p. 97. See also Kobeko, *Pavel Petrovich*, 136. The notes to the published correspondence contain substantial excerpts from Paul's letters to Catherine which provide a commentary on the trip.

[66] *SIRIO* 27, p. 105 n. 1; Kobeko, *Pavel Petrovich*, 137–41.

[67] Catherine to Grimm, 1 Sept. (os 1776, *SIRIO* 23, p. 59; Kobeko, *Pavel Petrovich*, 144.

decision to set down a series of instructions or conditions which Sophia was expected to fulfil and which could be taken as guide-lines for their lives together. Paul had no intention of falling under the spell of this second wife as he had done with his first. He intended to dominate this marriage; Sophia, soon to be Mariia, was willing that he should succeed. Paul's instructions do something else: they show a remarkable degree of maturity. He appears to be insightful about his own character and realistic about the role he was expected to play as well as the world in which he had to live. The memorandum was written to be read by Catherine and therefore sheds further light on how the relationship between them stood. It also reflects what Paul had learnt from his first marriage. The tone is assertive but dignified, and if it reveals a clear understanding of where his dangers lay, it also shows a considerable self-awareness.[68]

Paul's instructions for his fiancée were in the form of a series of suggestions and recommendations concerning her deportment and the sort of relationship they could expect or towards which they should strive. Paul urged Sophia Dorothea to take her religious duties seriously, to practise piety, and to be conscientious about attending services and observing required rituals.[69] This injunction owed something to his own strong religious bent, but it was rooted equally in his understanding of the general public's sensitivity to religious forms, particularly on the part of the ruling family. It was even more important, however, that Sophia Dorothea understand and accept the overmastering importance of the empress in everything relating to their lives. Catherine, as Paul presented her, was someone whose trust and guidance, freely given, could greatly ease the grand duchess's life. She was also the only person, apart from Paul himself, on whom Sophia Dorothea should rely for dispassionate, objective advice. This was plainly a warning. Catherine had complained that everyone advised Nathalia except herself, and that was unacceptable. Paul did no more than speak to reality when advising his new bride on the face which she should show her imperial mother-in-law, and in fact, he took his own advice seriously.[70]

Catherine's sensitivity to criticism and her suspicion of potential conspiracies appeared as well. It was best not to complain about the empress or to voice disappointments. If there were problems that had to be resolved, or if there were matters which the grand duchess did not understand, she was recommended to seek face-to-face

---

[68] 'Instruktsiia velikago kniazia Pavla Petrovicha velikoi kniagine Marii Fedorovne (1776)', ed. E. S. Shumigorskii, *Russkaia starina*, 93 (1898), 247–61. See Ragsdale, *Tsar Paul*, 51–5.
[69] 'Instruktsiia', 251–2.   [70] Ibid. 252.

explanations. Above all, she should avoid using go-betweens. Intermediaries had an ugly way of turning into conspirators or intriguers, and where the empress was concerned, it was imperative to keep away from third parties. Paul's wife was expected to be above reproach; more important, she was to understand that she had no 'personal goals' other than serving the empress. So long as she kept this point in mind, and adhered faithfully to it, she would be able to speak frankly and openly to Catherine, and this without fear.[71]

Nathalia's behaviour and the problems it generated were behind these injunctions, but Paul was speaking for himself as well. It was not just that Catherine dominated his world; he was also writing about what he believed to be the deference owed to majesty. What Paul recommended was not only what he showed to Catherine, however much he resented her right to demand it, but it was what he expected of the people who served him when he in turn became the ruler. There is no reason to think that he was being Aesopian, or simply pandering to Catherine's sensibilities. What he urged was, in fact, the style of behaviour which he followed in his own dealings with the empress, and while his anger at his impotence grew with the passing years, and his resentment at the injustice Catherine did him waxed in concert, he held firmly to these same principles in his relations with her.

The main part of the memorandum explored the terms of marriage. Paul was still smarting from his experience with Nathalia. If he had loved too well to be wise the first time, he intended to avoid repeating the experience. He pointed out that so far as their personal relations were concerned, love, or even a substantial affection, was largely a matter of chance, but even so their marriage could be a good one if they cultivated trust, friendship, and a sense of mutual obligation. Moreover, in these matters, Paul intended to lead, and what he presented Sophia Dorothea was a set of prescriptions which would enable her to win and hold his confidence and friendship. Here Paul spoke of good conduct, kindness, tolerance, and personal understanding. He confessed that he was not an ordinary person, that he was difficult, and that his wife should be prepared for this. She would have to accommodate unusual emotional demands, to 'arm herself with patience and meekness' so that she could tolerate his 'ardor and volatile disposition, and equally [his] impatience'. On the other hand, he intended to take her in hand and instruct her in everything. He would feel free to criticize her style of life, her dress,

---

[71] 'Instruktsiia', 252–3, 255, 257.

or any other thing, no matter how intimate or inconsequential it might seem, and she was expected to receive such criticism without offence. Paul admitted that his advice might well be wrong nine times out of ten, but there was always the chance that at least once he might be right. The deprecatory tone was typical of his adult style, and so also was the force of what he said. Whether he was right or wrong, Sophia was to take what he had to say with good grace. It was his place to advise, correct, or criticize; it was hers to accept. Paul softened these assertions with the further self-depreciating comment that, after all, he had 'some knowledge of the situation here', a fact which he thought made it likely that at least some of his advice would be useful. His concluding admonition, however, came from the heart. He wanted her to be on 'a completely friendly basis' with him (though without 'transgressing decency', a curious and possibly revealing qualification), and he expected her to tell him openly and frankly what she found unattractive or unlikeable. In this, as in her dealings with the empress, Sophia was always to deal with him, avoiding intermediaries. It was vital that she should never hear anything critical of him from a third party. Listening to such complaints from other people would be inconsistent with maintaining the distance that was necessary between individuals of their rank and the rest of society.[72]

This last point was one that concerned Paul deeply. He repeatedly warned Sophia against confiding in people, in giving anyone the opportunity to come close enough to act for her or against her. And he was preoccupied with the appearance of things. Sophia should weigh every action to be certain that it would embarrass neither of them, while asking whether anything she might do would give someone else a hold on her. Paul noted with some bitterness how ill-educated even court society was, to say nothing of the greater public, and how it tended, therefore, to fasten on trifling details which were then loaded with a significance all out of proportion to their substance. Even common people were easily offended, though they were inclined to respect people in authority. But they enjoyed attention, and they would take advantage of too kind or permissive an attitude towards them by multiplying their requests and their petitions of grievance. This was inconvenient and not to be encouraged.[73]

There were prescriptions for daily living. The couple would need to budget their expenditures and manage money thriftily. Purchasing on credit or through unauthorized channels had to be avoided, and it

[72] Ibid. 252–3.   [73] Ibid. 253, 255, 257, 259.

was necessary to keep careful records of all funds received and those disbursed. And the same regularity was to characterize the way their household ran.[74] Paul believed that well-established routines would protect them against 'our own fantasies, which frequently become caprices . . .' and would help them to establish themselves as models for others to emulate. This, as Father Platon taught, was a primary responsibility for princes. Where there was neither discipline nor routine, a kind of moral anarchy followed. To avoid this, Paul laid out a comprehensive schedule for receptions, meals, and other social activities. He also believed that schedules, once established, should not be altered, since the public considered change in the order of things as evidence of capriciousness and a lack of serious commitment.

Two kinds of etiquette were necessary, one for formal occasions (receptions and holidays), and the other for ordinary usage. This guaranteed that there would always be established rules, regardless of the circumstance. Duty played a large part in all of this. Paul admitted that formal receptions or similar functions were often monotonous if not downright boring. But they were necessary and when they were finished, he and his wife would be able to retire to their own apartments to enjoy their privacy in the certain knowledge that they had done what they were supposed to do.[75]

Regularity was essential in their private lives. Sophia was expected to rise early enough to discharge her morning duties and complete her toilette. Paul expected to be fully dressed by 10, and on ordinary days he would have a full schedule until noon. Sophia was to be ready for public appearances by noon on weekdays, and by 10.30 a.m. on Sundays. Included in her morning schedule was time for studies, with special attention, as Paul urged, to Russian language, history, and politics. Her time after lunch could be given over to general reading, music, and other useful or pleasurable occupations. Paul believed that Sophia would be wise to budget a few minutes every day to be entirely alone. She should not, however, use these private moments to entertain any individual or group which could be thought of as a private circle. The grand duchess should restrict her contacts to those with the people appointed to serve her, and thus avoid giving rise to gossip. (This comment was an oblique reference to Paul's first wife's habit of claiming her private moments in Razumovskii's company.) Paul described his own life as very regular, and he urged his fiancée to share that regularity. In his case, apart from everything else, he believed that such a life was essential to his health, and though Paul seemed to acknowledge that his own rigid

[74] 'Instruktsiia', 255–7.   [75] Ibid. 257–8.

regimen might pose some problems for Sophia Dorothea, it was also clear that he insisted on it.[76]

The memo showed one of Paul's most enduring characteristics: the need to establish a recognized routine or schedule in which each party was made fully aware of what was required. Uncertainty or lack of definition were dangerous. Just as he believed that it was imperative for every member of the army to know what was expected of him, so it was essential for Paul and his new bride to have everything clearly defined. This was not, however, a contract between equal parties. It was rather a set of rules, a body of law, in fact, laid down to regulate personal relationships. Paul explicitly recognized Catherine's dominant position; Sophia was expected to recognize his. There were reasons, explanations for what he legislated, but these were offered only as a guide for understanding, a suggestion of the problems which the rules were intended to solve. For Paul, a good world was an orderly world in which recognized authority governed. The regulations for his future wife provided a sample of how he thought larger and more complex organizations should be governed. This was Paul's *Domostroi*, his epitome of the relationships and obligations which govern a good household, and like *Domostroi*, it could be taken to demonstrate how he believed a good government, or a good society, would function.[77]

The memo produced no disagreements. Sophia Dorothea commented on the manuscript that she agreed with everything proposed, and that in fact the instructions went much further than they needed to have done. She laid this excess of zeal to Paul's bad experience in his first marriage, a point with which, in fact, he agreed. Nevertheless, everything was clear, and not least that it was Paul who intended to control the household and the marriage. The instruction was a bulwark against his falling into the dependency which marked his marriage with Nathalia. It also asserted his importance, his duties, his place, and his work. Sophia Dorothea was made to feel the significance of the man she was marrying as well as the importance of the post she was going to hold. It apparently did not occur to her that the document also revealed a profound insecurity and a nearly desperate insistence on rules to stabilize life. Paul recognized that he was a man of uncertain temperament, and that his wife should

---

[76] Ibid. 257–60.

[77] *Domostroi* was a collection of rules on religious observances and everyday behaviour attributed to Father Sylvester, an adviser to Ivan IV (the Terrible) in the middle of the 16th cent. It included homilies and the instructions of a father to a son, probably by Sylvester. Morane, *Paul Ier*, 183–4, compares Paul's instruction with *Domostroi*.

understand the problems which this created; neither he nor she could have been expected to understand the significance of Paul's memorandum as a hint of the emotional conflicts which underlay his passionate and tempestuous persona. Assertive, even aggressive in his prescriptions, Paul also showed an insecure, suspicious, and obsessive personality. It was this side of his character which eventually came to dominate.

The marriage was celebrated on 26 September/7 October 1776. Sophia Dorothea, now Mariia Fedorovna, proved to be everything that Paul and Catherine hoped for, and a bit beside.[78] She had wanted to come to Russia, she was enthusiastic about her marriage and delighted with her husband. Mariia Fedorovna found her life in Paul, and far from being interested in the great world, led him towards a comfortable domesticity. Catherine was greatly relieved. The disastrous first marriage could be entirely forgotten. Paul was finally married to a woman who was in no way threatening to the empress and was becoming deeply involved in setting up his household. The old order had been liquidated. Panin was in virtual retirement; Orlov and his followers were in eclipse; and whatever dangers Paul's majority may have posed were safely past. Catherine's position was more secure than ever; her best years lay just ahead, while Paul was now well launched on his long career of waiting for his mother to die.

[78] Catherine spoke of her passion for 'this delicious creature' and vowed that she was everything she could have hoped for. 'She has the figure of a nymph, the color of lilies and roses. Her skin is transparent, she is well proportioned, her walk is light and graceful. Her heart, like her character, is excellent and sweet and her face shows forth all the good qualities of her soul . . . In sum, my princess combines all the qualities which I would want to find in my son's companion . . . I am perfectly satisfied.' *SIRIO* 27, p. 117.

5
ON BEING GRAND DUKE AT HOME AND ABROAD: 1776–1783

During the decade from 1773 to 1783 Paul's situation was transformed. At the beginning of the period, he was the acknowledged heir and a person of recognized importance. He had been raised to maturity by one of the most powerful men in the empire, and he retained close ties with his governor after the household was dissolved. Catherine accepted her son's standing. She put herself on a footing of intimacy with him, she briefed him on affairs, and she mildly astonished court observers by giving Count Razumovskii and Prince Alexander Kurakin, Paul's nearest friends, appointments of some importance.[1] Paul's health and welfare, as in earlier years, remained a matter of concern for everyone with political interests in Russia, while after his first marriage, the intrigues and conspiracies which swirled around his small court attracted wide attention. By 1783, virtually none of this was true. Paul's court was drawing away from the great court into isolation. Personal relations between Catherine and Paul were strained to the breaking point. They never significantly improved. What status Paul retained owed entirely to Catherine's reluctance to change the succession, a decision which she repeatedly considered from as early as 1782.[2]

Several factors worked to produce these results. Paul was fitted by neither temperament nor training for the intensely competitive political world in which he had to survive. The Saldern affair had exposed him directly to some of the realities of court life, and he was able to turn it to his advantage. But he found obnoxious the manipulative and compromising techniques necessary to be successful. He saw himself as a man of principle who could stand apart from everyone else, disregarding what people might think in order to act according to what he knew was right. When his former tutor, Osten-Sacken, warned him that he was being criticized for unfairness to his personal servants, for ignoring Count Panin, and for overreacting

---

[1] PRO, SP/91/95, Gunning to Suffolk, 5/16 Oct. 1775.
[2] PRO, FO/65/8, Harris to Grantham, no. 50, 6/17 Dec. 1782, mentions the possibility.

when faced with minor disciplinary faults among the troops he had inspected at Riga, Paul responded sharply. Most of what was being said, he declared, was no more than malicious gossip, while the charge that he had been too harsh at Riga was pernicious. He had found dangerous conditions of disorder and indiscipline. The corrective measures he took, while stern, were also necessary. He was not, he wrote in some exasperation, always wrong, nor, more significantly, was he so situated that he had to trim what he did to fit what people expected: 'If I were in a position where I needed a party,' he wrote,

then I would have to be silent to spare certain persons, but being what I am [i.e. the future tsar] I can have no other party or interest than that of the state, and with my character, it is hard to see things going wrong, above all when negligence and personal interests are the cause of it. I would prefer to be hated for doing good than loved while condoning evil. I therefore hope that in the present instance, no one will complain of my severity or ingratitude.[3]

The attitude Paul struck honoured his probity and his mentors' teachings. In the absolute terms he meant and lived by, however, it was an invitation to disaster. Though grateful to Panin for his guardianship, Paul apparently had no idea how much his relatively favourable situation owed to the powerful position the Panin party held, or how to replace that influence as it faded away. He would make no effort to grant favours to win support; he would build no parties, nor would he encourage anyone to do so. He thought courtiers should support him as the common people did, because he was the heir, yet no one should expect preferential treatment because they supported him. He would give them justice, neither less nor more. And he expected the same from the one person whose sovereignty over him he recognized: the empress, his mother. But here both his instincts and his theories were wrong. Catherine was a political animal who knew better than most how to manipulate the people whose support she needed. Paul might ultimately become the tsar, but until he did, Catherine saw him as one integer in a political equation, and, as matters were turning out, not a particularly important one. She certainly had no intention of sharing her power with him (or with anyone else) and, as Count Panin's influence receded, Paul's leverage on his mother faded away.

[3] 'Pisma Pavla Petrovicha k Sakenu', no. 7, 8/19 Oct. 1776, *SIRIO* 20, pp. 411–12. When Osten-Sacken later asked to have a relative placed in Paul's regiment, Paul refused because an exception would have to be made. Ibid., nos. 8 and 9, 15/26 Apr. and 8/19 July 1776, pp. 412–14.

Potemkin was Paul's most serious competitor, nor was there any realistic hope for a long-term accommodation between them. They stood on opposite sides of nearly every major issue, hence any increase in Paul's influence would be won at Potemkin's expense. The favourite had every reason to frustrate Paul's ambitions and he was able to do so; Paul was powerless to cope with him. Given Potemkin's influence with Catherine, and Paul's stiff-necked refusal to countenance compromises, it was only a question of time until his *rapprochement* with his mother unravelled. When Ségur, the French minister to Russia, talked with him in 1787, he made the point that Paul could hardly have expected Catherine to include him in her inner circle when he was so adamant in his opposition to all her policies, domestic as well as foreign.[4] Ségur, of course, was entirely correct. Paul made no secret of his opposition to his mother's plans, and though she showed remarkable patience in dealing with him, she also kept him well away from anything sensitive. This suited Potemkin who seems to have lost no opportunity to undercut Paul with the empress. Not surprisingly, Paul learnt to hate the favourite while identifying Catherine as the principal impediment to his ambitions. Eventually he came to see her as the source of everything that was wrong with Russia. As the years passed, Catherine's critical attitudes towards Paul hardened to the point that she always expected the worst of him. Whatever faith she had that he could change dissipated during his long trip through Europe in 1781–2. She then began to question whether he should be allowed to succeed her, an issue which agitated her conscience (and reinforced his deepest fears) until the day she finally died.

Paul's second marriage began his adult life. The couple started what was to become a numerous family when Alexander Pavlovich was born on 12 December (os) 1777. A second son, Constantine, arrived eighteen months later. Five girls—Alexandra, Mariia, Catherine, Helene, and Olga—followed, beginning in 1783, and then two more boys, Nicholas in 1796 and Michael in 1798. All but Olga reached maturity. Paul was deeply moved by his parental role. When Mariia was pregnant with Alexander, he wrote to Father Platon that it was his fond hope that the coming child would resemble himself in his 'fervour for God and his love of country', and he swore that his first care would be 'to inspire these two sentiments in it'.[5] But he was

---

[4] Louis Philippe, comte de Ségur, *Mémoires ou souvenirs et anecdotes*, 3 vols. (Paris, 1826), iii. 524.

[5] (Quoted) Kobeko, *Pavel Petrovich*, 158; PRO, SP/91/101, Oakes to Eden, 18/29 July, 15/26 Dec. 1777. Oakes referred to Paul's joy 'as a man more than a

never given the opportunity. As soon as Alexander was born, Catherine claimed him to raise, and when Constantine arrived, he too became his grandmother's exclusive charge. The empress chose her grandsons' names, laid down the rules for their care, training, and eventually their education. Since girls, as she told Baron Grimm, interested her less than boys, Paul and Mariia were able to spend more time with the female members of the brood, and Mariia had more responsibility for raising them. The boys were another matter. Alexander was a future tsar; Constantine was to be the heir to a Byzantine succession state; both were far too precious to be left to their parents.[6]

When Catherine took control over Alexander and Constantine, she underscored Paul's real position in her court. His responsibilities were only ceremonial; even where his family was concerned, Catherine established the rules. Not too much should be made of this, however. Paul's instructions to his wife make it clear that he believed Catherine ruled the family and that it was imperative to recognize that fact, to accept it, and to avoid even the appearance of the contrary. Paul undoubtedly was disappointed with the turn events took, and he resented having no voice at all in planning his sons' education. (But this was no more than what was happening to him in military, administrative, or diplomatic affairs.) Moreover, he and Mariia were by no means isolated from their boys. Unlike Catherine's experience with Paul, they saw the children regularly and often, and so long as they remained at court, all were part of a family circle. There is no direct evidence to support the belief that Catherine's monopolizing of the education given to Alexander and Constantine was particularly wounding. The children of the state belonged to the state; Paul implicitly recognized the empress's right to do as she did. Curiously enough, in later years when the boys were adolescent, Paul had revenge of a sort when Alexander and Constantine voluntarily became part-time members of his private garrison, throwing themselves enthusiastically into the drills and

---

Patriot' at Alexander's birth and noted the absence of 'any scintilla of suspicion' similar to those 'which were so well founded upon a former occasion'.

[6] Kobeko, *Pavel Petrovich*, 158–9; Morane, *Paul Ier*, 204–10. Catherine wrote about her joy in Alexander and her plans for Constantine in her correspondence with Grimm. See *SIRIO* 23, pp. 136, 143, 147, 152, 158, 173, 184, 233, 266, etc. See pp. 497 ff. (18 Sept. (os) 1790) for her appraisal of her (then) 6 grandchildren and her admission to favouring the boys over the girls. Catherine also wrote to Gustave III describing Alexander as a baby and her arrangements for him. Her grandiose dream for Constantine was common knowledge and was ascribed to Potemkin. See PRO, SP/91/103, Harris to Weymouth, 25 May/3 June 1779.

manœuvres, and explicitly turning against their grandmother's views.[7]

What Paul actually did after he became well established in his second marriage was to discharge the routine functions which were his responsibilities and, together with Mariia, to refurbish or build up the properties they held. He also continued the studies and planning on public affairs which he began before his first marriage, while establishing such foreign contacts as he could. His interest in military reforms continued and deepened. This was reflected in his letters to Count Peter Panin in which he expanded on the military side to the political memorandum he had submitted in 1774.[8] There he had raised the issue of military costs and their effect on society. He had put himself on record as supporting firm discipline and a well-articulated chain of command. Sound organization, in his view, was essential to military success, and every individual serving, from the field-marshal to the common soldier, should know precisely what was required of him. The Prussian system fitted his dispositions exactly, though it was not yet clear how deeply he was committed to it.

There were larger problems to explore as well. Paul opposed aggression, but he believed a strong military system was essential to Russia's security. He favoured a standing force organized into a permanent system of internal defences oriented to each of the four frontiers Russia shared with potentially hostile peoples. The problem was that such an elaborate military system meant a heavy charge against the budget, while manning the defences would absorb productive forces needed on the land. To take up some of the economic slack, he suggested settlements which would combine agricultural and military functions, an early version of the military colonies, in fact. He also proposed using a portion of the existing military budget to recruit abroad. He thought Poles could be successfully recruited, though he believed they would be difficult to discipline. Recruitment in the Germanies would be preferable, and there his own status as a German prince (albeit landless: Holstein had been passed back to Denmark) would facilitate the process. The purpose of hiring mercenaries was to preserve needed peasant labour.

---

[7] See Prince Adam Czartoryski, *Mémoires du prince Adam Czartoryski et correspondence avec l'empereur Alexandre I*^{er}, 2 vols. (Paris, 1887), i. 107–8, and below, Ch. 6.

[8] 'Perepiska v.k. Pavla Petrovicha s gr. Petrom Paninym v 1778 g.', *Russkaia starina*, 33 (1882) 403–18, 739–64. See Kobeko, *Pavel Petrovich*, 167–77, and below, Ch. 6.

Paul's proposals were an invitation to further discussion. But his correspondents were reluctant to commit themselves, though they praised him for the effort he was making. Though obviously unsatisfactory, this was all Paul was able to elicit, and it was not until five years later, when Catherine gave him Gatchina, that he was able to put some of his ideas into practice. His diplomacy was marginally more successful. Through Alexander Kurakin, his unofficial chancellor, Paul maintained contact with the king in Poland, Stanislaus Poniatowski, and he pursued a correspondence with the heir to the Prussian throne, the future Frederick William II ('le gros Gu' in Catherine's dismissive phrase). The crown prince visited Petersburg in 1780. Catherine treated him perfunctorily, but Paul was attracted by his mystical and romantic style. The two became fast friends, beginning a clandestine correspondence through the Prussian minister in Petersburg, which continued until 1788. Catherine appears to have learnt about this connection while Paul was travelling abroad. She chose not to make an issue of it, though it further confirmed his commitment to Prussia at a time when Catherine's policies favoured Austria.[9]

What Paul and Mariia did accomplish was to create a court which was both separate and different from the great court. It was relatively small and intimate. It was also easy, informal, and graceful. Here Mariia led, developing plans for decorating their small palace at Kamennyi Ostrov, their apartments in the Winter Palace, and in 1777 beginning the long-term building project which produced the exquisite country seat they named Pavlovsk. This project took fourteen years to complete and absorbed a substantial part of the grand ducal budget. Pavlovsk was Mariia's favourite spot in Russia, her retreat, and after Paul's death, her home. Building it was an important project for their early years together, though Paul was never so involved as Mariia was. He found his place at Gatchina six years later.[10]

[9] For Kurakin's correspondence with the Polish king, *Arkhiv Kurakina*, 322–3, 325–6, 336–7, 386, 413–17 (all from 1788). On Paul and the Prussian crown prince, Morane, *Paul Ier*, 202–3. Goetz, the Prussian minister, asserted that Paul considered Frederick William 'his brother and a personally cherished friend' (12 Sept. (NS) 1780). See also ibid. 304–7 and below, Ch. 6. Sir James Harris reported that Catherine discovered the correspondence while Paul was abroad. Though she 'took great umbrage' she did nothing about it. PRO, FO/65/5, no. 184, Harris to Stormont, 7/18 December 1781.

[10] For details, Suzanne Massie, *Pavlovsk: The Life of a Russian Palace* (London, 1990), 3–60; Kobeko, *Pavel Petrovich*, 159–61; Morane, *Paul Ier*, 190–1; Shumigorskii, *Imperatritsa Mariia Fedorovna*, i. 149–51. For Catherine's comments, *SIRIO* 27, p. 115, and (to Grimm) 23, 16 Apr. (OS) 1779, p. 135. See Erik

Paul and Mariia were an excellent match, but there were limits to what even a good marriage offered. Mariia seems to have hoped that by filling Paul's days with domestic activity she would help him to find both an occupation and some personal satisfaction. The strategy worked up to a point, but Paul had far too much ambition and energy to be satisfied with what amounted to genteel retirement. Even in the early days he questioned what, in fact, he had ever done, and whether he would finally have the chance to make his mark. He complained to Father Platon that his life was barren, that he was doing no more than occupying himself, filling his time, and as his hopes for anything more were distant, his life was passing with little to show for it. Platon had compared Paul to Cyrus, but Paul, though he thanked him for the compliment, rejected the comparison. 'I have never done anything so glorious as he did; good intentions never count as great actions.' He bitterly described himself as using his time the way a baby would, for amusement and distraction. Even the sweat that bedewed his brow came from boredom rather than honest effort. So Platon should see there was no real comparison between such a life and that of Cyrus. 'When Cyrus rested, it was after having done great things and in preparation for doing more and greater. But when I seek repose or distraction, it is to escape my own sad thoughts and suffocating cares.' Platon rejected so despairing a view and urged Paul to find himself in work. The grand duke agreed that work was the way to rout melancholy, but he asked plaintively whether 'it is always in our power to fill our time?' There were those, himself included, who were eager to labour, yet were prevented from it, and so suffered cruelly from the emptiness of their lives.[11]

The most obvious issue between Paul and his mother in the years following Nathalia's death was the direction of Russian foreign policy. Count Panin had promoted close relations with Prussia as part of the 'northern system', a combination of powers which included the Scandinavian monarchies, Russia, and Prussia. By the later 1770s, however, this approach was falling out of step with Catherine's interests and ambitions. Russian meddling in Swedish internal politics, an aggressive policy in Poland leading to the first partition, and a growing interest in the empire's southern provinces called the alliance between Russia and Prussia into question. Catherine's personal dislike for Frederick the Great added to the

Amburger, *Ingermanland: Eine junge Provinz Russlands im Wirkungsbereich der Residenz und Weltstadt St. Petersburg-Leningrad*, 2 pts. (Vienna, 1980), 177, etc. for information on the imperial estates. Check index.

[11] 'Pisma Pavla Petrovicha k Platonu', *Russkii archkiv*, 2 (1887), letters of 19 June and 16 July (os).

strain. The most important factor lay in the south. The underlying impetus came from the potential for growth in territories Russia already held, most notably Ukraine and New Russia, where economic expansion and a burgeoning population put pressure on the frontiers with the Ottoman empire and led to demands for protection against Turkish border raids. The successful campaign against the Turks which was concluded by the treaty of Kuchuk Kainardji in 1774 fed Potemkin's bold vision of a giant Russian-dominated principality in the south. By the end of the decade, Catherine contemplated the partition of the Ottoman empire and the creation of a new kingdom, called Dacia, under a Russian prince. It was this imperial ambition which led her to name Paul's second son Constantine, orienting his education to Greek language, literature, and culture, and, in European politics, led her to move closer to Austria. From the mid-1770s on, the Prussian connection was losing out, and Count Panin, Frederick's foremost supporter in Russian political circles, found himself on the defensive.[12]

These developments directly affected Paul's situation. As Panin's pupil, and the best hope for the Panin party, Paul had accepted the pro-Prussian political orientation to which he added his own deep respect for Frederick and the Prussian ruling house. That this occurred at a time when Catherine was turning away from Prussia was Paul's misfortune. He not only placed himself firmly in support of a losing cause, but he stood in direct opposition to the plans which Catherine and Potemkin were maturing. This stance further reduced his usefulness. Catherine hardly needed to legitimize her opposition. She was having difficulty enough in breaking Panin's influence; to encourage it by involving Paul in her affairs would have been senseless.

Catherine's shift of political interest from the north to the south was behind the most important public event in the early years of Paul's marriage, the European tour he and Mariia took in 1781–2.[13] This was the only time he became directly involved in Catherine's

[12] See Madariaga, *Catherine the Great*, 187–236, 359–92; Ransel, *Panin Party*, ch. 9 and esp. 248–55; E. I. Druzhinina, *Severnoe pricheronomor'e v 1775–1780 gg.* (Moscow, 1959), E. Hösch, 'Das sogenannte griechische Projekt Katharinas II', *Jahrbücher für Geschichte Osteuropas*, NS 12 (1964), 168–206; Hugh Ragsdale, 'Montmorin and Catherine's Greek Project: Revolution in French Foreign Policy', *Cahiers du monde russe et soviétique*, 27/1 (1986), 27–44.

[13] Accounts of the journey appear in Shil'der, *Pavel I*, 143–76; Shumigorskii, *Imperatritsa Mariia Fedorovna*, i. 164–234; Kobeko, *Pavel Petrovich*, 208–52; Morane, *Paul Ier*, 211–67. Cf. Benckendorff, *La Jeunesse d'un tzar*, 163–233. This book generally follows Kobeko, but it omits some sections and adds others. The coverage of the trip to the west is much fuller and more detailed than the original.

foreign policy. The initiative was not his, nor was the purpose one which he approved. Nevertheless it drew him onto the stage of European events and provided him with a range of new experiences. This was particularly important since his direct knowledge of Europe was limited to his visit to Berlin in 1776. The impressions he collected helped to firm and mature his thinking. The trip also put him into the public eye, and some of the most valuable comments which we have on his character and deportment in this period of his life come from people whom he met abroad. Finally, by the time Paul returned, Catherine had given up any hope that he could be brought to her way of thinking. His stubborn commitment to Prussia, his persistent criticism of his mother and her advisers, and the clear evidence that his court contained a core of active opposition all contributed to the result. Les Secondats, as Paul and Mariia were designated in Catherine's correspondence with Grimm, returned from Europe in a state of high disfavour which finally moderated to a cool, sometimes contemptuous, disregard.

The precipitating cause for the trip lay in Catherine's desire for *rapprochement* with Austria. In the spring of 1780, she and Joseph II had met at Mogilev at his suggestion. The talks were productive, and when Joseph showed an interest in seeing more of Russia, Catherine invited him to visit Moscow and St Petersburg. In the course of further travels, the emperor met Paul and Mariia Fedorovna and saw the opportunity to promote a further and more intimate connection with Russia. He mentioned the possibility of finding a bride for his nephew, Franz, and discovered that Mariia's younger sister, Elizabeth, was the same age. When he returned to Vienna, Joseph did the necessary preliminary work, and then broached the idea of a marriage alliance to Catherine who responded enthusiastically.[14]

Joseph was less favourably impressed by Paul than by Mariia. He remarked that Paul, 'though not an imbecile', could hardly be compared with Mariia, whom he thought to be much the brighter and more able. He also thought it not unlikely that she would one day rule. Paul's behaviour during Joseph's visit was not calculated to charm. He was stiff, hostile, and uncompromisingly pro-Prussian, though he unbent somewhat before Joseph left.[15] When the marriage

---

[14] Alfred Ritter von Arneth (ed.), *Joseph II und Katharina von Russland: Ihr Briefwechsel* (Vienna, 1869), esp. the introduction, pp. v–viii. Catherine's 1780 letters to Paul and Mariia on the Mogilev trip and the meeting with Joseph are in SIRIO 9, pp. 39–63. See esp. the letters for 24 and 25 May (os) 1780, pp. 52–4.

[15] Adolph Beer (ed.), *Joseph II, Leopold II, und Kaunitz: Ihr Briefwechsel* (Vienna, 1873), Joseph to Leopold, 19 Feb. 1781, pp. 9–11; app. 1 (Memo on the current position of the marriage arrangements for Archduke Franz: 19 Feb. 1781),

alliance was proposed, Paul faced a dilemma. At base, the idea did not appeal to him—to approve it would compromise his Prussian loyalties—yet he was unwilling to oppose something about which Mariia was enthusiastic and which meant a brilliant connection for her family. Mariia herself claimed that she continued to support Paul's principles, but family came before politics, and she was both an exponent for and an expediter of her sister's marriage.

In the wake of Joseph's visit, Paul, who remembered his own trip to Berlin with particular pleasure, became restless and anxious for a change of scene. Joseph's informal suggestion of a visit to Vienna, opened the possibility to him of an extended tour of Europe, a prospect Mariia greeted with enthusiasm. She could dream of visits with her family, perhaps even a return to Montbeillard, and an excursion to Berlin. She regretted that she would have to leave her children, but that was the only drawback in view. Meanwhile, in her continuing correspondence with the emperor, Catherine found occasion to remark that Paul and Mariia might well visit Austria and Italy. She gave the impression that Paul initiated the idea and was pressing her for it. She also hinted that she was inclined to give in.[16]

The English ambassador, Sir James Harris, probably on Potemkin's authority, reported the same matter somewhat differently.[17] In his version, it was Catherine who engineered Paul's request. According to Harris, Catherine was anxious to have Paul go, both to cement relations with Joseph and to remove him for a time from Petersburg. (The final confrontation with Count Panin lay before her, and she may have preferred to have Paul, who would be Panin's partisan, out of the way.) Catherine also believed that if the suggestion for a long journey came from her, Paul's suspicions would be aroused, and he would reject it. To avoid that problem, she enlisted Prince Nikolai Repnin, the husband of Panin's niece, a distinguished diplomat, and a familiar of the young court as well as a long-time loyalist in the Panin party, to whisper in Paul's ear that if he wanted to travel, he had but to ask. There was an excellent chance that his request would be granted. After due consideration, Paul and Mariia, as this version goes, made the request, while Catherine, after an appropriate interval for weighing the idea's merits, agreed. So the matter was settled.

The trip, once broached, became a topic for comment and speculation. All manner of advantages were expected from it. Andrei

---

323–8. See also Alfred Ritter von Arneth (ed.), *Maria Theresia und Joseph II*, 3 vols. (Vienna, 1867–8), iii. 266–80.

[16] Morane, *Paul Ier*, 212–13.

[17] PRO, FO/65/5, no. 156, Sir James Harris to Viscount Stormont, 21 Oct./1 Nov. 1781 (25 fos.). Cf. Turgenev, *La Cour de Russie*, 363–72.

Samborskii, a priest who had lived abroad and would accompany Paul and Mariia as their chaplain, published an address to the empress in which he pointed out how sending her son and heir to Europe would demonstrate good faith and trust, win public support, enhance her reputation, and contribute to peace and the general welfare.[18] Within the family circle, it was agreed on all sides that Joseph was far broader in outlook and better informed for the extensive travels he had undertaken. In general, Paul agreed, remarking on the good fortune of people of his station who had the opportunity to travel and the taste for it. He wrote to Osten-Sacken that travel such as he contemplated could not fail to expand what he knew and understood and thus enhance his value to the fatherland. The trip was a duty which he ought to undertake.[19]

The itinerary was also matter for discussion. Catherine hoped to limit the visit to Austria and Italy, but Paul wanted to see Paris and to visit Berlin. Catherine promptly vetoed the Berlin idea, and she was reluctant about Paris. Eventually, however, she gave in. Agreeing to Paris made it easier for Paul to accept the prohibition on Berlin. Catherine also put Moscow off limits. Apparently she wanted no repetition of the enthusiastic reception her son had had there earlier. The final itinerary provided for visits to Poland, Austria, Italy and the papal states, France, including Paris, the Low Countries, and the Rhine principalities. For greater freedom of movement, Paul and Mariia were to travel incognito, though the decision that they would take virtually their entire household meant a vastly unwieldy entourage which had to be broken into three separate columns. The children were considered too young to travel and were to remain behind. The expanded itinerary and the large company of travellers meant a considerable increase in costs over the initial estimates. Catherine, however, was willing to bear that, and Paul, though he was disappointed at the prohibition on Berlin, was otherwise well pleased. Mariia was ecstatic.

The departure was set for mid-September. Posting stations had been arranged and everything was in readiness when Mariia and Paul changed their minds. They decided they could not go. What had happened was that the Prussian king, unable to change the decision bypassing Berlin, set out to abort the trip entirely. Count Panin was

---

[18] Andrei Samborskii, *Rech Eia Imperatorskomu Velichestvu po blagopoluchnom vozvrashchenii iz puteshestviia ikh Imperatorskikh vysochestvikh'* (St Petersburg, n.d.), 2 pp. From the Dimsdale collection.

[19] See 'Iz zapisok velikoi kniagini Marii Fedorovny (Conversations touchant le voyage, 19 et 26 Mai, 1781)', Shil'der, *Pavel I*, 542–3; Paul to Osten-Sacken, no. 28, 12/23 July 1781, *SIRIO* 23, p. 429.

his chosen instrument. Panin had withdrawn from the court in the spring, but he returned to make this final effort. One ploy was to convince Mariia that she should not leave her children for so long a time. Alexander and Constantine had only recently been inoculated, and Panin expatiated on the dangers of the aftermath while hinting at unforeseen disasters which Mariia could do nothing about if she were far away. Mariia was highly susceptible to such suggestions, and she quickly lost enthusiasm. Panin also had warnings for Paul. He hinted to him that he had been manœuvred into planning this trip and that there was any number of unpleasant consequences which could follow it. There would be nothing, for example, to prevent Catherine from taking Alexander to Moscow and presenting him to the people as the heir. And would not the emperor be well placed to prevent Paul from returning to Russia in case of need? Or in case Catherine should die while Paul was away, what was there to prevent Orlov and Potemkin from burying their differences and shutting Paul out of Russia forever? The point was that Paul had real interests to defend; his absence could only give comfort to his enemies.[20]

These interventions set off a crisis. Paul was worried, Mariia was frantic, and finally Paul gave in. He cancelled the plans that had been made; they would not go. But when he and Mariia faced Catherine, they found her adamant. She would accept neither their fears nor their decision. Presumably Paul never articulated his political concerns, but there were endless discussions concerning the children. Catherine's position was firm: the plans were already made and could only be changed at enormous inconvenience to everyone, while calling off the trip would make the worst possible impression abroad. The children had come through the first stage of their inoculation without complications, and Baron Dimsdale (whom Paul did trust) was on hand should any need arise. There was nothing to fear. For a time it was thought that Paul might have squeezed a concession on Berlin from Catherine, but even that did not happen. It became clear that Catherine insisted that they go. Paul accepted the decision with ill grace. Mariia hung on the brink of hysteria. When the moment for departure arrived, she had to be dragged to the carriage, and she fell into a deep faint as the vehicle finally rolled out of the courtyard. Paul was grimly silent. In her first letters to her 'dear children', Catherine acknowledged how difficult the parting was and urged

---

[20] PRO, FO/65/4, no. 137, Harris to Stormont, 17/28 Sept. 1781, and no. 156, 21 Oct./1 Nov. 1781; Turgenev, *La Cour de Russie*, 360–1 and esp. 368–70; Morane, *Paul Ier*, 214–17.

them, should they so desire, to come back at any time. It was an offer which could hardly be accepted.[21]

Both Paul and Mariia kept journals on the trip, though neither has been found. Nicholas I ordered that all Mariia's journals be burnt after her death in 1828; they were too revealing of family affairs.[22] Paul's journal simply disappeared. Both corresponded regularly with Catherine, but while her letters have been published, theirs have not, nor is their whereabouts currently known. Members of the party, most notably Lafermière, Paul's librarian, and baroness Oberkirch, Mariia's close friend, did write on the events they observed. Lafermière was not in the column travelling with Paul and Mariia, and his letters are only marginally useful, though his notes on Paul's enthusiastic reception in Paris, based on a contemporary literary journal, are helpful. Baroness Oberkirch did not join the party until it reached Paris, though for the latter part of the trip her memoirs are an important source. Political correspondents in the capitals visited wrote their impressions of 'les comtes du Nord' to their home governments and Catherine's diplomats kept her well informed. There are references to portions of this correspondence in the secondary literature. The only connected account of the trip appears in Catherine's letters where it is possible to see shadows of what Paul and Mariia were writing to her. Paul wrote less than Mariia did and only occasionally remarked on points which caught his mother's interest. What she wrote to him dealt largely with tasks he was expected to perform, or were conventional greetings for

[21] Thomas Dimsdale's wife, Elizabeth, witnessed the departure. In her diary, she called 'the day and the circumstances attending it [something] I shall never forget'. The grand duchess's distress at leaving her children 'affected everybody and so many people were crying I believe the carriages stood waiting for them near two hours'. Finally, Baron Dimsdale and two other gentlemen helped the grand duchess (who 'had hardly any strength') into the carriage. After they left, word came that scarcely a mile down the road the carriage stopped as the grand duchess had fainted. The grand duke, once she was recovered, 'said very seriously to her he could not bear it any longer and if she would not exert herself, he declared—upon his honor, he would immediately turn back'. This seems to have settled the matter, and all went well afterwards. When the uproar in the courtyard was at its height, Elizabeth Dimsdale noticed Catherine coolly walking in the garden. Far from crying, she 'very wisely said, why all this trouble about going on a journey they very much wished, and quite of their own advice'. Elizabeth Dimsdale, 'Diary of a Trip to Russia in 1781', Dimsdale collection. The diary has been recently published: *An English Lady at the Court of Catherine the Great*, ed. A. G. Cross (Cambridge, 1989). See esp. 64–5. Cf. Turgenev, *La Cour de Russie*, 361–3 and Catherine to Paul and Mariia, 21 Sept. (os) 1781, SIRIO 9, pp. 65–6. See also Catherine's letters for 1, 10, and 19 Oct. (os), SIRIO 9, pp. 68–74.

[22] Theodore Schiemann, *Geschichte Russlands unter Kaiser Nikolaus I*, 4 vols. (Berlin, 1904–19), ii. 286 and n. 2; Kobeko, *Pavel Petrovich*, 192–3.

birthdays and name days. The letters she addressed to Mariia, or to Mariia and Paul, were warm, informal, and informative. She was most likely to refer to points in Mariia's letters when she wrote to the pair as a couple, while her long descriptions of what Alexander and Constantine were doing seemed also to be written for the mother rather than the father.[23]

Vienna was the first major stop on the journey and the most important. Paul approached the Habsburg capital via Poland where Stanislaus Poniatowski gave him a warm and generous welcome. Poniatowski was favourably impressed with Paul, who found his Polish reception very much to his taste.[24] The approach to Vienna was more difficult. It was rumoured that Joseph was annoyed at the slow progress his Russian guests were making and that he had finally decided against meeting them. If so, he changed his mind, going literally the extra mile to accommodate his visitors. Apprised of their approach from Poland, he made a two-day journey to Troppau where he suddenly appeared to greet them and to accompany them to Vienna. Whether Paul and Mariia were thrown off-stride by Joseph's unexpected arrival, or whether Paul's brief visit to the Polish court had reawakened his prejudices towards Austria, the first encounter with the emperor turned out to be awkward and constrained. It required all Joseph's very considerable charm and social address to ease the situation, and he himself acknowledged that there had been some difficulty at first. He refused to consider the matter serious, however, and he reported that, by the time they reached Vienna, they were chattering with the ease of old friends.[25]

The rough spots Joseph so assiduously smoothed were not entirely political. Mariia was ill at ease in new situations, and there were overtones to the meeting with Joseph which made Paul uncomfortable. That it all passed off, and that the visit was a success, appears from Catherine's remarks, from Joseph's correspondence with his brother,

[23] For Lafermière's letters, *Arkhiv kniazia Vorontsova*, xxix. 177–296. He excerpted material from Bachaumont's *Mémoires secrets de la République des lèttres*, a literary paper which reported Paul's visit to Paris as 1782's leading event. See 'Tsesarevich Pavel Petrovich vo Frantsii v 1782 godu; iz zapisok Bashomont'a'. *Russkaia starina* (Oct.–Dec. 1882), 321–34. Baroness Oberkirch's *Mémoires*, 127–281, cover Paris, May 1782 and after. For Catherine's letters, *SIRIO* 9, pp. 64 ff.

[24] Shumigorskii, *Mariia Fedorovna*, i. 185; Benckendorff, *La Jeunesse*, 172–3; Kobeko, *Pavel Petrovich*, 208; Catherine to Paul and Mariia, 11 and 19 Nov. (OS) 1781, *SIRIO* 9, pp. 86–7, 89–92.

[25] PRO, FO/7/3, Keith to Stormont, nos. 140, 141, and 142, 3, 7, and 10 Nov. (NS) 1781. Kaunitz was the source for Keith's reports indicating Austrian annoyance with Paul's slow progress and the shortness of his projected stay. See also Kaunitz to Joseph (addendum by Joseph), 15 Nov. 1781, Beer, *Joseph II*, 107–8.

and, more objectively, from the fact that the travellers greatly extended their stay. Paul had informed Joseph by courier from Poland that he and Mariia would only be able to remain in Vienna a week or so.[26] Under the emperor's friendly influence, they relaxed, began to enjoy themselves, and then deferred their departure from the originally deposed 20 November (OS) until after Christmas. They were in Vienna for over six weeks.[27]

Joseph used his knowledge of Paul and Mariia to plan the events which took place during their stay. Count Kaunitz had suggested that a display of the empire's power, magnificence, and cultural leadership would most impress the grand duke and his wife, and he proposed to make the visit a vast festival featuring opera, dance, music, and theatre performed by the leading artists of the day. Around this centrepiece he would have arranged a series of brilliant receptions, dinners, and balls, together with military manœuvres and parades. He also suggested that there be no admission fee for the gala events to guarantee the largest possible attendance.[28] Joseph rejected this plan as too expensive, too difficult to arrange on short notice, but above all as inappropriate for these guests. He believed that Paul and Mariia were private people who had no liking for elaborate social events, who needed time to themselves, who would particularly value the opportunity to visit instructive sites and appreciate choosing what they might see.[29] He also knew that Paul took a deep interest in governmental affairs, and that he felt himself excluded from everything important. Thus one of the first things Joseph showed his visitor was his own work cabinet, how he handled his papers and

[26] See *SIRIO* 9, pp. 89–94, 98–104, 108–13, for indications of Paul and Mariia's pleasure with their treatment. See also Catherine's letters to Joseph, Arneth, *Joseph II*, 112–21. Keith's reports supported this view. PRO, FO/7/3, Keith to Stormont, nos. 146–9, 151, 154, 155, 158, 159, and 161, and FO/7/4, nos. 2, 3, and 6. These reports cover the entire period of Paul and Mariia's stay. Sir James Harris reported the story differently from Petersburg. On the basis of information from the Austrian ambassador, Count Cobenzl (presumably informed from Vienna), and Potemkin, Harris portrayed Paul and Mariia's letters as exercises in dissimulation, that Paul was displeased and offended in Vienna, that Panin was coaching him, and that Catherine was as yet unaware. The Harris reports say more about court politics in Petersburg than what Paul and Mariia were doing in Vienna. PRO, FO/65/5, Harris to Fox, 30 Nov./11 Dec. 1781; 7/18 Dec. 1781; FO/65/6, no. 6, Apr. 1782.

[27] The duration of the stay had been left open. PRO, FO/7/3, Keith to Stormont, no. 120, 12 Sept. (NS) 1781. Kaunitz informed Keith of the original arrangements. Catherine warned Paul against leaving too abruptly, and asked for a definite date. Letters of 1 and 7 Dec. (OS) 1781, *SIRIO* 9, pp. 92–8. She also apologized to Joseph. Letters of 7/18 Dec. and 28 Dec. (OS) 1781, Arneth, *Joseph II*, 115–17.

[28] Kaunitz to Joseph, 22 July 1781, Beer, *Joseph II*, 92–3.

[29] Joseph to Kaunitz, Beer, *Joseph II*, 95–6, 100–2; Arneth, *Joseph II*, u. *Leopold von Toscana*, i. 332–9.

correspondence, and what he thought was his own responsibility and what could be delegated. He went further. He showed Paul his secret correspondence, the diplomatic arrangements between Catherine and himself, and outlined the negotiations in progress concerning their common interests. Catherine was pleased when Paul reported his conversations with Joseph on the latter's work; she was much less enthusiastic about his allowing Paul to see confidential papers. She hoped that he was not too young and inexperienced to bear such a responsibility.[30]

Magnificence had its moments. The entrance into Vienna became a triumphal progress, a brilliant ball was given two days later, while another held on the first weekend at Schönbrunn attracted 4,000 guests.[31] But Joseph was also assiduous in helping his visitors to see what they wanted to see. And they wanted to see everything that would give them information about or insight into society, the workings of the economic system, health maintenance, army training, and the governing of the country. They were equally interested in religion and culture. They visited mines, salt-works, and factories; military encampments, government offices, hospitals, schools, and prisons; churches, museums, and shrines. They were anxious to meet and talk with important people, and throughout their visit the emperor remained their guide and personal commentator. Catherine was pleased and impressed with the reports she received. She wrote repeatedly to thank Joseph for the care and trouble he was taking, and to tell him how enthusiastic Paul and Mariia were about him, and how their letters sparkled with admiration for him. To Paul and Mariia, she exclaimed over their warm reception, commented on the varied sights they were seeing, and expressed her approval with Paul's report 'that he considers the time passed in Vienna as dedicated to instruction' and his further note that the last days of their stay were devoted to inquiring into interesting and useful matters. At this stage of the journey, Catherine had every reason to be pleased.[32]

---

[30] Catherine II to Joseph II, 1 Dec. (OS) 1781 and 3 Jan. (OS) 1782, Arneth, *Joseph II*, 113–14, 117–19.

[31] PRO, FO/7/3, Keith to Stormont, no. 146, 21 Nov. (NS) 1781 (on the arrival in Vienna), no. 147, 24 Nov. (NS) 1781, and no. 148, 28 Nov. (NS) 1781. Morane, *Paul Ier*, 223.

[32] PRO, FO/7/3, Keith to Stormont, no. 149, 1 Dec. (NS) 1781; no. 154, 12 Dec. (NS) 1781; no. 158, 22 Dec. (NS) 1781. Catherine to Joseph, Arneth, *Joseph II*, 113–20; Catherine to Paul and Mariia, 1 Dec. (OS) 1781, *SIRIO* 9, pp. 92–4; 3 Dec. (OS) 1781, pp. 95–6 (visit to the Wielitschka mines); 10 Dec. (OS) 1781, pp. 98–102; to Mariia on her comments on their reception in Vienna, the Schönbrunn, etc., 21 Dec.

Paul, by all accounts, was conducting himself well. He was also far less susceptible to influence than Joseph thought him to be. His basic political views (especially his commitment to Prussia and the principles he believed Prussia embodied) remained entirely unchanged by his Vienna experiences. Yet he stayed on good terms with Joseph, took every opportunity to learn from the experiences laid before him, and in every respect showed himself to be a balanced and mature representative for his country. On the last day of December, Sir Robert Keith noted on Paul's visit that 'there has appeared an uniform Propriety, and a laudable Hunt after Knowledge which argue a greater share of Judgement and Penetration than has usually been ascribed to that Prince', while just a month earlier Kaunitz spoke of Paul to Keith 'in Terms of Commendation, giving it as his sincere Opinion that the Talents and acquired Knowledge of that Prince greatly exceeded the Idea he had formed of them from general Reports—He said all Parties seemed pleased with the Happy meeting . . . .'.[33]

Apart from the very good experience Paul and Mariia had with Joseph, they could take pleasure in the reception Vienna accorded them. Their entrance into the city in Joseph's carriage set off impromptu celebrations, their public appearances invariably drew large and noisy crowds, while the Viennese press greeted them as if they were the most important people in the world. The *Wiener Zeitung* for 24 November poetically proclaimed the city's 'boundless joy', at having 'the great northern star himself' shining in all his majesty within Vienna's walls. And in another place the same paper's versifier asked expansively if anywhere there was a true patriot to be found whose heart did not leap up for joy at the way heaven itself had linked 'the gods of this world' with unbreakable bonds of friendship.[34]

It is obvious that authority encouraged these outpourings, yet they contributed measurably to the gala atmosphere and to the travellers' self-esteem. Such popular demonstrations were repeated virtually

(OS) 1781, pp. 103–4; 26 Dec. (OS) 1781, pp. 104–8; (Paul's comments) 23 Dec. 1781/3 Jan. 1782 and 4 Jan. (NS) 1782, pp. 108–10; 13 Jan. (NS) 1782, pp. 110–13.

[33] PRO, FO/7/3, Keith to Stormont, no. 148, 28 Nov. (NS) and no. 161, 31 Dec. (NS) 1781.

[34] Arneth, *Joseph II u. Leopold von Toscana*, i. 61–2. The poems are given in full: 'Die Freude Wiens ist unbegrenzt, | Gleich uns das Glück zu Theil geworden, | Dass selbst der grosse Stern aus Norden, | In voller Majestät in unsern Mauern glänzt.' (This appeared as a motto above the news columns.) In that same issue (24 Nov. 1781) was the following: 'Da schon der Himmel selbst die Götter diesen Erden, | Mit eu'gen Freundschaftstanden knüpft, | Kann der wohl noch also Patriot Erfunden werden, | Dem nicht das Herz für Freuden küpft?'

everywhere Paul and Mariia went, with the most enthusiastic reception coming in Paris where, for the duration of their stay, 'les comtes du Nord' were to all intents adopted as the city's own. (They attracted the least attention in Rome and Naples.) This enthusiasm compared favourably with the gala reception Paul had had in Berlin five years earlier, and with the warm receptions he had on those rare occasions when he went among the people at home. All this adulation from commoners and titled alike contrasted sharply with the way Paul felt that he was treated at his mother's court. And from Catherine's viewpoint, Paul's reception abroad was two-edged: she could find some gratification in the good image for Russia that all of this implied, but she could worry as well that Paul's head might be turned by so much adulation. Indeed, there were hints that she was being warned to this effect long before Paul turned homeward, and that she, in consequence was preparing to deflate him.[35]

Mariia's family *was* waiting when she and Paul arrived in Vienna. This touched her heart, heightened her pleasure, and gave her an occupation beyond sightseeing. She became involved in arranging the details of her sister's marriage to the archduke Franz, and she protested (with Paul's backing) when Frederick summarily dismissed her brother, Frédéric-Eugène, from the Prussian service. Momentarily, it seemed, there were grounds for alienating Paul from the Prussians. But this did not happen. Frédéric-Eugène was taken into the Russian service where later he became an issue between Paul and Mariia and Catherine.[36]

Paul held aloof from the marital politicking, even going so far as to leave the room when the marriage was discussed. The marriage, like the trip itself, was part of Catherine's evident determination to draw nearer to Austria. Paul disapproved. It was a measure of his devotion to his wife that he made no move to upset the agreement. It was Joseph's belief that he could win Paul's friendship and so wean him from Prussia. The second in no way followed from the first. Personal relations between the grand duke and the emperor seemed good throughout the entire stay. Joseph spent some of every day with his guests, arranged their daily sightseeing, introduced them to the people they wanted to meet, and looked after all their needs. When the Russian party finally departed Vienna on 4 January, Joseph accompanied them on the first stage of their journey towards Venice. He remained with them as far as Mürzzuschlag after several members, Mariia included, took the flu and had to stop at Wiener

[35] See below, Ch. 6.
[36] Shumigorskii, *Mariia Fedorovna*, i. 116; Arneth, *Joseph II u. Leopold von Toscana*, i. 121; Morane, *Paul Ier*, 225–6; Kobeko, *Pavel Petrovich*, 208–11.

Neustadt. While the sick rested, the healthy members of the party entertained themselves with Paul and Joseph singing duets. It may well have been their most harmonious moment.[37]

With his guests well launched on the next leg of their journey, Joseph took stock of the situation.[38] On the whole, he reported in a letter to his brother Leopold, the visit 'took the most advantageous turn', and he concluded, rather overoptimistically, that 'there can no longer be any doubt about the sincerity of the sentiments of friendship and confidence which have been established between them and myself'. So well did Joseph think everything had gone that he offered his experience to guide Leopold when Paul and Mariia visited him the following spring in Tuscany. His outline offers an interesting and rather sympathetic portrait of Paul and Mariia at the end of 1781.

The most serious problem the emperor saw was to win and hold the grand ducal couple's trust. These were people whom circumstance had made more suspicious than it was natural for them to be, and it was essential that they not be given the least excuse for thinking they were being fooled, misled, or manipulated, or that anything of importance was being concealed from them. Nothing pleased them better than to be allowed to see everything they wanted to see freely, without hindrance, and with no effort to disguise or hide such faults as might exist. Similarly, problems and controversial issues were best discussed openly and without reserve. They placed the highest value on frankness, honesty, and plain-speaking, were offended by the patent hypocrisies practised in the name of formal etiquette, and were determined to accept no special favours from any individual. They insisted on rigidly adhering to their incognitos, which were to be used even in private conversations; they wanted no extra attendants (a personal retinue travelled with them); and they were happiest to be received as old acquaintances with whom it was possible to speak openly and without reserve.

The tastes and style of living which 'les comtes du Nord' affected were as simple and regular as their interests were cultivated. They wanted to meet and talk with interesting people, both men and women of whatever class, who were distinguished by their wit and knowledge. This, as Joseph reported it, was not entirely disinterested

---

[37] Benckendorff, *La Jeunesse*, 179–81. The duet was airs from 'Orpheus et Alceste'. The stop at Wiener Neustadt is commonly cited; Joseph, however, wrote to Leopold that he accompanied the Russians as far as Mürzzuschlag. Joseph to Leopold, 10 Jan. 1782, Arneth, *Joseph II u. Leopold von Toscana*, i. 67.

[38] For the memo summarized here, see: app. 3, Arneth, *Joseph II u. Leopold von Toscana*, i. 332–9. Cf. Kobeko, *Pavel Petrovich*, 199–203.

since they appeared to believe that by consorting with, and favourably impressing, such people their own status in the public eye would improve. Nevertheless, despite this, and despite their nearly insatiable appetite for seeing everything of interest, they remained private people who needed time to themselves. They retired early and did not go out before 10 or 10.30 in the morning. Their free time was spent in recording their impressions and attending to a voluminous correspondence. Their tastes in food were simple—fruit compote was a favourite dish—and they drank only mineral waters. Paul liked to have maps, pictures, and plans of the places he was visiting; Mariia, who enjoyed music and flowers, was pleased to have a clavecin and bouquets in her rooms. She always carried a nosegay when she went out. Paul would not dance at all; Mariia danced but did not care for it. However, 'Military and naval matters were certainly one of their favourite occupations, as well as those concerning commerce, industry, and manufacturing . . .'. Joseph urged his brother to make every effort to facilitate their seeing whatever they wished in these areas. He also noted that Paul and Mariia had an abiding interest in how people lived and what the government was doing to ease or to improve their conditions of life. Joseph still valued Mariia above Paul, though he considered neither, even by the most sympathetic reading, inspired, brilliant, or in any way exceptional. They did, however, appear to be devoted to one another, dedicated to improving themselves, enlightened, and humane.

The Venetians knew nothing of Joseph's recommendations. When Paul and Mariia arrived there, they were overwhelmed by a full week of non-stop festival. In later years, Mariia recalled that they were dissatisfied and rather disappointed in Italy because the press of official events was so wearying and time-consuming that they had little opportunity to find out about everyday life.[39] In Venice there was no time for serious pursuits. Instead there were receptions, balls, spectacles, regattas, opera, theatre, and banquets. And, according to at least one participant, the dowager countess Ursinius (Orsini) et Rosenberg, the Russian visitors were unfailingly gracious and charming. She found in Mariia 'a perfectly blended combination of dignity and sweetness', a high degree of social finesse, and 'the most marked desire to pay attention to everyone, eagerly seizing every pretext that presented itself to say something personal and honest'. Paul was more tightly controlled, less demonstrative, more of a single piece, yet completely at his ease. He chatted with anyone who approached him, usually putting questions to them, but always

---

[39] Benckendorff, *La Jeunesse*, 184–5.

questions on things which he had already noticed and which his interlocutor could explain to him. At the theatre, the dowager countess thought Paul's comments on design and decoration to be appropriate, tasteful, and intelligent; she declared him to be well informed on the arts in general. Both he and his wife were cultured, interesting, and altogether admirable companions.[40]

The closing event of the Russians' stay was a vast spectacle and illumination during which Paul and Mariia were surrounded by the most distinguished people of the city who paid their compliments and received expressions of gratitude and appreciation from the visitors. The imperial pair outdid themselves in graciousness and address, while crowds of citizens pressed around them, filling the great San Marco square. The spectacle ended in a paean for Venice with the huge crowd, nobles and commoners alike, roaring out the 'Viva San Marco!' in a perfect frenzy of patriotic enthusiasm. All of this had an extraordinary effect on Paul who was swept away by the spirit of the moment and was heard to shout to someone in the midst of the din, 'Here is the effect of good government: this people truly is one family united!'[41]

Venice impressed and attracted Paul. Its rigidly hierarchical social structure, its combination of law and authority, and its long tradition of civic spirit appealed strongly to him. Mariia thought he was misled. There were so many public activities that he never had the opportunity to see the rottenness underneath the glittering exterior, nor the way the ordered state which so impressed him stifled the public in its actions.[42] Catherine, too, countered Paul's enthusiasm for the Venetian system remarking on the relative ease with which a small state could order its affairs. Large, complex systems (like Russia) were far more difficult. Paul did, apparently, comment on Venice's decline from its former glory. This was a subject which

---

[40] *Du séjour des comtes du nord à Venise en janvier MDCCLXXXII: Lettre de mme. la comtesse douairière des Ursins et Rosenberg, à m. Richard Wynne, son frère à Londres* (n.pl., 1782), 19–20, 22–3. The letter, which is over 70 pp., gives a detailed account of the visit and is dated 12 Feb. 1782. See also K. Nonni, *Descrizione degli spettacoli, e feste datesi in Venezia per occasione della venuta delle LL. AA. II. il Gran Duca, e Gran Duchessa di Moscovia, sotto il nome de Conti del Nort, nel Mese di Gennajo, 1782,* 2nd edn. (Venice, 1782). This 15-pp. pamphlet describes the places visited and the events attended. As frontispieces, there are engravings depicting Paul and Mariia; the portrayal of Paul is particularly fine.

[41] Ursins et Rosenberg, *Du séjour*, 68–71; Nonni, *Descrizione*, 11–12. Both record Paul's excitement and his exclamation, though Nonni gives it as 'Voilà l'effet du sage Gouvernement de la République. Le Peuple est une famille.' There is no reference to the republic in the Ursins text.

[42] Benckendorff, *La Jeunesse*, 184–5. See Mariia's letter to her youngest son, Grand Duke Michael, when he was travelling in Italy in 1819. SIRIO 5, p. 111.

Catherine thought it useful for him to consider. In her view, a society's decline owed to a concatenation of events, but she was certain that degradation of the spirit contributed in no small way. Paul's reaction is not recorded.[43]

From Venice the travellers' way led to Rome, then to Naples, back to Rome, and finally to Florence. Rome's antiquities were vastly exciting and they visited them all. Mariia was overwhelmed by the Pantheon, about which she wrote at length to Catherine. And both were fascinated by St Peter's. It was their first stop when they arrived on 25 January, and they went back next day. Then, having seen the Capitol, the Coliseum, and the attendant sights, they returned to St Peter's where Pope Pius VI was officiating at the mass. When he passed by, they stopped him and thanked him for the facilities he had made available to them in the states of the church. They then waited until the office finished to approach him a second time with 'all the marks of the most profound respect and the greatest humility'. Only then did they go to see the Raphael loges as well as the Vatican library and museum.[44]

In later years, when he was tsar, Paul offered the octogenarian Pius VI asylum in Russia. He also became embroiled with him over issues of ecclesiastical administration in the Catholic territories under Russian control, and over his own election as grand master of the knights of Malta. Even in the heat of these conflicts, however, he never lost the reverence for the Roman church which he exhibited on his visit in 1782. His formal religious instructor had declared Rome heretical and Orthodoxy the one true Christian community. Paul ignored this position. As a religious person with a broad and tolerant outlook, he found nothing unusual in showing the deepest respect for the pope and the Roman church. All, he was to remark much later and in a different context, were Christians, and so was he.[45] In this respect, he spoke a different language from Catherine who had no

[43] Catherine to Paul and Mariia, 14 Feb. (os) 1782, *SIRIO* 9, pp. 121–2.

[44] Benckendorff, *La Jeunesse*, 187–8. Pavlovsk, Paul and Mariia's country estate, reproduced in miniature the great arcade which bounds St Peter's Square. Norman Saul uses this to indicate Paul's strong interest in and orientation toward the Catholic west; it certainly suggests that St Peter's made a powerful impression. Saul, *Russia and the Mediterranean*.

[45] See Roderick E. McGrew, 'Paul I and the Knights of Malta', in H. Ragsdale (ed.), *Reassessment*, 44–75. See below, Ch. 8. Platon's catechism taught that Catholics were schismatic and heretical. *Pravoslavnoe uchenie* (1765), 81–4, on the historical authenticity of the Orthodox faith. Paul's remark that he was, after all, a Christian man was made to the duke of Serra Capriola; he would also claim that at heart he was a Catholic. See *Nonciatures de Russie d'après les documents authentiques: Interim de Benvenuti 1799–1803*, ed. M. J. Rouët de Journel, SJ, *Studi e Testi*, 194 (Vatican City, 1957), pp. xiii and 56–7.

sympathy for the pope or the Roman church. When Mariia described the visits to the sublime St Peter's, Catherine responded that the Pantheon, on which Mariia had also remarked, was 'more sublime than the church of St Peter itself'. She also congratulated Paul on the two kisses the pope imprinted on his cheeks. He could pride himself on possessing a rarity which hardly any Catholic took away from Rome. A few days later she was ridiculing the tale that the pope had heard heavenly voices directing him to Vienna (to negotiate with Joseph) while commenting acidly that the trip would be more valuable for his health than for his political interests. Later, she wrote to Grimm that she did not know whether or not her son had given the pope a beautiful fur, but she avowed she had one ready for him whenever he would send the pallium to (i.e. recognize) her archbishop of Mogilev. That Paul publicly paraded his reverential attitude towards the church was a way for him to draw the line between himself and his mother while showing his anti-Austrian bias as well. Whether he intended this effect is uncertain, though he could hardly not have known how it could be read.[46]

The two days spent in Rome were a prelude to a later three-week visit, but the immediate business of the travellers was to go to Naples. That visit was less than a success. Paul insisted on private accommodations; he wanted no debts of gratitude. But carnival was in full swing, and housing was hard to find. Worse, the Russian minister in Naples was Andrei Razumovskii. It was he who was responsible for local arrangements, including housing. When the two met, Paul controlled his anger until they were alone, and then poured out his pent-up fury. Razumovskii took his tongue-lashing, if not with good humour, at least with dignity, and was able to continue with his official duties. Paul, however, was unable to recover his spirits, began to sulk, and then turned mulishly uncooperative. He was withdrawn and rude to his hosts, Ferdinand III and Queen Caroline, both of whom he thoroughly disliked, and to avoid contact with them he went off sightseeing to Herculaneum, Pompeii, and Paestum. He was only prevented from visiting Mount Vesuvius by the extreme and unseasonable cold.[47]

---

[46] Catherine to Mariia and Paul, 18 Feb. (OS) and 27 Feb./6 Mar. 1782, *SIRIO* 9, pp. 122–4, 130–2. Catherine to Grimm, no. 108, 2 Apr. (OS) 1782, *SIRIO* 23, p. 235. On Catherine and the papacy, Paul Pierling, *La Russie et le Saint-Siège*, 5 vols. (Paris, 1896–1912), esp. vol. v.

[47] Lafermière to Vorontsov, Naples, 9 Feb. (NS) 1782, *Arkhiv kniazia Vorontsova*, xxix. 222–4; Wassiltchikow, *Razoumowski*, ii/1 71–3; Kobeko, *Pavel Petrovich*, 214–15; Morane, *Paul Ier*, 232–4. Morane repeated the assertion by the French minister in Naples, Clermont d'Amboise, that Paul drew his sword and had to be

Paul's discomfort in Naples became such that after a week he left suddenly for Rome without so much as taking leave of the king. None of this apparently disturbed Catherine whose letters remained friendly and interested.[48] Rome was much more to the grand ducal taste. Paul and Mariia went back to sightseeing and entered the art market. No catalogue of their purchases exists, though references to the decorations, paintings, and statuary they installed at Pavlosk and later at Gatchina make it apparent that they bought extensively. Catherine had hoped they would use her favourite agent, a German painter named Reiffenstein, but he was incapacitated with gout, and they turned to an Englishman named Jenkins. Catherine suspected that Paul was being victimized, and Grimm, when she wrote him about it, confirmed her fears. Jenkins, in his opinion, was a rascal who had literally decorated England with his trash. Paul, however, remained oblivious, nor is there any way of knowing whether, as Catherine claimed, there were more bastards than legitimate offspring among the treasures he sent home.[49]

Italy, apart from its antiquities, was a disappointment. The contrast between the condition of the people—their crowded livings, the poverty, the run-down look of the towns—and the beauty of the countryside initially excited comment and discussion. Eventually, however, it became depressing. St Peter's may have been thrilling, but the papal states were appalling. Paul wrote to Father Platon that he had come to believe that 'outside of pictures and other curiosities of that sort, there is nothing here [in Italy] to see'. Indeed, the Italian scene was such as to bring tears to the eyes, for it showed 'how far humanity can ascend under a good government', and how far it would fall when government was 'inept and brutal as it is in our days, with all due respect to the pope's infallibility'.[50]

In Tuscany, however, and especially in Florence, the clouds lifted. Paul and Mariia were impressed with the good order, prosperity, and beauty of this most beautiful of Italy's cities and regions. The Archduke Leopold was a governor worthy of study and emulation.

---

restrained from attacking Razumovskii. Wassiltchikow recounts a similar story which was a tradition in the Razumovskii family.

[48] See esp. Catherine's letter of 10 Mar. (OS) 1782, *SIRIO* 9, pp. 128–9. After Paul became tsar, he strongly backed these same Neopolitan Bourbons. See below, Ch. 9.

[49] Kobeko, *Pavel Petrovich*, 216; Catherine to Grimm, *SIRIO* 23, p. 154; Grimm to Catherine, 10/21 July 1782, *SIRIO* 44, p. 243; Morane, *Paul Ier*, 213–32.

[50] Mariia Fedorovna to La Harpe, 30 Apr. (OS) 1819, *SIRIO* 5, p. 111; Lafermière to Vorontsov, no. 19, 20 Mar. (NS) 1782, *Arkhiv kniazia Vorontsova*, xxix. 227; Paul to Platon, *Russkii arkhiv*, 2 (1887), 28.

Both waxed enthusiastic over the Tuscan court and their reception there. They were also pleased with what they saw of 14-year-old Archduke Franz, the future husband of Mariia's sister. Franz had not yet been told of his engagement; Leopold considered him too young, though Mariia was impressed with the maturity of his outlook. Catherine was happy with all of this. And the enthusiastic letters from Florence were reinforced by favourable reports from other sources on the impression they made. From her point of view, the visit to Tuscany was a striking success.[51]

Two months after Paul and Mariia left, Leopold drafted a long report to Joseph on their visit and what he thought he had learnt about them. Leopold was a fine administrator, a shrewd observer, and he wrote at length.[52] On the surface, his letter offered nothing but praise for what he described as the frankness, confidentiality, and friendliness Paul and Mariia showed him. Indeed, as he pointed out, he was surprised at how open they were, leaving literally nothing to the imagination when matters concerning them personally were discussed. In their very openness, however, Paul in particular revealed both ideas and an underlying character which were threatening to Austria's interests and which had troubling implications for his future subjects. Leopold made no comment on this aspect of his report; what he reported stood by itself.

Leopold was much taken with Mariia, with her 'sweetness, wit, talent and diligence', her deep attachment to her husband, and the 'friendly and cordial way they live together'. He approved of the religious spirit she showed during the Lenten season, and her commitment to the Greek faith. In his eyes, she was an altogether admirable young woman who supported her husband wholeheartedly. Paul impressed in other ways. Leopold saw him as a man of intellectual capacity who had a flair for grasping and coming to see all sides of complicated issues. He was also extremely suspicious. Leopold echoed Joseph's point that, in dealing with him, 'it is necessary to act openly, roundly, sincerely, and with justice'. He was struck with Paul's power and energy, 'the vigor in his way of thinking', and he predicted that he would be a very active ruler. He saw Paul as a man of commitment who, once he had taken a position, would not be easily moved from it, nor would he permit anyone to direct him. He was also certain that when he became tsar,

---

[51] Catherine to Paul and Mariia, 31 Mar. (OS) 1782, *SIRIO* 9, pp. 133–5, noting the letters from Rome and Florence. See also Benckendorff, *La Jeunesse*, 195–7; Kobeko, *Pavel Petrovich*, 220–1; Shumigorskii, *Mariia Fedorovna*, i. 114–24.

[52] For the report summarized here, see Arneth, *Joseph II u. Leopold von Toscana*, i. 114–24.

he would be 'even more severe and rigid for order, subordination without restriction, rule, and exactitude' than he was at present.

Paul appears to have said nothing about his situation in Catherine's court, or about the empress personally. But he spoke at length about how much he disapproved her internal reforms, 'all these great projects and innovations' which were going forward and which 'have more of appearance and name than of true solidity'. Nor was he backward about criticizing Catherine's plan 'for aggrandising herself at the expense of the Turks and refounding the empire of Constantinople'. Not only did he disapprove, but he would accept no argument at all for a monarchy so vast as Russia to conquer new territories. In his opinion, all such 'useless ideas of conquest serve only to acquire glory without bringing real advantage', and weakened the state which undertook them. This, of course, was the doctrine which he had summarized in his 1774 essay, and he connected it with another set of beliefs: his personal commitment to Berlin. For Paul, as Leopold described him, not only belonged heart and soul to Prussia, but identified that commitment with a conservative, peace-oriented policy.

Where Austria was concerned, Paul's remarks went beyond frankness. He complained repeatedly that, at his mother's insistence, he was kept under surveillance and that his mail was being held in Mantua. Leopold was unable to convince him that delays in the mail did not mean that the government was watching him. On larger questions, Paul gave it as his opinion that Austria had gained far more value from the partition of Poland than Russia had done. The implication was that an adjustment was in order. He also accused Austria of harbouring aggressive intentions in Italy, in the Germanies, and against the Ottoman empire. (Paul remained convinced of Austria's aggressive intent; this issue was critical in his troubles with Vienna during the war of the second coalition in 1799–1800.) He interpreted the current coalescence of Russian and Austrian interests as a pact for aggression. To this, it should be obvious, he would be firmly opposed; his political preferences lay with Prussia and peace.

As if reaffirming his own inalterable opposition to an Austro-Russian *rapprochement* were not enough, Paul charged that Austria had already bought and paid for the support of leading members of his mother's government, presumably to advance this ugly alliance. Leopold, he asserted, surely must know all about it since it was, after all, common knowledge, 'as was the day it was done, and the sums that were paid'. When the archduke protested his ignorance, Paul declared that he could inform him, and then listed the miscreants:

Prince Potemkin, Count Bezborodko, Catherine's secretary, Bakunin, the first commissioner for foreign affairs, Counts Simon and Alexander Vorontsov, and Morkov, the current Russian minister in Holland. His control slipped as the enormity of what he was describing overcame him. These men, in his eyes, were traitors, and he swore that as soon as he was tsar, he would uproot them from office, arrest them, and imprison them. Mariia, who was present at this conversation, confirmed everything her angry husband said.

What Leopold reported was a vintage example of how Paul reacted on issues where he disagreed. There were furious charges, threats of action, and claims of inside knowledge. How well informed he actually was is difficult to say. He had no access to what happened in Catherine's inner councils beyond what individuals might tell him or what he gleaned from gossip. He proved, however, to be an assiduous hoarder of this type of information. Leopold found him surprisingly knowledgeable on the court at Vienna, especially its civil and military employees, command levels of the army, family relationships, and general politics. When asked how they knew what they knew, Paul and Mariia revealed that in addition to their journals they kept notebooks in which they jotted down whatever they heard that was interesting. And they had been doing this for several years. They kept records of the conversations they had with important people, when they took place, where, and what was said. So, for example, when they wanted to discuss Franz's marriage to Elizabeth, they were able to take out their notebooks and read out how 'His Majesty the Emperor told us such and such a thing, the words themselves, the Monday in March, in what room, in the presence of what person, at what time of day or evening.' Not surprisingly, after this revelation, Leopold took special pains over what he said since he knew it was all going down in the Russians' notebooks and would be there to be called up against him at any time.

This portrait of Paul and Mariia had more depth and detail than Joseph's earlier appraisal. Leopold found Mariia an attractive person, and he thought the relationship between husband and wife exemplary. If there was any tension between them, it did not show. Paul was more difficult, more complicated, and clearly someone to be reckoned with. Leopold portrayed him as a careful, suspicious, and vengeful man, yet one whose anger was very near the surface, and who was as stubborn and unyielding on matters which he considered principle as it was possible for any person to be. He saw no willingness to compromise, though he identified a capacity for dissimulation, but in Leopold's opinion Joseph only deluded himself if he thought he had won any ground with Paul. The opinions the grand duke gave so freely were prima-facie evidence to the contrary.

Leopold accompanied 'les comtes du Nord' as far as Livorno where they spent Easter and visited the Russian fleet. In Milan they were entertained by the Litta family, a connection which later was important for Paul's relations with the knights of Malta, and they passed on through Turin towards Lyons. They had intended to visit Geneva, but political disorders there forced them to change their plan. They were given a gala reception by the citizens of Lyons where they visited the St. Étienne arms factories as well as various hospitals and prisons before leaving for Paris. At Fontainebleau Mariia's childhood friend Madame Oberkirch joined them to the grand duchess's great delight, and they made a triumphal entry into the city on 7 May taking temporary lodging with the Russian ambassador before moving into special accommodations on the ground floor of the Orangerie.[53]

Paris rather than Vienna was the high point of the trip.[54] Louis XVI and Marie Antoinette made every effort to welcome their Russian visitors, to make them comfortable, and to open society to them. Relations between the imperial pair and the royal couple began on an awkward note; with familiarity, however, the picture changed as Mariia overcame her natural reserve and disapproval of what she saw as Marie Antoinette's light and giddy ways. The king, who was virtually incomprehensible at the formal reception, finally mastered his shyness to put himself on warm personal terms with his guests. Paul seemed more than equal to any occasion. 'You see from whence I write you', he introduced a note from Paris to Osten-Sacken, 'that is to say in the midst of a whirlwind of people, of things, of facts' and he prayed that God would give him 'sufficient strength to be equal to it all'. However, he knew he had a front to maintain, and this was worth the effort, for 'when one labors a little on his reputation,

---

[53] Lafermière to Vorontsov, no. 21, Turin, 25 Apr. (NS) 1782, *Arkhiv kniazia Vorontsova*, xxix. 220 on the Geneva disorders and the itinerary change; for Catherine's comments, her letter to Paul and Mariia, 5 May (OS) 1782, SIRIO 9, p. 148. See also: Benckendorff, *La Jeunesse*, 197–8; Kobeko, *Pavel Petrovich*, 221–5; Oberkirch, *Mémoires*, 150 ff.

[54] Morane, *Paul Ier*, 244–58, covers the visit in detail, using French sources to good advantage. Cf. Kobeko, *Pavel Petrovich*, 221–32; Benckendorff, *La Jeunesse*, 197–217; Shil'der, *Pavel I*, 161–3; Shumigorskii, *Mariia Fedorovna*, i. 211–24. Baron Grimm accompanied the Russians around the city and reported their experiences to Catherine. See his letters of 16/27 May, 19/31 May, 5/16 June, 7/18 June, 10/21 June, 28 June/9 July, 10/21 July, 1782, SIRIO 44, pp. 214–24. Oberkirch, *Mémoires*, 154–220, is the most complete account of the visit and can be checked against Grimm.

neither fatigue nor wakefulness are frightening. One seeds to reap and everything is repaid.'[55] Both Paul and Mariia found the pace and crowds exhausting, yet they were treated with such consideration for their needs that they could only be charmed. Marie Antoinette had the instructions and admonitions which Joseph had prepared, and they were followed to the letter. Mariia found flowers and her clavecin in the Orangerie apartment; Paul was deluged with maps, plans, and guides for everything he wanted to see. Mercy d'Argenteau, the Austrian minister in Paris, made sure that the travellers were aware that it was Joseph whose influence produced these amenities.[56]

But Paris herself was ready to fête the Russians. Russia, and especially Catherine, were in high good favour thanks to the support the empress was giving France against England; the Armed Neutrality of 1780 was very popular. Shops worked Russia or the empress into their names, and one ingenious entrepreneur sold a blouse *à la russe* modelled on a little shirt Catherine had designed for Alexander. Catherine's high standing with the intellectual establishment was also helpful. Paul and Mariia were entertained at special sittings of the academy as well as at a reading, given by Beaumarchais himself, from the manuscript of his 'Mariage de Figaro'. There was scarcely a dissenting word: to be *à la russe* was to be à la mode, and for a month, Paul and Mariia rode the crest of a wave of popularity.

Paris fed Paul's monarchical appetites. The inner circle of the royal family, the counts of Provence and Artois, the duke of Orléans, and the prince of Condé, competed with one another in welcoming and entertaining the count and countess of the North. Condé made a particularly strong impression. Paul and Mariia spent forty-eight hours as his honoured guests at Chantilly, where nothing was spared in the way of luxury and comfort. The prince was reputed to be both a cultured gentleman and a brave warrior; Paul was enchanted with him. Not all the royal family was equally prepossessing. The duke of Chartres, later Philippe Egalité, made a bad impression with his gross manners and open disrespect for the king who, in Paul's opinion, was much too patient. 'If my mother had such a cousin', he remarked, 'he would not remain long in Russia', and he commented darkly that such divisions in the ruling family could be extremely dangerous to public order.

[55] Paul to Osten-Sacken, no. 37, 14/25 May 1782, *SIRIO* 20, p. 435.
[56] Morane, *Paul Ier*, 246. Morane quotes the Austrian ambassador, Mercy-Argenteau, who informed Joseph that he had made it his goal to let the Russians know that 'it is to the emperor [Joseph] that they owe what proves to be agreeable in this court'. (Quoted from) Arneth and Flammeront, *Correspondence secrète de Mercy-Argenteau*, i. 107 and 110 (Paris, 1889).

Paul wallowed in royalist sentiment. Even before he was formally presented, he travelled to Versailles to attend a service of installation for the order of the Holy Ghost. He was deeply impressed. And after he had his formal presentation at court, he went into the room where the three-month-old dauphin lay in his crib to tell the baby's governess that she must remember this day so that she could tell the dauphin in later years how the future tsar of Russia had visited and had vowed to maintain a connection with him which would bind their two countries long into the future. These sentiments were repeated with complacent approval throughout the court.

Before the court and society, Paul and Mariia appeared to good advantage. There were the inevitable comments on Paul's manners—people came to see the 'young Scythian', criticized his loud and disruptive voice (the approved court style was to speak in a soft murmur, virtually a whisper, while Paul spoke out roundly), and wondered that he was not more savage than he was. Carping aside, there was nothing especially scandalous to report. It was known that Paul's temper was quick, but it almost never showed, though there was one confrontation which titillated the public and set tongues wagging. Catherine's favourite architect, Clérisseau, wanted to greet Paul to express his gratitude for all the empress had done for him. When he was presented, however, there was such a crush that Paul misunderstood what the artist wanted, and thinking he was trying to promote a commission, responded brusquely that he had none to give and turned away. Clérisseau, wounded and angry, went away vowing that he would have satisfaction. When Paul learnt about his mistake, he determined to right matters and, seeing Clérisseau again, began to tell him what he would have said had there not been such a crowd. It was an attempt to make amends. The architect refused to accept Paul's lead, chose to take what he was saying as a further insult, and rejected Mariia's efforts to put things straight. Unable to make Clérisseau understand, and frustrated at the impasse, Paul finally walked away from it. Grimm apologized to Catherine for Clérisseau's behaviour, though suggested that whatever wrong he did arose from his profound respect for and gratitude to Catherine. He also thought Paul handled a difficult situation well.[57]

---

[57] For Grimm's account, his letter to Catherine, 24 Oct./4 Nov. 1782, *SIRIO* 44, pp. 283–6. Baroness Oberkirch reported the confrontation rather differently. She saw only one meeting (the 2nd) and described Clérisseau blocking Paul's way and demanding to know why Paul would not talk to him. Paul is said to have replied, 'Because I have nothing to say to you.' Clérisseau then charged Paul with ignoring him when they were both in Petersburg and asserted that he had written the empress to protest. Paul gave a wry smile and slipped past remarking, 'You can also write to

As Paul and Mariia improved on their relations with the king and queen, they began to confide their more private feelings. In Paul's case, this included complaints about Catherine and the way she treated him. There was a particular cause. There was a continuing correspondence between Prince Alexander Kurakin in Paul's retinue and Paul's partisans in St Petersburg who not only reported what was happening but commented on it. This correspondence did not escape Catherine's attention, and when one of the correspondents, a captain Bibikov, indulged in critical remarks about Potemkin and the empress, he was put under arrest. Orders were also prepared for Kurakin's immediate recall. Catherine icily informed her son (in Russian in an otherwise French text) that she had uncovered an intrigue against herself about which Paul should know and that she had taken steps to correct the matter. Later she expanded on her theme, rejected Kurakin's self-serving efforts to distance himself from Bibikov, and indulged in a sharp attack on gossip-mongers and disloyal servitors. The warning was unmistakable; Catherine would not tolerate even the appearance of a cabal among Paul's intimates. She hardly needed to say that Paul himself was not beyond her reach.[58]

Paul was both angry and helpless. Kurakin was a long-time friend and one of the few people who were intimate with him. There was no way to protect him, and losing him would be a painful blow. Small wonder then that he spoke bitterly of the circumstances under which he had to live in Petersburg, the hostile surveillance of which he was the object, the harassment which he suffered at the hands of Catherine's favourites, and the way that anything and everything to do with himself, his comfort, or his friends was open to attack. This was persecution, and he resented it. Marie Antoinette sympathized and asked if it was true that he could trust no one in the company

madame my mother that you prevented me from passing, monsieur! She will certainly thank you for that!' Oberkirch, *Mémoires*, 212. Grimm said that there were several versions, but in fact no one was near enough to the two men to hear. Oberkirch thought, as Grimm did, that Paul handled the situation well. Her comment, however, that 'M. le comte du Nord possesses a perfect tact and great power over himself' (p. 215), goes rather far, though throughout the trip Paul maintained an even and courteous demeanor. The one serious exception was in Naples.

[58] Catherine to Paul, 25 Apr. (OS) 1782, *SIRIO* 23, p. 145; 7 June (OS) 1782, *SIRIO* 23, pp. 157–9. For Bibikov's letter dated 1 Apr. (OS) 1782, Shil'der, *Pavel I*, no. xvi, p. 555. Given the severity of Catherine's reaction, the letter is rather innocuous. Harris, however, reported that Potemkin had been agitating Catherine against Paul, and that her suspicions were fully aroused. PRO, FO/65/6, Harris to Stormont, no. 14, 11/22 Feb. 1782.

which attended him. Paul replied that he would not dare to have so much as a poodle that was devoted to him because 'he would never leave Paris as my mother would have him thrown into the Seine with a stone attached to his neck'.[59]

Despite his grievances, Paul enjoyed the infinite variety which Paris offered. He and Mariia toured the city's sights and were warmly welcomed wherever they went. Grimm was jubilant over their reception; Madame Oberkirch added details. When Mariia, for example, attended a special session of the academy of sciences with Paul, she made an effort to quote something from what each academician whom she met had written. Her audience, not surprisingly, was astonished. The theatre was a special joy. The Théâtre-Français put on command performances of *The Gallant Mercury*, and, particularly appealing to Paul, *The Hunting Party of Henry IV*. He was so moved by the performance that he requested it be played again. They heard Rameau's *Castor and Pollux*, saw Mademoiselle Heinel, a celebrated dancer, in a pantomime called 'Ninette at Court', and viewed the Gobelins at Les Invalides. They visited Notre Dame, which Mariia thought overwhelming; they attended a session of the *parlement*, visited Louis XVI's retired financial minister, Jacques Necker (whose work Mariia strongly recommended to Paul), and looked in on the brilliant salons. They found the hospitals, asylums, orphanages, and prisons, and they went to the caserne to visit the garrison. They spent money freely. Paul paid the debts of several men incarcerated in debtor's prison and made large on-the-spot contributions to churches and hospitals. 'Les comtes du Nord', as Madame Oberkirch reported, would leave their rooms with purses stuffed with gold, and when they returned those same purses would be empty. Their generosity was warmly received, and one evening at the theatre they were treated to an ovation which lasted throughout the performance.[60]

[59] Morane, *Paul Ier*, 248, uses this incident to indict Paul for 'These invectives, these violent explosions' which could have seemed 'foreign and a little plebeian' in the muted atmosphere of Versailles. In fact, Paul behaved far better than this suggests and showed considerable control.

[60] Grimm to Catherine, 16/27 May 1782, for Beaumarchais's reading and the academy's sitting; 19/30 May for theatricals. He records that 'their [les comtes du Nord] popularity is a plague which has infected all Paris'. Their leaving (letter of 5/16 June) will be a loss; their success has been enormous, and Grimm cites it to pay further compliments to Catherine and the education she gave Paul. He reports how M. le Vergennes (the first minister) was overwhelmed with Paul, and wonders how he would contain himself were he to see Alexander and Constantine who undoubtedly far surpass their father. *SIRIO* 44, pp. 216–21. Oberkirch, *Mémoires*, on Beaumarchais, 168; on the academy, 169–70; on the theatre, 170–1; sightseeing, 177–84. See also 'Iz zapisok Bashomont'a'.

For this brief period, Paul and Mariia lived as they thought royalty should. They complained of fatigue, of the multiplying burdens of etiquette, but they lived their roles to the hilt. Finally, in early June after a month of high living, they reluctantly prepared to leave. They parted from the king and queen most cordially at Choisy, and went south to visit some of the Loire chateaux. From there they turned first west, then north through Maine, Brittany, and Normandy towards the Low Countries. Paris had been an extraordinary experience; everything thereafter was anticlimax.

Though Paul and Mariia took more than ordinary pains to visit institutions charged with caring for the poor, the destitute, and above all the ill, there is no sign at all that they related what they saw to more general social problems. They did complain about the state of the roads and the poor coaching facilities, but none of this was given any broader significance. Yet there is at least one hint that the changes occurring in French life did not entirely escape Paul, and that already in 1782 he was concerned about the direction French thought was taking. When he passed through Brittany on his way to Brest, he is supposed to have stopped overnight in the village of Chateaulin where he visited the church and talked with the abbé Lharidon de Penguilly. The conversation was wide-ranging, touching, among other things, on the destiny of a France in which a radically new orientation of ideas, 'which had not escaped the perspicacity of the future emperor during his stay in Paris', threatened all that was established and stable. Paul was greatly impressed with abbé Lharidon, and on the following day he returned to him and to the subject they had discussed the night before. He also proposed that if the catastrophe both feared were to happen Lharidon should seek asylum in Russia. Whether Paul remembered the incident or not, the abbé did, and when the revolution broke out he emigrated and was warmly received. He died in Russia, far away from France, a beneficiary of Paul's 1782 visit.[61]

Brittany, Normandy, and the Low Countries provided an interlude of relative ease after the intense experiences in Paris. Paul retraced Peter the Great's steps at Maasdam and Spa, was fascinated by the flat geometricity of the Dutch landscapes, and was reminded of Peter's lack of sympathy for the open and disorderly political system by which the Netherlands was governed. Peter's memory was never far from Paul's mind in the Low Countries, and this may help to account for the extraordinary anecdote Baroness Oberkirch recorded him telling in Brussels.[62] One evening in July, after Mariia had left

[61] T. Pilven, *Un tzar en Bretagne* (Rennes, 1892), 17.
[62] Oberkirch, *Mémoires*, 239–48.

the party, the talk had turned to premonitions, prophecies, and supernatural events. Paul contributed nothing to the conversation until the prince de Ligne asked him if Russia was exempt from wondrous occurrences. Paul said that there were such phenomena, that he had had some experience of them, but that he was reluctant to talk about them. Nevertheless, on being urged, he told of going out in Petersburg late one night attended only by Kurakin. As they strolled along, he became aware of a figure walking beside him, between himself and the wall. The night, in early spring, was pleasant, but Paul felt a deep chill on his left side. He called Kurakin's attention to the figure, but the prince said that no one was there. Paul insisted there was someone, and looked more closely to see who it might be. The figure was muffled to the eyes in its cloak, and wore a hat pulled down firmly over its forehead. When it spoke, it addressed him as 'Poor Paul', identified itself as someone 'who is interested in you', and declared that it was his wish that Paul not become 'too attached to this world, for you will not remain here long'. The apparition advised Paul 'to live justly if you wish to die in peace' and to remember that remorse was 'the sharpest torment of great souls'. It also predicted that Paul would see him again, and often, and then lowered its cloak to reveal the unmistakable features—'the noble brow and penetrating eye'—of Paul's great grandfather, Peter the Great. He disappeared just opposite the site Catherine later selected for Falconet's heroic equestrian statue of Peter. This, to Paul's mind, was as much cause for wonder as the apparition itself. He had never suggested that site to his mother; the phantom knew in advance and predicted it.

Kurakin never saw the apparition. He was uncomfortable while Paul was telling the story, and when asked for confirmation that 'something strange had happened', his reply was, 'So strange, monseigneur, that despite the respect I owe your words, I can only regard this fact as a trick of your imagination.' Paul was amused at the reply. He had only agreed to tell the story after everyone promised not to repeat it. Beyond his fear that it would frighten Mariia, he did not want to have such a story of ghosts, told by himself about himself, making the rounds of Europe. Yet he swore he believed in it, regardless of what Kurakin said, and he related how his left side seemed frozen, and how it took him hours in bed to get warm. And what might all this prove, the prince de Ligne asked sceptically. 'It proves', said Paul, 'that I will die young, monsieur.'

There is no confirmation in any other source that Paul told this tale in Brussels. Madame Oberkirch swore that she, at any rate, had never mentioned the story to anyone, though she felt that she could include it in her memoirs since by the time they might be published, the story would be no more than a bit of historical trivia. She did note, however, that at least twice during the remainder of the trip, Paul reminded her of their secret. The section of the memoirs describing the trip was written seven years after the events described and followed what the author called 'an exact and detailed journal', though that document has disappeared.[63] None of the other participants in the conversation have mentioned Paul's encounter with Peter, but nor is there a similarly detailed record of the trip kept by any member of the grand duke's inner circle. Madame Oberkirch died in 1803. At the time she wrote, however, Paul was still grand duke, and the prophecy was far from having been fulfilled. The Oberkirch memoirs, though hardly a literary or psychological monument, are reliable on the subjects which they cover; there is nothing inherently unbelievable in Paul's telling such a story; and he was, as was his wife, disposed to take dreams and portents seriously. Paul belonged to a generation of believers. The other world, the world beyond, had a powerful reality for them which was sanctioned by their religious faith. And at the very least, Madame Oberkirch's fitting the story to Paul, if that is, in fact, what she did, says something about the way she saw him, and what, on the basis of that exposure, she thought appropriate to him. More prosaically, as the source is more trustworthy than not, we can view this tale as more likely to have been told than not.

Travel was growing wearisome, and when the party crossed once more into Germany, public events marked by the inevitable punctiliousness and jealousy of place which the German princes affected made daily life increasingly troublesome. The arrival at Montbeillard brought relief and, for Mariia, unfeigned pleasure. A family person, she had returned home, and she exulted in it. Everyone in the party, Paul included, enjoyed the warmth, intimacy, and informality of the family setting; for a few brief days it was possible to relax. From Montbeillard, the pastoral beauty and menacing power of the Swiss Alps beckoned. Several excursions were made. Paul made a pilgrimage to Zürich to meet Lavater, the friend of Goethe, whose curious blend of philosophy, science, and pure mysticism made him one of the popular phenomena of the late eighteenth century. Lavater's 'science of physiognomy' assumed the presence of the divinity in every person, and claimed that the close study of faces revealed the degree of the divine presence. In time, Lavater held, as man progressed towards his perfection, his face would become the

[63] Oberkirch, *Mémoires*, 25.

image of the face of God. Paul talked with him at length, explained his own ideas, and listened with attention to this most theological of philosophers.[64]

Despite the joys Étupes and the surrounding region offered, it was time to go home. Paul was weary of travel—he had been ready to turn back while still in Italy—and there were dissonances which made him uncomfortable with Mariia's family, and even with Mariia herself. The Württembergers, once the marriage with Archduke Franz was proposed, became outspoken Habsburg partisans. Paul found this irritating. Moreover his wife, quite unconsciously, was diverging from him on related issues. Mariia always tried to stay in line with Paul's positions. But her gratitude to Joseph for working out her sister's marriage made her take a more sympathetic tone towards Austria than Paul did, though she continued to support his pro-Prussian views. Mariia also felt gratitude towards Catherine, and as their correspondence suggests, there was some warmth between the empress and her daughter-in-law. In fact, at a time when Paul was increasingly apprehensive about what was happening in Petersburg, and was both angry and worried about what his mother intended, Mariia was becoming more favourably inclined towards Catherine. Mariia always gave unstintingly of herself to Paul, but it is doubtful if she understood how deep his resentments ran, or how wounding he would find even the appearance of a difference of opinion between them on issues on which he held strong views. Both Catherine and Prussia were such subjects; Mariia and her family were on very dangerous ground.

The party left Montbeillard for Stuttgart where Mariia's eccentric and spendthrift uncle, Charles-Eugène II, ruling duke of Württemberg, planned an enormous fête in their honour. In both elaboration and expense (reputedly 350,000 florins were spent on it) it was the most lavish of the displays offered to the Russians, rivalling even the carnival in Venice, and it exhausted the travellers' last reserves of energy and patience.[65] The urge to go home was becoming overwhelming. Catherine was pressing them to return as quickly as possible, telling Mariia how much the children missed them and how they were looking forward to their arrival.[66] Paul was more than happy to agree. The party set out directly for Vienna, bypassing

[64] Lafermière to Vorontsov, no. 23, 7 Aug. (NS) 1782, *Arkhiv kniazia Vorontsova*, xxix. 236; Shumigorskii, *Mariia Fedorovna*, i. 228 ff.; Kobeko, *Pavel Petrovich*, 234–9; Morane, *Paul Ier*, 260–3; Oberkirch, *Mémoires*, 255–67.

[65] Baroness Oberkirch reported that the celebration was so wild that Paul only just escaped being hoisted aloft and borne about in triumph. *Mémoires*, 272–3.

[66] See *SIRIO* 9, pp. 170–94.

Munich where yet another fête was in preparation. Vienna now was the first stage on the road to Petersburg.

The second visit to Vienna was less satisfactory than the first. More than a year of touring had taken its toll, and Joseph fell ill towards the end of their stay. Though civilities were maintained, it was clear that the Russians were as happy to be on their way as the emperor was to see them go. To Catherine, Joseph solemnly asserted that the trip had done Paul and Mariia a great deal of good. He was sure that they were returning in a much more agreeable state of mind than that in which they had arrived. He hinted that their excessive distrust, suspicion, and other troubling features of their deportment owed to the kind of people who surrounded them, and he told Catherine, almost frankly, that peace in her own court depended on eliminating those people from Paul's entourage who stood by principles different from her own. This he considered essential 'for tranquillity and the domestic and private satisfaction of three persons to whom I am truly attached'.[67] In fact, Paul and Mariia had irritated Joseph by spurning his recommended route via Teschen in favour of one which took them across a corner of Prussian Silesia. Since this route, as the emperor noted on a file of work from Kaunitz, was recognized by all the couriers to be the worst, he could only conclude that the imperial couple was showing their weakness and subservience to those advisers 'who wish to honor the king of Prussia by having them see some villages of Prussian Silesia, not being able to go by way of Berlin'.[68]

Joseph did not bother to announce to Leopold that Paul and Mariia had left, though he wrote to him about related matters. Nor did any continuing relationship follow on the visit. In August 1783, Leopold mentioned that he saw from a letter Joseph had written to Count Cobenzl that the grand dukes of Russia were no longer writing to the emperor. He reported earlier that Mariia had written after leaving Florence, but that Paul never had, and now neither answered letters nor acknowledged services. Leopold's wife had arranged to have a snuff-box ornamented for Mariia Fedorovna to give to Catherine, and she had sent it at least three months before with a covering letter. There had been no response. Leopold affected not to be surprised at such gauche behaviour in view of what he had learnt of Paul's and Mariia's characters when they visited him. That she did not write to Joseph did surprise him, since she seemed to be in correspondence with virtually everybody in Italy. The only possible

---

[67] Joseph to Catherine, 6 Oct. 1782, Arneth, *Joseph II*, 161–3.
[68] Beer, *Joseph II*, 125.

conclusion was that Paul had remained true to his principles, and Mariia followed her husband.[69]

The echoes from the European trip are heard throughout Paul's later life. It was an experience which came at a critical time for him, and it had the effect of confirming and reinforcing both what he had been taught and what he was coming to believe. The aristocratic world came to life before his eyes with all its panoply and rich traditions. He saw an aristocracy more civilized, more sophisticated, and, as it appeared, more supportive of basic monarchical institutions than the Russian nobility was or could be, and his determination to remould the aristocracy in Russia according to the European model may well date from 1781-2. He also found evidence to support his belief that strong, enlightened government was essential to good public order, that the morality of the ruler and the ruling classes affected directly the condition of society, and that it was possible for a society of disparate classes to be united in a common spirit of commitment to secure society's welfare and progress. There is no evidence, however, that what he saw in Vienna made the slightest impression. Whatever he may have learnt from his observations, Paul remained firmly committed to Prussian ideals and organizational principles. Not even a year after his return from the west, he began constructing an elaborate model for society on his new estate at Gatchina. Both the spirit and the detail were wholly Prussian.[70] Perhaps the greatest revelation of this trip came from the warmth of his reception, and the willingness, even eagerness, of the people at the very apex of society to recognize and honour him. This was the treatment he thought he deserved, and it contrasted sharply with his nullity at home. It was cruel to give him, as Catherine had done, so harsh a reminder of just how helpless and dependent he was when he was at the peak of his Parisian triumph. But cruel or not, the fact was inalterable. So long as Catherine lived, the only life Paul had was the one she allowed him. Perhaps it was thoughts such as these which gradually displaced the bright European images in Paul's mind as his convoy crawled through the icy autumn rains and ubiquitous mud towards Petersburg.

[69] Leopold to Joseph [end of Aug. 1783], Arneth, *Joseph II u. Leopold von Toscana*, i. 170.
[70] The Gatchina estate will be treated in detail in Ch. 6.

6
THE LONG WAIT: 1783–1796

Paul and Mariia returned from Europe to a cold, even hostile, reception. Their first meeting with Catherine was very brief, and over the next several months she continued to show that she was out of countenance with them. The English minister remarked that 'From all I can learn, they [Paul and Mariia] are as displeased at their Reception as the Empress is sorry for their Return', and, a few days later, that 'nothing the Great Duke and Dutchess can do seems to please the Empress . . . who apparently made up her Mind to be displeased with them and insists on being so'. Indeed, the empress, it was said, was so irritated with her son that she was considering removing him from the succession, though there was no independent confirmation for this assertion.[1]

The reasons for Catherine's reactions were not far to seek. She was well aware that Paul, while abroad, not only criticized her foreign and domestic policies, but reprobated her style and her supporters. The Bibikov affair underlined the fact that Paul's household numbered many who were strongly critical of herself, her favourite, and her government, and though Count Panin was now entirely out of the political picture, the residues of his thinking remained green with her son and his supporters. Moreover, Catherine enjoyed not having to cope with Paul's ambitions and moods. Soon after his return there was talk of yet another journey for him, this time to England. Catherine was said to regret that he had not had the opportunity to see the English parliamentary monarchy, one of the political phenomena of the age, in action. It was also said that she had been so easy in his absence that an English journey would provide an admirable excuse for arranging for his being gone again.[2]

Catherine's hostility may also have been a reaction to Paul's popular successes abroad. The travellers had had enthusiastic

---

[1] Catherine's letters to Paul and Mariia as they approached Russia become notably cooler. See *SIRIO* 9, pp. 187 ff. For Harris's comments, PRO, FO/65/8, to Grantham, no. 44, 22 Nov./3 Dec. 1782; no. 50, 6/17 Dec. 1782.

[2] PRO, FO/65/9, Harris to Grantham, no. 60, 21 Dec. 1782/7 Jan. 1783. Talk of another journey continued over the next two years. See e.g. Paul to Osten-Sacken, no. 52, 24 Apr./5 May 1784, *SIRIO* 20, pp. 444–5.

receptions in Austria, France, Germany, and the Venetian republic, while for the most part the impression which they made on the courts where they were received was good. Catherine apparently believed that so much popular adulation combined with such friendly and respectful treatment from monarchs and the ruling classes was dangerously encouraging to Paul and Mariia's self-esteem. Even before their arrival, it was bruited in St Petersburg that 'the Flattery and Attention their Imp. Highnesses have received during their journey joined to the Experience and Knowledge they think they have acquired by travelling have raised them very high in their own Opinions and that their Vanity increases at every New Town they visit'. It was predicted that this would contribute to widening 'the Breach between them and the Empress', and in fact Joseph remarked sadly (on Count Cobenzl's authority) that Paul was going to find Petersburg even more disagreeable on his return than it was before his departure.[3]

Whether it was Catherine's belief that her children needed deflating, that was precisely the effect which her treatment of them had. Diminished, put on the defensive, made to feel that they were guilty of foolish or thoughtless behaviour, they were given no opportunity to enjoy their foreign triumphs at home. Mariia was particularly wounded when Catherine introduced a new and stringent dress code which required her to return over 200 boxes of French finery she could never wear. Contemporaries saw this as a particularly spiteful way for the empress to strike at her daughter-in-law, though the legislation could be rationalized as part of a new campaign against excessive expenditures on foreign luxuries. The grand duchess should, as Catherine noted, have been more prudent.[4] Certainly in the days following their return, Paul and Mariia behaved as if they were in disgrace, living in a kind of semi-retirement, appearing only as required, and avoiding all other social contacts. Harris seemed to be approving. 'The Conduct of the Great Duke and Dutchess since their return', he wrote, 'has been more discreet than could have been expected. They live almost entirely by themselves—have dismissed from their Society their former Friends, and seem as if they intend to be wholly guided by the will of the Empress alone.' And they were alone. Not only was Count Panin 'so weakened in his

---

[3] PRO, FO/65/8, Harris to Grantham, 23 Aug./3 Sept. 1782; Joseph to Leopold, 7 Aug. 1782, Arneth, *Joseph II u. Leopold von Toscana*, i. 126–31; Leopold to Joseph, [end of Aug.] 1782, ibid. 133.

[4] Kobeko, *Pavel Petrovich*, 249–61, for Catherine's reactions on the return home. See also Turgenev, *La Cour de Russie*, 379–82; Morane, *Paul Ier*, 268–70; Harris, *Diaries*, i. 488, ii. 15, 18–19.

intellect as to be no longer able to afford them either Support or Advice', but Paul now knew that he could trust no one as he had been 'betrayed by almost every Person who accompanied them in their Journey'.[5]

Though Count Panin was ill when Paul returned, he appears to have visited his former governor only three times. The first was immediately following his return; the second was just three days before Panin died. Paul implied in a letter to Count Saltykov that the second visit was made on the spur of the moment, following a social conversation with Saltykov in which his relationship with Panin had come up. He left the impression that Panin was well and the visit was of no consequence. He did, however, remark that he himself was so pleased and felt so optimistic that he became certain that this was a sign that some evil impended, and so warned his entourage. Word that Panin was critically ill arrived the next morning.[6]

In fact, this particular meeting was far more important than Paul's comments indicated. Panin had been working for some time on a major political reform project for the empire. Two years earlier, in 1781, he had drafted a preamble in which he not only catalogued 'the abuses of despotic rule', but affirmed the 'right of rebellions against tyrants', and outlined specific proposals for Russia. Panin, of course, had played a leading part in overthrowing Peter III and had contributed to the public justification for that revolution. Plainly, he was convinced that the revolution had gone awry, that manifold abuses required attention, and that structural changes were imperative to establish a constitutional order which could maintain the rule of law and serve the whole society. David Ransel, who, on the basis of recent Soviet authority, has unravelled these mysteries, reports that Panin originally intended for his proposals to reach Paul by way of his brother, General Peter Panin, but that the latter, troubled by their dangerous content, suppressed them. Paul, therefore, could not have seen them. When he visited Panin on the evening of 28 March (os) 1783, however, what he and Panin discussed was the substance of those proposals, with Paul taking notes. These notes have survived and, together with a more systematic draft which Paul completed several days later, provided a record of what Panin was thinking. They also contain important background for the political plans Paul formulated in 1788, and by extension for structural aspects of the

---

[5] PRO, FO/65/8, Harris to Grantham, no. 50, 6/17 Dec. 1782.
[6] 'Pismo k N. I. Saltykovu', *Russkii arkhiv*, 18 (1864), 943. See also Kobeko, *Pavel Petrovich*, 260.

legislative programme he introduced after Catherine's death in 1796.[7]

The talks with Panin covered current governmental abuses and compared what was happening in Russia with events elsewhere. Paul recorded that he and Panin agreed that it was necessary 'to bring the monarchical executive power indispensable to such a large state into conformity with the advantages of that freedom necessary to each estate for its preservation from the despotism either of the ruler himself or of some private [power]'. The first requirement to this end was to regularize the succession by establishing an 'immutable succession law'. Beyond the succession, there would be a new constitutional order which would observe the principle of separating the legislative, executive, and judicial powers. Panin also proposed establishing a new state council comprised of the heads of the departments of justice, revenue, finance, budget, commerce, navy, army, and foreign affairs. Such a council would be compatible with a ministerial form of government and would provide an administrative centre for developing and co-ordinating policies.

The senate, which was currently both a judicial body and the state's leading administrative institution, was to be turned into a supreme court which would possess powers of judicial review as well as being the empire's highest court of appeal. There were to be four branches (St Petersburg, Kazan, Moscow, and Glukhov) with each branch further divided into criminal and appeals departments. The seven members for each department were to be elected by the provincial nobility in the senate district, from among those members holding one of the first three ranks in the service hierarchy. The tsar would choose one of the three candidates the nobles nominated. The St Petersburg senate was to be superior to the others, with responsibility for settling cases they could not. Final decision lay with the tsar if the St Petersburg senate failed.

The senate's powers of review were to be extremely broad, covering all governmental matters except foreign affairs. As Paul summarized it, 'It is necessary that the Senate possess the right to make representations to the sovereign . . . concerning the establishment, amendment and nullification [of edicts] . . . relating directly to the administration and the people, such as those in the departments of

---

[7] This, and subsequent material, follows David Ransel, 'An Ambivalent Legacy: The Education of Grand Duke Paul', in Ragsdale (ed.), *Reassessment*, 9–12 and nn. 16–21. The quoted material is from Ransel. Ransel used materials uncovered and explicated by M. M. Safonov. See his 'Konstitutsionnyi proekt N. I. Panina— D. I. Fonvizina', *Vspomogatel'nye istoricheskie distsipliny*, vi (Leningrad, 1974), 261–80. Ransel follows Safonov. Cf. Shumigorskii, *Pavel I*, app.

revenue, finance, treasury, budget, commerce, and [army and navy] as regards taxation and recruitment.' Whether the senate's powers were intended to control the tsar himself, that he could be considered subject to the law, was left unsaid, though it appears from the earlier notes that one recognized purpose of the new order was to protect the rights of social groups against encroachment by the ruler or anyone else.

What reservations Paul may have had about what he was writing down are unknown. The right of rebellion in Panin's original preamble must have given him pause, especially when he stopped to reflect on the revolution of 1762, while the doctrine that the estates had inalienable rights ran against his own inclination to stress obligations. Yet much of what Panin had to say fitted with Paul's thinking. Certainly the need for a new law of succession had become an article of faith with Paul, while Panin's state council corresponded closely with Paul's predilection for centralization and the use of rationalizing mechanisms. The expanded senate limited to judicial inquiry and charged with overseeing administrative policies also could serve Paul's emphasis on disciplinary control and the need to police subordinate authority. This, of course, would have been a different emphasis from what Panin would seem to have had in mind.[8]

Clearly, there was much that Panin believed that Paul could not accept. It was a measure of his great respect for his old friend, adviser, and former governor that he ignored or rationalized the unacceptable while retaining the balance. Even in 1783 Paul's thinking on government was much closer to conventional autocratic practice than Panin's had become. And over the next thirteen years, this difference increased radically. Yet, even as tsar, Paul was to show the influence of Panin's ideas and would continue to use elements of the constitutionalist's vocabulary. By then, of course, Paul was already well launched into becoming the kind of monarch Panin most deplored. In 1783, it would have been difficult to believe that had Panin been alive eighteen years later, he would have sympathized with the men who organized to depose his former charge. Yet most assuredly he would have.

[8] Ransel ('Ambivalent Legacy', 12) properly stresses the unique character of this charter. At the same time, he goes too far when he refers to it as a 'personal written commitment to grant his subjects a constitution based on separation of powers and elected representation at the national level'. Apart from the documentary problem of intent, such ideas are at odds with Paul's previous and subsequent thinking, and Ransel makes the latter point himself. The most the evidence will bear is Ransel's earlier comment that the 1783 plan 'went as far as he [Paul] was ever to go in considering a constitutional order for Russia' (p. 12).

Panin died on 31 March (OS) 1783. Paul went to see him one final time in his last hours but found him unconscious. He also assisted at the burial service. In his letter to Saltykov he remarked that Panin's death affected everyone. 'Even his enemies were shamed into silence in the face of the general mourning', while the crowd at the burial ceremonies included a large number of people Paul had never seen with Panin, yet who had come to pay their respects.[9] Paul himself appeared to take his loss in stride. Indeed, the Panin family was said to have been hurt that he had stayed away so long. There were strong political reasons for him to do so, but it would also seem that Paul did not feel such losses very deeply. Preserving and completing Panin's last political testament, however, was an act of profound respect, homage in fact, to a man who had helped shape his life and to whom he was closely bound. Panin left a mark on Paul which Paul recognized and understood; unfortunately it was only a mark, and other influences were already obliterating it.

The very low profile Paul and Mariia maintained after their return accorded exactly with the position Catherine had defined for them in her court. There were the usual appearances as part of the court's routine, there were entertainments and galas, and there were occasions when the young court offered a banquet, a ball, or a spectacle. But this was literally all there was for them to do. They had no part in the state's political life. Paul was consulted on nothing, participated in nothing, and with the exception of his ritual role as grand admiral, had no part at all in the government. It was not just that he was discredited; it was as if, for political purposes, he simply did not exist. As he wrote Osten-Sacken, 'I do nothing political. I leave it to the gazettes. My role is to keep still.' Fitzherbert, the British minister who followed Harris, complained to his government that, while it was important 'to inquire into the political Dispositions and Views of the Great Duke', this was very difficult since 'he [the Great Duke] is kept in entire Ignorance as to all Matters of Government' and was also aware 'of the danger that might attend his seeming to concern himself on those Subjects'. And Fitzherbert concluded, understandably but erroneously, that Paul paid little attention to them.[10]

Mariia's situation was somewhat different. She, at least, could remain busy and involved. Her primary project was to complete Pavlovsk. This occupied her constantly for the better part of eight

[9] 'Pismo k N. I. Saltykovu', *Russkii arkhiv* 18 (1864).
[10] Kobeko, *Pavel Petrovich*, 266–7; Morane, *Paul Ier*, ch. 6, *passim*. Paul to Osten-Sacken, 8/19 June 1783, SIRIO 20, pp. 441–2; PRO, FO/65/14, Fitzherbert to Carmarthen, no. 39, 28 Feb. (OS) 1786.

more years. She also continued with her various crafts, a kind of stone lithography was her most successful medium, and she pursued her interests in charitable works. She read extensively and consulted endlessly with Paul on their plans for the future. She also bore children, five girls in nine years, and gave as much of her time as she was allowed to their raising. It was Paul who felt the burden of an occupationless existence most severely; it was also he who was least well prepared to deal with it.[11]

The great court offered nothing. Though Catherine maintained an iron hold over Paul and his family, she gave her son no standing and very little respect. He responded in kind, coming to affect an ironical and disapproving air in her presence, acting for all the world like a disgraced courtier.[12] He held ostentatiously aloof from the so-called alcove politics which so fascinated contemporaries and which had as their centrepiece the succession of handsome young men who made love to his mother, and he heartily detested those who reached and held the status of favourite. This feeling was reciprocated, though at least one, Mamanov, attempted, on Catherine's urging, to establish friendly relations with him. He failed. The most famous of the favourites, Grigorii Potemkin, did favours when he could for Paul and Mariia, including helping them with their debts. It was more common, however, for Catherine's favourites to denigrate Paul, or even to insult him. On one occasion when Catherine was discussing a point with Platon Zubov, the most influential of the favourites after Orlov and Potemkin, she asked what Paul's opinion was. He replied that he thought as Zubov did, whereupon Zubov mimed surprise and cried, 'Did I say something stupid, then?'[13]

Paul's perpetually being out of favour made a difficult life harder still for it was thought that one sure road to the empress's favour was to denigrate her son, or to report matters unfavourable to him.

---

[11] Shumigorskii, *Mariia Fedorovna*, i. 255–8; Morane, *Paul Ier*, 270–2, 337–58. For an intimate picture of Mariia Fedorovna at work on Pavlovsk, see her correspondence with her overseer, P. K. Küchelbecker, in Grand Duke Konstantin Nikolaevich, *Pavlovsk: Ocherk istorii i opisanie, 1777–1877* (St Petersburg, 1877), 519–52. Charles Cameron was the architect. See G. Lukomsky, *Charles Cameron, 1740–1812* (London, 1943), esp. 61–73. Heinrich Storch described Pavlovsk as standing 'Amidst the most charming productions of Flora ...'. He thought it a marvel of 'majestic simplicity, a monument of correct taste' whose overall effect was that 'nature and art have concurred to one sole end in this elysium'. H. F. Storch, *The Picture of St. Petersburg* (London, 1801), 79–81.

[12] Morane, *Paul Ier*, 299, quoting the Prince de Ligne, *Mélanges militaires*, 28 vols. (Leopoldberg, 1795–1805), xxv. 13.

[13] Morane, *Paul Ier*, 296–9; Kobeko, *Pavel Petrovich*, 293–9, 374; *Russkaia starina*, 17, p. 453.

Princess Dashkova, outspoken as usual, always refused invitations to events at Paul's residences because, as she told him, everything that was said or that happened there was reported to the empress, while he was kept informed of doings at the Winter Palace. She had no desire to be interrogated by the one or to be suspected as an informer by the other. It was no comfortable thing to be caught between the mother and the son; she had no intention of exposing herself to the danger.[14] What this meant was that Paul and Mariia really led two lives. Their official life at court was required of them; their real life was lived on their private estates.

In the 1780s, the domestic reforms which Catherine had begun in the preceding decade were finally completed.[15] They included a reorganization and redrawing of the guberniia system; creating district and municipal authorities using electoral principles and seeking to promote local initiatives; a system of local courts; comprehensive police regulations which covered everything from health requirements to security and order; an effort to legislate a stronger basis for mercantile development and to create the social elements of a modern constitutional order; the foundations of a new imperial educational system; and an effort to confirm particular groups, beginning with the nobility, in rights appropriate to their status in society. Foreign policy was directed towards consolidating newly acquired territories in the south while maintaining a firm hold on Poland. The annexation of the Crimea in 1783, the second Russo-Turkish war (1787–92), and the definitive partitioning of Poland in 1793 and 1795 were the high points; the outbreak of the French revolution in 1789, and the subsequent efforts by England, Austria, and Prussia to block France militarily, formed the frame within which Catherine manœuvred through the last decade of her reign. Though an outspoken opponent of the revolution, she contributed almost nothing to the struggle against it in Europe, and it was not until the year she died that a Russian relief army began to march west. Hostilities with Persia, another matter entirely, broke out at the same time.

For the most part, Paul was cool or openly hostile to what his mother was doing. And the longer he was kept waiting in the wilderness, the more comprehensive his opposition became. Had he had a part in forming or carrying out the various policies Catherine eventually implemented, his attitudes might have been different.

[14] E. R. Dashkova, *Mémoires, Arkhiv kniazia Vorontsova*, xxi. 262–264.
[15] Madariaga, *Catherine the Great*, esp. 277–324, 377–451. The second citation covers foreign policy issues. See Madariaga's notes and bibliography for specialized references on particular points.

Since he had not, there was not even a beginning point for compromise. Nor is there anything in what he did, said, or wrote to suggest that he was looking for a common footing. Where Paul was concerned, the fundamental problem was that it was he and not his mother who should have been making the decisions. It followed from this that the principles for which he stood, or the policies which he approved, were those which should have been implemented. It was this immovable conviction which helps to explain his intransigence, a factor which early frustrated even the minimal attempts Catherine made to work with him on political questions.

Most members of the diplomatic community balanced between offending Catherine by showing too much interest in Paul, and ignoring him completely. None, however, ran the risk of intimacy. Those few who penetrated even momentarily into his separate world found him ready to talk, and likely to rehearse all his troubles. Curt von Stedingk, the Swedish minister who came to Petersburg after the peace of Varela, found Paul so frank as to be embarrassing, and declared he hardly knew what to do with the confidences the grand duke showered on him.[16] The Count de Ségur, who represented France in Petersburg from 1785 to 1787, had a similar experience. When he arrived in Petersburg, Paul and Mariia greeted him warmly, remembering their own reception in Paris three years earlier. But their feelings cooled as he went from triumph to triumph to become one of Catherine's intimates. He lost Catherine's favour in the summer of 1787 and was recalled in the autumn. Leaving Petersburg, he passed near Paul's estate at Gatchina, and on an impulse stopped to pay his respects. Paul appeared to be expecting him, or at least was unsurprised by his arrival, and pressed him to stay the night. Ségur agreed, and the two men talked for hours. Paul, now that Ségur was no longer his mother's favourite diplomat, unburdened himself at length, complaining bitterly about the treatment he had had at his mother's hands, and discussing in the frankest way possible the implications of the succession rule in Russia. Ségur reported that he defended Catherine to Paul—he stressed Paul's independence and Catherine's magnanimity—and he claimed that he advised Paul on reform of the succession. Paul was utterly frank about his sense of isolation, his distance from the court, and the resentment he felt. He was more than frank, he was insistent, even compulsive about it.

---

[16] *Mémoires posthumes du feldmaréchal comte de Stedingk, redigés sur des lettres, dépêches et autres pièces authentiques laissés à sa famille, par le général comte de Björnstjerna*, 3 vols. (Paris, 1844–7), esp. i. 289 ff., for Stedingk's initial contact with Paul and Mariia. After five years, Paul seemed 'less ugly', though Mariia had visibly aged (p. 303). See also Kobeko, *Pavel Petrovich*, 334.

Once launched, he seemed unable to restrain himself, to hold anything back. He harped on the injustices he suffered, the mistakes his mother and her ministers were making, and his own powerlessness. Yet it was also clear, as it had been with Leopold of Austria five years earlier, that Paul was fully abreast of what was going forward, though he despaired over how long it would be before he would be able to do anything about it.[17]

Study, planning, observation, and certain contacts with the diplomatic community were hardly substitutes for being tsar. But they were what Paul had, and he worked to expand them. He took an increasingly active interest in military exercises, personally drilling the handful of troops assigned to his residences, and volunteering for service in the Crimea when it appeared that war was threatening. For a time it seemed that he would go, once Mariia, who was in the late stages of pregnancy, was delivered. Catherine then, however, changed her mind and refused his offer. His place, she told him, was in the capital with his family. She may also have thought about the problems that could arise were Paul to have to serve with Potemkin.[18] To take the sting from her refusal, or to divert his attention, she bought Orlov's estate at Gatchina from his heirs and presented it to Paul on the occasion of the birth of his first daughter, Alexandra. He and Mariia took up residence at Gatchina that very autumn. Suddenly he had a place, a kingdom in effect, to do with as he chose. For the next thirteen years, Gatchina was the centre of his world.[19]

The Gatchina estate had already achieved fame of a sort. In 1767, Orlov, probably at Catherine's urging, invited Jean Jacques Rousseau, then living unhappily in England, to come to Russia and to stay at Gatchina. This was a place, as Orlov wrote, that was distinguished for both its privacy and its great natural beauty. It would be an ideal haven for a man of sensitivity and sensibility. Rousseau declined with

---

[17] Ségur, *Mémoires*, ii. 534–7.

[18] Morane, *Paul Ier*, 272–3; Harris reported on 13/24 June 1783, that 'The Great Duke's Equippages are ready and he will join the Army as soon as the Great Duchess has lain in.' PRO, FO/65/9, no. 54, Harris to Fox. Harris does not explain why Paul did not finally go.

[19] Harris reported the Gatchina grant. PRO, FO/65/10, no. 75, to Fox, 8/19 May 1783. Kobeko, *Pavel Petrovich*, 267–82, 286–93, 349–409, describes Gatchina, court life there (to *c.*1787), and the military aspect. S. Kaznakov, 'Pavlovskaia Gatchina', *Starye gody* (July–Sept. 1914), 101–88 (I am indebted to Professor Ragsdale for bringing this piece to my attention); see also S. V. Rozhdestvenskii, 'Gatchinskaia votchina Pavla I', *Uchenye zapiski RANIION, Institut Istorii*, 6 (1928), 127–45; Shil'der, *Pavel I*, 186–7, 192–3; L. V. Ruzov and Iu. N. Iablochkin, *Gatchina* (Leningrad, 1959); V. Shvarts, *Prigorody Leningrada* (Leningrad, 1961).

thanks. He had grown too old, and Gatchina, while undoubtedly of great beauty, was too far from the sun.[20] What Rousseau rejected, Paul received with unadulterated joy. He fell in love with his new holding, invested it with every amenity necessary to its role as his country seat, and lavished hours on its decoration and development. Mariia saw Gatchina as a rival to Pavlovsk; she urged 'her faithful Küchelbecker' to make haste and not let the new holding overshadow hers.[21] In the end, the two estates were as different as their master and mistress: Gatchina expressed what Paul was and what he hoped to be as dramatically as Pavlosk reflected Mariia and her world.

Gatchina was a large estate which lay some twenty-six miles to the south of Petersburg on the main road to Moscow. The highroad was nearly two miles from the palace whose entrance was marked by monumental stone gates. The grant which Catherine made to Paul covered the village of Gatchina itself, the palace, its furnishings, decorations, and outbuildings, and the twenty villages which comprised the estate proper. To this were added the holdings of New-Skovoritska and Old-Skovoritska, together with their villages, woodland, and arable land. The region across which this vast estate sprawled is slightly hilly, with a fertile, well-watered, though somewhat sandy soil. It was considered good farming land, and especially favourable for animal husbandry. There was a valuable stone quarry near the village of Pudosta which provided building stone for both Tsarskoe Selo and Pavlosk. Stone from the Pudosta quarry was prized for its warm yellowish or ochre tones. A much harder and somewhat darker stone was quarried at Shchernitsa. The population of the Gatchina estates at the time Paul took possession has been given as 7,000, excluding the military garrison. Since there were more than 3,000 male souls registered on the estate, the total population was probably somewhat larger.[22]

[20] *Correspondance générale de J. J. Rousseau*, ed. T. Defou (Paris, 1931), xi. 325, for Orlov's letter dated 2 Jan. 1767. A London merchant, Alexander Baxter, delivered the letter to Rousseau at Wooten. Rousseau replied on 28 Feb. 1767. See Amburger, *Ingermanland*, p. 825 n. 64.   [21] Nikolaevich, *Pavlovsk*, 527.

[22] Kobeko, *Pavel Petrovich*, 267–82. There was at least one effort reported to increase it. In summer 1784, an overseer who needed additional labourers at Gatchina, and found it difficult to recruit them, let it be known that any serf who would contract 'during a given Period of Time' to work at Gatchina could then become 'a Burgher of that Place and be free forever from the Dominion of his former Master'. This word spread like wildfire through the neighbourhood and set off a migration of hundreds of obligated peasants and house servants to Gatchina. The government treated the movement as an incipient uprising, dispatched troops to restore order, and severely punished those peasants identified as ringleaders. See PRO, FO/65/11, no. 29, Fitzherbert to Carmarthen, 2 July (NS) 1784.

The palace or manor house with its colonnades and outbuildings, its parks, lakes, streams, and gardens, was a showplace, 'one of the most superb in Europe', as Heinrich Storch remarked in a contemporary description.[23] The original buildings were the work of the influential Italian architect, Rinaldi, and were constructed between 1766 and 1781, when he died with the complex still unfinished. Paul added substantially to the ensemble, working with his favourite architect, Vincenzio Brenna, in the years after his accession. There was relatively little building between 1783 and 1796 beyond the completion of what Rinaldi had started and adding the structures necessary for an expanded garrison. Paul also did extensive work on the gardens where his penchant for geometrical forms was matched by his botanical interests. Among his special plantings was a park of trees from other parts of the empire which became an arboretum, one of the earliest of its kind.[24]

The palace was a vast three-storied structure built in a basic classical style embellished with towers on two corners of the building. There were additional lower towers at each corner of the courtyard. The courtyard was formed by connecting the palace proper with its near outbuildings by two colonnaded walks. Viewed from the lake and garden side, the palace appeared to be a strongly fortified castle with gothic overtones. The setting, in fact, was quite romantic. Busts and statues of classical heroes, particularly Roman emperors and generals, were set in niches in the colonnades, while the palace interior was richly furnished and decorated with statuary, bas-reliefs, enormous hangings, and monumental pictures. Among these, a portrayal of 'The Rape of the Sabine Women' held pride of place. Portraits of Paul's heroes graced the walls: Peter the Great, Frederick II of Prussia, Sully, and in a niche a bust of Henry IV of France. Paul's personal library, now in excess of 40,000 volumes, was accommodated on another floor, while the living space available offered rooms for hundreds of people. Gatchina was built on a heroic scale; Paul found it fitted him exactly.[25]

Three settlements loosely linked lay beyond the palace grounds along the Porkhov highway. One, a sort of suburb, was composed of wooden houses with a few stone structures and housed court servants, artisans, and small merchants or shopkeepers. On the market-place itself, there was a bright, metal-roofed, two-storey hospital and church. The same building also housed an apothecary's shop and laboratory. Dwellings for the district physician and

[23] Storch, *Picture*, 80.
[24] Amburger, *Ingermanland*, 3–4, 491–500, 519–20.
[25] Kobeko, *Pavel Petrovich*, 267–82, on Gatchina.

paramedic or feldscher flanked the square. The largest structures in this complex, however, were the local school, a textile plant, and the artillery caserne. Beyond this suburb was the village of Gatchina proper. It was here that the bulk of the peasant population, largely of Finnish extraction and the Lutheran faith, was found. The village comprised two rows of well-built wooden cabins or cottages. In the middle of the street stood a new chapel which was shared by Lutheran and Catholic communicants. A third small community called Ingerburg was laid out in 1794 even further up the road towards Petersburg. This little town was made up of stone houses, several storeys high, some of which Paul had built. Others were constructed by high court officials, or even new factory owners and merchants, to provide additional accommodation away from the palace. These three settlements connected by a road formed a single district which was served by a special security watch, the streets were surfaced, and trees were planted along the side of the main road.

From the beginning of his tenure, Paul paid particular attention to the many needs of the people living on the estate. Regular church services for Orthodox believers were held in the court and hospital churches. There was a pastor to serve the German Lutheran community in Gatchina and in Pavlosk and Tsarskoe Selo (which were some thirteen miles away). A parish priest ministered to the small Roman Catholic population in Gatchina and Pavlosk. Beyond such spiritual needs, Paul also took the maintenance of the physical community under his direction. He provided upkeep for houses, public buildings, footpaths, and roads. He reorganized and expanded the police and fire watches, kept track of the personal fortunes of the merchants, artisans, and peasants who made their livings on his lands, and intervened personally in cases where people suffered financial set-backs, acquired debts beyond what they could handle, or, worst of all, fell into the hands of usurers. He reduced the dues of his peasants, provided loans when they were needed, and worked to improve the people's productivity and standard of living. A. A. Samborskii, who was the religious instructor for Paul's children, had studied the new agriculture in England. He founded an agricultural school at Pavlovsk in 1797 with Paul's support; they were carrying forward and institutionalizing a tradition begun at Gatchina over a decade earlier.[26]

There were other developments. Paul, like his mother, was concerned with medicine and public health, and he provided the best possible health-care facilities for his Gatchina dependants. The

[26] Amburger, *Ingermanland*, 522, on Samborskii.

hospital was built with close attention to advanced designs, and particularly the need to provide space, air, and sunshine. It contained more than one hundred beds which were distributed through wards, and there were single patient rooms when privacy or isolation were required. The hospital was available to all who needed its services, non-residents as well as residents. Feldschers, working under the supervision of the district physician, provided home treatment for those who did not go to the hospital, and there was a district midwife available to instruct expectant mothers and assist with births.

As with the health and security of his people, Paul set out to provide at least the rudiments of an education for every class of people and, as far as possible, to educate each group to the level appropriate to its social status. In addition to the regular school, there was a small pension or boarding school which took a few students to be prepared for higher education. At the foundling home, the soldiers' children were taught with the orphans to read and write. There were also opportunities to learn handicrafts, farming, and gardening. In some sense, the foundling school was an early vocational training centre, offering preparation for work in the various domainal industries at Gatchina. Paul was anxious to promote manufacturing. In addition to training, he subsidized housing for workers as well as providing land and loans for building factories. Three industries, apart from quarrying and agriculture, developed on the estate: the manufacture of glass and porcelain, textiles, and hat-making. Taken together, these industries made Gatchina an important early factory centre.

Paul's interest in agriculture and manufacturing, his concern for the welfare of his dependants, his emphasis on good housing, clean streets, security of person and property, and good medical care placed him squarely in the tradition of enlightened public service. Moreover, he accepted personally the responsibility for his dependants, spent his time and money to discharge that obligation, and used both his powers as landlord and his organizational skills to create an effective local administration. He also laid down rules for his dependants' behaviour, and he enforced them. He established a stringent dress code at Gatchina which forbade immoral or subversive styles, styles inappropriate to the wearer's class, and even interdicted the round hat. He used a passport system to identify strangers on his lands, and he instituted curfews, guard posts, and all the paraphernalia of a tightly organized, well-disciplined community. In all of this, he showed his kinship with the pervasive idea that it was the responsibility of authority to maintain order and the social services necessary to a good life. Broadly speaking, none of this was innovative or creative. European communities had taken up such burdens as a secular charge 300 years before; the tradition that governments on all levels were responsible for the health and welfare of the citizens had been central to continental political thinking for at least a century and a half; and these propositions formed a fundamental element in the political vocabulary of the Enlightenment. What makes Gatchina significant is both the high seriousness of Paul's commitment to the principles of social obligation, his activism in implementing those principles, and his heavy stress on control, discipline, and order. Gatchina was not only his little kingdom; it was also his miniature version of the 'well-ordered police state', and as such it demonstrates one very important dimension of what he intended to do with Russia once he became tsar.

Contemplating the social and economic aspects of Gatchina, there was actually little to choose so far as goals were concerned between Paul and his mother. The means, however, were vastly different. Paul was a thoroughgoing paternalist who would have no truck with local councils or initiatives. While he was open to his dependants' suggestions, they always remained in their state of dependency, and they were expected to accept his decisions, whatever they might be. What was done, he did, and if he saw an obligation to assist his people, he did so in his own way and according to his own rules. The principle of a tightly centralized administration, which was at the core of his later government, was already obvious at Gatchina. It stood at variance with the more complex legislative initiatives his mother had set in train, to reproduce social formations which had proved progressive in western countries and to encourage people to become involved in solving local problems. Paul considered himself the problem-solver, and so far as his influence and wealth would reach he would care for his people and guide them. This he considered to be his duty and his right.

But he would also claim that it was the duty of every noble landholder to be equally concerned with his dependants. If Gatchina contained in embryo what Paul intended for Russia, it was likewise a model for the way the landholding gentry should administer its lands and care for its people. That Paul ran up heavy debts, constantly overspending the allowances Catherine gave him as well as the income from his properties and enterprises, showed that he, in common with most of the landed gentry, could not bridge the gap between the costs of maintaining an aristocratic life-style and the relatively low productivity of their major assets.[27] Paul and Mariia

[27] M. Confino, *Domaines et seigneurs en Russie vers la fin du XVIIIe siècle* (Paris, 1963), and *Systèmes agraires et progrès agricole: l'Assolement triennal en Russie*

were chronically short of cash, Catherine refused to help, and their debts ballooned to between 600,000 and 800,000 rubles. Worse, Paul was victimized by his financial officer, a certain Baron de Borck, whose accounts over a two-year period were said to be short 500,000 rubles. He was thought to have diverted at least 300,000 to his own use.[28]

What gave Gatchina its special character and its notoriety in the 1790s was Paul's private army. This, of course, was something which went beyond normal estate management and bore directly on Paul's role as tsar-to-be. Paul had begun drilling his guards at Kamennyi Ostrov and then Pavlovsk much earlier, and he eventually established both an artillery range and a fortress on the latter estate. But neither of these places was militarized. Mariia's influence dominated Pavlovsk, while Kamennyi Ostrov was both too small and too near the Winter Palace to give Paul the scope he needed. Gatchina was another matter. Large in size and remote from both the capital and the imperial summer residences, it offered space and privacy. Over the thirteen years from the first autumn spent at Gatchina to the November night in 1796 when he rushed off to Petersburg to become the tsar, Paul made his favourite estate into a full-fledged military centre. He spent every autumn in residence there overseeing his annual grand manœuvres, but even while fulfilling his duties at the Winter Palace or Tsarskoe Selo, where the court repaired in summer, he slipped away as often as possible to Gatchina. Mariia was always at his side. And during the last two years before Catherine died, Paul was at Gatchina almost continuously.

Paul had two sets of cavalry quarters added to the estate's outbuildings, one near the animal preserve or *Tiergarten*, the other in the village by the main road. A large caserne for the infantry was constructed next to the palace on the left side. Barriers and sentry posts were set up at the entrances to the estate, guards patrolled the boundaries, and uniforms were required to be worn at all times by the men who were serving there. Though beautiful naturally, and beautified as only a late eighteenth-century residence for a ruling personage might be, Gatchina was also organized in a military

---

aux XVIIIe–XIXe siècles (Paris, 1969) for basic problems of the domainal economy. See also V. I. Semevskii, *Krestianskii vopros v Rossii v XVIII i pervoi polovine XIX veka*, 2 vols. (St Petersburg, 1888). On gentry debt, Jerome Blum, *Lord and Peasant in Russia from the Ninth to the Nineteenth Century* (Princeton, NJ, 1961), esp. chs. 18, 19, and 20. See below, Ch. 8.

[28] Kobeko, *Pavel Petrovich*, 346–9: Rostopchin to Vorontsov, 8/19 Dec. 1795, *Arkhiv kniazia Vorontsova*, viii 120; HHSA, Russland II Berichte, Carton 81, Cobenzl to Thugut, 27 Jan. (NS) 1795, and no. 42, apostille 5, 9 July (NS) 1795.

manner and maintained with the most rigid attention to details. Just as Paul himself was fastidious in his dress and would never appear in public other than carefully turned out with his boots, belts, and buttons polished and his uniform carefully brushed, so Gatchina was kept spic and span and always ready for inspection.[29]

Within the world Paul had built for himself, the military became his primary occupation, his profession, finally his obsession. It was all very well for him to plan for the day when he would become tsar, but that planning was meaningless without a force he could trust implicitly. More, the army at Gatchina was to be everything Paul believed both the regular army and the guards regiments were not. It was his conviction, which grew stronger over the years, that Catherine's generals and favourites used the army for their own purposes, condoned ill-discipline, turned a blind eye on the most corrupt practices, and altogether undermined the forces' effectiveness and spirit. His answer was to create the model for a new army which, once he had become tsar, would also become the nucleus for a reformed Russian army, and the main support for a refurbished Russian state.

The original Gatchina garrison was but a single company of marines. Over the next decade, Paul expanded that nucleus until there were more than 2,000 enlisted men with 130 officers. Both officers and men were recruited from the regular army. Since a posting to Gatchina was considered no favour, it was said with some justice that what Paul had was what others did not want or could not handle: the undisciplined, the incompetent, the misfits. But there was another way to see it. What Paul acquired were outsiders, men who did not fit into the smooth grooves of the established forces. This would be especially true of the officers. Significantly, general Sablukov described the Gatchintsi as Little Russians, ill-educated, uncultured, coarse, and loud.[30] There seems no reason to doubt the truth of his description. It was precisely such people whom Paul could mould, who might well owe him their careers, and who would be loyal to him above all. And in this respect, Paul was highly successful. An unusual *esprit* developed among the Gatchintsi. They were Paul's own, and they remained loyal to him. One of the few, if

---

[29] Kobeko, *Pavel Petrovich*, 394–409; P. Lebedev, 'Preobrazovateli russkoi armii v tsarstvovanie Imperatora Pavla Petrovicha', *Russkaia starina*, 18 (1877), 227–48.

[30] 'Reminiscences of the Court and Times of the Emperor Paul I of Russia up to the Period of His Death: from the Papers of a Deceased Russian General Officer [Sablukov]', *Fraser's Magazine* (Aug. 1865), 229. Prince Adam Czartoryski described the Gatchintsi as 'the discontented of the great court' and later, and more harshly, as 'ill-educated clowns'. *Mémoires*, i. 106–28.

not the only, laudatory reminiscences on Paul Petrovich in the years before he became tsar was published anonymously in Hamburg in 1797 from the papers of a Polish officer in Paul's service. What the author's anecdotes described was a man deeply concerned for the people whose lives he directed, a firm, sometimes harsh, but always just and humane man who would become a good as well as a strong ruler.[31] This, of course, was entirely at odds with the common view of Paul in the 1790s. Paul's people were different from those who inhabited the court and held commissions in the guards. This very difference in class background, culture, and above all training strengthened them in their ties to Paul; it also set them apart from those with whom they would have to work once Paul was tsar.

Paul's Gatchina squadrons were too small to provide the base he needed to dominate the court and the military. Yet the Gatchintsi included a number of men who became important after 1796. Among these, one of the best known was Count A. A. Arakcheev, a brilliant organizer and brutal disciplinarian who was probably the most famous officer to emerge from Paul's nest.[32] Arakcheev fitted the Gatchina mould. A man from the furthest reaches of the lesser gentry and a compulsive overachiever who was always an outsider, Arakcheev came to Paul with his early promising career virtually in ruins and with the ugly stench of scandal clinging to him. Paul recognized his capacities, ignored the past, and gave him the opportunity to mend his fortunes. Arakcheev responded with an intensity of commitment and unswerving loyalty which satisfied even Paul's exalted standards. He became Paul's ideal officer, a standard by which to measure others, and the very embodiment to observers of the essential Gatchina spirit. He was also generally despised.[33] It was typical of Paul to make no concessions to Arakcheev's commitment or dedication, and to punish him for even inadvertently

---

[31] Anon. *Anekdoten aus dem Privatleben der Kaiserin Catharina, Pauls der Ersten, und seiner Familie* (Hamburg, 1797).

[32] For Arakcheev with Paul, 1792–6, Kobeko, *Pavel Petrovich*, 404–9. Michael Jenkins, *Arakcheev: Grand Vizier of the Russian Empire* (London, 1969), provides a good general account of this enigmatic figure. The absence of notes lessens its usefulness.

[33] Morane, *Paul Ier*, 362–3; Shil'der, *Imperator Aleksandr Pervyi* i. 97; Sablukov, 'Reminiscences', 235, described Arakcheev as resembling 'a monkey in regimentals', while his countenance showed 'a singular mixture of intelligence and wickedness' Sablukov credited him with 'impartiality in administering justice' and 'Economy with public monies'. Countess Golovina referred to Arakcheev as 'a person called from the muck by the emperor', *Souvenirs*, 146. Mariia thought Catherine Nelidova (see below) a much better influence on Paul than 'such a brute as colonel Arakcheev', quoted in de Grunwald, *L'Assassinat*, 74.

stepping out of line. Arakcheev, in fact, was in domestic exile when the conspiracy against Paul matured; had he been called back to the capital twenty-four hours sooner, Paul's story might have ended very differently. Logistics and administration were Arakcheev's strengths (though his reputation from Gatchina was as an unforgiving and sadistic drill instructor). His battlefield achievements were nil, but he left an indelible mark on Russian history as the organizer and expediter of the often-condemned military colonies under Alexander I. The hereditary grand duke's dependence on Arakcheev during Paul's reign, and his continuing trust in him throughout his own, is by no means the least of the anomalies which cluster around the 'liberal' and 'enlightened' eldest son of Paul.[34]

Count Fedor Rostopchin was another of the Gatchina notables who played a significant role later. Rostopchin was a different kind of outsider, an individualist who was temperamental to the point of eccentricity, who affected to care for no one except his master whom he served loyally and with dedication, though hardly blindly. Rostopchin was well aware of Paul's weaknesses. He also believed that he himself was unappreciated and discriminated against by Catherine and her intimates, most particularly by Potemkin whom he cordially hated, and he affected to believe that he was virtually alone among the courtiers of his time in placing duty above self-interest. His comments on contemporaries were scathing. And his own account of how he won Paul's favour is appropriately cynical. While on detached service in Berlin, he won a large sum gambling at cards with a Prussian officer. The officer was unable to pay but gave him, in settlement of the debt, an elaborately finished and detailed army of toy soldiers, a veritable work of military art. Paul learnt of Rostopchin's 'army' when the latter returned to Petersburg and asked to see it. Rostopchin agreed. Paul was enthralled with the toys, and Rostopchin gave him the set on the spot. The gift moved Paul deeply and gave Rostopchin a powerful initial advantage. He also served Paul well, however, and though like Arakcheev he was punished when he offended, he became Paul's president of the college of foreign affairs and the man responsible for expediting foreign policy decisions in 1799 and 1800. Later, under Alexander, he was governor-general of Moscow when Napoleon invaded in 1812 and has been credited with starting the Moscow fire which helped to force the French withdrawal. Rostopchin was the most able of the

---

[34] See A. A. Kizevetter, 'Imperator Aleksandr I i Arakcheev', *Istoricheskie ocherki* (Moscow, 1912), 287–401.

Gatchintsi; he was also one who rose above the blinkered militarism which characterized the Gatchina style.[35]

Rostopchin and Arakcheev were, each in his own way, outstanding. More typical was General Steinwehr, a former Prussian officer who was garrison commander at Gatchina and assisted Paul in teaching the Prussian drill; General Lindener, a Pole who took a German name to impress his master; or General Nikolai Petrovich Arkharov. Neither Steinwehr nor Lindener distinguished themselves in any way, while Arkharov was a particularly stupid sycophant who catered shamelessly to Paul's disciplinary penchants and his mania for conformity. Arkharov was responsible for police functions at Gatchina and then served as governor-general of St Petersburg in the first year of Paul's reign. He was cashiered for an overzealous interpretation of Paul's own order to have the gates, portals, and sentry boxes of the capital painted. He so offended Mariia that it was actually she, in alliance with the redoubtable Catherine Nelidova, who engineered his fall and arranged the appointment of General Buxhoeweden, a relative by marriage of Nelidova's, in his place. Unfortunately, there were more Arkharovs than Rostopchins among the Gatchintsi, and relatively few made any significant mark.[36]

The master of Gatchina, Paul himself, was the central figure in the composition. He was the commander-in-chief and the most visible of all the officers. When in residence, Paul oversaw the daily inspections, planned the exercises, led units on manœuvres, administered the supply services, wrote a new infantry manual based on a Prussian version of 1766, and designed the men's uniforms. His example in everything military was Frederick the Great, and the Gatchina world was permeated with the Prussian spirit. The troops were tricked out in costumes modelled on what had been worn in Frederick's army: high boots, gauntlets, a tall pointed hat, and the hair set in wax and dressed with flour with a pigtail down the back. Even the guardhouses and the gates were painted in the Prussian style with

---

[35] There is no adequate biography of Rostopchin. The most substantial account available is A. El'nitskii, 'Fedor Vasil'evich Rostopchin', *Russkii biograficheskii slovar* (St Petersburg, 1918), xxvii. 238–305. See also J. M. P. McErlean, 'Fedor Vasil'evich Rostopchin', *Modern Encyclopedia of Russian and Soviet History* (Gulf Breeze, Flo., 1983), xxxi. 165–171, for a recent summary with current bibliography. Rostopchin's letters to Count S. R. Vorontsov reveal the man as well as circumstances in Paul's court. *Arkhiv kniazia Vorontsova*, viii. 37–457. See also Kobeko, *Pavel Petrovich*, 411; Morane, *Paul I*^{er}, 363–4.

[36] Kobeko, *Pavel Petrovich*, 399–401, for Paul's subordinates. See also de Grunwald, *L'Assassinat*, 60–1, on Steinwehr, Lindener, and Kannabeck. For Arkharov and his fall, Shumigorskii, *Nelidova*, 90–2; Heyking, *Aus den Tagen Kaiser Pauls*, ed. F. von Bienenmann (Leipzig, 1886), 49–50.

alternating stripes of orange, white, and black. Catherine banned the Gatchina uniform at court—even Paul was forbidden to wear one—since there was to be no competition with the established forces, and in the capital Gatchina was only the name of an estate. But Paul could ignore Petersburg. He marched and counter-marched his troops until their command of parade drill, the manual of arms, and battlefield manoeuvre was letter perfect. He was an alert officer, a strong disciplinarian, and a demanding leader. Most of all, he was absolutely certain of what he was doing, and he refused to be deterred by adverse opinion. At Gatchina, Paul ruled. The Gatchintsi were his army; Gatchina was his world; and so long as he remained there, he was busy, fulfilled, and almost happy.[37]

Catherine complained about the cost of Paul's activities, watched closely that he did not overstep the bounds of what she was willing to allow, and chafed at the time Alexander and Constantine were spending in his army. Yet she made no attempt to stop what her son was doing. The fact was that, for Catherine, Gatchina was a blessing. It engaged Paul's attention and kept him away from her. Since she was certain that his exercises were no threat to herself, she could afford to be indulgent. When Paul used his artillery range at nearby Pavlovsk, the thump of the guns was clearly audible at Tsarskoe Selo where Catherine, if she noticed it at all, would smile and perhaps remark that her son was playing at his games again.[38]

If Paul was entirely in command at Gatchina, a soldier's soldier doing his duty, in Petersburg he remained a supernumerary, a useless appendage to his mother's court who had no will of his own. In the spring of 1787, Catherine made a triumphal progress through her southern lands to visit the Crimea where she again met Joseph II. In planning this trip, she pointedly omitted Paul and Mariia from the entourage, though she announced that she intended to take her grandsons, Alexander and Constantine, with her. Paul and Mariia, who in fact were never directly told about the empress's plan, protested vehemently when they heard of it, with Mariia, in desperation, even calling on Potemkin for assistance. When Catherine remained adamant, they suggested that she take them, the parents, as well. This idea was rejected out of hand. At the last minute, however,

---

[37] Kobeko, *Pavel Petrovich*, 329 ff.; Morane, *Paul Ier*, 360–2. Morane stresses Prussian discipline; Kobeko notes Paul's interest in his men and their problems. His officers at Gatchina liked him for it. It was this side to Paul that the anonymous author of the *Anekdoten* stressed.

[38] Ségur underlined the freedom Catherine gave Paul, using the private army as a key example. He also claimed this showed how much she trusted him. *Mémoires*, ii. 534–5.

Constantine fell ill with chicken pox, and since Alexander had been exposed, both boys had to be left behind. Catherine accepted this defeat by nature philosophically, but she was unwilling for the parents to exploit it. She reminded Count Saltykov, who was in charge of her grandsons' education, that the parents were in no way to be permitted to interfere with the programme established for the boys. Their ideas or suggestions, as always, were unwelcome.[39]

The Turks read Catherine's visit as a threat, and the empress had hardly returned to St Petersburg before she received the news that the Russian ambassador and his staff had been arrested and incarcerated in the Seven Towers, the traditional way to announce a declaration of war. When Paul learnt that hostilities were beginning again, he petitioned Catherine to be allowed to go to the front.[40] His dream was to march off with his own army, but there was no likelihood that Catherine would ever permit that, and, in fact, her first response to his request was a flat no. Her argument was unchanged from four years earlier. Paul was the heir; his place was with his family, and he most certainly should not expose his life to the rigours of campaigning in foreign lands far from home. Paul, however, was importunate, and Mariia joined in. She even proposed that she should accompany her husband to the front. Catherine was scandalized at such an idea. She grumbled to Grimm that the Secondats gave her no peace over Paul's petition to go with the forces, and though she swore she would not, she gradually weakened.[41] Finally, with great reluctance, she agreed that Paul could go. Mariia, however, was going to have to stay at home. The arrangements were made, Paul's horses and equipment had been dispatched, and everything was in readiness. Then, at the eleventh hour, Catherine changed her mind, precipitating a violent quarrel with Paul. In this case, however, Catherine felt that she had due cause.

---

[39] Kobeko, *Pavel Petrovich*, 307–9; Morane, *Paul Ier*, 308–12; Shil'der, *Pavel I*, 199–208 and 556–8. For the correspondence between Catherine and Paul and Mariia before and during the trip, *SIRIO* 15, pp. 37–135. Fitzherbert reported Paul and Mariia's profound distress when they learnt accidentally that Catherine was taking Alexander and Constantine with her. PRO, FO/65/13, no. 56, 28 Nov. (NS) 1786; FO/65/15, 3/13 Jan. 1787, and 17 Jan. (NS) 1787. In Catherine's absence, Mariia was to report on the children's health and was required to have Catherine's permission for any steps she took to protect her daughters from infection. For Catherine's letters to Saltykov, Catherine II, *Sochineniia*, xii. 691–2.

[40] Paul to Catherine, 10 and 11 Sept. (OS) 1787, *Russkaia starina*, 8 (1873), 856; Kobeko, *Pavel Petrovich*, 320–1; Morane, *Paul Ier*, 315–17.

[41] Catherine to Grimm, 29 Nov. (OS) 1787, *SIRIO* 23, p. 429; Shil'der, *Pavel I*, 209.

The altercation broke out when one of Mariia's attendants was overheard to remark that the grand duchess was pregnant again. This news was carried immediately to Catherine who had not been told. She was deeply disturbed. When Paul and Mariia were travelling in Europe, there were rumours in the press that the grand duchess was pregnant. Catherine wrote immediately asking for the truth of the matter. The same occurred the previous spring when the Hamburg *Gazette* reported that Mariia was pregnant. Catherine, who was on her Crimean junket, wrote asking if this were true. As before, there were denials. Catherine believed that she of all people should be told first about something so intimate to her family, and so important to the state. She resented learning by hearsay. 'I think, my dear son,' she wrote on this occasion, 'that it is my right not to be informed of the grand duchess's pregnancies by inquiries or rumours in the town, nor to be the last to know.' And reminding him that she had asked him from Kiev about the same matter, she demanded to know from whence this pregnancy dated. Worst of all, she insisted that the permission she had already granted for him to go to the front had to be rescinded; for him to go exposed both his wife and the unborn child to unnecessary dangers. Paul was to put off his departure until Mariia had been delivered. Paul protested, but only half-heartedly; there was little he could say. He was, however, very angry, and not least for the bad impression his sudden change of plans was likely to create abroad. What must Europe think, he asked his mother bitterly, after it had been announced that he was going to the front, and then he was dragged back without any public explanation. Europe, Catherine remarked drily, would only think that he was her son and subject who did precisely what she required when she required it. The matter was closed.[42]

The child, the fourth of five daughters, was born in May, but by then another situation had developed. Gustave III of Sweden, seeing Russia occupied with the Turks, decided to strike directly at St Petersburg. This was war within earshot of the Winter Palace, and when Paul once more volunteered, Catherine agreed.[43] Paul treated

[42] *Russkaia starina*, 8 (1873), 856–72. Accounts vary. Frazer, the British consul, reported that Catherine had had a letter from Potemkin after which she wrote to Paul withdrawing her approval for his service, *alleging* his wife's pregnancy as the reason. A further communication from Potemkin cleared the way for Paul to join his forces, but by that time, the Swedish crisis had broken and Paul was already committed to that front. See PRO, FO/65/15, no. 4, Frazer to Carmarthen, 25 Sept. (NS) 1787; no. 24, 14 Dec. (NS) 1787; no. 25, Dec. (NS) 1787; no. 1, 4 Jan. (NS) 1788; no. 7, 2 Feb. (NS) 1788); no. 28, 10 June (NS) 1788. Cf. Kobeko, *Pavel Petrovich*, 322–4; Morane, *Paul Ier*, 317–18; Shil'der, *Pavel I*, 209–15.

[43] For Paul, Catherine, and the Swedish campaign, *SIRIO* 15, pp. 135–57 and

the matter seriously. He drew up his will and instructed Mariia on what she should do concerning the succession. He also put together a political testament in the form of an instruction or *nakaz* for his successor. This document, together with a decree on the succession and the letters to his wife, summarized Paul's political thinking before the onset of the French revolution. It also may be taken as a guide to the general principles and some of the specific legislation which he introduced as tsar eight years later.[44]

The instruction began by considering what form of government was best for Russia, and what was needed to realize it. Paul concluded, as his mother had in her more famous *Instruction* twenty-one years earlier, that 'there is no better form [of government] than autocracy, for it combines the strength of law with the executive dispatch of a single authority'. To provide advice, and otherwise to assist the autocrat in governing, he proposed the formation of a state council composed of the government's chief administrators, including the chancellor, the vice-chancellors for foreign affairs and justice, the state treasurer, and the ministers of naval affairs, finance, and commerce. The council, whose composition resembled Panin's council of 1783, was intended to be more than an *ad hoc* advisory body. It was the crown in a proposed reorganization of existing administrative colleges and councils into a centralized system of ministries. The focus was on the autocrat assisted by councillors of his own choosing. Law in this system was the codification and consistent application of the autocrat's will. All administrative organs bore responsibility for realizing that function.

The autocratic principle was fundamental to Paul's view of Russian government. The most serious constitutional deficiency which he saw inhibiting autocracy was the absence of a settled law of succession. In his mind, this meant a hereditary principle which could endow the ruler with unquestioned moral force. Only this could put an end to factional manœuvring and reduce the danger of palace revolutions. His own experience was obviously the starting-point for this conviction. By 1788 he was convinced that his mother had usurped what should have been his, and in doing so had opened the

esp. 150–3 for her approval. The uncertainty over whether Paul could go appears in Fitzherbert's reports. See PRO, FO/65/17, no. 2, 14 Jan. (NS) 1788; no. 7, 2 Feb. (NS) 1788; no. 35, 12 July (NS) 1788.

[44] For these materials, M. Semevskii, 'Materialy k russkoi istorii XVIII veka', *Vestnik evropy*, 2 (Apr. 1867), 297–330. For two recent appraisals, see Scharf, 'Staatsauffassung und Regierungsprogramm eines aufgeklärten Selbstherrschers', and Ransel, *Panin Party*, 282–9. See also Ransel, 'Ambivalent Legacy', 12–14, and Kobeko, *Pavel Petrovich*, 311–17.

door to the crassest forms of corruption and abuse. To remedy this deficiency, Paul (with Mariia) drew up a decree re-establishing the hereditary succession on the basis of male primogeniture, spelling out in uncompromising detail precisely how it would progress. He introduced this reform (dated 1788) at his coronation on Easter Sunday 1797.[45] He also instructed Mariia on what she should do if Catherine died while he was away, or if both he and the empress died. In the first instance, oaths of allegiance were to be sworn to himself as emperor and to Alexander as his heir. In the second case, Alexander would be declared emperor with Mariia as regent until he reached the age of 17 when he would rule in his own right. What Paul proposed was precisely the sort of settlement Panin urged on Catherine in 1762 which she refused.

The affirmation of autocracy and the hereditary succession placed Paul firmly in the modern absolutist tradition. His view of society and the ruler's obligations towards it showed a paternalistic and humanitarian emphasis with enlightened overtones. Paul envisioned society as a hierarchical construction of corporate entities or estates each of which—nobility, clergy, middle class, or peasants—performed a particular function. The nobility was the governing caste, the ruler's supporters, and bore the moral obligation of state service. (Peter III abolished obligatory service for the aristocracy in 1762, while Catherine had already legislated extensively to define nobiliary rights.) The clergy was responsible for society's spiritual welfare, while the peasants and the middle class represented the productive element. Each group needed to understand its function; hence there had to be an educational system which would 'instill a knowledge of the prescribed goals and the desire on the part of each person, according to his estate, to fulfill his duties for the common goal of society'. This approach, like the affirmation of autocracy and the advocacy of administrative centralization, was squarely in the mainstream of contemporary Russian thinking, and was the basis for the educational system institutionalized early in the reign of Paul's son, Nicholas I.[46]

---

[45] For the decree, *Polnoe sobranie zakonov rossiiskoi imperii* (hereafter *PSZ*), 1st ser., xxiv, no. 17910. See also Kobeko, *Pavel Petrovich*, 316–17. Catherine considered a similar law but never wrote it. See 'Otryvok sobstvennoruchnago chernago proekta manifesta Ekaterina II o prestonasledii', *Russkaia starina*, 12 (1875), 384–5.

[46] Paul's thinking on educating classes according to function parallels prescriptions offered *c*.1804 by Ivan Petrovich Pnin. See his 'Opyt o prosveshcheniia otnositel'no k Rossii', *Sochineniia* (Moscow, 1934), 121–61. Marc Raeff has trans. the essay for his *Russian Intellectual History*, 126–58. See esp. 147 ff. The Nicholaevan

Paul's views on government and social structure were enlightened in the sense that they involved a rational system and placed primary emphasis on every man's responsibility to serve the whole. Each person contributed according to the disposition of his caste; privilege arose out of function; the common welfare was what everyone served; and the ruler, though answerable only to his conscience and God, was truly the state's first servant. Moreover, the *nakaz* was heavily freighted with humanitarian concerns. Paul believed that the powerful had to be prevented from exploiting the weak, and he pointed specifically to the peasants' need to be protected against their often capricious overseers and gentry masters. He also considered the liquor monopolies a social liability and proposed their reduction. He thought that promoting mining and manufacturing would enable the state to replace revenues it might lose with the passing of the alcohol monopoly. He dilated on the social costs of unstable currencies, the need for effective domestic security systems, and a proper balance between military (external) and police (internal) protection. This returned to themes which he had addressed in 1774 and 1778. He argued the need for a moral approach to foreign affairs which eschewed aggression while defending the state's real interests, the maintenance of balance, order, and peace, and he recommended that Russia put her greatest emphasis on developing her own strength and supporting the northern alliance. His commitment to a Panin-like foreign policy remained unaltered.

The 1788 instruction plainly showed Paul's basic political thinking. His approach was paternalistic, humanitarian, and in the broad sense of the term, progressive. Allowing for the fact that at the time he wrote he was entirely outside the circle of power, his views on Russia and her future were thoughtful and should have augured well. That they did not was less a function of what he had learnt and what he believed than of the kind of man he had come to be. His problems were not a consequence of failures or achievements in education. Rather they arose from his having been raised to be a ruler, and then cut off from any role whatsoever in the life he should have led.

The Swedish campaign, the only active fighting Paul ever saw, proved to be wholly unsatisfactory. He was allowed to take his personal staff from Gatchina, but he was forced to leave his troops behind. Worse, he was to be only an observer, leaving all decisions to the regular command. The hastily chosen general for the Swedish front was Count Mussin-Pushkin, a man whose physical infirmities and advanced age reinforced a natural unwillingness to make

programme, as presented in the official decrees, is outlined in detail in Nicholas Hans, *History of Russian Educational Policy, 1701–1917* (London, 1931), 64–75.

decisions. Paul disagreed with virtually everything Mussin-Pushkin did, but he could only grumble to his aides or seethe in silence.[47] His one achievement was a grudging commendation from his mother when the Swedes approached him with cease-fire proposals, and he passed them on to constituted authority. Nevertheless, Paul did hear musket balls whistle past his ears (the Swedes apologized for firing on him), and thus could claim his baptism of fire.[48]

Whatever emotional rewards Paul may have won from his experiences at war were entirely personal and self-generated. His participation was not reported in the gazettes, and there was no decoration for him when he came home. This was surely Catherine's doing. And her own comment on his Swedish adventures was a little play she wrote entitled 'the Woeful Knight (*Gore-Bogatyr*) or The Hero of Misfortune', satirizing military heroics. Ostensibly its target was Gustave III, but the message could be applied equally well to Paul. Frustrated with what he saw in the campaign as monumental incompetence, and furious at his own impotence, Paul returned to Gatchina to resume drilling, manœuvring, and waiting for the time when it all would mean something.[49]

Paul returned from the wars to an explosive situation in his household which ignited the following year. Since at least 1785, his name had been linked with one of Mariia's maids of honour, Catherine Ivanovna Nelidova, who had actually joined the grand duke's court at the time of his first marriage.[50] After Nathalia's

[47] Mariia feared Paul's anger at the incompetence he saw around him, and she believed that Steinwehr stirred him up. See Mariia Fedorovna to Vadkovskii, *Osmnadtsatyi vek*, i. 411–13.

[48] On the Swedish campaign, see Paul's correspondence with Catherine, SIRIO 15, pp. 135–57. Kurakin described Paul's disgust with the Russian command. *Osmnadtsatyi vek*, i. 408–9. See also Kobeko, *Pavel Petrovich*, 324–9; Morane, *Paul Ier*, 320–2; Shil'der, *Pavel I*, 219–30. Paul's departure for and return from the front were barely remarked. See PRO, FO/65/16, Frazer to Carmarthen, no. 28, 10 June (NS) 1788; no. 50, 30 Sept. (NS) 1788. Ségur's reports were more informative. See Morane, *Paul Ier*, 321 nn. 1 and 2.

[49] Ségur, *Mémoires*, iii. 377, noted that Paul saw almost no combat as 'there was a great deal of threatening on both sides, but little fighting'. On the 'Woeful Knight', *Russkaia starina*, 3 (1874), 154; Morane, *Paul Ier*, 322. 'Gore-Bogatyr' was played before Paul on 31 Jan. (OS) 1789. A. V. Khrapovitskii, *Dnevnik*, ed. N. Barsukov (St Petersburg, 1874), 248. Catherine claimed that it took great courage to remain in Petersburg in earshot of the cannons' roar but, as Rostopchin assured Paul in 1800, she was ready to fly shamelessly to escape the Swedes. Paul agreed and noted on the report, 'and the horses were ready'. Kobeko, *Pavel Petrovich*, 330.

[50] Paul's affair with Catherine Nelidova is fully documented in Shumigorskii's *Nelidova* and his *Mariia Fedorovna*, i. 356–74, 401–23. Both books are rich in contemporary material including the correspondence of the two women. Dmitri de Benckendorff, *La Favorite d'un tzar: Catherine Ivanowna Nelidow, 1758–1839*

death, Nelidova became maid of honour to Mariia Fedorovna, and she travelled with the grand ducal entourage through Europe in 1781–2. What brought her and Paul together can only be conjectured. Propinquity probably had a great deal to do with it. The grand duke's court was an intimate one, and during the long stays at Pavlovsk and Gatchina, its members were inevitably thrown together. Entertaining themselves in isolation occupied much of the court's time as they organized and presented plays, recitations, ballets, pantomimes, and musical evenings. Even Paul occasionally took a hand or offered a word of advice. Nelidova, who had been educated at the Smol'nyi Institute for noble girls, was a competent musician, an accomplished dancer, and played a leading part in organizing and expediting the entertainments.[51]

Small, bright-eyed with a gamine smile, tensile, and alert, Nelidova was not considered particularly attractive—Catherine called her the little monster—but she was lively and energetic. She was also clever, witty, extremely verbal, and well-schooled. She was steeped in the sentimental idealism considered appropriate for someone of her sex and station which included strong religious feelings, belief in a pure, even sacrificial, love, honour, friendship, personal piety, and above all, a true heart. What attracted her to Paul, according to her major biographer, was respect for his effort to maintain a pious and harmonious family life in a dissolute society, sympathy for his position as the prince without a kingdom, and indignation at the shabby, contemptuous, and condescending treatment he had to suffer from inferiors who should have been his servants. Nelidova saw herself as Paul's protector as well as his companion and friend. She had never, as she told him in 1797 after twelve years of devoted

(Paris, 1902), is subtitled 'after Shumigorskii' and translates substantial parts of the Nelidova biography. Some parts are omitted, but material is added as well. There are no footnotes (Shumigorskii is fully annotated) nor does Benckendorff indicate where material is added or omitted. Only comparison with the Russian text reveals that. Both Morane, *Paul Ier*, 378–400, and Kobeko, *Pavel Petrovich*, 356–60, cover this crisis. Morane is preferable on the Nelidova affair. *Correspondence de Sa Majesté l'Impératrice Marie Feodorowna avec Mademoiselle de Nelidoff sa Demoiselle d'Honneur (1797–1801) suivre des Lettres de Mademoiselle Nelidoff au Prince A[lexandre] B. Kourakin*, ed. Princess Lise Troubetzkoy (Paris, 1896), is deficient in scholarly apparatus and editorial interpretation, but the letters are very useful. The Kurakin letters cover 1785–96. For letters from Nelidova to Paul beginning 23 Nov. (os) 1796, see: 'Iz bumag. E. I. Nelidovy', *Osmnadtsatyi vek*, i. 422–44.

[51] Kobeko, *Pavel Petrovich*, 286, 288–92. It was rumoured that Paul was pushed towards Nelidova (possibly on Catherine's urging) by suggestions that Mariia and Mme Benckendorff, her special friend, controlled his life. Nelidova was a counter to that influence. See Golovina, *Souvenirs*, 45–6, and 'Zapiski ken. F. N. Golitsyna', *Russkii arkhiv*, 1 (1874), 1287–8. Golovina's account is garbled.

caring, thought of him as a man; rather he was her sister, and dear to her withal.[52]

The attraction Paul found in Nelidova was precisely her openness and sympathy. She was a person who believed in him, who seemed to understand the way he felt, who was ready to support him, yet who would not hesitate to warn and criticize, who forced him to confront his mistakes, who urged him to live up to his potential and his position. Once the spark was struck, Paul's feelings, never well controlled, blazed up. No day could pass without his seeing and talking with Nelidova. She was essential to him. He demanded more and more of her time, and this she gladly gave. He was her prince, her tsar-to-be, but he was also 'this dear little Paul', a good man betrayed by the world in which he had to live. But she gave him more than sympathy, for she had temperament, personality, and flair. She was as quick as he was; she loved exaggerated, sentimental rhetoric; she spoke feelingly of love, honour, courage, and loyalty, the very virtues he extolled. They were, in fact, well matched.[53]

Paul believed he loved Nelidova, and he told her so. Their relationship, he wrote her when sending a devotional book, was particular to them, unique. He chose to honour her with a gift (the book) which would lead her to think of God, and he avowed that 'It is my way of showing love for those who are most dear to me'. This, he declared, was in no way criminal (a reference to gossipy critics), and he instructed her to open the book on impulse and at random: the words she read would have a special meaning. He concluded that 'God alone knows how dear you are to me. I call down on you His most holy benediction, and am everything for you, friend and servitor.'[54] From the Swedish front in 1788 he sent a hasty note: were he to die, at the moment of his death he would think of her, and in 1790, when he was seriously ill, he wrote the empress a letter in which he condemned those gossips who dirtied Nelidova's reputation, declaring that his love for her was innocent and pure, pointing out how alone and helpless she was in the world, and begging Catherine, should he die, to shelter and protect her.[55]

---

[52] Shumigorskii, *Nelidova* 15. Nelidova referred to Paul as her sister in an undated note, probably from 1797. See 'Iz bumag E. I. Nelidovy', *Osmnadtsatyi vek*, i (1868), 422–44.

[53] The reference to 'this dear little Paul' was in a letter to Vadkovskii which Nelidova wrote at Mariia's request. Such forwardness displeased Mariia. Shumigorskii, *Nelidova*, 18–20. For Nelidova's personality in contrast to Mariia's, and its appeal to Paul, ibid. 21–6; Shumigorskii, *Mariia Fedorovna*, i. 325–6.

[54] 'Iz bumag Nelidovy', no. 26, pp. 448–9.

[55] For the note from the front, Shumigorskii, *Nelidova*, 21. The letter to Catherine is 'Pismo v.k. Pavla Petrovicha k Imperatritse Ekaterine ob

Though gossip said it was otherwise, it is generally agreed that the bonds between Paul and Nelidova were as chaste as he insisted.[56] There was nothing of wooing or seduction. Rather they lived a chivalric romance carried on at a high pitch of verbal intensity with a cool disregard for the rest of the world. Undoubtedly there was an underlying and unresolved sexual tension which was heightened by the mutually imposed impossibility of any sexual fulfilment. The satisfactions in this relationship lay in the highly charged exchanges which it generated; sexual relations were on another and wholly inferior plane.

Given the standards of the age and the moral character of the Russian court, Paul and Nelidova were both unusually chaste. Paul, of course, was sexually experienced, but there were powerful checks on his adventuring. The first and most important was his contempt for his mother's favourites and the relationship which made them what they were. His personal style was in conscious contradiction with that of the great court. To keep a mistress who would have a favourite's power would run counter to everything he believed he stood for. It would also, and inevitably, destroy the particular relationship with Nelidova he enjoyed. In the second place, whether he reciprocated Mariia's love or not, Paul was, in his own special way, devoted to his wife. They lived intimately together, even sleeping together, as our anonymous anecdotalist remarked, like any ordinary married couple.[57] Even when their troubles were serious, they continued to cohabit, and Mariia carried through two pregnancies. All of this gave her great influence with Paul, which she was not always wise in using, but it also meant that Paul had a ready, comfortable, and submissive woman who was wholly satisfying to him. The third was Nelidova herself who seems to have had relatively little interest in establishing sexual relations with anyone. The

---

E. I. Nelidovoi', *Osmnadtsatyi vek*, i. 445–6. See also Mariia Fedorovna, *Correspondence*, ed. Troubetzkoi, pp. xxxiii–xxxv; Shumigorskii, *Nelidova*, 27; *Mariia Fedorovna*, i. 366.

[56] Though platonic, the relationship had its livelier moments. Sablukov records that one night, while on duty in the palace (Paul was then tsar), he saw Paul hurriedly leave Nelidova's rooms followed by a high-heeled woman's shoe which was flung at him and narrowly missed. Nelidova followed the missile into the hall, collected it, and returned to her room. 'Reminiscences: Part II', *Fraser's Magazine* (Sept. 1865), 303–4. (See *Russkii arkhiv* (1869), 1919–20.) Shumigorskii, *Nelidova*, 21–2, denies that there was any substance whatsoever to the rumours of a physical love affair. See also Chizh, 'Imperator Pavel I' 633 ff., who agrees.

[57] Anon., *Anekdoten*, 48. Mariia was said to use the time before sleep to tell Paul about people she thought were out of line and deserved punishment. Golovkine, *La Cour de Paul Ier*, 159–60.

Smol'nyi Institute where she lived from the age of 6 until she was 16 enforced a monastic discipline which, as far as is known, Nelidova never challenged. As a maid of honour, there were temptations, but Nelidova, who was neither rich nor beautiful, made a career of serving her mistresses. Her sharp tongue won her fame of a sort, though nothing that would encourage dalliance, and until she became Paul's friend, she was best known for her dancing. She was, in fact, one of the unapproachables who was never linked with any man.[58]

Four years younger than Paul (she was born in 1758), Catherine Nelidova was already 27 when he became interested in her. She was exactly 40 when their relationship ended definitively in 1798. This was no girl with an easily turned head, but a mature woman who had made her way virtually alone for more than a decade in a dangerously competitive environment. She never gave over being the dedicated servant of her mistress, the grand duchess, and through her the grand duke; she ostentatiously avoided even the appearance of accepting favours from anyone, most particularly Paul, and she gave every evidence of believing the exalted principles she preached.[59] In effect, transcending sex was Nelidova's best weapon. It kept her free of entangling, disruptive, and ultimately enslaving relationships (even with Paul she retained a very wide field of personal independence), and if she were ambitious, she may even have understood that for her sex was an inferior weapon to ply to win Paul's favour. Certainly she was clever—Rostopchin, who disliked her, dubbed her 'the little enchantress'—and she maintained her very special relationship with Paul for almost a decade. This in itself was a remarkable achievement in light of his volatility and the large number of influential people, beginning with Mariia herself, who tried to dislodge her. Always modest, unassuming, and apparently disinterested, she gave her enemies little opportunity, beyond gossip, to get at her. There is only one sign of a crack in the moral armour.

[58] Shumigorskii, *Nelidova*, *passim*; on the early years, pp. 2–15.

[59] Nelidova would accept small remembrances like a book. She rejected a large holding when Paul offered it, though she kept a porcelain service. 'Iz bumag E. I. Nelidovy', no. 1, 23 Nov. (os) 1796, p. 424. When Paul offered her mother 2,000 peasants, she insisted the number be reduced to 500 and protested that even that was unnecessary. Ibid., no. 3, 12 Dec. (os) 1796, p. 427. She often spoke of how happy she could be at Smol'nyi with a good library, her harp, and crayons, and the opportunity to watch young people growing up. Mariia Fedorovna, *Correspondance*, ed. Troubetskoi, 190–4. Shumigorskii considers these attitudes less self-abnegation than an idealistic unworldliness which suffused the whole of her life. *Nelidova*, 43–45. She seemed unable to understand someone so dissolute and self-indulgent as Prince Alexander Kurakin.

When Sir Charles Whitworth, the English minister to Petersburg, desperately needed favourable action on a tariff treaty early in Paul's reign, he gave a large bribe to Ivan Kutiasov, the tsar's wholly corrupt barber, *valet de chambre*, and confidant. He gave an even larger one to Catherine Nelidova.[60]

From the time of her marriage, Mariia Fedorovna had dedicated herself to serving Paul's best interests. She came to Russia prepared to find everything good in him, and she refused to be disappointed. Their marriage seemed strong, and if Paul was perhaps less enchanted with his wife in the early years than she was with him, he was on the best of terms with her and treated her with affection and consideration. With the passage of years, however, what had been pleasant palled. Mariia, with all her good qualities, was not a very interesting person. She was didactic, conventional, and rather unimaginative. She was not inclined to soar.[61] She hardly knew what to do with Paul and Nelidova, but she did see, as time passed, that 'the little one', as she called her rival, not only had a strong hold on Paul's affections, but that she was usurping functions which Mariia considered her own. Through the early years of the marriage, Mariia scarcely left her husband's side. She saw it as her duty to be with him, to listen to him, to plan with him, to admire him. As Paul increasingly turned to Nelidova, Mariia felt abandoned. She resented her rival, began to complain to her intimates, and even laid her problem before Catherine who neither understood nor sympathized. Her opinion was that Mariia had only to be patient; it was she who had the advantages of appearance and position. In time, Nelidova could only lose.[62]

The troubles began in 1789–90. Count Cobenzl, the Austrian ambassador, reported to Vienna in March 1790 that 'It has been

---

[60] PRO, FO/65/36, Whitworth to Grenville, no. 12, St Petersburg, 23 Feb. (NS) 1797. The dispatch is marked 'Most Secret'. The information on the bribes is in cipher. Kutiasov received 20,000 rubles, Nelidova 30,000 'on the footing of a [loan] ... for the purchase of a villa'. The payments were to be made on the exchange of ratifications.

[61] Shumigorskii, *Nelidova*, 15–16. Catherine remarked to Grimm, 7, 11, and 12 Oct. (OS) 1795, that Mariia read a great deal without understanding all that she read—she believed that culture, like having babies, was what a woman ought to do—and speculating on her granddaughters' futures, suggested ironically that if they were all named Mariia, then like their mother, 'they would have the same preoccupations with their complexions, they would eat enough for four and would know how to choose their readings with discrimination, after which they would become excellent bourgeois ladies for any country whatsoever'. *SIRIO* 23, p. 659.

[62] On the interview, 'Zapiski Mukhanovoi', *Russkii arkhiv*, 1 (1878), 308, with Catherine remarking: 'Look how beautiful you are; your rival is a little monster; stop torturing yourself and be sure of your charms.' Cf. Shumigorskii, *Nelidova*, 29.

remarked for more than a year that the grand duke in the interior of his household has often given way to humors and expressions of temperament which everyone who approaches him has to suffer; the grand duchess herself, despite her sweetness and her attachment for her husband, is often the target'. The reason for these 'disturbances and perturbations', Cobenzl wrote in May, was that 'the grand duke has all at once fallen in love with mademoiselle Nelidow, maid of honour for mme. the grand duchess . . . [whose] situation . . . is made more cruel since she loves the prince her husband, and yet it is before her eyes that he constantly speaks in the ear of mlle. Nelidow and openly pays court to her'. His treatment of the grand duchess 'with whom he appears to be entirely disgusted' is very rough, 'and so he is with everyone whom she honours with her confidence'. Matters scarcely improved. By August, Mariia was openly displaying her irritation. This led to sharp quarrels between Paul and Mariia whom Cobenzl described as 'presently extremely cold to one another'.[63]

Mariia had hoped to avoid a confrontation. Unfortunately she was carrying other heavy emotional burdens, and Paul's persistent public intimacy with Nelidova proved to be more than she could stand. The French revolution had destroyed her family's home and sent her parents into exile; she had failed to protect her brother, Frédèric Eugène, from Catherine who expelled him from the army without recognition of service for savagely mistreating his wife (even Mariia could not defend his behaviour); her sister, whose marriage she helped negotiate in 1781–2, died in childbed, while her favourite younger brother, who had just come to Russia and was commissioned to serve with Potemkin in the south, contracted a fever and died there. The Nelidova affair was one blow too many.[64]

In autumn 1790, tensions eased when Nelidova apologized to Mariia and Paul fell ill. Mariia was not prepared to make peace with Nelidova, though while nursing Paul assiduously she refrained from interfering in his daily talks with her. Her forbearance won her no advantage, however, for as Paul recovered his suspicious and uncertain temper reasserted itself, with the result that 'everyone

---

[63] HHSA, Russland II Berichte, Cobenzl to Kaunitz, no. 18, apostille 10, 22 Mar. (NS) 1790; no. 30, apostille 11, 9 May (NS) 1790; no. 54, apostille 8, 16 Aug. (NS) 1790.

[64] Kobeko, *Pavel Petrovich*, 336–7; Shumigorskii, *Mariia Fedorovna*, i. 277–85. The problem with Frédèric Eugène was a major scandal. See Shil'der, *Pavel I*, 193–9; Morane, *Paul Ier*, 323–33. Lafermière wrote to Count S. R. Vorontsov about the heavy blows Mariia sustained, especially her brother's death: no. 44, 3 Mar. (OS) 1790, *Arkhiv kniazia Vorontsova*, xxix. 274; 27 Aug. (OS) 1791, ibid. 277–80.

around him, and that without exception, is exposed to his incivility'. He continued to treat Mariia badly while favouring Nelidova.[65]

Once Mariia had shown her opposition to Nelidova, nothing that she did could make amends. Paul was furious, and aroused; he gave the matter no rest. He charged his wife with disloyalty, accused her of plotting with his enemies who were determined to deprive him of his rights, and insisted on making support for Nelidova a litmus test of loyalty to himself.[66] Mariia's supporters fell under heavy suspicion, were harried and threatened, until the most important of them, Madame Benckendorff (Mariia's bosom friend from Montbeillard) was driven to request that she be permitted to retire. She felt her continued presence was an obvious burden on Mariia. Lafermière, Paul's long-time servitor but a warm supporter of the grand duchess, also sought retirement to escape from what had become an intolerable situation. Violier, an artist whom Mariia employed, was expelled from the court when he declined to give up his apartment (which connected with Paul's rooms) to Catherine Nelidova, while the empress herself had to intervene to protect Count Nikita Petrovich Panin from her son's wrath when he refused to enlist under Nelidova's banner.[67]

Panin told the story in a letter to Count S. R. Vorontsov written in 1799. He had been appointed gentleman of the bedchamber to the grand duke in 1791, but when he went to take up his duties, he 'no longer found the union and concord in the imperial family' he had witnessed before. 'La Nelidoff already ruled', while the grand duchess was 'abandoned, mistreated, scorned by all those who wished to pay her [Nelidova] court'. Panin refused to play this game despite the fact that the grand duke made every effort to win him, 'employing first caresses, then coldness, then threats'. Panin was made to understand in various ways that his future status depended

---

[65] Conditions in the young court in the fall of 1790 are covered in some detail in Cobenzl's correspondence. See HHSA, Russland II Berichte, Carton 73, no. 68, 8 Oct. (NS) 1790; no. 73, apostille 2, 28 Oct (NS) 1790; no. 79, apostille 5, 24 Nov. (NS) 1790 (for the comment quoted).

[66] Shumigorskii, *Nelidova*, 35–7.

[67] HHSA, Russland II Berichte, Carton 73, Cobenzl to Kaunitz, no. 4, apostille 1, 19 Jan. (NS) 1791; Carton 74, no. 21, 21 Mar. (NS), 1791; Carton 75, no. 48, 12 July (NS) 1791 (the Violier incident); no. 72, apostille 8, 13 Oct. (NS) 1791; no. 80, 15 Nov. (NS), 1791 (on Mme Benckendorff); no. 82, 29 Nov. (NS) 1791 (discussing the factions in the Nelidova affair). Lafermière told Count Vorontsov that the summer of 1791 was extremely disagreeable owing to the persistent bickering in the young court. No. 97, 21 Sept. (OS) 1791, *Arkhiv kniazia Vorontsova*, xxix, 279–80. He was overjoyed that his severe rheumatism gave him an acceptable reason for retiring. No. 48, 17 Jan. (OS) 1793, ibid. 281–2.

on his current behaviour, that he was expected to show 'respect for la Nelidoff [and] scorn for the grand duchess'. He still refused, and as the pressure from intermediaries mounted, he requested an interview with Paul which took place in August 1791. Hard words were spoken on both sides which Panin made no attempt to repeat, but he claimed that his resistance drew down upon him 'from the emperor's [i.e. Paul's] own mouth these terrible words: *The road which you follow, monsieur, can only lead you to the window or the door.*' The point was unmistakable: Panin's career hung in the balance. Panin, however, claimed that he replied that he would not be deflected from the path of honour and left without waiting for Paul's words of dismissal.[68]

In 1799, Panin was already convinced that Paul had to be replaced, and was probably working towards that end. This letter should be read with that fact in mind. But even discounting it in those terms, it describes a situation fully documented in other sources. Where Nelidova was concerned, Paul expected co-operation and support. For the moment, Mariia was the enemy. And the very strength of his reaction inhibited Nelidova from taking action herself. If she abandoned the court, as she was increasingly inclined to do, she could reliably expect an even worse reaction from Paul. Nelidova appears to have held no animus towards those who supported Mariia, or towards Mariia herself. Yet she made no effort to appear as anything but Paul's nearest and dearest friend.[69] Eventually, however, the tension became too great for her, and when a new round of violent quarrels followed a public airing of the scandal in *Le Moniteur universel* (24 April 1792), she asked the empress for permission to leave her post and retire to Smol'nyi. The request was made on 25 June (OS) 1792. Catherine, however, withheld permission for fourteen months, and Nelidova remained in place. Nor did she leave immediately once she could, but rather, as Rostopchin put it, 'continues to live there [at court] and enjoys a success at the expense of the grand duke's dignity while exposing him to universal blame'.[70]

[68] Count N. P. Panin to Vorontsov, 19 Apr. (OS) 1799, *Arkhiv kniazia Vorontsova*, xi. 70–1; *Materialy dlia zhizneopisaniia grafa Nikity Petrovicha Panina (1770–1837)*, ed. A. Brikner, 7 vols. (St Petersburg, 1888–92), i. 105–8.

[69] Shumigorskii, *Nelidova*, 27–8. When Mme Benckendorff recruited Mme Rzhevskiia-Alomova against Nelidova, Mme Rzhevskiia, who claimed to feel real pity for Mariia, still spoke openly to Nelidova who never showed the least sign of taking offence. Moreover, she must not have said anything to Paul for he continued to treat Rzhevskiia in a friendly way. 'Zapiski Rzhevskoi', *Russkii arkhiv* (1871), 41.

[70] Rostopchin to Vorontsov, *Arkhiv kniazia Vorontsova*, viii. 80; Shumigorskii, *Nelidova*, 46.

But Paul was angry over Nelidova's decision to leave, and even more upset when his mother finally agreed. He only began to accept the situation when Nelidova promised she would come regularly to visit at Gatchina, and to stay as long as she could. The result was that, while officially her connection with Paul's court had ended, matters went back on the same footing as before. Nelidova remained the central figure in the grand duke's society.[71]

In 1790, Mariia had apparently decided that she could not resist Nelidova, and though she rejected her maid of honour's tentative approach the following year, she took a passive line. For three years, from 1791 to 1794, she not only coped with Nelidova's presence, but put up as well with Paul's constant sniping interspersed with angry attacks. Her purpose was to maintain at least a vestige of familial harmony, but her success was minimal. Nelidova's request to retire seemed to promise a resolution, though Paul's angry reactions showed how far there was to go. Nevertheless, when Catherine finally agreed to Nelidova's departure, Mariia could only have been relieved. It then gradually dawned on her that nothing had really changed, that Nelidova was still the cuckoo in her nest, and that there was literally no way to get rid of her. Faced with an apparently endless quarrel, Mariia took the only road open to her and offered to make up with Nelidova, who was only too happy to agree. The resulting alliance was a strange one, but it calmed the grand duke's court, restoring something of the harmony that had been known before 1789. Mariia, though at first resentful and bitter, gradually came to accept Nelidova, and in time these two women forged a deep friendship which lasted until Mariia's death in 1828. The war was definitely finished; nothing comparable to it was to agitate Paul and his court until 1798.[72]

In 1791, the English minister, Charles Whitworth, who paid less attention to family affairs than did Cobenzl, and was less well informed concerning them, none the less made the astute observation that while Paul's conduct towards Mariia 'is generally reprobated' he also thought that the empress 'may not be sorry to see an Union

[71] Shumigorskii, *Nelidova*, 36–41, 45–6. Cobenzl reported Paul's furious reaction when Catherine agreed to Nelidova's request and his determination to boycott the court. HHSA, Russland II Berichte, Carton 78, Cobenzl to Kaunitz, no. 56, 1 Oct. (NS) 1793. His sulk continued that autumn. Ibid., no. 57, 4 Oct. (NS) 1793; no. 61, 20 Oct. (NS) 1793; no. 70, 10 Dec. (NS) 1793. He relented, then retreated again when Nelidova was excluded from court occasions. She then joined him and Mariia at Gatchina 'where he enjoys the satisfaction of living under the same roof virtually the whole day with her [Nelidova]'. Carton 79, Cobenzl to Kaunitz, no. 13, 11 Mar. (NS) 1794.
[72] Shumigorskii, *Nelidova*, 47–51.

destroyed which placed Their Highnesses in so favorable a Point of View'. He connected this speculation with Catherine's rumoured determination to replace Paul 'of whose Capacity for Government she entertains but a very mean Opinion' with his son, Alexander, in the succession.[73] Catherine did nothing to assist Mariia during the Nelidova crisis. Worse, it is alleged that she contributed to the conflict between Paul and Mariia by insinuating to Paul through Osten-Sacken that Madame Benckendorff and Lafermière dominated Mariia on whom Paul had become dependent.[74] But Catherine was not the only one to find an opportunity in Paul's troubles. It was during this period that his barber and personal attendant, Ivan Kutaisov, emerged as an increasingly influential person. He showed his new power when, as Paul became suspicious (or bored with) the alliance-in-virtue between Nelidova and Mariia, he was able to point Paul at another young woman, Mademoiselle Verigina, whom the grand duke approached before he realized that she was engaged to Sergei Pleshcheev. The Verigina scandal, which enraged Nelidova and sent her scurrying back to Smol'nyi in 1796, was short-lived, and by the time it was over Paul was convinced that Nelidova was the only honest person in the capital, certainly the only person whom he could trust. After Catherine's death, and with Mariia's wholehearted assistance, he cajoled Nelidova back to court where, for something over eighteen months, she and Mariia played a critically important role.[75]

Mariia's motivation in seeking Nelidova out and allying with her went beyond mere household peace. She knew, as well as anyone, the antagonism which marred Paul's relations with his mother. She had lived with his bitterness literally since their marriage, and she knew as well how much emotional capital Catherine had invested in her oldest grandchild. Without an established law of succession, Paul's becoming emperor (and her mounting the throne with him as his empress) depended on whether Catherine would permit Paul's designation as heir apparent to stand. Mariia also knew that Paul was his own worst enemy. Throughout their life together she had tried always to be with him, to cushion him against damaging

[73] PRO, FO/65/22, Whitworth to Grenville, no. 61, St Petersburg, 23 Nov. (NS) 1791.
[74] 'Zapiski kn. F. N. Golitsyna', *Russkii arkhiv* (1874), 1287–8; Shumigorskii, *Nelidova*, 29. See above and n. 48.
[75] Shumigorskii, *Nelidova*, 51–5 and following; see below, Ch. 7. On Kutaisov, *Russkii biograficheskii slovar*, ix. 616–17. For a modern summary, Hugh Ragsdale, 'Ivan Pavlovich Kutaisov', *Modern Encyclopedia of Russian and Soviet History*, xviii. 206–7. Kutaisov appears prominently in the literature on Paul's life and reign; there is, however, no study of him.

shocks, to help him control his emotions, and especially to curb his temper. In this she performed a necessary function—in the early days it was Panin and Paul's tutors, later Andrei Razumovskii, Osten-Sacken, even Casper Saldern, who worked at this chore—and on the whole she had been successful. Or she was until Nelidova appeared. One of her many griefs with Nelidova was that favourite's unfortunate determination to underline Paul's rights, to encourage him to protect what might be taken from him, and to assert himself in dealing with the empress. (Curiously, Paul's first wife, whom Nelidova liked as well as served, was thought to have pressed the same position.) This, in Mariia's opinion, was not at all what Paul needed. She wanted to see Paul and Catherine on good terms. She was particularly concerned that he avoid irritating the empress, and that he not act irresponsibly, unpredictably, or uncooperatively. By opposing Nelidova, however, she lost her standing with her husband and became herself a disruptive influence. Only Nelidova exerted any control over Paul and, as Mariia saw it, her influence would only make Paul worse. Allying with Nelidova could bring peace to the family, improve Paul's image, and put Mariia in a position where, through Nelidova, she could contribute to guiding and controlling her husband. There was a very real danger, or so she thought, that if she failed in this, Paul would lose his future, and so, of course, would she.[76]

This family drama was played out against a new political background dominated by the revolutionary upheavals in France, the rapid spread of revolutionary ideas in Europe, and the fumbling efforts of Britain, Austria, and Prussia to reverse what was happening. Paul reacted strongly to the news from France. He became the revolution's most outspoken opponent in the Russian court, he began to judge the behaviour of other states according to their willingness to act against this new and terrifying force, and he made resistance to revolutionary influences his personal first priority. In the beginning, he and Catherine spoke the same language. Soon, however, her failure to match her anti-revolutionary rhetoric with effective military support for the allies fighting France created a new issue between them, and when she chose to move against Poland in 1793 rather than support the war in the west, Paul virtually broke off relations with her. During the last three years of her life, he appeared at court as seldom as possible, and in 1795–6 hardly at all.[77] It was

[76] Shumigorskii, *Mariia Fedorovna*, i. 402–3; *Nelidova*, 47–55.
[77] Ségur reported consternation at the Russian court when the Bastille fell, but in the town, merchants and businessmen as well as some 'young men of more elevated class' greeted the news enthusiastically. Paul was horrified from the beginning.

this behaviour Mariia believed she had to reverse; judging from what she wrote, however, she saw only the personal issues and not the political questions. Paul could believe that he now stood alone in a new and special sense. No one seemed to see the dangers he saw, and especially the need to take steps against revolutionary subversion in Russia itself. By 1795, he had come to the conclusion that it would not be possible to reverse events in France; it was entirely too late. The important thing was to build up internal defences against the revolution, to avoid policies which would generate public disorder, and to work towards establishing a new balance of power which could contain and eventually reduce the French position in Europe. Yet Paul himself could do none of this; the only place he had some freedom to act was Gatchina, and there he did what he could.

Paul's political writings, together with what he did both at Gatchina and after he became tsar, provide a relatively clear picture of his view of revolution. At base, he believed that social disorders were a direct consequence of actions which destroyed the natural, that is the organic, relationships necessary to a healthy society. To enlarge one segment or function of society at the expense of the rest, inevitably distorted the entire composition, and to the extent that such distortion bore heavily on other portions of society, there was dissatisfaction and the potential for violence. Rulers who failed to understand the practical limits on what they did could create instability and thus endanger society's very existence. Reason had its role in preserving harmony, balance, and internal peace. Beyond this, each element of society had particular functions or obligations to fulfil. The monarch and the governing aristocracy were responsible for creating good order and protecting those incapable of protecting themselves. Just as productive functions required peasants, labourers, and merchants to create wealth and expedite its exchange, so it was necessary to have landowners, military officers, and administrators, together with all of their servants and supporters, to promote security. The ruler was responsible for the whole and directed it from the apex of the political and social pyramid. If the monarch were morally flawed and incapable of controlling or directing his subordinates, or if the subordinates proved immoral and used their

---

Stedingk asserted in 1791 that the grand duke would arm every Russian to restore the French monarchy. *Mémoires*, i. 179. Golovkin quoted Paul as saying that the revolution so upset him that 'I only think in a fever and talk in a transport'. *La Cour de Paul Ier*, 122. Paul talked freely to Count Cobenzl about his feelings, urged Austria to act against France, and praised her when she did. His despair when the coalition failed, and his anger with his mother's policies, were expressd openly and publicly. For a summary of this material, McGrew, 'A Political Portrait', esp. 507–9.

positions of trust to benefit themselves at the expense of other members of society, perversion would enter in with the potential to destroy the entire social fabric. In France, the monarch lost control, the aristocracy failed in its duties, and new men, whose moral perceptions had been warped by subversive doctrines, seized leadership. France was a horrifying example of the disastrous consequences which followed on moral disorder, self-indulgence, and disloyalty.

Paul believed in control and discipline. He lived by schedule and routine, he hated disorderliness, and any hint of insubordination brought swift retaliation. All these characterstics were raised to new orders of magnitude in the light of what had happened in France. He believed that Russia needed to be ready to repel the revolution as it spread to the east. More, it was essential for Russia to put her own house in order to prevent or suppress revolutionary upheavals. Here he saw real danger. He had long thought that Catherine's aggressive foreign policies threatened Russia's internal stability. He was convinced as well that the rule of favourites had turned the state administration into a morass, while the army, by his standards, was unready to fight. Above all, there was a great and crying need for leadership. He saw himself and his Gatchina cadres as the answer to these problems. He drove himself and his men furiously in an unremitting search for that total submission of the individual to discipline which he believed led to perfection in execution and absolute commitment to cause and leader. 'Always the disciplinarian,' as Count Cobenzl reported in 1793, 'the grand duke has redoubled his efforts in this regard since the revolution in France. The slightest failure in manœuvre or drill, a servant's error, the least mistake, in fact, ignites his wrath and brings down the most severe punishments on the miscreants.'[78] No one was spared, for what Paul was doing at Gatchina was in preparation for the day when he would rule in Russia. And if that day never dawned, he at the very least could feel that he had done everything in his power to meet his obligations. Gatchina was his model community; it was also his preparatory school for a new generation of leaders, and his first step towards reversing Russia's descent into chaos.

As the *émigré* nobility filtered into Russia from France, Paul found active support for his ideas. Count Esterhazy, who arrived in

[78] HHSA, Russland II Berichte, Carton 77, no. 9, apostille 5, Cobenzl to Cobenzl, 19 Feb. (NS) 1793; Carton 79, no. 40, apostille 6, Cobenzl to Thugut, 25 July (NS) 1794; Kobeko, *Pavel Petrovich*, 407–8; Rostopchin to Vorontsov, 14 Apr. and 6 July (OS) 1793, and 28 May (OS) 1794, *Arkhiv kniazia Vorontsova*, viii. 67, 71, 76–7, 93–4; 'Zapiski kn. F. N. Golitsyna', *Russkii arkhiv* (1874), 1307; de Grunwald, *L'Assassinat*, 79–80.

Petersburg in 1791, was thought to be especially influential in agitating him against the revolution and, in league with the other *émigrés*, to encourage him in his most despotic tendencies.[79] In fact, Paul was fully armed for reaction without the *émigré* influences, and, paradoxically, it was the *émigrés* themselves, or rather an influential faction among them, who encouraged Catherine to remove Paul from the succession. The reasoning was that Paul was too extreme, too violent, and too unpredictable; Alexander would be more amenable to their influence.[80]

Certainly Paul's severity and punctiliousness were cause for apprehension. In July 1793 Count Rostopchin, who was close to Paul and favoured by him, wrote that 'One cannot watch without pity and horror everything the elder grand duke is doing; it could be said that he invents ways to make himself hated and detested; he has it fixed in mind that he is scorned, that he is shown no respect, and beginning from that point, he fastens on everyone and punishes without distinction.' With his little private army, 'he imagines himself to be the deceased king of Prussia', he holds daily parades, manœuvres every Wednesday, and 'the least sign of delay or error will unhinge him and send him into a passion'. No one, Rostopchin went on, was immune from punishment, and anyone who had to serve in his vicinity was at risk. Personally, Rostopchin hoped to stay as far away from him as circumstances permitted.[81] A year later, the situation was unchanged with Paul 'always in bad humour, his head full of visions, surrounded by people the most honest of whom deserve to be beaten, and convinced that the Jacobins are everywhere'. He reported that Paul recently punished four officers for wearing their queues too short, a demonstration, or so Rostopchin asserted, that they affected a rebellious spirit.[82] But this was 'our way', that is, the Gatchina way, and it had been practised for over a decade.

[79] Kobeko, *Pavel Petrovich*, 372–3; Morane, *Paul Ier*, 368–71. For Esterhazy's account of and reflections on his experiences in Russia, see *Mémoires du comte Valentin Esterhazy*, ed. Ernest Daudet (Paris, 1905), chs. 10 and 11. See also *Lettres du comte Valentin Esterhazy à sa femme, 1784–1792*, ed. Daudet (Paris, 1907), esp. the section titled 'La cour de Russie sous le règne de Catherine'. Though Paul and Esterhazy were close, at least initially, there is relatively little on Paul in either the *Mémoires* or the letters. Golovkin considered Esterhazy a bad influence on Paul. He referred to him as one of those whose actions were responsible for bringing on the revolution in France, and then compounded his sin by insisting that 'It is only by spilling blood in time that one prevents troubles in a great monarchy.' *La Cour de Paul Ier*, 123.   [80] Kobeko, *Pavel Petrovich*, 367–8; Morane, *Paul Ier*, 413.

[81] Rostopchin to Vorontsov, 6 July (OS) 1793, *Arkhiv kniazia Vorontsova*, viii. 76–7.

[82] Rostopchin to Vorontsov, 28 May (OS) 1794, ibid. 93–4; Stedingk, *Mémoires*, i. 202–3 ('People say that he is mad but he is not'), 404, 511.

The fact was that bruising and concussive as Paul's affair with Catherine Nelidova was, and brutal as his discipline was known to be, these developments only reinforced a reputation which he had already developed. Angry, depressed, complaining, moody, and unpredictable, Paul was widely disliked and even feared a little when the 1790s dawned. His behaviour over the next six years added substantially to this unprepossessing image. Nor were Mariia's fears about the succession groundless. There had been speculation for years about whether Catherine would allow Paul to succeed her. After Alexander was born, she had a viable alternative. Catherine's dislike for Paul and her conviction that he lacked the capacity to govern grew steadily through the 1780s. At the same time, her attachment to Alexander deepened. In his grandmother's eyes, Paul's eldest son was everything that his father was not and never could be, and she fell into the habit of referring to Alexander's future reign as if Paul did not exist.[83]

Catherine appears not to have done anything about Paul's status until 1787, when, after her return from the Crimea, she began to study the regulations governing the succession to the throne and how they had come into effect. This was her normal approach to any project, but she was forced to put her work aside when the Russo-Turkish war broke out.[84] Four years later, she took the problem up again, though from a different angle. Still unprepared to draw up a document, she announced the decision that Alexander should marry as soon as possible. The grand duke was only 15, but Catherine considered him old for his years. He was affianced in 1793 and wed to a 15-year-old princess of Baden-Baden who became the grand duchess Elizabeth Alexievna.[85]

---

[83] For Catherine's attachment to Alexander, see her correspondence with Baron Grimm, *SIRIO* 23. In 1792, she told Grimm that Alexander was going to marry and that she was looking forward to great-grandchildren from him (then aged 14) and his chosen bride. And she went on: 'My Alexander will be married and in time crowned with all the ceremonies, all the solemnities, and all the public celebrations possible; he will pass by in splendour, magnificence, and grandeur; oh, how happy he will be, and how happy one will be with him!' No. 213, 14 Aug. (OS) 1792, p. 574. Paul, in this vision, is ignored, while it would appear that Catherine would be present to enjoy her grandson's triumph.

[84] See Khrapovitskii, *Dnevnik*, entries for 20 and 25 Aug., pp. 46 and 47. The entries only show that the succession issue was under discussion when the war broke out.

[85] See Grand Duke Nicolas Mikhailowitch, *L'Impératrice Elisabeth: Épouse d'Alexandre Ier*, 3 vols. (in 5 bks.) (St Petersburg, 1908–9); id., *L'Empereur Alexandre Ier: Essai d'étude historique*, 2 vols. (St Petersburg, 1912); Shil'der, *Aleksandr I*.

At this point, the *émigrés* took a hand. Led by Choiseul-Geoffier (former French ambassador to Constantinople), Esterhazy, and the prince of Nassau-Siegen, a conspiracy was formed to draw Alexander's favourite tutor, Frédéric Caesar LaHarpe, into a plan 'to spare Russia the reign of a new Tiberius [Paul]'. Counting on LaHarpe's affection for Alexander as well as on his republican tendencies, it was thought he would agree to arouse the grand duke against his authoritarian father in the name of Russia's welfare. Catherine, who must have approved what was going forward, interviewed LaHarpe on 18 October (OS) 1793. She spoke in inferences, but he saw at once where she was going and did his best to prevent her from unveiling her plan. In the end he was successful and, after two hours of conversation, was able to escape without facing the issue directly. She apparently understood that his evasions meant rejection, but they parted on good terms, and she took no steps against him. He left Petersburg just over a year later. Paul apparently knew what LaHarpe did, for later, when Russian forces invaded Switzerland, he wrote Paul to intercede for his country and reminded the tsar of the service he performed in 1793. Paul acknowledged his debt.[86]

Catherine may have made at least two other attempts to clear the way for Alexander. In June 1796, when Mariia was recovering from the birth of Nicholas, Catherine approached her with a proposal in writing to exclude Paul from the succession in Alexander's favour. All Mariia had to do was sign. Mariia refused, though she seems never to have told Paul, who only learnt of this transaction after he was tsar. He interpreted Mariia's failure to inform him as evidence that she sympathized with Catherine's intentions, a totally mistaken conclusion.[87] Catherine's other effort was with Alexander himself. She approached him with the proposal in order to be certain that, if she acted, he would accept the change. Alexander was adept at avoiding binding commitments. He had had a lifetime of balancing between his father and his grandmother without offending either. He

---

[86] Kobeko, *Pavel Petrovich*, 366–70. Kobeko believes that even had LaHarpe made the effort, Alexander would not have agreed. He was disgusted with politics as well as the situation in Catherine's court, and he respected as well as feared Paul. He also shared some of Paul's interests, in particular the military. Ibid. 370–2; Czartoryski, *Mémoires*, i. 94–111, and below, Ch. 7.

[87] Baron M. Korf, 'Materialy i cherti k biografii imperatora Nikolaia Igo i k istorii ego tsarstvovaniia', *SIRIO* 98 (1896), 9–10. The story, reported by Anna Pavlovna on the authority of her husband, the prince of Orange, was supposedly told him by Mariia Fedorovna after Alexander's death in 1825. Grand Duke Nikolai Mikhailovich is sceptical about the story as well as Shil'der's conclusion that Alexander took an oath of loyalty to Paul before Arakcheev. See *L'Empereur Alexandre I*er, i. 3–4.

was also at a stage of his life when he was showing great distaste for the demands politics and politicians made on him. In this case, he was able to evade the issue, neither openly agreeing to nor flatly rejecting what Catherine proposed. His grandmother must have been satisfied that he would co-operate, however, for it appears that she then had instruments drawn up which announced Paul's exclusion from the succession and Alexander's elevation to it as of 1 January (OS) 1797. Paul was to be sent into exile at the castle of Lohde in Lithuania. Of course none of this happened. Catherine died on 6/17 November 1796, and Paul allegedly found and destroyed the documents. Alexander said nothing, remaining loyal to his father for about three and a half years.[88]

During the last two years of Catherine's life, Paul was seldom seen in Petersburg. With peace in his own household, he was content to remain at Gatchina drilling his soldiers and administering the estate. In earlier years, Catherine insisted that he appear for formal court functions. As their relations worsened, and as she grew older, she abandoned these efforts, and left him largely to himself. The last important event in which he participated at court was the aborted announcement of his eldest daughter's betrothal to the king of Sweden.[89] Since this was one of the few occasions when Catherine was publicly humiliated, Paul might have been expected to have enjoyed the scene. In fact, however, his sympathies were with his mother. The issue was whether the grand duchess would become Lutheran, as the Swedes insisted, or whether she might remain Orthodox in private life while performing her public functions as a nominal Lutheran. This last was Catherine's position, but the young Gustave IV, who was a religious enthusiast if not a fanatic, never accepted it, though Russian negotiators thought he had. Neither Prince Zubov nor Count Morkov, who were charged with the negotiations, clarified the point with their opposite numbers, and when the nuptial agreement was presented to the king to sign, he refused. Catherine, the court, and the diplomatic community were gathered waiting for him to appear so the marriage could be announced, but he never did. After several hours and numerous

---

[88] Shil'der, *Aleksandr Pervyi*, i. 128; Nicolas Mikhailowitch, *Alexandre Ier*, i. 2. Catherine approached Alexander on 17 Sept. (OS) 1796; he responded with a vague letter acknowledging something which Shil'der believes was the proposal to set Paul aside.

[89] The following account is based on Kobeko, *Pavel Petrovich*, 410–21. Cf. Shil'der, *Pavel I*, 269; Morane, *Paul Ier*, 422–31. Rogerson, Catherine's English doctor, provided a detailed eyewitness narrative for S. R. Vorontsov in London. *Arkhiv kniazia Vorontsova*, xxx/8. 66–8.

whispered consultations, it had to be admitted formally and publicly that there would be no betrothal that night. Catherine retired in a state of fury seldom seen, and Paul, who had come unexpectedly to the ceremony, returned to Gatchina. Though pleased that Zubov and Morkov had gone wrong, Paul agreed with his mother's position and sympathized with her anger.

Paul had no way of knowing it, but his long wait was almost finished. It was time enough and the pressures were building. He knew that Catherine was seriously considering removing him from the succession; he may have been told that the documents had already been drawn up. Every day that passed was a moment of danger he had survived; each new day that dawned brought with it the possibility of arrest, incarceration, exile, or even murder. The melancholy histories of Ivan VI and Peter III offered little comfort. Paul had known those stories from childhood, had lived through the crises that generated them, and had learnt to link his fate with theirs. His Gatchina troops offered no real protection if his enemies were determined, and Paul was not cut out to lead a popular uprising. He also had a sense of his own destiny, and a fatalistic attitude towards it. So he worried and waited, and lived his life as he knew it. It was the best that he could do.

The long wait ended in the evening of 6/17 November 1796. On the morning of 5 November Catherine suffered a massive stroke. She was found lying helpless and partially paralysed on the floor of her dressing room. She appeared to recognize her valet, tried to raise her hand as if to point towards her heart, and then slipped into a coma from which she never woke. She died thirty-six hours later at about 9.45 p.m. on 6 November. She was 67 years old. Though it had been apparent for more than a year that her energies were flagging, her sudden death was a rude shock. Her health, considering her age, was good, though she had suffered for some time from poor kidney function which produced gross swelling in her legs and abdomen. Moreover, as a result of the aborted Swedish marriage, she had been under intense nervous strain in the early autumn and showed an uncharacteristic tendency towards melancholy and pessimism. It is also likely that settling the succession question weighed heavily on her. But her spirits had improved markedly and she was in cheerful good form on the morning of her attack. As soon as her physicians saw her, however, they knew she was beyond their help, and the decision was taken to send Count Nicholas Zubov, the favourite's brother, to carry the news to Paul at Gatchina. If the empress's inner circle knew that Paul had been excluded, they apparently decided to act as if they did not know. The other alternatives are that the empress's decision was still a secret, or that it had not been taken.[90]

Paul, as usual, had spent the morning on parade. He dined with Mariia Fedorovna and several friends at the Gatchina mill, and then relaxed over coffee. The after dinner conversation turned on his visions of the night before when he dreamt of being lifted up and out of bed by some unknown force. The dream recurred. Mariia swore she had had the same experience, and it was in an excited, even exalted, state of mind that they turned back towards the castle. On the way, they met a hussar bringing word that Count Nicholas Zubov had come with important news and was waiting at the palace. Paul was shaken. Zubov was the enemy. His appearance could only be threatening, and a confirmation of the feelings Paul's subconscious had raised to the surface during the night. He caught at his wife's hand, 'My dear,' he gasped, 'we are lost', and then recovered to ask 'how many Zubovs' there were. When he learnt there was only one, that this was not a party sent for him, he calmed himself sufficiently to go to meet the messenger, who knelt to greet him. The message was succinct: his mother was on the verge of death, and he was urgently required at the Winter Palace. Too distraught to make the arrangements himself, Paul paced feverishly until the coaches were ready. He had waited all his life for this moment. Now that it had arrived, he could hardly contain himself.[91]

The early November night was drawing in when the carriages finally swept out on the road to Petersburg. For Paul, the auspices

---

[90] Madariaga, *Catherine the Great*, 577–8, describes the last hours. See also Count Fedor Rostopchin, 'Le Dernier Jour de la vie de l'impératrice Catherine II et le premier jour du règne de l'empereur Paul Ier', *Œuvres inédites du comte Rostoptchine*, ed. Countess L. Rostoptchine (Paris, 1894), 3–38. The same document has been published in *Arkhiv kniazia Vorontsova*, viii. 159–74. The account was written as a letter to Count S. R. Vorontsov and was dated 15 Nov. (OS) 1796. It is valuable, especially for Paul's actions immediately following Catherine's death. E. Melchior de Vogüe compared Rostopchin's description with Saint-Simon on the death of Louis XIV. See *Le Fils de Pierre le grand, Mazeppa, un changement du règne* (Paris, 1884), 293–5. See also, Golovine, *Souvenirs*, 136–41. Rogerson to Vorontsov, no. 10, 25 Nov. (NS) 1796, *Arkhiv kniazia Vorontsova*, xxx. 75, wrote about Catherine's death but gave few details. Rogerson was also the source for Whitworth's report on Catherine's death. PRO, FO/65/35, no. 57, Whitworth to Grenville, 18 Nov. (NS) 1796. Grand Duchess Elizabeth described her feelings of despair and loss on Catherine's death in a letter to her mother, 7/18 Nov. 1796. See Nicolas Mikhailowitch, *L'Impératrice Elisabeth*, i. 233, no. 119.

[91] Nikolai Osipovich Kotliubitskii, 'Rasskazy', *Russkii arkhiv* (1866), 1309; Sanglen, 'Zapiski', *Russkaia starina*, 36 (1882), 468; Rostopchin, 'Le Dernier Jour', 7–10; de Vogüe, *Le Fils de Pierre*, 318–25; Morane, *Paul Ier*, 433–4; Kobeko, *Pavel Petrovich*, 420; Shil'der, *Pavel I*, 277–8; Waliszewski, *Paul Ier*, 99–100.

were good and were growing better. Messenger after messenger met the party with news from the court. There was no sign of resistance, no vestige of an attempt to rally to his son. Every indication was that he had already been accepted in St Petersburg as Catherine's successor. The blow he had every reason to expect was not going to fall. When the horses were changed at the posting station at Sophia, Count Rostopchin, who had ridden out from the capital, met the party and was invited to ride in Paul's carriage. It was a beautiful night, sharp and clear, and the stars were bright. It was, as Rostopchin later described it, a great and portentous time. He was so overcome with all it meant that impulsively he seized Paul's hand and cried out, 'Monseigneur, what a moment for you!' Paul responded with a firm, warm grasp and declared that God had upheld him through forty-two years and 'Perhaps he will give me the strength to support the state to which he destines me; I hope for everything from His good will.'[92] The terror Paul had felt when Zubov was announced was now past; he arrived in the courtyard of the Winter Palace at 8.30 in the evening, a determined and confident man, entered the palace, and went straight to his mother's apartments. Catherine, whose stentorian breathing was the only sign that she was still alive, had been stretched out on a pallet mattress. Paul passed by her, giving no sign, to disappear into an inner apartment where he remained secluded from the public's view until she expired.

As the news of Catherine's stroke filtered through the capital—there was no general announcement—courtiers gathered in the corridors and on the stairways of the Winter Palace. The prospect these people faced was daunting. Catherine had governed Russia for thirty-four years. Many of those waiting for news had grown old in her service; most had known no other ruler. They knew Paul as well. He had been a fixture at court for more than two decades, passing, like the courtiers themselves, from youth to middle age. Few remembered how promising and attractive he had been when he first emerged from Panin's care. What they knew was what they now saw: a sulking, choleric man who had withdrawn from society, who had been constantly at odds with the empress, and who was best known for the scandals that swirled through his household, the thuggishness and nullity of his favoured servitors, and his own punctiliousness, paradomania, and unpredictable temper. There was fear for the future, especially among those whom Catherine had particularly favoured. It was confidently expected that Platon Zubov would be purged at the first opportunity; no one wanted to be seen in his

---

[92] Rostopchin, 'Le Dernier Jour', 16.

company, and the formerly all-powerful favourite found himself unable, or so Rostopchin reported, to get so much as a glass of water.[93] Count Cobenzl, the Austrian ambassador, spoke for many when he told his government that, while Paul had always treated him well, he very much feared that his close relationship with the dying empress would seriously limit his future usefulness. But Cobenzl was one who saw good in Paul, and he mustered some measure of brightness in the midst of the general gloom by arguing that history offered a number of examples of men who were far better as rulers than they had promised to be as heir apparent. He suggested that Paul might be of that number. The tone of his dispatches, however, belied his optimism; this was a faint hope indeed.[94]

Paul made no announcements, no public gestures, on his arrival. Catherine was the empress until she died. In private, however, he took steps to assure his position. He began to interview members of the current administration as well as distinguished people in the court. He had to organize a government. He also went through the pending correspondence and, in company with Count Bezborodko (or possibly either Prince Platon Zubov or even Count Rostopchin) began to inventory his mother's private papers. It was while doing this task that he is supposed to have found Orlov's note reporting Peter III's death, the unsigned letter purportedly from his wife agreeing that Alexander should rule in his stead, Catherine's will, and the draft of her decree removing him from the succession. This last was either torn into pieces or thrown into the fire.[95]

Paul and Mariia rested but slept little during the night of 5 November. The grand dukes Alexander and Constantine, together with their wives, joined the watchers early, and during the night Paul appeared briefly for prayers. Catherine's colour came and went. In

[93] Rostopchin, 'Le Dernier Jour', 27–8.
[94] HHSA, Russland II Berichte, Carton 84, Cobenzl to Thugut, no. 72, 25 Nov. (NS) 1796, and apostille 3. Whitworth was more positive, noting that 'both the head and the heart of the new Sovereign are good', and if he were sometimes capricious or morose, he had been given ample cause. PRO, FO/65/35, Whitworth to Grenville, no. 57, 18 Nov. (NS) 1796; McGrew, 'Political Portrait', 509–11.
[95] There is no undisputed evidence that Catherine disinherited Paul. And what happened while Catherine lay dying is unclear. The court journal states specifically that her papers were sealed on the morning of 6 Nov. under the care of Grand Duke Alexander, Count Bezborodko, and the procuror-general, Samoilov. Platon Zubov was a witness. See Waliszewski, *Paul Ier*, 104, citing *Osmnadtsatyi vek*, i. 484. It is reasonable that Paul inventoried the papers before that moment, and that would have been the time when the offending documents were destroyed. That is the argument suggested here. See I. I. de Sanglen, 'Pavel i ego vremia', *Russkaia starina* (1882–3); Golitsyn, 'Rasskazy', 643; Shil'der, *Pavel I*, 282; Rostopchin, 'Le Dernier Jour', 24–5; Morane, *Paul Ier*, 415–17.

the early hours, there were moments when some thought that she was recovering, or that she would at least awake; there was no substance for such hopes, however, though the empress's body resisted death. The long hours dragged by; all business was suspended, and with the exception of the muted sobbing of an ancient attendant and the dying woman's rasping breath, there was silence in the chamber. Finally in the evening of the second day, the rhythms of the breathing changed, the entire family gathered for the last moments, there was a heavy groan, a cry, and Catherine died. Paul, at last, had come into his inheritance.

7
TSAR REFORMER

Paul entered on his inheritance quietly. Neither peals of bells nor cannonades announced him. To have indulged in public celebrations (as was done when his mother seized the throne) would have insulted the memory of a deceased ruler and was unnecessary to the investiture of a legitimate heir. Or so Paul declared.[1] Legitimacy and the revolution of 1762 were very much on his mind. Even as the oath of allegiance was administered he noticed that Count Alexis Orlov, a central figure in the conspiracy thirty-four years earlier, was not present to be sworn. He did not want Orlov to forget that 23 June. When the ceremony was ended, he sent two of his most trusted subordinates, Fedor Rostopchin and General Nikolai Petrovich Arkharov, to find him. There was nothing sinister in his absence. Though still physically active, Orlov was 80 years old and feeling the burden of his years. He had maintained the vigil as long as he could through Catherine's last hours, but fatigue finally drove him home and into bed. It was there Paul's emissaries found him. Arkharov wanted to put him under arrest and drag him back to the palace, but Rostopchin stopped him. Once Orlov had been made to understand what had happened, he insisted on taking the oath at once. He did so in a loud voice before an ikon in his bedroom.[2]

When Paul was told about what had happened, he declared himself relieved. He would not have wanted to begin his reign without such an important person at his side. Count Cobenzl, who reported this remark, was unimpressed. He believed that Paul feared Orlov was conspiring against him and that he showed an excessive timidity where no danger existed.[3] But Cobenzl missed the point. Singling out Orlov called attention to what had been done in 1762 and who had done it. This was the first in a series of reminders of the

---

[1] HHSA, Russland II Berichte, Carton 84, no. 72, apostille 4, Cobenzl to Thugut, 25 Nov. (NS) 1796; Shil′der, *Pavel I*, 285 ff.

[2] Rostopchin, 'Le Dernier Jour', 33–8; *Arkhiv kniazia Vorontsova*, viii. 158–74. Cobenzl summarized the story in HHSA, Russland II Berichte, Carton 84, no. 75, apostille 4, 7 Dec. (NS) 1796.

[3] HHSA, Russland II Berichte, Carton 84, no. 75, apostille 4, Cobenzl to Thugut, 7 Dec. (NS) 1796.

crime with which Catherine's reign began. Others were even more pointed. Both Prince Bariatinskii, who was marshal for the court, and the former captain Passek, currently governor-general of White Russia, were removed from office and later exiled. Bariatinskii had been in the conspiracy's inner circle and was implicated in Peter's death at Ropsha; it was Passek's arrest which precipitated the *coup*. And Princess Dashkova, the flamboyant heroine of the rush to Peterhof, was ordered to leave her Moscow estates to rusticate in the wilds near Novgorod. Exile, she was told, would allow her to meditate her misdeeds in 1762.[4]

While the remaining conspirators felt the edge of Paul's vengeance, those people who had been loyal to Peter and who had suffered exile for their pains, were amnestied, recalled to the capital, and loaded with honours. In Paul's eyes, they were heroes.[5] But his final word on 1762 was an elaborate funeral ceremony for which Peter III's body was to be exhumed and brought by the man who killed him to lie in state beside the wife who overthrew him. Initially, Paul had intended to give Catherine the same treatment she had given Peter, burying her in the Nevskii monastery cemetery rather than in the crypt of the Peter-Paul fortress where Russia's rulers traditionally lay. When Peter died, the excuse given for denying him burial with his peers was that he had never been formally crowned. That, of course, was not true of Catherine, and a Nevskii burial would have been an open statement that she had had no right to rule. Although this was what Paul believed, he was brought to see that he was going too far.[6] The announced decision, therefore, in place of disgracing Catherine, restored Peter to the public as her equal. But Paul intended more than that. As the ceremonies unfolded, they were seen to call attention to the former tsar rather than the empress, that it was he rather than she who was honoured and mourned.[7]

[4] Ibid. no. 72, apostille 1, 25 Nov. (NS) 1796; Czartoryski, *Mémoires*, i. 128–30; PRO, FO/65/35, no. 62, Whitworth to Grenville, 5 Dec. (NS) 1796. See also: Masson, *Mémoires secrètes*, 206–7; Dashkova, *Mémoires*, 319–20.

[5] Stockholm, Riksarkivet, Diplomatica Moscovitica, vol. 456, Stedingk to the king, 14/25 Nov. 1796. Stedingk's reports are more sympathetic to Paul and his purposes than those of other diplomats. See also: Masson, *Mémoires secrètes*, 200–1; Golovkine, *La Cour de Paul I*^{er}, 127–8. Andrei Vasil'evich Gudovich, one of those recalled, wrote his impressions to Count S. R. Vorontsov in London. *Arkhiv kniazia Vorontsova*, xxiv. 254–5.

[6] HHSA, Russland II Berichte, no. 72, apostille 11, Cobenzl to Thugut, 25 Nov. (NS) 1796. For the decree ordering Peter exhumed, *PSZ*, vol. 24, no. 17537, 9 Nov. (OS) 1796.

[7] The point was clear and painful to Catherine's partisans. See e.g. Grand Duchess Elizabeth to her mother, 2/13 Dec. 1796, Grand Duke Nicolas Mikhailowitch, *L'Impératrice Elizabeth*, i. 240; Golovine, *Souvenirs*, 144, 148.

Peter's neglected grave lay in a distant part of the cemetery and was only found with difficulty. Paul personally attended its opening and made an occasion of the exhumation. Just fragments of the corpse and its accoutrements remained, but Paul spoke tenderly over them, kissed an ancient gauntlet, and wept. He had never, he was reported saying through his tears, lost sight of his duty to give his august father the last rites owing to him, and now that God had granted him the power and the means to do so, he was eager to discharge this obligation.[8] A solemn procession brought the remains to the Winter Palace. Count Stedingk, the Swedish ambassador, wrote to his government:

I have just witnessed the most august, melancholy, and in every respect compelling ceremony I have ever experienced ... the transfer of the body of Peter III from Newsky to the palace ... The order, the silence, the deep and moving chants, the number of persons forming the cortège, the mixture of ancient and modern forms, and the imperial family, walking from the Alexander Newsky, following the casket, with no marks of distinction (the emperor having declared that all honors on this day were for the deceased emperor) all that created a total impression which truly moved the soul ...[9]

In the funeral cortège, Bariatinskii and two or three others, survivors of the conspiracy (one source mentions Passek), drew the coffin, while Count Orlov walked behind it carrying Peter's crown. The remains were placed in the great hall of the Winter Palace where they lay together with those of Catherine prior to burial in the crypt.[10] Nobody could miss what was being said. The double funeral was an extraordinary stroke of political theatre which effectively removed Catherine from the centre of attraction. When queried about it, however, Paul affected to believe that he had done nothing unusual. 'My mother,' he remarked with characteristic irony, 'having been called to the throne by the voice of the people, was too busy to arrange for my father's last rites. I am remedying that oversight.' This, and indeed all he had done, was, he asserted, undertaken in a spirit of filial piety, and represented no more than the duty a son

---

[8] HHSS, Russland II Berichte, Cobenzl to Thugut, no. 75, apostille 2, 7 Dec. (NS) 1796; Masson, *Mémoires secrètes*, 198–200; Golovkine, *La Cour de Paul Ier*, 125–6.

[9] Riksarkivet, Diplomatica Moscovitica, vol. 456, Stedingk to the king, 2/13 Dec. 1796.

[10] Stedingk, Cobenzl, and Whitworth all described the event. See above citations. See also: Golovine, *Souvenirs*, 144–8, for funerary details; cf. Czartoryski, *Mémoires*, 128–30. Orlov protested his role, but Paul shouted at him, and he marched with dignity.

owed to his father.[11] Paul had made his point. He ruled by right as Peter's son.

There were other injustices to correct. In 1792, Catherine had leading members of the then illegal freemason societies interrogated. The focal point for the investigation was the eminent publisher and writer, N. I. Novikov, whose press in Moscow had published books declared to be contrary to religion and public morality, and who was known to have been a leading Russian mason. When Novikov's premises were raided, copies of books published at his press which had been banned eight years earlier were found. This was used to justify his immediate arrest and interrogation. Twelve questions were put to him which he was to answer in writing. Of these, two focused on alleged masonic links with Paul and with Paul's close associates, N. V. Repnin, Alexander Kurakin, and S. I. Pleshcheev. The charge was that Novikov and his circle had attempted to draw Paul into a foreign, in this case Prussian, masonic association. It was alleged that the contact between the masons in Moscow and the grand duke in Petersburg was a certain Bazhenev, an architect, who personally carried books of a mystical and devotional nature to Paul. Confronted with a written statement from Bazhenev, Novikov pled 'his heartfelt remorse for this deed worthy of the severest punishment'.[12]

There was (and is) no direct evidence that Paul ever joined a masonic society, and while Bazhenev undoubtedly delivered a packet of books directly to Paul, the grand duke kept himself clear of any involvement with the group beyond that contact. Novikov's confession was to a hoped-for goal and he paid heavily for it. He was sentenced to fifteen years' incarceration in the Schlüsselburg fortress. Indeed, the sentence seemed surprisingly heavy since other prominent

---

[11] HHSA, Russland II Berichte, Carton 84, Cobenzl to Thugut, no. 72, apostille 13, 25 Nov. (NS) 1796. Paul concluded a later conversation on the funeral by saying, 'I hope, mr. ambassador, that you approve of what I am doing. I fulfill my obligations; heaven will judge the rest.' Ibid., Cobenzl to Thugut, no. 75, apostille 1, 7 Dec.(NS) 1796. Cobenzl had reservations and was troubled, but Charles Whitworth remarked that rehabilitating Peter III 'may in the opinion of some be considered as a severe judgement on the memory of his [Paul's] Mother; but it is by the public laid to the account of filial piety; and in fact serves to render the commencement of His Reign still more popular'. PRO, FO/65/35, no. 62, Whitworth to Grenville, 5 Dec. (NS) 1796. See also the reports by Tauentzien to Berlin and Völkersham to Dresden in Shil'der, *Aleksandr I*, i (appendix), 354, 357.

[12] W. Gareth Jones, *Nikolay Novikov: Enlightener of Russia* (Cambridge, 1984), ch. 8, pp. 123–48 treats Novikov and the masonic order; for the investigations and imprisonment, pp. 183–215. Cf. Eidel'man, *Gran'vekov*, 48 and Madariaga, *Catherine the Great*, 527–9. The leading Soviet account of Novikov's work and significance is G. Makogonenko, *Nikolai Novikov i russkoe prosveshchenie* (Moscow, 1951).

Moscow masons—Prince N. N. Trubetskoi, A. M. Turgenev, and I. V. Lopukhin—were simply exiled to their estates, and Lopukhin was excused from even that penalty on grounds of his father's ill health. Novikov's comparatively severe sentence has been taken to suggest that Catherine was settling scores with a long-time critic and journalistic adversary, though it has also been argued recently that the sentence was a 'tribute' exacted by zealous police officials who saw the offences involved as more serious than the empress did.[13] Whatever the explanation, Novikov spent over four years in confinement. When the empress died, S. I. Pleshcheev, one of the masons in Paul's inner circle and a close friend of Mariia Fedorovna, joined with others in urging Novikov's release. Paul agreed, though unlike his treatment of Peter III's partisans, he made no gesture towards Novikov, and later he renewed the prohibitions against the masons as a dangerous influence. Whatever sympathy he had for the movement had long since evaporated.

The new tsar also took up the case of Alexander Radishchev whose *Journey from Petersburg to Moscow*, completed in 1788 and published in 1790, limned the brutality and corruption of contemporary Russia in the most powerful terms.[14] The book portrayed the moral price serfdom exacted from peasants and landlords alike, prophesying that unless the institution was abolished and its victims recognized as free men, revolution would follow. Catherine saw the book as a dangerously subversive tract, was incensed that it escaped censorship, and then denigrated it by ascribing it to a frustrated favour-seeker who had been forbidden the court. The book was impounded, its author imprisoned, interrogated, and condemned to be taken in chains to Nerzhinsk on the Chinese border and there beheaded. Catherine commuted this brutal sentence to ten years' hard labour in Nerzhinsk, and Radishchev was launched on a six-year journey into oblivion. Count Alexander Vorontsov, his protector and intercessor, won some mitigation of his condition and when Catherine died urged Paul to release the writer from his sentence. Paul did so, permitting Radishchev to return to European Russia and reside on his lands. It remained to Alexander I to allow him to return to Petersburg.[15]

---

[13] Jones, *Novikov*, 214.
[14] Alexander Radishchev, *Journey from Petersburg to Moscow*, ed. and trans. Roderick Thaler (Cambridge, Mass., 1958), which includes Catherine's marginalia; Allen McConnell, *A Russian Philosophe: Alexander Radishchev, 1749–1802* (London, 1959).
[15] McConnell, *Radishchev*, 106–22, 163–76.

It is unlikely that Paul ever read the *Journey*. Had he done so, he would have found much with which to sympathize. He had long since argued the necessity for protecting those who had no power against those who had a great deal, and he could well have accepted the portrayal of abuses in Catherine's Russia. That, after all, was fundamental to his thinking, as was the danger which moral corruption posed to contemporary Russian life. His solutions, of course, were quite otherwise, and the levelling tendencies, a constant subtext throughout the book, stood in diametric opposition to his own hierarchical values. Since far less radical books were wholly banned during Paul's reign, and much less critical persons imprisoned or exiled for their alleged Jacobin coloration, the relief Paul granted Radishchev was undoubtedly a product of his willingness to see and act against the injustices in what his mother had done. The judgement was on her rather than the author or his thought.

In the same vein, Paul declared his lack of sympathy for Catherine's Polish policies. He had long maintained cordial relations with Stanislaus Poniatowski, Poland's much maligned and disregarded king, and once tsar he accepted Poland's external debts as a charge on the Russian treasury, honoured Stanislaus, and invited him first to Petersburg and then to participate in his coronation at Moscow. He also ordered the release of 12,000 Polish prisoners taken in 1795 who were performing forced labour in Russia, and in a highly emotional scene, freed first Kosciusko and then the fiery patriot, Ignaz Potocky. Though wholly unwilling to consider reconstituting Poland—the deed was done and other states' interests were involved—Paul was anxious to free and indemnify those Poles languishing in Russia. Later, especially where Potocky was concerned, he admitted he had been wrong, and urged the Austrian government to redouble its efforts to lay that dangerous rebel by the heels. In 1796, however, he could afford to see his Polish prisoners as men of honour and patriots who had been wronged and to whom restitution was owed.[16]

Putting the record straight by righting some of Catherine's wrongs established Paul at the opposite end of the political spectrum. And by identifying himself openly and unreservedly with Peter III, he signalled a new political departure as well. It was Paul's conviction that, had his father lived, he would have disciplined both the army and society, establishing masculine military principles to counteract the corruption, indolence, and self-indulgence he

---

[16] Shil'der, *Pavel I*, 318–21; Czartoryski, *Mémoires*, 134–6; Golovkine, *La Cour de Paul Ier*, 138–9; HHSA, Russland II Berichte, Carton 88, Cobenzl to Thugut, no. 48, apostille 6, 9 Sept. (NS) 1798.

considered inseparable from women's rule. The bridge connecting father and son was 'prussianism', that is, the belief that Prussia offered the best model for Russia to follow. There was, however, one marked difference between Peter and Paul. Peter had considered Frederick the Great master as well as mentor, and was ready to enlist Russia under the Prussian banner. When he abandoned Austria to make peace with Prussia after Elizabeth died, however, Peter showed a far more radical commitment to Berlin's foreign policies than Paul, at least after 1789, could even contemplate. This tsar, as the Austrian ambassador assured his government, might be 'very Prussian in everything related to discipline for the soldiers and in all the military regulations, but not at all where his political system is concerned'. Paul had been profoundly offended by 'the odious conduct' of the Prussian court during the Turkish war (1787–92), nor could he support a government 'which shows itself the friend of the French revolutionaries'. Whitworth agreed, quipping that 'the particularity of the Emperor for Prussia extends no further than to the hat or coat', and then, a month later, reporting more soberly that everything in Petersburg had become Prussian in form as Prussia was held to be the only example for civil and military institutions worth following. Moreover, Paul, as Cobenzl insisted, had no ambitions to rival Frederick as a commander; his policies were pacific; he was not interested in military glory.[17]

The immediate task Paul faced when he arrived in Petersburg was to organize his government. He began on this while Catherine was still breathing; the results gradually became clear over the next three weeks.[18] Despite the general apprehension, there was nothing like a purge of the empress's leading officials. Count Ostermann, the aged vice-chancellor, was elevated to chancellor, though it was understood his duties were to be formal, while the ubiquitous count Arkadii Ivanovich Morkov, about whom Paul had serious doubts, was permitted to remain in the college of foreign affairs. He was given no responsibilities, however, and after a misunderstanding with the tsar

[17] HHSA, Russland II Berichte, Carton 84, Cobenzl to Thugut, no. 72, apostilles 3 and 17, 25 Nov. (NS) 1796; PRO, FO/65/35, no. 58, Whitworth to Grenville, 21 Nov. (NS) 1796; ibid., no. 68, 25 Dec. 25 (NS) 1796; HHSA, Russland II Berichte, Carton 84, Cobenzl to Thugut, no. 75, 7 Dec. (NS) 1796.

[18] Here the Austrian reports are particularly helpful. See: HHSA, Russland II Berichte, Carton 84, Cobenzl to Thugut, no. 72, apostilles 1, 3, 11, 13, 15, 25 Nov. (NS) 1796; no. 74, 2 Dec.(NS) 1796; no. 75, apostille 5, 7 Dec. (NS) 1796; no. 78, 18 Dec. (NS) 1796; no. 79, apostille 2, 26 Dec. (NS) 1796. Whitworth's reports, though less detailed on new appointments, parallel and confirm Cobenzl's. See PRO, FO/65/35, no. 60, Whitworth to Grenville, 26 Nov. (NS) 1796; no. 64, 13 Dec. (NS) 1796; no. 65, 16 Dec. (NS) 1796; no. 68, 25 Dec. (NS) 1796.

over the terms of his resignation, was ordered into exile on his lands.[19] The most visible hold-over from the previous reign, Platon Zubov, was treated surprisingly well, retaining his marshal's baton, a guards command, and some administrative duties. Even these proved too much for him to handle to Paul's satisfaction, however, and following a scandal involving a weapons order which he failed to execute, he was given permission to travel abroad. It was Zubov who was indirectly responsible for Paul's dismissal of Peter von der Pahlen as governor of Kurland, a development which, though unimportant at the time it happened, may have been the first event in the tortuous series which led finally to the tsar's murder.[20]

The most distinguished figure from Catherine's government to join Paul's inner circle was Count (soon-to-be-Prince) A. A. Bezborodko who performed the chancellor's functions and, once Ostermann retired, became chancellor in name as well as in fact. His influence was felt in virtually every corner of the central government, though his primary emphasis was on foreign relations. Bezborodko was precisely the sort of man the new administration needed. Thoroughly experienced in both domestic and international affairs, he was also an adroit politician who was able to defend his interests and maintain his balance in the constant and complicated struggle for preference that went on without interruption in Paul's court as it had done in Catherine's.

Paul, it will be remembered, had denounced Bezborodko to Archduke Leopold as one of Catherine's servitors who had been bought by Austria. That charge apparently was forgotten in 1796 when he needed a strong and experienced minister. That Bezborodko opposed Potemkin, his earlier protector and mentor, before the latter's death in 1791, and carefully avoided Prince Zubov in the aftermath, may have improved Paul's opinion of him. He was known to be a thoroughly competent official with an extraordinary memory for detail, and the ability, when necessary, to accomplish an immense quantity of work in a relatively short time. He was also greedy, corrupt, and lazy. Yet with two decades of experience to add weight to his judgements, Bezborodko could influence Paul when he chose to, acting as a brake on the tsar's tendency to rush to extremities.

---

[19] For Morkov's story, Rogerson to Vorontsov, 25 Nov. (NS) 1796, *Arkhiv kniazia Vorontsova*, xxx. 76–7; Rostopchin to Vorontsov, 25 Nov. (OS) 1796, ibid. vii. 174; HHSA, Russland II Berichte, Carton 84, Cobenzl to Thugut, no. 72, apostille 3, 24 Nov. (NS) 1796; no. 79, apostille 2, 26 Dec. (NS) 1796.

[20] HHSA, Russland II Berichte, Cobenzl to Thugut, no. 3, 10 Jan. (NS) 1797; Elisabeth to her mother, 29 Jan./10 Feb. 1797, Nicolas Mikhailowitch, *L'Impératrice Elisabeth*, 243; Baron Heyking, *Aus den Tagen Kaiser Pauls*, 42.

Cobenzl, who knew him well and worked with him closely, considered him the balance wheel in Paul's government, and the only official capable of playing that role. He was also the only member of Paul's inner circle—apart from the tsar himself—who had developed a plan for reshaping the central government and could speak to the issue of constitutional reform on both theoretical and practical grounds.[21]

The appointments which Paul did make showed his entirely natural disposition to have men he trusted in strategic positions in his government. Military appointments and promotions came first. On 7 November (OS), after declaring himself chief of all the regiments of guards, Paul named Alexander and Constantine respectively colonel of the Semenovskii and Izmailovskii regiments, both active appointments, and the infant grand duke Nicholas titular colonel of the Horse Guards. Arakcheev, now colonel, became city commandant, while six of Paul's intimates became his adjutants: Major-Generals S. I. Pleshcheev and I. I. Shuvalov; Fedor Rostopchin as a newly commissioned brigadier; Colonel G. G. Kushelev, Major N. O. Kotliubitskii, and a page of the bedchamber, Catherine Nelidova's younger brother, whose scandalously rapid rise to adjutant-general showed that favouritism was alive and well in Paul's new court.

The next day Count N. I. Saltykov, who had succeeded Panin as governor of Paul's household and was vice-president of the war college under Catherine, was promoted to field marshal, while Brigadier Rostopchin and Colonels Kushelev, Arakcheev, and Obolianinov were all raised to the rank of major-general. Lieutenant-Colonel Kologrivov became a colonel. Prince N. V. Repnin was promoted to field marshal on 9 November (OS), General Melissino, Arakcheev's mentor and protector, became general-in-chief on 11 November (OS), and the following day Count I. G. Chernyshev became field marshal with responsibility for the fleet. He would take over as president of the college of naval affairs.[22]

---

[21] See N. Grigorovich, 'Kantsler kniaz A. A. Bezborodko v sviazi s sobytiiami ego vremeni', *SIRIO* 26 and 29 (1879 and 1881), esp. 29, pp. 347–416. Bezborodko was uncertain of his reception from Paul, but was put at ease and given the task of preparing the accession manifesto. Rostopchin, *Œuvres inédites*, 20–2. His influence with Paul grew steadily from that point. HHSA, Russland II Berichte, Carton 84, Cobenzl to Thugut, no. 72, apostille 1, 25 Nov. (NS) 1796; Carton 85, no. 5, 18 Jan. (NS) 1797; Carton 89, no. 60, 6 Nov. (NS) 1798. Cobenzl considered Bezborodko indispensable. See ibid., no. 61, apostille 4, 14 Nov. (NS) 1798. For Bezborodko's reform memo, see app. 18, N. Grigorovich, op. cit., pp. 643–6; for an English trans., Marc Raeff, *Plans for Political Reform in Imperial Russia, 1730–1905* (Englewood Cliffs, NJ, 1966), 69–74.

[22] Shil'der, *Pavel I*, 289–90.

Subsequently Rostopchin and Arakcheev were named adjutant-general and inspector-general of artillery respectively, while General Arkharov was given the post of governor-general for the St Petersburg district, with responsibility for enforcing a new and stringent social discipline. Rostopchin would have preferred a position in the civil administration, but Paul insisted that the military was where he was most needed. Arkharov shared Paul's drill-master's mentality, and had been charged with enforcing police regulations at Gatchina. Arakcheev had already made his reputation as a disciplinarian and administrator who was devoted to his imperial master.[23]

In the central administration, Paul appointed his old friend and long-time correspondent, Prince Alexander Kurakin, vice-chancellor. Kurakin's younger brother, Alexis, became procuror-general. As vice-chancellor, Alexander Kurakin initially was the ranking official in the college of foreign affairs. He made very little of the position, however, satisfying himself with acting as Paul's spokesman to the diplomatic community. His younger brother did much more. The procuror-general became responsible for co-ordinating the work of a much enlarged senate, and served, in effect, as first minister for the interior. Observers were unimpressed with Alexis Kurakin's capacities, but Paul trusted him, and he had backing from both Mariia Fedorovna and Catherine Nelidova. In this case the empress and her friend were justified in their support and the critics were wrong. Kurakin proved to be an energetic official who served Paul well during the most important legislative period of his reign.[24]

Within the court, the dominant political faction at the outset was a loose coalition of friends, relations, and sympathetic supporters gathered around Mariia Fedorovna and Catherine Nelidova. The Kurakins were intimates of this circle and provided a direct channel between it and the central administration. Bezborodko, though more

[23] P. S. Lebedev, 'Preobrazovateli russkoi armii', 241–7, for Rostopchin, Arakcheev, and the military reforms; Rostopchin to Vorontsov, 8/19 Dec. 1795, *Arkhiv kniazia Vorontsova*, viii. 115–23. After the decree reorganizing the army (29 Nov. (OS) 1796) Rostopchin requested and received a civil appointment. *Œuvres inédites*, 19 and n. 1. For Arakcheev's career, A. A. Kizevetter, 'Imperator Aleksandr I i Arakcheev', *Istoricheskii ocherki*, 287–401, and esp. 308–62. On Arkharov, Shumigorskii, *Nelidova*, 83, 85–6, 90.

[24] On the procuracy-general and Kurakin's role, Klochkov, *Ocherki pravitel'stvennoi deiatel'nosti*, 224–70. Whitworth recorded a common judgement, however, when he wrote that the tsar had confided basic revenue policy to the younger prince Kurakin who is 'unequal to the Task himself, and wanting even the Merit of making a judicious choice of such as might assist him'. PRO, FO/65/38, Whitworth to Grenville, no. 64, 14 Dec. (NS) 1797.

distant, was also careful to remain on friendly terms with its main members. Ultimately, he was to conspire in its fall, but during the first eighteen months he worked with and through it. Known as 'the empress's party', this group was primarily active on domestic issues. There, however, it was highly influential, so much so, for example, that when Count Jakob Sievers, the director of canals and waterways, needed support for his projects, he made his appeal to Mariia Fedorovna. The Dutch banker, Robert Woot, Paul's informal but highly influential counsellor on fiscal matters, was an intimate of this circle. His connections were through his close friend, Baron Nicolay, a long-time member of Paul and Mariia's household, and Alexis Kurakin, with whom he collaborated on the Bank of Assistance for the Nobility. Paul gave Mariia responsibility for the empire's charitable institutions, and they had regularly discussed domestic policies and conditions before he became tsar. He was in no way unwilling to hear his wife's opinion on such matters, and she regularly advised him. The result was that, with Alexis Kurakin in the procuror-general's office, the empress's party had substantial direct influence on governmental decisions. The collapse of this party, the scattering of its members, and Mariia's retreat into political isolation, were main events in the *bouleversement* of Paul's government in the summer of 1798.[25]

Catherine Nelidova was thought to be the most influential individual in the empress's party. This, of course, was a resumption of her earlier role. Nelidova returned to Smol'nyi shortly before Catherine's death, and it was only by dint of great exertion by both Paul and Mariia that she was brought again to leave her retreat. Before the new year dawned, she was once more established as the tsar's personal mediator *par excellence* and directrix of the imperial conscience. Everything was not just as it had been, however, for while Paul remained susceptible to her influence, there were indications that he had begun to tire of the constant moral pressure she put on him. Their relationship had lasted more than a decade, and given the emotional intensity involved in it, it could be expected to wear thin. It required surprisingly little to convince Paul that she should go during the crisis summer of 1798.[26]

---

[25] The alliance between Mariia Fedorovna and Catherine Nelidova was the backbone of the empress's party. Shumigorskii, *Nelidova*, 64–131. Waliszewski, *Paul Ier*, ch. 6, *passim*, describes the circle around Paul, including the empress's party, but without connecting it to domestic politics. On Mariia's domestic policy interests, Blum, *Sievers Denkwürdigkeiten*, iv. 413–19, 421. On Robert Woot, McGrew, 'Politics of Absolutism', and below, ch. 8.

[26] Shumigorskii, *Nelidova*, 64–131.

It would be difficult to speak of any organized opposition to the empress's party, but at least two men, Rostopchin and Ivan Kutaisov, remained aloof, and the latter used whatever opportunities came his way to undermine its position. Kutaisov was a Turk who had been captured while still a boy and brought to Petersburg where he became Paul's personal barber and valet. He also became a confidant who eventually supplanted all others in private influence with his master. Kutaisov's day, like that of Rostopchin, was still in the future. Both men considered themselves at odds with the empress's party, Rostopchin from an exaggerated distaste for courtiers of any and all sorts, Kutaisov from ambition and an intriguing spirit. Neither could be considered the leader of a faction, though each in his own way became an important influence on events.[27]

The young court, headed by Grand Duke Alexander and his wife Elizabeth, was of little account politically during the first three years of Paul's reign. This was true despite the presence, at various times, of such notable personalities as Prince Adam Czartoryski and Count Paul Stroganov, or the enlightened diplomat-administrator (and Bezborodko's nephew) Viktor Kochubei. By the time Alexander was willing to listen to proposals for displacing his father, these men, together with Nikolai Nikolaevich Novosil'tsev, the fourth member of what became Alexander's secret committee in 1801, were in exile or living abroad.[28] At the beginning of Paul's reign, therefore, Alexander's household was essentially a lighter and more graceful adjunct of the main court, though the relationship was not without strain. Elizabeth was often at odds with Mariia, who was as authoritarian in her way as Paul was in his, and while Paul considered Elizabeth attractive—she seems to have reminded him of Nathalia, her aunt and his long dead first wife—he failed to understand her and was often harsh with her. He thought her and Constantine's wife flighty, immature, and irresponsible, exemplars of a younger generation which simply did not understand what was required of them. He saw it as his duty to put them straight, to discipline them, and Mariia fully supported his views.[29]

---

[27] Heyking, *Aus den Tagen Kaiser Pauls*, 114, placed Bezborodko in the opposition as well. After the collapse of the empress's party, Bezborodko and his supporters dominated the court. HHSA, Russland II Berichte, Carton 89, no. 60, Cobenzl to Thugut, 6 Nov. (NS) 1798. On Kutaisov and Rostopchin, Shil'der, *Pavel I*, esp. ch. 11, pp. 285–340. See also above, Ch. 6 n. 32 on Rostopchin.

[28] Shil'der, *Aleksandr Pervyi* i. 166–74; Grand Duc Nicolas Mikhailowitch, *Le Comte Paul Alexandrowitch Stroganov*, 3 vols. (Paris, 1905).

[29] Nicolas Mikhailowitch, *L'Impératrice Elisabeth*, 234–7 and esp. 244–6. Rostopchin was responsible for perlustrating Elizabeth's letters. See also Golovine, *Souvenirs*, 140–71 and esp. 157, for severity with Elizabeth and Anne. Varvara

Where Alexander and Constantine were concerned, Paul held them close and in a state of dependence. Constantine resembled his father both in his irascible temperament and in his interest in military affairs. It was said that he was his father's favourite, though if this was true, it had no political consequences. Alexander was a different matter. Paul's treatment of him was the exact reverse of what he himself had suffered at Catherine's hands. He literally loaded his son with civil and military duties, creating a burden which Alexander was barely able to carry, and then only with the unofficial assistance of General Arakcheev. This strange alliance between the man who exemplified the Gatchina spirit and the enlightened heir began before Catherine's death, was reinforced by Paul himself, and continued through the rest of Alexander's life.[30]

Before her death, Alexander was entirely disenchanted with his grandmother's court and the sickly sycophancy practised by the people who dominated it. So disgusted was he that he declared, in a well-known letter to Count Kochubei written some six months before Catherine died, that he intended to withdraw from political life entirely and, with his wife, to 'renounce this scabrous place' to rusticate on the banks of the Rhine. He could do no less, he declared, since maintaining a clear conscience was a first principle with him (presumably an impossibility in his present and future circumstances), while accepting a task which was patently beyond his powers would never allow him any peace. (The implication that he believed he was destined to succeed to the throne, and soon, is unmistakable.)[31] When Catherine died, Alexander welcomed his father's accession and threw himself enthusiastically into his new duties. Perhaps he was relieved to be free of his grandmother, and he seems to have been certain that his father would bring a new and better day to Russia.[32] His own situation changed radically as he became, at least in appearance, his father's primary aide, but he soon discovered that what he had were heavy responsibilities with no power of independent

Golovina was a partisan of Catherine and Elizabeth; though the latter turned against her, Golovina remained her supporter.

[30] Shil'der, *Aleksandr Pervyi*, i. 111–32, 161–90. Czartoryski, *Mémoires*, i. 107–9; Kizevetter, 'Imperator Alesandr I i Arakcheev', 362–72.

[31] 'Pismo velikago kniazia Aleksandra Pavlovicha k kniaziu Viktoru Pavlovichu Kochubeiu ot 10-go Maia 1796 gode', Shil'der, *Aleksandr Pervyi*, i, app. XI, pp. 276–8.

[32] Fedor Golovkin reported that Alexander 'expected to see the heavens open when his father became tsar' while displaying an almost indecent delight 'that he would no longer have to obey an old woman'. *La Cour de Paul Ier*, 151–2. This echoes Czartoryski's gentler judgement on Alexander's (and Constantine's) alienation from Catherine at the end of her life. *Mémoires*, i. 107–11.

decision. Moreover, Paul's fixation on discipline and punishments troubled him. Though he lived in fear of his father's temper, he tried to intercede with him, much as Nelidova did, in favour of individuals who needed help, and he gained thereby a reputation for understanding and compassion which stood at odds with his father's manner. Paul's reign was little more than five weeks old when Cobenzl commented on this contrast, noting that it was the grand duke's constant occupation to soften his father's harshness, that he had been successful in winning reprieves for many officers, and that he had even been able to protect them by keeping knowledge of their slips from coming to the tsar's attention.[33] Beyond such occasional humanitarian interventions, however, there is no sign that Alexander had the slightest influence with Paul politically. And while he was uncomfortable with what was happening in Russia, he showed no inclination to challenge his father, or to encourage those who might. He did talk privately with close friends about the plans they were going to implement when he was finally tsar, and he wrote to LaHarpe, his old tutor, that he had abandoned his idea of emigrating. Even so, he described conditions as abysmal despite his father's promising beginnings, and he solicited LaHarpe's counsel on establishing 'a free constitution' in Russia. Given the differences between Paul and Alexander, the young court should have contained the seed of an opposition, while Alexander was the best if rather distant hope for anyone who wanted to look beyond his father. But this vague orientation hardly defined an effective resistance, nor was Alexander's circle a faction in any meaningful political sense. The grand duke lacked both patronage and power; he had no independent position, and he had neither the means nor the will to manipulate Paul.[34]

Paul, in fact, had matters very much in hand. His enemies from the past had been easily scattered, his heir was docile, his wife was loyal and involved in supportive work on his affairs, and he was able to put together a government which, if not brilliant, contained capable men who were willing to accept and follow his lead. Moreover, he knew exactly where he intended to take the country. He had spent

[33] HHSA, Russland II Berichte, Carton 84, Cobenzl to Thugut, no. 79, apostille 2, 26 Dec. (NS) 1796. When Dietrichstein's credentials were not in order, he went to Alexander who had become the tsar's mediator. Ibid., Carton 86, Dietrichstein to Thugut, no. 49, apostille 1, 13 Aug. (NS) 1797. Cobenzl believed that Paul idolized his son and that this accounted for the grand duke's success with his father. Ibid., Carton 89, Cobenzl to Thugut, no. 61, apostille 4, 14 Nov. (NS) 1797.

[34] 'Pismo tsesarevna Aleksandra Pavlovicha Lagarpu', Gatchina, 22 Sept./8 Oct. 1797, Shil'der, *Aleksandr Pervyi*, i, app. xv, pp. 180–2. See also ibid. 161–5. Cf. Shil'der, *Pavel I*, 367–70 and 370–1 n. 1.

years watching abuses multiply and errors compound. By the time Catherine died, he was wholly blind to her achievements and out of sympathy with her goals. Russia, as he saw her, was in desperate straits; it was his obligation to deal with the problem, and that as rapidly as possible. The failure to do so could only lay the country open to a revolution. Cobenzl was shocked at the depths of Paul's pessimism and his obsession with the revolutionary threat. But he put the best possible face on the matter, explaining to Chancellor Thugut that it was Paul's political inexperience and his lifelong exclusion from public affairs which were at fault. In time, the tsar would surely come to understand that, despite certain abuses and insufficiencies, the Russian system was sound. He only hoped that before that realization dawned, Paul might not do real damage to the country by enforcing far more severe corrections than conditions warranted.[35] In fact, Cobenzl scarcely understood the situation at all. It was Paul's intention to make a revolution to prevent a worse one. Bolstered by his own legitimacy, and backed by people he thought he could trust, Paul did, in fact, set out to change everything at once. Any errors he made could be corrected as he went along, nor did he see any need for further reflection. He had spent two decades thinking and planning; the time for action had come.

It was characteristic of Paul to embark on a radical refurbishing of Russia's governing institutions without any public explanation of what he was doing. Beyond the formal announcement of Catherine's death and his own accession, there was no manifesto, no ringing declaration of principles to identify the issues he intended to confront, or to define the goals he hoped to realize. He saw no need to justify himself. It was not just that the problems were self-evident; Paul firmly believed it was his right to declare what had to be done; society's role was to accept and obey. There was matter enough to absorb. A regular torrent of ukases, rescripts, manifestos, and verbal orders spewed out during the first weeks, nor did the flood abate until well into 1798. Dmitrii Troshchinskii, who served as state secretary under Catherine, Paul, and Alexander (and who drafted Alexander's accession manifesto after Paul was murdered) estimated that some 48,000 orders, rules, and laws were issued in the first calendar year of Paul's reign.[36] The vast majority dealt with minor matters, but the effect was of a revolution sweeping away everything familiar. A powerful sense of urgency suffused the capital. Paul drove himself and his subordinates unmercifully. He insisted on a regular

[35] HHSA, Russland II Berichte, Carton 84, Cobenzl to Thugut, no. 72, apostille 17, 25 Nov. (NS) 1796.
[36] Ibid., Carton 87, Dietrichstein to Thugut, no. 6, apostille 6, 29 Jan. (NS) 1798.

work schedule, lengthened official office hours, and, himself an early riser, called meetings for 5.30, 6.00, and 7.00 a.m. It was not unusual for special assignments or even routine tasks to occupy officials until late at night with an early morning reporting session still ahead. There was no repose, no time for reflection, Rostopchin reported bitterly, distractedly, yet proudly, no chance to catch a breath or write a proper letter.[37] And the laws came tumbling out, helter-skelter, first in tens, then hundreds, and finally, before the first rush was over, in thousands. It was a stunning performance, but what was most stunning of all was that the basic outlines of what Paul intended to accomplish were in place before the court left Petersburg for Moscow and the coronation at the end of February. Subsequent legislation refined, codified, or expanded on what was begun in the first five months, but there were no new directions. Paul had long known how he wanted to correct Russia's course; he only needed the opportunity to begin.

Though domestic matters dominated, there was a major shift in foreign policy which in some sense explained the reforms that were simultaneously taking shape. Immediately on Catherine's death rumours began to circulate that Paul intended to withdraw the military support his mother had tendered Austria for the struggle against France. A relief force was already marching west, and a new recruitment had been announced. At first, Count Ostermann, speaking for the government, denied the rumour, but in fact the decision had already been taken: the relief force was called back and the recruitment cancelled.[38] Paul justified this decision on the grounds that 'he regarded the Russian army as too badly ordered to be able to act and the Russian empire as too saturated with democratism to dare to undertake anything'. In such circumstances, to begin his reign with a campaign abroad, no matter how just or necessary it might be, would be unwise. The new regime needed to consolidate itself.[39] Though the Austrian ambassador was dis-

---

[37] On the atmosphere of urgency and Paul's work schedule, ibid., Carton 84, Cobenzl to Thugut, no. 75, apostille 5, 7 Dec. (NS) 1796; Rostopchin to Vorontsov, 25 Feb. (OS) 1797, *Arkhiv kniazia Vorontsova*, viii. 176–8; de Grunwald, *L'Assassinat*, 108.

[38] HHSA, Russland II Berichte, Carton 84, Cobenzl to Thugut, no. 72, apostilles 3 and 8, 25 Nov. (NS) 1796. See below, Ch. 9.

[39] Ibid., no. 72, 25 Nov. (NS) 1796. See also: PRO/65/35, Whitworth to Grenville, no. 57, 18 Nov. (NS) 1796; ibid., no. 62, 5 Dec. (NS) 1796. Cobenzl believed these judgements were so obviously wrong that the first moments of the reign would serve to correct them. This proved not to be the case as Paul later argued the same points in two long conversations with Cobenzl justifying his policies. See: Carton 84, Cobenzl to Thugut, no. 10, 13 Feb. (NS) 1797; Carton 85, no. 29, 4 May (NS) 1797.

appointed, Paul's cancelling the recruitment and the recall of his troops which preceded it won general approval as a boon to the people and a very promising first step. And when this step was taken in conjunction with his decision to withdraw from Persia while seeking an accommodation with the Ottoman empire, it became quite clear that Russian foreign policy was to progress along very different lines than it had followed under Catherine. Such pacific gestures led the English minister to the dark conclusion that now 'this Country bids fair to lose a great part of the Consideration which the profound views and exalted Character of the late Sovereign attached to it'. He also had the grace to note that it might be 'uncandid to give an opinion of a Reign of three weeks', and it could be added that Russians did not share his concerns. Paul's retrenchment on Catherine's last commitments was well received.[40]

For contemporaries, reform was too mild a word to describe the changes Paul brought to Petersburg. Overnight, there was a new look and a new spirit. Everything became overtly military. Strange officers in unfamiliar uniforms strode purposefully about cracking their heels, jingling their sword chains and their spurs, and dressed in the modes in vogue early in the reign of Frederick the Great. This gave the court an alien atmosphere, almost, it was said, as if one had fallen asleep in Petersburg to awake in Potsdam, or worse, as if the Russian capital had been overrun, and this was an army of occupation. 'In short,' as Whitworth remarked on Paul's first day, 'the Court and the town is [sic] entirely military, and we can scarcely persuade ourselves that instead of Petersburg we are not at Potsdam.'[41]

---

[40] Rostopchin told Cobenzl that suspending the recruitment and ending the Persian campaign were intended to benefit the public; the public, as Cobenzl reported, warmly approved. HHSA, Russland II Berichte, Carton 84, no. 72, apostille 17, 25 Nov. (NS) 1796. See also: Riksarkivet, Diplomatica Moscovitica, volume 456, Stedingk to the King, 9/20 Nov. and 12/23 Nov. 1796; Masson, Mémoires secrètes, 194–5; Rogerson to Vorontsov, 25 Nov. (NS) 1796, Arkhiv kniazia Vorontsova, xxx. 80. S. R. Vorontsov, impressed with what he heard from Petersburg, praised Paul's good beginning and specifically his cancelling the recruitment. S. R. Vorontsov to A. R. Vorontsov, London, 9/20 Dec. 1796, Arkhiv kniazia Vorontsova, x. 3. Whitworth was critical, but reported the popularity of Paul's actions. PRO, FO/65/35, Whitworth to Grenville, no. 64, 13 Dec. (NS) 1796.

[41] Ibid. no. 58, 21 Nov. (NS) 1796. 'Everything', Whitworth wrote two weeks later, 'is now military, and that most minutely.' Ibid., no. 62, 5 Dec. (NS) 1796. See also Riksarkivet, Diplomatica Moscovitica, vol. 456, Stedingk to the king, 7/18 Nov. and 9/20 Nov. 1796. As Cobenzl wrote, 'In general it would appear that everything is to be put on a military footing and with a severe discipline.' HHSA, Russland II Berichte, Carton 84, Cobenzl to Thugut, no. 72, apostille 4, 25 Nov. (NS) 1796.

When first the grand dukes and then the tsar appeared formally before the court, they looked, as one observer reported, 'like old portraits of German officers walking out of their frames', but anyone who was tempted to laugh sobered quickly when the tsar himself took the morning review. He obviously expected something different from and better than what he observed. He 'bowed, puffed, and blew [snorting through his nose: a sign of great annoyance] as the guard marched past, shrugged up his shoulders and shook his head to show his displeasure'. These troops failed to measure up, and for more than two hours, the new tsar harangued, hectored, and cajoled. This was Paul the drill-master, a role he relished and faithfully performed nearly every working day of his reign.[42]

Three days later (10 November (OS) 1796), Paul's own army from Gatchina reached the capital. The tsar rode out to meet it and lead it back to the great square before the Winter Palace where he put it through the drill. These soldiers marched to his orders; they knew what he wanted, and he was clearly proud of them.[43] Observers were quick to notice that each of the Gatchina units bore the name of one of the regular guards regiments. Paul himself led the detachment called Preobrazhenskii, Alexander led the (Gatchina) Semenovskii, while Constantine commanded the Ismailovskii. The Gatchina troops, in fact, had become the guards, and the standing regiments were to be integrated with them, a prospect which the guards that were viewed with fear and loathing. Sablukov (then with the Horse Guards) remembered the Gatchintsi as Little Russians, coarse of speech and crude of manner, men whose very appearance offended their proudly aristocratic comrades. But the Gatchintsi were the favoured ones, and their resentful rivals soon realized that any controversy, any word of criticism, was reported immediately to higher authority, and often reached the tsar himself. The men from Gatchina were the new élite and the example that others were to follow. Nor was this just the guards. The entire army was to learn the Prussian drill, at which the Gatchina troops were already proficient, and for those officers who needed help, night classes were held at the Winter Palace. Eventually, Paul intended to eliminate the guards as

---

[42] Sablukov, 'Reminiscences: Part I', 228; PRO, FO/65/35, Whitworth to Grenville, no. 58, 10/21 Nov. 1796.

[43] HHSA, Russland II Berichte, Carton 84, Cobenzl to Thugut, no. 72, apostille 11, 25 Nov. (NS) 1796; Sablukov, 'Reminiscences: Part I', 228-9; Riksarkivet, Diplomatica Moscovitica, vol. 456, Stedingk to the king, 12/23 Nov. 1796; Czartoryski, Mémoires, i. 127.

they had been known while reorganizing the whole of Russia's forces. It was this process which began in that initial review.⁴⁴

By the end of the first week, Paul's new order was in place in Petersburg. The city was sealed. Barriers with guard mounts appeared at all the city gates, guard posts were established on major thoroughfares and at the entrance to public buildings, curfew was imposed, and an internal passport system was enforced. This, however, was only the beginning. Paul disapproved of virtually everything about life as it was lived in the capital. He set out to correct what he found offensive. New regulations prescribed the way people were to dress, travel, and deport themselves. The police were everywhere and zealous to do their job. The slightest variation from what was acceptable resulted in immediate arrest and punishment. Cobenzl reported on 7 December (NS) that wearing round hats was forbidden to people not in traditional Russian dress, and 'the police grab them off the heads of anyone they encounter wearing them in the streets'.⁴⁵ No explanations were accepted. The city became a social minefield. People were afraid to set foot in the streets lest they violate some new regulation of which they had not heard. Theoretically, foreigners were exempt from the dress codes, but even they were at risk since the police were not inclined to discriminate. The foreign element, diplomats included, soon learnt that it was wiser to conform than to run the risk of arrest. The result of all this, as Whitworth reported, was that

The ease and tranquillity of the late Reign are lost with Her from whom they deriv'd . . . A spirit of reform extending to persons as well as things has spread an universal alarm . . . Every hour is mark'd with a new Ukase . . . for the purpose of introducing a change in some established custom. A most severe and exact discipline is introduced into every department both civil and military, and this with such a degree of rigour, as has even absolutely chang'd the face of society.⁴⁶

---

⁴⁴ Sablukov, 'Reminiscences: Part I', 228–9; Christopher Duffy, *Russia's Military Way to the West: Origins and Nature of Russian Military Power* (London, 1981), 201–5; Shil′der, *Pavel I*, 285 ff.; *Aleksandr I*, i. 139 ff.; *Histoire anecdotique*, 28 ff.; Masson, *Mémoires secrètes*, 207–8, for slighting remarks on the Gatchintsi and the bitterness of guards officers toward them. See also Golovkine, *La Cour de Paul Ier*, 127–8.

⁴⁵ HHSA, Russland II Berichte, Carton 84, Cobenzl to Thugut, no. 75, apostille 5, 7 Dec. (NS) 1796.

⁴⁶ PRO, FO/65/35, Whitworth to Grenville, no. 62, 5 Dec. (NS) 1796. Cf. Shil′der, *Pavel I*, *Aleksandr I*, and *Histoire anecdotique*. See also HHSA, Russland II Berichte, Carton 84, Cobenzl to Thugut, no. 75, apostille 5, 7 Dec. (NS) 1796.

Absolutist through Catherine was, she had never used the state's powers in quite this way, though she did impose sumptuary laws (as in 1782) and even forbade large cravats which covered the chin. But she was no social disciplinarian in the sense in which Paul set out to be. Like a stern father with rumbustious children, he laid down rules for public conduct, and he expected them to be obeyed. If the people refused to listen, or if they forgot, they were punished. Society was to be taught to behave the way soldiers learnt their drill. There was, however, one important difference: the manual of arms and the military code were precise and finite. Society had no such handbook. Orders were given and enforced hour by hour. Sometimes they were published, and sometimes not, and there was no comprehensive summary of the radical restrictions on dress, for example, until early in 1798. It was the subjects' responsibility to keep abreast, though even the enforcers could not stay fully informed. This condition, of course, added substantially to the anxiety in people's lives.[47]

There was a marked class bias in Paul's social regulations. The rules on dress and behaviour aimed primarily at the wealthy, the well-born, the privileged. This was consistent with his conviction that years of permissiveness under female rulers of doubtful legitimacy had fostered self-indulgent and socially irresponsible attitudes, especially among the nobility. It was their style of life which required attention. But this vision of a corrupted upper class was joined to the idea (already long institutionalized at Gatchina) that regulation and discipline were good in themselves. Every citizen, regardless of class, was expected to observe the rules and derive benefit from them. Street traffic was to move slowly and decorously; the dashing troika was banned, and only German harnesses were permitted. If these rules were a step towards safer streets, especially for pedestrians, regulations on clothing had an ideological bent. Men's dress was changing all over Europe, but Paul connected change in clothing style with disorder and contempt for authority. The most obvious referent was those styles popular in France. In fact, however, Paul challenged the whole of contemporary male chic. Old forms were favoured over new: breeches and stockings, buckled shoes, powdered hair tied in a queue or bag were permitted; trousers, frock-coats, round hats (except, as we saw, with native Russian dress), top boots, and laces on shoes or breeches were prohibited. Hair had to be combed back off the forehead, and there were rules as well for the height of collars, styles in neckcloths, and how servants should be dressed. Some of the regulations belonged to an announced

[47] The comprehensive dress code appeared 13 Jan. (OS) 1798. *Russkaia starina*, 3 (1870), 532 ff.

attack on 'luxury', a code word for aristocratic wastefulness and high living, but all such rules at base were intended to bring society more closely into conformity with what Paul deemed acceptable behaviour and appearance.[48]

None of this was a new departure for Paul. He had enforced a similar code for years at Gatchina. And it was this which made his choice of General Arkharov as military governor-general for Petersburg especially important. It was Arkharov who had been responsible for enforcing the Gatchina regulations. He knew Paul's thinking, and he believed, probably with some justice, that he could anticipate what the tsar might want. His zeal in promoting his master's cause made enforcement even more severe than the regulations warranted and the police won fame of a sort for their unrestrained, often violent, and usually mindless handling of violators.[49] Paul himself, however, offered the leading example of the severity which his new order demanded, and nowhere was it more apparent than in his treatment of his officers. Nothing which offended seemed to escape his attention: his penchant for finicking detail was amply matched by his determination to punish any aberrations. 'In general,' Cobenzl wrote in late December, 'the slightest error committed by an officer on parade, even a small irregularity in the spontoon salute, is punished either by transfer to a country regiment which results in reducing him [the culprit] two ranks, or by expelling him entirely from the service, or even in some cases making him a common soldier.' Not surprisingly, he also reported that 'more than half the officers in the guards have already voluntarily resigned'.[50]

It is obvious from contemporary sources that people hated what was happening to them. Paul, however, ignored those reactions. Sure

---

[48] HHSA, Russland II Berichte, Carton 84, Cobenzl to Thugut, no. 75, apostille 5, 7 Dec. (NS) 1796. After describing the prohibition on cabs in the palace courtyard, negroes or domestics costumed in military-style uniforms riding behind the nobles' carriages, and the use of six-horse teams, Cobenzl remarked that it was the tsar's intention 'to institute great reforms to diminish luxuriousness'. Stedingk made the same point. Riksarkivet, Diplomatica Moscovitica, vol. 456, Stedingk to the king, 9/20 Nov. 1796. Sablukov, 'Reminiscences: Part I', 228, remembered these rules as dating from the first day. See also Czartoryski, Mémoires, i. 141.

[49] Shumigorskii, Nelidova, 82–90.

[50] HHSA, Russland II Berichte, Carton 84, Cobenzl to Thugut, no. 79, apostille 2, 26 Dec. (NS) 1796. Sablukov confirmed both the severity of the order and the officers' flight from it. 'Reminiscences: Part I', 236–7. He also suggested that the army in Catherine's time was slack and needed discipline. Ibid. 231 n. This was a common judgement. See Aleksandr Mikhailovskii-Danilevskii, Istoriia voiny Rossii s Frantsieiu v 1799 gody, i. 28–31. Czartoryski considered the guards self-serving and self-indulgent, and Count Stedingk called them 'the worst troops in the empire'. De Grunwald, L'Assassinat, 58.

in his own mind of what he now was doing, and in full control of the forces necessary to enforce his will, he simply went ahead. And in general he succeeded. The style of life introduced during the first days characterized the entirety of his reign. There was no relaxation from first to last. Indeed, the opposite was more nearly true, a fact which undoubtedly accounts for the spontaneous celebrations which greeted the news that he was dead. On the other hand, the degree and kind of resistance which Paul's regulations generated should not be exaggerated. Indeed, grumbling apart, there was virtually none. People accepted the new order; realistically, they had no other choice. Hence new uniforms were fitted, sewn, and worn in a matter of hours; frock-coats disappeared or were turned into emergency cloaks by slashing scissors, while even round hats could be folded and pinned to form a tricorn. Whitworth, who had to modify his own headgear to avoid police harassment, remarked on the absence of any strong reactions to Paul's new regulations which, in other countries, might not have been 'entirely free from danger'. However, in Russia, thanks to 'the character of the people, and that spirit of subordination which yet prevails, scarcely a murmur is heard'.[51] One of the most troublesome rules required passers-by, regardless of age, sex, or station, whether on foot, horseback, or in carriages, to stop, dismount if necessary, and kneel down when meeting the tsar or any member of his immediate family. The police were particularly alert to oversights, and this was a rule on which Paul himself was adamant. Even this, however, came to be accepted as one of life's inconveniences—short of martyrdom there was no way effectively to protest it—though individuals soon learnt when and where the tsar was most likely to appear and to avoid those times and places.[52]

More positively, Paul's new government needed personnel, and the tsar was willing to be a generous master. Catherine had lavished gifts on certain individuals who were important to her. Paul did so too— the people on whom he most depended, Bezborodko, the Kurakins, Arakcheev, were richly rewarded—but he also spread his gifts broadly, pouring literally millions of rubles in salaries, pensions, and land grants over hundreds of persons in his service. His generosity,

[51] PRO, FO/65/35, Whitworth to Grenville, no. 62, 5 Dec. (NS) 1796.
[52] Czartoryski, *Mémoires*, i. 132–47. When Kotzebue was returned from his Siberian exile to status and preferment, he lived in perpetual fear of violating some one of Paul's rules. Whenever he went out, he looked out for the emperor so that he could get down in time from his coach. Kotzebue, *The Most Remarkable Year*, ii. 251–2. This was in autumn 1800. See also: Poletika, 'Zapiski', *Russkii arkhiv* (1885), 319–20; Golovine, *Souvenirs*, pt. 2, pp. 142–59; Masson, *Mémoires secrètes*, 207 ff.

especially in light of a virtually bankrupt treasury, was stunning. The point, however, was to buy loyalty while reinforcing the nobility's dependence on the crown. So the troops continued to march, and if they were fortunate enough to have an officer experienced in the Prussian drill, they flourished. And the same individuals who retailed stories about the tsar's tyrannical inconsequence, or told with horror how he raged on the parade ground, competed fiercely for posts in the new administration, or preened themselves on finding their names on the current honours list. But this was as it should be, and observers applauded. Whitworth emphasised how harsh and demanding Paul was, but he also pointed out 'that what might be deemed severe is so tempered with the most scrupulous attention to the wants and even comfort of the Public, and with such signal marks of liberality that the rigour is not felt'. Such tributes to Paul's astuteness in building a base for support while enforcing a thoroughly unpopular regimen were considered hopeful for the future.[53]

Ironically, the only violent protests Paul's new policies occasioned occurred among the peasants, a class he was determined to protect. Between Catherine's death in November and the end of the year, the authorities recorded 55 separate peasant uprisings in addition to at least 2 protests, in which petitions were presented, where there was no violence. The activity escalated with the new year as an additional 119 outbreaks occurred, and 58 more collective petitions were presented. Most of the protests occurred between January and March, and they represented the most widespread peasant unrest since the Pugachev revolt two decades earlier. They also far outstripped the record for incidents of peasant violence compiled over the next quarter century. The underlying causes for these demonstrations were rooted in peasant resentment against their condition as serfs, while the official reporting reveals both the contempt and fear the peasants aroused in the people responsible for controlling them. Paul himself, however, appears to have provided the immediate trigger to the uprising when he required all his subjects, non-privileged as well as privileged, to swear allegiance to him. This had not been done before, and what made it inflammatory

---

[53] PRO, FO/65/35, Whitworth to Grenville, no. 62, 5 Dec. (NS) 1796; HHSA, Russland II Berichte, Carton 84, Cobenzl to Thugut, 18 Dec. (NS) 1796; no. 79, apostille 2, 21 Dec. (NS) 1796. Cobenzl worried about cost—the treasury faced 1,300,000 rubles in disbursements with but 200,000 rubles on hand—and reported growing consternation that Paul was granting lands with peasants inside Russia (rather than in border territories or new lands), something Catherine avoided doing for even her greatest favourites.

was the widespread belief among the peasants that the land was theirs, and that gentry ownership, and the powers it conferred, were temporary. Someday, it was said, the tsar-father would release his people and restore their heritage.[54]

The new oath of allegiance appeared to replace the gentry's authority with that of the tsar. At least some peasants heard it that way and began to celebrate their 'emancipation', refusing any longer to obey their noble overlords or the officials who enforced the nobles' rights. In most places, the euphoria quickly passed, and the people bowed to reality. But in some places, where relations were already strained and there were grievances outstanding, there were confrontations, violence, and finally military interventions to restore order. To add to the problem, some state peasants granted by Paul to private individuals protested their change in status. Even so, the levels of violence and bloodshed were low, certainly in no way comparable to the Pugachev bloodletting, though Paul was forced to reaffirm in the strongest possible terms the gentry's authority over its peasants, and the necessity for the peasants to accept that authority.[55]

Even as a declared friend of the people, Paul could in no way condone disorder or disobedience. But he also fitted the riots into his own special view of the world and used them to justify decisions he had already taken. In his mind the riots supported his conviction that Russia was in danger of a revolution and needed both a period of peace and the reforms he was rushing into effect. Social disorder, in his thinking, was a consequence of moral failure, and in particular the pursuit of individual interests without regard for the common good. For some persons, so strong was this motivation that they were willing actively to foment unrest to win their goals. This, he thought, was the case with the peasant risings. Paul was certain that the riots proved the existence of a conspiracy to embarrass, undermine, or even overthrow him. As he explained the point, past rulers whose legitimacy was questionable had not dared require the peasants to take the oath. Since he was legitimate, the problem did not arise. His enemies, however, had misrepresented the oath to the people, and in doing so aroused hopes that could not be fulfilled. This disappointment, engendered by intriguers who hoped to injure him, caused the revolt. When asked if these miscreants were, in fact, Jacobins, domestic carriers of that most dangerous of revolutionary infections,

[54] S. N. Valk, *Krestianskoe dvizhenie v Rossii v 1796–1825 gg* (Moscow, 1961), 18, for a tabular presentation of data on peasant outbreaks from 1797 to 1825. Documents on the 1796–7 uprising appear on pp. 62–154.

[55] PSZ, no. 17769, 29 Jan. (os) 1797, vol. 24, pp. 305–6; Shil'der, *Pavel I*, 327–35; Shumigorskii, *Pavel I*, 101 ff.

Paul unhesitatingly said no. The people he had in mind were familiars of the court who had been his enemies for years. It was they who had planted 'unwonted hopes' among the people and were responsible for the violence that followed.[56]

Disciplining society produced the most immediate effects and provided the most visible signs of Paul's new order. They were, however, only a part of his total legislative effort. Paul disagreed fundamentally with what he understood of Catherine's policies. His primary criticism was that there was inadequate control over what individuals did in her name while institutional changes had too often favoured special interests. In the event, society as a whole was the loser. This view was in no way unique to Paul, and there was substantial evidence to support it. The country staggered under an immense burden of debt, inflation soared as paper money values declined, tax collections lagged, both the army and the navy were in disorder, substantially undermanned and in desperate need of attention, while the central government seemed to be paralysed. Advancing years had taken a heavy toll on Catherine's political powers, while the favourite, Platon Zubov, lacked both the skills and the drive to give the government direction.[57] Contemporaries who saw the picture so wondered at the decay which lay beneath the surface of so brilliant a reign, but Paul, ignoring brilliance, focused on what he saw as wrong and how to correct it. His prescription was to reawaken a sense of social responsibility and respect for order. To achieve this it was not only necessary to have responsible people in charge, it was imperative to establish institutions, and relations among institutions, which would promote discipline and control. The emperor and his officials were responsible for the state's affairs.

[56] Paul offered this explanation to Cobenzl who reported it as if in the tsar's own words. HHSA, Russland II Berichte, Carton 84, Cobenzl to Thugut, no. 10, 17 Feb. (NS) 1797. His reports on the uprisings themselves emphasized the oath issue. See ibid., no. 8, apostille 9, 8 Feb. (NS) 1797; no. 9, 14 Feb. (NS) 1797. Whitworth divided the blame between the peasants for thinking the oath of allegiance freed them, and Paul for having granted crown peasants to private persons. Unlike Cobenzl, he also stressed revolutionary doctrines as a cause, indicting that 'common enemy of all regular Governments' which preaches 'the doctrines of disobedience and of revolt wherever they can insinuate themselves' and declaring that 'no permanent peace or security can be looked for until the seed of sedition, which from France, threatens every other country, however remote it may be, shall be fairly plucked out by the root'. PRO, FO/65/35, Whitworth to Grenville, no. 8, 14 Feb. (NS) 1797. Paul agreed in principle, but he refused to blame Jacobins or the revolution for his troubles: the peasants were misled by his personal enemies.

[57] Riksarkivet, Diplomatica Moscovitica, vol. 456, Stedingk to the chancellor, 5/16 Mar. 1796; ibid., Stedingk to the king, 9/20 Nov. 1796. For Austrian citations, see above, n. 42.

And everyone, in the end, had to answer to the emperor. Paul would tolerate no independent fiefdoms in his Russia, and no class of citizens could claim exemption from the tsar's authority. Prescriptive rights, especially those set down by Catherine in the charters to the nobility and the town-dwellers in 1785, were unacceptable. Paul believed that the tsar ruled; society received the benefit of that rule.[58]

The primary institutional thrust of Paul's thinking was towards a radical centralization of power with all governing channels leading to the tsar.[59] Paul himself, however, was no Philip II or even Nicholas I, and he made no effort to maintain personal control over the government's day-to-day functioning. Indeed, he made it abundantly clear that it was his chosen subordinates who were expected to deal with the substance of governmental decision, and to that extent he delegated authority freely. Military affairs, in all their ramifications, and foreign policy were the two fields which he dealt with personally. For the rest, he wanted subordinates on whom he could rely. In this respect, Count Dietrichstein reported a telling exchange. The issue was the fiscal situation, but Paul, when queried about it, snapped angrily that he really knew nothing, that unlike his mother he was not interested in long reports or memoranda, and that he left such things to his procuror-general whose responsibility they were.[60]

Delegating authority did not mean that Paul allowed his subordinates autonomy. On the contrary, he kept close track of what they did, and when he was displeased, he punished them severely. Fear of what the tsar might discover, and recognition that his spies were everywhere, were powerful barriers to peculation (or independent initiative) throughout the whole period. The more important effect of delegating authority, however, was to create the need for an institutional focus for the government, a body, in effect, where the tsar's leading administrative officials reviewed policies, worked out

[58] See M. V. Klochkov, *Pravitel'stvennoi deiatel'nosti*, 109–42, for a thoughtful overview of Paul as a legislator. The contrast of Paul's approach with Catherine's, and the rationalizing and centralizing tendencies, appear in pp. 143–60. See also Shumigorskii, *Pavel I*, 81–126. Shil'der is much less satisfactory for Paul's legislative programme.

[59] Klochkov, *Pravitel'stvennoi deiatel'nosti*, 407–33 and 'prilozhenie', nos. 3, 4, 5, pp. 588–94, for nn. and tables. Klochkov stresses rationalization, particularly the retrenchment of unnecessary employees and promoting productivity and efficiency. The structural reorientation was towards centralized control and closer contact for the tsar with local affairs.

[60] HHSA, Russland II Berichte, Carton 86, Dietrichstein to Thugut, no. 49, apostille 1, 13 Aug. (NS) 1797. Cf. PRO, FO/65/38, Whitworth to Grenville, 14 Dec. (NS) 1797. The delegation of power on financial matters (while the tsar allegedly spent his time on parade, army uniforms, and ceremonials) was considered a weakness.

problems, advised the ruler, and received his orders or decisions. Count Panin had urged the establishment of a state council at different stages in his career, though the council he had in mind, particularly at the end of his life, was neither a mere board of advisers, nor a mechanism for realizing the tsar's will. It was a governing body in its own right. Paul's emphasis was different. While he understood the importance of counsel and advice, his concern was that his will be executed. The state council which he established, using an institution Catherine had organized and then let slip, was to serve that end. In doing so, it became the nerve-centre for his government. Its membership included the presidents of the administrative colleges, the chancellor and the vice-chancellor, and the procuror-general of St Petersburg and Moscow. At first, Paul sat regularly with the council. Whether he met with it or not, however, he kept close contact with it through his procuror-general.[61]

The council was particularly active during Paul's first year, holding fifty-eight sittings to discuss budgetary matters, tariffs and taxes, currency values and exchange rates, the further development of waterways, and the expansion of grain reserves as a barrier to famine. Foreign policy questions arose, though most commonly in the context of the domestic issues which they posed, while matters pertaining to the law and the courts were handled in the senate. The council had no executive or administrative responsibilities. Those resided in the colleges, the holy synod, the departments or expeditions, and the gubernii. The state council was a co-ordinating body and, as Paul used it, it was primarily important in the early stages of his reign. After the first year, as the colleges and administrative departments gained strength, the council was less commonly called upon. In 1798, the number of sessions dropped off to twenty-four, there were twenty-two in 1799, and in 1800 the council met just six times. This last, it should be added, may well speak less to constitutional efficiency than to the deterioration of the governing system as Paul isolated himself from state affairs while concentrating governmental powers first in Count Rostopchin, and finally, and most disastrously, in General Peter von der Pahlen. Through 1799, however, the state council was central to the operation of the government, and in the first year, it was the institution of primary resort.[62]

The other institution at the centre of Paul's system was the governing senate which performed both judicial and legislative

[61] Klochkov, *Pravitel'svennoi deiatel'nosti*, 160–80.
[62] Ibid.

functions.[63] It reviewed specific cases or complaints, including alleged crimes against the state; it studied the basis in previous law for new regulations in process of being drafted; it was charged with continuing and completing the draft of a law code; and it acted as a kind of judicial conscience for the empire. This emphasis on the senate was new. When Paul ascended the throne, the senate slumbered, though Catherine had worked on plans for its development through the last five years of her life. By 1796, the senate had fallen far behind in its work. Its 272 administrative officers and 46 members were submerged under a load of 14,231 undecided cases, and the number was growing daily. This situation, in Paul's eyes, was intolerable. He increased the number of senators to 90, ordered a substantial reorganization, and enlarged the staff to 782. The new senate comprised seventeen separate departments and had a role to play in virtually every aspect of Russian political life except foreign policy and military affairs. This expanded competence more than tripled the case-load which increased from 13,317 in 1796 to 42,223 in 1800. The organization, however, became increasingly efficient and productivity rose. In 1797 20,838 cases were decided, and that number improved to 44,480 in 1800. Unresolved cases reached a high of 18,881 in 1798, and then, despite the massively increased amount of work, fell at the end of the following year to 13,381. With the case-load more than tripled, by 1800 the new senate had fewer unresolved cases than had been the case in 1796.[64]

Paul reorganized the senate in the first two months of his reign. That it achieved the levels of productivity that it did testified to the pressure he exerted and to the efforts of two procurors-general, Prince Alexis Kurakin and Count Peter Lopukhin. Oblianinov, who held the post in Paul's last days, was, unfortunately, wholly incompetent. By then, however, the government was disintegrating. After Paul's death, the situation changed dramatically. By 1805, senate personnel had ballooned to over 10,000 workers who completed less work than was done by a tenth of their number under Paul. It would appear to have been the importance which Paul attached to the institution, and his determination to make it perform, that activated his procurors-general and accounted for the difference between the senate in his time and later.[65]

[63] On the senate, ibid. 180-223. As in the case of the council, Klochkov provides bibliography as well as a summary of the authorities whose work he contravenes.
[64] Ibid. 217-22.
[65] Ibid. 224-70, for the procuracy under Paul. See also the chapter on the governing senate, pp. 180-223. Klochkov avoids judging the quality of decisions, restricting himself to issues of organization, economy, and productivity. Studies

As a boy, Paul accepted the idea that the rule of law separated civil from barbarous societies. That same thought continued to shape his adult thinking. But his views on what constituted the rule of law now ran in quite different channels from the liberal-constitutional principles Panin was promoting at the end of his life.[66] For Paul, law was legitimacy, regularity, and order. It meant systematic, predictable government, and it was wholly compatible with autocracy. The legitimate sovereign, in Paul's thinking, was the source of law; it was important for the sovereign to know that existing laws were interpreted and applied; it was also the monarch's right, his duty, in fact, to judge the judgement: to change the law if that were necessary. When Paul would strike himself on the chest and declare, 'Here is the law!', he spoke what he believed was the literal truth. And when he chose to ignore precedents or statutes, or to short-circuit the judicial process, he considered that his right. Bad law was there to be changed. Peter's succession law fell into this category. So did Catherine's regulations on local government, the statute establishing the gubernii. And so did the nobles' rights and exemptions. Paul recognized no law superior to himself; it was enough that God's law guided him and that he would have to answer to God for what he did on earth.[67]

Beyond the state council and the senate, the actual governing of Russia was carried on through a variety of central and provincial

analysing the quality of decision-making hardly exist at all, though Baron Heyking's memoirs throw some light on the subject, especially the procedures followed. His verdict was mixed, though it would appear that he set very high standards of performance. It would also appear that Paul, though vitally interested, interfered very little. *Aus den Tagen Kaiser Pauls*, 16–24, 27–8, 30–3, 35–8 (appraisals of colleagues), 56–8 (appraisal of the senate), 58–72, 75–89, 90–1, 96–103, 105–7.

[66] See above, Ch. 6.

[67] Richard Wortman, *The Development of a Russian Legal Consciousness* (Chicago, 1976), argues that the respect which western countries showed for the law, judges, and lawyers was reserved in Russia for the state. The autocrat's will was superior to any law. See: introduction and ch. 1, *passim*. This was precisely Paul's position. Codification of the law was necessary for regularity and predictability. George Yaney, *The Systematization of Russian Government* (Urbana, Ill., 1973), suggests that regularity and order were desiderata rather than accomplishments, though they figured largely in the descriptions of 18th- and 19th-cent. forms. Russia in Paul's day was far from realizing a government of laws; Paul's rationalizing approach was in the mainstream of theorizing about government, and his council and senate reforms attempted to create institutions compatible with regularity and system. But governing, as even Heyking shows, was very much a matter of individuals acting. Heyking, on the whole, approved of what Paul did in his first 18 months. Then the tsar fell under bad influences. The latter period corresponds, of course, with Heyking's own fall from favour. See *Aus den Tagen Kaiser Pauls*, pts. 1 and 2 *passim*; esp. pp. 13–14 for a general assessment.

bodies. When Catherine reorganized the local governing system in 1775, she explicitly undertook to bring government as close as possible to the areas for which it was responsible, to involve the people served by her complex system of government (guberniia) and district (uezd) courts and councils in selecting personnel and even serving (with various restrictions on eligibility) in the different offices. One consequence of the reform was radically to increase the number of governing institutions and the number of people staffing them; another was to displace to the gubernii functions normally associated with the central administration. There was considerable opportunity for confusion, and, objectively speaking, by 1796 a thoroughgoing review of the system was in order. What it received was a wrenching shift intended to make it run in very different channels from those it was created to fit.[68]

In Paul's eyes, Catherine's system for local government was a disaster. He spoke slightingly of it to Archduke Leopold in 1782, nor did he change his opinion over the next fourteen years. By the time Catherine died, the reorganization of provincial and local government was high among his priorities. Paul's criticisms, largely visible through the reforms he undertook, were by no means unsubstantial. He considered the system too complex to be effective, much too costly, and far too profligate of the ruler's authority. There was insufficient oversight from the central administration; functions which properly belonged to the central government, and were better performed there, had been dispersed among the gubernii; and the system had been legislated without any regard for cultural variety and with no provision for preserving local laws and customs. Catherine had co-opted local grandees in support of a uniform application of Russian laws. Paul was determined substantially to modify that outcome in selected areas of the empire. He also intended to reduce the size of the local government establishment and hence its costs while replacing elected citizens in the courts and councils with appointed officials. In the end, as decentralization was a primary theme in Catherine's reform of local government, recentralization dominated Paul's revisions.[69]

Work on reorganizing the guberniia system began immediately. The first stage of the reforms was completed in 1797, though the reorganization of municipal authorities, prefigured in the new arrangements for governing Petersburg and Moscow, was only codified in 1800. The number of gubernii was reduced from fifty to forty-one with one separate administrative district; five courts were

[68] The appraisal here rests on Madariaga, *Catherine the Great*, 277–324.
[69] Klochkov, *Pravitel'stvennoi deiatel'nosti*, 413–28.

eliminated from the guberniia system and two more from the district; and the number of serving officials, as well as the costs for government functions, were substantially reduced.[70] A number of central administrative colleges, eliminated by Catherine because they duplicated guberniia functions, were restored. The most notable were the colleges for mining, manufacturing, and commerce to which Paul also added a central commission for economic affairs. In 1797, to administer the imperial family's holdings, Paul established the first ministry in Russian history. A ministry for commerce followed in 1800, while throughout the central governing apparatus, collegial presidents and department heads took on the attributes and responsibilities of ministers. The move away from the decentralized, guberniia-based administration of Catherine's day coincided with and supported ministerial authority at the centre. These were the immediate precedents for Russia's definitive move to a ministerial government under Alexander I in 1802. There was no cultural or historical precedent in Russia for what Catherine attempted. Paul, however, with his emphasis on the tsar-autocrat, and the clustering of governmental functions at the centre, was fully in tune with at least 200 years of Russia's institutional development. Undoubtedly this helps to account for the ease with which he dismantled Catherine's system, and it was Paul's version of the centralized state that lived to shape the nineteenth century.[71]

The aspect of Paul's reforms which ran counter to the centralizing tendency was his willingness to use local forms in newly acquired districts of the empire. Eleven gubernii were recognized to be different from the rest of Russia. They included Belorussia, Volynia, Vyborg, Kiev, Kurland, Latvia, Lithuania, Little Russia, Minsk, Podolia, and Estonia. As far as possible in these areas, local forms similar to those provided for in the reforms of 1775 and modified by legislation in 1796 and 1797 were used. In fact, Paul gave away less in substantive authority than it appeared. Military and financial affairs remained firmly in the hands of the central government, and in any conflict between the autocrat and the locality, it was the autocrat whose will prevailed.[72] Yet Paul was clearly more mindful of minorities than either Catherine or his nineteenth-century successors. The gubernii listed, for example, contained the whole of Russia's relatively new Jewish population. The Jews, however, had occupied their lands for many generations, and over the years they had worked out various agreements with their Christian neighbours protecting rights in property, access to markets, landholding, and commercial

[70] Klochkov, *Pravitel'stvennoi deiatel'nosti*, 416, 588–95.
[71] Ibid. 396–406, 402.   [72] Ibid. 414.

ventures, and defining tax liabilities. Paul insisted on the validity of these engagements, firmly resisting Polish and Russian pressures to undercut the privileges guaranteed to the Jewish communities. He applied the same tolerant and enlightened principles to the various religions in this region.[73] Tolerance was not an invitation to self-government, however, and he in no way intended the different religious groups to be free of imperial control. If they were permitted their local laws, it was because he allowed it. He did not, for example, accept the protests of the Catholic community when a Lutheran was chosen *oberprocurator* for the holy synod with administrative responsibility for all religious groups within the empire; he rejected the claim that the pope or his representative should have a voice in choosing officials who dealt with Catholics; and he refused to exempt papal communications, bulls included, from imperial censorship. Undoubtedly Paul's separate policies for the western provinces created anomalies and contradictions; equally they showed him to be surprisingly sensitive to religious difference and made him the most progressive of Russia's rulers on rights of minorities in the empire.[74]

The problems of local government impinged on another sensitive area: the rights of the nobility. This included both exemptions from tax and corporal punishment, and powers of self-government. Paul went as far as he could in removing the protections which nobles and other privileged groups could claim under Catherine's regulations. He modified the prohibitions in the 1785 charter on corporal punishment to the nobility to the point that they were meaningless, and while he left the nobles free of taxation on their lands, nobles carried the expense of local governing bodies, while the Bank of Assistance for the Nobility contained a compulsory feature which forced indebted nobles to use it and hence to subject themselves to its severe repayment schedules. The effect approached taxation.[75] The noble assemblies, which served as instruments for self-government, meanwhile, were permitted to exist, but under the

---

[73] See Matthias Rest, *Die russische Judengesetzgebung von der ersten polnischen Teilung bis zum 'Položenie dlia evreev'* (Wiesbaden, 1975). Paul's 'localist' policies plainly benefited the Jewish settlements; codifying the rules, and ultimately russifying them, weakened the Jewish position.

[74] On Paul and the Roman church, Journel, *Litta* and Benvenuti, *Studi e testi*, 167 and 194. For a summary of leading ideas, see his 'Paul Ier de Russie et l'Union des églises: Documents inédites', *Revue d'histoire ecclésiastique*, 54/4 (1959), 838–63. See also: Pierling, *La Russie et le Saint Siège*, v, pp. iii–iv and 177–334; Heyking, *Aus den Tagen Kaiser Pauls*, for the importance attached to traditional legal forms for the Baltic provinces and Poland.

[75] The bank was intended to benefit the state treasury. See below, Ch. 8.

central government's oversight. Participation in local government was redefined as one of the noble's obligations, and so Paul hoped they would come to see it. On the other hand, Paul forthrightly reasserted the serfholding aristocracy's hold over their peasants. The nobility was an essential element in his conception of the imperial system, but he believed Catherine had gone too far in promoting its autonomy, rights, and self-government. He set out to redress that balance, giving the landholding class a continuing and vital role while reducing its privileges.[76]

Virtually everything we have discussed so far was done *ad hoc*. Paul obviously had thought long and hard about what he wanted, but he brought almost nothing in finished form with him to the throne. As far as Russia's governing machinery was concerned, he acted essentially as a problem-solver, a pragmatist who considered himself sufficiently well informed on the existing government apparatus to adjust it to serve his purposes. Over time, various of his judgements were modified, and in some cases, local government is one example, the changes were codified into detailed legislation. In no case, it should be added, did Paul retrench on the positions taken. Though the quality of his decisions declined, he remained consistently within the legislative framework established in the first days of his reign.

Significantly, Paul understood that the rationalized governing mechanisms which he wanted to implement required specially trained personnel. To that end, on 14 January (OS) 1797, he embarked on one of his very few positive educational reforms, decreeing the foundation of a school for training men for government service.[77] The school he proposed was to admit only children of the gentry who were at least 12 years of age, with places to be allotted on the basis of competitive examinations. The original decree provided for just twenty-seven students. The number later was increased to fifty. Of the original appointees, twelve were destined for the senate, four for the heraldry office, four for the master of requests, and seven

---

[76] More attention has been given to Catherine's emancipation of the nobility than to Paul's revision of their rights. See Robert E. Jones, *The Emancipation of the Russian Nobility, 1762–1785* (Princeton, NJ, 1973); Paul Dukes, *Catherine II and the Russian Nobility* (Cambridge, 1966); Madariaga, *Catherine the Great*, 295–8. Madariaga's discussion of local government shows the way Catherine integrated the nobility into the governing process. See esp. 282–6. Paul's revisions of nobiliary rights and functions are well summarized in Klochkov, *Pravitel'stvennoi deiatel'nosti*, 434–501. See also S. A. Korf, *Dvorianstvo i ego soslovnoe upravlenie za stoletie 1762–1856* (St Petersburg, 1906).

[77] *PSZ*, vol. 24, series 1, no. 17707, 1 Jan. (OS) 1797 and no. 17733, 14 Jan. (OS) 1797.

for the colleges. The curriculum was intended to be practical, aiming at training rather than education, though some general studies were thought necessary. The four-year course included Russian calligraphy, clerical writing, arithmetic, the short catechism, general (universal) history, advanced catechism, world geography, and eventually geometry, trigonometry, Russian history, Russian geography, and logic. In the final year, legal studies, drawing, and German language were added. Academic work was combined with practical assignments in the offices for which the students were destined, and progress through the system was by examination. Acceptance into the school carried civil rank (titular iunker), while on graduation the successful candidate was named collegiate iunker. This school was the predecessor of an institution founded in 1805 which became the imperial school of law. In Paul's day, it enjoyed huge popularity as an entry point into the civil service for young men who would normally have entered the army, but who were unhappy with its current prospects. Paul was disturbed that civil administration could be preferred to military service, and he ordered stringent controls over admission. Even without that problem, the iunker school was no more than a useful beginning on a major problem to which Paul and his sucessors gave inadequate attention.[78]

Budgetary questions were a matter of primary concern. Debt was rising, the treasury was empty, and immediate action was essential. Paul's response took several forms. First, the administrative and military changes he introduced were intended to reduce state expenditures. This was particularly true of the local government reforms, and to a marked degree he succeeded.[79] He also believed that it was essential to consolidate and begin to pay off Russia's gigantic foreign debt, and to encourage frugality and savings among the profligate nobility. Further, the state had to be weaned from its dependence on paper money, the value of the ruble had to be reestablished, and state receipts had to be enlarged to permit a balanced budget. A beginning was made on each of these points at

[78] J. Frederick Starr argues that in the 19th cent. Russia was significantly undergoverned in part because trained personnel was not available in the provinces. See his *Decentralization and Self-Government in Russia* (Princeton, NJ, 1972). Heyking was unimpressed with the quality of people serving in the senate and considered himself fortunate to recruit two competent assistants. *Aus den Tagen Kaiser Pauls*, 35–8, 40–1. L. H. von Jakob, who served in the central administration during Alexander's reign, noted that a cameralist style of government was virtually impossible for Russia given the absence of adequate numbers of trained people. See his memoirs, trans. and ed. David and Karin Griffiths, *Canadian-American Slavic Studies*, 9/4 (Winter 1975), esp. 526–8 on carelessness with appointments.

[79] Klochkov, *Pravitel'stvennoi deiatel'nosti*, 414–6, 589–94.

once, and to dramatize his determination to reduce the paper money in circulation, he caused assignats to the amount of one million rubles (some say five million) to be burnt on the great square before the Winter Palace. He also appointed a trustworthy court banker, A. I. Vasiliev, and set up a special commission to deal with finance and commerce. Work began on consolidating foreign debt with Robert Woot of Amsterdam's Hope and Company, Russia's major foreign creditor, while a series of tax and tariff increases were introduced. The most creative piece of fiscal legislation in Paul's reign, the Bank of Assistance for the Nobility, was not completed until December 1797, and will be discussed below, but even without that Paul's obvious concern over Russia's financial situation, and his clear determination to do something about it, was considered a healthy sign and spoke well for him.[80]

The other side to the picture was that, while determined, Paul was not particularly well informed on money matters or the economy in general, while he shared many of the attitudes that helped to multiply public and private debt in Russia. As grand duke, he was never able to live on the admittedly penurious stipend his mother gave him. He was a prince, and he wanted to live as a prince; economizing was not in his nature, and it contradicted the ideas of magnificence he associated with kingship. Beautifully run as Gatchina may have been, it was not an economic success, and Paul's debts mounted steadily. As tsar, though he saw the need to deal with fiscal problems, he thought it more important to settle substantial allowances on his wife and on his sons, to plan grandiose building projects—Gatchina literally blossomed after he became tsar, and he laid out plans for an elaborate new palace in Petersburg—and to multiply ceremonial occasions at the court. The treasury might be empty but rich gifts for his supporters were essential, and in the very first month of his reign, he accepted the debts of the defunct Polish priory of the knights of Malta, moved the foundation to Petersburg, and settled a large endowment on it for the future, as well as giving it quarters and salarying its local leadership. All this was charged against state receipts.[81] Free spending to acquire or create beauty, grandeur, and

---

[80] Klochkov, *Pravitel'stvennoi deiatel'nosti*, 168–72, 174, 384–9. For an excellent summary on money and credit see Klaus Heller, *Die Geld- und Kreditpolitik des russischen Reiches in der Zeit der Assignaten, 1768–1839/40* (Wiesbaden, 1983), 52–68 (for Paul's reign).

[81] The family allowances were raised immediately, with the empress to have 50,000 rubles per annum, Alexander 200,000, Grand Duchess Elizabeth 100,000, Constantine, 100,000, Grand Duchess Anne, 70,000, Grand Duke Nicholas, 100,000, and the grand duchesses Alexandra, Helen, Mariia, Catherine, and Anna, 60,000 each. Before Michael's birth in 1798, the family allowances had reached

the habiliments of power was essential to Paul's idea of himself. He had to be free to make the grand gesture, and he needed wealth to buy his nobles' support. Paul's beginning on Russia's fiscal problems was promising. He cared, and he was prepared to do something. It was also apparent, however, that his vision was one-sided, incomplete, and he did not have any clear idea of policy alternatives which offered a way out of the economic traps implicit in monarchical ideology. His first efforts at dealing with the intractable budget issue drove living costs up and brought widespread and vociferous protests. But that was only a beginning. Fiscal problems continued to plague him throughout most of his short reign.[82]

The army was Paul's own speciality. His daily drills, the *Wachtparade* modelled on Frederick the Great's example, became a central occasion which no officer dared miss, for not only was the password for the day announced, but commendations and reproofs were given, while policy decisions and new legislative departures were declared. All the tsar's orders and comments, hastily taken down by his adjutant for the day, were worked up to be published in *Peterburgskyia vedemosti*, the official gazette, or were set out by the appropriate chancellor as decrees. To assist him in his military administration, Paul combined the functions of the chancellory for artillery and fortifications, the commissariat, and the so-called *proviant* under the war college to which he appointed Count Nikolai Saltykov as president. In fact, the college's authority was much abridged, and limited to routine administrative functions, while a new institution, His Imperial Highness' Mobile Military Chancellory, was set up to co-ordinate military administration. Its powers were broad, extending into civilian affairs, and it moved about with the tsar. The inspectorates for cavalry, infantry, and artillery became primary channels for informing Paul about everyday conditions in the army across the country—young officers from the Gatchina pool served as observers and were hated as spies—while the general staff

1,370,000 rubles annually. *PSZ*, vol. 24, series 1, no. 17560, 17 Nov. (OS) 1796. On financial support for the knights of Malta, McGrew, 'Paul I and the Knights of Malta', 48–9 and Ch. 8 below.

[82] Despite his announced determination to balance the budget, Paul's government ran an increasing deficit from 1797 to 1800. Expenditures increased from *c.*76 to 81 million rubles per annum. Receipts lagged expenditures by 23 to 26 million rubles. There was an attempt to establish a silver base for the assignat and to stabilize the number of assignats in circulation at 53,595,600 rubles. Neither effort succeeded. Assignats in circulation increased to above 212 million rubles. Heller, *Geld- und Kreditpolitik*, 58–60; *SIRIO* 45, pp. 73 ff. The main revenue sources were poll tax (14,390,155); crown peasant *obrok* (14,707,921); alcohol tax (18,089,393); and customs receipts (5,978,289). Waliszewski, *Paul Ier*, 254–8.

was abolished in favour of yet another special body which reported directly to Paul, the Suite of His Imperial Highness Concerning the Affairs of the Quartermaster. This group was relied upon to assist in campaign planning, but its members performed a variety of other services for the tsar including inspections, arranging journeys, and carrying out special diplomatic as well as military missions. When Paul was outlining his ideas for military reform over two decades earlier, he had stressed the importance of the ruler's playing an active role in the direction of the army. It was that function that these institutions served. Paul was in personal charge.[83]

Such concentrated attention on all aspects of military life gave it clear priority over all other subjects. Apart from the two to three hours Paul spent on the parade-ground daily, a full 40 per cent of all his legislative enactments between 6 November (OS) 1796 and his coronation, on 5 April (OS) 1797, dealt with military subjects. His first official word, following the announcement of Catherine's death and his own accession, was the *prikaz* cited above which dealt with his own position *vis-à-vis* the guards, the role of his sons, and the personnel of his personal suite.[84] The most important items in the early military legislative record were the regulations for the infantry and cavalry dated 29 November (OS) 1796.[85] The infantry rules were based on (and in part simply translated) a Prussian manual first drafted in 1726, revised by Frederick in 1757, published in English translation in 1759, and in French in 1760. There were no further revisions and Paul appears to have used the 1760 edition. The rules dealt with drill and etiquette, the minutiae of a military culture. Some portions of Frederick's code had to be adjusted to fit with specific Russian needs—Paul himself, for example, approved leaves while in the Prussian regulations unit commanders could perform this function—but the overall effect was to establish an army organized according to Prussian principles. Even more than the overt Prussianism, however, the regulations are a monument to a mentality fascinated by particulars, and with the need to order them, codify them, so that they could be taught and enforced. But this, too, was in accord with the spirit of the original. The regulations were drafted 'so that no

[83] Duffy, *Russia's Military Way*, 200–8.

[84] *PSZ*, series 1, vol. 24, no. 17531, 7 Nov. (OS) 1796. Shil'der, *Pavel I*, 289, for the order read at the first *Wachtparade*. For the period to 21 Dec. (OS) 1796, 139 decrees, rescripts, or ukases are listed in the collected laws: 59 dealt with military matters. This understates the intensity of attention to military questions since the *Polnoe sobranie zakonov* is neither comprehensive nor definitive. See Raeff, *M. M. Speransky*, ch. 11 and esp. pp. 326–31 on the problems of compiling the collection and its final character.

[85] *PSZ*, series 1, vol. 24, no. 17588, pp. 26–212.

event of however small importance can at any time happen in reference to which His [Prussian] Majesty has not published a certain rule of conduct'. No clearer statement of Paul's intentions could be possible.[86]

Paul's army was to be a new model: stern, ascetic, controlled. Every effort was made to obliterate the special favours officers had come to consider their right and to make their military duties their primary concern. The correct uniform for each individual was to be worn at all times. Indefinite leaves were cancelled; officers were expected either to rejoin their regiments or leave the service. Generals were ordered to restrict themselves to a single aide-de-camp (Zubov alone had deployed 200) while stringent rules against using junior officers for any purpose other than soldiering were drawn up and enforced. Regimental names were changed from geographical regions to those of commanding officers (soldiers were known to complain that they did not know to what unit they belonged when the general's name was unfamiliar), while administrative changes and reforms in provisioning methods cut off a major source of illegal income for unit commanders and gave some guarantee that the men would receive the supplies and equipment designated for them.[87] The code of military conduct was revised and then revised again, broadening categories of offence and introducing more severe punishments. And then there were the uniforms. The comfortable and commodious clothing Potemkin had favoured was abolished. The infantry was dressed in the old Prussian style with a high conical hat, hair plastered with a noisome compound of wax, grease, and powder, and a long pigtail attached behind. So difficult were these styles that every unit had to have hairdressers and the men were known to spend an entire night before parade preparing their coiffures. There were blunt, stubby shoes for the feet, while long tight leggings were buttoned to above the knees.[88] Everything was tight—coat, breeches,

---

[86] *Regulations for the Prussian Infantry...* (London, 1759), 422. Paul, Kushelev, and Rostopchin had worked on the infantry regulation for application at Gatchina. Rostopchin was made responsible for bringing the Gatchina regulations up to date for application to the Russian army generally. This took just over 3 weeks of hard work. Much of the Prussian original was retained, including Frederick's injunctions to the good soldier: how he should bear himself, how he should look people in the eye, and how he should always be neat, clean, and a credit to the regiment. The most comprehensive analysis of the regulation in the context of Paul's military thinking and policies is Petr Lebedev, 'Preobrazovteli russkoi armii'. Lebedev is critical of Paul's approach.

[87] Shil'der, *Pavel I*, 289 ff.; Shumigorskii, *Pavel I*, 131–45; de Grunwald, *L'Assassinat*, 115–19; Duffy, *Russia's Military Way*, 200–8.

[88] Duffy, *Russia's Military Way*, 200–8.

leggings—and free movement was difficult. An English observer described the Russian army in Holland in 1799 as 'exactely the stiff, hard, wooden machines . . . as the Russians of the Seven Years War'. With dress and equipment unchanged, 'They waddled slowly forward to the tap-tap of their monotonous drums', and when repulsed, 'they waddled slowly back again'.[89] It was a cruel description and should be set against the reports of heroism and sheer brilliance achieved, especially under Suvorov in Italy and Switzerland, but it also conveys dramatically the appearance and style of Russia's prussianized forces. (It also indicates the continuity of western German influence to which Paul returned.) Suvorov, whom Paul tried to win over, rejected the reforms wholesale. Battles, as he well knew, were not won by fancy dress; hair powder did not fire, pigtails were hardly bayonets, and the whole business of the new army was absurd. Prussians, in his vivid phrase, were lousy and stank; for him, a pure-blooded Russian who had suffered no defeats, Frederick, who had, was no apt example. Paul had no choice; Suvorov was permitted to retire. Arakcheev was more the sort of man Paul needed, while Suvorov, an authentic Russian hero, was relegated to his estates until the Austrians suggested that he be made generalissimo in the joint effort in 1799.[90]

Yet as with so much else, what Paul intended and did with the army had its praiseworthy side. Military administration improved to the point that in 1799 the empire was able to carry on simultaneously naval operations in the Black Sea, the Aegean, the Mediterranean, and the English Channel; mount a joint amphibious attack with the British on Holland; and deploy land forces across the Balkans, through the Germanies north of Switzerland, and in Italy.[91] The problems the Russians met owed to diplomatic failings and parti-

---

[89] Sir Henry Dumbary, quoted Duffy, *Russia's Military Way*, 205.

[90] Paul's confrontation with Suvorov was described in the Saxon minister's correspondence. When brought the new regulations for exercises and uniforms, Suvorov agreed that his teacher had come, but that he was too old to learn and that 'hair curls are not cannons nor soldiers' pigtails bayonets'. Shil'der inserts other and widely cited versions of the quip. Suvorov, Völkersham reported, won no praise for his wit, but was ordered to Petersburg and dismissed. 'Materialy dlia istorii tsarstvovaniia imperatora Pavla I', Völkersham correspondence, no. 6, 13/24 Feb. 1797, Shil'der, *Aleksandr Pervyi i*, i. 360–1. De Grunwald portrays Suvorov angry and speaking the famous words directly to Paul: 'Sire, there is powder and powder; curls are not cannon, a pigtail is not a bayonet, and I, I am not a Prussian but a pureblood Russian . . . I put myself higher than the deceased king of Prussia for I, with God's help, I have never lost a battle.' *L'Assassinat*, 119.

[91] For an excellent account which recognizes the achievements of Paul's government without minimizing the corruption and inefficiency, esp. after 1798, see Saul, *Russia and the Mediterranean*, 25–154. See below, Ch. 9.

cularly Paul's omission of logistical and provisioning agreements in advance. And the troops, allowing for one disastrous collapse in Holland, fought extremely well. How much owed to Paul's reforms and how much was in spite of them is hard to tell, though improved organizational and administrative discipline was an important factor. Nor were Paul's goals in the reforms he undertook either minor or unimportant. He intended to bring the army under the tsar's personal control and did; he set out to eliminate the tyranny of senior officers and colonels (something he achieved by substituting his own tyranny over them); he intended to make the officers recognize their professional obligations and to curb their licentious behaviour, especially their wildly excessive drinking and gambling, and in this, briefly at any rate, he succeeded. Finally, he wanted to improve the lot of the common soldier to which end he increased pay, enlarged the garrison schools, and established a military orphanage. On the other hand, he drilled and manœuvred the men unmercifully until rumblings from the ranks and desertions brought him temporarily to lighten the daily load.[92] The punishment code became an increasingly serious problem. Paul might say, as he did in the 1796 regulation, that 'The soldier must always be regarded as a human being, for almost anything can be attained through friendly dealings. Soldiers will do more for an officer who treats them well, and receives their trust, than for one whom they merely fear.'[93] Yet the system he introduced and enforced was extremely harsh, first on the officers, but eventually on the men. He forgot his own injunctions. The best that Paul intended and achieved was to bring order, control, and discipline into the system. At least, he made it extremely difficult for any senior officer to become an independent despot over his men. The orderliness he achieved was the other side to the harsh methods he used to keep everyone in line.

The 1796 military code was not the only major piece of legislation Paul brought with him to the throne. Another was a detailed exposition of the relationships obtaining within the imperial family, the titles appropriate to each person, the properties each possessed, and the administration of those properties.[94] This decree, in fact, turned the imperial family into an institution located at the centre of the socio-political system. Like the military regulations, it was done in loving detail with collateral relationships spun out and the most careful distinctions in rank, priority, and title. It was this enormous document which provided the context for the succession manifesto announced at the coronation; it was also to carry out the family

[92] Duffy, *Russia's Military Way*, 207. [93] Quoted, ibid.
[94] *PSZ*, series 1, vol. 24, no. 17906, 5 Apr. (OS) 1797, pp. 525–69.

regulation that the ministry for apanage was founded. A further statute codified the rules governing the knightly orders in the tsar's gift.[95] This decree covered ranks, robes, and insignia; administration and financing; the day of the year each order was celebrated; the day appointed for celebrating all knightly orders; the events at which the orders were expected to participate, and much more. Long before Paul became the protector of the knights of Malta, much less that order's grand master, he had legislated a comprehensive code institutionalizing four existing chivalric orders as an integral part of his court's society. These were symbols of the first importance.

Contemporaries reporting on Paul's first months in office gave his efforts mixed reviews. The prussianization of the Russian army and the influence of the Gatchina outsiders were sore points, as was the severity of the discipline introduced in society and the military. On Paul himself, it was generally agreed that he was inexperienced but wanted to do right, that 'he had a good heart', and that there were abuses to reform. He was severely criticized, however, for the extraordinary amount of time he lavished on seemingly unimportant details, for 'versatility', that is, the inability to hold to a steady and consistent course of action, for the lack of system in the reforms he announced, and for his apparently ungovernable temper. When enraged, there was no telling what he might do, though once the fury was over, he seemed ashamed and willing to make amends.[96]

The foreign diplomats are invaluable for seeing Paul as a political man. They knew that they had to satisfy him personally, yet they found that he was often inaccessible. They leave little doubt that he was frustrating and difficult to work with, that he was inclined to sudden and unexpected reactions, that he had a violent temper, and that, in the political sense of the term, he was wholly inexperienced. His style of speaking was sometimes allusive to the point of being incomprehensible, he was no respecter of persons, he could be vindictive, self-righteous, and often ridiculous. What in general they failed to grasp was that Paul knew where he intended to take Russia, that he had a well-defined sense of what constituted Russia's interests, and in what kind of world those interests would be best

---

[95] *PSZ*, series 1, vol. 24, no. 17908, 5 Apr. (OS) 1797, pp. 569 ff.
[96] McGrew, 'Political Portrait', 511–18. Shil'der, 'Materialy', *Aleksandr Pervyi*, i. 353–71, gives reports from different Prussian representatives as well as the Saxon minister. Paul's destructive behaviour is a main theme in memoirs by Czartoryski, Mme Golovina, Golovkin, Masson, Orlov, Derzhavin, Golitsyn, Dashkova, and even Sablukov, as well as in the correspondence of Grand Duchess Elizabeth, Rostopchin, and Rogerson. The memoirists (except for Sablukov) are unfriendly witnesses; the diplomats, though by no means uncritical, give a more balanced view.

served. He was by no means so inconsiderable as his contemporaries pictured him, and he had much more to offer than 'a good heart'.

There is no doubt that Paul was an enthusiast, a fanatic even, where the military was concerned, and his interest in the details of whatever fascinated him was endless. He was, moreover, compulsive about getting things right. And once the forms or rules were established, he insisted, regardless of how petty they might be, that they be observed. In the early days of his reign he showed both energy and capacity in his attack on a governing system which he believed was too easily manipulated by special interests and was insufficiently responsive to the ruler's will and the people's interests. These were not 'bagatelles'. Paul gave his concentrated attention to reforming the Russian system in his image, expunging what he thought was unworkable or contradictory while emphasizing those institutions which supported the kind of autocracy he believed that Peter had built, and that Peter's successors had buried. By coronation day, Paul had established the kind of state he intended to govern and the methods by which he would rule it.

Paul had completed the first stage of his legislative agenda by the time he left for Moscow to be crowned. The coronation was to take place on Easter Sunday, 5/16 April 1797, and revealed yet another side to the new tsar's political personality. Paul believed in the efficacy of symbols. It was imperative for him that he pass through the rituals of becoming tsar, and that court and people be fully involved in the process. His asceticism showed clearly in his military reforms, in his effort to restrain the luxurious living style of the great nobility, and in the simple personal morality of service and obligation which he preached. But he also saw himself at the centre of a brilliant figuration, the beloved and exalted monarch whose power and benevolence supported and enlightened a grateful people. What could be more moving than the ritual celebration of installing such a ruler? It was in this spirit that Paul approached his coronation. He missed no opportunity to play variations on the pageantry of monarchy, to place himself before and among his people, to receive their plaudits, to bask in their adoration, or to call for those formal expressions of respect and loyalty he believed were owing to him. For Paul, the coronation marked the realization of his fondest hopes, the final public ratification of what he knew he was, and what he had endured so much to become. It had to be magnificent.

The choice of Easter for the event was hardly accidental.[97] This

---

[97] Golovkine, *La Cour de Paul Ier*, 139, asserts the conscious choice as fact. Golovkin was master of ceremonies for the coronation. Paul announced his coronation on the day Peter III and Catherine were buried; the exact date was not

greatest of the church's holidays which celebrated resurrection was appropriate for sanctifying a ruler dedicated to his motherland's rebirth, her salvation from the long era of moral decay and social disorder in which she languished. Paul's religiosity, always important in his private life, literally took wing with his elevation to the tsardom. Even before leaving Petersburg, he experimented with a sacerdotal role, learning the priest's function in offering the mass and hearing confession. It seems to have been his idea that he might say the former at his coronation after hearing the latter from his family and retainers. He realized, however, that to burst upon the world in this new guise required preparation, so he considered beginning his performances at the cathedral of Our Lady of Kazan in Petersburg. The justification for the role he sought was the tsar's designation as head of the Russian church; the holy synod diverted him by respectfully reminding him that no person twice married was eligible under canon law to perform sacerdotal rituals. Paul accepted the ruling and gave up practising his responses. But when he appeared at the cathedral of the Annunciation on the Kremlin to be crowned, he wore a short religious vestment similar to a bishop's cope as part of his ceremonial dress. Nor did he put his *dalmatique*, so called, aside when he appeared on the parade-ground. The combination of uniform tunic, high Prussian boots, and a cope conveyed the mixture of secular and ecclesiastical functions which Paul saw as his; as with so many of his effects, it also made him slightly ridiculous.[98]

The transfer of the court to Moscow began in January with the departure of the first guards regiments. It was effectively completed with the arrival of the imperial family at Catherine's palace of Petrovskii, a dour gothic structure outside the city which lacked both architectural distinction and charm of setting, on 15 March (OS). The court remained there in some discomfort until after the formal entrance into Moscow on 28 March (OS). Since accommodation on the Kremlin was inadequate, Paul, his immediate family, and his entourage needed a city residence. Count Bezborodko offered, and Paul later bought, his recently acquired palace in a removed and charming sylvan setting. The tsar immediately ordered the trees felled

given until later. On the coronation, Shil'der, *Pavel I*, 341–51; Shumigorskii, *Pavel I*, 121–4; Waliszewski, *Paul I*ᵉʳ, 126–9. Contemporary accounts include Golovkine, *La Cour de Paul I*ᵉʳ, 139–46; Golovine, *Souvenirs*, 160–71; A. Golitsyn, 'Zapiski', *Russkii arkhiv* (1886), 12, 143. See also: *Russkaia starina*, 33 (1882), 214; *Istoricheskie vedomosti*, 69 (1887), 349.

[98] Shumigorskii, *Pavel I*, 121–2; Waliszewski, *Paul I*ᵉʳ, 127; Golitsyn, 'Zapiski', 143; Golovkine, *La Cour de Paul I*ᵉʳ, 149–50. Golovkine claimed that, according to Platon, Paul's religiosity was more a matter of his head (policy) than his heart.

so that a parade-ground could be built. He took up residence after his triumphal entry, and then used the palace until he left the capital early in May.[99]

It was traditional for the ruler awaiting coronation to remain outside the city until his formal entrance into it. Paul, however, used the transparent device of the official incognito to make daily excursions into Moscow. Sometimes the court accompanied him, sometimes only his familiars.[100] In earlier days, Catherine had worried about Paul's courting popularity with the crowd in Moscow. He was encouraged to restrain himself. There was no reason now to do so, however, and he missed no opportunity to show himself to the people and to receive their cheers. Relaxed and at his ease in a large open carriage, he appeared again and again in the streets, and the enthusiastic crowds would follow him back to Petrovskii where they ringed the palace round. Paul was comfortable in Moscow. It was his city, he had always been popular there, and if ordinary people enthusiastically welcomed his every appearance, the Moscow gentry, who had shown a strong aversion for Catherine and especially her aggressive foreign policies, looked to him as their best future hope. Later this enthusiasm waned—one reporter spoke of the turn beginning during the coronation visit—but on the surface, at any rate, it was in full flood and gave Paul's presentation of himself legitimacy and support.[101]

The preparations for the official entry began on 25 March (OS) when a richly costumed cortège of mounted heralds led by General Arkharov progressed from Petrovskii through the Tver gate to the Kremlin proclaiming the tsar's coming. This ritual was repeated on 26 March (OS). On 28 March (OS) the Saturday before Palm Sunday, the entire route from Petrovskii to the Kremlin to the Bezborodko Palace was lined with soldiers. The procession set out at noon led by mounted cossacks and hussars, followed by leading members of the Moscow nobility riding in carriages and attended by their sons on horseback. The horse guards and cavalier guards were next, in full regalia, followed by Paul attended by Alexander and Constantine

[99] On Petrovskii and the living arrangements, Golovine, *Souvenirs*, 160 ff. See also Shil'der, *Pavel I*, 323–5 and Waliszewski, *Paul I*^{er}, 126–7.

[100] Golovkine, *La Cour de Paul I*^{er}, 126, for the schedule of events before the official entry. See also Shil'der, *Pavel I*, 341–7.

[101] Count Brühl believed that 'Whatever may be the demonstrations of this city [Moscow] in favour of their sovereign, there is general discontent; it even exists in the provinces and the army'. 1/12 May 1797, Shil'der, 'Materialy', *Aleksandr Petvyi*, i. 365. Robert E. Jones documents Moscow's more favourable disposition towards Paul and the opposition to Catherine's foreign policies. 'Opposition to War and Expansion in Eighteenth Century Russia.'

and his personal aides. Court functionaries rode in the next carriages, and then came Mariia attended by one daughter, Helen, and her daughter-in-law, the grand duchess Elizabeth. Other members of the family were ill, while the baby Nicholas had been left in Petersburg. The ladies of the court and another regiment of guards completed the procession.

The parade moved slowly with Paul setting the pace. Dressed in a simple uniform, he ambled along on the now ancient white horse given him by the prince de Condé at Chantilly in 1782. The pace gave Paul maximum exposure to the cheering crowds. Fedor Golovkin, who was master of ceremonies for the event, recorded that it took four hours for the procession to reach the Kremlin; another observer noted that the procession was organized by noon and disbanded at the Bezborodko Palace at 8.00 p.m. It was a bitterly cold day which made the slow pace hard to bear, and such officials as were required to ride horseback and were unaccustomed to it added an unexpected (and undoubtedly unwelcome) comic touch as they struggled to keep their seats. The following day, Palm Sunday, the heralds rode out again, this time to announce the coronation, now just a week off. And throughout Holy Week there was a succession of public ceremonies at which the tsar assisted which included blessing the guards' flags (Nelidova personally brought a new set sewn by the girls at Smol'nyi), a ritual footwashing, the preparation of holy oils, and on Good Friday, the re-enactment of Christ's progress to Calvary. Rehearsal for the coronation ceremony also began on Good Friday under Paul's personal direction.[102]

Coronation day dawned early. The courtiers began to gather at 5.00 a.m.; the ladies of the court appeared at 7.00. The procession to the cathedral moved at 8 o'clock. The ceremonies continued through the morning and into the afternoon. Gabriel, the metropolitan of Moscow, officiated. He was assisted by Archbishop Platon, Paul's former instructor in religion and long-time friend and correspondent. Platon should have taken the ceremony, but Paul was irritated with him for his refusal to accept honours offered to him, and for his reluctance to come to the capital and to take on new official duties.[103] So it was that when Paul arrived wearing a sword, it was Gabriel rather than Platon who ordered him to remove it before entering the holy precinct. It was a tense moment, a confrontation in fact, that ended with Paul obeying without a word. This was the first coronation at which both an emperor and his empress were crowned.

[102] Golovkine, *La Cour de Paul Ier*, 142–4; Golovine, *Souvenirs*, 162–4; Shil'der, *Pavel I*, 342–3; Waliszewski, *Paul Ier*, 126–7.
[103] Papmehl, *Platon of Moscow*, 72.

Though frustrated in his plan to perform the service, Paul did crown Mariia. Looking on among the honoured guests were Stanislaus-August, the former king of Poland, and Lorenzo Litta, the papal nuncio. Paul had thought to rally the deposed princes of Europe at his coronation; Stanislaus was the only one who came. Litta was more significant. His presence not only signalled Paul's commitment to the traditional institutions of pre-revolutionary Europe, but it showed as well his very favourable disposition towards Catholicism. Catherine had refused to allow the nuncio to come any nearer than Warsaw; his presence at the coronation marked the opening of a new era in Russo-papal relations.[104]

With the ceremonies completed, Paul stepped forward to present three special manifestos. One was the decree drafted in 1788 which both he and Mariia had signed, re-establishing an hereditary succession in Russia, identifying Alexander as Paul's heir and successor, and spelling out the descent of power in detail according to the principle of male primogeniture.[105] With this law, the always questionable idea legislated by Peter the Great that the tsar should choose his own successor was overthrown, and a condition fertile for political intrigue eliminated. The succession manifesto was an important step toward a regularized political system and the rule of law; as such it was probably the single most important decree Paul promulgated.

The second decree was of another character entirely. It dealt with the knightly orders which the government supported. What caused comment was that only four of six active orders were included. St Andrew, St Catherine, St Alexander Nevskii, and St Anne were subsidized; the two orders created by Catherine, St Vladimir and St George, were omitted.[106] The order of St George was a soldiers' order which Paul wanted to refuse to recognize. He had nothing but contempt for what he termed 'Potemkin's army', and he carried this prejudice to such lengths that he was prepared to ignore any distinction won by men who served in it. Shortly after his accession he had ruled that the day for the order of St George, 26 November, would not be celebrated. Catherine Nelidova had challenged this decision, pointing out that what he proposed was monstrously unfair to men who had served their fatherland well and faithfully, and for whom the order was recognition of their sacrifices. To treat them as

[104] Golovkine, *La Cour de Paul Ier*, 144–5; Golovine, *Souvenirs*, 165–6; Waliszewski, *Paul Ier*, 126–9.
[105] *PSZ*, series 1, vol. 24, no. 17906, treated the imperial family; no. 17907 set the succession and was dated 1788.
[106] Ibid., no. 17908.

Paul intended to do was impolitic, morally repugnant, and wholly unworthy of him. Paul gave in only to take the more serious step of excluding the order from further state recognition and support. Again Nelidova successfully intervened. The order of St George was reaffirmed later in the week in a decree which referred to its oral promulgation earlier at the coronation. The order of St Vladimir, however, was not restored until 1802.[107]

The third decree concerned peasant work obligations and reflected Paul's long-standing determination to be an advocate for the lowly against the powerful. In contrast with other legislation for the period, however, and especially in comparison with the forceful reaffirmation of gentry authority over their peasants in January, it was a very modest contribution. The decree suggested that gentry landowners ought not to claim more than three days' labour from serfs performing *barshchina* on their lands. To do so meant that peasants were forced to desperate expedients to find the time to cultivate their own holdings, including working on Sundays. Holy writ declared Sunday a day of rest for all; to create a circumstance which forced people to violate God's law was wrong.[108]

Though the occasion gave it weight, this was a very gentle word in the ear for Russia's landholders. It was also, however, more than was usually said. Paul intended to improve conditions, to see that the peasants' rights were protected, and that the landholders did not exploit them. He was also, however, firmly committed to the existing social order. He was not willing to see the peasants lose what he believed the system guaranteed them; but he did not intend to change the system. The decree on labour obligations was entirely consistent with enlightened support for traditional Russian political and social values. That he was willing to defend the weak hardly argued that he hoped to free them, or that he even envisioned that as a worthwhile future goal.[109]

Following the coronation, Paul, Mariia, and their entourage retired to the Kremlin Palace to dine in state, to receive their subjects' congratulations, and to preside over the announcement of benefices

---

[107] Shumigorskii, *Nelidova*, 67–9. For the letter, *Osmnadtsaty vek*, iii. 425–6. See also Rogerson to Vorontsov, 10 June (NS) 1797, *Arkhiv kniazia Vorontsova*, xxx. 86–7 n. 1.

[108] *PSZ*, series 1, vol. 24, no. 17909. Confino, *Domaines et seigneurs*, 232, notes correctly that this was an invitation rather than an order.

[109] Klochkov, *Pravitel'stvennoi deiatel'nosti*, 501–27 for Paul's peasant policies; pp. 528–84 are an exhaustive analysis of the manifesto on 3-day *barshchina*. Klochkov emphasizes the protective and progressive character of Paul's legislation and therefore, unlike Confino, considers the manifesto a significant break in the serf tradition.

in honour of the occasion. These last were considerable: 167 individuals received land, peasants, promotions, new titles, pensions, and decorations; 82,000 male serfs were assigned to individual nobles together with thousands of acres of land. The largest and richest grants by far went to Bezborodko and the Kurakin brothers, the men closest to Paul in his handling of affairs. The Kurakins, long-time friends of Paul's, were also favourites with Nelidova whose influence in the grants seemed pervasive. Bezborodko, however, was not among Nelidova's favourites, though he had done very well with Paul from the beginning. Whether this owed to the tsar's appreciation for his statesmanlike qualities, or his gratitude for Bezborodko's alleged co-operation in finding and destroying Catherine's testament removing him from the succession, has never been decided. That Paul was grateful to him was obvious. Bezborodko was given the title of prince, two estates, a total of 16,000 souls, and when Count Ostermann retired sixteen days later, he was named imperial chancellor as well.[110]

What may be more significant than any individual grant, however, was the breadth of Paul's generosity which reached deep into both military and civil ranks. Almost, it seemed, there was something for everyone, though inevitably, even in such a downpour, there were some who stayed dry.[111]

There is only one recorded protest. The next to last benefice was for Ivan Kutaisov who was given the rank of gentleman of the bedchamber, fourth class. Kutaisov thought he should have had more and made the uncharacteristic mistake of telling Paul so. The tsar's reaction was an explosion of fearsome rage, a blow, and expulsion from his presence with the certainty of exile. Ironically, it was Catherine Nelidova who intervened to save Kutaisov for the day when his intrigues would contribute to her exile and the collapse of the empress's party.[112]

Despite Paul's delphic utterance on three-day *barshchina*, the peasants were clear losers in the benefice game. The decree itself made new problems for some, since in the Ukraine, for example, only two days' work was required; Paul's suggestion could be used to justify a heavier burden. But this was by no means the worst of it. The honours list affected tens of thousands of lives, and this hardly for the better. The 82,000 souls distributed on 5 April were in

---

[110] Shil'der, *Pavel I*, 344–6, 565–72. Cf. Waliszewski, *Paul Ier*, 130; Golovkine, *La Cour de Paul Ier*, 143–7.

[111] Golovkine claimed that he alone received nothing. He did not know why, nor was Nelidova able to enlighten him or correct the oversight. Ibid. 146 n. 1.

[112] Heyking, *Aus den Tagen Kaiser Pauls*, 45–6; Shumigorskii, *Nelidova*, 81.

addition to 50,000 set aside for the knightly orders and numerous gifts given at the time of his accession. In the end it was estimated that well over 150,000 male souls passed into the gentry's hands between Catherine's death and Paul's coronation.[113] When the figure is raised to account for wives and children, the number of people involved would be a conservative 400,000, and the total might well have been above half a million. The peasants taken were largely state peasants who paid a relatively modest 3 ruble quitrent (the average *obrok* paid to gentry owners at the end of the eighteenth century was 6 rubles) and whose terms of obligation were considered to be less onerous than those of gentry serfs. If anything, state peasants appeared to be nearer to enjoying the freedoms of independent farmers than gentry serfs and were cited by early economists to demonstrate a gradual movement toward a free peasantry in Russia.[114]

Catherine and her predecessors had avoided granting state peasants to the nobles, but Paul found several reasons for doing so. According to Cobenzl, the tsar calculated that giving 100,000 state peasants to his nobles would only cost the treasury 300,000 rubles in income while conferring a benefit twice as large, and in those areas where the quitrent was higher than the average, about three times that amount. This was a worthwhile prize indeed.[115] Paul insisted on rich rewards to celebrate his accession and coronation. With the treasury virtually empty, granting state peasants offered a painless way to accomplish his end. Once the decision was taken, other advantages were discovered as well. It was argued that low *obrok* and minimal restrictions encouraged state peasants to leave the land

---

[113] The estimate is Cobenzl's. See HHSA, Russland II Berichte, Carton 85, Cobenzl to Thugut, no. 29, apostille 9, 4 May (NS) 1797. It is not clear what is included in the total. The grants listed aggregate only 79,292, while Shil'der gives a figure of *c*.82,000. For his version of the numbers and the honours list, see *Pavel I*, prilozhenie 23, pp. 565–72.

[114] Semevskii, *Krestianskii vopros*, 52–3 and app. 9, pp. 593–5 for data on 'average' *obrok*. Confino, *Domaines et seigneurs* and *Systèmes agraires*, is excellent on problems of innovation, change, and development viewed from the perspective of landowners and peasants. Heinrich Storch, a disciple and popularizer of Adam Smith who was close to the imperial family, considered the gentry better masters than they were portrayed, but he also regarded state peasants as evidence of, and a model for, further progress towards freedom. For his ideas and career, and for further material on contemporary views of agriculture, the peasants, and development, see Roderick E. McGrew, 'Dilemmas of Development: Baron Heinrich Friedrich Storch (1766–1835) on the Growth of Imperial Russia', *Jahrbücher für Geschichte Osteuropas*, NS 24/1 (1976), 31–71.

[115] HHSA, Russland II Berichte, Carton 85, Cobenzl to Thugut, no. 29, apostille 9, 4 May (NS) 1797.

where their labour was needed. Moreover, it was said that state peasants were particularly unproductive. It was asserted, for example, that the consolidation of ecclesiastical peasants with state peasants at the beginning of Catherine's reign worked to the overall disadvantage of agricultural production as the state peasants corrupted the work habits of those peasants formerly on church lands.[116]

In a curious variation on these themes, and to show that the transfers were ultimately to the advantage of the peasants themselves, it was also pointed out that while state peasants were subject to low *obrok*, they were at the mercy of corrupt government overseers who could be expected to demand additional and wholly illegal payments. This abuse, which was considered difficult to identify and eradicate, would disappear when the state peasant became a gentry serf.[117] If there was any validity to these arguments, and critics were doubtful, it was quite clear that Paul had moved to strengthen the bond between the tsar and his nobility in the most traditional way possible: by grants of land and the people necessary to work it. That he did so by alienating a state resource at a time when it was desperately needed, and at a cost in popular resistance and violence, only attests to the importance which he attached to this aspect of his policies.

With honours distributed, ceremonial recognition for the newly consecrated tsar went forward, and this process bade fair never to end. Seated on their respective thrones, and surrounded by their family together with the first gentlemen and ladies of the empire, Paul and Mariia received society's formal congratulations. The process went on for hours as the master of ceremonies, knowing full well what had to be done to please and satisfy the tsar, sent every available individual through the line with those persons holding multiple appointments making a separate appearance for each position held.[118] The ceremonies took hours, but Paul and Mariia were seen to be enjoying every moment and were loath to see them end. Indeed, during the month that followed, these scenes were repeated as often as possible on the barest of provocations. At the end of the period Count Cobenzl wrote Vienna in some exasperation,

As for ceremonial, I must again add that the emperor has prolonged by four days his stay at the Kremlin and multiplied so far as it has been possible the occasions for grand etiquette and representations on the throne. He has received successively in imperial dress the felicitations of the diplomatic

---

[116] Ibid.   [117] Ibid.
[118] Golovine, *Souvenirs*, 167–9; Golitsyn, 'Zapiski', *Russkii arkhiv*, 3 (1886), 143.

corps, of all the classes of the nobility, men and women, and of all the officers of the garrison as well as the guards. It is unbelievable to what degree Paul I loves great ceremonies, the importance which he attaches to them, and the time which he employs for them. The post of Grand Master for this section has become one of the most significant in the empire.[119]

Mariia was said to remark that Catherine's hand was inflamed and swollen it was kissed so often and with such enthusiasm when she was crowned, but that her own, though weary, showed no such signs. She was disappointed. Paul was as punctilious about the ceremonies as he was pleased with the results. He insisted that when a courtier knelt, his knee should be heard to hit the floor sharply (like a musket butt hitting the ground during the manual of arms) and the kiss on the hand had to be firm and well defined: no mere brushing of the lips would do. Ultimately, a new ceremony was devised to bring the long-drawn process to an end. Paul and Mariia were again seated in full regalia on their respective thrones and then were stripped, piece by piece, of their symbols of office—crown, sceptre, orb, mantle—until they were left in their everyday clothes while the signs of their power were returned to the treasury. At least one self-confessed sceptic found this ceremony curiously moving.[120]

The coronation festivities gave Paul a triumph of another sort. It was traditional on such occasions to give the people a feast with roasted meats and unlimited wine. More often than not such affairs ended in drunken brawls with serious injuries and even deaths. Paul deplored such violence, but he hated in any way to diminish the people's enjoyment or frustrate their expectations. On one of his rides through the city, he found himself surrounded by a huge crowd and thought to remind them of how badly they behaved at public festivals. The response he heard was that, on such occasions, the authorities treated the people like dogs, and they responded in kind. Paul declared that under him matters would be different. The people would be treated like human beings, with dignity and respect. Tables would be provided with regular places so the celebrants could sit down and be served. And he gave orders to that end on the spot. Tables to accommodate 60,000 people were laid on Tuesday 7/18 April. This was to be the celebratory feast. The places were filled, and though the celebrants had to sit several hours before the tsar, who was attending mass, gave the signal to commence, order and a festive air were maintained. There were no fights or riots; those for whom there was no room were turned away. Respect and liking for

[119] HHSA, Russland II Berichte, Carton 85, Cobenzl to Thugut, no. 29, apostille 9, 4 May (NS), 1797.
[120] Golovkine, *La Cour de Paul Ier*, 148.

Paul undoubtedly had something to do with the way the peace was kept. But so also did the careful organization of the affair, the provision of adequate quantities of food and drink served only when the feasters were seated and ready, and careful control over the quantity as well as the timing of the service. Squads of soldiers and police were available if needed, but they proved to be unnecessary. The coronation feast for the people of Moscow was a triumph for the tsar.[121]

The coronation ended Paul's first six months as tsar. It was a period of extraordinary activity and accomplishment. From the hour of his accession Paul moved swiftly and with determination to achieve his goals. No opposition had an opportunity to form, and he recruited a government which melded old and trusted followers with hold-overs from the previous reign. His uncertainties seemed to cease when he became tsar. He had realized his destiny, and it was only as time passed, as he had to live with the consequences of his decisions, that euphoria died, and his personal as well as his political burdens multiplied. In the beginning, however, Paul was strong, active, and engaged. He had a programme which he proceeded to legislate and a style of governing which he established. Both differed from the major emphases in Catherine's reign yet, at least initially, both fell within the boundaries of political practice as contemporaries understood it. The tolerances, however, were narrow. Paul's largest problem was to build strong, supportive alliances within governing society. This was essential if his political programme was to have any potential for influencing Russia's long-term development. It was also something that was difficult for him to understand and execute. It was apparent, for example, from the first day that his new military policies would cause serious discord; the only effective answer was to develop an officer corps with a stake in the new system which was loyal to Paul and his ideas. Though this proved to be his Achilles' heel, there was really nothing at the beginning of his reign which predicted the way it would end. Indeed, the beginning was better than most people feared it would be and, objectively speaking, it made a good start on establishing the groundwork for a viable if thoroughly paternalistic and authoritarian era. Catherine was now long gone. A new order had been established which, despite Paul's personal fate, gave characteristic shape to autocratic Russia in the nineteenth century.

[121] HHSA, Russland II Berichte, Carton 85, Cobenzl to Thugut, no. 25, 20 Apr. (NS), 1797.

8
THE BANK, THE COURT, AND THE KNIGHTS OF MALTA: 1797-1798

By the end of 1797, Paul could look back with some satisfaction on what he had accomplished. His enemies were scattered, he had firm control over the army and the state administration, and the outward traces of his mother's reign had all but disappeared. His personal life was in good order. Relations with Mariia Fedorovna were on an acceptable footing; his sons were allied with him and working at his side. Best of all, the men he had chosen to lead the government had so far proved worthy of his trust; the state's affairs were prospering. The peasant uprisings of the past winter were finished and showed no signs of breaking out again. Governmental reforms were moving steadily ahead and, while finances posed serious problems, there were plans in preparation to deal with them. Progress in the military was especially gratifying to Paul, though he was troubled by evidence of discontent in the ranks, and he resented the large number of officers' resignations. None the less, he could well believe that he had drawn Russia back from the brink of disaster, that the most dangerous moments were past, and that his reformed version of the autocracy was well launched.

There could be no doubt in anyone's mind about who was responsible for the changes that had taken place. Paul led ostentatiously; his impress was unmistakable. He made no concessions to people's feelings and sought no compromises. On the contrary, he seemed to be determined to challenge his opposition, to show himself just as he was, without adornment, and to force people to accept him. In line with his own maxim that he would rather be hated for doing what he knew to be right than loved while avoiding his responsibilities, he had moved directly into the positions he intended to occupy. And through the first years of his reign, he successfully held his ground. The contrast with Peter III's situation could hardly have been greater. Within six months of his accession, a powerful conspiracy existed which, when it needed, could mobilize the most influential groups in Russia in support. No such conspiracy confronted Paul. However uncomfortable people may have been with his style and the repressive atmosphere he created, there was no social group with sufficient coherence to act against him, his legislation gave rewards to every important segment of society, while his excesses were most deeply felt by individuals. The major difference, however, was that Paul had no rival to rally an opposition; there was no Catherine to challenge him. Alexander was far from ready to play such a role; the empress was her husband's most devoted subject; and Paul himself had succeeded in creating a government which combined people from Catherine's time with whom he could work with his own Gatchina cohort. As a result, though his initial assault on Catherine's Russia generated criticism, some of it severe, there was no base on which anyone could build serious opposition, nor was there to be for nearly three more years. Paul had begun well, even brilliantly; the problem would be to sustain the level he initiated.

The reforms introduced in April 1797 reorganized the institutions under which Russia was governed and by means of which she was protected. In the autumn of that year, Paul turned in a different direction. The government was short of money and heavily indebted to foreign lenders. The ruble was weak on the international exchange, reflecting the debasement of Russian currency values through a virtually unrestricted outpouring of paper money (assignats), while the levels of gentry indebtedness had never been higher. This last was considered a major impediment to agricultural development and a threat to the stability of the landholding class. All of these conditions were of concern to Paul. Financial problems were most immediately distressing, though the condition of the gentry was the long-term problem he considered most important. To deal with finances Paul had already ordered increased taxes and fees, but he had also accepted heavy new charges on the budget, and he needed new sources of state income. He was understandably taken, therefore, with the suggestion that the gentry's debts could be capitalized to provide a new source of state income and a plan worked out which would discharge existing foreign accounts, absorb excess assignats (thus improving the ruble's exchange value), and provide additional cash for the treasury. The long-term gain in the plan was that gentry debts could be reduced if not eliminated, while there was the potential for introducing a new spirit of thrift among Russia's financially feckless landowners. All these advantages were to be won by creating a new land bank for the nobility.[1]

Paul himself was uninformed on fiscal matters, but political economy was one of Mariia's strong interests which she shared with

[1] See McGrew, 'Politics of Absolutism' and S. Ia. Borovoi, 'Vspomogatel'nyi bank', *Istoricheskie zapiski*, 44 (1953), 206–30.

Baron Nicolay, a long-time member of the household. Mariia supported Alexis Kurakin who, as procuror-general, had overall responsibility for imperial finances, and he in turn worked closely with A. I. Vasiliev, the court treasurer. It was this group which promoted the plan for the bank. Its originator and prime mover, however, was Robert Woot, the Dutch financial agent who came to Russia representing Hope and Company of Amsterdam and London.[2] In the 1790s, Hope became the Russian government's main credit source. They also held a substantial share of the outstanding debt of the defunct Polish monarchy and had made private loans to Paul when he was grand duke. Woot's original mission in Russia was to convince Catherine that she should honour Poland's debts. He failed in this, but he met Paul and made a favourable impression. Both Kurakin and Nicolay became his friends and sponsored him with Mariia Fedorovna. Woot gained Bezborodko's support as well. When Paul became tsar, he agreed to Woot's requests and invited him to work out a plan. He did so in conjunction with Kurakin and Vasiliev; Mariia looked on approvingly. From the beginning, the Bank of Assistance for the Nobility was unequivocally linked with the empress's party.

Paul offered the bank as a solution to the deeply rooted problem of gentry indebtedness. He gave no hint that other purposes lay behind it. In the preamble to the decree, he referred to his obligation to watch over his subjects' welfare, 'to assure their tranquillity, to procure for them every means of prosperity, and to guarantee . . . good faith and harmony in their mutual engagements'. He pointed to the large number of noble families 'groaning under the weight of debts transmitted to them from generation to generation . . . or contracted through their own negligence'. These people had failed to use the imperial banks to ease their burdens, and having piled debt on debt, disordered their own and their creditors' affairs. Worse, 'unable to escape from the extremity of falling into the hands of grasping usurers, they multiply the number of those deadly blood-suckers while . . . preparing for their innocent posterity the

---

[2] Kurakin drafted the proposals but Woot was the originator. For contemporary evidence, HHSA, Russland II Berichte, Carton 87, no. 6, 29 Jan. (NS) 1798, Viazzoli memo: 'It is Voute [sic] who has furnished the plan for the afore-mentioned bank.' See also ibid., Dietrichstein to Thugut, apostille 1, 1 Feb. (NS) 1798, remarking on Woot's role in revising the original statute, and Carton 88, no. 11, 27 Feb. (NS) 1798. See also Storch, *Cours d'économie politique*, iv. 35, where Woot is identified as the author, though not by name, and S. R. Vorontsov to A. R. Vorontsov, 4/15 Mar. 1799, *Arkhiv kniazia Vorontsova*, x. 41–2. Borovoi, 'Vspomogatel'nyi bank', 211, stresses Kurakin's role in underlining his point that the bank favoured the great landholders.

melancholy prospect of falling into poverty'. The bank would remedy these ills. The nobility, Paul hoped, would recognize 'our determination to save them and their descendants from the dangers menacing them', and would make good use of the means offered so as to 'recover its properties from the hands of avid usurers', pay its debts, and once it has 're-established its name in honour', to expand its economy in all its forms, and, above all, 'curtailing in its dwellings the superfluous expenses that are the consequence of the imagined needs of Luxury', to commit itself to moderation in its life while transmitting to 'its most distant posterity' the fruits collected in the present reign.[3]

The problem Paul addressed was real and of long standing. The conventional wisdom (which he accepted) was that the gentry was deeply in debt because it lacked discipline in its daily life and had given itself up to the pursuit of luxury and soft living without regard for cost. There was a sliver of truth in these convictions, though, in fact, as an explanation for gentry indebtedness, they were grossly over-simplified. The domainal economy, on which the gentry landowners were dependent, was surprisingly effective in maintaining subsistence, but it generated little surplus. It was a conservative economy dominated by a risk-averse peasant culture which the gentry, though often educated to other values, accepted perforce. The result was a relatively secure economy but one which yielded small disposable incomes. For a few great landholders with tens of thousands of serfs (a tiny fraction of the gentry class) the domainal economy produced real wealth, though even this was hardly sufficient to support the opulent style of living such lords aspired to, while for the great majority, low income levels left a difficult choice: the *dvorianin* could live like a peasant, or he could borrow to make up the difference between his returns and the costs of the way he wanted to live. The gentry went both ways, though a large enough proportion chose indebtedness for this to become a major feature in Russian economic life.[4]

The eighteenth-century economy was expanding and expensive. Cultural westernization created a growing demand for imported

[3] *PSZ*, series 1, vol. 24, no. 18274. Cf. *Manifeste de la banque d'hypothèque établie pour la noblesse* (St Petersburg, 1798). See also *PSZ*, series 1, vol. 25, no. 18383. Cf. *Réglemente de la banque impériale d'hypothèque établie pour la noblesse* (St Petersburg, 1798). The French versions circulated in Petersburg and were found filed with the Whitworth correspondence in the Public Record Office, London (Kew).

[4] For gentry credit problems and government responses: Blum, *Lord and Peasant*, 379–84; Confino, *Domaines et seigneurs*, 136–83; Borovoi, 'Vspomogatel'nyi bank', 207–10.

products and a broadening range of consumer goods, while inflationary monetary policies, themselves a response to international economic changes and the heavy demands of war, conspired to increase the noble's need for money. The state, rather than permitting private money-lenders to fatten at the nobles' expense, began early in the century to provide inexpensive credit. In 1729, a *Monetnaia kontora* or monetary bureau had been set up to help nobles redeem pledges they had made to pawnbrokers, and four years later, it was authorized to make loans secured by jewellery, gold, or silver. The first bank for nobles was organized in 1754 with a capital of 750,000 rubles, a figure which ballooned over the next thirty years to six million rubles without beginning to satisfy the demand. A government loan bank absorbed the nobles' bank in 1786, adding another five million rubles in capital, while between 1769 and 1785 a variety of institutions from the assignat bank to foundling homes and the charity boards of provincial governments were given the right to lend their idle funds to the gentry. The provincial noble assemblies created in 1785 were also permitted to set up banks for the local nobility. Despite the shortage of capital in the Russian economy, the interest rates in all these public institutions remained throughout the century a modest 6 to 8 per cent, whereas private rates ran three or four times as high. The banks subsidized the nobility's spending, and the nobility borrowed to the limits of the capital available. By 1792, the government loan bank had twenty-two million rubles in outstanding loans, and the level of private indebtedness could only be guessed. Repayment was slow, new loans were made to cover old debts, thereby increasing the demand for credit, and the mass of indebtedness grew steadily.[5]

The Bank of Assistance for the Nobility fitted into the tradition of providing the nobility with credit assistance, thus preserving the symbiotic relationship between the gentry, who received their lands and peasants from the ruler in return for service to him as the autocrat. But Paul intended to go further than his predecessors. He not only provided credit, he clearly intended this credit to be used to reduce indebtedness, to force landowners to practise thrift and orderly financial management, and to bring their spending into line with their incomes. In the event of the failure of these efforts, the current generation of noble landowners could be punished by having their properties sequestered and the whole of the income from those lands devoted to debt reduction. The next generation would be

[5] McGrew, 'Politics of Absolutism', 106. For an interesting contemporary comment on the bank and credit problem, PRO, FO/65/28, Whitworth to Grenville, no. 43, 10 Aug. (NS) 1794.

protected since the sequestered lands would remain the owners' property to be restored to full possession or inherited once the debt against them was discharged. Nor was it to be left to the indebted landowner to decide if he would take a loan. Even private creditors could force him to borrow to clear up his debts, while loans to cover indebtedness to state institutions were virtually automatic. The gentry, profligate and self-indulgent for seventy-five years, were now to be called to account, forced to put their financial houses into order, and made to be thrifty, savings-minded, and sober in their lives.[6]

Woot's basic plan was a scheme for massive debt consolidation. There was no upper limit on the amount of money it could advance. Originally Alexis Kurakin suggested one hundred million rubles for the bank's capital. Even that enormous sum was considered inadequate, however, and the bank's creators left it that it would be open for two years during which time loans would be made in the amount of collateral presented to it. The ceiling, in fact, was no ceiling.[7] Loans were made in a special scrip which could only be used to pay debts. Creditors had to accept the scrip, though in fact, they could not spend it.[8] Apparently it was assumed that creditors would hold the scrip to maturity, collecting the 5 per cent interest which it paid. Acceptable though this may have been to institutional creditors, the merchant community raised such a storm that two days after the plan was announced this provision was changed.[9] People who had to accept the scrip were allowed to exchange it for assignats. But even this was not wholly satisfactory. The scrip was considered an inferior tender and was discounted 25 per cent on emission. Creditors, however, still had to accept it at face value in discharge of debt. Especially for private creditors, the bank meant a forced settlement of what was owed them at a 25 per cent discount. Predictably they continued to complain.[10]

Paul apparently believed that, though his primary target was the gentry, the bank would be a benefit for private persons victimized by

[6] Borovoi, 'Vspomogatel'nyi bank', emphasizes the contribution the bank made to the gentry's well-being. My point is that the intention of the bank was to discipline the gentry, and that this intention failed owing to changes in the bank plan. Borovoi's point on Kurakin's influence, especially on the administrative rules, is well taken.

[7] Borovoi, 'Vspomogatel'nyi bank', 212; ukaz, art. 39, *PSZ*, series 1, vol. 24, no. 18274 (hereafter, *Ukaz*).

[8] *Ukaz*, article 28.

[9] *Ukaz*, preamble; art. 29; McGrew, 'Politics of Absolutism', 110.

[10] McGrew, 'Politics of Absolutism', 115–16; Storch, *Cours d'économie politique*, vi. 35–41.

the nobility's financial irresponsibility. When the merchants complained, he moved swiftly to solve the problem. Having done so, however, he insisted that creditors had been protected and specifically warned debt-holders against dunning their noble clients. They were to be quiet and peaceable, secure in the knowledge that their tsar had come to their rescue. If they were not, and persisted in agitating for what they were owed, they would be declared 'blood-sucking usurers', their claims would be forfeit, and they would face punishment under the usury laws.[11] Paul intended to reinforce the sanctity of contracts, a fundamental necessity for the economic development of any modern society. Yet he treated the interests of merchants and artisans cavalierly, and he made it abundantly clear that while the nobility required disciplining, they should be protected as well. Possibly his own experiences of being always short of money and embarrassed by his debts underlay his warnings against harassing those who owed; more likely it showed his deep preference for a tranquil, ordered society. Certainly he had little sympathy for aggressive capitalists, though he accepted the need to encourage conditions in which capitalism could flourish and the economy could grow.

The heart of the bank proposal concerned the gentry. The bank had the power to make forced loans which were secured by specifically identified parcels of land. The value of the land was set according to its productivity. The scale of measurement was arbitrary. The empire was divided into four classes of land. The unit of measure was the male serf whose work was valued at 40, 50, 65, and 75 rubles moving from class four to class one. A class one estate of 500 serfs thus had a mortgage value of 37,500 rubles. The average *obrok* (quitrent) paid by Russian serfs at the end of the eighteenth century has been estimated at between 5 and 6 rubles. Interestingly enough, at the time the bank was legislated, another decree using the same quadripartite division of the empire set *obrok* for state peasants at 3½, 4, 4½, and 5 rubles. The figure was last established in 1783 at a flat 3 rubles.[12]

---

[11] *Ukaz*, art. 37 and 39; McGrew, 'Politics of Absolutism', 113–14.

[12] McGrew, 'Politics of Absolutism', 110–11. The classes are given in app. B to the *Ukaz*. Borovoi, 'Vspomogatel'nyi bank', 221, provides tables on the number of peasants pledged from each guberniia. Average *obrok* is an inexact concept. Semevskii suggested 5 rubles as the average yearly quit-rent at the end of Catherine's reign, but he also noted that *obrok* was rising. Semevskii, *Krestianskii vopros*, 52–3 and app. 9, pp. 593–5. Borovoi cites Semevskii's data for the 6 ruble figure. 'Vspomogatel'nyi bank', 215. Paul increased *obrok* for state peasants. *PSZ*, series 1, vol. 24, no. 1827, 18 Dec. (OS) 1797. See Klochkov, *Pravitel'stvennoi deiatel'nosti*, 518.

The enormous disparity between the rent which noble landlords would receive and the value which the crown assigned their lands meant forced loans which would absorb most of the rental income which even the best class of holding produced. The 37,500 ruble mortgage mentioned above would carry an 8 per cent (later 6 per cent) initiation fee which would be deducted at the time the loan was made, though the 6 per cent interest was calculated against the total amount of the loan. In the first five years, the annual cost in interest would be 2,250 rubles. Principal reductions were to begin in the sixth year at 20 rubles per thousand, rising by fives to 80 rubles per thousand in the last year of the loan.[13] Assuming a high average *obrok*, the landowner would take in just 3,000 rubles per year. Interest alone would absorb virtually the whole of that amount. And when principal reductions began, the total bill would be over three times the *obrok* income. Even if the *obrok* paid was double the average, there would be no way for a landholder to meet his obligation; a forced loan at this level would make confiscation almost inevitable. Small wonder that the plan was greeted with dismay.[14]

The loans were not intended to be voluntary. Moreover, there is no indication at any point in any of the bank decrees that the issue of ability to pay was ever raised. The provisions for validating collateral involved no more than determining if the land existed where it was stated to be, if it did in fact belong to the person applying, and whether there was already debt attached to it. There was no provision for reviewing the debtor's financial status. The land was enough to justify the loan. Loans made against factories were no different. Valuation depended on previous production, but ability to meet repayment schedules was not included in the evaluation process.[15] The law was intended to reschedule existing indebtedness and force its discharge. Those persons most deeply in debt faced the certainty that their holdings would be sequestered and managed by the bank.

---

[13] *PSZ*, series 1, vol. 24, no. 18274, art. 11, p. 825 and app. G, p. 831.
[14] Public reactions to Paul's bank proposals were reported in detail. Gentry fear of dispossession was especially strong. See: HHSA, Russland II Berichte, Carton 87, Dietrichstein to Thugut, no. 1, 22 Dec. 1797/2 Jan. 1798 and annex; no. 3, 29 Dec. 1797/9 Jan. 1798; no. 5, apostille 1, 29 Jan. (NS) 1798. See also memo of consul general for economic affairs, Viazzoli, 29 Jan. (NS) 1798, in Dietrichstein, no. 6, same date. Cf. PRO, FO/65/38, Whitworth to Grenville, no. 64, 14 Dec. (NS) 1797 and FO/65/39, Whitworth to Grenville, no. 68, 9 Jan. (NS) 1798.
[15] *PSZ*, series 1, vol. 24, no. 10274, art. 31 and vol. 25, no. 18383 (*Réglemente*), cover procedures.

There was little mercy for defaulters. A borrower in default had just ten days before substantial penalties were assessed. An additional 1 per cent of the outstanding loan balance was to be levied for the first month in arrears. A further 2 per cent was added for the second month, and another 3 per cent for the third. At the end of three months, if default continued, the bank could apply to the provincial assembly in the guberniia where the land was located to have the property taken over and managed to satisfy the debt. Until twenty-five years passed, or the debt was satisfied, the bank retained control. The owner received no income from the property, and was not even permitted to visit it. Once the debt was satisfied, however, the owner or his heirs resumed possession of the land.[16]

So savage were the provisions of this plan that it is tempting to see a further motive behind it. An indebted noble confronting a forced loan which would absorb the whole of his income and claim his land until his debt was satisfied did have some options. He could sell his land to pay his debts, and many appear to have done just that prior to the plan's formal announcement. New loans from private sources were another alternative, though it was not easy to find such money, and if it was to be found, it would be extremely expensive.[17] The third and most intriguing possibility was for nobles receiving *obrok* to shift to labour dues (*barshchina*) and undertake to develop a more productive agriculture. Obviously Paul and his advisers thought there was far more value in the land than the rental system yielded. They were also biased towards the *barshchina* relationship precisely because it emphasized production on the land and did not encourage peasants to enter other occupations. The bank plan provided a five-year period when only interest was assessed, a time which would permit the gentry to reorganize their operations before the full weight of the repayment schedule fell on them. Paul said that he expected the nobility to use this opportunity to improve their domestic economy, and it may well have been that the bank was the rod which he hoped would beat them into better and more profitable ways. But if that were the case, the intention remained a secret one. There is no evidence, apart from extending a close reading of the bank decrees, to support the position, though coercing the gentry to find ways to realize a better return from lands would be entirely consistent with Paul's thinking. Practically speaking, if any such intent were there, the structure of the plan worked against it. This was a proposal to

[16] *Ukaz*, arts. 30 and 31.
[17] Dietrichstein reported in detail on the scramble for alternatives. HHSA, Russland II Berichte, Carton 87, Dietrichstein to Thugut, no. 6, apostille 1, 29 Jan. (NS) 1798.

reduce existing debt; there was no provision for new money to foster agricultural innovations. Even so, had the plan worked, bringing the gentry's personal debt to a lower level would have been a desirable first step towards further development in agriculture. Though Paul never claimed that he was using the bank to reshape the domainal economy, the plan had an interesting potential for that purpose.

The merchants' outcry, which forced a shift to free convertibility of bank scrip when the plan was first announced, led to further changes, all of which were summarized in a supplementary revision to the original decree.[18] The revised plan was easier to use and resolved some outstanding problems. Apart from free convertibility, the initiation fee was reduced by 2 per cent (administrative costs were lower than expected), borrowers were allowed to pay their interest entirely in bank scrip, and the interest due was calculated from the date the loan was made rather than from 1 March, the date the bank opened. These, however, were minor adjustments. Free convertibility was the most important change and it created a very serious problem. Since the bank's founders had put no upper limit on the amount of scrip that could be issued or exchanged, with free convertibility, issuing scrip was the same as issuing new assignats. The practical effect was to offset all Paul's efforts to reduce the amount of paper money in circulation. Between March 1798 and October 1799, Russian landholders pledged 708,050 serfs to receive nearly forty-one million rubles in scrip. Over half this amount was exchanged immediately for assignats, and by 1802, when the bank was reorganized, only three million rubles still remained in scrip. The bank had increased the number of assignats in circulation by some thirty-eight million rubles in just eighteen months. Inevitably, the paper ruble dropped in value, losing a further fifteen silver kopecks (from $79\frac{1}{3}$ to $64\frac{1}{3}$) while prices continued to rise.[19]

The bank's results, at first glance, seem wholly negative. It not only contributed to weakening the currency, but as a method for debt consolidation it was a flat failure. During its life, the total volume of gentry debt actually increased. Despite the tens of millions of rubles loaned, every other lending agency in Russia showed a significant increase in the amount of debt outstanding, while budget books for

[18] See *PSZ*, series 1, vol. 25, no. 18718, 25 Oct. (OS) 1798. The criticism and revision were discussed in HHSA, Russland II Berichte, Carton 88, Dietrichstein to Thugut, no. 1, 1 Feb. (NS) 1798; no. 12, 2 Mar. (NS) 1798. The report on the revised plan is no. 61, 14 Nov. (NS) 1798, and contains a published copy of the manifesto of 25 Oct. (OS) 1798, which revised the plan.
[19] Borovoi, 'Vspomogatel'nyi bank', 224 ff.; E. Amburger, *Geschichte der Behördenorganisation Russlands von Peter dem Grossen bis 1917* (Leiden, 1966), 212.

individual families reveal a sharp upward swing in personal obligations.[20] The plan neither regularized the gentry's finances nor offered the moral gain Paul hoped for. This point is important. The bank reflected Paul's deep ambivalence about the Russian nobility. The society he envisioned assumed a committed, loyal aristocracy which served. The nobility he saw in Russia was self-indulgent, egoistic, corrupt, and untrustworthy. How to discipline it to improve its character was an underlying theme in much that he did. The bank was to contribute by forcing the aristocracy to give up debilitating luxuries, to pay attention to their estates, to pay their debts, and to spend no more than their incomes warranted. The benefit in all this was the moral improvement which the whole society would enjoy. This, however, did not happen. What did happen was that the gentry were forced to pay what amounted to an undeclared tax on their indebtedness. This was not announced, but it was intended since that is the way the plan was constructed. Given Paul's perspective and the treasury's needs, forcing the nobility to pay such a tax was obviously appealing; that the ultimate price would be a further adulteration of the currency was something he was unable, or unwilling, to foresee.

The bank's operating principles were both sophisticated and cynical. The initiation fee covered all costs; no appropriations from state funds were necessary. More significantly, previous banks (and indeed most lending institutions) made loans from already existing funds. The nobles' bank relied on neither existing nor anticipated receipts; there was no capital pool of any sort. Debtors paid the bank as if it had advanced them money under an agreement secured by their lands. What actually happened, however, was that debtors received a sum of money which they were obligated to repay in twenty unequal instalments together with interest for twenty-five years. But there had been, in fact, no loan of principal; there was only scrip issued against the stated value of the landowner's holdings. If the original version of the bank had held, and the bank scrip had remained limited to the discharge of debt with circulating currency used to pay debt interest, the plan probably would have avoided the explosive rise in paper money it generated since the nobility's creditors would have provided the value which the scrip represented.[21] This, however, was wholly unacceptable to the merchant community.

[20] Borovoi, 'Vspomogatel'nyi bank', 217–27.

[21] This position was commonly accepted in the empress's circle and was asserted by Baron Nicolay in defence of Woot. Nicolay claimed that the revised plan was the opposite of what Woot recommended and this drove the exchange down. Nicolay to Alexander Romanovich [Vorontsov], 19 Sept. (os) 1798, *Arkhiv kniazia Vorontsova*, xxii. 79.

With free convertibility, the state became the source of value which the loans required by issuing additional paper money. This was obviously undesirable, but there was some offsetting gain. The bank substantially increased the treasury's income. An estimated three million rubles were collected on loan premiums. Every piece of scrip the bank accepted in discharge of obligations carried the 5 per cent interest payment for which the borrower was liable and which would continue for twenty-five years. There were also fees and profits from discount and exchange functions. During the eighteen months it was open, these sources brought in between ten and fifteen million rubles before loan interest and return of principal had even begun. Paul and his advisers had found a new and relatively easy way to increase government receipts without having recourse to a direct tax on gentry land. In the end, though gentry debt spiralled and the currency suffered, the treasury gained.[22] This was undoubtedly intended, though the price was very high. What was not intended was that the bank would become a windfall for the richest landed proprietors. Yet that too happened. Alexis Kurakin, his brother, and a few great landlords like them, used the bank as a source for ready money. The ploy was to mortgage lands which they wanted to retain but whose income they were willing to forgo. They received the inflated amounts allowed under the bank's mortgage schedule, and then made no effort to repay the loan. The worst that could happen was that they would not receive their rents; since they already had a cash advance far in excess of what they gave up, the problem was hardly pressing.[23]

Paul knew that the plan was being abused. When he revised the operational code in the fall of 1799, he included a sharp warning to those people who were exploiting the bank for their own purposes. But he did nothing further about it. Rules for the bank's administration had been worked out in such detail that even the placement of chairs and the demeanour expected of an applicant were stipulated, but apart from demonstrating a compulsive interest in administrative details, these regulations were of little importance. On the other hand, substantive decisions on validating properties as securities, sequestering defaulters' lands, or granting petitions for forced loans were passed on to the provincial assemblies in the territories where those lands were located. This meant that it was the gentry

[22] McGrew, 'Politics of Absolutism', 116–18 and 124 n. 46. Borovoi, 'Vspomogatel'nyi bank', 218 ff., provides information on who received loans, the amounts involved, and the repayments.

[23] Borovoi's point, that the nobility gained handsomely from the plan, is correct. This was not, however, the intent. Cf. Golovkine, *La Cour de Paul Ier*, 159.

themselves rather than state bureaucrats who made decisions about the way the bank would be applied, turning the regulatory decree into an empty exercise in legal formalism.[24]

The bank of assistance became a major scandal. Woot, in particular, was roughly handled. Count S. R. Vorontsov considered him an unscrupulous rascal and 'archswindler'. Count Dietrichstein, an influential member of the Austrian delegation, despised him. It was Dietrichstein who reported a conversation at the British minister's residence in which Woot, preening in front of a company of Dutch and English merchants, asserted that Russia was a veritable Peru inhabited by apes and that any merchant who had only doubled or tripled his capital over fifteen years must be a regular imbecile. Nor did he hide what his own intentions were. When asked why he organized the bank the way he did, he replied that it offered the only hope his employers had for recovering their loans to Russia. The bank was created to pay off Hope and Company.[25] The Swedish minister, Curt von Stedingk, who went out of his way to warn his government against Woot's schemes, reported that the link between Hope and the bank of assistance was an agreement to consolidate Poland's debts into a single loan of 88,330,000 Dutch florins. The bank would generate the funds to meet this obligation at the expense of Russian merchants and gentry. Woot himself was said to have prospered extravagantly from the arrangements which he made. His fee for establishing the bank was reputed to have been one million rubles, and before the bank opened, he was buying outstanding gentry loans at discount to collect in full when the bank was ready for business.[26] On every side, it appeared that Paul's new bank existed to serve special interests, particularly Woot's and the firm he represented. When Viazzoli, the Austrian consul-general for economic affairs, was offered an appointment as court banker, he flatly refused. His work would have been with the bank of assistance, an institution which he described as patently fraudulent, and one no honest man would dare to put his name to. Such an appointment

---

[24] For the regulatory aspect, *PSZ*, series 1, vol. 25, no. 18383 (*Réglemente*) and Borovoi, 'Vspomogatel'nyi bank', 217–27.

[25] HHSA, Russland II Berichte, Carton 87, Dietrichstein to Thugut, no. 6, apostille 1, 29 Jan. (NS) 1798; Carton 88, no. 7, 1 Feb. (NS) 1798. S. R. Vorontsov to A. R. Vorontsov, no. 58, Dec. 1802, *Arkhiv kniazia Vorontsova*, viii. 185; HHSA, Russland II Berichte, Carton 87, no. 41, 18 Apr. (OS) 1798, pp. 206–7.

[26] Riksarkivet, Diplomatica Moscovitica, vol. 459, Stedingk to the king, apostille, 19/30 Mar. 1798, provides details on Woot's activities. None of this information appears in Borovoi. The Hope archives, which would be invaluable, are not available.

could only be an invitation to serious trouble.[27] Charles Whitworth summed up the position when he remarked that Paul's officials working on finances 'alarm the Publick ... by Establishments equally subversive of publick Credit as that of Individuals, for the relief of whom they are pretended to be instituted', and he concluded cuttingly that if only Paul were as willing to combat 'the common Enemy' as he was to challenge his own subjects, 'the Fate of Europe might be yet redeemed'.[28]

The bank was Paul's only attempt at a comprehensive solution to fiscal and economic problems, though individual legislative acts showed that he took his obligations to improve conditions in the empire seriously. One of his most fruitful moves was to approve an extensive canal-building project in the north of Russia and to appropriate the funds for the first link. Mariia contributed money from her personal fortune towards continuing construction during the war year of 1799, and the plan was taken over by Alexander I and completed by 1810. The resulting system was one of the most elaborate in the world and contributed strongly to the economic vitality of the Russian north. Indeed, so successful was it that in the early nineteenth century it made railroad development quite unnecessary.[29] Paul also renewed the policy of building government grain storage facilities to be filled against future dearth, ordered clarification of bankruptcy procedures, reduced the price of salt, renegotiated tariff agreements with England, and forbade the sale of peasants in Little Russia separate from the land.[30] Not everything of this sort that was attempted was successful—the granaries were built and then ignored—but Paul's legislative record bore out his announced determination to pay attention to his people's prosperity and to protect the helpless against the powerful. His most important attempt to affect the way society functioned went wildly awry, however, and it is difficult to discern any clear economic policy in the legislation passed. This owed in part to the growing importance of foreign policy issues in 1797 and 1798.

[27] HHSA, Russland II Berichte, Carton 87, Viazzoli memo in Dietrichstein to Thugut, no. 6, 29 Jan. (NS) 1798. See also Count P. V. Zavadovskii, no. 122, 23 Dec. (OS) 1797, *Arkhiv kniazia Vorontsova*, xii. 190.
[28] PRO, FO/65/39, no. 68, 9 Jan. (NS) 1798.
[29] See R. E. Jones, 'Getting the Goods to St. Petersburg', *Slavic Review*, 43/3 (Fall 1984), 431–2. Cf. Karl Blum, *Ein russischer Staatsmann* [Sievers], iv, bk. 12, pp. 418–21 and *passim*.
[30] See Klochkov, *Pravitel'stvennoi deiatel'nosti*, 481–569, for Paul's social policies. For a summary, de Grunwald, *L'Assassinat*, 109–12. The decree against selling peasants in Russia without land was promulgated on 16 Oct. (OS) 1798. See Klochkov, pp. 524–5.

Though Paul clung to a neutralist or non-aligned stance officially, his deep antagonism toward the revolution, and his dismay when peace negotiations failed to contain French aggression, led him towards an increasingly activist position in the months following his coronation. In autumn 1797, he renewed the recruitment cancelled on his accession, and by 1798 he was working openly for an alliance with Austria, England, the Neapolitan Bourbons, and the Ottoman Turks.[31] He also invited *émigrés*, displaced in the recent hostilities, to find refuge in Russia; installed the future Louis XVIII with a subsidy at Mittau; accepted the *émigré* army which the prince de Condé led; and gave a handsome settlement to the small Polish priory of the knights of Malta whose lands had come to Russia in the partitions. Of these latter moves, those concerning the knights of Malta were the most significant both for what they revealed about Paul and for their bearing on the political crisis which attended the second coalition and the war with France.[32]

On Sunday 29 November/10 December 1797 a special delegation from the knights of St John of Jerusalem, the knights of Malta, made its ceremonial entrance into St Petersburg. The party came to express the order's gratitude for the settlement Paul had offered them the previous year and to name him protector of the order, a dignity he would share with the German (holy Roman) emperor, and the king of the two Sicilies. This was a gala occasion rich in the formal ceremonies Paul loved. The entire Russian court led by the imperial family received the knightly emissaries, and after Paul was invested with his new dignity—dressed for the occasion in the costume of the order—the grand cross of Malta was bestowed on Mariia, while Paul himself knighted the grand dukes Alexander and Constantine. The chevalier Maisonneuve, annalist for the knights in Russia, described the scene, hailing it as a return to the golden days of Henry IV and Charles V when the first gentlemen of every realm were knights of

---

[31] Paul's foreign policy will be discussed in detail in Ch. 9.

[32] See McGrew, 'Paul I and the Knights'. Saul, *Russia and the Mediterranean*, places the issue in its political context. Comte Michel de Pierredon, *Histoire politique de l'ordre souverain de Jérusalem (Ordre de Malte) de 1789 à 1955*, 2 vols. (Paris, 1956), i, chs. 3–10, pp. 23–218, is generally reliable on the order's political history and contains an excellent selection of documents for Paul's period. The best material on relations between Russia and the Vatican, fundamental for the Malta problem, are the *Nonciatures de Russie*, ed. Rouët de Journel. His introductions to the documents are fine historical studies; the documents themselves are the best published sources available on Russo-papal relations in 1797–1803 and include data of the first importance for understanding Paul's interest in and relations with the knights of Malta.

Malta. Paul was delighted to keep such company, and he willingly gave the needs of the Russian priory his close personal attention.[33]

Paul had been fascinated with the knights of Malta since his early years. Catherine gave him the abbé Vertot's monumental history of the order when he was 10. It was among his favourite books, and he continued to study the order's traditions and institutions into adulthood. He had the knights' seal put up over the door of the estate hospital at Gatchina, and Maisonnueve himself praised his knowledge of the order and its rules.[34] There were also long-standing political connections between the knights and Russia. Diplomatic relations in much of the eighteenth century had been generally good, and Malta played a part in westernizing Russia's naval forces. Beginning in 1698, and continuing until 1767, Russian naval cadets took training at La Valletta, so that when Sweden attacked Russia in 1788, it was natural for Catherine to request an officer from Malta to assist the Russian fleet. The order sent Count Giulio Litta.

When Paul and Mariia had visited Italy in 1782, they were entertained by the Litta family in Milan. When Giulio was dispatched to Petersburg in 1788, he sought Paul out and was warmly welcomed. Litta gained an excellent record in the war and because of his knowledge of Russia and its court, he was returned to Petersburg in 1796 to negotiate with Catherine over the knights' lands in Poland. Paul was prepared to extend to Litta a welcoming

---

[33] McGrew, 'Paul I and the Knights', 50; Chevalier Joseph de Maisonnueve, *Annales historiques de l'ordre de St. Jean de Jérusalem depuis l'année 1725 jusqu'au moment présent* (St Petersburg, 1799), 94–105. Maisonnueve was Louis XVI's chamberlain and was appointed minister plenipotentiary for the knights of Malta in Berlin and Warsaw. In Paul's reign, he was the order's chargé d'affaires in St Petersburg. His *Annales historiques* were published by the imperial press and may be considered official. Stedingk also reported the ceremonies and commented on their importance: Riksarkivet, Diplomatica Moscovitica, vol. 458, Stedingk to the king, St Petersburg, 10/21 Nov., 18/29 Nov., 27 Nov./8 Dec., and 4/15 Dec. 1797. Charles Whitworth thought such displays wasted everyone's time and showed a notable weakness in Paul: PRO, FO/65/38, Whitworth to Grenville, no. 64, St Petersburg, 14 Dec. (NS) 1797.

[34] McGrew, 'Paul I and the Knights', 45; Shumigorskii, *Pavel I*, 17–18, 107; Kobeko, *Pawel Petrowitsch*, 133–4; Zubow, *Paul der Erste*, 24–5. The history was l'abbé de Vertot, *Histoire des chevaliers hospitaliers de S. Jean de Jérusalem, appellés depuis chevaliers de Rhodes, et aujourd'hui chevaliers de Malthe*. The 1st edn. was published in Paris in 1726. Paul's version was probably the 4th (1755) in 13 bks. of narration to 1568, with a chronological summary in one bk. from 1568–1725, and a 15th book giving the knights' governing institutions and political procedures. The history is political and military, pointedly excluding supernatural or miraculous events. The work went through 14 edns., the last in 1853. Maisonnueve, *Annales historiques*, 44–5, asserted Paul's knowledge of the history and institutions of the order.

hand, but Catherine was otherwise inclined. The knights, to protect their interests in France (unsuccessfully as it happened), had sent a representative to wait on the revolutionary government. Catherine considered this act tantamount to recognizing the republic and refused to hear Litta's case. She treated his brother, Lorenzo, who was papal nuncio and archbishop of Thebes, even more harshly. He had come to negotiate the status and treatment of Russia's Roman Catholic subjects. Catherine allowed him to approach no nearer than Warsaw.[35]

When Catherine died, Paul made amends. He informed Count Litta through Kurakin on the day after Catherine's death that he would arrange the knights' affairs in Poland very much to their advantage, and he invited Lorenzo Litta to Moscow for the coronation. Afterwards, he was to come to Petersburg to begin formal talks. At a time when everyone was working feverishly on reforms, both Paul and his first minister found time for the problems of the Polish priory. Kurakin, though apologetic for the delay, was able to outline a basic plan when he talked with Litta on 19/30 December, and a convention was completed and signed on 4/15 January 1797.[36] Litta had been instructed to agree to nothing which might compromise the order's constitution or embarrass the knights politically. He claimed to have fulfilled that part of his instructions, asserting that the agreement he had been offered was exemplary and should show other Christian monarchs 'how worthy it is for them to support our existence and our splendour, and how much it is to their interest to assure by our conservation the preservation of all the Nobility of Europe which is, and which will always be, the best support for thrones and monarchies'.[37]

[35] McGrew, 'Paul I and the Knights', 45–7. See A. A. Aliab'ev, 'Snosheniia Rossi s Mal'tiiskim Ordenom do 1789 g.', *Sbornik Moskovskago glavnago arkhiva ministerstva inostrannykh del*, 5 (1893), 175–218; Giuseppi Greppi, *Un gentiluomo milanese guerriero-diplomatico, 1763–1839: Appunti biografici sul Bali Conte Giulio Litta-Visconti Arese* (Milan, 1896), esp. chs. 2 and 3; Litta, 'Depeshi grafa Litty, poslannika Mal'tiiskago ordena v Peterburge, pisannyi v kontse 1796 i nachale 1797 goda', ed. A. F. Buchkov, *SIRIO* 2 (1868), 175–218 and introductory essay, 164–75. See also Pierredon, *Histoire politique*, i. 1–67; Journel, *Litta*, esp. pp. vi–viii.

[36] 'Depeshi Litty', no. 51, 6/17 Nov. 1796, p. 188; nos. 56 and 57, 2/13 and 12/23 Dec. 1796, pp. 190–2; no. 59, 19/30 Dec. 1796, pp. 199–206. Greppi, *Giulio Litta*, 94–6; Journel, *Litta*, pp. vii–xii, xxvi–xxviii; 'Convention entre Sa Majesté Impériale de toutes les Russies et l'Ordre Souverain de Malte et Son Altesse Eminentissime Monseigneur le Grand Maître', Maisonnueve, *Annales historiques*, 48–71; *PSZ*, series 1, vol. 24, no. 17708, 4 Jan. (OS) 1797.

[37] 'Depeshi Litty', no. 61, 7/18 Jan. 1797, pp. 209–37; Greppi, *Giulio Litta*, 98–9. Greppi underlines the point that the agreement conformed to the order's rules; he

Certainly what Paul offered was rich, especially in light of Russia's difficult financial situation. He agreed to accept all past dues owed by the Polish priory to the treasury at Malta as legitimate claims on the imperial purse and set up the machinery to pay them. He proposed to move the Polish grand priory to Petersburg and enlarge it from six to ten commanderies. He pledged himself personally to oversee and protect the new foundation, and he outlined an annual budget for the priory which he guaranteed to the amount of 300,000 Polish florins (90,000 rubles). The priory was to be renamed the grand priory of Russia, but only the tsar's Roman Catholic subjects were eligible to enter and serve in it. Paul had insisted that no one of the ten commanderies could be held by other than a subject of the tsar; he then proposed to the grand master that the first commandery go to Count Giulio Litta.[38]

Paul initiated this settlement and laid down the conditions; Litta had only to receive it. The agreement provided the clearest possible evidence of Paul's commitment to support the order; it also demonstrated that Russia now was on equal terms with all other European monarchies. As Litta wrote, 'it was the intention of His Majesty, the Emperor, that the Order of Malta be established here in such a way as to accord to it in Russia the same lustre and consideration it enjoys on the lands of other powers'.[39] Indeed, Paul's ambition for the Russian priory went further than even Litta could approve. The tsar declared his hopes that a Russian *langue* could be created. He rejected as beneath Russia's dignity Litta's suggestion that the Russian priory should be affiliated with the catch-all Anglo-Bavarian *langue*. This question, which involved complex legal and constitutional issues, was left open for later discussions.[40] On the constitutional side, however, Paul pledged himself to protect the religious freedom of the Catholic knights and to observe the order's traditions, constitution, and regulations. These phrases were intended to allay the fears of traditionalists at La Valletta and in Rome who were sceptical about the status of their order in a non-Catholic

also noted that the order could reject the convention if there was a conflict with the constitution. Journel, *Litta*, pp. vii–xii, xxvi–xxviii, thought the 'flood of gold' Paul poured over the knights was corrupting and a factor in the Littas' ultimate failure.

[38] 'Convention', *passim*; 'Depeshi Litty', no. 61, *passim*. McGrew, 'Paul I and the Knights', 48–9.

[39] 'Depeshi Litty', no. 61, 7/18 Jan. 1797, pp. 219–21; Greppi, *Giulio Litta*, 100.

[40] A *langue* or 'tongue' was the largest regional grouping in the knights' organizational structure. There were 8 *langues* at the time of the French revolution. Priories and commanderies were subordinate to *langues*, with commanderies being divisions of priories. Paul sought a more elevated position for the Russian priory by suggesting that it become a *langue*.

country and under the protection of a ruler who headed both the Russian state and the Russian Orthodox church.[41]

Litta knew Paul well. He urged the grand master to accept the agreement and to see to its swift ratification without quibble or qualification. Everything that had been won could be lost were the order not to act expeditiously. Moreover, the tsar should be rewarded for his benevolence. Litta suggested that an appropriate gift would be an ancient cross of Malta, preferably one that had belonged to one of the order's great grand masters such as de l'Isle-Adam, la Vallette, or d'Aubusson. A gift of that sort would particularly appeal to a man of Paul's sensibilities, and while there might be problems in actually finding such a precious relic, Litta was sure one would be found, 'above all if one searches with the full intention of finding it'. For, as he pointed out with the epistolary equivalent of a wink, 'Your Excellency knows better than I that it is faith that produces miracles.'[42]

Paul's proposals for reconstructing the Polish priory were warmly received. Ferdinand Hompesch, the newly elected grand master, presented them to the sacred council on 7 August. It was the council which recommended that Paul be made a protector of the order. This was a dignity which he had not sought, but it was one which he was delighted to receive. Litta was named ambassador extraordinary and charged with presenting the tsar with his new title, the venerable cross of Malta (which had indeed been found), and a ceremonial coat of arms.[43] This ceremony took place in Petersburg on 29 November/10 December 1797. The prince de Condé, who already headed the *émigré* army in Russia, was named grand prior of the Russian grand priory. It was also announced that Count Giulio Litta, his embassy accomplished, would remain in Petersburg as Paul's adviser on matters relating to the knights of Malta. Litta was on loan from the order; his appointment was in Paul's gift, and it gave him direct access to the tsar.

From this time forward, the knights of Malta, or more precisely the Russian grand priory of the knights of Malta, occupied a central place at court and in the tsar's sentiments. Paul made no attempt to interfere in the order's affairs in Europe. Litta may well have hoped that he would do so, but if that were the case, he was disappointed. Like the European monarchs he admired, however, Paul distinguished

---

[41] 'Convention', preamble, 49; arts. xi and xii, p. 58.
[42] 'Depeshi Litty', no. 61, 7/18 Jan. 1797, pp. 210, 230–3.
[43] Greppi, *Giulio Litta*, 106–7; cf. Pierredon, *Histoire politique*, i, chs. 3–9. Pierredon criticizes Hompesch and his council but does not attach great weight to the convention as something destructive of the order.

the knights in his society and promoted their interests assiduously. His generosity seemed limitless. He gave the priory sumptuous housing and a chapel, he proposed to build a priory church, and he richly endowed the order's chaplaincy which was given to the papal nuncio, Lorenzo Litta. Yet open-handed as he was, he was also careful to observe the order's established rules and regulations. Even the deceased Rohan, who had warned Litta against the Russians, could hardly have objected to the way Paul dealt with the Russian grand priory. This situation changed after Paul became grand master ten months later. Apart from complaints about time wasted in ceremonial functions, and the growing influence of the *émigrés*, the knights' arrival generated little reaction. There was concern when the convention was signed that France might consider it an act of aggression. Those fears proved groundless, however, though Bonaparte, who intercepted the original convention on its way to Malta, used it to justify expropriating the Italian priories' dues for the use of the French army.[44]

The empress's party encouraged Paul's support for the *émigré* aristocracy, including the generous settlement with the knights of Malta. Mariia, who profoundly resented the republicans' seizure of Württemberg and her family's exile, was a particularly outspoken advocate who went beyond charity to urge active intervention to destroy revolutionary institutions and to restore the dispossessed princes, including the king of France, to their former status. Nelidova shared her feelings and supported her views. Paul, though sympathetic with Mariia's basic position, was not yet ready to shift the fundamentally neutralist policy with which his reign began, while the chancellor, Prince Bezborodko, opposed the empress's position as inconsistent with Russia's current needs and capacities. The growing number of *émigrés* in Russia, particularly in the capital, and their potential influence with Paul through Mariia and her friends, worried him, and this raised a larger question: the disproportionate influence which the circle around Mariia and Nelidova wielded on all governmental issues. Though chancellor, Bezborodko found himself at a disadvantage. He was reported to be considering retirement, though in fact what he set in train was a classic court intrigue whose purpose was to overturn and replace the faction currently in power.[45]

Though Mariia was the ostensible centre for the empress's party, her influence rested on Nelidova's special relationship with Paul. If Nelidova could be separated from the tsar, and a new favourite who

[44] Frederick W. Ryan, *The House of the Temple: A Study of Malta and its Knights in the French Revolution* (London, 1930), 244–5.
[45] Shumigorskii, *Nelidova*, 110–20; *Pavel I*, 148–50; Shil'der, *Pavel I*, 383 ff.

lacked her commitment to the empress installed, Mariia's position would be greatly weakened. And if Paul could be made to believe that his wife and her ally were using him to promote their own interests and those of their followers—that they were, in fact, a party—it was more than likely that anyone the empress had supported would become suspect. Events favoured this approach. Paul was deeply disturbed by the uproar which the bank of assistance set off and which would not abate. Dietrichstein noted that 'one does not dare to speak loudly about these [financial] innovations' for the emperor was determined to identify and punish critics. The empress confided 'that she knew some people who spoke ill of the bank, but that she would not wish to name them lest she lose them'.[46] There was a further dangerous rumour that Mariia herself had benefited hugely when the bank opened, and had even sent funds abroad, some of which had gone to her family. The remainder was presumably for her own use.[47] That her intentions may have been charitable was really beside the point. That particular story, had it reached Paul's ears with any authority, could well have made Bezborodko's intrigue unnecessary. It was also reported that Paul had removed the bank from Kurakin's care and that it was Bezborodko himself who was working with Woot on revisions. This was a clear victory for the chancellor, a break, in fact, in the empress's circle's monopoly on domestic policies, and it is entirely possible that Alexis Kurakin would have been dismissed in the summer of 1798 whether there had been an intrigue or not.[48]

In addition to Bezborodko, Fedor Rostopchin was critical of the empress's faction and despised Nelidova. But he was not well enough connected, or sufficiently adept at the court's political games, to organize an effective intrigue. He was, however, willing to second Bezborodko. But the key to the conspiracy was Paul's barber and personal valet, Ivan Kutaisov, who had been close to Paul for years, and who was known to be able to affect his master's feelings. Kutaisov had reason to be grateful to Nelidova for her protection when Paul rounded on him after the coronation. He also saw her, however, as an impediment to his ambitions, a rival, in fact, for the tsar's favour. He may also have believed what he finally told Paul,

---

[46] HHSA, Russland II Berichte, Carton 87, Dietrichstein to Thugut, no. 6, apostille 1, 29 Jan. (NS) 1798; Golovkine, *La Cour de Paul Ier*, 158.

[47] For Dietrichstein's report on the 6 million rubles(!) Mariia was supposed to have received, HHSA, Russland II Berichte, Carton 88, Dietrichstein to Thugut, no. 7, 1 Feb. (NS) 1798. Dietrichstein asked for special instructions on this issue.

[48] HHSA, Russland II Berichte, Carton 88, Dietrichstein to Thugut, no. 10, 23 Feb. (NS) 1798; no. 11, 27 Feb. (NS) 1798.

that neither Mariia nor Nelidova were truly devoted to him and that they manipulated him for their own ends.[49]

Paul was vulnerable. He was hypersensitive to any suggestion that he was not personally in charge, that anybody else controlled him, and he had long harboured the wholly irrational suspicion that Mariia might one day be tempted to 'play Catherine's role'.[50] And there was another problem. He was again becoming restless with his marriage. During the coronation he had shown an inclination 'to act the gallant' with young women of the court who were flattered and pleased and encouraged his attention. This was blatant enough to worry Mariia and Nelidova who urged an early departure from Moscow.[51] That problem took on another dimension with the grand duke Michael's birth in January of 1798.

Mariia's labour was particularly prolonged and difficult and was followed by a severe fever and profound depression. There was great uncertainty over her recovery, and when she did get well, she was strongly advised not to become pregnant again.[52] Mariia reluctantly accepted this opinion and Paul agreed. Abstinence from intercourse was the only certain guarantee for the empress's future well being. In the face of these developments, Paul, if anything, became more solicitous of Mariia's welfare. In preparation for her mother's approaching visit to Russia, he began to have a special wooden residence constructed in the gardens at Pavlosk. Mariia was still mourning her father's recent death; she was all the more anxious to see her mother. The news that her mother had suddenly died in early March was crushing. Mariia fell ill and was pronounced too unwell to accompany Paul when he left for Moscow and an inspection tour through Kazan and the eastern provinces early in May. Nelidova also remained in Petersburg.[53]

With neither Mariia nor Nelidova present, Bezborodko's cabal had a free hand. They made the most of their opportunity. Paul

[49] Heyking, *Aus den Tagen Kaiser Pauls*, 112–14; Shumigorskii, *Nelidova*, 117–18.

[50] Masson recorded Paul's using this phrase when he observed Mariia and Prince Kurakin speaking privately: 'You wish, madame, to make friends for yourself, and to prepare yourself to play Catherine's role, but know that you will not find me a Peter III.' *Mémoires secrètes*, i. 325–6 n. 1. The alleged exchange occurred before Paul became tsar.

[51] HHSA, Russland II Berichte, Carton 85, Cobenzl to Thugut, no. 29, apostille 14, 4 May (NS) 1797; Golovine, *Souvenirs*, i. 169.

[52] Baron Nicolay reported details of the birth to S. R. Vorontsov. 3/14 Feb. 1798, *Arkhiv kniazia Vorontsova*, xxii. 59–61; Shumigorskii, *Nelidova*, 120–2; PRO, FO/65/40, Whitworth to Grenville, no. 36, 21 Aug. (NS) 1798, 'Most Secret and Confidential'.

[53] Shumigorskii, *Nelidova*, 121–2.

returned in June having acquired a new mistress, Anna Lopukhina, and with the firm determination to strip Mariia of her political standing, to put Nelidova out of his life, and to rid himself of the people in his government who belonged to their party. The only circumstantial account of how it happened, that of Baron Heyking, identified Kutaisov as the main actor. As Heyking told the story, Paul, as always, received a warm welcome when he came to Moscow. He was moved by it, and being moved, he ruminated privately with Kutaisov on why it was that he was so well appreciated there, while in Petersburg he was always criticized. Kutaisov responded that that hardly surprised him. Paul immediately wanted to know what he meant. Kutaisov affected to be unwilling to speak further. The tsar demanded an answer; Kutaisov agreed to provide it if Paul would promise not to repeat what he was told. The promise given, Kutaisov explained himself:

Sire, it happens that here [in Moscow] you are seen as you truly are, good, magnanimous, and sensitive, while in Petersburg it is said, if some grace is extended: it is the empress or Frl. Nelidow, or even, Sire, it is the Kurakins, who have extracted it from you. So it is whenever you do good, but if you punish, it is you alone [who does it].

Paul pondered, absorbed, and then enquired, 'Thus it is said that I let myself be governed by both those women?' To which Kutaisov replied, 'Even so, Sire'. Paul's answer, as he sat down and began to write, was 'Ah, my ladies, I will show you whether I am governed!' Kutaisov, at this point, threw himself at his master's feet, pleading with him to take care, to dissimulate his purposes toward those two women. Paul agreed. The rest of the plot unfolded quietly; Mariia and Nelidova remained unaware of the changes which were approaching as Paul came home.[54]

Subsequent to this exchange (the following day, according to Heyking) Paul was brought to notice Anna Lopukhina at a court ball. She was one of those who caught his eye the previous year. This time, however, she intended to let him see her interest in him, and a bystander connected with the conspiracy was then to remark to Paul that he seemed to have made a conquest. Paul was pleased but noted that she was only a child; not such a child, came back the response, for she would soon be 17. Matters moved rapidly from that point. Paul was captivated, charmed, and finally, infatuated. Anna conquered his imagination. While Kutaisov pursued negotiations with her stepmother, Paul abandoned all pretence of carrying on business,

[54] Heyking, *Aus den Tagen Kaiser Pauls*, 112–17; the material quoted is on p. 115.

even slighting the manœuvres he was supposed to review; the officers in charge, from Marshal Saltykov down, were stunned at the offhand and uncritical approval their efforts won. The negotiations continued until the morning Paul was to leave; the word that all was satisfactorily arranged arrived as he waited impatiently in his carriage. The new romance was set.[55]

Paul concealed his intentions from Mariia. His letters to her on the return trip contained no hint of what he had done. The Lopukhin household was to remove to Petersburg. Paul went on his inspection tour, returning to Pavlosk by a circuitous route the third week in June. He was met by Mariia and Nelidova who found him cold and hostile; he announced that his stay would be brief, a sure sign of his displeasure. Mariia reacted tardily to the situation, attempting to re-establish their relationship on its old footing of intimacy. Paul simply refused: he claimed to have no taste for what was offered; he no longer needed or wanted a sexual relationship. That aspect of their marriage had atrophied. Mariia, apprised of Lopukhina's approach, wrote to her forbidding her to come any nearer. This desperate and clumsy ploy only angered Paul. Nelidova, who had returned to Smol'nyi, rushed back to intervene one more time: she met a scornful rebuff. And on one pretext or another, her friends and relations began to be dismissed. Buxhoeweden was removed as governor-general of Petersburg; his replacement, Kutaisov's candidate, was General Count Peter von der Pahlen. Alexis Kurakin lost his position as procuror-general and was assigned to the senate; his replacement was Anna Lopukhina's father. Alexander Kurakin was retained as vice-chancellor until the fall when he was replaced by Count Viktor Kochubei, ambassador to Constantinople and Bezborodko's nephew; Rostopchin, who had left the government under a cloud in January, was restored to his former status. Baron Heyking was sent home in September; Neledinskii, Pleshcheev, Nelidova's brother, Arkadii, and a host of others were reassigned, reduced in rank, or sent away. Nelidova herself voluntarily followed the Buxhoewedens into exile at Lohde in Lithuania. She remained there until 1800. Mariia was left in isolation, forbidden any contacts outside the family circle except those necessitated by her formal duties.[56]

The dissolution of the empress's party took place over the period from July to October 1798. Mariia's fall came at the beginning and

[55] Shumigorskii, *Nelidova*, 126–8; Heyking, *Aus den Tagen*, 113–16.
[56] Shumigorskii, *Pavel I*, 157, for Paul's rejection of Mariia; *Nelidova*, 128–47, covers the break-up with Nelidova, the consequences for the court, and gives generous selections from Nelidova's correspondence with Paul. See also Shil'der, *Pavel I*, 387–95.

was accompanied by stormy scenes reminiscent of the quarrels in Paul's household in the early 1790s. Finally, with great dignity, she wrote her husband urging him, whatever his feelings might be, not to abuse her in public. To do so was profoundly wounding and only diminished his standing. Paul accepted her point, and a sort of peace descended.[57] But his suspicions, once aroused, were not easily quieted. He referred openly to Mariia's faction as Jacobins, and made the astonishing claim that had they not held him back, he would have taken an active role in the struggle with France much sooner.[58] His suspicions also turned against his eldest son. Alexander may have attempted to defend his mother and so lost his father's regard.[59] Whether that is so or not, by November it was known that Paul's favourable attitudes to his heir had changed dramatically, and his new hostility took in his son's friends and associates. Even Viktor Kochubei, the new vice-chancellor, was affected. Ironically, Kochubei was inclined to believe that the empress involved herself in matters which should not have concerned her, and that her party had overreached itself. But his connections with the grand duke made him suspect in Paul's eyes, and even his uncle's influence was insufficient to restore him to Paul's good graces. Kochubei served as vice-chancellor until August 1799, but never was given the opportunity to deal with policy issues. Paul distrusted him, he was unhappy in his position, and finally resigned.[60]

The fall of the empress's party broke major lines of continuity. Paul's relations with Mariia stabilized, though she never regained her previous status as his confidante and councillor. Nelidova's influence,

---

[57] Shumigorskii, *Nelidova*, 132–4.

[58] These comments were made to Cobenzl when he had his first audience with Paul after returning from negotiating with Bonaparte. HHSA, Russland II Berichte, Carton 88, Cobenzl to Thugut, no. 48, 9 Sept. (NS) 1798. Cobenzl was stunned by assertions so obviously contradictory of fact.

[59] Golovkin reported a dramatic confrontation between Paul and Alexander on 25 July (OS) 1798 at 10.00 a.m. When Paul ordered Alexander to inform the empress that she must never again be involved in political affairs, Alexander refused, and Paul is supposed to have cried, 'I thought that I had only lost my wife, but I see that I have also lost my son', on which Alexander fell at his father's feet and wept. When Paul mistreated Mariia, however, Alexander intervened to save her from serious harm, though he could not prevent Paul from locking her up in isolation for three hours. Golovkine, *La Cour de Paul Ier*, 174–6.

[60] HHSA, Russland II Berichte, Carton 89, Cobenzl to Thugut, no. 61, apostille 4, 14 Nov. (NS) 1798; no. 64, 23 Nov. (NS) 1798; no. 67, 18 Dec. (NS) 1798; Carton 90, no. 1, apostille 2, 4 Jan. (NS) 1799; no. 20, apostille 3, 22 Mar. (NS) 1799; no. 36, apostille 12, 17 May (NS) 1799; no. 57, apostille 7, 31 July (NS) 1799; no. 63, apostille 1 [n.d.: *c.*23 Aug. (NS) 1799]; Kochubei to S. R. Vorontsov, *Arkhiv kniazia Vorontsova*, xviii. 149–50: Shumigorskii, *Nelidova*, 136–7.

a potent factor in Paul's life for over a decade, was completely ended. For a time there was some fear that, if she returned to Petersburg, she might re-establish her ascendancy, and a close watch was kept on her correspondence, especially with Mariia. There was even an order forbidding her return. When it became clear that nothing remained for these two women, that they were politically harmless, the surveillance ended and the order was withdrawn. Paul himself agreed to Nelidova's return to Petersburg in 1800.[61]

Politically speaking, the new order should have belonged to Bezborodko, but events had overtaken him. He was unable to prevent Paul from accepting the grand mastership of the knights of Malta, he failed to stem the *émigrés*' expanding importance at the court, and he found himself presiding over plans for an active and far-reaching intervention against France. Paul was launching a great crusade; Bezborodko's role was to facilitate it. The chancellor was at the end of his career. His health was poor and growing worse. He was forced to take leave, to seek treatments, and he died in April 1799. His carefully laid and brilliantly executed plan to unseat the empress's party was his last and most dramatic achievement, though so successful was he in concealing his role that Count Cobenzl, who considered himself close with Bezborodko, firmly denied that the chancellor had anything to do with the fate of the empress's party.[62]

The new power structure was a curious one. Within the court, Ivan Kutaisov was Paul's adviser and confidant. His influence with the tsar was substantial, and he became everybody's fixer. Wholly corrupt, he seems to have had little interest in policies or, in the broadest sense, politics. But he did have the tsar's ear and enjoyed an extraordinary intimacy. Anna Lopukhina, the *maîtresse en titre*, was Paul's romantic dream. She appears to have had no political influence at all, though she did, on occasion, urge opinions on him. Her best weapon was her tears; nothing further from Nelidova's sentimental, emotionally charged rhetoric on duty and the need to be true to one's best self could be imagined. Paul celebrated Lopukhina: he decked the court and reuniformed the army in her colours. He declared her a grand cross of the knights of Malta, watched by her bed when she was ill, and magnanimously gave her away in marriage when she declared she had lost her heart. As with Nelidova, Paul's relationship with Lopukhina (or Gagarina as she became) was believed to be platonic. Some hinted that her marriage with Pavel Gavrilovich Gagarin was to dampen Paul's ardour. If so, it would appear to have

[61] Shumigorskii, *Nelidova*, 158–9.
[62] HHSA, Russland II Berichte, Carton 88, Cobenzl to Thugut, no. 48, apostille 5, 9 Sept. (NS) 1798.

been successful. Nevertheless, Gagarina remained a central figure in Paul's circle, and when he built the Michael Palace, there was an apartment for her which connected by an interior passage with his own rooms. For all that, it could hardly be said that Gagarina rivalled Nelidova as a figure in Russian history. She was an anecdote rather than a legend, and had relatively little effect beyond showing her imperial suitor at a considerable disadvantage. She died in childbed four years after Paul's murder.[63]

Lopukhina's father, who became procuror general in the place of Alexis Kurakin, proved to be honest and hard-working, though his influence was in no way comparable to the younger Kurakin's. A sound administrator, Lopukhin remained in the background where he worked at the routine tasks of his appointment. The situation scarcely favoured anything else. While Kurakin was procuror general, domestic policy occupied the centre of the political stage. Foreign policy dominated Lopukhin's time, and he had no part to play there.[64] Viktor Kochubei, the new vice-chancellor, played a passive part for reasons we have already mentioned. He was subordinate to Fedor Rostopchin who emerged as an important personage in the college of foreign affairs, and, after Bezborodko's death, a dominant one. Indeed, Rostopchin and von der Pahlen, a candidate Kutaisov had strongly urged on Paul, became the most

[63] Shumigorskii, *Nelidova*, 148–9; Golovine, *Souvenirs*, 200–3, 205–6, 218; Golovkine, *La Cour de Paul Ier*, 181–5 and 183–4 n. 1. Cobenzl reported Paul's affair with Lopukhina in detail; his dispatches, together with a special summary which Dietrichstein prepared, offer the most comprehensive contemporary evidence available. The relevant references are: HHSA, Russland II Berichte, Carton 89, Cobenzl to Thugut, no. 61, apostille 4, 14 Nov. (NS) 1798 on Paul's public courtship of Lopukhina and her resistance to him; no. 65, apostille 3, 10 Dec. (NS) 1798 on her influence over court entertainments; Carton 90, no. 4, apostille 6, 29 Jan. (NS) 1799, on the court and the army wearing her colours; no. 6, apostille 6, 29 Jan. (NS) 1799, on her illness and Paul's suspending business to sit with her; Carton 93, 'Relationen Dietrichstein von Russland: Oktober-Dezember, 1799', Biala, 26 Nov. (NS) 1799, 'Notices de la cour de Russie et le personnel de l'Empereur', which contains Paul's sworn oath that he had never been unfaithful to either of his wives, a description of the tsar's public pursuit of Lopukhina and his mounting frustration in it, and the circumstances of his approving Lopukhina's marriage to Gagarin; no. 7, Cobenzl to Thugut, 21 Jan. (NS) 1800, and no. 10, apostille 3, 31 Jan. (NS) 1800, on the permission for Lopukhina to marry and the marriage. Charles Whitworth's sole report on the Lopukhina affair deplored Paul's public pursuit of her and praised him for gaining control of his feelings and approving her marriage with Gagarin. PRO, FO/65/46, Whitworth to Grenville, no. 14, 21 Feb. (NS) 1800.

[64] Klochkov, *Pravitel'stvennoi deiatel'nosti*, 224–70, discusses Lopukhin in the procuror-general's office. Heyking reported that Lopukhin's quiet, retiring style did not suit Paul, and that he was overlooked and undervalued. *Aus den Tagen Kaiser Pauls*, 136.

powerful officials in the government, though Nikita Petrovich Panin, called back from the embassy in Berlin, became a significant rival to Rostopchin despite poor personal relations with the tsar. Through the war years of 1799 and 1800, the last three named formed the backbone of Paul's government, while in its last phases, von der Pahlen became a sort of grand vizier as Paul concentrated all lines of authority in his hands.[65]

While the fall of the empress's party brought about a major shift in governing personnel, it had relatively little effect on policy. The reforms begun at the start of the reign continued to evolve toward the centralized political system outlined in the last chapter. There was no relaxation of either military or social discipline; if anything, it intensified. In international affairs, Paul continued to move towards confrontation with France at the same time as redoubling his efforts to underwrite resistance on every level to Jacobinism and the corrosive effects of modernity. He also continued to resist (though with mixed results) abuses of power and position within Russia, while dismantling nobiliary privileges which either had been sanctioned by tradition, or set up in law. Whether viewed from the perspective of policy or ideology, the fall of the empress's party brought no significant changes. If anything the level of competence in the inner administration rose and, ironically enough, the most serious loss may well have been Mariia Fedorovna's voice on domestic affairs.

The events which we have described coincided with Paul's stunning decision to accept 'election' as grand master of the knights of Malta. Nothing that had gone before prepared opinion for this departure, and once it had happened there was little enthusiasm for it. It all began with Napoleon Bonaparte's decision to invade Egypt in the summer of 1798. He justified taking Malta on strategic grounds, primarily to secure his supply lines, though the British were able to neutralize the island's effect by blockading and putting it under siege. The plans for attacking Malta had existed for some time, and when the French fleet appeared off La Valletta in June, French agents had been in place since January. Their help, however, was hardly necessary. The handful of knights in their fortress offered almost no resistance. On 12 June the French occupied the port and the castle, almost literally without firing a shot.[66]

---

[65] Ibid. 117–19 for Kutaisov's part in Pahlen's rise.
[66] Pierredon, *Histoire politique*, i. 140–94, for a detailed account of the background, planning, and seizure of Malta. Pierredon provides the official French account, Ferdinand Hompesch's account, and accounts by knights who supported the order. Pierredon's is by far the best and most comprehensive coverage available.

The news that La Valletta had surrendered reached Petersburg early in July. There was no reaction, however, for nearly six weeks. Then, on 26 August/6 September, the Russian grand priory, without any warning, set off a political bomb. Protesting in the strongest possible terms, it levelled a burning indictment of incompetence, cowardice, and treason against Grand Master Ferdinand Hompesch, and in a long supporting document, presented evidence alleged to have originated with eyewitnesses of impeccable credentials proving that he was guilty as charged. This broadside concluded by asserting that 'the truth has revealed to us Ferdinand Hompesch accused and convicted of improvidence, cowardice, and treachery' and that 'We, Knights of the Grand Priory of Russia and others present in St. Petersburg regard Ferdinand Hompesch as disqualified from the rank to which we have elevated him, and by virtue of our own rules, we consider ourselves absolved from the obedience which we would [otherwise] owe him as our Chief.' The Petersburg priory invited the other *langues* and priories of Europe to join them in this renunciation, while for the immediate future the Russian priory 'threw itself into the arms of our August and Sovereign PROTECTOR Paul I'. The priory called on Paul to make his will known, promised him its obedience, and urged him 'to extend his generous protection over all the members of our Order who, in these unhappy circumstances, remain faithful to the unchanging foundation of our institution, RELIGION and Honour'.[67]

Of all the foundations in Europe, only the Russian priory reacted to Bonaparte's attack on Malta in this way. For most, the issue was French violation of neutral rights, though certain individuals were critical of Baron Hompesch's policies and behaviour.[68] Some of this material filtered into Russia through the summer, though the official envoy from the imperial government to the knights, the chevalier O'Hara, reported personally to Paul in July emphasizing French

[67] 'Protestation du Grand Prieuré de Russie' and 'Manifeste du Grand Prieuré de Russie', Maisonnueve, *Annales historiques*, 170–4, 174–90. Pierredon reprints these documents. *Histoire politique*, i. 339–40, 341–9. See also *Actes du chapître du Grand Prieuré de Russie* (St Petersburg, 1798). Printed by the imperial press, this collection also includes Paul's *ukaz* of 10/21 Sept. 1798 (his response to the protest); his proclamation as grand master, 27 Oct./7 Nov. 1798; his acceptance decree, 13/24 Nov. 1798; and the decree (in Latin) establishing St Petersburg as the knights' headquarters, 21 Dec. 1798/1 Jan. 1799. Giulio Litta sent this very rare publication to the pope. It is filed with Pius VI's correspondence. See Archivio Vaticano, Nunziature Polonia-Russia, no. 344/1, fo. 89, Pius VI to Bali Giulio conte Litta, Florence, 5 Nov. 1798.

[68] McGrew, 'Paul I and the Knights', 51–2, and pp. 69–70 nn. 47, 48, and 49; Pierredon, *Histoire politique*, i. 221, 336–9, 349–51, 361–4.

duplicity and affirming Hompesch's loyalty and commitment. Paul accepted O'Hara's reports calmly and with every evidence of gratitude for them. O'Hara knew, however, that there were deeper currents running, that his report was not welcome to Count Litta, and that what he told Paul was either disbelieved or simply set aside.[69] The fact was that Giulio Litta, Paul's adviser on the knights' affairs, saw the fall of Malta as an opportunity to be seized. It was he who drew up the denunciation which the Russian grand priory published, twisting and fabricating evidence to support the view that Hompesch had betrayed his trust. The purpose of the denunciation was to make the case that Hompesch had no right to the order's loyalty, that he was, therefore, no longer grand master, and then to propose Paul in his stead. Litta's reasons for this action were twofold: Paul believed in the order and was the best hope for the future; and with Paul as grand master, Litta's future would be richly assured. Denouncing Hompesch was the necessary first step toward realizing Litta's plan.[70]

Whether Paul himself suggested that he could be grand master, or whether it was Litta who broached the subject to him, is unknown. It is more likely that the idea originated with Litta and that it was he who convinced a willing Paul that the proposal was practical. It is also likely that this took place before the denunciation was published. Certainly Paul's response to the charges and the plea for support was warmly sympathetic. He accepted and affirmed the fact that Hompesch was guilty as charged and was no longer the order's head; he offered St Petersburg as the knights' new international capital, their home until Malta could be restored to them; and he took the order under his personal protection.[71] Litta's brother, the papal nuncio, immediately forwarded all the documents in the case

[69] Colonel O'Hara's account of his interview with Paul appears in a letter to his brother, Charles O'Hara, written on 23 Aug/4 Sept. 1801, from St Petersburg. The letter is in the papers of Colonel Anthony O'Hara, National Library of Ireland, Dublin, where it was found by Professor A. G. Cross of Cambridge Univ., who permitted me to use it. The account, though written three years after the event, corroborates the fragments of evidence already known and fills a gap in the documentation. I am grateful to Professor Cross for this material. For the documentary context, and the story as known previously, see McGrew, 'Paul I and the Knights', 53 and 71 n. 58.

[70] The opinion on Litta's role is unanimous. See: Anthony O'Hara to Charles O'Hara, 23 Aug./4 Sept. 1801; Riksarkivet, Diplomatica Moscovitica, vol. 460, Stedingk to the king, 18/29 Mar. 1799; PRO, FO/65/42, Whitworth to Grenville, no. 13, 13 Mar. (NS) 1799; l'abbé J. F. Georgel, *Mémoires pour servir à l'histoire des événemens de la fin du dix-huitième siècle depuis 1760 jusqu'en 1806–1810* (Paris, 1818), vi. 188–9; Pierredon, *Histoire politique*, i. 218–19.

[71] *Ukaz*, 10/21 Sept. 1798, Maisonnueve, *Annales historiques*, 192–3.

to Rome with an approving covering letter which elicited a strongly supportive response from the pope. Pius VI accepted the Russian priory's position that there was a case for Hompesch to answer; in fact, he had already suspended the grand master from his duties pending an investigation of the circumstances of Malta's fall. He also accepted Paul's offer of St Petersburg as the knights' new capital, and he thanked the tsar warmly for extending his personal support and protection. Indeed, he went further. In the event that it was necessary to choose a new grand master, he suggested that the candidate might well come from the Russian grand priory of which he had a very high opinion. What he did not say was that the vacancy already existed. On the contrary, he pointed out that the constitution of the knights of Malta was such that while a priory could bring charges against a grand master, no single priory had the power to remove one. The point was made unambiguously, though without special emphasis, but Odescalchi, the papal secretary, repeated it in his covering letter. There was no possibility of error. So far as the pope was concerned the Russian grand priory had drawn an indictment against Ferdinand Hompesch. It was up to the order as a whole to judge.[72]

There is little question that the papal nuncio and Giulio Litta himself had assured Paul that the pope would accept the Russian priory's deposition of Hompesch, and that he would agree to Paul's election as grand master. Certainly that was the assumption behind the next move. On 27 October/7 November 1798, the Russian grand priory again appealed to Paul. After referring to the parlous state in which the order of St John now found itself, the members of the Russian priory, explicitly claiming to speak with the voice of the entire order, called on Paul to become their leader and accept the grand mastership they proferred. Paul's acceptance was published six days later.[73]

This exchange completed a process which began at the end of August, and probably had been agreed at that time. Whether the pope's letters arrived before or after the offer was tendered is not clear. They had probably come by the time Paul accepted, however. Precisely when they arrived is less important than the fact that the Littas entirely suppressed the pope's reservations concerning the Russian grand priory's proceedings, and at the time Paul was

[72] The materials from Russia, though without Litta's letters, are in Archivio Vaticano, Polonia–Russia, vol. 344/I, fo. 89, Pius VI to (G.) Litta, 17 Oct. 1798, and 5 Nov. 1798. For Vatican letters to Litta, Pierredon, *Histoire politique*, i, no. 55, Pius VI to bailli Litta, 17 Oct. 1798, pp. 360–1; Journel, *Litta*, no. 126, p. 269.

[73] Maisonnueve, *Annales historiques*, 197–200; Pierredon, *Histoire politique*, i, nos. 61 and 63, pp. 366–9.

accepting the grand mastership, put out word that letters from the Vatican had arrived that gave full approval to what the Russian priory had done. Indeed, Stedingk reported as fact that the bailli de Litta had received a letter from the pope

in which he [the pope] approves all the measures taken by the Priory of Russia against the Grand Master; and he exhorts at the same time the Knights to choose among themselves one of their number who can replace the Grand Master. It would appear certain that the Emperor, at the prayers of the Priory of Russia, will accept the position of grand master, and we have already seen him in recent days taking over the functions of the Order in Russia.[74]

The impression given was that Paul's election to the grand magistracy had papal sanction. This, of course, was totally untrue, as was the statement that the pope accepted the Russian priory's deposition of Baron Hompesch. Presumably the Littas believed that the pope, in light of the advantages Paul could give the order, and the favourable conditions he could create for the church in the Russian empire, would not cavil at what had been done and would ratify the tsar's new dignity. It was not, in fact, an unreasonable wager, nor were the consequences of losing it especially dire. Whether Paul was warned that this was the case and simply acted as if he were not, or whether he was kept entirely in the dark, is not known. The Vatican sources suggest the latter. Indeed, it would appear that Paul had no idea of what the pope's actual position was until sometime in February 1799, when he set it out in an unciphered memo to Lorenzo Litta which the Russian government was intended to intercept.

The intercepted letter technique allowed the Vatican to inform the Russian government unofficially of the pope's actual position while avoiding the necessity for a formal declaration on either side. As a method of damage control, it was reasonably successful. As soon as Paul was informed, he dismissed Giulio Litta from his post as lieutenant to the grand master and exiled him to his wife's estates. Lorenzo Litta was ordered out of Petersburg at once with the proviso that he was not to stop until he had crossed the Russian frontier. The complex negotiations on which he had been engaged concerning the status of Catholics in the Russian empire, and which were going far less well than he had been led to believe, were simply dropped. Formal diplomatic relations were not broken, but there were no further negotiations between Russia and the Vatican until after the death of Pius VI and the election of Pius VII. When they were taken

[74] Riksarkivet, Diplomatica Moscovitica, vol. 459, Stedingk to the king, 19/30 Nov. 1798; McGrew, 'Paul I and the Knights', 56 and 72 nn. 76 and 77.

up again late in 1800 they covered explicitly the thorny problem of Paul's grand mastership, and they were well in train when he was killed in March 1801. It should be added that Paul's reaction to the pope's stand was surprisingly mild. This does not, however, justify the conclusion that he had prior knowledge that refusal was likely or even possible.[75]

The Littas' motives for urging Paul to accept the grand mastership and concealing the pope's position need detain us no further. Paul's intentions are another matter. Until autumn 1798 he was content to act as the order's protector, and it was still essentially in that guise that he responded to the denunciation of Hompesch. Whatever transpired between him and Litta from the end of August to the start of November can only be conjectured. What he did when he became grand master, however, is a matter of record. Despite his repeated assertions that he recognized an obligation to maintain the forms and traditions of the order intact, Paul announced on his election what amounted to the order's transformation.[76] The organization was thrown open for membership to nobles of all religious faiths by creating a second Russian priory which was simply enormous. The Orthodox priory, as it came to be known, comprised ninety-eight commanderies and was large enough to accommodate the whole of the eligible Russian nobility. At the same time, and in total disregard for both precedent and written rule, Paul appointed serving officials for the order, his own sacred council, from among the high officials of the imperial Russian administration. By these steps, Paul changed the character of the order from a sovereign, autonomous entity under the nominal oversight of the pope to a Russian imperial institution with associated branches in various foreign countries. No such reorientation of the order would have been possible had Paul remained protector. Being grand master as well as tsar, however, he was able to do whatever seemed appropriate to him.

It is likely that the suggestions for what Paul could do by becoming grand master originated with Giulio Litta. They appealed, however, to Paul's activist bent. The knights of Malta, reformed and revived, as he wrote to the pope in December, were integral to his plans for confronting and defeating revolutionary Jacobinism. He was, he reminded his holiness, in the process of making diplomatic and

---

[75] McGrew, 'Paul I and the Knights', 57–8; Greppi, *Giulio Litta*, 128–30, 641–2 ff.; Journel, *Litta*, pp. lviii–lxix, and *Benvenuti*, pp. viii–xi; Pierredon, *Histoire politique*, i. 230–5.

[76] 'Paul I of Russia: Ukaz: 29 November/10 December, 1798' (British Library Pamphlet filed under Paul I); cf. *PSZ*, series 1, vol. 25, no. 18766, 29 Nov. (os) 1798.

military commitments to that end, and he also recalled that he had invited Europe's displaced nobility to come to Russia where he was building a bastion against the destructive forces of the modern world. To defeat those forces was his announced intent and one which, when realized, would render a 'signal service to the Universe'. It was for this great enterprise that he was taking over the knights, mobilizing the *émigrés*, and inviting the pope's participation.[77]

There was more. From Paul's perspective, the knights would make a critical contribution to his continuing struggle within Russia against subversion and error. As an ancient and respectable order embodying the best of monarchical Europe's values, the knights would serve as a model for raising the moral consciousness of the Russian nobility. This most dangerous yet necessary class would be made stronger and more reliable by association with and induction into a body whose 'laws and statutes . . . inspire love of virtue, contribute to strong morals, strengthen the bonds of subordination, and offer a powerful remedy against thoughtless love of novelty and unbridled license in thinking'. The knights were a society which had always provided 'a means for states to increase [their] strength, security, and glory', and in Russia he believed that the order would 'Offer to OUR faithful nobility a further motive to stimulate the love of glory . . . and the practice of actions useful to the Fatherland and agreeable to its sovereign.' The knights, in sum, were another means to further Paul's moral revolution.[78]

The effects of Paul's decision were soon felt in international politics where the Malta issue proved to be divisive and an impediment to co-operation. Its consequences for Russian society, however, were minor, though much was made of it at court. Paul put the knights at the centre of ceremonial life, lavished his time and the treasury's scarce resources on its affairs, and became thoroughly enmeshed in the details of its administration. He appeared to consider the knights the most precious jewel in his imperial crown, and he conferred its symbols as his highest mark of favour.[79] His enthusiasm, however, was not shared. The knights of Malta was an

[77] Paul I to Pius VI, 14/25 Dec. 1798, Pierredon, *Histoire politique*, i, no. 68, pp. 375–7; Journel, *Litta*, no. 146, pp. 299–300; 'Appel de . . . Paul I', Pierredon, no. 69, pp. 377–9; Maisonnueve, *Annales historiques*, 257–61.

[78] 'Appel de . . . Paul I', 379–83, esp. 383; Ukaz, 1–2.

[79] British policy did not permit its representatives to accept foreign knighthoods, but when Paul conferred the order of Malta on Whitworth, the ambassador pleaded with his government to make an exception. A refusal, regardless of the reason given, would be taken by the tsar as 'not only unfriendly but a presumption that His [Britannic] Majesty does not perfectly adopt his [Paul's] views'. PRO, FO/65/45, Whitworth to Grenville, no. 115, 27 Dec. (NS) 1799.

alien body with no connection to Russia beyond Paul's eccentric predilections; moreover, the order's business was a constant distraction from what was considered to be the tsar's proper interests. Prince Bezborodko told Cobenzl privately that in his opinion 'everything done here relative to the order of Malta was illegal, and that the emperor having no interest [to serve] in taking on himself this grand magistracy should have limited himself to being the Protector of the Order and working to maintain it and restore it to its former state'. Both Kochubei and Rostopchin, though at odds on other matters, shared Bezborodko's view of Paul's magistracy, and far from seeing any benefit were in constant fear of new troubles which the tsar's infatuation with the order might set off.[80] It was Countess Golovina, however, who not only noted Paul's intense preoccupation with the knights, the extravagances he perpetrated in their name (which qualified the ennobling effect of his chivalric style), but commented on the bitterness and resentment which followed on his using the Malta cross as virtually his unique symbol. 'The nation', she wrote, 'was shocked to see its Emperor more proud of being grand master of the order of Malta than of being sovereign of Russia.'[81]

It soon became clear that Paul's radical changes in the structure of the order were not going to be followed by any serious functional reforms. Though war was coming, he made no attempt to exploit the knights' rich military heritage, nor did he draw the society around him as a new praetorian guard. In other hands, the order might have been revitalized as a crusading *oprichnina*, modelled on Ivan the Terrible's fierce guardians, and so a scourge for uncooperative nobles, or it could have emerged as a dedicated political priesthood, monarchical activists who could serve as a counterweight to revolutionary freemasonry or, more appropriately still, the hydra-headed Jacobin menace. But Paul's imagination did not reach in this direction. He looked to a modern army into which even the guards regiments were to be integrated, while the knights of Malta were to make their contribution by embodying the forms and symbols of the traditions which the reformed army was defending. It was what the order stood for that was meaningful to Paul and that he believed he was grafting onto the Russian body politic. When he stressed the importance of the order to his plans, it was always as a moral force.

---

[80] Cobenzl reported Bezborodko's comment in Dec. 1798; Kochubei talked with him about the Malta problem the following July. HHSA, Russland II Berichte, Carton 89, Cobenzl to Thugut, no. 65, apostille 5, 10 Dec. (NS) 1798; Carton 92, no. 49, apostille 1, 3 July (NS) 1799.

[81] Golovine, *Souvenirs*, 202–3.

The knights stood for the kind of world in which he believed, hence it was enough for him that the order existed and had come under his control. He took pride in it, identified with it, and enjoyed wielding its symbols and leading its rituals. By taking control of it and bringing it into Russia, he could envision himself bringing Russia nearer to his ideal.[82]

The bank of assistance for the nobility, the fall of the empress's party, and Paul's election as grand master of the knights of Malta were all events which took place against a background of heightening international tension and intensifying diplomatic activity. The neutralist, even pacifist, tone which had marked the reign's first months was already fading in autumn 1797, and by 1798 had become a thing of the past. Long before Malta fell, Paul had committed himself to maintaining at least a minimum level of support for Austria and England, and he clearly identified Jacobinism with French expansion and a direct threat to political stability in Europe. Before looking at these matters in detail, however, it would be useful to review Paul's situation at the end of 1798. It obviously was vastly different to what it had been in the period following the coronation.

Though Paul's popularity with the general population remained strong, his standing with the privileged classes was low, while politically, two years as tsar had begun to show his weaknesses. None were unexpected, though the good beginning he had made in the first five months may have led some people to believe that the future could be better than it proved to be. That his was a harsh and repressive regime had come to be taken for granted. And it was to grow worse. Its most serious effects continued to be felt by the military, and especially the officer corps. A high volume of resignations temporarily defused a potentially explosive situation, though it was apparent that Paul made service extremely difficult. Increased taxes, rising prices, a deteriorating currency, and the special burdens imposed on merchants and landholders by the bank of assistance generated complaints and protests, but nothing occurred

[82] See Baron F. I. Brunov [Brunnow], 'Aperçu des principales transactions du cabinet de Russie sous les règnes de Catherine II, Paul I, et Alexandre I', *SIRIO* 31 (1881), 197–416, but esp. 233–9. The essay was written for Grand Duke Alexander Nikolaevich in 1838 and emphasizes the role Paul hoped the knights would take in resisting revolutionary influences. Tsar Nicholas I recorded on the MS (p. 234 n. 1) that this was the first time that he really understood what his father intended. Cf. Baron Michel de Taube, *L'Empereur Paul I de Russie, grand maître de l'ordre de Malte et son 'grand prieuré' russe de l'ordre de St. Jean de Jérusalem* (Paris, 1955), and 'Le Tsar Paul I et l'ordre de Malthe en Russie', *Revue d'histoire moderne*, 5 (1930), 161–77, esp. 167–8, 171.

that was remotely comparable to the peasants' uprising at the beginning of the reign. The most serious complaints came from privileged and literate sources; the group which most worried Paul was both the one he was most at pains to discipline (or inspire), and it was also the group which was most critical of him. No conspiracies were hatching, however, and none would develop until later in 1799.

Both the bank for the nobility and the Malta question raised serious doubts about Paul's effectiveness. In each case he deferred to the opinions of self-interested foreigners—Robert Woot in the case of the bank and Giulio Litta on the knights of Malta—and this with results that could only be deplored. The bank had seriously adverse effects for all but a very few people; Paul's enthusiasm for grandiose, all-encompassing solutions led him astray. Nor was he protected by the men whom he had made responsible for fiscal matters, notably Alexis Kurakin, while even the empress defended the proposals and the men who made them. Paul was forced to revise what was proposed, and in the process made the plan more useful for those who hoped to abuse it.

In parallel fashion, the Malta question and Paul's courtship of Nelidova's successor strongly indicated that the tsar's volatile and impetuous character could lead him to use his powers in wholly inappropriate ways. To some degree, both helped to make him ridiculous. Made to order for caricature, Paul lacked *gravitas*. Unlike his son, Nicholas I, he was in no way the model of a monarch.[83]

Relatively little of significance changed over the period from May 1797 to November 1798, yet the impression is left of a ruler whose judgement was as uncertain as it was swift. Given what Paul was trying to do in the first five months of his reign, the quality of his decisions was high. Certainly the legislative programme which he introduced applied systematically the vision of how Russia should be governed which he had developed over his long years as grand duke. In 1798, such a proposition would be indefensible. Apart from disciplinary aspects and the machinery of repression, it would be difficult to identify any significant themes in the increasingly sporadic bursts of legislative activity which marked the period, while the commitments that were made, though reflective of Paul's values,

---

[83] Nicholas V. Riasanovsky, *Nicholas I and Official Nationality in Russia* (Berkeley, Calif., 1966), ch. 1, shows how Nicholas appeared to be what a monarch should be. He had presence, a commanding eye, a strong frame, and an air of authority. The absence of a commanding presence undoubtedly made Paul appear to be less than he was; his behaviour enhanced that impression. People hated him, but they also learnt to be contemptuous of him. This contributed to his downfall. See below, Ch. 10.

were of doubtful quality and betrayed a tendency towards irrelevance. This is not to suggest that his mind was deteriorating or that he was suffering the loss of Nelidova's personal gyroscope. Rather it is to say that Paul had already done what he was prepared to do, that the more he was forced to extemporize, the more likely he was to slip, and ultimately that the way he wanted to approach the world was rather different from the way most of his contemporaries did. Here the evidence offered by his attitudes towards and hopes for the knights of Malta in Russia is particularly telling. But diplomacy and war, major concerns from the summer of 1798 to the end of his reign, posed even more difficult questions than reordering the imperial government and reforming the behaviour of the nobility. Paul was to have some dramatic moments on the international stage, and it is to those that we now shall turn.

9
PEACE AND WAR: 1797–1801

Though domestic questions dominated the first year of Paul's reign, foreign policy was never far from his mind. When he came to the throne, the drama of the first coalition against revolutionary France was in its last act. Prussia, never an enthusiastic participant, had withdrawn in 1795 to take up what proved to be an unshakeable neutrality. Britain and Austria soldiered on though without much hope until Catherine dispatched an auxiliary force of 60,000 men to support her beleaguered allies. Though firm in her determination not to interfere with the internal situation in France (this was not a crusade to overthrow the republic), she believed that a victory for the monarchists was essential to stem the spread of revolutionary influence.[1] The movement of Russian troops lifted allied morale and kindled a new enthusiasm for the war, but all that died with Catherine. Immediately on ascending the throne, Paul recalled all Russian forces outside the country, and, after a momentary hesitation, cancelled the recruitment which had been ordered earlier in the autumn.[2] These actions coincided with the fall of Mantua, Austria's last foothold in northern Italy, and were followed by a French invasion of Austria itself. Paul had made it dramatically clear that he was not bound by his mother's policies and that, as he noted on the Austrian ambassador's memorandum of protest, he and he alone would decide what Russia's interests were and how they would best be served.[3]

Two armies were withdrawn in those first days, the auxiliary force destined to assist Austria, and an invasion army under Valerian

---

[1] F. F. Martens, *Recueil des traités et conventions conclus par la Russie avec les puissances étrangères*, 15 vols. (St Petersburg, 1874–1909), ix/x. 411–13, xiii. 247–8. See also ii. 192 ff., vi. 163 ff., x. 363 ff.

[2] See above, Ch. 7.

[3] Aleksandr Mikhailovskii-Danilevskii and Dmitri Ivanovich Miliutin, *Istoriia voiny Rossii s Frantsieiu v 1799 gody* (St Petersburg, 1852), i/1. 23–4. Mikhailovskii-Danilevskii wrote vol. i, pt. 1, of this standard study of the war in 1799. D. M. Miliutin completed vol. i and wrote vols. ii–v. Cited hereafter as *Voina . . . 1799*. Cf. Martens, *Recueil des traités*, ii. 282–3 and HHSA, Russland II Berichte, Carton 82, Cobenzl to Thugut, no. 72; no. 72, apostilles 8 and 17, 25 Nov. (NS) 1796; no. 75, 7 Dec. (NS) 1796.

Zubov which had been launched at Persia. The second indicated a major policy change. Paul was firmly opposed to wars of expansion. He had been a critic of his mother's policies *vis-à-vis* Turkey, the Black Sea, and western Asia since the end of the first Russo-Turkish war. In his view, peace, negotiations, even alliance would better serve Russia's expanding Levantine interests than confrontation. This point of view had substantial support both inside the foreign policy establishment and in society, and it led directly to co-operation with the Porte in resisting French expansion in the eastern Mediterranean. It led as well to a diplomatic resolution of Russian problems with Persia.[4] The withdrawal from the war with France was a different matter. Paul accepted the idea that French expansion endangered Russian interests, but he also believed that his country was in no condition to fight a foreign war, nor would she be until the army and the governing establishment had been extensively reformed.[5] Of the two threats, he considered the danger of a domestic breakdown the more immediate. Even with French troops on Austrian soil and Vienna at risk, he refused Austria's pleas to dispatch 12,000 men under the mutual defence treaty of 1795. Your best hope, he told Cobenzl on that occasion, is to end the fighting as quickly as possible and negotiate a settlement. He rejected the idea that the moral effect of even a token Russian intervention would influence the French, and when he learnt a few days after this conversation that Austria and France had in fact reached a preliminary agreement at Leoben, he was well pleased.[6] Again, during the summer when Austria wanted to repudiate the peace and return to the battlefield, he warned the government that if they did so, they would fight without Russia. 'Think carefully', he urged Cobenzl, 'before you recommence the dance.'[7] Yet through all of this, Paul claimed to stand as Austria's ally, and early in 1797, he provided her cover against Prussian interference in Germany by moving three regiments of infantry with their cavalry support onto his western frontier. He also informed

---

[4] Muriel Atkin, 'The Pragmatic Diplomacy of Paul I: Russia's Relations with Asia, 1796–1801', *Slavic Review*, 38/1 (Mar. 1979), 60–74; ead., *Russia and Iran, 1780–1828* (Minneapolis, 1980); Robert E. Jones, 'Opposition to War and Expansion'; Hugh Ragsdale, 'Russia, Prussia, and Europe in the Policy of Paul I', *Jahrbücher für Geschichte Osteuropas*, 31/1 (1983), 81–118, esp. 81–2 and 86–7. See also Saul, *Russia and the Mediterranean*, 67–8.

[5] See above, Ch. 7.

[6] HHSA, Russland II Berichte, Carton 85, Cobenzl to Thugut, no. 30, Moscow, 17 May (NS) 1797.

[7] Ibid., Carton 86, no. 44, St Petersburg, 20 July (NS) 1797.

Berlin of his determination to protect Austria's interests at a time when she would have difficulty protecting them herself.[8]

When Paul refused to make an armed intervention before Leoben, there was still the possibility that he could mediate between Austria and France. He had also been approached, as he informed Cobenzl, by the French government through Prussia. Vienna feared, as Cobenzl's comments made clear, that Prussia would become involved in the mediation, but Paul swore that he intended to do no more than use Prussia as a channel to communicate with France.[9] He also assured the Austrian ambassador that he would only deal indirectly with the French and that there was no question of his recognizing the current republican regime. This last was something less than frank. Cobenzl, who found the approaches through Berlin threatening, suggested alternative ways to establish contact with the Directory's representatives, including using Count Razumovskii, the Russian ambassador in Vienna. Paul, however, insisted that indirect contact through Prussia was best and most consistent with his own dignity.[10]

A few days later Count Bezborodko, Paul's chancellor, informed Cobenzl that Prince N. V. Repnin was to go to Berlin carrying a letter from Paul which promised 60,000 Russian troops for Austria's assistance in case France did not make peace on reasonable terms. It would also urge Prussia to support the sanctity of the German constitution and assert that Russia could not view any further weakening of Austria with less than alarm. All this was very well, as Cobenzl told Bezborodko, for the future, but it was no help for the present, and he confessed to Thugut that Repnin's pro-Prussian attitudes worried him. He concluded morosely that 'It is unfortunately only too true that our ally in no way fulfils what the urgency of present circumstances and the intimacy of the bonds between us demand'. However, he continued, 'no matter how afflicting this state of things may be, as it is impossible to change them, it is necessary to draw out of these demonstrations whatever we can to use against our enemies'. It was this hope that helped him to appear to be better satisfied with what he was told than he actually was.[11] Had he known the substance, however, of the instructions Paul had prepared for Prince Repnin, he would have been even less encouraged.[12]

[8] Ibid., Carton 85, no. 29, Moscow, 4 May (NS) 1797; Ragsdale, 'Russia, Prussia, and Europe', 82–3.
[9] HHSA, Russland II Berichte, Carton 85, Cobenzl to Thugut, no. 29, Moscow, 4 May (NS) 1797.   [10] Ibid.
[11] Ibid. The conversation with Bezborodko followed the talk with Paul by two days.
[12] The summary of Paul's letter to the Prussian court which Bezborodko gave Cobenzl contained only a fraction of the negotiating instructions Repnin received.

Paul's instructions, though they would have disappointed the Austrians, showed a surprisingly flexible and pragmatic approach to achieving peace. His position on the revolution in France had long since shifted from the rabid interventionism which marked his views at the beginning of the revolutionary period. During his conversation with Cobenzl he recalled how

> until 1793 he had been so enraged against all the French revolutionaries . . . that society made fun of him, yet throughout that entire time he had never ceased to represent to the empress the necessity for sending troops to your [i.e. Austria's] assistance, that that was the only way to unite the Prussian and the Austrian operations, and that until then [1793] one could successfully have destroyed the democracy and reestablished the monarchy, but that after that time, the matter became impossible and when the empress announced her resolution to send 60,000 men [to Austria's aid] he told her, 'Madame, it is too late, you can no longer do anything.'[13]

Consistent with this approach, the Repnin instructions indicated Paul's willingness to recognize the republic (assuming that a 'reasonable' settlement was possible), and his territorial recommendations took into account what France had achieved since the war began in 1792. There was no sign of returning France to her pre-war boundaries, nor was there any mention of restoring the Bourbons. Paul reiterated his determination, however, to protect the integrity of the German empire, and he opposed further annexations on the left bank of the Rhine. The Alps on the Italian frontier would make an acceptable French border and would allow France to retain Savoy and Nice. He was also prepared to accept French annexation of the Austrian Netherlands, while he held that the Stadholder should be re-established in Holland under Prussia's guardianship. Despite his concern for the German empire, he was willing for Austria to be compensated for her losses with a portion of Bavaria or by annexing secularized imperial lands. He also indicated that if contact could be quietly arranged with the French representative in Berlin, preferably at his request, it would be possible to advance peace talks further. This, too, went beyond what Paul had told Cobenzl he was willing to do.[14]

The peace signed at Leoben (18 April 1797) made Paul's plans moot and ended Prince Repnin's mission before it started. But France

For the instructions, see Mikhailovskii-Danilevskii, *Voina* . . . *1799*, i. 34–42; cf. Martens, *Recueil des traités*, vi. 250–1. Ragsdale, 'Russia, Prussia, and Europe', 83, summarizes the high points.

[13] HHSA, Russland II Berichte, Carton 85, Cobenzl to Thugut, no. 29, Moscow, 4 May (NS) 1797.
[14] Mikhailovskii-Danilevskii, *Voina* . . . *1799*, i. 34–7.

was interested in the new tsar and had requested the court at Berlin to investigate the possibility of meetings with the Russians. Paul jumped at the chance, sending Count Nikita Petrovich Panin to Berlin as his special emissary. The Repnin instructions became Panin's. Paul indicated that, if asked, he would consider mediating a general European settlement, though this was not a point to be pursued aggressively. Conversations between Monsieur Caillard, the Directory's ambassador to Berlin, and Count Panin followed which came to no conclusion. The agreement they discussed was generally unexceptionable and built on previous commercial and political arrangements. There was, however, no meeting of minds over one clause which stipulated that neither contracting party would support the enemies of the other. This clause, if accepted, would have required Paul to withdraw support from the aristocratic victims of the revolution, many of whom had taken refuge in St Petersburg. Open though his negotiating stance may have been, he was not ready to abandon the *émigrés*. Having reached impasse, Caillard and Panin had to wait for new instructions. During this lull, France and Austria signed the treaty of Campoformio (6/17 October 1797). Subsequently, the negotiations died as Paul turned to military intervention in response to new evidences of French aggression.[15]

France was not Paul's only diplomatic interest in this period. While shielding Austria, he had also reached out to Berlin. Immediately on his accession, he sent a special emissary to Friedrich Wilhelm II with a warm personal message. The Prussian king was pleased and dispatched Count Brühl to Petersburg charged with greetings and congratulations. Paul then wrote again inviting Prussia's co-operation with Russia and recalling previous close personal and political relationships.[16] Paul hoped to draw Prussia back into the alliance with Russia, Britain, and Austria. He recognized the rivalry between Vienna and Berlin as another threat to European stability; he hoped, as we have seen, to use Berlin's relations with France to open channels to Paris; and all disclaimers aside, he felt nostalgia for the times when the Prussian connection was an anchor in the north. But the Prussian government continued to disappoint, and Paul's efforts to write a Russo-Prussian agreement failed. The Prussians twisted and turned, but in the end, their neutrality, their distrust of Austria,

---

[15] Mikhailovskii-Danilevskii, *Voina* . . . 1799, 27–8, 44–5. For the text of Caillard's note dated '7 ventôse, an v' (25 Feb. 1797), ibid. 370–1 n. 41; 375–7 n. 51 concerns the Caillard negotiations. See also Ragsdale, 'Russia, Prussia, and Europe', 84–5.

[16] Mikhailovskii-Danilevskii, *Voina* . . . 1799, i. 25–6; 368 n. 37 for Paul's letter to the Prussian king; 370 n. 40, for Paul's comments to Stepan Kolychev, his representative in Berlin.

and the security which they found in their current relationship with France, militated against any agreement at all.[17] Nevertheless, Paul showed remarkable persistence. He continued working on relations with Prussia through the summer of 1798, and then returned to the charge a year later as part of his planning with England for their joint attack on Holland. And when the second coalition broke down during the autumn and winter of 1799–1800, he turned once more to Berlin, this time in the context of establishing a new 'northern system'. Only then did the relationship which had escaped him over the preceding three years develop, though in the event it proved to be less than satisfactory.[18]

Paul's first diplomatic steps accomplished relatively little beyond encouraging Austria to settle with France. Though he was willing to mediate between Austria and France, or Austria and Prussia, he was not asked to do so; his suggestion for a congress at Leipzig was ignored (he himself had scotched the idea of a meeting at Berne as being too far from Russia); he played no part in the negotiations and settlement at Campoformio; and though a guarantor of the German imperial constitution and a proponent of its integrity, he was not invited to the congress at Rastadt which took up how Campoformio was to be applied to the Germanies. With no territorial interests and no army on the scene, Paul stood apart from the main diplomatic action. Nor did this situation change until the following year when he put Russia's naval and military forces into play against France, and took a leading part in arming the second coalition. Even then, however, the political initiative escaped him as, despite substantial and largely successful military contributions, the main impetus for political decisions remained with Vienna, London, and Paris.

Both the English and the Austrian correspondents discounted Paul's explanation for his withdrawing military support, suggesting that he lacked the energy or even the courage to take up Catherine's role.[19] Whether Russia was in fact in danger of a revolution is

[17] Ragsdale, 'Russia, Prussia and Europe', for Russo-Prussian relations. His article contains new material from East German archival holdings. On efforts to win Prussia to the coalition, Mikhailovskii-Danilevskii, *Voina* . . . 1799, i. 113–15; 464 n. 176 and 464 n. 177.

[18] Ragsdale, 'Russia, Prussia, and Europe', and Martens, *Recueil des traités*, vi. 250–95; Miliutin, *Voina* . . . 1799, iii. 127–31 and 355–6 n. 181, v. 164–5, and 425–7 nn. 1 and 2, 168–9 and 428–9 n. 6, 251–4, and 258–60. See below.

[19] HHSA, Russland II Berichte, Carton 84, Cobenzl to Thugut, no. 72, 25 Nov. (NS) 1796; no. 75, 7 Dec. (NS) 1796; Carton 85, no. 29, Moscow, 4 May (NS) 1797; Carton 86, no. 44, 20 July (NS) 1797; Carton 86, Dietrichstein to Thugut, no. 49, apostille 1, 13 Aug. (NS) 1797. PRO, FO/65/35, Whitworth to Grenville, 18 Nov. (NS) 1796; no. 64, 13 Dec. (NS) 1796; 65/37, no. 24, Moscow, 3 May (NS) 1797; 65/

doubtful, but Paul believed the danger was real, and he refused to consider any new commitments until those conditions had been set right. He used the peasant uprisings at the beginning of his reign to show how right he was to withdraw from the war in the west, and even at the time of his coronation, he declared that he was still far too involved to be able to consider adventures outside Russia.[20] Whether his diagnosis was correct, and whether his treatment did, in fact, cure the diseases he identified, is beside the point. Paul himself made Russia's foreign policy; until he was satisfied, nothing further could be done. Satisfaction, however, came surprisingly early. Less than a year after his accession he told the English minister that he believed his reforms had taken hold, that the army was ready, and that Russia was prepared to play an active part once more in the affairs of Europe.[21] The atmosphere in the capital reflected this change of view. In place of the earlier pacifism, a new belligerency stirred; Paul's officers seemed to be ambitious for war, though there was some question whether the regular soldiers, who had been drilled and manœuvred to exhaustion, shared their superiors' enthusiasm.[22]

At the same time as this newly martial spirit appeared, Paul identified himself explicitly with the people and symbols of the *ancien régime*. After Campoformio, the prince de Condé's *émigré* army needed a home. Paul gave it one, though he took the precaution of splitting the force and establishing its components in the western provinces far from either Moscow or Petersburg. He worried that Jacobins might be hiding among the aristos, so once the Condé army was settled within fortress Russia, he forbade further immigration, first of Frenchmen, and then of all foreigners, without his express consent. Cobenzl, when he saw the decrees, complimented him on his

38, no. 46, 8 Sept. (NS) 1797; 65/47, 19 Sept. (NS) 1797) no. 51, 10 Oct. (NS) 1797. In this last Whitworth held that 'Fear alone, is and ever will be, the secret but undoubted groundwork of his [Paul's] Policy' and Russia will inevitably lose 'the consideration' won under Catherine. Whitworth was less sceptical of the need for domestic reform than Cobenzl was, though he discounted the dangers of a revolution.

[20] See especially Cobenzl's conversations with Paul: HHSA, Russland II Berichte, Carton 84, Cobenzl to Thugut, no. 10, 17 Feb (NS) 1797; Carton 85, no. 29, Moscow, 4 May (NS) 1797; no. 30, Moscow, 17 May (NS) 1797) no. 44, St Petersburg, 20 July (NS) 1797.

[21] HHSA, Russland II Berichte, Carton 84, Dietrichstein to Thugut, no. 59, apostille 1, 13 Oct. (NS) 1797.

[22] Ibid.; PRO, FO/65/38, Whitworth to Grenville, no. 53, 17 Oct. (NS) 1797. The occasion for the military demonstrations was a sudden quarrel with Sweden which was soon over. Three days earlier, however, Whitworth informed London that the tsar had taken a very firm, even threatening, line with Prussia. Ibid., no. 52, 14 Oct. (NS) 1797.

foresight in a hazardous situation.²³ Campoformio also forced the displacement of Louis XVIII. Paul gave him 200,000 rubles for current expenses, arranged a regular subsidy, and rescued him from Braunschweig to install him on Russian territory in the castle at Mittau.²⁴ This was also the time when the Polish priory of the knights of Malta became the Russian grand priory and was moved under imperial protection to St Petersburg. And when, early in the next year, Pius VI was driven out of Rome, Paul offered him asylum.²⁵ Paul's view of himself as a defender of legitimacy and the old order was hardly new. What was new was his willingness to fight. This came from his satisfaction with the army reforms. He continued to negotiate, but it was clear that war in defence of the established system had become thinkable.

No single incident was responsible for drawing Paul from peace towards war, though the root of it was France's expanding power position and the failure of diplomatic measures to set any effective limit on it. Campoformio troubled Paul. It was an agreement which he feared would create further instability and it showed a threatening disposition by France to intrude on the eastern Mediterranean. Even before the treaty was signed, French forces had occupied the Ionian islands, and in September they seized the Russian consul at Zanta. Until this matter was resolved, Paul broke off contact with the French in Berlin. Campoformio ratified French control over the Ionian islands. It also partitioned the former Venetian republic, in part to satisfy Austrian demands for compensation. Moreover, with the treaty signed, the French government seemed less interested in maintaining contact with Russia, and while the meetings at Rastadt were organized, Napoleon began campaigning again in Italy. Rome was occupied in February and a Roman republic declared. The possibility that Italy would become French and Jacobin was frighteningly real. During the spring, a major concentration of military and naval power at Toulon added to the uncertainty, and when Bonaparte slipped away from the British blockaders to seize Malta, it was still uncertain what he intended. The campaign in Egypt, disastrous though it was for the French fleet, firmly established Bonaparte as a threat to Turkish, Russian, and British interests. It also removed him for the time from proximity to Paris.

---

[23] Mikhailovskii-Danilevskii, *Voina* ... *1799*, i. 49–51, 54–6, 381 n. 62. HHSA, Russland II Berichte, Carton 88, Cobenzl to Thugut, no. 48, 9 Sept. (NS) 1798. The comments were offered nearly two years after the event when Cobenzl had returned from his special assignment negotiating peace with the French.

[24] Mikhailovskii-Danilevskii, *Voina* ... *1799*, i. 51–2.

[25] See above, Ch. 8.

Meanwhile, the French satellite republic in the Netherlands gained a new constitution and was drawn closer to Paris, while French forces entered Switzerland and announced the formation of a Helvetian republic.[26]

French action in the Mediterranean drew Russia and the Ottoman empire closer together. Paul had no interest in expanding at the expense of the Porte, while France, which had acted as a counterweight to Russian influence in the Levant in Catherine's time, had become a primary threat to Ottoman interests. The French in Italy and the Adriatic were likewise a threat to Russia's burgeoning Black Sea trade. The result was a natural conjunction between Russia and the Ottomans which Paul blessed and which produced combined operations against the French position in the Ionian islands months before a Russo-Turkish treaty was signed on 3 January 1799. French expansion in general impressed Paul as a continuing threat to Europe, but their action in Italy and the Mediterranean impinged on rulers and principalities Paul had promised to protect, while endangering Russian economic interests of significant dimension. French aggressiveness was responsible for shifting Paul from his peaceful stance towards war; French pressures on Italy and the Levant were particularly important.[27]

Prussia refused to join the coalition which took shape in 1798, and England, though she signed a treaty with Russia on 29 December, made no new agreements with Austria. The English considered Austria's peace with France (Leoben, Campoformio) a violation of the agreements under which they served in the first coalition. They also shared Paul's desire to have Prussia in the new coalition and favoured Berlin at Vienna's expense. Austria, on her side, struck an early agreement with Naples (20 May 1798) but signed no additional treaty with Russia.[28] Nor were there preliminary negotiations to define war aims. Paul in 1798 was as anxious to fight the French as he had been determined earlier to remain at peace. This is not to say that he had no purpose in mind as he clearly did though, unlike his purposes in his earlier diplomacy, his goals were broad: to overthrow whatever the republic had established and restore traditional authorities. And, if the war could be carried into France, the republic

[26] Mikhailovskii-Danilevskii, *Voina* . . . *1799*, i. 57–81 and 336–64 nn.; Ragsdale, 'Russia, Prussia, and Austria', 85–7.

[27] See Norman E. Saul, 'The Objectives of Paul's Italian Policy', in H. Ragsdale (ed.), *Reassessment*, 31–43; Saul, *Russia and the Mediterranean*, 54–65. For developing Russian economic and cultural contacts with the Mediterranean before Paul, see ibid., ch. 1, *passim*. Cf. Stanislavskaia, *Russko-angliiskie otnosheniia*, and E. V. Tarle, *Admiral Ushakov na Sredizemnom More, 1799–1800* (Moscow, 1948).

[28] Ragsdale, 'Russia, Prussia, and Europe', 87.

overthrown, and monarchy re-established, the war would be a total success.[29] This was 'the good cause' (*la bonne cause*) to which presumably all the allies were committed, and it was in the service of *la bonne cause* that Paul emerged as the coalition's leader. As Whitworth wrote from Moscow, 'It would be impossible for me to give you a reasonable idea of the zeal of His Majesty the Emperor for the good cause and of his extraordinary desire to contribute by all means in his power to its success.'[30] Paul was committed and determined; he had embarked on a crusade.

Austria was Paul's nearest ally and the state with which he had to work most closely. Vienna had pressed him for support in 1797, and seemed reluctant throughout the negotiations with France to make peace. The Rastadt conference provided an opportunity for dragging matters out that Austria seized upon, and as Paul turned away from his efforts to promote a general peace in favour of going to war, his thinking meshed once more with that of Austria. Yet their approaches, and the assumptions behind them, remained very different. And therein lay the seed of their future troubles.

Baron Thugut, the Austrian chancellor who controlled both politics and military policy, hated France and was an outspoken opponent of revolutionary principles. He was also, however, uncertain that Austria had the means to defeat the French, and he was aware of the heavy price his country had paid in the course of the wars beginning in 1787. The loss of the Netherlands at the beginning of the revolutionary period had been a heavy blow; the expulsion from Italy, which was completed at the end of 1796, was equally painful. It was also cautionary. Though Thugut was committed to recovering as much of what had been lost as possible, and gaining compensation for what could not be recovered, he was unwilling to endanger unnecessarily either the forces at his command, or the territories he still controlled. This produced a careful, conservatizing approach to military operations, and a calculated weighing of interest in forming political commitments. If France could be successfully invaded, a revolution raised, and the monarchical system restored, Thugut's—and Austria's—ultimate hopes would have been realized. But in any choice between a solid if limited gain and the

---

[29] Mikhailovskii-Danilevskii, *Voina* . . . 1799, i. 108–11; 455–6 n. 161 and 457 n. 165. Martens, *Recueil des traités*, ii (Austria and Russia), 198–213; x (England and Russia), 408–41.

[30] (Quoted) Ragsdale, 'Russia, Prussia, and Europe', 87–8, from Martens, *Recueil des traités*, ix. 425.

more remote possibility of total victory, Thugut was prepared to choose the first.[31]

The way Austria intended to approach this war appeared before the general hostilities began. Ferdinand IV of Naples, bedazzled by the array of support he thought he had—Russian, Austrian, British, even Turkish—attacked the French in Rome. His offensive, ill-prepared at best, stalled, a counterattack was mounted, and the French rolled over Naples, driving the king, his court, and government into exile at Palermo. Ferdinand, on the strength of a formal alliance with Austria, appealed to Vienna for help when the tide turned. He was refused. The explanation was that Naples had acted unilaterally; therefore there was no obligation involved. Moreover, Austria was still preparing and was unable to divert forces to help.[32] Paul, however, leapt to Naples's assistance, diverting a column under General Rehbinder across the Balkans to the Dalmatian coast where the Neapolitans were to take responsibility for shipping the troops to Italy.[33] These forces arrived long after the fighting finished and played no part at all in liberating Naples later in the campaign. Their dispatch was a gesture of solidarity with a brother monarch and the fulfilment of a promise for support. The contrast between Paul's warmly supportive if quixotic gesture and Thugut's coldly rationalist refusal to act could hardly have been greater.

The truth was that the basis on which Paul chose to go to war differed in fundamental ways from Austria's. Russia, as Paul repeatedly emphasized, had no territorial interests. She was fighting to stop French expansion, to free territories under French control, and to re-establish rulers who had lost their thrones. Austria agreed with these goals but always with the proviso that she had definite territorial interests, and that those interests were supported by previous agreements and were vital to her future security and prosperity. In the event of conflict, they would take precedence over restoring deposed princes or recovering lost lands. Indeed, a comprehensive restoration of the old order in Italy would seriously compromise Austria's claims for compensation. Unfortunately, none of this appears to have been discussed prior to the opening of the

[31] Miliutin, *Voina* . . . *1799*, ii. 153–8. Cf. A. von Vivenot, 'Thugut und sein politisches System', *Archiv für Österreichische Geschichte*, 43 (1870).

[32] Mikhailovskii-Danilevskii, *Voina* . . . *1799*, i. 118–21, 465–7 n. 178; Miliutin, *Voina* . . . *1799*, i. 151–2. Though Austria did not provide Naples support, they counted on the backing of both Sardinia and Naples in Italy, and it was the Austrian general, Mack, who led Naples's army against Rome.

[33] Mikhailovskii-Danilevskii, *Voina* . . . *1799*, i. 118–21; 465–7 n. 178 and esp. n. 168.

campaign. Paul did request a statement of war aims from Thugut in December 1798, and he made the same request more pressingly the following summer.[34] He failed in both cases. There was, in fact, no meeting of minds on the political issues which the war posed and, at least where Italy was concerned, Paul found himself with no alternative to accepting what the Austrians wanted and did. Curiously enough, despite the incompatibility of war aims between Russia and Austria, the issues which caused the greatest friction were military, while the final break occurred over a particularly egregious affront to Russian honour.[35]

The terms on which Paul supported Austria gave all the advantage to Vienna. Combined operations were governed by a defensive alliance written in 1792 and renewed in 1795 which was only marginally applicable to the situation in 1798. According to this treaty, the two contracting powers agreed to provide support in the event that one or the other was invaded. If the invasion occurred at a point too far removed from the ally's boundary to make direct assistance practical, a subsidy equivalent to the stipulated 12,000 troops was to be paid. If Russia were to support Austria, as soon as the Russian forces crossed the frontier Austria accepted responsibility for supplying them. The Austrians then could use the Russian troops as they were needed. The Russians were, in fact, auxiliaries supporting the Austrian army, and their commanders were to follow the orders of the Austrian authorities over them. The English ambassador urged Paul formally to declare Russia a full partner in the coalition rather than restricting himself to an auxiliary role. This was, in fact, the tsar's intention, but Bezborodko supported by Kochubei dissuaded him from doing so. The ostensible reason was that such a declaration should await the settlement of all arrangements including subsidies. A new treaty with Austria would then have to be negotiated. This was not done, and the effect was that Paul allowed the Austrians to define how and for what purposes the Russian troops could be used.[36]

---

[34] Ibid. 115. See below.

[35] Paul blamed Austria, and specifically Archduke Charles, for the Russian defeat at Zürich, but the event which led him definitively to abandon Austria was the gratuitously insulting behaviour of the Austrian general Fröhlich towards Russia's flag and forces at Ancona. The point is discussed in detail below. For a recent broad review of the diplomatic issues in the coalition's failure, see Paul Schroeder, 'The Collapse of the Second Coalition', *Journal of Modern History*, 59 (1987), 244–90. The military issues are discussed in A. B. Rodger, *The War of the Second Coalition, 1798–1801: A Strategic Commentary* (Oxford, 1969).

[36] Martens, *Recueil des traités*, ii. 198–213, 271–7, 280–1, 358–72. The 1792 treaty is given on pp. 198–213. Cobenzl reported the dispute between Paul and his

Vienna unconsciously compounded the problems of co-operation by suggesting a Russian commander for the allied armies campaigning in northern Italy. The original choice for this command, the brilliant 26-year-old prince of Orange, had died unexpectedly. The prince of Württemberg was considered and rejected, and the only other Austrian commander of sufficient stature and experience, the archduke Charles, was scheduled to lead the imperial armies in Germany. Joseph, the archduke palatin of Hungary, was temporarily installed, but his inexperience disqualified him from sole command. The idea of appointing an Austrian general to oversee the archduke palatin was considered, but none of the Austrian field commanders were thought to have the standing to perform the task. The English minister, Sir Morton Eden, suggested to Count Razumovskii that he might recommend the very distinguished Russian general, Count Alexander Suvorov, to oversee the archduke palatin and serve as commander of the combined Austrian–Russian forces in Italy. The idea was well taken by Thugut and the Austrian leadership, and Razumovskii offered it to Paul as their idea which he recommended. Though the idea of a Russian commander appealed to Paul, Suvorov posed a problem. He had been openly dismissive of Paul's military reforms and, in fact, had been retired to his lands in a state of mild disgrace. But Paul did not hesitate long. Suvorov could be an excellent choice. He was well known to the Austrian command and was respected. And Paul had a high opinion of his ability, so much so that he had gone out of his way to attempt to win him to his ideas. He put aside whatever reservations he had, called Suvorov to St Petersburg, gave him his instructions, and set him on the road to Vienna where he arrived to a thunderous public welcome on 14 March (NS) 1799.[37]

advisers over the full participation issue; Bezborodko was unsympathetic to the war, and chose this way to restrain Paul's 'dangerous enthusiasms'. HHSA, Russland II Berichte, Carton 89, Cobenzl to Thugut, no. 64, 23 Nov. (NS) 1798.

[37] Mikhailovskii-Danilevskii, *Voina* ... *1799*, i. 122–3. For Razumovskii's letter to Paul (20/31 Jan. 1799), 471 n. 188. See also Wassiltchikow, *Razoumowski*, ii/1. 296–8. Razumovskii was already regarded as too pro-Austrian, and it was thought Kolychev was about to replace him. Wassiltchikow (ibid. 292) asserts that the Suvorov suggestion saved Razumovskii from being recalled. For Suvorov's arrival in Vienna, ibid. 306–10. For an excellent modern treatment of Suvorov, his career, and his role in the second coalition, see Philip Longworth, *The Art of Victory: The Life and Achievements of Generalissimo Suvorov* (London, 1965), 236 ff. *A. V. Suvorov: Sbornik dokumentov*, ed. G. P. Meshchariakov, 4 vols. (Moscow, 1949–53) provides rich documentation on military and biographical questions. See also N. M. Korobkov, *Generalissimo Suvorov: Sbornik dokumentov i materialov* (Ogiz, 1947), esp. 221–318.

Suvorov was an established commander of the first rank. The Austrians recognized this by withdrawing the archduke palatin entirely from the Italian command, replacing him with Suvorov, and making the Russian general an Austrian field-marshal. This was to eliminate any controversies about precedence or seniority which might arise with the Austrian general officers whom he would command. Suvorov reported to, and received his orders from, Emperor Francis II. His real superior, however, was the *Hofkriegsrath* or Aulic council, which not only controlled policy decisions, but which interfered in tactical matters. Thugut, who fancied himself as both a strategist and a tactician, controlled the *Hofkriegsrath*, and he expected to oversee the field armies and the generals in charge. Suvorov, therefore, was in fact subordinate to Thugut. Since the Russian ambassador in Vienna, Count Andrei Razumovskii, belonged to Thugut's circle and supported the chancellor's ideas, Suvorov's only recourse in case of disagreement would be to write to Petersburg. Any serious difference of opinion thus would become a diplomatic issue.[38]

Temperamentally, Suvorov and Thugut were ill-assorted. Suvorov was as mercurial as Thugut was dogged, and as dismissive of forms as the chancellor was punctilious. In his seventies, Suvorov was famous for his eccentricity, even clownishness, and he attracted animosity and loyalty in almost equal parts. He was an exponent of speed, manœuvrability, and the bayonet charge, and his rapid dashes left his Austrian observers breathless. Nothing further from the Austrians' conservative plod could be imagined. These were differences which guaranteed friction. Nor did the problems end there. Suvorov's view of why the war was being fought fitted Paul's rather than Thugut's thinking. Suvorov was a deeply religious man, a strong legitimist, and a bitter enemy of Jacobinism. He saw himself in Italy as a liberator who would destroy the alien and atheistic system France had imposed, and whose duty it was to bring back the people's religion and their legitimate rulers. He believed that he was fighting a people's war, and he exulted in the public uprisings against the French which accompanied the allies' march.[39] Suvorov was to praise the Austrians who fought beside his Russians, and he was generous in giving credit to Austrian officers. But there was almost no common ground between himself and Vienna. His character, and the victories he won, made the arrangements under which Austria

---

[38] Mikhailovskii-Danilevskii, *Voina . . . 1799*, i. 139–41; Miliutin, *Voina . . . 1799*, i. 151–7, provides a thoughtful if partisan appraisal of Thugut.

[39] For Suvorov's character, Longworth, *Suvorov, passim*, and esp. 247, for conflict with the Austrians on outlook and goals.

and Russia fought essentially unworkable. Suvorov was much more than an auxiliary or a mercenary. He dominated a scene in which he was supposed to play a subordinate role.

A series of irritating controversies plagued Russia's relations with Austria from the beginning. As soon as the main column of Russian troops under General Rosenberg reached the frontier, there was a quarrel over provisioning. The 1795 agreement required the Austrians to supply their Russian auxiliaries, but there were no settled guidelines on the quantity or character of food and fodder. When the Russian advance units met their Austrian commissariat, General Rosenberg protested that what the Austrians intended to provide was less than Russian troops normally received and was of poor quality. Paul, when informed, ordered him to halt his advance and, when a satisfactory resolution was not immediately forthcoming, to return the troops to their bases inside Russia. This controversy became a full-scale diplomatic crisis which absorbed a crucial six weeks before it was settled.[40]

Paul's election as grand master of the knights of Malta further muddied the diplomatic waters and strained relations with Austria. The election was obviously controversial, but Paul forced the issue by making acceptance of it a test of loyalty to himself. Spain was one victim. An object of suspicion because of its close ties to France, Paul ordered the Spanish chargé out of Petersburg and subsequently, when the Spanish court followed suit, declared war. The declaration spoke only to Spain's French connections, but it was noted that Paul had learnt that the Spanish court intended to reject his election as grand master. The declaration of war was a diplomatic presumptive strike intended to smother the anticipated protest.[41] Bavaria, which had only recently re-established the order after earlier secularizing the lands of religious foundations, was similarly reluctant to approve

---

[40] For the provisioning crisis from Cobenzl's side, HHSA, Russland II Berichte, Carton 89, Cobenzl to Thugut, Kouvert 20 Sept.–10 Oct. (NS) 1798, pp. 1–64. Whitworth considered the crisis evidence of the 'changeableness' of Paul's character and the amount of grain involved 'trifling'. He thought Austria originated the problem, and that it provided evidence of the 'unaccountable conduct' of the Austrian government which was 'constantly calling for assistance, but little disposed to satisfy those from whom they can receive it'. PRO, FO/65/41, Whitworth to Grenville, no. 46, St Petersburg, 4 Oct. (NS) 1798. Miliutin, *Voina* ... 1799, i. 102–7, took the provisioning crisis much more seriously.

[41] Stedingk gave the knights of Malta question considerable weight in appraising Paul's foreign policy. On the declaration of war against Spain, see Riksarkivet, Diplomatica Moscovitica, vol. 460, Stedingk to the king, 14 July/4 Aug. 1799. Paul's action against Spain, where Russia had at best a tenuous relationship, was particularly revealing. Cf. HHSA, Russland II Berichte, Carton 92, Cobenzl to Thugut, no. 57, 31 July (NS) 1799.

Paul's election. Baron Hompesch's brother was influential at Munich and kept the issue alive. Paul ordered the Bavarian attaché, Baron Reuchlin, to leave Petersburg immediately after learning of Bavaria's opposition, and he followed this with threats that he would settle the matter by ordering Rosenberg's corps to invade. The Bavarians, caught between Austria's claims for compensation at their expense and Paul's threats, chose to placate the tsar. A special delegation was chosen to go to Petersburg to recognize Paul as grand master and to convey the elector's support and good wishes. Paul accepted the gesture, rewarded the Bavarians by declaring them friends and allies, and promised them protection against Austrian claims. Bavaria responded by offering a special force of 20,000 troops to support the alliance.[42]

The most dangerous problems which the Malta issue posed to the alliance, however, stemmed from the reluctance of the Bohemian priory, which lived under the protection of the court at Vienna, to accept Baron Hompesch's deposition and Paul's election. The controversy developed during the spring and summer of 1799 at the same time as friction over the conduct of the campaign in Italy was mounting towards a crisis. The stance of the Bohemian priory was critical. With the French priories gone, the Bohemian priory was the largest and most influential in Europe. For it to quibble at Paul's election was potentially more damaging even than the pope's opposition, which, by the Russian interpretation at any rate, could be offset by an affirmative role in his favour of a majority of the priories and *langues* free to vote and voting.[43] Moreover, the Bohemian priory was firmly identified with the German emperor and the Austrian government, that is, with Paul's primary ally in the struggle against France. For a negative to originate there would seriously embarrass the tsar while proving to him that Austria was deficient

---

[42] On background to the Bavarian incident, Miliutin, *Voina . . . 1799*, i. 157 and 510 n. 14; ii. 155–6 and 161–2 The Bavarian incident is reviewed in detail in a report Count Stedingk sent his court by special courier to avoid Paul's secret police: Riksarkivet, Diplomatica Moscovitica, vol. 460, Stedingk to the king, 18/29 Mar. 1799. See also: PRO, FO/65/42, Whitworth to Grenville, no. 13, 13 Mar. (NS) 1799; HHSA, Russland II Berichte, Carton 89, Cobenzl to Thugut, no. 65, apostille 5, 10 Dec. (NS) 1798; no. 67, 18 Dec. (NS) 1798; Carton 91, no. 36, apostille 14, 17 Mar. (NS) 1799. See also Archivio Vaticano, Polonia–Russia, vol. 344/VI, fo. 26, Maggio–2 ottobre (NS) 1802 [sic: 1798–1802] for the preliminary agreement of 6 July 1799 and the formal convention of 29 July 1799. Baron Flachslander wrote that there was no choice but to agree terms with Paul and that this was made necessary 'By the interest of the Church, perhaps that of the Order', a sentiment which Archbishop Albi accepted.

[43] McGrew, 'Paul I and the Knights', 55–9, esp. 57.

in loyalty and goodwill. Both the government in Vienna and the allies' representatives in Petersburg hoped to avoid any such outcome. This was accomplished initially by putting off a public declaration when it was apparent that the decision would go against Paul. Baron Hompesch had come from the Bohemian priory, and had a wide circle of friends at the Austrian court. Consequently, when he sought refuge after the fall of Malta, he went to Trieste where he lived under Austrian protection. While in exile, he continued to style himself grand master of the knights of Malta, though (as noted above), the pope had earlier suspended his appointment until a full investigation of the charges against him could be made.[44] Such pretensions infuriated Paul who regarded Hompesch as a traitor to the order who had been charged and deposed. When Paul learnt that Baron Hompesch was not only using his title but had sent a formal deputation to Malta as representatives of the grand master, his anger boiled over. He declared that Francis II himself was responsible for controlling Hompesch's behaviour, and he demanded that the emperor either force Hompesch to give up his pretensions and live as a private citizen, or expel him from the imperial domains. If the emperor refused to discipline this wayward subject, Paul announced that he would have no choice but to withdraw his forces from the coalition.[45]

Paul's complaint and the threat it carried produced a flurry of disclaimers in Vienna. The alternatives, however, were clear, and the emperor forced Hompesch to choose between expulsion and resignation. The former grand master formally resigned his offices and titles.[46] This was a satisfying victory, but it still left the problem of recognizing Paul's election to be solved. This was handled in the same way, with the Austrian government applying strong pressure to the recalcitrant knights while announcing to the Russians that the priory would approve. The capitulation was reluctant, but eventually it was possible to organize a delegation of knights to carry the priory's decision to St Petersburg. The fact of the priory's acquiescence apart, the delegation's appearance offered the opportunity for one of those dramatic ceremonials so dear to Paul's heart. It was, however, less than a wholehearted affirmation that the delegation brought, for their presentation at no point contained the title 'grand master of the knights of Malta'. The Bohemian priory numbered many who were willing to recognize Paul's protection, support, even his leadership,

---

[44] Ibid.
[45] Miliutin, *Voina* . . . *1799*, iii. 223–4.
[46] Pierredon, *Histoire politique*, i, documents 76 and 77 for the curt order of Francis II to Hompesch and the latter's resignation.

but who balked at giving him the full title. Their ruse was discovered before the official audience took placed and was declared totally unacceptable. Another crisis loomed; without explicit recognition that the tsar was, in fact, grand master, Paul would dissolve the coalition and recall his troops. It was Cobenzl who virtually bludgeoned the delegates into using the hated formula. The alliance had been saved again.[47]

Malta became an important issue because Paul considered it to be so. Long after the question of whether he was or was not grand master had been settled, he urged Bonaparte to use his influence with the Spanish court to win the approval that had escaped him there. There was nothing in this but his own need to be recognized by everyone in the role he had accepted. Though uncomfortable with what they did, the government in Vienna was willing to agree to his claims; Russian armies were far more important to the matters at hand than who wore the grand master's robes. This is not to say that the Austrian court was wholly disengaged. When Paul appointed a Russian citizen to represent the knights in Vienna he was reminded that it was customary, even a matter of right, that the Bohemian priory nominate for this post. He never understood the point—to his mind his power as grand master was no less absolute than his powers as tsar—but he finally agreed to Count St Julien, a distinguished member of the Bohemian priory who had won his favour, as the appointee. The priory agreed to the appointment, and the issue was resolved by avoiding a clash over what the grand master's rights were.[48] The Austrians, and particularly Baron Thugut, were far less flexible on questions of military policy and the political future of northern Italy. There they gave away nothing, preferring in the end to lose future Russian support rather than abandon the political advantages the Russian armies had already given them. It was this policy, short-sighted as it was, that contributed to alienating Paul from the coalition after one short season of campaigning and left the Austrians to face a revived France alone in 1800.

The erosion of Austro-Russian relations in 1799 developed out of the campaign itself. Following France's easy victory over Naples, the war turned against her to become a triumphal march for the allies.

[47] Cobenzl's correspondence tells the story of the Bohemian priory, its efforts to circumvent Paul, and the steps Cobenzl took to force them to co-operate. HHSA, Russland II Berichte, Carton 91, Cobenzl to Thugut, no. 42, 11 June (NS) 1799; Carton 92, no. 49, apostille 1, 3 July (NS) 1799; Carton 92, no. 60, 9 Aug. (NS) 1799; no. 62, 16 Aug. (NS) 1799.

[48] Cobenzl also negotiated this matter. See HHSA, Russland II Berichte, Carton 92, Cobenzl to Thugut, no. 49, apostile 1, 3 July (NS) 1799; no. 62, 16 Aug. (NS) 1799; no. 63, apostille 2, 23 Aug. (NS) 1799.

Italy was swept clear of republican armies and the administrators they had installed, the French were driven off their island conquests in the Adriatic and the Mediterranean, the French fleet, savaged at the Nile, was unable to prevent the British from controlling access by sea to the battle zones in Europe or in western Asia, while Suvorov, who seemed unbeatable, conquered northern Italy. The government in Paris was in disorder, and a vast overhaul of both governing and military operations, the latter literally in the face of the enemy, was carried out. The unrest continued, however, until Napoleon Bonaparte, returned from his losing campaign in Egypt, seized control in the *coup d'état* of Brumaire, 18 October 1799.[49]

Despite French weaknesses, Suvorov's Italian victories had no counterpart on the Rhine or in Switzerland. The archduke Charles won one major engagement at Zürich, but for nearly three months he did nothing, despite the fact that allied forces held a numerical advantage over the French.[50] Then, at the end of August, following his overwhelming victory at Novi, Suvorov was ordered to regroup, to reduce the fortresses he had left behind, while his plan for an invasion over the coastal mountains into France was rejected. A new grand strategy, with which Paul agreed, was put into effect. Suvorov was ordered into Switzerland where his forces were to join two other Russian armies under Rimskii-Korsakov and Rehbinder supported by the prince de Condé's *émigrés*. The Russians were to leave northern Italy where they were to be replaced by an Austrian occupation force. Archduke Charles would fall back from Zürich while the Russians moved in to fill the positions held by the imperial German forces which would move on to the Rhine. These moves were to co-ordinate as well with an Anglo-Russian invasion of Holland.[51]

Though at the beginning of the campaign Thugut rejected the idea of the Russians basing themselves in Switzerland, he now supported the same idea as part of what was to develop as a massive allied assault on France proper with the Russian armies linking the two

---

[49] Miliutin, *Voina* . . . 1799, iii. 7–22 for a summary of the allied victory (vol. ii, *passim*, covers the campaign in detail), and iii. 23–45 for the Prairial revolution and its effect on the military situation. The description of Suvorov's victory over Joubert and the reformed French forces at Terzo, Orva, and Novi (beginning 1/12 Aug. 1799) follow pp. 30–65. For Bonaparte's *coup*, v. 236–9.

[50] Miliutin, *Voina* . . . 1799, ii. 318–44, for background to the Swiss campaign and the Austrians' very delicate approach.

[51] Ibid. 7–201, esp. 141–4. For Paul's enthusiastic reception of the new plan, see his letter to Suvorov, 4/15 Aug. 1799, p. 144, and to Razumovskii, same date, pp. 386–7 n. 212. The overall plan is given in Razumovskii's report to Paul, 31 July (NS) 1799, pp. 381–3 n. 211, and in Thugut's letter to Cobenzl, pp. 383–6.

main segments of the imperial forces and launching an invasion through Franche Comté. It was believed that uprisings in the Netherlands, along the Rhine, and in France itself would follow the invasion, and that this would bring down the shaky republican government and open the way to re-establishing the French monarchy.[52] More practically, at least for Austria, the new programme effectively removed the Russians from northern Italy where they had become an embarrassment to Austrian ambitions, especially in Piedmont, while eliminating the thorny relationship with Suvorov which had already created severe strains between Vienna and St Petersburg. But what had been friction and bad feeling in Italy turned into a mortal crisis in Switzerland. Within six weeks of Suvorov's last major victory, the Russian armies had been beaten, and Suvorov's column narrowly escaped total annihilation. What happened was that the archduke Charles left Zürich before the Russian forces could meet, giving the French general, Masséna, a marked numerical advantage over General Korsakov whom he attacked and defeated. Korsakov withdrew from Switzerland leaving Suvorov, who had just stormed over the St Gottard, marooned with a scant 16,000 troops at Muttenthale and completely surrounded. The French confidently expected his surrender. Though losing half their numbers, Suvorov's Russians fought their way out of the trap, finally joining with the remaining Russian forces near Glarus. But the whole of Switzerland was in French hands. Paul laid the blame squarely on the Austrians, and so the breakdown of the alliance began.[53]

Combined operations under the best of circumstances are difficult. In the case of Russia and the Austrians, they proved to be particularly so. Suvorov found himself serving several masters. Though his orders came from the emperor himself, it was the court military council and Chancellor Thugut who laid down the basic policy lines, gave orders to the Austrian officers ostensibly under Suvorov's command, and revised Suvorov's plans for campaign. Moreover, Suvorov found that

---

[52] Ibid., n. 211, Razumovskii to Paul, and Thugut to Cobenzl; n. 212, Paul to Razumovskii. Paul believed that 'if we occupy ourselves constantly and single-mindedly in making war on the French, one can believe that within a year France will once more be governed by a king. For it is this that I intend' (p. 386).

[53] Ibid. iii. 152–89 for the Austrian failure to join with the Russian forces in Switzerland. Miliutin blames Thugut and his political agents rather than Archduke Charles. For the military consequences, Suvorov's invasion of Switzerland, and his escape, see ibid. iv. 30–68; Korsakov's defeat at Zürich, pp. 69–107; the Swiss campaign up to Paul's decision to withdraw Suvorov, pp. 108–52. For a summary account, Longworth, *Suvorov*, 270–89. At this point, for Paul, Suvorov was a hero and a genius; no blame attached to him. See Paul's rescript, 29 Oct./9 Nov. 1799, Miliutin, *Voina . . . 1799*, iv. 164.

Austrian generals were reluctant to support him, that they were much slower to react, even when co-operative, than he was accustomed to expect, and that they would either contradict or ignore his orders. Supplies were a constant problem, and whenever he complained to Vienna, his complaints had no apparent effect. The problems worsened as the summer wore on until finally he took his case to Paul. In an angry letter which resonated through the next several weeks, he declared his griefs. He was receiving no cooperation from Vienna, politicians and generals alike seemed determined to put barriers in his way, so much so that it was becoming virtually impossible for him to fight the war. If this situation could not be changed, it would be better for him to be relieved of his commission and recalled.[54]

Apart from professional jealousies and a tendency to denigrate the Russians for their backwardness, and their general for his madcap style, the Austrians believed they had grounds for concern. It was widely thought that Suvorov's successes owed more to luck than craft, that his headlong tactics were an invitation to disaster, that his rapid marches exhausted the troops, and that his unwillingness to sit down and besiege fortresses left dangerous strong points in his rear.[55] The most important problem, however, was the conflict in goals between Suvorov and Baron Thugut. This took concrete form when Suvorov, following the liberation of Turin, called for the people to greet the return of the Sardinian monarchy to Piedmont, personally invited the king and his heir to return, and called for the army of Piedmont to join with his own. He was immediately informed by Vienna that none of this was acceptable, that the Sardinian monarchy had forfeited its rights in the agreement it had signed with the French permitting it to retreat to Cagliari, and that it was normal practice for such a territory to be occupied and its future determined at a peace conference. This case was urged on Paul, who had agreed with Suvorov's call for the Sardinians' return, and Paul accepted the

[54] Suvorov's complaints corresponded with his August victories. Despite his successes, his plans were rejected and the Austrians diverted forces from his command. Emperor Francis II wrote to Suvorov on 29 July/9 Aug., Miliutin, *Voina* ... 1799, iii. 73–9. Suvorov protested, but to no avail. Ibid. 81–2. For the text of the emperor's letter, ibid. 338–40 n. 110; Suvorov's appeal and a new campaign plan are given in ibid. 341–2 n. 111. His complaints to Paul (routed through Rostopchin) were dated 5/16 and 7/18 Aug. 1799. Ibid. 83–4.

[55] In the beginning, Suvorov refused to discuss his plans with the *Hofkriegsrath*. Miliutin, *Voina* ... 1799, i. 140. For problems in Austro-Russian co-ordination, ibid. ii. 29–42. See also Suvorov's plan and Francis II's negative reactions, ibid. 314–17, and 591–3 n. 121. For comments on Suvorov's 'luck' and complaints about the speed of his marches, ibid. 323–6, 334.

Austrian view. He instructed Suvorov to rescind his invitation to Charles Emmanuel and his brother, the duke of Aosta, and he directed Suvorov to accede to the establishment of an occupying administration. He also, however, demanded that Razumovskii, his ambassador in Vienna, query the Austrian government on precisely what their demands were, and he proposed that a general conference be held to clarify the issues involved.[56]

Suvorov's complaints were minor irritations in comparison with the issues which Piedmont and the future of Italy posed. Paul was fully committed to defending the integrity of the Neapolitan and Sardinian monarchies and to restoring them to the territories they had lost. He had no intention, as he pointedly told Razumovskii, of destroying the present French government only to allow another state to replace it as an aggressor against the weaker states he was supporting.[57] This declaration was plainly a warning to Austria. Thugut's position was that while Austria had no quarrel with the Italian rulers as such, she also required indemnification for the heavy losses she had suffered when the Netherlands were taken from her and for the unequal territorial settlement which occurred when Poland was partitioned the second time without her participation. It had been secretly agreed, or so Thugut asserted, that Austria was to be so compensated, but he also pointed out that it was precisely those agreements which made it undesirable for a congress to be held at Petersburg or anywhere else. Only the powers involved needed to be consulted. He also suggested that England would not care to have a review of the acquisitions she had made in the east and west Indies which had so greatly enlarged her control over international commerce. And it was also made clear—Razumovskii stressed the point—that great powers decided international political issues. It would be a major error to permit Sardinia or the kingdom of the two Sicilies to sit down with Russia, Austria, and Prussia.[58]

Paul found himself at a severe disadvantage in this exchange. He laid down demands; the Austrians were to give over talking in

[56] On the return of the Sardinian monarchy and the problem of Piedmont, Miliutin, *Voina* . . . 1799, iii. 226–7, 445–7 nn. 312–13. For Thugut's position, ibid. 227–8 and especially his instructions to Cobenzl, 448–9 n. 315. Paul accepted Thugut's position and instructed Suvorov accordingly. Ibid. 450 n. 318 and 224–30. On Paul's congress proposal and Thugut's reaction, ibid. 240–1.

[57] Miliutin, *Voina* . . . 1799, n. 339, Paul to Razumovskii, 31 July (os) 1799, pp. 465–6.

[58] Ibid. 462 n. 336 for Paul's demand (15/26 July 1799) for a discussion of points of settlement and a congress. Razumovskii conferred with Thugut and reported the results on 15/26 July. Ibid. 463–4 n. 337. Razumovskii's report of 18/29 Aug. 1799 is a comprehensive summary of the Austrian position. Ibid. 469–73 n. 347.

generalizations and state specifically what they required to meet what they thought was owed; he broadened the discussion to include a supposed challenge to assistance Württemberg was promising the Russians; and he asserted the need for Austria to join herself to the Russo-Turkish alliance. Thugut ignored the first point, flatly rejected the last, and suggested that Paul saw a problem where no problem existed on the second.[59] Moreover, throughout the entire exchange, both he and the emperor simply denied that there was any problem between the government and Suvorov, that they had scrupulously observed the terms of the field-marshal's appointment, and that if there had been difficulties involving specific generals, the matter should be looked into.[60] In sum, on neither the military nor the political issues did Paul make any headway whatsoever. When Thugut proposed that all the Russian forces join together in Switzerland, Paul was as pleased at having them once more under his orders and far from Vienna as the Austrians were happy to be rid of them. But Paul was now thinking in terms of working with his other allies, not Austria, and the situation in Switzerland hastened him towards a decision whose roots were set in the controversy over Italy.[61]

Though he envisioned a strong Russian presence in Switzerland, Paul became more and more concerned as word of the archduke Charles's rapid and apparently premature withdrawal reached him.[62] The tsar had studied the terrain and realized how far the Russian forces were apart and in what danger they stood. He protested to Vienna, but received no satisfaction. Indeed, even before the news arrived on 10/21 October of General Korsakov's defeat, Paul was seriously weighing a break with Austria. Moreover, he had already replaced Razumovskii in Vienna with Stepan Kolychev who made no

---

[59] Miliutin, *Voina*... 1799, pp. 249–50 and 477–80, 483–4, nn. 357, 358, 362.
[60] Ibid. 247–9, 469 n. 346.
[61] Ibid. 253 and Rostopchin to Cobenzl, 3/14 Sept. 1799, p. 480 n. 358; Paul to Suvorov, 4/15 Sept. 1799, pp. 480–1 n. 359. Rostopchin remarked on 25 Aug./5 Sept. that the emperor (Paul) was now determined to preserve Europe from both the French and the Austrians, or, as would be more accurate in the latter case, from Baron Thugut (pp. 481–2 n. 360).
[62] Ibid. 261–2; for Paul's deep disappointment with the campaign's outcome, see his letter to Suvorov, 16 Sept. (OS), pp. 489–90 n. 372. Thomas Wickham, the British minister plenipotentiary in Switzerland and a close observer of the campaign, deplored the archduke's withdrawal and the absence of co-ordination between Russian and Austrian forces. He suggested that archduke Charles was also disappointed, but that he had been 'forced' to withdraw. What forced him was not specified. Wickham to Suvorov, 22 Aug. (NS) and 9 Sept. (NS) 1799, pp. 398–401 n. 242 and 407–8 n. 252.

effort to explain or even to present the Austrian position. If Razumovskii was Thugut's creature, Kolychev was the chancellor's enemy.[63] Nor was the news that did reach Petersburg encouraging. Austria had begun to negotiate towards a separate peace using Spain as her intermediary, while in Italy, Vienna was already integrating Piedmont into the Austrian system. Public discontent there was running high, and the Austrians were facing angry public demonstrations. The bad news from Zürich only confirmed Paul's mounting fears. Though he did not yet know of Suvorov's travail, he wrote to Emperor Francis on 11/22 October that their arrangement was at an end, and when the Russian forces did complete their rendezvous in Switzerland, he ordered them into winter quarters.[64]

The Austrians, faced with Paul's decision, made a serious attempt to overturn it. Assuming (quite incorrectly as it happened) that the tsar had decided in haste, they hoped to give him the leisure to change his mind. The archduke Charles wrote to Suvorov deploring the decision and urging that it not be allowed to be said that a single set-back caused so redoubtable a warrior to sheath his sword; the British government added its voice, with the king himself arguing for the continuation of the coalition, while in both Vienna and Petersburg the British and Austrian delegations alike pressed for continued cooperation. Paul's initial response was that he was 'determined entirely to break off the alliance with the Vienna court', and he made the point explicitly that so long as Thugut was chancellor, there could be no mutual trust and hence no co-operative action.[65] But no sooner had he expressed this view than he began to relent. He indicated that he was willing to continue with the war if Thugut were dismissed and if the political boundaries of 1798 were recognized. Indeed, despite Russian tentatives to Berlin (the counterpart to Austria's efforts to promote a separate peace through Spain), for a brief period it seemed that the worst of the crisis was past and that the coalition might survive the winter to fight again in the spring.[66] These hopes were dashed, definitively as it turned out, by yet another Russian–Austrian incident, and one in which the Russians were plainly the injured party. Appropriately, this incident occurred in Italy and involved once more the anomalous position the

[63] Ibid. iv. 207–20; Kolychev to Suvorov, 19/30 Sept. 1799, pp. 363–4 n. 197; Paul to Emperor Francis II, pp. 220 and 388 n. 238.
[64] Ibid. 209–14, 220, 388 n. 238.   [65] Ibid. 223–4, 227–8.
[66] Ibid. v. 169–89. The decision to continue produced a wave of new instructions. Ibid. 173–4, 432–3 n. 13. Whitworth's correspondence shows the British delegation oscillating between despair and joy, as Paul first denied the alliance, then relented, then denied it again. PRO, FO/65/45, Whitworth to Grenville, nos. 107, 108, 109, 113, 28 Nov. 3, 5, and 24 Dec. (all NS) 1799.

Russians occupied as auxiliaries. It involved as well a particularly arrogant Austrian general who made a positive virtue of humiliating his Russian and Turkish allies.

The crisis which ended the Austro-Russian alliance occurred over the seizure of Ancona, an important port and naval facility on the Adriatic coast north-east from Rome.[67] The port had been blockaded by a combined Russo-Turkish fleet. It was attacked on the land side by an Austrian army. When the garrison finally surrendered, however, the terms were negotiated by the French commander with General Fröhlich, an Austrian officer who arrived at the very end of the siege. The Russians were in no way consulted on the terms, or even recognized in the negotiations. When the French flag over the port was lowered, the Austrian was run up in its place. A Russian landing party claimed the right to display the tsar's standard as well. The Russian flag no sooner flew than the Austrians pulled it down and drove the Russians off the quay. Fröhlich's actions were reported at once to Paul who demanded satisfaction. While the Austrians shuffled, Paul once more declared the alliance terminated and sent definitive orders for the return of his troops.[68] The allies again rallied in an effort to convince Paul that he should not leave the coalition. This placed Thugut in a particularly difficult situation. He was unwilling to see Russia restored to an active role, but he worried that if a complete break ensued Paul would establish a relationship with Prussia. At first, therefore, he denied that Paul had any grounds for complaint—he had been misinformed over what actually happened at Ancona. Then he shifted ground and agreed that General Fröhlich should be tried in a disciplinary court presided over by Prince Ferdinand of Württemberg. Russia was invited to have an official observer at the proceedings and General Miloradovich was chosen.[69] General Fröhlich was found guilty of an offence against the Russian flag and was suspended from the service; two other generals present at Ancona (Skall and Küsevich) were recalled to Vienna to answer for their actions; the major and two lieutenants Fröhlich had left in charge of the works faced court martial. This, however, did not satisfy Paul who considered the punishments too light for the crimes committed. Vienna, however, was unwilling to go further, though Prince von Fürstenberg was sent as a special emissary with personal letters from the emperor, the empress, the archduke palatine and his

[67] On Ancona, Miliutin, *Voina* . . . 1799, v, ch. 74 *passim* and pp. 413–22 nn. 137, 140, 142; on Paul's reactions, pp. 191–2, 452 n. 40.

[68] Suvorov's definitive order to return was dated 27 Dec. 1799/8 Jan. 1800. Miliutin, *Voina* . . . 1799, v. 188–9.

[69] Ibid. 192–3, 453 nn. 42, 43, 44.

wife, Paul's daughter, Alexandra. Von Fürstenberg was not granted an audience, the letters were handed to Count Rostopchin, and the Ancona affair remained unsettled.[70]

When Admiral Ushakov's report arrived detailing the Ancona events, Paul immediately forbade Count Cobenzl to appear at court. The prohibition, which was to last until the tsar was satisfied, was never lifted. Paul then requested Kolychev to inform Vienna that he had reason to be discontented with Cobenzl's conduct and that his continued presence in St Petersburg could only prove deleterious to the conduct of affairs.[71] Cobenzl found himself under a form of house arrest, surrounded by police spies, and cut off from the rest of the diplomatic community. Paul made it clear that he regarded anyone who visited Cobenzl with deep suspicion, and that they would be subject to reprisals. 'When I do not see the ambassador', he was reported to have said, 'I do not want my subjects seeing him.' Both the comte de Choiseul and the marquis de Lambert were exiled from the capital after calling on Cobenzl, and this was taken as positive proof that having any contact with him was foolhardy in the extreme. Whitworth, who had stood well with Paul, may, by defending Cobenzl in the interests of the alliance (personally he loathed the Austrian), have given cause for his own recall which Paul secretly requested on 1/13 February 1800.[72] Unable in so straitened circumstances to do any work, Cobenzl requested that he be relieved of his duties and left St Petersburg in May. The Austrian government suggested that Paul exercise a veto over any new ambassador to be appointed, though what they hoped to do was clear the way for Cobenzl's reappointment, possibly with the cover that he had left Petersburg 'to take the waters'. Paul, however, had come to the conclusion that no Austrian ambassador was needed until the Ancona matter was settled. He ordered Kolychev to return to Petersburg, and by the spring of 1800, diplomatic relations were all

---

[70] Ibid. 193.
[71] Ibid. 191–2; Paul's rescript to Kolychev, 30 Jan./11 Feb. 1800, p. 452 n. 41 PRO, FO/65/45, Whitworth to Grenville, no. 115, 31 Dec. (NS) 1799; HHSA, Russland II Berichte, Carton 93, Cobenzl to Thugut, no. 92, 29 Dec. (NS) 1799.
[72] HHSA, Russland II Berichte, Carton 94, Cobenzl to Thugut no. 12, 11 Feb. (NS) 1800; ibid., apostille 1; no. 13, apostille 2, 15 Feb. (NS) 1800; no. 18, 8 Mar. (NS) 1800; no. 19, 17 Mar. (NS) 1800, reports that Cobenzl has had a formal order through Panin that all official contacts between Austria and Russia are severed until the Ancona affair has been settled; no. 20, 21 Mar. (NS) 1800, noted Whitworth's fall from favour; the rumour that Paul had requested Whitworth's recall did not surface until 15 April (NS). See Cobenzl to Thugut, no. 26. The request was actually made in Feb. Miliutin, *Voina* . . . 1799, v. 196–9.

but suspended. By summer, Paul was arming his frontiers against his former ally.[73]

Paul's relations with his other major partner in 'la bonne cause', England, followed a different course, though the end, a virtual diplomatic break by the summer of 1800, was the same.[74] By autumn 1800, England had displaced Austria as the primary target for Paul's animus, and the two countries were effectively at war when Paul died. In some respects, this shift was even more radical than the change in relations with Austria. There was also less justification for it though, as we shall see, there was a certain logic to its development once the alliance with Austria broke down.

Britain and Russia were much closer together at the beginning of Paul's reign than Britain and Austria. Whitworth was particularly well treated by Paul and remained influential until the end of 1799. Despite the recall of forces in 1796, Paul promised continued Russian naval support for the British home fleet, a promise which he faithfully fulfilled, while the trade agreement completed in 1797 not only favoured the entry of British goods, but was also virtually silent on the knotty question of observing neutral rights which had forestalled an earlier agreement with Catherine. Whitworth deplored Paul's pacifism at the beginning of the reign, and strongly supported his mounting belligerency in 1798. His government encouraged Paul to take a leading role in the coalition against France, and as the war developed it became apparent that Britain and Russia had a common outlook on why the war was being fought. The British were prepared to promote popular uprisings against the Jacobins and saw the purpose of the war to be the destruction of the republican system and the re-establishment of the French monarchy. Paul was unenthusiastic about their support for the comte d'Artois—his commitment to Louis XVIII was still clear and unambiguous—but this was not a troublesome issue. British observers supported the Russian position in the controversies with Austria, British naval units co-operated effectively with Russian land forces at Genoa, and Russia approved of the strong support Nelson gave Ferdinand IV at Naples.[75]

---

[73] Miliutin, *Voina* . . . *1799*, v. 192–3.
[74] The following overview is based on Martens, *Recueil des traités*, x. 408–41, xi. 1–10, together with the Whitworth correspondence: PRO, FO/65/35–47. Whitworth supported the British position effectively until his fall from favour in winter 1799–1800. See also Miliutin, *Voina* . . . *1799*, iii. 124–51, for detailed coverage of the background to the campaign in Holland; the campaign itself is treated in vol. v.
[75] Miliutin, *Voina* . . . *1799*, ii. 368–91, iii. 140–4, 217–18. Nelson turned against Russia in 1800. Ibid. v. 201 and 459–60 n. 56.

When the English first proposed a joint Anglo-Russian attack on Holland in May 1799, Paul responded enthusiastically. Though he was already making a heavy contribution to the common cause—he claimed 100,000 men already outside the country—the only question he felt he could legitimately raise was how much more it was possible for him to do. He finally settled on seventeen battalions with artillery. He did have some reservations when he learnt that the duke of York, George III's second son, was to head the expedition, but he went no further than expressing a hope that the choice might fall on someone else. The arrangements, however, moved ahead rapidly. A treaty was drawn up and ratified, and operations were under way by the end of August. Though Britain intended, if possible, to capture the Dutch fleet, there was no hidden agenda such as Austria pursued in Italy. Rather, with allied forces moving into place along the Rhine, there were high hopes that the assault on Holland would clear the Netherlands and open the way to an attack on France.[76]

The first stage of the manœuvre went well, with a landing on the Texel, a barrier island controlling the northern approach to Holland, accomplished early in September. This put the allies in position to neutralize the Dutch fleet. The subsequent campaign, however, was plagued by bad weather, poor co-ordination of Russian and British units, and unexpectedly fierce resistance from Dutch and French troops alike. The Russian command botched an early morning assault during which two Russian regiments exchanged volleys unaware that they were killing their comrades; Russian officers complained that the British gave them insufficient backing and, while the Russians fought well after breaking and running in the confusion of the first attack, they never recovered what had been lost. Nor did the invaders' fortunes improve. As the weather worsened and the invading army remained pinned down, the British command concluded that the entire operation had no future and negotiated an armistice. The Russians were not included in these parlies, although the British praised Russian behaviour under fire. The Russians had taken the majority of casualties: 1,800 Russians were killed or wounded in the first engagement; overall Russian casualties formed nearly three-quarters of all allied losses, and the French took some 5,000 Russians prisoner. What had begun well ended ill, and when Paul learnt the cost of the operation, he was stunned. This, of course,

---

[76] Ibid. iii. 124–51. The project was first mentioned by Lord Grenville in a letter to Whitworth on 3 May (NS) 1799. Ibid. 363 n. 177. On Paul's response, Martens, *Recueil des traités*, x. 428–9.

came in addition to the crushing defeat Korsakov had suffered at Zürich.[77]

The Dutch disaster was a mirror image of the Italian–Swiss débâcle. In the latter, the Russian army performed well until Zürich, and even that defeat was less the fault of Russian arms than it was of Austrian policy. The political failure involved was as massive as the military successes and far more influential. In the Dutch campaign, it was the army that failed, and Paul, shaken by this news, dismissed Generals Hermann and Arbanev, publicly censured the units involved in the Bergen fiasco, and refused to replace their standards.[78] The duke of York, Count S. R. Vorontsov, and even King George III intervened to praise the Russian soldiers for their courage and to quiet Paul's rage and disappointment. Eventually they succeeded. The punishments were reduced, and there were some promotions and decorations. The defeat still stung, however, and while Paul blamed his own people, he refused to exculpate the English. He particularly questioned the leadership and judgement of the duke of York, and made it a condition of future operations that he have nothing to do with Russian troops. His rage rekindled when he heard about the abysmal conditions his soldiers suffered when they returned from Holland to England. Held for weeks on shipboard because the British were unwilling to have them on shore, they were finally settled on the Channel Islands of Jersey and Guernsey in makeshift camps without adequate facilities or supplies.[79] This treatment was shabby by any standard, though when General Essen pressed it with the tsar, Count Vorontsov feared that Essen's charges would further fuel Paul's anger against England, and so effectively did he malign the general that Paul, who had earlier promoted and decorated him for his Dutch campaign, expelled him from the service. When Essen was vindicated, Paul took his revenge on the British leadership by ordering Vorontsov to take back the Russian medals given to Lord Duncan and Vice-Admirals Ripon and Mitchell. There were, in sum, bruises from the Dutch adventure, but there was nothing that would not heal, and new plans were put forward for the next campaigning season. The attack on Holland and

---

[77] On the campaign, Miliutin, *Voina . . . 1799*, v. 8–92. Though not a success, the British acquired a good part of the Dutch fleet; for the Russians, however, the campaign was a disaster. Of 17,000 men embarked at Reval, just 10,539 returned healthy; there were 3,308 sick and wounded.

[78] Miliutin, *Voina . . . 1799*, v. 92–4.

[79] Ibid. 173–4; 432–3, instructions to Count S. R. Vorontsov, 21 Nov./1 Dec. 1799; 193 and 453 n. 46.

its defeat strained relations between Russia and England, but hardly endangered the alliance.[80]

The allies had missed a golden opportunity in the summer of 1799. By the autumn, when the Directory was overthrown and Napoleon took power, the flow of events had already turned against them. The new government's policies accelerated the change. Bonaparte was determined to liquidate the revolutionary extremes of the Jacobin era; Brumaire was a conservative revolution. Conciliatory towards the *émigrés* and the church, Napoleon also began diplomatically to probe the monarchies allied against him. He wrote directly to Francis II and George III, a move which was received with suspicion and official disdain, although it was already apparent that Austria, at any rate, would have to negotiate. He also indicated to Prussia, a country with which France continued to maintain diplomatic relations, that he would welcome contact with St Petersburg, and later he proposed to return the Russian prisoners in French hands without a quid pro quo. He hoped for further discussions.[81]

Paul's experiences with Austria and England had forced him to review his political thinking. His injuries, especially at the hands of the Austrians, led him to ignore the victories won in northern Italy and the Mediterranean to concentrate on the set-backs in Switzerland and what he interpreted as Austria's betrayal. When he finally recalled his forces from the west, disengaging in every theatre of operations, he was left without a position from which to negotiate. He sulked, irresolute, through the winter and spring of 1800. He avoided contact with foreign representatives, and, as he had done in the last years of Catherine's reign, appeared infrequently at court. What he decided on during this period in the wilderness was to reconstitute the northern alliance. He completely abandoned Austria, and in February 1800, he requested London to recall Whitworth. He had already extended tentatives to Prussia, Denmark, and Sweden. The English minister was not replaced, and as Paul drew nearer to the Scandinavian countries, relations with London rapidly deteriorated. In the mean time France under Bonaparte reconquered Italy, undoing in a single campaign what Suvorov had accomplished the year before. Paul, it was said, was cheered when the news came of the drubbing the Austrians took at Marengo (14 June 1800), but his new

---

[80] Ibid. 194–6.
[81] The best and most recent work on Napoleon and Paul is Hugh Ragsdale, 'Was Paul Bonaparte's Fool?' *Reassessment*, 76–90; *Détente in the Napoleonic Era: Bonaparte and the Russians* (Lawrence, Kan., 1980); 'Russia, Prussia, and Europe', 106 ff. Miliutin's richly documented coverage is still useful. See *Voina . . . 1799*, v. 237–45, 264–81.

diplomacy was passing a milestone of its own: there was a modest defensive alliance with Prussia, actually the renewal of an agreement made by Catherine in 1792, and both Denmark and Sweden were seeking Russian ties to secure the Baltic and their maritime interests against England. By summer 1800, Paul had completely abandoned the policies he pursued so enthusiastically in 1798 and 1799. His next step was to improve on the opening to France which Bonaparte offered.[82]

Of Russia's allies in 1799, it was Austria which proved to be the insurmountable barrier to Paul's continuing in the war. Once he had decided to break with her, and to withdraw his forces from western Europe, the military and political reasons for maintaining the alliance with Britain became less pressing. For the English, bringing Russia into the land war in Europe against France had been a matter of prime necessity. Austria, by herself, was inadequate to the task; with Russian support, a victory was possible. When the alliance began to disintegrate in autumn of 1799, the English made every effort to retrieve the situation. George III himself strongly urged Paul to reconsider, and a campaign was mounted through Lord Minto in Vienna, Whitworth in Petersburg, and Thomas Wickham with Suvorov in Germany. These efforts succeeded to the extent that Stepan Kolychev reopened discussions with Thugut in Vienna, and Paul agreed to new planning for the spring campaigns, though his Russian forces were to be independent of both the British and the Austrians. Ancona ruined this effort, though when Paul recalled Suvorov at the start of the new year it still appeared possible for him to work with England. Various plans were mooted, though it was apparent that Paul was less interested than before in his London connections.[83]

Paul had been deeply affected by the failures in Switzerland and Holland, by the devious behaviour of the Austrians, and by the rather contradictory signals he had from London. Though still their ally, Paul found he had grievances against the English, and when they began to question whether they would pay the amount of subsidy promised for the service of his troops, he was outraged. The English claimed that he had failed to send the full complement promised in

[82] Ragsdale, 'Russia, Prussia, and Europe', esp. 97 ff. Cf. Ole Feldback, 'The Foreign Policy of Tsar Paul I, 1800–1801: An Interpretation', *Jahrbücher für Geschichte Osteuropas*, NS 30/1 (1982), and *Denmark and the Armed Neutrality: 1800–1801: Small Power Policy in a World War* (Copenhagen, 1980). Both Ragsdale and Feldback use Miliutin extensively. See *Voina* . . . 1799, v. 163–70, 425–7 nn. 1 and 2, 427 n. 5 (also in *PSZ*, vol. 25, *ukaz* to the senate, 5/16 Nov. 1799), 428–9 n. 6.

[83] Miliutin, *Voina* . . . 1799, v. 168–89, 429–30 n. 8, 431 n. 11, 432–3 n. 13.

the treaty; Paul insisted that the count should have been by units rather than numbers of men and that he had fulfilled the spirit and intent of the agreement.[84] Though hardly earth-shaking, this dispute, on top of those arising from the campaign itself and the issue of the way the Russian troops were housed, gave further cause of irritation to a man already beset on every side. But what ultimately proved most influential in determining Paul's relations with England was his new relationship with Denmark and Sweden. Drawing Prussia into an alliance against France was entirely acceptable to London; but as Paul constructed what he hoped would become a northern alliance, he also committed himself to defending neutrals' rights on the high seas. That position put him on a collision course with England.

Neutrals' rights, as we noted above, played no part in the 1797 Anglo-Russian commercial treaty, while during 1798 and 1799 Russian vessels had co-operated with the British fleet blockading the continent. Those vessels were withdrawn, however, when the Russian fleet sailed home. Defending neutral rights—the re-establishment of the League of Armed Neutrality of 1780—became part of the cement for the new northern alliance, and British seizures of neutral shipping became a critical issue for the Russian government. One crisis in late summer was settled without difficulty, but the English refused to stop interfering with neutral vessels, and when another Swedish intercept was taken back to England, Paul made a formal protest. The protest was rejected, and Paul closed the English trading factories at St Petersburg. English vessels were impounded with the goods they carried, and British seamen and merchants were put under arrest.[85] This crisis, too, was resolved by negotiation, but worse was yet to come. Russian hostility towards England and Paul's interference with the blockade convinced Lord Nelson, who was in charge of the siege of French-held Malta, that the island should not be given back to the knights of Malta, i.e. to the Russian tsar. This was a decision which was strongly opposed in London where it was feared that interfering with Malta would push Russia beyond the point of no return. The troubles over the blockade were serious enough. To make an issue of Malta would make the Russians enemies indeed.[86]

---

[84] Miliutin, *Voina* . . . *1799*, v. 197.

[85] Ibid. 252–62, 495 n. 125, 496 n. 127; Ragsdale, 'Russia, Prussia, and Europe', 110–12; Feldback, 'Foreign Policy of Paul I', esp. 20–1 ff. On the first Russian embargo, see the reports of Stephen Shairp to Lord Grenville, PRO, FO/65/47, 1 Oct. (NS) 1800. The reports comprise eleven items addressed to various correspondents, Grenville included, written in the course of Shairp's mission in Sept. 1800.

[86] Miliutin, *Voina* . . . *1799*, v. 260.

It was generally understood that in the event that Malta fell to the English, it would be occupied by Russian, English, and Neapolitan troops. When Nelson took Malta, however, he announced that he intended to hold the island until a peace conference could determine its disposition. He denied the claim of the knights of St John on the island. The basis of his denial was a charter from the time of Charles V which he was supposed to have found, which contained the clause that if the knights lost the island its ownership would revert to the ruling house of Naples. Whatever the merits of this argument and the document on which it was based, Nelson acted on it. Paul took an extremely serious view of this action; he considered it tantamount to a declaration of war and struck back at once. He impounded all British ships in Russian ports, sent the crews to detention camps, and took traders hostage to be held until he had received satisfaction.[87] He also began to prepare the Baltic against a British attack. Prussia, in effect, was ordered to mobilize against Hanover, and Paul looked to his own coastal defences as well as strengthening his borders against Austria. Britain took counter measures. A fleet under the command of Nelson and Parker entered the Baltic, bombarded Copenhagen, and, having forced the Danes to surrender, set sail for Petersburg.[88] These events unfolded over the first months of 1801, but by the time the fleet headed for the Russian capital, Paul was dead, and his son hastened to make his peace with England.

The dramatic deterioration of Anglo-Russian relations paralleled a *rapprochement* with France. Bonaparte's original offer to release the Russian prisoners of war was met with Paul's rather cool response that he could only accept on the understanding that these troops would swear not to fight against France. He wanted to avoid any imputation of a conditionless gift. However, the ice was broken and negotiations for a further understanding began in Berlin.[89] Though Napoleon had defeated Austria at Marengo and cleared the allies out of Italy, no final settlement was at hand, nor would there be one until after the French victory at Hohenlinde at the end of 1800. An agreement with Russia was desirable to pressure Austria further. Moreover, the clash between England and Russia was to Bonaparte's advantage, while, from Paul's standpoint, French support would add measurably to his ability to withstand an English assault. But there was a deeper attraction. Paul saw Bonaparte as liquidating the

[87] Miliutin, *Voina* . . . *1799*, v. 260 and 496 n. 128.
[88] Ibid. 260–2, 282–4, 497–8 nn. 130–1, and 507–8 n. 156.
[89] Ibid. 264–5; Ragsdale, 'Russia, Prussia, and Europe', 104–5; 'Bonaparte's Fool', 82. Ragsdale argues convincingly that Paul kept his head and, contrary to the common perception, was not swept away by Bonaparte's advances.

revolution, re-establishing a sound conventional political and social order in France—a monarchy in everything but name—and if Bonaparte was willing to negotiate on terms favourable to the rights of German and Italian princes, Paul was willing to approach agreement with him. Russian conditions were presented, a common ground for talks existed, and Paul entered into a personal correspondence with Napoleon. General Sprengtporten was sent to receive the Russian prisoners who, freshly armed and accoutred, were to be used to garrison Malta once the island had been recovered from the English. Paul then sent Stepan Kolychev, now vice-chancellor, to treat with France. Bonaparte hoped to have him present for the final settlement with Austria at Lunéville, but he travelled too slowly and the agreements were signed before he arrived. No formal treaty was struck between Russia and France, however, owing to Paul's sudden death. There is, of course, no way of telling where all this would have led had Paul lived, though there are some tantalizing hints.[90]

As the coalition broke up, Paul was seeking a better basis for Russian policy. Rostopchin is said to have remarked to him that Russia had spent men and resources in the recent war to gain nothing of value, a charge with which Paul was forced to agree, and he invited Rostopchin to put his ideas on paper. Earlier, Count Panin had outlined a set of principles for Russia to follow which, in fact, presented the position Paul pursued through 1800. What Rostopchin proposed was more dramatic: a reversion to the Greek project of Catherine, including the partition of the Ottoman empire. Paul's notes showed a favourable reaction though, in fact, the policies he followed during the last months of his life reflected a less radical approach than the Rostopchin memo suggested, though admittedly the picture is unclear.[91] He did, however, take one important and

[90] Miliutin, *Voina* . . . *1799*, 265–79, 499–500 n. 136. For Paul's personal notes to Bonaparte, p. 500 n. 137. For Sprengtporten's reports, p. 502 n. 141, p. 503 n. 144. See also: Ragsdale, 'Russia, Prussia, and Europe', 101–18; cf. Feldback, 'Foreign Policy of Paul I', 26–34. Feldback insists that Paul was pursuing hegemony; the argument, while interesting, is less convincing than Ragsdale's.

[91] Count Nikita Petrovich Panin was vice-chancellor and Rostopchin's rival. His memoir, presented 21 Sept. (os), argued the destructive effects of an Austrian collapse and urged Paul to offer a new intervention with the proviso that the small states, Bavaria, Württemberg, Naples, and Sardinia, would be guaranteed their integrity. Panin leaned towards England and Prussia. See *Materialy Panina*, ed. A. Brikner, v. 610. The Rostopchin memo, properly called 'notorious', was submitted about the same time. See *Russkii arkhiv*, 16/1 (1878), 103–10. Paul followed neither, charting his own course. His marginalia, however, seem to suggest that he approved of the Rostopchin memo when he read it. To 'approve' and to build a policy, of course, are different matters, but Ragsdale offers an interesting though possibly overelaborate explanation, claiming that while the memoir is genuine,

dramatic step. He organized and dispatched a column of cossacks to attack British India. Russia was exposed to Britain's naval forces, but Britain's colonial holdings offered an inviting target. If this attack, hasty and ill-prepared though it was, was intended to be part of a larger Franco-Russian campaign to redraw the maps of Europe and western Asia, it might have represented the next stage in Paul's planned co-operation with Napoleon. There is no convincing evidence that this was the case, however, and the most that can be said about the effort was that it showed some prescience on Paul's part concerning Britain's vulnerabilities. It also prefigured an orientation for Russian policy which was to become familiar in the nineteenth century.[92]

By 1801, the breakdown of the coalition was complete. Russia was effectively at war with England, a new northern system was coming into being, and *rapprochement* with France was advancing. There was also progress on the Malta question. Napoleon had agreed that Malta, once free from England, should be returned to Paul and the knights of St John, while the tsar's campaign for recognition as grand master was a secular success. The pope's approval, however, continued to elude him. The new pope, Pius VII, seemed no more forthcoming on the question than his predecessor had been, though a strong minority within the church urged recognition. This faction reasoned that, as Paul was a determined defender of religious values and monarchical legitimacy, his recognition as grand master would be a major gain for the church and the interests it was sworn to defend, and that such an achievement would more than justify whatever compromises were necessary to achieve it. One possibility

Paul's 'approval' is not: *Détente*, 117–19. Feldback entirely rejects Ragsdale's suggestion, regards the approval as genuine, and considers the memoir to be an important document for understanding Paul's foreign policy decisions. See 'Foreign Policy of Paul I', 24 n. 30. The position here is that, whether Paul approved or not, he did not conduct his policies according to the principles Rostopchin urged.

[92] The attack on India is sometimes used to show Paul's lack of control over himself and political realities at the end of his reign. See e.g. Shil'der, *Pavel I*, 417–19. Ragsdale thinks that the suggestion for the attack came from Napoleon and was part of his larger plan which included closing the continent to British trade. See *Détente*, ch. 5. Muriel Atkin, 'The Pragmatic Diplomacy of Paul I', thinks that the expedition to India was based on widely held strategic assumptions. She rejects the idea that the plan was essentially French and, while it may have been ill-judged and ill-timed, considers it a viable option. See also her *Russia and Iran*, 42–52. Saul, *Russia and the Mediterranean*, 148–9, presents the attack on India as a logical extension of Russian geo-political thinking which, especially in the context of French movements in support, made sense. Saul cites the very interesting H. Sutherland Edwards, *Russian Projects against India from Czar Peter to General Skobeleff* (London, 1885).

was to secularize the order, and this was under serious consideration. A more radical approach considered using Paul to bring about a reunification of the western and eastern churches.

At the end of 1800, these issues took on new life. Serra Capriola, the Neapolitan minister in Petersburg, acted as the intermediary with Rome, and Paul is supposed to have formulated proposals of major significance which were on their way to the Vatican when he was killed. What those proposals were is not known, though there is a persistent story that he converted to Roman Catholicism and was prepared to act in the role of unifier. Paul did claim sympathy with the Roman church and he acknowledged the pope's leading role, but he was also demonstrably a firm defender of the tsar's authority over ecclesiastical matters of all communions in Russia. If he had become a Catholic to win papal recognition for his grand mastership of Malta, he would undoubtedly have been a most radical gallican. There is, however, no evidence beyond rumour that he did convert, nor is there anything more than circumstance to support speculation on where his negotiations with the papacy were leading. That such negotiations were in train is unquestionable, however, and they serve as testimony to the importance he continued to attach to his grand mastership and papal recognition for it.[93]

Prior to the *rapprochement* with Napoleon, the prince de Condé's little force of *émigrés* separated from the Russian army to move to Austrian territory. It is not clear whether this was inadvertence or policy, but no effort was made to reclaim them for Russia.[94] Paul remained firm in his support for the Italian and German princes whose rights he considered to be integral to the stable European community which he envisioned, but he abruptly ended his patronage of Louis XVIII. That unfortunate was simply told to go; his subsidy was too burdensome. Backing a claimant to the French throne made no sense when Paul had found so satisfactory an associate in Bonaparte who performed the functions of a legitimate ruler even if he did not bear the title. The fact was that Louis XVIII had become an embarrassment to the new course Russian policy was following. With that touch of pragmatism which showed repeatedly in Paul's policy approaches, he disembarrassed himself of an unwanted burden.[95]

[93] McGrew, 'Paul I and the Knights', 63–4 and 74–5 nn. 107–17; Pierling, *La Russie*, v. 290–328, esp. 316–28

[94] Miliutin, *Voina* . . . *1799*, v. 212–14 and 473–7 n. 83.

[95] Ragsdale, 'Russia, Prussia, and Europe', 114–15. Ragsdale points out that there is no documentary evidence to show why Paul moved against Louis XVIII when he did. L'abbé Georgel, however, was unequivocal: Paul expelled Louis XVIII

The policy shifts Paul initiated in 1800 had gained in substance by the end of the year, but they were still very much in process when his reign ended on the night of 11/23 March 1801. His successor retrenched on the major issues, re-establishing friendly relations with England and Austria, withdrawing from the Malta question, retreating from the developing association with Bonaparte, and taking up a neutral stance. Within a year the war was finished and a general peace signed at Amiens. The extent to which foreign policy may have played a part in the successful conspiracy to end Paul's reign is a subject for our next chapter. Paul's conduct of external affairs, however, bears directly on the question of his character and competence, and it is fundamental to appraising the significance of his reign.

Viewed abstractly, Paul's foreign policy followed a remarkably consistent line to the end of 1800. He focused his attention on Europe, and he identified Russia's vital interests with establishing the foundations for a lasting peace. Achieving that end involved recognizing the legitimate interests of all the European states, and where those interests collided, to negotiate compromises. To further those goals, it was important for him to maintain active diplomatic relations with every state, including those for which he had limited sympathy or with which there was no common ground of agreement on which to build. France, Denmark, and Sweden fell early into one or another of these categories. He was willing to go to war, but only when he could do so without endangering the society he governed, and when there appeared to be no alternative for it. Though predisposed to the traditional hereditary monarchy, Paul was prepared to deal with individual states on the basis of what they did rather than what they were. He fought France because the Directory continued to expand, not because it was republican. A restrained republican government, willing to accept the established interests of other societies and to participate in building up a peaceful European community, was acceptable. An aggressive republic which refused to limit its ambitions and which undermined or overthrew the governments around it not only had to be blocked, but should be overthrown. Unquiet and aggressive monarchies also had to be controlled, however, and made to conform to the requirements of a stable and peaceful Europe. Peace, order, and the acceptance of the principles needed to realize them weighed more heavily with Paul than the forms governments took. In this respect his approach was pragmatic, even realistic.

to authenticate his new ties with Bonaparte. *Voyage à St. Pétersbourg* (Paris, 1818), 485–6, see also 328–30.

Interwoven with the idea of maintaining Europe as a stable community, however, was a firm commitment to traditional values and a fundamental hostility to revolutionary ideology. Paul fought this battle inside Russia with every weapon at his command. He attempted to seal the country against subversive people and ideas, and when he could, he pressured other states to purge themselves of radical ideas and contacts. It was in part this issue which created friction between Denmark and Russia at the beginning of Paul's reign, militating against any early reconstruction of a northern system, and it showed dramatically in Paul's insistence that the free city of Hamburg close the radical political clubs active there as a prerequisite for diplomatic and economic ties. A mounting conservative tendency eased the way to incorporating both into Paul's new system in 1800. So far as the major powers were concerned, France aside, ideological questions played little part. Prussia maintained a neutral stance and diplomatic relations with France, but in no way leaned towards republicanism. England was firmly anti-republican as was Austria though, as we saw, Austria placed her particular interests ahead of the campaign to restore the French monarchy. Both Sardinia and Naples were firmly anti-republican and anti-French, as was the Ottoman empire. Sweden occasionally seemed ambivalent, and Paul worried about internal disorders there which might not be effectively controlled, as well as an unhealthy open-mindedness in relations with France. Spain, though monarchical, was committed to France, while Bavaria shifted from one side to the other. The reasons had little to do with ideology as such and a great deal to do with propinquity and power politics.

Paul's position as a defender of established values at home was more radical than that of his contemporaries, and when he went to war against the French his rhetoric was powerfully and uniformly legitimist. Clearly he considered an activist revolutionary government in France extremely dangerous to European order. Protecting the institutions of the old order was a necessity in the face of rampant revolutionary threats. Hence, succouring the knights of Malta supported an important symbol of the old order with which Paul identified. His election as grand master, however, created a new situation. The refusal to recognize his status denigrated him personally. This was wholly unacceptable. The issue was not truly ideological—republican versus monarchical—but one of regard and loyalty. Paul expected recognition. To refuse it insulted his person and his majesty, and he was prepared to exact a heavy price for any such refusal. The knights of Malta, in Paul's mind, embodied the best of the old order and deserved his patronage. Once elected grand master, he projected an important role for them inside Russia, and he spoke of them as a rallying point for the campaign against the revolution abroad. Neither idea proved effective, though the gigantic Russian priory provided a beginning for the moral reform of the nobility that Paul hoped to see. In the war against the revolution, however, the knights were a persistent embarrassment, the hidden reef on which diplomatic ventures unexpectedly ran aground and occasionally foundered. The recognition issue became inseparable from the question of friendship for or opposition to Russia. Paul made it so, and this in turn made recognition a diplomatic issue in its own right, and a necessary precondition for building the alliances aimed against the revolution.

For the brief period Paul was active on the European scene, he attempted to open new directions in Russian foreign policy. In all of his efforts, he showed himself to be disinterested. He had no territorial claims to make; he offered himself as a mediator and, more actively, as a guardian for the interests of those threatened by powers greater than themselves, and by events beyond their control. The Europe Paul wanted to see was one in which each state would be safe, in which there was justice for the smaller principalities as well as protection. He wanted to see the tide of revolutionary conquest rolled back, and he sought like-minded states to give him support in what he purposed. The ideas he pursued became the writ of post-Napoleonic Europe; what he failed to create at the end of the eighteenth century, Metternich finally realized between 1815 and 1848.

But Paul was no Metternich and Russia was not Austria. Paul was a poor negotiator. Since he made no claims, he put no price on his co-operation but rather offered it as a starting-point. He had no leverage over his opponents. He was inclined to be soft and over accommodative when he needed to be hard—his dealing with Austria in the late spring and early summer of 1799 is a critical case in point—and when he turned hard, he became destructively so. His reaction to English 'perfidy' and the new war he brought on as a result is a good example. Paul compromised when he should have been firm and turned adamant when compromise was indicated. The circumstances suggest that these turns were dictated less by what the situation demanded than by the way he felt about what was happening. Whatever high principles he expressed, he was most likely to react strongly when his own position was compromised and his will countered. He was most successful in areas where he was least involved—the middle east, for example. He was least successful where his relations with other states were most intimate and most likely to involve assaults on his ego. From a standpoint of foreign policy, Paul defined a new approach, but he fell short of what he set out to accomplish. His influence on the settlement which took shape at the end of 1800 was relatively small, and he dragged Russia into a conflict with England which offered no advantage at all. In concrete terms, Paul's domestic programmes were more successful than his foreign policy. His diplomacy put his country at serious risk, and as 1801 dawned there was little hope for a favourable resolution so long as he lived. He was not fated to live long.

10
THE END OF THE BEGINNING

On 7 November (OS) 1800, Paul had ruled Russia for precisely four years. During that time, he had reorganized the empire's governing institutions to fit his conception of a centralized, chain-of-command administration; he had imposed his authoritarian values on the court and the country; he had reshaped the army to conform with the Frederickian example he admired; he had attacked budget deficits, foreign debt, and currency problems, and having identified revolutionary subversion as the major issue of the day, he had built barriers against foreign influences while instituting comprehensive controls on thought and social behaviour. In a liberalizing age, Paul stood as a committed conservative who turned to militaristic and authoritarian measures to preserve the established social system. And he followed the same mode in diplomacy where he set himself to defend traditional institutions, to protect the European community against uncontrolled change, and to underwrite a stable political order. Through the summer of 1799, these efforts enjoyed a remarkable degree of success, crowned by Suvorov's stunning victories in Italy. The defeats that followed in Switzerland and Holland, however, the collapse of the alliances with Austria and Britain, and the confused attempts to build a new diplomatic system conspired to obliterate Paul's earlier achievements, to highlight his personal eccentricities, and to intensify resentment at his repressive and unpredictably authoritarian style. All this raised once more, in the most pressing way possible, the question of whether he was competent to rule. A conspiracy to overthrow him in favour of Grand Duke Alexander formed during the dark days of 1800. It matured in the late autumn of that year and mounted a successful *coup d'état* the following March.[1]

---

[1] The basic sources on the conspiracy, the *coup*, and the murder are: *Tsareubiistvo 11 Marta 1801 goda: Zapiski uchastnikov i sovremennikov* (St Petersburg, 1907, 1908); Theodore Schiemann (ed.), *Die Ermordung Pauls und die Thronbesteigung Nikolaus I, neue Materialen* (Berlin, 1902); id., *Zur Geschichte der Regierung Paul I und Nikolaus I*, 2nd edn. (Berlin, 1906), which presents the same material as *Die Ermordung Pauls* . . .; Leo Loewenson, 'The Death of Paul I (1801) and the Memoirs of Count Bennigsen', *The Slavonic and East European Review*, 29

The End of the Beginning 323

The conspiracy of 1800–1 was in the traditional mould of eighteenth-century Russian palace revolutions. Sixty-eight participants have been identified, though the actual total may have been much higher. The organizer and leader, General Count Peter von der Pahlen, was a soldier and administrator of long standing who had become Paul's most trusted official and controlled security arrangements for the Petersburg district. Pahlen planned the uprising, recruited the other participants, won the approval of Grand Duke Alexander for the *coup* attempt, and organized the assault on the Michael Palace. He had the backing of the commanders of the Preobrazhenskii and Semenovskii guards regiments, while the attack force itself was drawn from a pool of disaffected officers, some of whom were out of service, and all of whom despised Paul. There were close ties with Catherine's reign. Pahlen gave the most visible role to Prince Platon Zubov, whose gigantic younger brother, Nicholas, was also prominent in the assault and may have been the first to lay violent hands on Paul. Another Zubov, Valerian, marched with Pahlen and the second force. The tactical commander for the primary group which invaded Paul's bedchamber was a Hanoverian general, Leo Bennigsen, whom Pahlen had particularly wanted at his side. Bennigsen was an experienced officer, a cool head, and a wholly reliable man. The success or failure of the attack came to rest with him.

Pahlen's *coup* was directed specifically at Paul.[2] Organized in a matter of weeks between November and January, it exploited bitterness in the officer class and gave expression to the insecurity, even terror, which Paul inspired in the army, among his courtiers, in his family, and in the state administration. The jubilance and spontaneous celebrations occasioned in St Petersburg by the official announcement that Paul had died of an apoplectic stroke and that Alexander ruled was a striking testimonial to how burdensome his reign had become and what a relief his sudden death was. As the Swedish ambassador remarked, 'everyone rejoices'.[3] The fact that no

---

(Dec. 1950), 212–32; Sablukov, 'Reminiscences: Part II'; Czartoryski, *Mémoires*, i, ch. 8; *Memoiren des Herzogs Eugen von Württemberg*, 2 vols. 3 pts. (Frankfurt, 1862), 'Jungend Erinnerungen' i. 74–156; and Heyking, *Aus den Tagen Kaiser Pauls*.

[2] See James J. Kennedy, jun., 'The Politics of Assassination', in H. Ragsdale (ed.), *Reassessment*, 125–45. Cf. Eidel'man, *Gran'vekov* which links the 1801 *coup* with the revolts in 1762 and 1825 as part of an emerging protest against autocracy rooted in liberalizing constitutionalist ideals.

[3] Riksarkivet, Diplomatica Moscovitica, vol. 465, Stedingk to the king, St Petersburg, 15/27 Mar. 1801; Grand Duke Nicolas Mikhailowitch, *L'Impératrice*

one betrayed the plot, though it was widely known and even more widely suspected, suggests how little loyalty or even sympathy Paul had come to command. But the revolt was in no sense a national uprising or a social revolution. It was a carefully organized *coup* which avoided confrontations with potential loyalists and which aimed at presenting the world with an accomplished fact. In this the conspiracy's leaders succeeded brilliantly; they left no basis for a counter stroke. At the same time, they made no pretence of investing the *coup* with any broader significance than removing a dangerously incompetent ruler in favour of his legitimate successor.[4]

In the hours prior to the assault on the Michael Palace, there was talk about what the revolution might mean, and whether a step was being taken on the road to a new political order. But the level of ideological consciousness (as opposed to anger with the tyrant) was relatively low. The conspirators' purpose was to depose Paul in favour of Alexander who was expected to relax his father's most egregrious control measures, to place a limit, as Sablukov put it, on despotism, and to save the fatherland.[5] Neither Pahlen, nor Nikita Panin before him, proposed in talking with Alexander to limit the tsar's power through a constitution, or to reconsider the structural reforms Paul had introduced. Those issues simply did not arise. The primary justification for the revolt was the immediate damage Paul was doing and threatened to do. In this respect, the *coup* of 1801 was more nearly similar to that of 1762, where the issue was Peter III, what he had done and was doing, than it was to the Decembrist revolt in 1825. In 1762, once they had won, Catherine and her circle presented themselves as both a reform party and the protectors of Russia's indigenous heritage. They also claimed a broad constituency for their actions. The Decembrists, of course, went much further. They not only set out to topple Nicholas I, but they had formulated elaborate plans for turning the autocracy into either a revolutionary republic or a constitutional monarchy. Dreams of such fundamental changes played no part in 1801, and would have been anachronistic in 1762.[6]

Elisabeth, i. 170, Elizabeth to her mother, 13/25 Mar. 1801; Czartoryski, *Mémoires*, i. 230; Welianinow-Sernov, 'Die Ermordung', Schiemann (ed.), *Die Ermordung Pauls I*, 32.

[4] See Bennigsen's brief description of the case Pahlen made to Alexander, Loewenson, 'Death of Paul I', 222–3; 'Iz zapisok grafa Lanzherona', *Tsareubiistvo 11 marta 1801* (1907), 134–6.

[5] Sablukov, 'Reminiscences', 323.

[6] For the central ideas of the Decembrist societies, *Vosstanie dekabristov: Materialy*, 8 vols. (Moscow, 1925). The most striking single work to come out of the

The 1801 *coup* was not, however, a revolution without a rationale. Justifying the overthrow of the tsar gave a certain philosophical tone to the conspiracy, a vocabulary in effect, which spoke to the orientation of the rebels. French revolutionary thinkers had little resonance for this cabal, but Enlightenment values of the pre-revolutionary era found expression in the common view that Paul had become a tyrant, a personal despot, who daily overstepped the boundaries of legitimate authority and made a mockery of his responsibilities as a ruler. For these latter-day Romans, and so they styled themselves, to bring down such a monarch was a moral obligation.[7] Moreover, though this was not a revolution to change the system, it did promote certain expectations. An autocracy whose functioning was predictable and orderly and which guaranteed security of persons and property (especially that of the nobility) was what the people who organized against Paul sought. This hope, to the degree that it was expressed, was put in terms of a return to Catherine's values, a promise which Alexander stammered out to the Semenovskii immediately after Paul's death, and Dmitri Troshchinskii made the central point in his final version of the accession manifesto in which the new tsar pledged to 'govern the nation according to the laws and court of the august Catherine the Great, our Grandmother, whose memory for us and for the entire fatherland will always be dear'.[8] But little energy was spent on developing a position. The position was assumed. With Paul removed, the new regime had to be better, freer, more humane. The fundamental problem for the conspiracy's leaders was Paul and how to remove him without destroying themselves. It was he they held responsible for the whirlwind threatening Russia from abroad, and for creating a situation within the country in which there was no security of person or position. Matters could only improve if Alexander became tsar; it was enough to accomplish that.

Though opposition to Paul had existed from his first day in office, it lacked any rallying point and was dissipated in carping criticism or,

movement was P. I. Pestel, *Russkaia pravda: Nakaz verkhovnomu vremennomu pravleniiu* (St Petersburg, 1906). The Decembrists were both more politically aware and intellectually sophisticated than the conspirators in 1801; they also had an organizational existence for more than 8 years.

[7] Loewenson, 'Death of Paul I', 226; 'Iz zapisok Lanzherona', *Tsareubiistvo* (1907), 144; Eugen von Württemberg, 'Bemerkungen', *Die Ermordung Pauls I*, 84; Ernst von Wedell, 'Aufschlüsse über die Ermordung des Kaisers Pauls I', *Die Ermordung des Pauls I*, 73; Shil'der, *Pavel I*, 466–9, quoting N. P. Panin to S. R. Vorontsov, *Arkhiv kniazia Vorontsova*, xi. 112.

[8] HHSA, Russland II Berichte, Carton 95, app. to no. 16, Locatelli to Trautsmandorff, St Petersburg, 15/27 Mar. 1801.

more effectively, in resignations from service followed by rustication on family estates or travel abroad. Those dismissed from service swelled the ranks of the disaffected. Alexander, after greeting his father's accession with enthusiasm, became disenchanted, and their relations deteriorated rapidly, particularly after the fall of the empress's faction in 1798. At that time Paul had accused Mariia and the Kurakins of actively plotting to overthrow him. A year later his suspicions were unrelieved, and it was reported that the empress had twice been placed under house arrest. Alexander tried to defend his mother but only succeeded in angering Paul.[9]

Count Dietrichstein not only recorded Paul's animus against his son and wife, but went on to remark that in any other country Paul's way of conducting his affairs would have caused a revolution. But Paul, as Dietrichstein saw him, enjoyed several advantages. The honours which he lavished with a prodigality unknown before had won him the support of a nation avid for rewards, while his victories in Europe, achieved cheaply but with enormous éclat, had substantially strengthened his standing. Nor was there any immediate alternative to his continuing in power. The empress was forbidden by the new succession law to succeed her husband, while the heir, Grand Duke Alexander, had as his most notable personal traits a certain sweetness and patience of character and was altogether too weak a person to challenge his father. These circumstances went a long way, in Dietrichstein's opinion, toward guaranteeing Paul against a revolution that would deprive him of his throne.

There were two possibilities which might alter the situation and produce the change so many hoped for. The first was that 'among all [Paul's] victims would be found one man who was both desperate and vindictive' who would sacrifice himself to destroy the tsar. That this had not happened was a commonly expressed source of wonder, while the conviction that it had to come about, and soon, 'forms a primary topic of conversation in every society from the first to the last', and served as another indication of the low esteem in which the

---

[9] HHSA, Russland II Berichte, Carton 93, le comte de Dietrichstein-Proskacy, Major-General of Engineers, 'Notices sur la cour de Russie et le personnel de l'Empereur', Biala, 26 Nov. (NS) 1799. Dietrichstein, a member of the special delegation Thugut sent to Petersburg for the archduke Joseph's marriage, had been in Russia earlier, had married a Shuvalov, and had excellent personal connections in Grand Duke Alexander's circle. His long and very frank appraisal, written at white heat as soon as he crossed the Russian border, reflects on the way Paul was viewed by what was becoming a hostile opposition.

tsar was held. The second possibility was that if Paul were to engage in some act of severity toward his eldest son, even

without going so far as to make him suffer the fate of the unhappy tsarevich [Alexis, son of Peter the Great who died at his father's order if not by his hand], perhaps doing no more than simply restricting his liberty, it would give the signal for a rebellion by the guards regiments where there certainly are to be found some Orlovs, Passeks, and Bariatinskiis [activists in Catherine's *coup*] who would think that so offensive a sovereign ought not to survive.

Dietrichstein's prediction was close to what happened and reflected what society appeared to expect; at the time that he wrote, however, Paul was in no particular danger.

The foundations for the conspiracy were laid in the spring and early summer of 1800. The man responsible was Count Nikita Petrovich Panin, the nephew of Paul's governor and the son of Paul's earliest military mentor.[10] Nikita Petrovich had served as Paul's special emissary to Berlin in 1798 and 1799. When his extended negotiations to bring Prussia into the coalition foundered, Paul recalled him in October 1799 to replace Viktor Kochubei as vice-chancellor and a member of the college of foreign affairs. Panin was a cool, remote, rather haughty man with a markedly legalistic bent to his mind, an appreciation for English constitutional practices, and an unexpected preoccupation with paranormal phenomena (he was fascinated with mesmerism) and the occult. He was by no means a favourite of Paul's. We have seen how they clashed violently in 1792 when Paul demanded that Panin give his allegiance to Nelidova rather than Mariia, and that it was Catherine who protected him against her son's threats when he refused.[11] Even so, his undoubted capacity, if not his person, was appreciated, and Paul chose him for the delicate and difficult post in Berlin. But he won no favours on his return to Petersburg. Fedor Rostopchin monopolized Paul's attention and dominated the college; Panin served as little more than a functionary, carrying messages to and from the foreign embassies, and almost never saw the tsar. This had been his predecessor's fate as well and had contributed to his decision to leave the government.

Panin's sympathies were entirely engaged with the coalition, but he was hardly in place before the mounting controversy over Austria

---

[10] On Panin, see *Materialy Panina*, ed. Brikner; id., 'N. P. Panin', *Russkii biograficheskii slovar*, xiii. 205–11; Prince A. B. Lobanov-Rostovskii summarizes Panin's role: 'Graf Nikita Petrowitsch Panin', in Schiemann (ed.), *Die Ermordung*, 1–8 (in Russian, pp. 261–8).

[11] *Materialy Panina*, ed. Brikner, i. 105–8. See above, Ch. 6.

threatened its foundations. He did what he could in the winter of 1799–1800 to support the English minister's efforts to prevent a break between Russia and Austria, or at least to preserve the Anglo-Russian connection.[12] But Panin was politically powerless and could only watch helplessly when the coalition fell apart in the spring of 1800. He also came to the conclusion, however, that the real danger for Russia and the coalition was less Austrian duplicity than Paul's dangerously unsettled personality. He commented bitterly on the uncomfortable atmosphere which the master's dark and violent moods produced, and it would appear that he came to share the English minister's opinion that Paul, for practical purposes, was dangerously disturbed, and that it was this that was at the root of the difficulties he was creating. As he wrote to Count Vorontsov concerning this time, 'Here nothing has changed; the master's melancholy and bad temper make rapid progress, and it is always ill-humour which decides everything in the administration as in [foreign] politics.'[13]

Panin was well acquainted with Whitworth and saw him regularly at the home of Olga Zherebtsova, Platon Zubov's sister and Whitworth's mistress. Whitworth is often included as a conspirator with Panin, though the evidence is largely circumstantial.[14] But he was certainly in a position to discuss with Panin the details of the English solution to the political problems posed by George III's periodic bouts of dementia, while his own views on Paul's mental state expressed an opinion which was probably widely held and commonly discussed among the Zubovs and which Panin, as he showed in his talks with Alexander, had come to accept. In March 1800 Whitworth wrote to his government:

I can easily conceive Your Lordship's surprise at the repeated instances I have for some time past had to record of the inconsistencies and apparently unaccountable conduct of this court: but when Your Lordship is acquainted with the real situation of affairs, and confirmed in what it is possible you may have suspected, nothing which has passed will appear unnatural, and

[12] PRO, FO/65/44, Whitworth to Grenville, no. 75, 22 Aug. (NS) 1799; no. 94, 10 Oct. (NS) 1799; no. 109, 5 Dec. (NS) 1799; 65/46, no. 22, 2 Apr. (NS) 1800; HHSA, Russland II Berichte, Carton 93, Cobenzl to Thugut, no. 10, apostille 3, 3 Jan. (NS) 1800.

[13] Quoted, Shil'der, *Pavel I*, 469. For Whitworth's reiterated fears on Paul's mental stability, see PRO, FO/65/45, Whitworth to Grenville, no. 101, 1 Nov. (NS) 1799; no. 109, 5 Dec. (NS) 1799; no. 111, 13 Dec. (NS) 1799; no. 113, 24 Dec. (NS) 1799; 65/46, no. 14, 21 Feb. (NS) 1800.

[14] See e.g. Shil'der, *Pavel I*, 466–9; Zubow, *Paul der Erste*, 66–8; de Grunwald, *L'Assassinat*, 174–5. Kenney, 'Lord Whitworth and the Conspiracy', provides the most recent evidence on Whitworth's role.

we shall be equally prepared for everything which is to come. The fact is, and I speak it with regret, that the Emperor is literally not in his senses. This truth has for many years been known to those nearest to Him, and I have myself had frequent opportunities of observing it. But since he has come to the Throne, his disorder has gradually increased and now manifests itself in such a manner as to fill everyone with the most serious alarm. This is the fatal cause of every thing which has passed, and to this we must impute the deviations which we have yet to lament. The Emperor's actions are guided by no fixed rules or principles; consequently nothing is, or can be, stable. I have for motives which are too obvious to be dwelt upon, endeavoured as long as possible to conceal this fatal principle of all our disappointments. I have never for a moment lost sight of the importance of reaping all the benefit we could from his Character; and I have kept within my own breast the anxieties under which I have laboured. The truth must however at last be divulged. We must know what we are to depend upon, but we must at the same time not forget that the Emperor, such as He is, is the despotic sovereign of a powerful Empire, of one connected by Nature with Great Britain; and that from which alone we can procure the means of maintaining the ascendancy of our naval power.[15]

The question of Paul's mental stability was never very far away throughout the last decade of his life. As early as 1792, according to Fedor Golovkin, Platon Zubov was heard to remark that Paul was, in fact, quite mad, to which Catherine was said to reply in a thoughtful way that while they (she and Platon) might know that, the truth was that unfortunately he was not mad enough to threaten the state (and hence, presumably, to justify restraining him).[16] We noted earlier that both Mariia Fedorovna and Catherine Nelidova worried over the violence of Paul's reactions and the effect they had on the public, and that they made every effort not only to modify his behaviour through pleading and exhortation but to shield him against experiences which might ignite his rage.[17] Paul's furious temper was legendary, though it was observed that in its aftermath he would become quite rational again and even make amends for any excesses he might have committed.[18] Yet the minister of Sardinia, who was

---

[15] PRO, FO/65/46, Whitworth to Grenville, no. 17 (duplicate), 18 Mar. (NS) 1800. The dispatch contained an unremarkable report *en clair* while the secret report was written between the lines of the regular report in invisible ink. There is no evidence that Paul's government (or Paul himself) ever read this letter; Paul's request for Whitworth's recall antedated it by more than six weeks.

[16] Golovkine, *La Cour de Paul Ier*, 120.

[17] The point is discussed at length in Ch. 6 above.

[18] See: HHSA, Russland II Berichte, Carton 84, Cobenzl to Thugut, no. 79, apostille 2, 26 Dec. (NS) 1796; Prinz Eugen von Württemberg, 'Jungend Erinnerungen', 79 ff. After Prinz Eugen's first conversation with Paul, which went well, General Dibich muttered, 'Thank God, he [Paul] was in good spirits . . .'. But when Prinz

favourably disposed to Paul, put all qualifiers aside and told his government, at the time that Whitworth was writing, that Paul was intermittently, though definitely, insane; the occasional character of his condition meant that it was possible to deal rationally with him when the fit was not on him.[19]

Paul knew perfectly well what was said about him and the impressions he had made. He explained to Count Stedingk that his protracted absences from official functions were his gift to the court: since his appearance and behaviour so terrified people, the best he could do was to avoid them. 'What . . . would you have me do?' he complained, 'It is said that I am a terrible man, insupportable. I do not wish to frighten anyone. I cover myself with my cloak and I hide . . .'.[20] He recognized that there were those who thought him mad. He was certain that his mother had believed this and took it seriously enough to consider excluding him from the succession. But, as he argued to Dietrichstein, 'even if they think me mad, do they think that 24 million people and my allies are [mad] as well?' Cobenzl reported that Paul often said things of this sort since he was convinced that 'the deceased empress wanted to make him appear to be mad' and even tried to enlist Count Pushkin, who was responsible for Paul's court, to support the charge. Pushkin refused, and when Paul became tsar he showered him with gifts to show his gratitude.[21] For many observers, however, Paul's diplomatic revolution as well as his personal behaviour between summer 1800 and spring 1801 confirmed Catherine's fear. Just over a month before Paul was killed, Count S. R. Vorontsov wrote to N. N. Novosil'tsev from the safety of Richmond-on-Thames a despairing little parable of a ship driving before a storm with a madman in command who had locked the crew below, and an attractive young first officer who, with the crew, could overcome the mad master and save the ship if he only would. Such urging and instruction as outsiders (like the author and his correspondent) might make were in a language which the principals failed to understand; Novosil'tsev might think, even under these circumstances, that there was hope for ship, master, and crew, but Vorontsov could see none and expected the worst.[22]

Eugen spoke brightly and unwittingly of Immanuel Kant, he was treated to a frightening example of Paul's movement from good spirits to anger.

[19] Shil'der, *Pavel I*, 462 n. 2.
[20] Riksarkivet, Diplomatica Moscovitica, vol. 464, Stedingk to the king, 30 Mar./11 Apr. 1800.
[21] HHSA, Russland II Berichte, Carton 86, Cobenzl to Thugut, no. 38, apostille 2, 24 June (NS) 1797; Dietrichstein's report is in annexe 2 to Cobenzl's dispatches.
[22] S. R. Vorontsov to N. N. Novosil'tsev, 5 Feb. (NS) 1801, *Arkhiv kniazia Vorontsova*, xi. 381; Shil'der, *Pavel I*, 465–6.

If Panin took some ideas from Whitworth for dealing with the problems Paul posed, the only allies he actually recruited were two personal friends, Admiral Joseph Ribas, and the governor-general of St Petersburg, Peter von der Pahlen. Ribas, beyond the moral support he offered, was virtually useless in political intrigue, not least because his own reputation had been significantly compromised.[23] Pahlen, however, was another matter. As governor-general he had access to Alexander, which Panin did not, and he was in a position to arrange secret meetings as well as to offer a safe channel for written communications. Pahlen fell in with Panin's ideas immediately. Distantly related, they had met in 1795 when Pahlen was governor-general at Riga, and a warm friendship ensued.[24] But friendship apart, Pahlen had substantial reasons to listen closely to Panin's plans. When Paul became tsar, he had reviewed what he knew of the officials serving him. Pahlen, possibly because he had won favour with Catherine and enjoyed the Zubovs' protection, attracted his attention. One evening he closely questioned Baron Heyking, who had only recently joined Paul's inner circle, about how Pahlen was regarded in Kurland. Heyking knew Pahlen personally, indeed, he was dining with him when the news of Paul's accession arrived in Riga, and he was both well connected and thoroughly familiar with the political situation. His response, that the great majority of the population was satisfied with Pahlen, apparently failed to quiet Paul's suspicions, and Pahlen was removed from his post as governor-general and given an army command. While this transaction was in process, one of Arkharov's police spies reported secretly that Pahlen, contrary to Paul's explicit orders, received and entertained Platon Zubov. The report was misleading, but Paul took it at face value, dismissed Pahlen from his military appointment, and ordered him into exile on his estates. When Pahlen wrote seeking to set the record straight, Paul refused to receive the letter. The matter, at least so far as he was concerned, was closed.[25]

Pahlen was determined to mend his fortunes. He campaigned for reinstatement, won Kutaisov's backing, and in autumn 1797 was appointed commander of the Horse Guards. So assiduous was Kutaisov on Pahlen's behalf that Paul began to wonder just what sort of paragon this man was, and whether dismissing him had been an error. The new command was the answer. It also brought Pahlen into direct contact with Paul who not only exercised the troops, but

[23] Waliszewski, *Paul Ier*, 571–2, 575.
[24] *Materialy Panina*, ed. Brikner, i. 152. Panin wrote to his wife on 8/19 July 1795, urging her to give some attention to the Pahlens as 'they are my friends'.
[25] Heyking, *Aus den Tagen Kaiser Pauls*, 16, 29, 42, 53.

regularly upbraided their commander. Pahlen took it all, remarking after one especially savage dressing-down that he was like a doll with a weight in the base: no matter how violently he might be shoved or thrown, he always came right side up. He was a survivor, but he was something more as well. He was determined to be Paul's perfect servitor, the man who could be relied upon always to do exactly what his master ordered, and that without question. When his son ran afoul of Paul's regulations and faced punishment, Pahlen, to the tsar's surprise, made no effort to intervene: rules were rules, and the young man might benefit from the lesson. With this attitude, to which he clung devotedly, and with Kutaisov's continued support, Pahlen flourished. When the empress's party fell in summer 1798 and Buxhoeweden was dismissed as governor-general of Petersburg, Pahlen received the post; he was on his way to becoming the most powerful official in the empire.

Pahlen could well have settled on a course of revenge when Paul dismissed him at the beginning of his reign. Certainly he was not neutral towards this tsar, though he kept his feelings well buried beneath a jovial imperturbability which won him many friends and much admiration. But after the *coup*, and speaking in private, he declared without qualification that he had always hated Paul and that, despite his rapid advancement, he felt he owed him nothing.[26] Such a statement helps to explain his tenacity in positioning himself so that the tsar's life lay literally in his hands. But there was more to it than that. Pahlen's continued exposure to the tsar on an increasingly intimate basis convinced him that neither his personal career nor the future of the empire would be secure so long as Paul governed. As he told Baron Heyking some six weeks after Paul's murder, and then repeated to General Langeron three years later, it was necessary to understand how dangerous Paul had become. Elevating Alexander to the throne was the only means for protecting the imperial family from the terrible fate Paul was planning for them, for preventing further atrocities against the nobility and the serving class, and for preserving Russia from the revolution which Paul's continued reign would surely bring. Hatred apart, Pahlen presented himself as a disinterested state servant acting to protect society. It requires no great insight, however, to realize that the man who could successfully promote a new tsar could expect to have unusual opportunities open to him, and during the brief period Pahlen served Alexander I, he appeared to be a man who was fully savouring the power he had won.[27]

[26] Ibid. 229.
[27] Ibid. 226–30; 'Iz zapisok grafa Lanzherona', *Tsareubiistvo* (1907), 134–6.

The balance among altruism, ambition, and revenge in Pahlen's motivation will always be obscure. His caution, however, or his gradual acceptance of the need to remove Paul, is quite clear. In the beginning, he did no more than bring Panin and Alexander together. He did not assume a leader's role until five months later, and indeed he could not had he wished. In August 1800, he was removed as governor-general in favour of General Svechin and sent into the interior to organize defence forces against the possibility of an Austrian attack. He returned to Petersburg at the end of October to resume his old post. It was at that time that he began actively to organize a *coup d'état*, and when Panin left in December he became the conspiracy's leader.

Sometime in June, Pahlen had arranged what was to become a series of secret meetings between Panin and Alexander. Panin took to the conspiratorial role with enthusiasm, carrying a dagger and watching out for lurking spies. The grand duke, on the other hand, was nervous and had trouble concentrating on what he was told, so fearful was he of discovery and exposure.[28] What Panin argued was essentially that Paul should not be permitted to continue ruling, that his judgement was wholly unreliable, and that he was committing atrocities against his loyal servitors. He had become a threat to Russia's stability and Europe's peace. Nor was he at ease with himself or his world. What the tsar needed above all else was to be relieved of the burdens of government and left in some quiet retreat. If he continued in his public role, he could only grow worse. The problem could be solved if Paul would abdicate his powers, preferably to a regency in his name directed by Alexander as his son and heir. In the event of him refusing to abdicate, he could legitimately be placed under restraint while the regency was established for him.[29]

Panin appears to have developed these ideas at length; he also claimed never to have promoted a *coup d'état*, to have had nothing to do with the conspiracy that took Paul's life, and, most important of all, to have firm evidence that Alexander had not only listened to

[28] See Zubow, *Paul der Erste*, 73–5. Panin warned Alexander a spy might be following them, and the terrified grand duke shrieked. Panin thought that Alexander's chagrin at showing his fear may have poisoned their relationship and contributed to his later fall. Zubow cites Rosenzweig, the resident minister of Saxony in Petersburg, who had the story directly from Panin. The original report is in the Dresden state archives, but a German trans. of it appeared in Fr. Bühlau (ed.), *Geheime Geschichte und Rätselhafte Menschen* (Leipzig, 1858), 58 ff. See also *Aus allen Zeiten und Länden* (Brunswick, 1882), and R. R. [Alexander Brückner], *Kaiser Pauls I. Ende 1801* (Stuttgart, 1897).

[29] 'Aus den Papieren des Grafen N. P. Panin', Schiemann (ed.), *Die Ermordung*, 53–6.

him, but had agreed to what he proposed.[30] All this, of course, was recorded long after the fact, when Panin was protesting against his dismissal and exile for participating in the conspiracy. In fact, it was he who took the first steps, though Pahlen eventually pre-empted the leadership and turned the conspiracy from an exercise in constitutional law to a palace revolution.

The grand duke met with Panin, listened to his arguments, and waited. While he did not, at least initially, approve of what was presented to him, he did not reject it, nor did he betray Panin to Paul. Panin's dismissal in November 1800 and his subsequent exile had nothing to do with his tampering with the grand duke. It followed the challenge he threw down to Rostopchin by questioning the direction of Paul's foreign policy. By autumn 1800, it should be recalled, Paul was prepared to fight England over neutral rights and the Malta question, and Austria over Italy, central Europe, and European Turkey. The tsar was aroused and unforgiving. Though Sweden, Denmark, and Prussia appeared to offer support of varying strength and reliability, the warmest diplomatic prospect was accommodation with Napoleonic France. It was this position that Panin challenged, and through it Rostopchin's dominance in the college of foreign affairs. He lost. His memorandum outlining a more conventional policy for Russia in Europe was disregarded. He was dismissed as vice-chancellor in early November and ordered to join the senate in Moscow. Those orders, however, were rescinded before they could be implemented as Panin was expelled from the service and sent into exile on his estates. Rostopchin had won a total victory.[31]

Whitworth had left Petersburg the preceding May; Ribas died suddenly on 16 November (os). Of the original 'conspiracy' only Pahlen and the grand duke Alexander remained. But Pahlen, whether because of what Paul was doing in his foreign policy, his turn to increasingly cruel punishments for his subordinates, the threat his own ambitions faced from Paul's unpredictable irascibility, or for a combination of these motives, actively took up organizing a *coup*. His argument to Alexander was that it had become imperative to remove Paul, while the grand duke, faced with multiplying evidence of his father's animosity and malign intent towards himself, his mother, and his brother, began to agree, though he was always to

[30] 'Aus den Papieren des Grafen N. P. Panin', Schiemann (ed.), *Die Ermordung*, 53–6.
[31] Panin's account of his confrontation with Rostopchin was given to I. M. Muraviev-Apostol to be conveyed to Count Vorontsov in London. See I. M. Muraviev-Apostol to S. R. Vorontsov, 16 Feb. (os) 1801, *Materialy Panina*, ed. Brikner, ch. 3, v. 616–24; *Arkhiv kniazia Vorontsova*, xi. 161–7.

claim that he insisted that his father should not be harmed. Certainly Paul was not to be killed.[32] Such reservations might have carried weight with Panin who was, after all, seeking a legal transition. But they carried next to no weight with Pahlen who focused on the essential point: Paul's removal. If this could be done without physically injuring the tsar, while maintaining order and political continuity, well and good. But Paul would be sacrificed if that were necessary. And that would appear to have been what Pahlen expected, and possibly preferred. He provided virtually nothing in the way of safeguards for protecting the tsar when the conspirators seized him, while the sort of people he recruited and gave the task of capturing the tsar made it unlikely that Paul would escape with his life.[33] What Pahlen needed from Alexander was his acquiescence in the *coup* attempt. Once it had happened the grand duke would be implicated and an ally, willing or unwilling, of the successful conspirators. This Pahlen was able to accomplish. What he did not foresee was Alexander's profoundly guilty reaction which made him susceptible to his mother's fixed determination to avenge her husband. Organizing the conspiracy was easy compared with harvesting its fruits. Pahlen succeeded admirably as an organizer; he was destroyed in the aftermath.

The conspiracy conjoined two issues. Panin emphasized Paul's incompetence, his lack of control, and the atrocities (figurative and literal) his condition produced. Pahlen continued to use Panin's approach when he had to deal with Alexander, but when he recruited the men who made the revolt, he stressed Paul's despotism, cruelty, and harsh disregard for the security, loyalty, and status of his subordinates. It was this latter theme that dominated by the time the attack on the Michael Palace was mounted.[34] And when the word went out, it was that the tyrant was dead and Russia could breathe again. Viazzoli, the Austrian consul-general, was in Riga when word was brought to him of the way Paul ended 'his detestable career'.

---

[32] Czartoryski, *Mémoires*, i. 234–6.

[33] De Grunwald, *L'Assassinat*, 185–6 notes the violence-prone among Pahlen's conspirators. Czartoryski recorded Alexander's horror at his father's death, but asked if he should have been surprised; the men who attacked Paul hated him. *Mémoires*, i. 254. Pahlen had promised to preserve Paul's life if possible, but he also declared that that would be very difficult. R. R. [Brückner], *Kaiser Pauls Ende*, 104.

[34] Czartoryski, *Mémoires*, i. 249–50; Ernst von Wedell, 'Aufschlüsse über die Ermordung des Kaisers Pauls I' (depositions of Bennigsen and Zubov, 1812), Schiemann (ed.), *Die Ermordung*, 79–80; 'Iz zapisok Lanzherona', *Tsareubiistvo* (1907), 114–15; 'The Death of Paul I', 227; 'Iz zapisok Fonvizina', *Tsareubiistvo* (1907), 166–7; 'Neizdannoe sochinenie Avgusta Kotsebu', ibid. 336–9; Welianinow-Zernow, 'Die Ermordung Pauls', Schiemann (ed.), *Die Ermordung*, 30.

Claiming to use 'expressions generally employed in Russia', Viazzoli described how Paul, 'by his extravagances, his cruelties, his madnesses, his brutalities, his terror . . . horribly compromised Russia [and] pushed his empire to the brink of the precipice'. And this after having 'wearied and insulted the entire nation', while almost 'overturning the political system of Europe'. Paul regarded himself 'as a god on earth' and 'betrayed and humiliated or degraded all those sovereigns who depended on him whom he considered and deemed his subjects'. But, worst of all, 'after having exercised the excess of despotism, and having reigned with a sceptre of iron, Paul I turned his rage and his fury toward his wife and his own son, the successor to the throne, whom he wished, it is said, to imprison and knout'. The *coup* was necessary 'to prevent this horror and to deliver Russia from the monster who had contemplated sacrificing innocence and virtue'. Viazzoli had been told that there was a plan to declare Paul mad, to seize his person, and secure him. But this plan was laid to prevent the civil war Paul's actions were threatening, and was undertaken by 'certain persons' (not to be named here) who invited officers of the guard into the secret and mobilized a considerable body of soldiers. And his account of the attack on Paul's bedroom conveys the certain impression of an execution. Though Paul begged for his life, 'two officers seized their scarves, threw them around Paul I's neck, and strangled him'. The conspirators appear in this account as tyrannicides, and in the aftermath of Paul's death that was their preferred portrayal of themselves.[35]

Though it played little part once the *coup* began, the conviction that Paul was mentally disturbed, that he was literally not in his senses, has remained green, since it both explains the extremities in his behaviour and helps to blur the moral edges of his murder.[36] This

---

[35] HHSA, Russland II Berichte, Carton 95, 'Rapport: Viazzoli à Trautsmandorff', Riga, 22 Mar./3 Apr. 1801. Viazzoli, the former Austrian consul-general, was a long-time resident of St Petersburg who was forced to leave when the Austrian legations were closed. He was well connected in both governmental and commercial circles (he was invited to join the government at the time of the opening of the Bank of Assistance for the Nobility), and as is obvious from the tenor of this report, he shared the opposition view of Paul as an unspeakable tyrant. His account of Paul's murder corresponds closely with those of the participants with two exceptions: he portrays Paul defending himself with a sword, and begging for mercy on his knees before two officers seized and strangled him. In a postscript dated a week later Viazzoli reported as hard fact that the leaders of the *coup* revealed their plans to Alexander and that the grand duke, while insisting that his father's life be spared, agreed to the attack.

[36] Shil'der, *Pavel I*, 462–6; Shumigorskii, *Pavel I*, 179–83, 184. Waliszewski, quoting primarily the sources Shil'der used (including Whitworth's letter cited above), accepts the idea that Paul was 'demented', but puts it in the same category as

has been particularly important for Alexander's apologists. It must be added here, however, that in clinical terms there are no certain or even substantial grounds for considering Paul insane.[37] But then the men who called him mad were not speaking clinically. What they expressed was their repugnance for behaviour that seemed to have no grounding in reason, that was extreme, contradictory, highly charged emotionally, and at odds with what they saw as normal. And when such outrageous behaviour not only threatened the status of leading personages who had to depend on him, but put the very security of the empire itself at risk, it was easy to say that the tsar had taken leave of his senses, that he was, in fact, mad, and that the public welfare demanded that he be removed from power and rusticated before he brought disaster down on everyone.

Though Paul was probably not certifiable, there is substantial evidence that he behaved irrationally and unpredictably, that he had a vicious temper, that he was capricious, headstrong, suspicious to an extraordinary degree, fearful, dependent, vengeful, and perverse. Though subject to persuasion by people he claimed to trust, he recognized no limits on what he was empowered to do, while the quality of his decisions, and even the attention he was willing to give to the jobs at hand, fluctuated greatly. A constitutional system, or even strong advisers, would have gone far towards shielding him against the consequences of his own emotional turbulence. But no constitution existed in Russia which could serve that function, and by the spring of 1799, Paul had lost the last councillor who was willing to try to restrain him. He had thrown off his wife's influence during the preceding year, and with that he lost Nelidova's dedicated

---

the dementia exhibited by revolutionary extremists in France. What he suffered was a sort of disease of the age, or one for which the age offered other examples. This in no way denied the extremities of Paul's behaviour. *Paul Ier*, 523–32. This conclusion is not far from Eidel'man's view that the disease from which Paul suffered was an excess of autocracy.

[37] V. F. Chizh, 'Imperator Pavel I', 289–90, for Paul's character type. Pt. ii *passim* deals with symptoms, while pt. iii applies the psychological analysis to Paul's policies, his relations with women, and the conspiracy. Hugh Ragsdale, *Tsar Paul and the Question of Madness: An Essay in History and Psychology* (Westport, Conn., 1988), only gets to the technical issues of Paul's emotional character after briefing his life, analysing him as an examplar of the Enlightenment, and discussing what 'madness' meant at the end of the 18th cent. Ragsdale finds that while Paul was not clinically insane, he was emotionally unbalanced and pathologically compulsive. He avoids Chizh's reductionism, suggesting that while Paul's personality helps us to understand his behaviour and contemporaries' reactions to it, it is not an explanation in itself. See also Ragsdale, 'The Mental Condition of Paul', *Reassessment*, 17–30.

friendship as well. Both had laboured hard to modify the way he made decisions and their substance. The people who remained close to Paul and who were able to influence what he did were either self-interested (Kutaisov and Pahlen), non-political and essentially superficial (Lopukhina-Gagarina), or convinced that implementing what the master wanted was their basic task (Rostopchin and Arakcheev).

Denmark's Christian VII or Britain's George III would have been sick men even if they had not been monarchs. This, however, was not so true of Paul. The burdens and frustrations of his office intensified his destructive tendencies, while his position and the power he wielded magnified his personality problems into major political issues. Had Paul never risen above grand duke, his behaviour might have been embarrassing, but it would hardly have been significant. As the tsar, however, what he felt and thought were instantly translatable into action, and as they were, he crossed the boundary beyond what could be tolerated; he went beyond reason. Whether in the larger scheme of things Paul's policies were defensible or even laudable, he terrified, infuriated, and traumatized the people who were around him. For those who experienced him that way, it was easy and natural to declare that he was out of his mind. And if he was sometimes better than others, this hardly altered the fact that his reactions could never be trusted.

Though the patterns of Paul's behaviour are beyond argument, not everyone reacted to them as Panin, Whitworth, Pahlen, or the Zubovs did. And even among those people who recognized his flaws, there was no unanimity on the need for his removal. In Paul's case, more is known about his enemies than about those who accepted him for what he was and tried to avoid confrontations with him, or actively supported him and the policies he introduced. General Sablukov, whose memoirs are one of the more useful sources we have for the events of 1801, avoided becoming involved in the plot, though he knew that something was going to happen. He was thought to be a loyalist, but he kept his suspicions to himself, and to that extent he aided the plotters. After Paul was killed, Sablukov was one of a number of officers who were outraged by what had happened and were quick to challenge the *coup*'s supporters. Pahlen was sufficiently disturbed by the open quarrels that followed to propose a banquet of reconciliation. His position, naturally enough, was that what was done was done, and that it was time to put the past away in favour of unity and a common effort. Sablukov refused at first to attend, and others would have joined him. He changed his mind when Pahlen made a personal plea, though in the event it was

The End of the Beginning

clear that there was a considerable residue of hostility between the factions.[38]

How many Sablukovs there were we have no way of knowing. His memoirs suggest, however, that there was at the very least a substantial number of officers (without including the despised Gatchintsi) who remained loyal to Paul despite everything he did. There were certainly men of that stripe in the government. Fedor Rostopchin had nothing but scorn for those courtiers who scanted their responsibilities to the heir when he was grand duke, nor did Rostopchin give Paul anything less than devoted service then and throughout his reign. Rostopchin's critics knew that he was clever and considered him an unworthy intriguer who knew how to manipulate the system. No one, however, questioned his loyalty.[39] Arakcheev was another whose devotion to Paul was unqualified and unquestioned, who saw himself primarily as the tsar's servant, and who accepted whatever the tsar ordered. Arakcheev may have had a ghastly reputation, but he was a superb organizer and administrator, and he was wholly Paul's man.[40]

For the Sablukovs, Rostopchins, or Arakcheevs, the flaws in Paul's personality, the treatment he meted out to subordinates, even the decisions he made, paled to insignificance before the fact that he was tsar and had the right to expect his subjects' undivided loyalty, regardless of what he did. This, of course, was Paul's own position, and he had lived by it scrupulously throughout his long apprenticeship under Catherine. Nor was this attitude limited to the tsar and his circle. Even people who had felt the sting of his lash showed evidence of it. Augustus von Kotzebue's memoirs record a story worthy of Kafka; the playwright was seized on returning to Russia with his family and, without any charge or explanation, exiled to Siberia.[41] His description of his travels as a prisoner across European Russia

---

[38] Sablukov, 'Reminiscences: Part II', 302–27.

[39] Countess Golovina remarked that when Rostopchin left the government Paul lost a man who 'truly loved him'. She insisted that Pahlen worked for at least a year to drive a wedge between Paul and Rostopchin, that he had Kutaisov's support, and that Rostopchin's dismissal just before Paul's murder was their triumph. *Souvenirs*, 248–52.

[40] On Arakcheev's loyalty to Paul, see above, Ch. 6. A study of the men of Paul's persuasion under Alexander I would be valuable for understanding the political history of that reign.

[41] August von Kotzebue, *Das merkwürdigste Jahr meines Lebens*, 2 vols. (Berlin, 1801). An English trans., faithful to the German original, appeared the following year: *The Most Remarkable Year in the Life of Augustus von Kotzebue: Containing an Account of his Exile into Siberia and of the other Extraordinary Events which Happened to him in Russia, Written by Himself*, trans. Benjamin Beresford, 3 vols. (London, 1802).

and what he saw of others who had run afoul of Paul's laws is chilling and graphic. More, he was never to find out why he was exiled, what he had done, or said, or written that accounted for his fate, and he was released in exactly the same way: without any explanation. Paul made amends once Kotzebue was back in Petersburg, granting him an estate and appointing him to head the German theatre (which was unsuccessfully competing with Madame Chevalier's French troupe). He also received various commissions indicative of trust, including one to catalogue the contents of the newly finished Michael Palace. At no time in this long and sometimes painful account did Kotzebue criticize Paul, though he had harsh words for some of his subordinates. He was terrified, of course, that he would again offend in some way and be sent away, but this was different from reprobating the tsar. The tsar did what he had to do; Kotzebue neither blamed him nor showed resentment at his own fate. The description which he wrote later of Paul's death, far from gloating, presents Paul in rather a more favourable light (Prince Andrei Lobanov-Rostovskii calls it apologetic) than other similar pieces, and Kotzebue goes out of his way to note Paul's good standing with the common soldiers while suggesting that with his death the people had lost a protector. Certainly there is no hint that he believed Paul deserved what happened to him.[42]

Panin's inability to organize an effective conspiracy or to win Alexander to his plans should make it apparent that Paul's overthrow was hardly inevitable. What might have happened had he arrested and imprisoned Mariia and his elder sons, established a new succession, and entered a shooting war with England can only be speculated. What is clear is that in autumn 1800 no effective plan to remove him existed. And, as matters then were, for one to have taken shape against the will of a loyal security chief (which General Svechin actually was) and without the grand duke's agreement would have been almost impossible. Paul, for all that he was both eccentric and despotic, was firmly in control. What destroyed him was Pahlen's defection. Without Pahlen, the greatest threat to Paul's future was the possibility of defeat and a foreign invasion, and, paradoxically, an invasion with the resultant surge of loyalty to tsar

---

[42] 'Neizdannoe sochinenie Avgusta Kotsebu ob imperatore Pavle I', *Tsareubiistvo* (1907), 269–363. While the great, the educated, society in fact, celebrated and wrote clever rhymes, 'The people and the soldiers said "He was our Father".' (363). See 'Dopolitel'nyia primechaniia kniazia A. B. Lobanova-Rostovskago k zapiske Kotsebu', *Tsareubiistvo* (1908), 412–23. The 1907 edn. in the British Library has only a part of Lobanov-Rostovskii's notes on Kotzebue. Kotzebue's contribution in the 1908 edn. covers pp. 315–411.

and fatherland might even have strengthened his position. The future, however, was in Pahlen's hands, and he began to shape it on his return to Petersburg from the front.

On 1 November (OS) 1800, an *ukaz* appeared granting amnesty to those officers and officials whom Paul had dismissed and exiled.[43] The decree was published only six days after Pahlen's return to Petersburg and was probably promulgated at his insistence and with the support of Ivan Kutaisov. Pahlen needed support. He was particularly anxious to have the Zubovs back, both for their symbolic importance as representatives of Catherine's reign and the nobles she favoured, and for the assistance they could offer in recruiting among the guards. Ivan Kutaisov had a special reason for adding his importunities to Pahlen's suggestions: Platon Zubov was said to be interested in marrying Kutaisov's daughter. He had been encouraged to look that way by his sister, Olga Zherebtsova, with the idea of gaining Kutaisov's favour for the Zubov faction. However it was brought about, Paul welcomed the Zubovs back, appointed Platon to the directorship of the first cadet corps, and his brother, Valerian, to the third. Nicholas Zubov received a regimental command. General Leo Bennigsen was another for whom the amnesty opened up what appeared to be a new future. Pahlen encouraged him to return to Petersburg and suggested that the tsar was eager to greet him and to make amends. In fact, this was in no way true. Bennigsen returned only to be ignored; this made him ripe for Pahlen to recruit him, a goal the governor-general had had in sight from the start.[44]

Paul's habit, and possibly his policy, of exiling people who had been dismissed had prevented the build-up of any large dissatisfied group in the capital. In October 1799, when it appeared that the city was going to be overrun by unemployed officers and clerks, the product of rationalizing policies as well as dismissals for cause, Paul ordered these potential indigents out of the city and forbade their lingering in the neighbourhood.[45] There were no means to provide

---

[43] *PSZ*, series 1, vol. 25, 1 Nov. (OS) 1800, nos. 19625 and 19626.

[44] Shil'der, *Aleksandr Pervyi*, i. 214; *Pavel I*, 470–1; Heyking, *Aus den Tagen Kaiser Pauls*, 198–200; 'Iz zapisok Lanzherona', *Tsareubiistvo* (1907), 137–8, where Pahlen explains his need for the Zubovs and Bennigsen and how he played on Paul's romantic sensibilities to get the amnesty.

[45] HHSA, Russland II Berichte, Carton 93, Dietrichstein, 'Notices sur la cour de Russie . . .' recorded this move and commented that Paul's exile policies filled the provinces and Moscow with his opponents while Petersburg remained free. His estimate that there were 14,000 people in this category seems wildly exaggerated. Eidel'man, *Gran'vekov*, 100–13, shows that the numbers of Paul's victims, as far as they can be verified in court papers, were far smaller than contemporary

for their needs, while their presence was a source of instability. When the exiles returned in 1800, however, no preparations were made for their coming, and some were destitute. All expected at least some help in finding employment, if not full reinstatement, but that Paul did not intend. The resulting disappointment and bitterness contributed to the capital's uncertain atmosphere, while Pahlen found himself with a virtually bottomless reservoir of men willing and ready to assist in overturning the tsar in power.[46]

It remains unclear just when Alexander agreed to the *coup*. Czartoryski remarked that the grand duke resisted for about six months, which suggests that he accepted what had to be done by the end of December or early in January. Prince Eugen stated flatly that the grand duke made his decision on 23 January/3 February 1801. There is nothing inherently unreasonable about that date, nor is there any corroboration for it.[47] And it remains possible that Alexander was positively inclined but still uncertain in early March. If so, there may be substance to the story that Pahlen 'betrayed' him, Mariia, and Constantine to Paul just days before the attack, thereby receiving written orders from the tsar to arrest the empress and the two grand dukes as well as other members of the conspiracy.[48] Alexander's capitulation would then have followed Pahlen's showing him this document. However this matter is resolved, it is beyond question that Alexander knew what Pahlen was doing in November and December and was plainly implicated. At the end of the period he contributed to planning the attack, suggesting the night of 11 March rather than

commentators, memoirists, etc. asserted. How complete the 'paper trail' may be is another and critical question yet to be answered.

[46] Heyking, *Aus den Tagen Kaiser Pauls*, 198–200.

[47] Czartoryski, *Mémoires*, i. 235; Prinz Eugen von Württemberg, 'Jungend Erinnerungen', 137.

[48] Pahlen's account of the confrontation with Paul on 7 Mar. (os) 1801 given to Langeron makes no mention of an arrest warrant or other enabling document. 'Iz zapisok Lanzherone', *Tsareubiistvo* (1907), 139–40. Heyking refers to an authorizing document. *Aus den Tagen Kaiser Pauls*, 217. Welianinov-Zernov gives a 3rd version in which Pahlen presents Paul with a list of conspirators headed by Mariia Fedorovna and followed by the two grand dukes together with their wives. Paul then drew up an *ukaz* ordering the empress and both grand duchesses into a monastery while Alexander and Constantine were to be locked up in a fortress. With this *ukaz* in hand, Pahlen went directly to Alexander and won his permission to remove Paul from the throne. Welianinow-Sernow, 'Die Ermordung Pauls', Schiemann (ed.), *Die Ermordung*, 23–4. This version was widely distributed. It is the one repeated in Bennigsen's memoirs, 'The Death of Paul I', 224, and in one form or another appears in most of the accounts set down by people contemporary with the events who relied on 2nd or 3rd hand information. Our account will follow Langeron and Heyking.

9 or 10 March because elements of his own Semenovskii regiment, of whose loyalty he was certain, would be on duty in the palace.[49] Constantine may have suspected that a plan was in train to remove Paul in favour of Alexander, but he was not involved because he was considered too unreliable to share the conspirators' secrets. On the night of the murder, Alexander told Sablukov that both he and Constantine were under arrest; this, however, did not prevent Constantine from sleeping soundly until Zubov called him to go to his brother, the emperor.[50] Alexander's wife, Elizabeth, considered her father-in-law a tyrant and Russia delivered from an intolerable despotism when he fell, though she deplored his death. It is probable that she knew nearly as much as Alexander at the end of 1800 and sympathized whole-heartedly with the idea of a change. Mariia, on the other hand, appears to have known no more than her fears. She had no part, even indirectly, in what happened; the *coup* and her husband's death exploded her world.[51]

The one person in Paul's inner circle about whom little is said is Ivan Kutaisov, yet he appears in the events described with irritating regularity. Following his early fall from favour, Pahlen was Kutaisov's protégé, continuing to rise with Ivan's backing when the fall of Mariia's faction delivered major influence into the Turk's hands. Baron Heyking considered Pahlen, Kutaisov, and Rostopchin to be closely linked until February 1801 when Rostopchin fell into eclipse, possibly with Pahlen's connivance. But Kutaisov and Pahlen virtually rose in tandem between 1798 and 1801. Throughout this period, Kutaisov was Paul's familiar, an intimate with almost unlimited scope, a companion whose corruption, though immense, was simply ignored. Kutaisov figures almost not at all in the stories of the *coup*. One partial exception is the suggestion described above that the Zubovs manipulated him. There is also the tale that on the eve of the

---

[49] 'Iz zapisok Lanzherona', *Tsareubiistvo* (1907), 140.

[50] Ibid. 145–7 for Constantine's account with explanatory notes. Sablukov's exchange with Alexander in Constantine's presence appears in his 'Reminiscences: Part II', 314–15.

[51] Waliszewskli, *Paul Ier*, 635, offers no direct evidence but argues on the basis of Elizabeth's behaviour that she was in on the secret of the conspiracy. On Mariia's reactions on the night of the murder, see Princess Daria Christoferovna Lieven, 'Pauls Tod', Schiemann (ed.), *Die Ermordung*, 35–52. See also Kotzebue (whose source was Princess Lieven), 'Neizdannoe sochinenie Avgusta Kotsebu', *Tsareubiistvo* (1907), 340–3. Elizabeth, who stayed with Mariia, described her reactions in her letter to her mother, 13/25 Mar. 1801, Grand Duke Nicolas Mikhailowitch, *L'Impératrice Elisabeth*, 269. See also Heyking, *Aus den Tagen Kaiser Pauls*, 222–3; Golovine, *Souvenirs*, 260–1; Prinz Eugen von Württemberg, 'Bemerkungen', Schiemann, *Die Ermordung*, 86–8; von Wedell, 'Aufschlüsse', ibid. 80–2.

coup a sealed letter denouncing the conspirators and exposing their plans was surreptitiously handed to Kutaisov. Since he was occupied at that moment, he either put the letter in his pocket and forgot it, or threw it down on his desk. In any case it was not opened until after the *coup* occurred and Paul was dead. Kutaisov slipped away from the palace on 11 March to take refuge with a friend. Given his association with and support for Pahlen, and his well-developed system for acquiring information and exerting influence, it is difficult to believe that he was unaware of the plot, though there is nothing to connect him with it directly.[52]

Paul lived always with the apprehension that plots were taking shape against him and that his enemies, sooner or later, would succeed. This fear may well have been behind the curious story we saw him tell in 1782 of meeting Peter the Great who warned him of an early death, and it links closely with his father's fate and his ultimate realization that he lived among enemies. Potemkin was the *bête noire* of his later years, while at the time of his accession it was the Zubovs whom he found especially threatening. He also took steps to neutralize and punish the relics of that 1762 conspiracy. The fear that he would be assassinated was with him from the time he became tsar and infected the people around him. In summer 1797 his hypersensitivity to the possibility of an attack set off near riots at Pavlovsk, and he was known to remark with satisfaction on the devoted loyalty of one officer or another who had saved him from 'a severe sore throat', his euphemism for strangling.[53] Shortly before his death, while riding in the palace garden, he had a severe attack of shortness of breath. He pulled up his horse and with every sign of discomfort and alarm complained of feeling suffocated, unable to breathe, and in imminent danger of dying. 'Won't they [have the chance to] strangle me?' he gasped. In the long reaches of the night

---

[52] Heyking, *Aus den Tagen Kaiser Pauls*, 177, 186, 213, for the rise in tandem of Kutaisov and Pahlen; Heyking considered them, with Rostopchin, the most powerful men in the realm. Rostopchin's dismissal and exile less than three weeks before the *coup* removed a major impediment to Pahlen's plans. Langeron, 'Iz zapisok Lanzherona', *Tsareubiistvo* (1907), 151, declares that Kutaisov was not in the plot. D'Allonville, *Mémoires*, viii. 7, identified the author of the letter to Kutaisov betraying the plot as Prince P. V. Meshcherskii; Kotzebue, 'Neizdanoe sochinenie', *Tsareubiistvo* (1907), 343–4 n. 2; Golovine, *Souvenirs*, 256. Kutaisov took refuge in the house of S. S. Lanskoi.

[53] HHSA, Russland II Berichte, Carton 86, Cobenzl to Thugut, no. 38, apostille 2, 24 June (NS) 1797; no. 44, apostille 12, 20 July (NS) 1797. For the false alarm and its consequences at Pavlovsk, ibid., Carton 84, Dietrichstein to Thugut, no. 54, apostille 10, 20 Sept. (NS) 1797; cf. Shumigorskii, *Nelidova*, 96–9.

when he was sleepless he would wander in his nightclothes through the palace checking and rechecking the guard posts.[54]

Paul disliked the Winter Palace for its associations with his mother and regarded it as insufficiently secure. Within days of his accession he had decreed the building of a new palace on the site of the old Summer Palace, which had burnt down.[55] Named after the archangel Michael, who is supposed to have appeared in a vision to a soldier on guard and chosen the site, this new construction, the work of Brenna, Paul's favourite architect, was to embody the spirit of the new reign and provide a secure haven for the ruler. The building, shaped to be both palace and fortress, was surrounded by a deep moat across which there were four drawbridges. With the gates barred and locked, the bridges raised, and the public rooms and connecting corridors under guard, Paul could feel himself secure. The building was rushed to completion in just over four years. A huge pile in the Renaissance mode with enormous public rooms and galleries to house Paul's art treasures, the Michael Palace was occupied on 1 February (OS) 1801. Paul was warned that the structure was not ready, that the plaster was still green, and that there would be unacceptably high humidity levels. The building needed six months, and better a year, for the masonry and plaster to dry. But Paul ignored all that, moving court and family from the Winter Palace into a structure where the moisture froze on the walls and vast clouds of mist obscured the public rooms when they were fully occupied. The Michael Palace, today the 'Engineer's Castle', was a joke and a scandal, but Paul paid no heed. In his eyes, its inconveniences were temporary, it was magnificent, and it was secure. He now had a counterpart in Petersburg for Gatchina.[56]

---

[54] Sablukov, 'Reminiscences: Part II', 313. For Paul's sleepless nights, HHSA, Russland II Berichte, Dietrichstein, 'Notices sur la cour de Russie...', Biala, 26 Nov. (NS) 1799.

[55] *PSZ*, series 1, vol. 24, no. 17571, 20 Nov. (OS) 1796; HHSA, Russland II Berichte, Carton 82, Cobenzl to Thugut, 7 Dec. (NS) 1796. In addition to a new theatre, 'there is also talk of building a new palace in place of that for summer which was in wood, and for which the plans were already made in advance'.

[56] Princess Lieven, 'Pauls Tod', Schiemann (ed.), *Die Ermordung*, 34–5, relates the story of the angelic inspiration for the palace and its name. She refers the story to the spring of 1797; in fact, the orders for the building were laid down several months earlier. See also: British Library, Tab. 487c, Vincenzio Brenna, *Designi dell'Imperial Palazzo S. Michele...*, 2 folio volumes, 1800(?); I. N. Vozherianov, 'Mikhailovskii zamok, dvorets imperatora Pavla I v S.-Peterburge v 1800–1801', *Russkaia starina*, 39 (1883), 651–2. Kotzebue, *The Most Remarkable Year*, iii. 11–73, describes the Michael Palace and its contents on the eve of Paul's death. He was charged with inventorying the objets d'art.

Pahlen's conspiracy played itself out in the Michael Palace. Paul was as exposed there as he would have been anywhere. On one occasion, when he was being particularly vivid about what he would do to the French revolutionaries, Catherine told him that he was no better than a ferocious beast and that he should know that it was impossible to fight ideas with cannons. In a variation on this, Paul was to discover that walls, moats, and gates were no protection against men determined to destroy him. So far as security was concerned, Pahlen was in possession of all the passwords and could go where he pleased, while Paul's adjutant, Argamakov, who had the freedom of the tsar's personal apartments and reported to him directly early in the morning, was a member of the conspiracy. Finally, on the night of the attack, Paul himself dismissed the Horse Guards stationed outside his bedchamber. Pahlen undoubtedly inspired this order and it was probably crucial. General, then Colonel, Sablukov was in command, and Pahlen himself later declared that he was the one officer the conspirators feared. Had Sablukov and his unit been in place, the initial attackers, a ragtag of officers from different units and without regular support, could have met severe resistance. As it was, Paul left two lackeys in hussar costume to guard his antechamber.[57]

Gustave IV of Sweden made a brief visit to Petersburg at the end of December and left at the beginning of January. Pahlen chose 15 March (OS) as the date for the *coup*; another tyrant was to fall with the Ides of March, but when it appeared that Paul was becoming suspicious, the date was moved up. Though Paul and Pahlen remained on the best of terms in these last days, there were hints and hairbreadth escapes which could only worry the conspirators. One story which Pahlen told found him in Paul's presence with a letter from the grand duke for Panin on his person. Paul teased him with hiding love letters and came towards him as if to rummage through his pockets. Pahlen recoiled, warning Paul that he used tobacco and that his handkerchief was soaked with it. Paul turned away with an expression of disgust. A variation on this story, told by Zubov and Bennigsen in 1812, had Pahlen facing Paul with two papers in his pocket, one orders for the day which Paul needed to see, the other a list of the members of the conspiracy. Paul rallied Pahlen on what he was carrying and demanded to see it; with two papers under his fingers, Pahlen produced the innocent order.[58]

[57] Sablukov, 'Reminiscences: Part II', 313–16, 319.
[58] 'Iz zapisok Lanzherona', *Tsareubiistvo* (1907), 136–7 for the tobacco story. The variant appears in von Wedell, 'Aufschlüsse', Schiemann (ed.), *Die Ermordung*, 77.

Shortly before the *coup*, the most dangerous confrontation occurred when Pahlen reportedly entered Paul's cabinet for his normal start-of-the-day conversation and found the tsar in a state of indignation and alarm. He turned towards his governor-general and demanded to know whether he had taken part in the *coup* of 1762. Pahlen admitted to being in service in Petersburg but reminded Paul that he was then very young and knew nothing. But they had discussed all this before; what brought it up at this point? What brought it up, Paul responded, was that it was going to happen again, that there was, in fact, a plot afoot which aimed at overthrowing him, and that Pahlen, who was responsible for his security, was doing nothing. Though Pahlen had undoubtedly prepared himself for such a moment, to have it actually happen shook him. It also raised him to unexpected heights of inventiveness. He coolly informed Paul that he knew about the conspiracy, that he was familiar with the people involved, and that, in fact, he himself was a member of it. But he could see no point in worrying Paul with such matters until it was time to act. Pahlen then took the initiative, arguing that there were substantial differences between Peter III's case and Paul's, and that all of these attested the support and even affection that Paul enjoyed. This contrasted with his father who had never been crowned and who was viewed, unlike Paul, as a German rather than a Russian. Moreover, Paul was just a child when Peter was overthrown, thus making it easy for his mother to appear in his place, but now he was a man with 20-year-old children. Paul accepted these arguments but warned that they could not afford to drowse. In other variations of this conversation, including one from Pahlen, Paul became excited and demanded action, arrests, fetters, and gibbets. At this Pahlen pulled a very long face and then told the tsar how shocked he was going to be when he learnt who his enemies were. He showed Paul the names, with the empress and the elder grand dukes at the head of the list. Arrest warrants were written out on the spot, though their implementation was to be delayed.[59]

What Pahlen had acquired, assuming that the basic story is true, were documents to show Alexander that would either level his last defences or at the least shore up his determination. It was also obvious that Paul had learnt something independently. It was now imperative to move quickly. Earlier, Paul had attempted to write to

---

[59] 'Iz zapisok Lanzherona', *Tsareubiistvo* (1907), 139–40. Even in this version Pahlen reported to Alexander that there was no time to lose. The Heyking version, which was related within weeks of the event (though published much later) was earlier than the Langeron version. See above, n. 48 for references and a summary of the Heyking and Velianinov/Zernov accounts.

Arakcheev and General Lindener without informing Pahlen, asking them to return to Petersburg at once. Pahlen intercepted the letters and took them to Paul. No letter was to go out without Pahlen seeing it; he chose to ask whether these were forgeries. Pahlen, when assured that they were not, arranged to have the letters sent in the normal way; he also gave orders that, should Arakcheev reach the city barriers, he was to be held there until Pahlen could see him. He was stopped the evening the *coup* took place.[60]

On 10 March (OS), presumably because of what he had learnt recently from Pahlen, Paul was in an extremely bad mood all day. Following the afternoon concert, he shut himself away for longer than usual, and then reappeared to confront Mariia and his older sons. With no word spoken, he went through what had become a recognized ritual of rage, crossing his arms, breathing heavily through his nose, and glaring silently at his wife, at Alexander, and at Constantine in turn. The evening meal was a trial. The atmosphere was heavy with hostility and fear, and at the end of it Paul left the table and the room without a word. Mariia was weeping quietly as the family silently withdrew.[61]

One particularly pointed anecdote from this time underlines Paul's suspicions of Alexander and suggests what the grand duke's future might have been. It has Paul walking into Alexander's room and discovering Voltaire's *Brutus* lying on the table open to the last page with the concluding lines, 'Rome is free: it is enough . . . let us thank the gods!' Paul saw this as a provocation and sent Kutaisov to Alexander with a history of the reign of Peter the Great. The section on tsarevich Alexis's treason and punishment was marked, and Kutaisov, in Paul's name, ordered the grand duke to read it. (In a somewhat different version, Paul himself brought Alexander a copy of the *ukaz* condemning Alexis for his crime and enquired if he knew about it.) Alexis's interrogation under torture and his death were something for Alexander to ponder on.[62] By this time, whatever Paul may have known, Alexander was hopelessly implicated in the plot, and this probably helps to account for his behaviour on the night of the *coup*. When Sablukov came to Constantine's rooms in connection

---

[60] Heyking, *Aus den Tagen Kaiser Pauls*, 216; Kotzebue, 'Neizdannoe sochinenie', *Tsareubiistvo* (1907), 326; Welianinow-Sernow, 'Die Ermordung Pauls', Schiemann, *Die Ermordung*, 27–8. See Shumigorskii, *Pavel I*, 203–4; Shil'der, *Pavel I*, 473–4; Waliszewski, *Paul Ier*, 597–8.

[61] Prinz Eugen von Württemberg, 'Jungend Erinnerungen' 127–8, who gives the date as 9 Mar. Cf. Shil'der, *Pavel I*, 483; Waliszewski, *Paul Ier*, 604.

[62] Shil'der, *Pavel I*, 479 and n. 3. Princess Lieven is the source for the story that Paul sent Kutaisov with the history. She places the story several days before Paul's death.

The End of the Beginning 349

with regimental business, Alexander was there, but with Paul nearby, 'he crept about like a frightened hare', and when Paul came in, ran away 'like a lamplighter', and 'sneaked again towards us like a crouching pointer' after Paul left. He was terrified, while Sablukov, if the language is any guide, was disgusted.[63]

If Paul's mood was bad on 9 and 10 March (OS) he was reportedly in good spirits throughout 11 March. Struck at dinner by Alexander's dismal looks, he asked if he were well and urged him to pay attention to his health, a particularly ironic remark considering what he presumably was planning for his son. He was later understood to say that a terrible time was at hand when blood would be shed and heads would roll, even some that had been very dear to him. He played with his younger children, visited the guard post outside his rooms where he talked briefly with Sablukov, and then went on to spend the balance of his evening with Anna Gagarina before retiring.[64] He acted like a man who had his world under control, who was either completely unconscious of what was happening, or who thought he had covered himself against all eventualities. The latter is probably closer to the truth.

While Paul was going through his normal evening routine, the final preparations for the *coup* moved ahead. Arrangements had been made for a carriage to be waiting near the palace, presumably to take Paul to his place of detention.[65] The conspirators, without Pahlen who had to be at court, gathered at Colonel Talyzin's apartments at the Winter Palace. Talyzin commanded the Preobrazhenskii guards. Many officers were in full uniform, and the supper, which had begun early in the evening, first turned into a celebratory gala and then a drinking bout. There was high glee at the prospect of a new tsar, serious argument about the possibility of a new political order, excited talk about constitutions, and even a proposal to wipe out the imperial family and start afresh. All this had been thought and talked about earlier. The three Zubov brothers were there, together with Colonel Depreradovich, a Serb, who was commander of the Semenovskii regiment. Dmitri Troshchinskii was one of the few civilians present; he had already drafted the abdication and the announcement of Alexander's accession; he would need to redraft the statement when Paul was killed.[66]

---

[63] Sablukov, 'Reminiscences: Part II', 314.
[64] Shil'der, *Pavel I*, 484–91; Waliszewski, *Paul Ier*, 610–11.
[65] Welianinow-Sernow, 'Die Ermordung Pauls', Schiemann (ed.), *Die Ermordung*, 28; Kotzebue, 'Neizdannoe sochinenie', *Tsareubiistvo* (1907), 357.
[66] The 1st version that Troschinskii wrote, according to Zubov and Bennigsen, stated that 'The emperor, in consequence of illness, has named grand duke

Predominantly military, the crowd was also young: 40 per cent of the conspirators who have been identified were under the age of 30, and several were in their teens. The largest single age group, however, fell between 30 and 40, the generation to which the Zubovs belonged. The conspirators, as James Kenney has demonstrated, represented a cross-section of the top layer of the Russian aristocracy at the end of the eighteenth century with descendants of Rurik and Gedimin rubbing shoulders with service nobles, untitled Muscovites of ancient lineage, and eighteenth-century parvenus. There were six senators in the conspiracy (three of them Zubovs), while officers from the regiments of guards numbered forty-five, virtually two-thirds of the conspirators identified. Significantly, General Bennigsen was the only regular army officer present and, with von der Pahlen, made up the whole of the German contingent. At least a dozen of the conspirators were closely connected with Grand Duke Alexander; another ten were relations or associates of the Zubovs. Many of the men had personal grievances against Paul, either for an act committed against them individually, against a member of their families, or against the regiment in which they served. There was profound anger at Paul's disregard for nobles' rights, especially the prohibitions on physical punishment, and everyone shared the conviction that Paul had gone far beyond what was possible for loyal subjects to accept; he had become an oppressor, a tyrant, and a burden which they were determined to remove.[67]

The basic plan was to force Paul's abdication or to arrest and retire him in Alexander's favour. There was uncertainty about the resistance that could be expected, and what should be done if Paul refused to abdicate or submit peacefully to his arrest. When Pahlen arrived half an hour before midnight, he stood before his comrades in full uniform and toasted the new tsar they were going to have. He then went over the plans, dividing the men into two groups. One under Platon Zubov and Leo Bennigsen was to enter the palace

Alexander as co-regent.' Von Wedell, 'Aufschlüsse', Schiemann (ed.), *Die Ermordung*, 77.

[67] Kenney, 'Politics of Assassination', 127–35. Kenney's argument, that the nobility was responsible, appeared in an anonymous tract on Paul published abroad just after his death. The author, like Kotzebue, sympathized with Paul's policy approach, and claimed that the tsar's intent was to force Russia's irresponsible grandees to accept his authority, the rule of law in fact, and stop exploiting their positions at the people's expense. The nobility struck back. See *Paul der Erste, Kayser von Russland, von einem unbefangenen Beobachter* (Leipzig, 1801), 80 pp. The author also blamed Paul himself for making his enemies' success possible. See also von Wedell, 'Aufschlüsse', Schieman (ed.), *Die Ermordung*, 72–6; Heyking, *Aus den Tagen Kaiser Pauls*, 229–31, for Zubov and Bennigsen on their motives.

through a postern gate. The other, under his own command, was to secure the front of the palace, cutting off Paul's alternative escape route. Units of the Preobrazhenskii and the Semenovskii were to hold the circumference of the palace; seizing Paul, however, was entrusted to Bennigsen and Zubov with perhaps a dozen officers in support. Pahlen made it perfectly clear that removing Paul was the first priority: if it could be done peacefully and with his agreement, so much the better; if he resisted, he would have to be taken by force. It is Kotzebue who has Pahlen responding to a question about what should be done should Paul resist with the aphorism, 'As everybody knows, to eat an omelette requires first breaking the eggs . . .'. He stopped well short of ordering Paul's death, though he also emphasized that, once the *coup* was under way, there was no turning back. Pahlen himself remained sober as did Leo Bennigsen. Platon Zubov's condition is not certain. Most of the rest were at the dangerously disorderly stage of being drunk, though the cold air and the brisk march from the Winter Palace to the Michael Palace must have had a sobering effect.[68]

The conspirators controlled the approaches to the palace, though co-ordination between the attacking groups broke down. Bennigsen and Zubov, with Argamakov leading the way, crossed the moat and entered the palace before Pahlen and his group were in place. Indeed, whatever delayed them, Pahlen's company was at least fifteen minutes behind that of Bennigsen and Zubov, not reaching the tsar's apartments until well after Paul was dead.[69] Paul must not have known that he was under attack until one of his servants in the outer chamber shouted a warning. The uproar in the antechamber meant that one escape route was closed. The enemy, whoever it was, was already at hand. Mariia's adjoining apartment offered a second way out. That door, however, had been locked on Paul's own orders. Finally, there was a secret trapdoor under his work table, but there was no time to open it. Paul fled his cot to hide behind a Spanish screen as Bennigsen and Platon Zubov broke in. Zubov, on seeing the empty bed, cried out that the bird had flown; Bennigsen, placing his hand in the covers, commented that it could not have gone far: 'the nest is still warm'. The room was enormous and filled with dark

[68] Kotzebue, 'Neizdannoe sochinenie', *Tsareubiistvo* (1907), 333; Velianinov-Zernov reports the drunken exaltation of the conspirators before the attack, but limits Pahlen's comments to logistical matters following a champagne toast to the new tsar, Alexander. 'Die Ermordung', Schiemann (ed.), *Die Ermordung*, 28–9.

[69] Bennigsen, 'Death of Paul I', 227. Why Pahlen was so late is matter for speculation. It may just have been a mix-up; it is also possible that he held off appearing so that, if the *coup* failed, he could amend his fortunes by arresting the conspirators and emerging as the tsar's defender.

shadows which the conspirators' candle scarcely affected. But when the moon broke from behind a cloud and poured its silvery light through a large window, Paul's bare feet and legs beneath the screen came into view.[70]

Only Platon Zubov and Bennigsen were actually in the room when Paul was discovered, though there were some men in the antechamber. Bennigsen formally pronounced Paul under arrest on the authority of Emperor Alexander. He also claimed to have told Paul that his life would be spared, but that he must not resist. He then began to check the other doors in the room while he repeated the declaration that Paul was under arrest on Alexander's orders. The tsar had difficulty taking in what was being said. He repeated the words, queried what they meant, and then, as he gained control over himself, demanded to know what he had done to deserve what was happening to him. By this time, other officers were pushing in and one answered Paul's question with 'You have tortured us for four years!' while others took up the charge. At this point, Platon Zubov precipitously left the room, possibly simply to inform Alexander on the floor beneath about what had happened.[71]

Bennigsen remained with two or three others, standing over Paul who neither surrendered nor defended himself. This brief lull was shattered when a new group of men, seven or eight in number, who had become separated from the leaders, burst into the bedchamber and, apparently under the impression that Paul was resisting, overthrew the screen, knocked over the light, and hurled themselves on the tsar. Paul was dragged down, struggled back up, and then was driven to the floor again. In the struggle his head slammed against the bronze capital of his marble-topped work table with such force as to crush his cheek and damage his eye. In the mêlée, Bennigsen rushed out to find a lamp, shouting the while at Paul not to resist, but by the time he had found a light and returned, the furious officers had choked the life out of the tsar with a guardsman's sash and were savaging the body. Paul had fought back desperately, at one point thrusting his fingers between the sash and his neck, and was heard to

---

[70] None of the people who actually killed Paul have left a record. Of the conspiracy's leaders, Pahlen had not yet arrived; Platon Zubov left early, and Bennigsen, as indicated, went out of the room after Zubov left and before the actual murder. See ibid. 226–7. The account Zubov and Bennigsen gave von Wedell in 1812, though explaining more fully Zubov's sudden departure, added nothing to clarifying the murder scene. See von Wedell, 'Aufschlüsse', Schiemann (ed.), *Die Ermordung*, 78–80.

[71] Bennigsen, 'Death of Paul I', 225–7; von Wedell, 'Aufschlüsse', Schiemann (ed.), *Die Ermordung*, 78–80.

cry out to be spared, to be given a moment to pray.[72] Ia. F. Skariatin and I. M. Tatarinov, captain and lieutenant respectively and both in their twenties, probably strangled Paul; N. I. Bibikov, a colonel in his thirties, won fame of a sort for seizing Paul by the hair and banging his head on the floor; in some versions Nicholas Zubov is credited with knocking Paul down by hitting him in the face with a heavy gold snuff-box. Some claimed that just before he died, Paul mistook an officer in a red uniform for his second son, Constantine, and begged him for mercy. When Bennigsen returned, he found a crumpled, battered corpse. After checking to be sure that there was no life in it, he ordered it laid out on the cot and covered with a cloak.[73]

Paul's life ended as his fantasies and dreams foretold. He died a victim. His death immediately set in train, however, the process of accommodating what had happened. Taking the oath to Alexander was the first order of business, but before that could be done, the guards had to be convinced that Paul was actually dead. Some units refused to go ahead until witnesses from the ranks had viewed the corpse and swore that the tsar was dead. There was no question on this point, for as one soldier who saw Paul shortly after his death put it, the emperor was 'very dead'.[74] As far as the guards were concerned, the fact of Paul's death weighed more heavily than the manner of it, and when Alexander hesitatingly declared, against the evidence seen by those who viewed the corpse, that Paul had died of apoplexy, no voice was raised.

The men who killed Paul celebrated what they had done, and briefly they were lionized. But only briefly. Valerian Zubov early

---

[72] Ibid.

[73] The violence done to the corpse is not recorded in the eyewitness accounts, though there is evidence aplenty from those who saw the corpse afterwards. There are hints as well that Paul was still living, though barely, when the murderers finished with him, and that the doctor who discovered a spark of life swiftly extinguished it. See PRO, FO/65/48, Lord St. Helens to Hawkesbury, 19/31 May 1801; 'It is added that when a Surgeon who lived in the Palace examined the body, and declared that he was not absolutely without some chance of recovery, some further and more violent means were immediately used to render it impossible.' D'Allonville, *Mémoires*, viii. 87: 'An English surgeon, who had prevented the empress from flying to the aid of her husband, was called, and he gave the last blow to the emperor by cutting his arteries.' Countess Golovina described the corpse lying in state as looking like a painted doll, so extensive was the repair necessary to conceal the wounds to the head, face, and neck. *Souvenirs*, 164. Curt von Stedingk confirmed the description. Riksarkivet, Diplomatica Moscovitica, vol. 465, Stedingk to the king, 14/26 Mar. 1801.

[74] Sablukov, 'Reminiscences: Part II', 317–18. Sablukov himself arranged for the men to see Paul's corpse when they appeared reluctant to take the oath to Alexander without positive evidence that Paul was dead.

complained to Adam Czartoryski that Alexander, unlike Catherine, had no sense of gratitude and refused to recognize those friends to whom he owed his throne.[75] And, fundamentally, Zubov was right. Though there was never an investigation of 11/12 March and the official story of Paul's death from apoplexy went unaltered, both Pahlen and Panin spent the balance of their adult lives in exile, while Platon Zubov, though serving briefly on Alexander's governing council, never penetrated the inner circles of power again and spent a good part of his time abroad. Bennigsen enjoyed a distinguished military career in the wars against Napoleon, but most of those involved in the conspiracy were simply lost to view. Certainly nothing like the Orlovs' influence or N. I. Panin's commanding role after 1762 emerged in the wake of 1801. Alexander turned to other friends and other advisers. Similarly, however, there was nothing comparable to Nicholas's systematic and unforgiving suppression of the Decembrists whose leadership was hanged while those found guilty of conspiracy were sent into what he intended to be a permanent exile. Many of the men who plotted against Paul were able to put the event behind them, and only a few were punished. The truth was that Alexander, for all the tears he shed, was a conspirator too, but a reluctant one. Catherine rode into Petersburg in triumph; she had plotted and won, and her friends profited from her victory. But Alexander had to be pushed to act at all, and when he realized what had happened, he was devastated. Nearly his first words to the returned Czartoryski were, 'Oh, if only you had been here, I never would have done it!'[76] His revulsion at his father's murder (he knew precisely the grisly scene played out before and after Paul's death) and his own guilt for the part he played prevented him from distinguishing the men who lifted him to the throne, while his complicity made any investigation or formal punishment of the conspirators impossible. He lived with this moral burden, and suffered from it, for the rest of his life.

Beginning on 12 March (OS), Russians, especially in the capitals, had a new freedom to celebrate. Paul's cramping rules on dress and behaviour were forgotten. The police, a dominant presence throughout his reign, slid into relative obscurity, and the process of eliminating four years of repression began. The motto of this new order was *imperium et libertate*, and Alexander called together his secret committee to discuss reforms. Yet while the new tsar anxiously awaited the return of his friends from abroad, he had also re-

---

[75] Czartoryski, *Mémoires*, i. 227–9.   [76] Ibid. 223.

established relations with Arakcheev, whom he distinguished and gave a leading role, while on the morning following Paul's death the *Wachtparade* commenced as though the master were still living.

Though many Russians, especially in the court and army, had every reason to forget Paul, in fact what Paul did over the four years and three months he ruled was fundamental to what Russia became in the first half of the nineteenth century. His reforms established a strongly centralized governing system focused on the tsar, introduced military principles into the nascent bureaucracy, reshaped the army and the military administration, regularized the succession, institutionalized the imperial family, and delivered a death blow to Catherine's innovations in local government. These contributions lasted. Indeed, the concentration and rationalization of power in the central government expanded under Alexander, most notably in the reorganization of the colleges into ministries, and continued in Nicholas's reign. The enormous proliferation of offices and officials which occurred in the first half of the nineteenth century contradicted Paul's commitment to political parsimony, but the autocracy's smothering paternalism, a reinvigorated police and censorship, active suppression of controversial opinion, and, especially in the capital, the persistent intrusion into people's private lives, were all entirely consistent with the style of government Paul practised.

In an enlightened age, Paul's radical efforts to police society shifted the debate over the degree of internal control that was necessary and desirable sharply to the right. There was, moreover, substantial support for his view of what constituted subversion, and by Nicholas's time a good part of what Paul had done in the name of protecting society fell within the limits of acceptable governmental practice and had become institutionalized. The liberalizing tendencies of Alexander's early years, themselves in part a reaction to the more egregrious of his father's repressive efforts, proved temporary and succumbed to that increasingly powerful conservative thrust which had first found systematic expression in Paul's policies. That such conservatism became institutionalized in an era when other European states were developing both radically expanded economic capacity and the more open if disorderly societies in which growth thrived, was the starting-point for Russia's comparative retrogression already apparent at mid-century.

In effect, Paul legislated the essential shape which the autocracy's governing institutions took for its last 116 years. And it was also he who shifted the way the state's power was to be employed, who defined, in fact, the preservationist orientation which characterized the next fifty years. This was a brand of conservatism which went beyond confronting Jacobins or godless democrats. Rather, it was the fundamental idea that structural changes in society were undesirable, that stability was the primary social value, and that the state's powers should be used essentially to support and improve what was established and sound. Though Paul invoked Peter the Great and identified with him as a legal activist, he had a very different conception of the purposes for which state power should be used. And this involved different perceptions of Russia as a historical society. Where Peter saw a backward polity in desperate need of mobilization and change in the direction of advanced European societies, Paul saw what he considered to be a viable society victimized by its ruling class. Peter used the powers at his command to reorder, to reorganize, and to force the acceptance of new ways. Paul saw no such need. Rather he set out to reform abuses and to make the existing order workable. Peter and, more subtly, Catherine were innovators determined to change Russia, to make her different than she was, and better. Paul, confronted by an era of profoundly unsettling changes, used his powers to preserve, ultimately to perfect, what already existed. Under his successor, this conservatizing approach, buttressed by social philosophies which extolled the virtues of natural and unforced growth, burgeoned and flourished. It was Nicholas who achieved the most complete realization of the way Paul thought; it was also in Nicholas's reign that the realization dawned that Russia was in a parlous state internally, that she was no longer competitive with the leading European powers, that wide-ranging political reforms (which bore more than a passing resemblance to what Catherine had attempted seventy-five years earlier) were essential, and that serfdom, the autocracy's cornerstone for two and a half centuries, would have to go. Russia, as she had been constituted, as Paul conceived of her and tried to keep her, was no longer capable of holding her place in the modern world.

In this way, the influence of the man so brutally murdered on 11/12 March remained, though Paul himself was carefully forgotten. Whatever else Paul may have been, he was in tune with fundamental imperatives shaping Russian history. Tsarist absolutism, as he interpreted it, was far closer to the country's established traditions than Catherine's sophisticated enlightenment, and it is therefore not surprising that it was his rejuvenated autocracy rather than her creative innovations which survived. But Paul was also different, or rather, his reign marked a new emphasis, for he was the first of a series of Russian rulers to attempt to cope with a radically modernizing world through an essentially conservative ideology.

Though his life ended ignominiously in the half light of his cavernous bedchamber, his reign marked a turning point, the hinge of Russia's modernity, and a striking introduction to the way official Russia was to respond to the challenges of the nineteenth century.

BIBLIOGRAPHY

A. ARCHIVAL MATERIAL

Archives du ministère des affaires étrangères, correspondance politique, vols. 140–1 (1800–2).
Archivio Vaticano, Nunziatora Polonia–Russia, vols. 343-A-344 (1793–1802).
Dimsdale Papers, Baron Thomas Dimsdale's Russian Visits, 1768 and 1781, Private Collection, Royston, Hertfordshire.
Haus,- Hof,- und Staatsarchiv (Vienna), Russland Relationen, Berichte II, Cartons 70–96 (1790–1802).
Public Record Office, State Papers, Russia, Vols. 58–104; Foreign Office, General Correspondence, Russia, vols. 1–48 (1790–1802); General Correspondence, Austria, vols. 3–4 (1781–1782).
Riksarkivet (Stockholm), Diplomatica Moscovitica, vols. 456–65 (1796–1801).

B. PUBLISHED SOURCE COLLECTIONS

Arkhiv gosudarstvennago soveta: Sovet v tsarstvovanie Imperatora Pavla (St Petersburg, 1888).
Arkhiv kniazia F. A. Kurakina, ed. M. I. Semevskii and V. N. Smolianinov, 10 vols. (Saratov, 1890–1902).
Arkhiv kniazia Viazemskago, ed. Count S. D. Sheremetev, 5 vols. (St Petersburg, 1899–1909).
Arkhiv kniazia Vorontsova, ed. Petr Bartenev, 40 vols. (Moscow, 1870–95).
Chteniia v obschchestve istorii i drevnostei rossiiskikh pri Moskovskom Universitete (Moscow, 1845–1916).
Drevenia i novaia Rossiia (St Petersburg, 1875–1881).
The Dropmore Papers: The Manuscripts of J. B. Fortescue Preserved at Dropmore, ed. Walter Fitzpatrick, 7 vols. (London, 1892–1910).
Istoricheskii vestnik (St Petersburg, 1880–1917).
Kamer-fuerskii tseremonial'nyi zhurnal (1796–1801).
M. I. Kutuzov: Sbornik dokumentov, ed. L. G. Beskrovnyi, 5 vols. (Moscow, 1950–6).
Martens, F. F., *Recueil des traités et conventions conclus par la Russie avec les puissances étrangères*, 15 vols. (St Petersburg, 1874–1909).
Materialy dlia zhizneopisaniia grafa Nikity Petrovicha Panina (1770–1837), ed. Aleksandr Brikner, 7 vols. (St Petersburg, 1888–92).

Bibliography

Nonciatures de Russie d'après les documents authentiques, Nonciature de Litta, 1797–1799, Interim de Benvenuti 1799–1803, ed. M. J. Rouët de Journel, SJ, *Studi e testi*, 167 and 194 (Vatican City, 1943 and 1957).
Osmnadtsatyi vek: Istoricheskii sbornik, ed. Petr Bartenev, 4 bks. in 2 vols. (Moscow, 1868–9).
Polnoe sobranie zakanov rossiiskoi imperii, 1st ser., xxiv–xxvi (St Petersburg, 1830).
Quellen zur Geschichte der Kriege von 1799 und 1800, ed. Hermann Hüffer (Leipzig, 1900–1).
Raeff, Marc (ed.), *Plans for Political Reform in Imperial Russia, 1730–1905* (Englewood Cliffs, NJ, 1966).
—— *Russian Intellectual History: An Anthology* (New York, 1966).
Rastopchine [Rostopchin], Comte Andrei, *Matériaux en grand partie inédite pour la biographie future du comte Theodore Rastopchine rassemblés par son fils* (Brussels, 1864).
Russkii arkhiv (Moscow, 1863–1917).
Russkaia starina (St Petersburg, 1870–1918).
Sbornik imperatorskago russkago istoricheskago obschchestva (St Petersburg, 1867–1917).
Schiemann, Theodore (ed.), *Die Ermordung Pauls und die Thronbesteigung Nikolaus I, neue Materialen* (Berlin, 1902).
—— *Zur Geschichte der Regierung Paul I und Nikolaus I*, 2nd edn. (Berlin, 1906).
Scott, James Brown (ed.), *The Armed Neutralities of 1780 and 1800: A Collection of Official Documents* (New York, 1918).
Senatskii arkhiv, i (St Petersburg, 1879).
Suvarovskii sbornik, ed. A. V. Sukhomlin (Moscow, 1951).
A. V. Suvorov: Sbornik dokumentov, ed. G. P. Meshcheriakov (Moscow, 1949–53).
Generalissimus Suvorov: Sbornik dokumentov i materialov, ed. N. M. Korobkov (Orgiz, 1947).
Tsareubiistvo 11 Marta 1801 goda: Zapiski uchastnikov i sovremennikov (St Petersburg, 1907, 1908).
Turgenev, Alexandre Ivanovich (ed.), *La Cour de Russie il y a cents ans, 1725–1783: Extraits des dépêches des ambassadeurs anglais et français*, 3rd edn. (Leipzig, 1860).
Admiral Ushakov: Sbornik dokumentov, ed. R. N. Mordvinov (Moscow, 1951–6).
Vivenot, Alfred von (ed.), *Vertrauliche Briefe des Freiherrn von Thugut* (Vienna, 1872).
Vremia Pavla i ego smert: Zapiski sovremennikov sobytiia 11-go Marta 1801 goda (Moscow, 1908).

C. CONTEMPORARY CORRESPONDENCE, MEMOIRES, HISTORIES, AND BELLES LETTRES

Actes du chapître du grand prieuré de Russie (St Petersburg, 1798).
Alexander Pavlovich, grand duke and tsar, 'Pisma imperatora Aleksandra I i drugikh osob tsarstvyaiushchago doma k F. Ts. Lagarpu', *stornik imperatorskago russkago istoricheskago obshchestua* 5 (1870), 1–121.
Allonville, A. I., le comte de, *Mémoires tirés des papiers d'un homme d'état*, 8 vols. (Paris, 1831–4).
Anon., *Anekdoten aus dem Privatleben der Kaiserin Catharina, Pauls der Ersten, und seiner Familie* (Hamburg, 1797).
—— *Ausführliche Beschreibung der Reise Seiner Kaiserlichen Hoheit des Grossfürsten von Russland Paul Petrowitz von St. Petersburg an den Königl. Preuss. Hof nach Berlin, nebst den dabey vorgefallenen Feyerlichkeiten und Freudensbezeigungen, wie auch der Reise Ihra* [sic] *Kaiserl. Hoheit der Prinzessin Sophia Dorothea Augusta Louisa von Würtemberg-Stuttgard, verlobten Braut des Grosfürsten von Berlin nach St. Petersburg* (Berlin, 1776).
—— *Konchina imperatritsy Ekateriny Vtoryia: Istoricheskoe i statisicheskoe: Kratkoe nachertanie o Nei, i o Rossii v Eia tsarstvovanie* (Moscow, 1801).
—— *Konchina rossiiskago imperatora Pavla I, kharaktera novago imperatora Aleksandra Pervago* (Moscow, 1802).
—— *Paul der Erste, Kayser von Russland, von einem unbefangenen Beobachter* (Leipzig, 1801).
—— *Zhizn, svoistva, voennayia i politicheskiia delniia rossiiskago imperatora Pavla I, general-feldmarshala kniazia Potemkina-Tavricheskago, i kantslera kniazia Bezborodki* (St Petersburg, 1805).
Asseburg, Freiherr Achatz Ferdinand von der, *Denkwürdigkeiten* (Berlin, 1842).
Bachaumont, Louis Petit de, 'Zapiski: Tsesarevich Pavel Petrovich vo Frantsii v 1782 g.', *Russkaia starina*, 36 (1882), 321–34.
Bennigsen, Count Levin A. G., *Mémoires du général Bennigsen*, 3 vols. (Paris, 1907–8).
Bennigsen, Rudolph von, 'Des Generals Grafen von Bennigsens Brief an den General von Fock über die Ermordung Kaiser Paul I.', *Historische Vierteljahrschrift*, 4 (1901), 57–69.
Bolotov, Andrei Timofeevich, *Pamiatnik protekshikh vremen ili kratkie istoricheskie zapiski o byvshikh proizshestviiakh i nosivshikhsia v narode sluchaiakh* (Moscow, 1875).
—— 'Zapiski: Prodolzhenie opisaniia zhizni Andrei Bolotova, opisannoe samym im dlia svoikh potomkov', *Russkaia starina* (June 1899), 535–76.
Boshniak, A. K., 'Razskazy starago pazha o vremeni Pavla I', *Russkaia starina*, 33 (1882), 212–16.

Bray, François-Gabriel, chevalier de, 'La Russie sous Paul I', *Revue d'histoire diplomatique*, 23 and 24 (1909 and 1911), 580–607 and 559–90.
Brenna, Vincenzio, *Designi dell'Imperial Palazzo S. Michele*, 2 folio vols. (n.pl. [British Library Collection] 1800?).
Cabres, Sabathier de, *Catherine II: Sa cour et la Russie en 1772* (Berlin, 1862).
Catherine II, grand duchess and empress, 'Bumagi imperatritsy Ekateriny II, 1744–1788', *Sbornik imperatorskago russkago istoricheskago obshchestva*, 27 (1880), 573 pp.
—— 'Bumagi imperatritsy Ekateriny II khraniashchiasia v gosudarstvennom arkhive', *Sbornik imperatorskago russkago istoricheskago obshchestva*, 13 (1874), 448 pp.
—— *Correspondence of Catherine the Great with Sir Charles Hanbury Williams*, ed. the earl of Ilchester (London, 1928).
—— 'Imperatritsa Ekaterina II: Istoricheskie materialy khraniashchiesia v biblioteke dvortsa goroda Pavlovska', ed. Grand Duke Konstantin Nikolaevich, *Russkaia starina*, 8 (1873), 649–90; 690; 9 (1874), 37–56, 277–300, 473–512.
—— *Mémoires de l'impératrice Catherine II écrits par elle-même*, ed. Alexander Herzen, 2nd edn. (London, 1859).
—— 'Otryvok sobstvennoruchnago chernago proekta manifesta Ekaterina II o prestonasledii', *Russkaia starina*, 12 (1875), 384–5.
—— 'Perepiska Ekateriny II s baronom Fridrikhom Melkiorom Grimmom', *Sbornik imperatorskago russkago istoricheskago obshchestva*, 23 (1878), 705 pp.
—— 'Perepiska s v.k. Pavlom Petrovichem i v.k. Mariei Feodorovnoiu, 1787–1792', *Russkaia starina*, 7/12 (1873), 853–84.
—— *Sochineniia*, ed. A. N. Pypin, 12 vols. (St Petersburg, 1901).
Chichigov, Admiral P. V., *Imperator Pavel I v zapiskakh admirala P. V. Chichigova*, ed. K. Voenskii (St Petersburg, 1909).
—— *Mémoires de l'amiral Tchitchagoff* (Paris, 1861).
Choiseul-Gouffier, Mme la comtesse de, *Historical Memories of the Emperor Alexander I and the Court of Russia*, trans. Mary B. Patterson (London, 1904).
—— *Réminiscences sur l'empereur Alexandre Ier et sur l'empereur Napoleon Ier* (Paris, 1862).
Chul'kov, M., *Istoricheskoe opisanie rossiiskoi kommertsii pri vsekh portakh i granitsakh ot drevnikh vremen do nyne nastoiatsago*, 7 vols., 21 pts. (St Petersburg, 1781–7).
Corberon, Marie Daniel Bourée, baron de, *Un diplomat français à la cour de Catherine II, 1775–1780: Journal intime*, 2 vols. (Paris, 1901).
Czartoryski, Prince Adam, *Mémoires du prince Adam Czartoryski et correspondance avec l'empereur Alexandre Ier*, 2 vols. (Paris, 1887).
Dal, Vladimir Ivanovich, 'Rasskazy o vremenakh Pavla I', *Russkaia starina* (Sept. 1870), 294–6.
Dashkova, Princess E. R., *Mémoires de la princesse Dashkaw: D'après le manuscrit révue et corrigé par l'auteur*, ed. Petr Bartenev, *Arkhiv kniazia Vorontsova*, xxi. 7–365.

Denisov, Ataman Adrian Karpovich, 'Zapiski: Istoriia kazaka donskago, atamana Adriana Karpovicha Denisova, 1763–1841', *Russkaia starina* (May–Aug. 1874), 1–45; (Sept.–Dec. 1874), 379–409, 601–41; (Jan.–Apr. 1875), 27–49, 237–71, 467–9.

Derzhavin, Gavril Romanovich, 'Zapiski', *Sobranie sochinenii Derzhavina*, vi (St Petersburg, 1869).

Dimsdale, Elizabeth, *An English Lady at the Court of Catherine the Great*, ed. A. G. Cross (Cambridge, 1989).

Dimsdale, Baron Thomas, *Thoughts on General and Partial Inoculation, Containing a Translation of the Two Treatises Written when the Author was at Petersburg, and Published there, by Command of Her Imperial Majesty, in the Russian Language* (London, 1776).

—— *Tracts on Inoculation Written and Published at St. Petersburg in the Year 1768 by Command of Her Imperial Majesty, The Empress of All the Russias, with Additional Observations on Epidemic Small-Pox, on the Nature of that Disease, and on the different Success of the various Modes of Inoculation* (London, 1781).

—— 'Zapiski barona Dimsdelia o prebyvaniu ego v Rossii', *Sbornik imperatorskago russkago istoricheskago obshchestva*, 2 (1868), 295–322.

'Diplomaticheskaia perepiska angliiskikh poslov i poslannikov pri russkom dvore, 1770–1776', *Sbornik imperatorskago russkago istoricheskago obshchestva*, 19 (1876), 523 pp.

'Diplomaticheskaia perepiska avstriiskikh poslov i poslannikova pri russkom dvore, 1762–1771', *Sbornik imperatorskago russkago istoricheskago obshchestva*, 18 (1876), 478 pp.; 46 (1885), 728 pp.; 109 (1901), 622 pp.

'Diplomaticheskaia perepiska frantsyzskikh predstavitelei pri dvore imperatritsy Ekateriny II, 1762–1772', *Sbornik imperatorskago russkago istoricheskago obshchestva*, 140 (1912), 686 pp.; 141 (1913), 588 pp.; 143 (1913), 622 pp.

'Diplomaticheskaia perepiska prusskikh poslannikov pri russkom dvore, 1767–1774', *Sbornik imperatorskago russkago istoricheskago obshchestva*, 37 (1883), 664 pp.; 72 (1891), 566 pp.

'Diplomaticheskiia snosheniia Rossii s Frantsiei v epokhu Napoleona I.', ed. Aleksandr Tachevskii, *Sbornik imperatorskago russkago istoricheskago obschchestva*, 70 (1890), 763 pp.

Dmitriev, Ivan Ivanovich, *Vzgliad na moiu zhizn: Zapiski deiatel'nago tainago sovetnika Ivana Ivanovicha Dmitrieva*, ed. M. A. Dmitriev (Moscow, 1886).

Dolgorukii, Prince Ivan Mikhailovich, 'Kapishche moego serdtsa ili slova vsekh tekh lits s koimi ia byl v raznykh otnosheniiakh v techenii moei zhizni', *Russkii arkhiv* (Jan.–May 1890), suppl.

Engelgardt, Egor Antonovich, *Zapiski* (Moscow, 1867).

Ermolov, Aleksei Petrovich, 'Rasskazy', *Chteniia v imperatorskom obshchestve istorii i drevnostei rossiiskikh* (Oct.–Dec. 1863), 214–32.

Esterhazy, Count Valentin, *Mémoires du comte Valentin Esterhazy*, ed. Ernest Daudet (Paris, 1905).

—— *Lettres du comte Valentin Esterhazy à sa femme, 1784–1792*, ed. Ernest Daudet (Paris, 1907).
Filosof, General Mikhail, 'Ob'ialenie generala Mikhaily Filosofa o volneniiakh krestian v 1797 g.', ed. G. K. Repinskii, *Russkaia starina*, 36 (1882), 351–4.
Fonvizin, Denis, *Sobranie sochinenii Fonvizina*, 2 vols. (Moscow, 1959).
Fonvizin, M. A., 'Zapiski', *Russkaia starina* (Mar.–Apr. 1884), 31–66; (May–June 1884), 281–302.
Foussadier, G. 'Extrait des maladies survenus à Son Altesse Imperiale [Paul Petrovich] depuis Sa Naissance jusqu'à ce jour' (23 Septembre (OS) 1768), Dimsdale Papers, A-38.
Garnovskii, Mikhail Antonovich, 'Zapiski', *Russkaia starina* (Jan.–Apr. 1876), 9–38, 237–65, 471–99, 687–720; (May–Aug. 1876), 1–32, 207–38, 399–440.
Georgel, l'abbé J. F., *Mémoires pour servir à l'histoire des événemens de la fin du dix-huitième siècle depuis 1760 jusqu'en 1806–1810*, vi (Paris, 1818).
Golitsyn, Prince A. N., 'Razskazy kniazia A. N. Golitsyna: Iz zapisok Iu. N. Barteneva', *Russkii arkhiv*, 24 (1886), pt. 1/369–81; pt. 2/52–108; 305–83; pt. 3/129–66.
—— 'Rasskazy pro Ekaterinu, Pavla, Aleksandra, Nikolaia i ikh sovremennikov', *Russkii arkhiv* (1866), 305–33.
—— 'Rasskazy', *Russkii arkhiv* (1869), 621–44.
Golovine, Countess Varvara Nikolaevna, *Souvenirs de la comtesse Golovine, 1766–1821*, ed. K. Waliszewski (Paris, 1910).
Golovkine, Count Fedor, *La Cour et le règne de Paul Ier* (Paris, 1905).
—— *Zapiski*, trans. and ed. E. S. Shumigorskii (St Petersburg, 1900).
Grech, Nikolai Ivanovich, *Zapiski moei zhizni* (St Petersburg, 1886).
Grimm, Baron Frederick Melchior, 'Mémoire historique sur l'origine et les suites de mon attachement pour l'impératrice Catherine II, jusqu'au décès de S.M.I.', *Sbornik imperatorskago russkago istoricheskago obshchestva*, 2 (1868), 324–93.
—— 'Pisma barona Melchiora Grimma k imperatritse Ekaterine II (Lettres de Grimm à l'Impératrice Catherine II), 1764–1791', *Sbornik imperatorskago russkago istoricheskago obshchestva*, 33 (1881), 534 pp.
—— 'Pisma Grimma k imperatritse Ekaterine II (Lettres de Grimm à l'impératrice Catherine II)', 2nd expanded edn., *Sbornik imperatorskago russkago istoricheskago obshchestva*, 44 (1885), 834 pp.
Gudovich, A. V., 'Pismo A. V. Gudovicha k grafu S. R. Vorontsovu ob otnosheniiakh k Pavlu Petrovichu', *Arkhiv kniazia Vorontsova*, 24, pp. 254–5.
Harris, James, 1st earl of Malmesbury, *Diaries and Correspondence*, 4 vols. (London, 1844).
Heyking, Baron Karl Heinrich von, 'Imperator Pavel i ego vremia', *Russkaia starina*, 56 (1887), 365–94, 783–815.
—— *Aus den Tagen Kaiser Pauls: Auszeichnungen eines kurländischen Edelmanns*, ed. Friedrich von Bienemann, 1838 (Leipzig, 1886).
Il'inskii, Nikolai Stepanovich, 'Iz zapisok', *Russkii arkhiv* (1879), 377–434.

Iskander [Alexander Herzen], *Istoricheskii sbornik vol'noi russkoi tipografii v Londone*, ii (London, 1861).
Jakob, L. H. von, 'M. M. Speranskii as Viewed in L. H. von Jakob's Unpublished Autobiography', tr. and ed. David and Karin Griffiths, *Canadian-American Slavic Studies*, 9/4 (Winter 1975), 481–541.
Joseph II, Leopold II, und Kaunitz: Ihr Briefweschel, ed. Adolph Beer, 2 vols. (Vienna, 1873).
Joseph II und Katharina von Russland: Ihr Briefwechsel, ed. Alfred Ritter von Arneth (Vienna, 1869).
Joseph II und Leopold von Toscana: Ihr Briefwechsel, ed. Alfred Ritter von Arneth (Vienna, 1872).
Maria Theresia und Joseph II, ed. Alfred Ritter von Arneth, 3 vols. (Vienna, 1867–8).
Karamzin, Nikolai Mikhailovich, *Memoir on Ancient and Modern Russia*, ed. and trans. Richard E. Pipes (Cambridge, Mass., 1959).
Khrapovitskii, A. V., *Dnevnik, 1782–1793*, ed. Nikolai Barsukov (St Petersburg, 1874).
Khvostov, Vasilii Semenovich, 'Zapiski', *Russkii arkhiv*, 3 (1870), 559–608.
Kochubei, Prince V. P., 'Pisma kniazia V. P. Kochubeia k grafu S. R. Vorontsovu', *Arkhiv kniazia Vorontsova*, 18, pp. 1–295.
Komarovskii, Evgraf Fedorovich, 'Iz zapisok', *Russkii arkhiv* (1867), 220–48, 521–76, 748–88, 1276–1230.
Kotliubitskii, Nikolai Osipovich, 'Rasskaz', *Russkii arkhiv* (1866), 1301–31.
Kotzebue, August von, *Das merkwürdigste Jahr meines Lebens*, 2 vols. (Berlin, 1801).
—— *The Most Remarkable Year in the Life of Augustus von Kotzebue; Containing an Account of his Exile into Siberia and of the other Extraordinary Events which Happened to him in Russia, Written by Himself*, trans. Benjamin Beresford, 3 vols. (London, 1802).
Kurakin, Prince Alexander Borisovich, *Souvenirs d'un voyage en Hollande et en Angleterre à sa sortie de l'université de Leyde, durant les années 1770, 1771, et 1772* (St Petersburg, 1815).
Labzina, A. E., *Vospominaniia Anny Evdokimovny Labzinoi, 1758–1828* (St Petersburg, 1914; Newton, Mass., 1974).
Lafermière, German, 'Pisma Lafermera k bratiam grafam Vorontsovym', *Arkhiv kniazia Vorontsova*, 29, pp. 177–298.
LaHarpe, Jean-François, *Correspondence littéraire addressée à Son Altesse Impériale Mgr. le Grand Duc [Paul] Aujourd'hui Empereur de Russie, et à M. le comte Schowalow, chambellan de l'Impératrice Catherine II, depuis 1774 jusqu'au 1789*, 4 vols. (Paris, 1801).
Lebrun, Mme Marie-Anne-Elizabeth [Vigée], *Souvenirs*, 3 vols. (Paris, 1835–7, 1869).
Litta, Count Giulio, 'Depeshi grafa Litty, poslannika maltiiskago ordena v Peterburge, pisannyia v kontse 1796 i nachale 1797 goda, ed. A. F. Bychkov, *Sbornik imperatorskago russkago istoricheskago obshchestva* 2 (1868), 164–274.

Lubianovskii, Senator Fedor Petrovich, 'Vospominania', *Russkii arkhiv* (1872), 98–185, 450–533.
Maisonnueve, Joseph de, *Annales historiques de l'ordre souverain de St. Jean de Jérusalem depuis l'année 1725 jusqu'au moment présent* (St Petersburg, 1798).
Maistre, Joseph de, *Mémoires politiques et correspondance diplomatique de Joseph de Maistre avec explications et commentaires par Albert Blanc*, 2nd edn. (Paris, 1859).
Manifeste de la banque d'hypothèque établie pour la noblesse (St Petersburg, 1798).
Mariia Fedorovna, grand duchess and empress, *Correspondance de Sa Majesté l'Impératrice Marie Feodorowna avec Mademoiselle de Nelidoff sa Demoiselle d'Honneur (1797–1801) suivre des Lettres de Mademoiselle de Nelidoff au Prince A[lexandre] B. Kourakin*, ed. Princess Lise Troubetzko (Paris, 1896).
—— 'Sobstvennoruchnyia pisma velikoi kniagini Marii Fedorovny (v posledstvu imperatritsy) k baronu Karlu Ivanovichu Sakenu poslanniku pri datskom dvore (1781–1783), *Sbornik imperatorskago russkago istoricheskago obshchestva*, 20 (1877), 397–404.
Masson, Charles-Francois-Philibert, *Mémoires secrètes sur la Russie et particuliérement sur la fin du règne de Catherine II et la commencement de celui de Paul I*, 2 vols. (Amsterdam, 1800).
—— *Lettre d'un francais à un allemand servant de réponse à M. de Kotzebue et de supplement aux 'Mémoires', suivie d'un précis historique de la déportation et de l'exile de l'auteur* (Paris, 1802).
Mertvaga, Count Dmitrii Borisovich, 'Zapiski', *Russkii arkhiv* (1867), suppl., 355 pp.
Mirovich, V. Ia. [Delo Mirovicha], *Osmnadtsatyi vek*, 1 (1868), 357–87.
Mukhanova, Mariia Sergeevna, 'Iz zapisok', *Russkii arkhiv* (1878), 209–16, 299–329.
Nelidova, Ekaterina Ivanovna, 'Iz bumag E. I. Nelidovy', *Osmnadtsatyi vek*, i (1868), 422–44.
Nicolay, Baron A. L. [Nikolai, Ludwig Heinrich], *Die Beiden Nicolai: Briefwechsel zwischen Ludwig Heinrich Nicolay in St. Petersburg und Friedrich Nicolai in Berlin, 1776–1811*, ed. Heinz Ischreyt (Lüneburg, 1989).
—— 'Pisma barona Andreia Lvovicha Nikolai k grafam Vorontsovym', *Arkhiv kniazia Vorontsova*, xxii. 3–120.
Nonni, K., *Descrizione degli spettacoli e feste datesi in Venezia per occasione della venuta delle LL. AA. II. il Gran Duca e Gran Duchesse di Moscovia, sotto il nome de Conti del Nort, nel Mese di Gennajo 1782*, 2nd edn. corrected and amplified (Venice, 1782).
Oberkirch, Baroness de, *Mémoires de la baronne d'Oberkirch sur la cour de Louis XVI et la société française avant 1789*, ed. Suzanne Burkard (Mercure de France; Paris, 1970).
Panin, Count N. I. 'Vsepoddanneishee pred'iavlenie slabago poniatiia i mneniia o vospitanii ego imperatorskago vysochestva gosudaria velikago

kniazia Pavla Petrovicha: Zapiska grafa N. I. Panina, 1760 g.', ed. T. A. Sosnovskii, *Russkaia starina*, 36 (1882), 313–20.

Panin, Count N. P., 'Pisma grafa N. P. Panina k grafu S. R. Vorontsovu: Tsartsvovanie Pavla Petrovicha', *Arkhiv kniazia Vorontsova*, xi. 1–122, 161–7.

Paul Petrovich, Grand Duke and Tsar, 'Bumagi iz arkhiva dvortsa v g. Pavlovskoe', ed. prince P. A. Viazemskii, *Sbornik imperatorskago russkago istoricheskago obshchestva*, 9 (1872), 194 pp.; 15 (1875), 174 pp.

—— 'Instruktsiia velikago kniazia Pavla Petrovicha velikoi kniagine Marii Feodorovne (1776)', ed. E. S. Shumigorskii, *Russkaia starina*, 93 (1898), 247–61.

—— *Paul I of Russia: Ukaz: 29 November/10 December, 1798* (St Petersburg, 1798; British Library).

—— 'Perepiska v.k. Pavla Petrovicha s gr. Petrom Paninym v 1778 g.', *Russkaia starina*, 33 (1882), 403–18, 739–64.

—— 'Pisma Pavla Petrovicha k Platonu', *Russkii arkhiv*, 2 (1887).

—— 'Pisma velikago kniazia Pavla Petrovicha (v posledstvie Imperatora Pavla I) k baronu Karlu Ivanovichu Sakenu poslannika pri datskom dvore, 1772–1784', *Sbornik imperatorskago russkago istoricheskago obshchestva*, 20 (1877), 405–46.

—— 'Pismo v.k. Pavla Petrovicha k Imperatritse Ekaterine ob E. I. Nelidovoi', *Osmnadtsatyi vek*, i (1868), 445–6.

—— 'Pismo k N. I. Saltykovu', *Russkii arkhiv* 18 (1864), 943.

—— 'Reskripty i vysochaishiia poveleniia imperatora Pavla Petrovicha k grafu N. P. Paninu v bytnost ego poslannikom v Berline, 1797–1799', *Arkhiv kniazia Vorontsova*, 11, pp. 259–85.

—— 'Tsesarevich Pavel Petrovich: Istoricheskie materialy v biblioteke dvortsa goroda Pavlovska', ed. Grand Duke Konstantin Nikolaevich, *Russkaia starina*, 8 (1873), 649–90, 853–84; 9 (1874), 37–56, 277–300, 473–512, 667–84.

—— 'Ukazy, poveleniia i reskripty: 1796–1801', ed. K. A. Viskovatov, *Russkaia starina*, 33 (1882), 443–8.

—— 'Ukazy, rasporiazheniia i rezoliutsii imperatora Pavla, 1799–1800 gg.', *Russkaia starina*, 8 (1873), 622–34.

—— 'Vysochaiskia poveleniia i ukazy S.-Peterburgskim voennym gubernatoram', *Russkaia starina*, 5 (1872), 235–56; 33 (1882), 191–205.

Pestel, P. I., *Russkaia pravda: Nakaz verkhovnomu vremennomu pravleniiu* (St Petersburg, 1906).

Pishchevich, A. S., 'Zhizn Aleksandra Semenovicha Pishchevicha im samym opisanaia', *Chteniia v imperatorskom obshchestve istorii i drevnostei rossiiskikh* (1885), 1, pp. 1–112; 2, pp. 113–273.

Platon (Levshin), archbishop of Tver, *A Sermon Preached by Order of Her Imperial Majesty on the Tomb of Peter the Great in the Cathedral Church of St. Petersburg* (London, 1770).

—— *La Doctrine orthodoxe ou la théologie chrétienne abbregée à l'usage de Son Altesse Impériale, Monseigneur le Grand-Duc Paul Petrowitz,*

Prince Impérial de toutes les Russies, trans. Symeon Mathieu (St Petersburg, 1776).
—— *Pravoslavnoe uchenie ili sokrashchennaia khristianskaia bogosloviia dlia upotrebleniia ego imperatorskago vysochestva presveteleishago vserossiiskago naslednika, blago vernago gosudaria tsesarevicha i velikago kniazia Pavla Petrovicha* (St Petersburg, 1765).
—— *The Present State of the Greek Church in Russia or a Summary of Christian Divinity* (Edinburgh, 1814).
Poletika, Petr Ivanovich, 'Vospominaniia', *Russkii arkhiv* (1885), 305–36.
Poroshin, Semon Andreevich, *Zapiski, sluzhashchiia k istorii Ego Imperatorskago Vysochestva Blagovernago Gosudaria Tsesarevicha i Velikago Kniazia Pavla Petrovicha naslednika prestolu Rossiiskago* (St Petersburg, 1844).
—— *Zapiski*, . . . (St Petersburg, 1881).
—— *Zapiski, sluzhashchiia k istorii ego imperatorskago vysochestva blagovernago gosudaria tsesarevicha i velikago kniazia Pavla Petrovicha*, 2nd enlarged edn., *Russkaia starina*, 30 (1881), pp. i–iv, 2–147; 31 (1881), 149–403; 32 (1881), 406–635.
Radishchev, Alexander, *Journey from Petersburg to Moscow*, ed. and trans. Roderick Thaler (Cambridge, Mass., 1958).
Reckert, K. K., *Wintergemählde*, 2nd improved edn. (Berlin, 1777).
Réglementes de la banque impériale d'hypothèque établie pour la noblesse (St Petersburg, 1798).
Regulations for the Prussian Infantry Translated from the German Original with Augmentations and Alterations made by the King of Prussia since the Publication of the Last Edition. To which is Added the Prussian Tactick; Being a Detail of the Grand Manœuvre, as performed by the Prussian Armies, tr. William Faucitt (London, 1759).
Reimers, Heinrich, 'Peterburg pri Imperatore Pavle Petroviche v 1796–1801 gg.', *Russkaia starina*, 39, pp. 43–74.
Ribop'er, Aleksandr Ivanovich, 'Zapiski', *Russkii arkhiv* (1877), 460–506.
Rogerson, John, 'Pisma pridvornago vracha Rozhersona k grafam Vorontsovym', *Arkhiv kniazia Vorontsova*, 30, pp. 49–184.
Rostopchin, Count Fedor Vasil'evich, *Œuvres inédites du comte Rostoptchine*, ed. Countess Lydie Rostoptchine (Paris, 1894).
—— 'O politicheskikh otnosheniiakh rossii v poslednie mesiatsy Pavlovskago tsarstvovaniia', *Russkii arkhiv*, 16/1 (1878), 103–10.
—— 'Pisma grafa F. V. Rostopchina k grafu S. R. Vorontsovu', *Arkhiv kniazia Vorontsova*, 8, pp. 37–457.
—— *Poslednii den Imperatritsa Ekateriny II i pervyi den tsarstvovaniia Imperatora Pavla I* (Moscow, 1864).
—— *Sochineniia*, ed. A. Smirdina (St Petersburg, 1853, 1869).
Rousseau, Jean Jacques, *Correspondance générale*, ed. T. Dufour, vol. xi (Paris, 1931).
Runich, Dmitrii Pavlovich, 'Sto let tomu nazad: Iz zapisok D. P. Runicha', *Russkaia starina* (Oct. 1896), 281–319.

Sablukov, General N. A., 'Reminiscences of the Court and Times of the Emperor Paul I of Russia up to the Period of His Death', *Fraser's Magazine for Town and Country*, 72 (1865), 222–41, 302–27.

—— *Zapiski N. A. Sablukova o vremenakh Pavla I i o konchine etago gosudaria* (Leipzig, 1902).

—— *Zapiski N. A. Sablukova o vremenakh Imperatora Pavla i konchina etago gosudaria*, ed. K. Voenskii (St Petersburg, 1911).

Samborskii, Andrei, *Rech Eia Imperatorskomu Velichestvu po blagopoluchnom vozvrashchenii iz puteshestvia ikh Imperatorskikh Vysochestvikh*, Dimsdale Collection (St Petersburg, n.d.).

Sanglen, Iakov Ivanovich de, 'Pavel i ego vremia', *Russkaia starina* (Oct.–Dec. 1882), 442–98; (Jan.–Mar. 1883), 1–46, 375–94, 539–78; (Apr.–June 1883), 137–50.

Ségur, Louis Philippe, comte de, *Mémoires ou souvenirs et anecdotes*, 3 vols. (Paris, 1826).

Seider, Fedor Nikolaevich, *Todeskampf am Hochgericht oder Geschichte des unglücklichen Dulders F. Seider, ehemaligen Predigers zu Randen in Estland* [sic], *von ihm selbst erzählt, ein Seitenstück zum 'Merkwürdigsten Jahr meines Lebens' von Aug. von Kotzebue* (Hildesheim, 1803).

Shishkov, Admiral Aleksandr Semenovich, *Zapiski, mneniia i perepiska admirala Shishkova* (Berlin, 1870).

Sievers, Count Jakob Johann, *Ein russischer Staatsmann: Des Grafen Jakob Johann Sievers Denkwürdigkeiten zur Geschichte Russlands*, ed. Karl Ludwig Blum, 4 vols. (Leipzig, 1857).

Stählins, Jakob von, *Aus dem Papieren Jakob von Stählins*, ed. Karl Stählin (Königsberg, 1926).

Stedingk, Count Curt von, *Mémoires posthumes du feldmaréchal comte de Stedingk, redigés sur des lettres, dépêches et autres pièces authentiques laissés à sa famille, par le général comte de Björnstjerna*, 3 vols. (Paris, 1844–7).

Storch, Heinrich Friedrich, *Cours d'économie politique ou exposition des principes qui déterminent la prosperité des nations*, 6 vols. (St Petersburg, 1815).

—— *Historisch-statistische Gemälde des russischen Reiches am Ende des achtzehnten Jahrhunderts* (Riga, 1797–1802).

—— *The Picture of St. Petersburg* [*Gemählde von St Petersburg*] (London, 1801).

Tatishchev, D. P., 'Pisma D. P. Tatishcheva k grafam A. R. i S. R. Vorontsovym', *Arkhiv kniazia Vorontsova*, 18, pp. 307–53.

Tuchkov, S. A., *Zapiski Sergeia Alekseevicha Tuchkova, 1766–1808*, ed. K. A. Voenskii (St Petersburg, 1908).

Turgenev, Aleksandr Mikhailovich, 'Zapiski: 1772–1801', *Russkaia starina* (July–Sept. 1885), 365–90; (Oct.–Dec. 1885), 55–82, 247–82, 473–86.

Ursins et Rosenberg, la comtesse douairière, *Du séjour des comtes du nord à Venise en janvier MDCCLXXXII: Lettre de mme. la comtesse douairière des Ursins et Rosenberg, à m. Richard Wynne, son frère à Londres* (n.pl., 1782).

Vadkovskii, F. F., 'Iz bumag Fedora Fedorovicha Vadkovskago', *Osmnadtsatyi vek*, 1 (1868), 408–21.
Vertot, l'abbé de, *Histoire des chevaliers hospitaliers de S. Jean de Jérusalem, appellés depuis chevaliers de Rhodes et aujourd'hui chevaliers de Malthe*, 14 edns., 15 vols. (Paris, 1726–1853).
Vigel, Filipp Filippovich, *Zapiski*, 7 vols. (Moscow, 1891–3, 1928).
Volkonskii, Prince Petr Mikhailovich, 'Rasskazy zapisannye s ego slov A. V. Viskovatym v ianvare 1845 g.', *Russkaia starina* (May 1876), 176–90.
Vorontsov, Count S. R., 'Pisma grafa S. R. Vorontsova k baronu A. L. Nikolai', *Arkhiv kniazia Vorontsova*, 22, pp. 485–536.
—— 'Pisma grafa Semena Romanovicha Vorontsova k bratu ego grafu Aleksandru Romanovichu, 1796–1804 gody', *Arkhiv kniazia Vorontsova*, 10, pp. 3–90.
—— 'Pisma grafa Semena Romanovicha Vorontsova k grafu F. V. Rostopchinu', *Arkhiv kniazia Vorontsova*, 8, pp. 513–62.
—— 'Pisma grafa S. R. Vorontsova k N. N. Novosil'tseva', *Arkhiv kniazia Vorontsova*, 11, pp. 379–95.
Vosstanie dekabristov: Materialy, 8 vols. (Moscow, 1925).
Württemberg, Prince Eugen von, *Aus dem Leben des kaiserlich russischen Generals der Infanterie Prinz Eugen von Württemberg aus dessen eigenhändigen Aufzeichnungen so wie aus dem schriftlichen Nachlass seiner Adjutanten*, ed. Freiherr von Helldorff, 2 vols. (Berlin, 1861).
—— *Memoiren des Herzogs Eugen von Württemberg*, ed. Freiherr von Helldorff, 2 vols., 3 pts. (Frankfurt, 1862).
Zschokke, Heinrich (ed.), 'Zur Geschichte der Verschworung gegen Paul I. und der Thronbesteigung Alexander I.', *Überlieferungen zur Geschichte unserer Zeit* (Jan.–June 1819), 340–52.

D. SECONDARY SOURCES, INCLUDING REFERENCE WORKS, GENERAL HISTORIES, BIOGRAPHIES, MONOGRAPHS, AND ARTICLES

Adamcyzk, Theresia, *Fürst G. A. Potemkin: Untersuchungen zu seiner Lebensgeschichte* (Einstelten, 1936; Osnabrück, 1966).
Alexander, John T., *Autocratic Politics in a National Crisis: The Imperial Russian Government and Pugachev's Revolt, 1773–1775* (Bloomington, Ind., 1969).
—— *Catherine the Great: Life and Legend* (New York, 1989).
—— *The Bubonic Plague in Early Modern Russia* (Baltimore, 1980).
Aliab'ev, A. A., 'Snosheniia Rossii s Mal'tiiskim Ordenom do 1789 g.', *Sbornik Moskovskago glavnago arkhiva ministerstva inostrannykh del*, 5 (1893), 175–218.
Almedingen, E. M., *So Dark a Stream: A Study of the Emperor Paul I of Russia, 1754–1801* (London, 1959).
Amburger, Erik, *Geschichte der Behördensorganisation Russlands von Peter dem Grossen bis 1917* (Leiden, 1966).

Amburger, E., *Ingermanland: Eine junge Provinz Russlands im Wirkungsbereich der Residenz und Weltstadt St. Petersburg-Leningrad*, 2 pts. (Vienna, 1980).
—— 'Madame Bielke, eine Korrespondentin Katharinas II', *Jahrbücher für Geschichte Osteuropas*, NS 35/3 (1987), 384–9.
Antoshevkii, I. K., *Derzhavnyi orden Sv. Ionna Ierusalimskago imenuemyi Maltiiskim v Rossii* (St Petersburg, 1914).
Atkin, Muriel, 'The Pragmatic Diplomacy of Paul I: Russia's Relations with Asia, 1796–1801', *Slavic Review*, 38/1 (Mar. 1979), 60–74.
—— *Russia and Iran, 1780–1828* (Minneapolis, 1980).
Bailleu, Paul (ed.), *Preussen und Frankreich von 1795 bis 1807* (Leipzig, 1881–7).
Bain, R. Nisbet, *The Daughter of Peter the Great* (Westminster, 1899; New York, 1970).
—— *Peter III Emperor of Russia* (Westminster, 1902; New York, 1971).
Balaeva, S. N., and Pomarnatski, A. V., *Gatchina* (Moscow, 1952).
Baranovich, A. I. et al. (eds.), *Ocherki istorii SSSR: Period feodalizma: Rossiia vo vtoroi polovine XVIII v.* (Moscow, 1956).
Barskov, Ia., 'Proekty voennykh reformykh tsesarevicha Pavla', *Russkii istoricheskii zhurnal*, 3–4 (1917), 104–45.
Bartlett, R. P., 'Catherine II, Voltaire and Henry IV of France', *Newsletter: Study Group on Eighteenth Century Russia*, 9 (1981), 41–50.
—— 'J. J. Sievers and the Russian Peasantry under Catherine II', *Jahrbücher für Geschichte Osteuropas*, NS 32/1 (1984), 16–33.
—— et al., *Russia and the World of the Eighteenth century* (Columbus, 1986).
Benckendorff, Dmitri de, *La Favorite d'un tzar: Catherine Ivanowna Nelidow, 1758–1839* (Paris, 1902).
—— *La Jeunesse d'un tzar* (Paris, 1896).
Bernhardi, Theodor von, 'Die Ermordung des Kaiser Paul I. von Russland am 23 März 1801', *Historische Zeitschrift*, 3 (1860), 133–68.
—— 'Die Ermordung von Kaiser Paul', *Preussische Jahrbücher*, 1 (1858), 420–8.
Berti, Giuseppe, *Russia e stati italiani nel Risorgimento* (Turin, 1957).
Bil'basov, V. A., *Geschichte Katharina II*, trans. M. von Pezold, 2 vols. (Berlin, 1891).
Blum, Jerome, *Lord and Peasant in Russia from the Ninth to the Nineteenth Century* (Princeton, NJ, 1961).
Borovoi, S. Ia., 'Vspomogatel'nyi bank', *Istoricheskie zapiski*, 44 (1953), 206–30.
Brückner [Brikner], Alexander, *Katharina die Zweite* (Berlin, 1883).
—— *Potemkin* (St Petersburg, 1891).
—— *Smert Pavla I. So statego V. I. Semevskago* (St Petersburg, 1907).
Brunov, Baron F. I., 'Aperçu des principales transactions du cabinet de Russie sous les règnes de Catherine II, Paul I, et Alexandre I', *Sbornik imperatorskago russkaga istoricheskago obshchestva* 31 (1881), 197–416.
Case, Lynn M., and Thomas, Daniel H. (eds.), *Guide to the Diplomatic Archives of Western Europe* (Philadelphia, 1959).

Charpentier, Marivic, 'Le Tsar implacable: Paul Ier', *Les Œuvres libres* (Paris, 1952), 203–30.
Chechulin, N. D., *Ocherki po istorii russkikh finansov v tsarstvovanie Ekateriny II* (St Petersburg, 1906).
Chizh, V. F., 'Imperator Pavel I: Psikhologicheskii analiz', *Voprosy filosofii i psikhologii*, 8 (1907), 221–90, 391–468, 585–678.
Confino, Michel, *Domaines et seigneurs en Russie vers la fin du XVIIIe siècle* (Paris, 1963).
—— *Systèmes agraires et progrès agricole: L'Assolement triennal en Russie au XVIIIe–XIXe siècles* (Paris, 1969).
Daudet, Ernest, *L'Histoire de l'émigration*, 3 vols. (Paris, 1904–7).
Donnert, Erich, *Russia in the Age of Enlightenment*, tr. Alison and Alistair Wightman (Leipzig, 1986).
Druzhinina, E. I., *Severnoe prichernomor'e v 1775–1780 gg.* (Moscow, 1959).
Duffy, Christopher, *Russia's Military Way to the West: Origins and Nature of Russian Military Power, 1700–1800* (London, 1981).
Dukes, Paul, *Catherine II and the Russian Nobility* (Cambridge, 1966).
Dzhedzhula, K. E., *Rossiia i velikaia frantsuzskaia revoliutsiia kontsa XVIII veka* (Kiev, 1972).
Easum, Chester V., *Prince Henry of Prussia, Brother of Frederick the Great* (Madison, Wis., 1942).
Edwards, H. Sutherland, *Russian Projects against India from Czar Peter to General Skobeleff* (London, 1885).
Efimov, D. P., *Imperator Pavel Pervyi po Shilderu i vospominaniiam sovremennikov* (Moscow, 1907).
Eidel'man, N. Ia., *Gran' vekov: Politicheskaia borba v Rossii konets XVIII–nachale XIX stoletiia* (Moscow, 1982).
—— 'Obratnoe providenie: Istoricheskii ocherk', *Novy mir*, 5 (1970), 226–41.
El'nitskii, A., 'Fedor Vasil'evich Rostopchin', *Russkii biograficheskii slovar*, xxvii (St Petersburg, 1918), 238–305.
Engel, Claire-Elaine, *Histoire de l'ordre de Malte* (Geneva, 1968).
—— *L'Ordre de Malte en Mediterranée, 1530–1798* (Monaco, 1957).
—— *The Knights of Malta: A Gallery of Portraits* (New York, 1963).
Feldback, Ole, *Denmark and the Armed Neutrality 1800–1801: Small Power Policy in a World War* (Copenhagen, 1980).
—— 'The Foreign Policy of Tsar Paul I, 1800–1801: An Interpretation', *Jahrbücher für Geschichte Osteuropas*, NS 30/1 (1982), 16–36.
Fleischhacker, Hedwig, 'Porträt Peter III', *Jahrbücher für Geschichte Osteuropas*, NS 5/1–2 (1957), 127–89.
Florinsky, Michael, *Russia: A History and Interpretation*, 2 vols. (New York, 1955).
Freeze, Gregory L., 'The *Soslovie* (Estate) Paradigm and Russian Social History', *American Historical Review*, 91/1 (Feb. 1986), 11–36.
Fuye, Maurice de la, *Rostopchin, européen ou slav?* (Paris, 1937).

Gardie, countess B. de la, *Un ambassadeur de Suède à la cour de Catherine II*, 2 vols. (Stockholm, 1919).
Garrard, J. G. (ed.), *The Eighteenth Century in Russia* (Oxford, 1973).
Gatchina: Gosudarstvennoe izdatel'stvo izobrazitel'nogo iskusstva (Moscow, 1958).
Geisman, P. A., and Dubovskii, A. N., *Graf Petr Ivanovich Panin, 1721–1789: Istoricheskii ocherk voennoi i gosudarstvennoi deiatel'nosti* (St Petersburg, 1897).
Geyer, Dietrich, 'Der Aufgeklärte Absolutismus in Russland: Bemerkungen zur Forschungslage', *Jahrbücher für Geschichte Osteuropas*, NS 30/2 (1982), 176–89.
—— '"Gesellschaft" als staatliche Veranstaltung: Bemerkungen zur Sozialgeschichte der russische Staatsverwaltung im 18. Jahrhundert', *Jahrbücher für Geschichte Osteuropas*, NS 14/1 (1966), 21–50.
—— 'Staatsausbau und Sozialfassung: Probleme des russischen Absolutismus am Ende des 18. Jahrhunderts', *Cahiers du monde russe et soviètique*, 7 (1966), 366–77.
Giesemann, Gerhard, *Kotzebue in Russland: Materialen zu einer Wirkungsgeschichte* (Frankfurt-am-Main, 1971).
Gitermann, Valentin, *Geschichte Russlands*, 3 vols. (Hamburg, 1949).
Gleason, Walter J., *Moral Idealists, Bureaucracy, and Catherine the Great* (New Brunswick, 1981).
—— 'Political Ideals and Loyalties of some Russian Writers of the early 1760s, *Slavic Review* 34 (Sept. 1975), 560–75.
Gosudarstvennye arkhivy SSSR: Kratkii spravochnik (Moscow, 1956).
Greppi, G., *Un gentiluomo milanese guerriero-diplomatico, 1763–1839: Appunti biografici sul Bali Conte Giulio Litta-Visconti Arese* (Milan, 1896).
—— *Révélations diplomatiques sur les relations de la Sardaigne avec l'Autriche et la Russie pendant la première et la deuxième coalitions* (Paris, 1859).
Grigorovich, Nikolai, *Kantsler kniaz Aleksandr Andreevich Bezborodko v sviazi s sobytiiami ego vremeni*, Sbornik imperatorskago russkago istoricheskago obshchestva, 26 (1879), 649 pp., and 29 (1881), 736 pp.
Grimsted, P. K., *Archives and Manuscript Repositories in the USSR: Moscow and Leningrad* (Princeton, NJ, 1972).
Grosjean, George, *La France et la Russie pendant le Directoire* (Paris, 1896).
Grunwald, Constantine de, *Alexandre Ier, le tsar mystique* (Paris, 1955).
—— *L'Assassinat de Paul Ier tsar de Russie* (Paris, 1960).
Hans, Nicholas, *History of Russian Educational Policy, 1701–1917* (London, 1931).
Heier, Edmund, *L. H. Nicolay (1737–1820) and His Contemporaries* (The Hague, 1965).
Helbig, Georg-Adolf-Wilhelm von, *Russische Güstlinge* (Tübingen, 1809).
Heller, Klaus, *Die Geld und Kreditpolitik des russischen Reiches in der Zeit der Assignaten (1768–1839/43)* (Wiesbaden, 1983).

Hoffman, Peter, *Russland im Zeitalter des Absolutismus* (Vaduz, 1988).
Hösch, E., 'Das sogenannte griechische Projekt Katharinas II', *Jahrbücher für Geschichte Osteuropas*, NS 12 (1964), 168–204.
Istoriia pravitel'stvuiushchego senata za dvesti let, 1711–1911 gg., 2 vols. (St Petersburg, 1911).
Jahn, Peter, *Russophilie und Konservatismus: Die russophile Literatur in der deutschen Öffentlichkeit 1831–1852* (Stuttgart, 1980).
Jenkins, Michael, *Arakcheev: Grand Vizier of the Russian Empire* (London, 1969).
Jones, Robert E., 'Getting the Goods to St. Petersburg: Water Transport from the Interior 1703–1811', *Slavic Review*, 43/3 (Fall 1984), 412–33.
—— 'Jacob Sievers, Enlightened Reform, and the Development of a "Third Estate" in Russia', *Russian Review*, 4 (1977), 424–37.
—— 'Opposition to War and Expansion in Late Eighteenth Century Russia', *Jahrbücher für Geschichte Osteuropas*, NS 32/1 (1984), 34–51.
—— *Provincial Development in Russia: Catherine II and Jakob Sievers* (New Brunswick, 1984).
—— *The Emancipation of the Russian Nobility, 1762–1785* (Princeton, NJ, 1973).
Jones, W. Gareth, *Nikolay Novikov: Enlightener of Russia* (Cambridge, 1984).
Journel, M. J. Rouët de, SJ, 'L'Imperatore Paolo I e la riunione delle Chiese', *La civiltà cattolica*, 3 (1959), 604–14.
—— 'Paul Ier de Russie et l'union des églises: Documents inédites', *Revue d'histoire ecclésiastique*, 44/4 (1959), 838–63.
Kaznakov, S., 'Pavlovskaia Gatchina', *Starye gody* (July–Sept. 1914), 101–88.
Keep, John L. H., 'Paul I and the Militarization of Government', in Hugh Ragsdale (ed.), *Paul I: A Reassessment of His Life and Reign* (Pittsburgh, 1979), 91–103.
—— 'The Russian Army's Response to the French Revolution', *Jahrbücher für Geschichte Osteuropas*, NS 28/4 (1980), 500–23.
Kenney, James J., jun., 'Lord Whitworth and the Conspiracy against Paul I: The New Evidence of the Kent Archive', *Slavic Review*, 36 (June 1977), 205–19.
—— 'The Politics of Assassination', in Hugh Ragsdale (ed.), *Paul I: A Reassessment of His Life and Reign* (Pittsburgh, 1979), 104–24.
Kizevetter, A. A., 'Imperator Aleksandr I i Arakcheev', *Istoricheskie ocherki* (Moscow, 1912), 287–401.
Kliuchevskii, V. O., *Kurs russkoi istorii: Sochineniia v vosmi tomakh*, i–v (Moscow, 1956–9).
Klochkov, M. V., *Ocherki pravitel'stvennoi deiatel'nosti vremeni Pavla I* (Petrograd, 1916).
Kobeko, Dmitri, *Der Cäsarewitsch Paul Petrowitsch, 1754–1796* (Berlin, 1886).
—— *Tsesarevich Pavel Petrovich, 1754–1796*, 2nd edn. (St Petersburg, 1883).

Konstantin Nikolaevich, Grand Duke, *Pavlovsk: Ocherki istorii i opisanie, 1777–1877* (St Petersburg, 1877).
—— *Pavlovsk*, 4 folio issues (St Petersburg, 1899).
—— 'Semen Andreevich Poroshin', *Russkii vestnik*, 8 (1866), 421–55.
Korf, Baron M. 'Materialy i cherti k biografii imperatora Nikolaia Igo i k istorii ego tsarstvovaniia', *Sbornik imperatorskago russkago istoricheskago obshchestva*, 98 (1896), 1–100.
Korf, Baron S. A., *Dvorianstvo i ego soslovnoe upravlenie za stoletie 1762–1856* (St Petersburg, 1906).
Korsakov, A. N., 'Votsarenie Imperatora Pavla', *Istoricheskii vestnik*, 17 (1896), 495–535, 921–66.
Koval'chenko, I. D., *Russkoe krepostnoe krest'ianstvo v pervoi polovine XIX v.* (Moscow, 1967).
Kovalevskii, P. I., 'Imperator Petr II, Imperator Pavel I', *Psikhiatricheskie eskizy iz istorii*, 1 (1909), 61–172.
Kupriianov, I., *Kratkii ocherk zhizni Eia Imperatorskago Velichestva blazhennoi pamiati gosudaryni Imperatritsy Marii Feodorovny* (St Petersburg, 1869).
Lebedev, Petr, *Grafy Nikita i Petr Paniny* (St Petersburg, 1863).
—— 'Preobrazovateli russkoi armii v tsarstvovanie Imperatora Pavla Petrovicha, 1796–1801', *Russkaia starina*, 18 (1877), 227–60, 577–608.
LeDonne, John P., 'Indirect Taxes in Catherine's Russia: The Salt Code of 1781', *Jahrbücher für Geschichte Osteuropas*, NS 23/2 (1975), 161–90.
—— 'Outlines of Russian Military Administration, 1762–1796', *Jahrbücher für Geschichte Osteuropas*, NS 31 (1983), 321–47; 33 (1985), 175–204; 34 (1986), 188–214.
—— *Ruling Russia: Politics and Administration in the Age of Absolutism, 1762–1796* (Princeton, NJ, 1984).
Liashchenko, P. I., *History of the National Economy of Russia to the 1917 Revolution*, tr. L. M. Herman (New York, 1949).
Lincoln, W. Bruce, *In the Vanguard of Reform: Russian Enlightened Bureaucrats, 1825–1861* (De Kalb, Ill., 1982).
—— 'The Russian State and its Cities: A Search for Effective Municipal Government, 1786–1842', *Jahrbücher für Geschichte Osteuropas*, NS 17/4 (1969), 531–41.
Loewenson, Leo, 'The Death of Paul I (1801) and the Memoirs of Count Bennigsen', *The Slavonic and East European Review*, 29 (Dec. 1950), 212–32.
Longworth, Philip, *The Art of Victory: The Life and Achievements of Generalissimo Suvorov, 1729–1800* (London, 1965).
—— *The Three Empresses: Catherine I, Anne and Elizabeth of Russia* (London, 1972).
Lukomsky, George, *Charles Cameron, 1740–1812* (London, 1943).
—— *Pavlovsk et Gatchina en dessins du poète russe V. A. Joukovsky, 1783–1852* (Paris, 1921).
McConnell, Allen, *A Russian Philosophe: Alexander Radishchev, 1749–1802* (The Hague, 1964).

McErlean, J. M. P., 'Fedor Vasil'evich Rostopchin', *Modern Encyclopedia of Russian and Soviet History*, ed. Joseph L. Wieczynski (Gulf Breeze, Flo., 1983), xxxi. 165–71.

McGrew, Roderick E., 'A Note on Some European Foreign Office Archives and Russian Domestic History', *Slavic Review*, 23 (1964), 531–6.

—— 'A Political Portrait of Paul I from the Austrian and English Archives', *Jahrbücher für Geschichte Osteuropas*, NS 18/4 (Dec. 1970), 503–29.

—— 'Dilemmas of Development: Baron Heinrich Friedrich Storch (1766–1835) on the Growth of Imperial Russia', *Jahrbücher für Geschichte Osteuropas*, NS 24/1 (1976), 31–71.

—— *Encyclopedia of Medical History* (New York, 1985).

—— 'Paul I and the Knights of Malta', in Hugh Ragsdale (ed.), *Paul I: A Reassessment of His Life and Reign* (Pittsburgh, 1979), 44–75.

—— 'The Politics of Absolutism: Paul I and the Bank of Assistance for the Nobility', in Hugh Ragsdale (ed.), *Paul I: A Reassessment of His Life and Reign* (Pittsburgh, 1979), 104–24.

Madariaga, Isabel de, *Russia in the Age of Catherine the Great* (New Haven, Conn., 1981).

Makogonenko, G., *Denis Fonvizin: Tvorcheskiy put* (Moscow, 1961).

—— *Nikolai Novikov i russkoe prosveshchenie* (Moscow, 1951).

Manfred, A. Z., 'Voiski soiuza s Rossiei, 1800–1801', *Istoriia SSR*, 4 (1971), 38–59.

Manning, Bruce W., 'Russian Military Innovation in the Second Half of the Eighteenth Century', *War and Society*, 2 (May 1984), 23–41.

Massie, Suzanne, *Pavlovsk: The Life of a Russian Palace* (London, 1990).

Mavrodin, V. V., *Krestianskaia voina v Rossii*, 3 vols. (Leningrad, 1961).

Mazour, A. G., *The First Russian Revolution: The Decembrists* (Berkeley, Calif., 1937).

Mikhailovskii-Danilevskii, Aleksandr, and Miliutin, Dmitri Ivanovich, *Istoriia voiny Rossii s Frantsieiu v 1799 gody*, 5 vols. (St Petersburg, 1852).

—— *Geschichte des Krieges Russlands mit Frankreich unter der Regierung Kaiser Pauls I im Jahre 1799*, trans. C. Schmitt, 5 vols. (Munich, 1856–8).

Milioukov, Paul, et al., *Histoire de Russie*, 3 vols. (Paris, 1932).

Mironov, B. N., 'Eksport russkogo khleba vo vtoroi polovine XVIII- nachal XIX v.', *Istoricheskie zapiski*, 93 (1974), 157–71.

Modern Encyclopedia of Russian and Soviet History, ed. Joseph L. Wieczynski, 54 vols. with suppl. (Gulf Breeze, Flo., 1976–90).

Morane, Pierre, *Paul Ier de Russie: Avant l'avènement: 1754–1796* (Paris, 1907).

Narotchnitski, A., et al., *La Révolution française et la Russie* (Moscow, 1989).

Neumann, Franz, *The Democratic and the Authoritarian State* (Glencoe, Ill., 1957).

Nicolas Mikhailowitch, Grand Duke, *Le Comte Paul Alexandrowitch Stroganov*, 3 vols. (Paris, 1905).

Nicolas Mikhailowitch, *L'Empereur Alexandre Ier: Essai d'étude historique*, 2 vols. (St Petersburg, 1912).
—— *L'Impératrice Elisabeth épouse d' Alexandre Ier*, 5 vols. (St Petersburg, 1908–9).
Nol'de, A. E., 'Pravitel'stvuiushchii senat v tsarstvovanie Pavla I', *Istoriia pravitel'stvuiushchego senata za dvesti let* (St Petersburg, 1911), 695–779.
Okenfuss, Max J., 'Education and Empire: School Reform in Enlightened Russia', *Jahrbücher für Geschichte Osteuropas*, NS 27/41 (1979), 41–68.
Okuny, Semen Bentsionovich, *Ocherki istorii SSSR: Konets XVIII–pervaia chetvert' XIX veka* (Leningrad, 1956).
Oliva, L. Jay, *Misalliance: A Study of French Policy in Russia during the Seven Years War* (Berkeley, Calif., 1968).
Oliver, Daria, *Elisabeth de Russie (fille de Pierre le Grand)* (Paris, 1962).
Panchulidzev, S. A., *Istoriia Kavaliergardov, 1724–1899*, 2 vols. (St Petersburg, 1899–1901).
Papmehl, K. A., *Metropolitan Platon of Moscow (Petr Levshin, 1737–1812): The Enlightened Prelate, Scholar, and Educator* (Newtonville, Mass., 1983).
Pashkov, A. I., *Istoriia russkoi ekonomicheskoi mysli*, i/1 and 2 (Moscow, 1955, 1958).
Pavlovsk: Pamiatniki russkoi khudozhestvennoi kultury (Moscow, 1952).
Pierling, Paul, *La Russie et le Saint-Siège*, 5 vols. (Paris, 1896–1912).
Pierredon, Count Michel de, *Histoire politique de l'ordre souverain de Jérusalem (Ordre de Malte) de 1789 à 1955*, 2 vols. (Paris, 1956).
Piggott, F. T., and Ormond, G. T. W., *Documentary History of the Armed Neutralities* (London, 1919).
Pilven, T., *Un tzar en Bretagne* (Rennes, 1892).
Pinter, W. M., and Rowney, D. K. (eds.), *The Bureaucratization of Russian Society from the Seventeenth to the Twentieth Centuries* (Chapel Hill, NC, 1980).
Polievktov, M. A., *Proekt soiuza Rossii s sardinskim korolevstvom v tsarstvovanie imperatora Pavla I* (St Petersburg, 1902).
Predtechenskii, A. V., *Ocherki obshchestvenno-politicheskoi istorii Rossii v pervoi chetverti XIX veka* (Moscow, 1957).
R. R. [Aleksandr Brikner], *Kaiser Pauls I. Ende, 1801* (Stuttgart, 1897).
Raeff, Marc, *Michael Speransky, Statesman of Imperial Russia* (The Hague, 1957).
—— 'Les Slaves, les allemands, et les lumières', *Canadian Slavic Studies*, 1/4 (1967), 521–51.
—— *Origins of the Russian Intelligentsia: The Eighteenth Century Nobility* (New York, 1966).
—— 'Pugachev's Rebellion', in Robert Foster and J. P. Greene (eds.), *Preconditions of Revolution in Early Modern Europe* (Baltimore, 1970).
—— 'The Domestic Policies of Peter III and His Overthrow', *American Historical Review*, 75/5 (1970), 1289–1310.

—— 'The Well-Ordered Police State and the Development of Modernity in Seventeenth- and Eighteenth-Century Europe: An Attempt at a Comparative Approach', *American Historical Review*, 80 (1975), 1221–43.
—— *The Well-Ordered Police State: Social and Institutional Change through Law in the Germanies and Russia, 1600–1800* (New Haven, Conn., 1983).
—— *Understanding Imperial Russia*, tr. Arthur Goldhammer (New York, 1984).
Ragsdale, Hugh, 'A Continental System in 1801: Paul I and Bonaparte', *Journal of Modern History*, 42 (1970), 70–89.
—— *Détente in the Napoleonic Era: Bonaparte and the Russians* (Lawrence, Kan., 1980).
—— 'Ivan Pavlovich Kutaisov, 1759?–1834', *Modern Encyclopedia of Russian and Soviet History* (Gulf Breeze, Flo., 1980), xviii. 206–7.
—— 'Montmorin and Catherine's Greek Project: Revolution in French Foreign Policy', *Cahiers du monde russe et soviétique*, 27/1 (1986), 27–44.
—— (ed.), *Paul I: A Reassessment of His Life and Reign* (Pittsburgh, 1979).
—— 'Russian Influence at Lunéville', *French Historical Studies*, 5 (1968), 274–84.
—— 'Russia, Prussia, and Europe in the Policy of Paul I', *Jahrbücher für Geschichte Osteuropas*, NS 31/1 (1983), 81–118.
—— 'The Mental Condition of Paul', in Hugh Ragsdale (ed.), *Paul I: A Reassessment of His Life and Reign* (Pittsburgh, 1979), 17–30.
—— *Tsar Paul and the Question of Madness: An Essay in History and Psychology* (Westport, Conn., 1988).
—— 'Was Paul Bonaparte's Fool? The Evidence of Neglected Archives', in Hugh Ragsdale (ed.), *Paul I: A Reassessment of His Life and Reign* (Pittsburgh, 1979), 76–90.
Ransel, David L., 'An Ambivalent Legacy: The Education of Grand Duke Paul', in Hugh Ragsdale (ed.), *Paul I: A Reassessment of His Life and Reign* (Pittsburgh, 1979), 1–16.
—— 'Count Petr Ivanovich Panin (1721–1789)', *Modern Encyclopedia of Russian and Soviet History* (Gulf Breeze, Flo., 1982), xxvi. 218–21.
—— *The Politics of Catherinian Russia: The Panin Party* (New Haven, Conn., 1975).
Rest, Matthias, *Die russische Judengesetzgebung von der ersten polnischen Teilung bis zum Položenie dlia evreev (1804)* (Wiesbaden, 1975).
Riasanovsky, Nicholas V., *Nicholas I and Official Nationality in Russia* (Berkeley, Calif., 1966).
Rice, Tamara Talbot, *Elizabeth, Empress of Russia* (New York, 1970).
Rodgers, A. B., *The War of the Second Coalition, 1798–1801: A Strategic Commentary* (Oxford, 1964).
Rozhdestvenskii, S. V., 'Gatchinskaia votchina Pavla I', *Uchenye zapiski RANIION, institut istorii*, 6 (1928), 127–45.
—— *Stoletie goroda Gatchiny, 1796–1896* (Gatchina, 1896).
Russkii biograficheskii slovar, 25 vols. (St Petersburg, 1896–1918).

Ryan, Frederick W., *The House of the Temple: A Story of Malta and its Knights in the French Revolution* (London, 1930).
Safonov, M. M., 'Konstitutsionnyi proekt, N. I. Panina–D. I. Fonvizina', *Vspomogatel'nye istoricheskie distsipliny*, 6 (1974), 261–80.
—— *Problema reformykh v pravitel'stvennoi politike Rossii na rubezhe XVIII i XIX vv.* (Leningrad, 1988).
Samoilov, V. I., *Vnutrenniaia i vneshniaia politika Pavla I* (Khlebnikovo, 1946).
Saul, Norman E., *Russia and the Mediterranean, 1797–1807* (Chicago, 1970).
—— 'The Objectives of Paul's Italian Policy', in Hugh Ragsdale (ed.), *Paul I: A Reassessment of His Life and Reign* (Pittsburgh, 1979), 31–43.
Scharf, Claus, 'Staatsauffassung und Regierungsprogramm eines aufgeklärten Selbstherrschers', in E. Schulin (ed.), *Gedenkschrift Martin Göhring Studien zur Europäische Geschichte* (Wiesbaden, 1968), 91–106.
Schiemann, Theodore, *Geschichte Russlands unter Kaiser Nikolaus I*, 4 vols. (Berlin, 1904–19).
Schmidt, Christian D., 'The Further Study of Paul (Werner Phillip in Verehrung zugeeignet)', tr. David and Karin Griffiths, in Hugh Ragsdale (ed.), *Paul I: A Reassessment of His Life and Reign* (Pittsburg, 1979), 147–69.
Schnitzler, Johann-Heinrich, *La Jeunesse de l'Impératrice Maria Feodorovna jusqu'à son mariage* (Colmar, 1864).
Schroeder, Paul, 'The Collapse of the Second Coalition', *Journal of Modern History*, 59 (1987), 244–90.
Ségur, Count Anatole de, *Vie du comte Rostopchin, gouverneur de Moscou en 1812* (Paris, 1871).
Semevskii, M., 'Materialy k russkoi istorii XVIII veka (1788 g.)', *Vestnik evropy*, 2 (Apr. 1867), 297–330.
Semevskii, V. I., *Krestianskii vopros v Rossii v XVIII i pervoi polovine XIX veka*, 2 vols. (St Petersburg, 1888).
—— *Krestianskii vopros v tsarstvovanie Imperatritsy Ekateriny II* (St Petersburg, 1903).
Shebaeva, M. F. (ed.), *Ocherki istorii shkoly i pedagogicheskoi mysly narodov SSSR, XVIII v.–pervaia polovina XIX v.* (Moscow, 1973).
Shil'der [Schilder], N., *Histoire anecdotique de Paul Ier* (Paris, 1899).
—— *Imperator Aleksandr Pervyi*, 4 vols. (St Petersburg, 1897–8).
—— *Imperator Pavel I: Istorikobiograficheskii ocherk* (St Petersburg, 1901).
—— 'Russkaia armiia v god smerti Ekateriny', *Russkaia starina* (Mar. 1895) 147–66; (May 1895), 185–202.
Shtrange, M. W., *Demokraticheskaia intelligentsiia Rossii v XVIII veke* (Moscow, 1965).
—— *Russkoe obshchestvo i frantsuzskaia revoliutsiia 1789–1794* (Moscow, 1956).
Shumigorskii, E. S., *Ekaterina Ivanovna Nelidova (1758–1839): Ocherk iz istoril imperatora Pavla* (St Petersburg, 1898).
—— *Imperator Pavel I: Zhizn i tsarstvovanie* (St Petersburg, 1907).

—— *Imperatritsa Mariia Fedorovna*, 2 vols. (St Petersburg, 1892).
—— '1800 god', *Russkaia starina* (Jan.–Mar. 1913), 37–54, 263–79; (Apr.–June 1913), 223–36.
—— 'Pavel I', *Russkii biograficheskii slovar* (St Petersburg, 1902), xiii. 4–64.
Shvarts, V., *Prigorody Leningrada* (Leningrad, 1961).
Solov'ev, S. M., *Istoriia Rossii s drevneishikh vremen*, 15 vols. (Moscow, 1963).
Soloveytchik, George, *Potemkin: Soldier, Statesman, Lover and Consort of Catherine of Russia* (New York, 1947).
Somma, Carlo di, *Une mission diplomatique du marquis de Gallo a Saint-Pétersbourg en 1799* (Naples, 1910).
Spiridonakis, Basile (ed.), *Mémoires et documents du ministère des affaires étrangères de France sur la Russie* (Quebec, 1962).
Stanislavskaia, A. M., *Russko-angliiskie otnosheniia i problemy Sredizemnomor'ia, 1798–1807* (Moscow, 1962).
—— *Rossiia i Gretsii v kontse XVIII–nachale XIX veke: Politika Rossi v Ionicheskoi respublike, 1798–1807* (Moscow, 1976).
Starr, J. Frederick, *Decentralization and Self-Government in Russia* (Princeton, NJ, 1972).
Storch, P., *Putevoditel po sad i gorodu Pavlovsku* (St Petersburg, 1845).
Stupperich, Robert, 'Die zweite Reise des Prinzen Heinrich von Preussen nach Petersburg', *Jahrbücher für Geschichte Osteuropas*, 3 (1938), 580–600.
Tarle, E. V., *Admiral Ushakov na Sredizemnom More, 1799–1800*, (Moscow, 1948).
Tatishchev, Sergei S., 'Paul I et Bonaparte', *La Nouvelle Revue*, 47 (1887), 631–65; 48 (1887), 41–58; 49 (1887), 233–60, 745–85.
Taube, Michel de, *L'Empereur Paul I de Russie, grand maître de l'ordre de Malte et son 'grand prieuré russe' de l'ordre de Saint-Jean-de-Jérusalem* (Paris, 1955).
—— 'Le Tsar Paul I et l'ordre de Malthe en Russie', *Revue d'histoire moderne*, 5 (1930), 161–77.
Torke, Hans Joachim, 'Autocratie und Absolutismus in Russland-Begriffsklärung und Periodisierung', in Uwe Halbach, Hans Hecker, and Andreas Kappeler (eds.), *Geschichte Altrusslands in der Begriffswelt Ihrer Quellen: Festschrift zum 70. Geburtstag von Günther Stökl* (Stuttgart, 1986).
—— 'Das russische Beamtentum in der ersten Hälfte des 19. Jahrhunderts', *Forschungen zur osteuropäischen Geschichte*, 23 (1967), 7–346.
Troitskii, S. M., *Finansovaia politika russkogo absoliutizma v XVIII veke* (Moscow, 1966).
—— *Rossii v XVIII veke* (Moscow, 1982).
Tucker, Clara J., 'The Foreign Policy of Paul I', Ph.D. dissertation, Syracuse Univ. 1965.
Valk, S. N., *Krestianskoe dvizhenie v Rossii v 1796–1825 gg.* (Moscow, 1961).

Vasil'chikov [*see also* Wassiltchikow], A. A., *Semeistvo Razumovskikh*, 5 vols. (St Petersburg, 1880–94).
Venturi, Franco, 'Italo-Russkie otnosheniia s 1750 do 1825', *Rossiia i Italiia: Iz istorii russko-italianskikh kulturnikh i obshchestvennykh otnoshenii* (Moscow, 1968).
Vogüe, viscomte E. Melchior de, *Le Fils de Pierre le Grand, Mazeppa, un changement de règne* (Paris, 1884).
Vozherianov, I. N., 'Mikhailovskii zamok, dvorets imperatora Pavla I v S.-Peterburge v 1800–1801', *Russkaia starina*, 39 (1883), 651–2.
Waliszewski, K., *La Dernière des Romanov: Elizabeth Ier, impératrice de Russie, 1741–1762* (Paris, 1902).
—— *Le Fils de la grande Catherine: Paul Ier, Empereur de Russie: Sa vie, sa règne, et sa mort: 1754–1801*, 3rd edn. (Paris, 1912).
—— *Le Roman d'une impératrice: Catherine II de Russie d'après ses mémoires, sa correspondance et les documents inédits des archives d'état*, 3rd edn. (Paris, 1897).
—— *Paul I of Russia* (London, 1913).
Wassiltchikow, A. A., *Les Razoumowski*, French edn., A. Brückner, 3 vols. (6 bks.) (Halle, 1893–4).
Wortman, Richard, 'Images of Rule and Problems of Gender in the Upbringing of Paul I and Alexander I', in Ezra Mendelsohn and Marshall S. Shatz (eds.), *Imperial Russia, 1700–1917: State, Society, Opposition: Essays in Honor of Marc Raeff* (De Kalb, Ill., 1988), 58–75.
—— *The Development of a Russian Legal Consciousness* (Chicago, 1976).
Yaney, George, *The Systematization of Russian Government* (Urbana, Ill., 1973).
Zhukovich, P., 'Zapadnaia Rossiia v tsarstvovanie imperatora Pavla', *Zhurnal ministerstva narodnago prosveshcheniia* (June 1916), 183–226; (Aug. 1916), 207–63; (Oct. 1916), 175–86.
Zubow, Valentin graf, *Zar Paul I. Mensch und Schicksal* (Stuttgart, 1963).

INDEX

abdication (proposed for Paul I) 5, 7, 333, 349, 350
absolutism 16, 356
absolutist 14
absolutist tradition 167
abuses (in Catherine's Russia) 146, 197, 206
Academy of Sciences (Paris) 136
accession (of Alexander I) 206, 349, 353
accession (of Paul I), *see* Paul I: accession
accession manifesto (Alexander I) 206, 325, 349
administrative centralization 167
administrative colleges 218, 222
administrative interests 39
administrative officials 217
administrators 181
Adriatic Sea 290, 300, 306
advanced European societies 356
Aegean Sea 230
Aepinus, Franciscus Maria Ulricus Theodorus 53
agriculture 155, 156, 253
agricultural development 245
alcohol monopoly 168
d'Alembert, Jean La Rond 41, 48
Alexander I, grand duke and tsar 28, 50, 76, 116, 118, 133, 163, 164, 196, 200, 206, 209, 222, 235, 340, 347, 350, 352, 353
    and 1801 *coup* 1, 2, 6–7, 333–5, 342–43
    birth 107
    and Catherine 108–9
    and Arakcheev 161
    and succession 167, 179, 183, 184–6, 190
    court and influence 203
    attitudes to Paul 204–5
    as heir and successor 237
    and alienation from Paul 268
    as alternative to Paul 324
    and Catherine's heritage 325
    as danger to Paul 326–7
    and Paul's alleged insanity 336–7
    and Paul before the *coup* 348–9
    and his guilt at Paul's murder 354
    and Paul's heritage 355
Alexis Petrovich, tsarevich 327, 348
Alps 285
Amiens (peace of) 318
amnesty (for Paul's exiles) 341
Amsterdam 226
ancien régime 288
Ancona 306–7, 312
Anglo-Bavarian *langue* 261
Anglo-Russian commercial treaty (1797) 313
Anglo-Russian campaign (in Holland) 309–10
Anglo-Russian connection 328
Anglo-Russian relations 308–14
Anna Pavlovna, grand duchess 107
Anne of Brunswick 20
Anne of Holstein-Gottorp 20
Anne of Courland (Kurland), empress of Russia 20, 75
Annunciation Cathedral 234
Aosta, duke of Sardinia 303
apoplectic stroke (alleged cause of death for Paul I) 1, 323
apoplexy 353
Apraksin, S. F. general count 36
Arakcheev, A. A., general count 5, 200, 201, 213, 230, 338, 348, 355
    character and career 160–1
    and grand duke Alexander 204
    and loyalty to Paul I 339
Arbanev, general 310
Argamakov, P. V. general 346, 351
Arkharov, Nikolai Petrovich, general 162, 192, 201, 212, 235, 331
Armed Neutrality, League of (1780) 133
army 17, 197, 216, 244, 278, 283, 322, 355
    at Gatchina 159
    and need to reform 182, 207

army (cont.):
  and German style 209
  ready for war 288–9
  and 1801 coup 323
  see also military
artisans 155, 250
Artois, count of 133, 308
asceticism (in military reforms) 233
Asseburg, A. F. baron von 83, 84
assignat bank 248
assignats 226, 253
asylums (of Paris) 136
Atkin, Muriel 13
d'Aubusson, Pierre (grand master of the knights of Malta d. 1506) 262
Aulic council 295, see Hofkriegsrath
Austria 144, 150, 180, 198, 199, 258, 279, 286, 287, 309–11, 314, 315, 318, 320, 322, 327–8, 334
  in second coalition 10–11
  relations with Russia (1755–6) 35
  and Paul's western tour 114–15, 122
  Paul's bias against 129, 140
  relief force denied to 207
  military support for withheld 282, 283–4
  relations with Britain, Prussia, Russia 290
  joins Russia against France 291–3
  and knights of Malta 296–9
  and Swiss débacle 300–1
  and Suvorov 302–4
  and breakdown in Russian relations 304–8
  and end of alliance 312
Austrian Netherlands 285
Austro-Russian defense treaty (1795) 283
authoritarianism 17, 322
autocracy 12, 244, 324
  in Paul's thinking 166–7
  and law 220
  seen by Paul as Petrine 233
  and conspirators' vision of 325
  in the nineteenth century 355–6
autocrat 16, 222
autonomy (denied Paul's subordinates) 217
autopsy (on Nathalia Alexievna) 92
auxiliary force (for Austria) 282

Baden-Baden 184
Bakunin, Peter Vasil'evich 131
balance (necessary in domestic affairs) 168
Balkans 230, 292
Baltic 312, 314
bank for nobles (1754) 248
Bank of Assistance for the Nobility 202, 223, 226, 246–56, 279, 280
bankruptcy (proceedings clarified) 257
banks (subsidize nobility) 248
Bariatinskii, Fedor prince 41, 80, 193, 194, 327
barshchina 238, 239, 252
Bavaria 285, 296–7, 319
Bazhenev, V. I. 195
Beaumarchais, Pierre Augustin baron de 133
Belorussia 222
benevolence (and monarchy) 233
benefices (at coronation) 238–9
Benkendorff, Anna Iuliana countess 176, 179
Bennigsen, Leo (Leontii Leont'evich) (Leon August Teofil) general 2, 323, 341, 350, 352, 353, 354
Bérenger, (French *chargé d'affaires*) 74
Bergen (Holland) 310
Berlin 113, 114, 122, 130, 141, 161, 198, 271, 289, 290, 305, 327
  and Hesse–Darmstadt marriage party 83–4
  and Paul's visit to (1776) 96–7
  eliminated from tour itinerary (1781–2) 115–6
  and Repnin instructions for 284–5
  and Panin mission to 286
  as channel for negotiations with Bonaparte (1800) 314
Berne 287
Bernouilli, Daniel 75
Bestuzhev (-Riumin), A. P. chancellor 21, 35, 36
Bezborodko, A. A. count, prince, chancellor 203, 213, 234, 270, 284, 293
  named Austrian agent by Paul 131
  and Catherine's edict on succession 190
  in Paul's government 199–200
  and empress' party 201–2, 263–5, 269

and rewards 239
and Robert Woot 246
on Paul as grand master 278
Bezborodko palace 235, 236
Bibikov affair 135–6, 143
Bibikov, N. I. colonel 353
Bibikov, P. A., *see* Bibikov affair
Bielfeld, J. F. baron 48
Bielke, MMe. 82, 84
Bil'basov, V. A. 25, n.7 25–6
Biron (Bühren), Ernst Johann count, general, regent 20
Black Sea 230, 283, 290
blockade 313
boarding school (at Gatchina) 156
Bobrinskoi, Alexei 30
Boerhaave, (court physician) 92
Bohemian priory of the knights of Malta 297, 298–9
Bonaparte, Napoleon 263, 272, 299, 312, 317, 318, 354
and seizure of Malta 271
and French expansion 289
and Brumaire 300
conservative policies 311
and *rapprochement* with Russia 314–15
and Paul's attack on India 316
Borck, baron de (financial overseer for Paul) 158
la bonne cause 291, 308
Bossuet, Jacques Bénigne bishop 48
boundaries (France, pre-war) 285
Bourbons 285
Braunschweig 289
Brenna, Vincenzio (architect) 154, 345
Britain 180, 282, 286, 308, 309, 312
see also England
British interests 289
Brittany 137
Brühl, Karl Adolph count de (Prussian envoy) 286
Brumaire (18 October 1788) 300, 311
Brunswick faction 20, 21, 74
Brussels 137, 138
Buckingham, (English ambassador) 33
Buckingham, George Villiers first duke of 49
budget (imperial) 218, 225, 245, 322
bureaucracy (state) 12, 13, 355
bureaucrats 256

Buxhoeweden, F. F. count, general 162, 267, 332
caesarean section 92
Caillard, A. B. (Directory minister to Berlin) 286
Campoformio (peace of) 286, 287, 288, 289, 290
cameralist tradition 64
canals 202, 257
canon law 234
capital (investment) 248, 254
capitalism 250
Caroline queen of Naples 127
caserne (of Paris) 136
Castera, J. H. 25
Castor and Pollux 136
catechism (for Paul) 61
Catherine I empress of Russia 19
Catherine II grand duchess and empress of Russia 8, 9, 12, 16, 17–18, 34, 47, 48, 51, 53, 56, 58, 65, 66, 69, 81, 82, 83, 84, 87, 89, 91, 97, 100, 103, 104, 110, 117, 118, 120, 122, 125–6, 127, 128, 129, 130, 131, 133, 134, 138, 140, 141, 142, 148, 149, 151, 152, 158, 161, 163, 167, 170, 171, 175, 182, 183, 192, 199, 200, 204, 206, 207, 208, 219, 220, 235, 240, 245, 246, 287, 308, 312, 315, 323, 327, 331, 339, 355, 356
as bride to grand duke Peter 21
relations with Peter 22–3, 37–8
and Paul's paternity 24–7
motherhood 28–30
political activity 35–7
coup d'état (1762) 39–41, 324
coup and Paul 42–3
and Paul's sexual initiation 57
relations with Paul 70–2, 77–8, 105, 106, 107, 135–6, 143–4
Paul's loyalty to 73
and marriage question 73–4
and Ivan VI's death 74
preventing small pox 75–6
and Paul's illness (1771) 77
her critics 79
Pugachev revolt 80
and Paul's first marriage 84–6
and Nathalia's death 92–4
arranging the second marriage 95

Catherine II (*cont.*):
  impressions of Sophia Dorothea 98–9
  and Paul's sons 108
  instigates western tour 112–16
  domestic and foreign policies 150
  contrasted with Paul 157, 211, 213, 243
  second Crimean trip 163
  and refuses Paul's service in Turkish war 164–5
  Paul on Swedish front 165
  denigrates Paul's service 169
  and Nelidova affair 174, 177, 178–9
  diverges from Paul on French revolution 180–1
  removing Paul from the succession 184–6
  and failed Swedish alliance 186–7
  death 187, 190–1
  funeral rites shared with Peter III 193–5
  injustices corrected 195–7
  and problems Paul corrected 216–7, 220, 224, 237
  and granting peasants 240–1
  and knights of Malta 259, 260
  her auxiliary force for Austria recalled 282
  as model for 1801 conspirators 325
  on Paul's mental state 329, 330
  criticizes Paul's views on subversives 346
  coup (1762) contrasted with 1801 354
  see also Sophia Augusta Frederika of Anhalt-Zerbst
Catherine Pavlovna grand duchess 107
catholicism 237
catholics 223, 275
ceremonial 226, 236, 241–2, 258, 277, 298
censorship 3, 196, 223, 355
central administration 201, 221
central authority 7
central commission for economic affairs 222
central Europe 334
central government 199, 200, 216, 220, 221, 222, 355
centralized state 221, 271, 355
centralization 147, 217, 355
chain-of-command administration 322
de Champeaux (French diplomat) 25–6
chancellor 199, 218, 239, 263, 284
chancellory for artillery and fortifications 227
Channel Islands 310
Chantilly 133, 236
charitable institutions 202
charity boards 248
Charles Augustus of Holstein, bishop of Lübeck 19–20
Charles (of Austria), archduke 294, 300, 301, 304, 305
Charles-Eugene II of Württemberg 140
Charles I (of England) 49
Charles V (of the Holy Roman Empire) 258, 314
Charles Emmanuel (of Sardinia) 303
charter of nobility (1785) 217, 223
charter of municipalities (1785) 217
charters 4
Chartorizhkaia, Sophia 57
Chateaulin 137
Chartres, duke of (Philippe Égalité) 133
Chernyshev, I. G. count 200
La Chétardie, le marquis de 20
Chevalier, MMe. de (comedienne, Kutaisov's mistress) 340
children of gentry 224
chivalry 17
chivalric style 278
Choglokova, Mme. (personal overseer to Catherine) 26
Choglokova, Vera Nikolaevna 56–7
Choiseul-Geoffier, count de 185, 307
Choisy 137
Christian community 10, 126
Christian faith 17
Christians 126
Christian VII (of Denmark) 338
church (Russian orthodox) 39, 234
churches 154–5
church lands 241
citizen 211
civil administration 201
civil service 225
class bias (in Paul's legislation) 211
clergy 167
Clérisseau, Ch.-L. (architect) 134
Cobenzl, count Louis de (Austrian

ambassador to St Petersburg) 141,
  144, 269, 278, 287, 288–9, 299
on Nelidova scandal 174–5
on Paul as disciplinarian 182, 212
on Paul at his accession 190
and Alexis Orlov's oath 192
and Paul's commitment to Prussia
  198
approves Bezborodko 200
on Paul and Alexander 205
and Paul's fears of revolution 206
and dress regulations 210
on granting state peasants to nobles
  240
and preoccupation with ceremony
  241–2
tries to prevent withdrawal of relief
  force 283
concerning Paul's approaches to
  Prussia 284
isolated in St Petersburg and recalled
  307
on Catherine and Paul's 'madness'
  330
code of military conduct 229
Coliseum 126
collateral (for loans) 249, 251
college of foreign affairs 161, 198, 270,
  327, 334
collegial presidents (and ministerial
  functions) 222
colleges 225, 355
Comenius, John Amos 44
les comtes du Nord 117, 123, 132, 136
commissariat 227
commission on finance and commerce
  226
common soldier 231
commanderies (of knights of Malta)
  261, 276
commerce 222
competitive examinations (for Iunker
  school) 224
Condé, Louis Joseph de Bourbon prince
  de 133, 236, 258, 262, 288, 300,
  317
confiscation (of defaulters' land) 251
conservative (values) 16, 322, 355–6
conspiracies:
  against Paul 1, 5–6, 7, 8, 13, 14, 17,
    318, 322, 323, 324, 325, 327–36,
    338, 346, 347, 348, 349
  conspirators (1801) 3, 5, 324, 336,
    349, 350–1, 354
  for Elizabeth (1741) 19, 20
  against Peter III (1762) 38–9, 42–3,
    344
  against Catherine 71, 79–80, 93
  and peasant rising (1796–7) 215–16
  against Paul and Peter III contrasted
    244–5
  and the empress' party 264
Constantine Pavlovich, grand duke 28,
  76, 107, 108, 112, 118, 163, 164,
  190, 200, 204, 209, 235–6, 258,
  342, 343, 348, 353
Constantinople 130, 185, 267
constitution 13, 324
constitutional government 6
constitutional law 334
constitutional monarchy 324
constitutional order 150
constitutional orientation 13
constitutional reform 200
constitutional system 337
constitutions 349
constitutionalism 79
consumer goods 248
contracts (sanctity of) 250
control (as political necessity) 182, 216,
  231, 324
  see also discipline
controls (on thought and behaviour)
  322
Copenhagen 314
de Corberon, baron de 92
corporal punishment 223
coronation (Paul I) 167, 197, 231, 255,
  264, 265, 288
coronation banquet 242–3
corrupted upper class 211
corruption (and women's rule) 197–8
cossacks 316
court (politics) 8, 39, 72, 77, 86–7,
  196, 209, 233, 264, 277, 322, 355
courtiers 189, 323
courts (legal) 218, 221–2
credit (availability) 248
creditors 249, 250, 254
Crimea 150, 152
crotchets 92
crusade (against France) 291

cultural variety 221
currency 168, 218, 245, 253, 254, 255, 279, 322
Czartoryski, Adam prince 203, 342, 354

Dacia 112
Dalmation coast 292
dalmatique 234
Dashkova, E. R. princess 38, 79, 150, 193
dauphin 134
debt 216, 225, 226, 251, 253
debt consolidation 249, 253
debtors 254
debt reduction 248
Decembrist revolt 13, 79, 324
Decembrists 354
decentralization (under Catherine) corrected 221, 222
default 252
delegated powers (by Paul) 217
democratism (in Russia) 207
democrats 355
democracy 285
Denmark 311, 312, 313, 318, 319, 334
departments (governmental) 218
Depreradovich, N. I. colonel 349
desertions 231
despot (Paul as) 325
despotism 324, 336, 343
development (economic) 14
developing societies 12
Diderot, Denis 48
Dietrichstein-Proskacy (Austrian) count, major-general of engineers 217, 256, 264, 326–7, 330
Dimsdale, Thomas doctor and baron 54, 75, 76, 116
diplomacy 13, 279, 281, 322
diplomatic relations 259
diplomatic system 322
Directory (French) 284, 286, 311, 318
discipline 16, 147, 182, 184, 205, 211, 216, 231, 233, 271, 280
  see also control
discount (on Bank scrip) 249, 255
disloyalty (Paul's view of) 182
disobedience 215
disposable income (of landowners) 247
disorder 215

disorderliness 182
dispossessed princes 263
district authority (local government) 150
district (*uezd*) courts and councils 221
  see also courts
district physician 154, 156
domainal economy 247, 253
domainal industries 156
domestic policy (Paul I) 202, 270
Domostroi 103
dress code 144, 156, 210, 211
drill (military) 211
Duncan, Adam admiral and viscount 310
dvorianin (gentry landowner) 247
  see also gentry
dynastic marriage 19

ecclesiastical peasants 241
economic capacity 355
economic development 250
economic growth 14
economic policy 257
economy 247
Eden, Sir Morton 294
education (at Gatchina) 156
educational reforms 224
educational system 150
Egypt 271, 289, 300
Eidel'man, N. Ia. 13–14
elected citizens 221
electoral principles 150
Elizabeth Alexievna, grand duchess and empress 184, 203, 236, 343
Elizabeth Petrovna, grand duchess and empress 19–20, 22, 25, 26, 28, 30–1, 36–7, 46, 57, 72, 73, 198
Elizbeth of Württemberg 113, 131
'emancipation' 215
émigrés 16, 162–3, 185, 258, 262, 263, 269, 277, 286, 288, 300, 311, 317
emperor (Paul) 216, 217
empress' party (Mariia Fedorovna) 201–2, 203, 239, 246, 263, 264, 267–9, 271, 279, 326, 332
enforcement (of regulations) 212
England 59, 133, 150, 258, 279, 287, 318, 319, 321, 334
  and realignment of Europe (1756) 35
  Paul should visit 143

and second coalition 290
and Dutch campaign (1799) 308–10
relations with Paul deteriorate 311–14
and vulnerability of India 316
see also Britain
English Channel 230
enlightened absolutism 12
enlightened absolutist 14
enlightened age 355
enlightened autocrat 13
enlightened government 6, 142
enlightened public service 156
Enlightenment 13, 157, 356
Enlightenment values 325
Essen, Ivan Nikolaevich general 310
estates (*soslovie*) 167
Esterhazy, Valentin count 182–3, 185
Estonia 222
Étupes 140
Eugene of Württemberg, prince 342
Europe 10, 154, 165, 180, 181, 211, 272, 277, 279, 290, 300, 312, 316, 318, 319, 320
European community 11, 317, 322
European monarchies 261
European order 319
European Russia 339
European stability 286
exchange (currency) 218, 255
exiles (domestic) 342
expeditions (administrative) 218

faction 203, 263
factional politics 12
factories 156, 251
Falçonet, Étienne Maurice 138
famine 218
farming 156
fatherland 324
favourite (Paul) 263–4
favourites (Catherine) 149, 182
fees (Bank loans) 245, 251, 253, 254, 255
feldscher 155, 156
female rulers 211
Fénélon, François de Salignac de Mothe 44, 48, 64
Ferdinand III of Naples 127
Ferdinand IV of Naples 292, 308
Ferdinand of Württemberg prince 306

feudalism 10
fiefdoms 217
Finland grand duchy of 48
first coalition 282, 290
first Russo-Turkish war 80, 283
fiscal issues 13, 202, 217, 222, 226, 227, 244, 245
Fitzherbert (English envoy) 148
fleet 200
Florence 126, 128, 129
Fontainebleau 132
Fonvizin, D. I. 79
foreign accounts 245
foreign affairs 168
foreign debt 225, 226, 322
foreign diplomats 232–3
foreign influence 322
foreign lenders 245
foreign governments 71
foreign luxuries 144
foreign policy (Russia) 8, 13, 111–3, 150, 168, 207–8, 217, 218, 219, 257, 270, 282, 318, 334
foreign policies 182
foreigners 280
foreign war 283
foundling home 156, 248
France 10, 19, 59, 150, 207, 258, 260, 263, 269, 282, 283, 284, 287, 295, 296, 297, 299, 311, 312, 313, 314, 316, 334
in diplomatic realignment (1756) 35
and Paul's European tour (1781–2) 115, 133, 144
Paul's reaction to revolution in 180–2
Paul's new approach to 285–6
expansion of 289–90
in allied strategy (1799) 300–1
and assault on Holland 309
in Paul's diplomatic thinking 318
Frances II German emperor 295, 297, 298, 305, 311
see also Franz archduke of Austria
Franche Comté 301
Franco-Russian campaign 316
Franz archduke of Austria 113, 122, 129, 131, 140
see also Frances II
Frederic-Eugene of Württemberg 122, 175

Frederick II (the Great) of Prussia 35, 60, 83, 95, 97, 98, 111, 112, 115–16, 154, 162, 198, 227, 228
Frederick William II of Prussia 110, 286
free convertibility (of Bank scrip) 253, 255
free peasantry 290
French aggression 279, 283, 285, 286, 289, 290, 319
French monarch 319
French monarchy 301, 308
French revolutionaries 285
French revolutionary thinkers 325
freedom 14
freemasons 195–6
freemasonry 278
Fröhlich, Michel (Austrian general) 306
frondeurs 5
frontier (Italian) 285
frugality 225
Fürstenberg, prince von (Austrian special envoy) 306–7

Gabriel, Moscow metropolitan 236
Gagarina, Anna Petrovna 349
  see also Gagarina-Lopukhina, Anna Petrovna; Lopukhina, Anna Petrovna
Gagarin, Pavel Gavrilovich 269–70
The Gallant Mercury 136
gallican 317
garrison (of Paris) 136
garrison (Moscow) 242
garrison schools 231
Gatchina 84, 110, 128, 142, 151, 166, 168, 169, 170, 178, 186, 204, 232, 245, 259
  Orlov invites Rousseau to 152–3
  description of 153, 154
  facilities and occupations 154–6
  political culture under Paul 156–7
  and domainal system 157–8
  and Paul's army 158–60
  Paul as master of 162–3
  and Paul's view of revolution 181–3
  police regulations for 201
  forces arrive in Petersburg 209
  model for social discipline 211–12
  and economy 226
Gatchintsi 159–60, 162, 163, 209, 339

Geneva 132
general staff 227–8
Genoa 308
gentry 235, 240, 245, 247, 248, 249, 250, 252, 254, 255–6
gentry debt 245–9, 251, 253, 255
gentry landholders 157, 238
gentry masters 168
gentry ownership 215
George III of Great Britain 309, 310, 311, 312, 328, 338
German constitution 284
German emperor 258
German empire 285
German (imperial) constitution 287
German (imperial) land 285
German (imperial) princes 139
German theatre (St Petersburg) 340
Germanies 130, 230, 287
Germany 139, 144, 283, 312
Glarus 301
glass factory (at Gatchina) 156
Gobelins (in Paris) 136
God's law (as ruler's guide) 220
Goethe, J. W. von 139
Golovina, Varvara Nikolaevna countess 278
Golovkin, Fedor count 51, 236, 329
Gore-Bogatyr 169
governing council 354
government loan bank (1786) 248
government receipts 255
governor-general (Moscow) 161
governor-general (St Petersburg) 212, 331, 332, 333, 347
grand magistracy of the knights of Malta 175, 278
grand master of the knights of Malta 126, 262, 271, 274, 276, 298, 299, 316, 319
grand mastership of the knights of Malta 269, 278, 317
grand prior of the Russian grand priory of the knights of Malta 262
grain reserves (anti-famine measures) 218, 257
Greek faith 129
Greek project 112 n. 12, 315
Grimm, Frederick Melchior baron de 86, 95, 108, 113, 127, 128, 134, 136, 164

Gross Jägersdorff (battle of) 36
growth (economic) 355
guards 4, 19, 20, 38, 39, 71, 159,
    209–10, 212, 228, 242, 278, 327,
    350, 353
guard posts 156, 210
guberniia 150
    see also Paul I grand duke and
    emperor: reorganization of
    government
Guernsey (isle of) 310
Gunning, Sir Robert (English envoy)
    84–5, 86, 88
Gustave Adolph, crown prince of
    Sweden 44
Gustave III of Sweden 165
Gustave IV of Sweden 186, 346

Hamburg 319
handicrafts (at Gatchina) 156
Hanover 35, 314
Hapsburg partisans 140
Harris, Sir James (English envoy)
    114–15, 144
hat-making (at Gatchina) 156
Heinel, Mlle. (dancer) 136
Helen Pavlovna grand duchess 107,
    236
Helsinki 48
Helvetian republic 290
Heraldry office 224
Henry IV of France 49, 61, 98, 154,
    258
Henry of Prussia prince 92, 95, 96
Herculaneum 127
hereditary monarchy 318
Hermann, I. I. (Russian) general 310
Hesse-Darmstadt 83, 90
Heyking, Karl Heinrich baron von 266,
    267, 331, 332, 343
hierarchical (society) 17
His Imperial Highness' Mobile Military
    Chancellory 227
Hofkriegsrath 295
    see also Aulic council
Hohenlinde 314
Holland 230, 231, 285, 287, 309, 310,
    312, 322
    see also Netherlands, Low Countries
Holstein 21
holy synod 218, 234

Hompesch, Ferdinand baron and grand
    master of the knights of
    Malta 262, 272, 273, 275, 276,
    297, 298
Hope and Company (Amsterdam) 226,
    246, 256
Horse Guards 200, 331, 346
hospital (Gatchina) 154
hospitals (of Paris) 136
honours list 239
housing 156
Hume, David 48
The Hunting Party of Henry IV 136

ideology 16
ideological consciousness 324
ideological questions 319
Ides of March 346
illegal payments (to overseers) 241
immigration 288
imperial control 223
imperial family 213, 222, 231–2, 323,
    332, 349, 355
imperial finances 246
imperial school of law 225
imperium et libertate 354
imported products 247–8
inalienable rights 147
India (British) 316
individual interests (and social disorder)
    215
indolence (and women's rule) 197
incognito (les comtes du Nord) 235
income (landowners') 252
income (state) 245
infantry regulations 228
inflation 216
influenza 77
Ingerburg 155
international politics 271, 277
    see also diplomacy
initiative (individual) 217
innovation 27, 356
inoculation 75–6
Ionian islands 289, 290
inspectorates (military) 227
instruction (*nakaz*) 1788 168
insubordination 182
intelligentsia 14
international exchange 245
interest (rates) 248, 249, 251, 254, 255

intrigue (court) 264
invasion army (Persia) 282–3
l'Isle, Adam Philippe Villiers de (grand master of the knights of Malta d. 1534) 262
Italy 10, 114, 130, 140, 141, 230, 282, 290, 305, 311, 314, 322, 334
   Mariia and Paul disappointed in 124, 128
   and Bonaparte 289
   as issue between Austria and Russia 291–3, 299, 304, 309
   and Suvorov 294, 295
   French expelled from 300
   Russian withdrawal from 301
Iunker school 224–5
   see also school for administrators, imperial school of law
Ivan Antonovich 74
   see also Ivan VI, emperor of Russia
Ivan VI emperor of Russia 20, 21, 24, 38, 71, 187
   see also Ivan Antonovich
Ivan IV (the Terrible) tsar of Russia 3, 278
Izmailovskii guards regiment 39, 200, 209

Jacobin menace 278
Jacobin (orientation) 197, 289, 311
Jacobinism 8, 271, 276, 279, 295
Jacobins 8, 183, 215, 268, 288, 308, 355
Jenkins (art dealer, Rome) 128
Jersey 310
Joseph archduke palatin of Hungary 294, 295
Joseph II of Austria emperor of Germany 115, 121, 127, 129, 131, 133, 140, 144
   and origin of Paul's western tour (1781–2) 113–14
   on Paul and Mariia 118–20, 122–4, 141
Journey from Petersburg to Moscow 196–7
   see also Alexander Radishchev
judicial process 220
judicial review 146
Julius Caesar 49

Kamennyi Ostrov 47, 110, 158
Kamenskii, M. F. colonel, later field marshall 60
Karamzin, Nikolai Mikhailovich 3, 7
Kaunitz, W. A. von count 119, 141
Kazan cathedral 39
Kazan 265
Keep, John L. H. 12–13
Keith, Sir Robert (English envoy) 32–3, 121
Kenney, James J. junior 350
kibitka 4–5
Kiev 165, 222
king of the Two Sicilies 258
kingdom of the Two Sicilies 303
Kliuchevskii, V. O. 10
Klochkov, M. V. 11–12, 14, 15
knightly orders 232, 237–8, 240
knights of Malta 132, 226, 232, 269, 280, 281, 289, 319
   ceremonial entry into Petersburg 258
   previous relations with Russia 259
   and Paul's settlement 260–2
   and Paul's 'election' as grand master 271–5
   transformation under Paul 276–7, 279
   and controversies over 296–9
   and the break with England 313–14
   see also knights of St John of Jerusalem, Malta
knights of St John of Jerusalem 49, 258, 314, 316
   see also knights of Malta
Kobeko, Dmitri Fomich 9
Kochubei, Viktor Pavlovich count 203, 204, 267, 268, 270, 278, 293, 327
Kologrivov, A. S. colonel later general 200
Kolychev, Stepan Alexeevich 304–5, 307, 312, 315
Korsakov, A. M. general 301, 310, 314
   see also Rimskii-Korsakov, A. M.
Kotliubitskii, N. O. major 200
Kosciusko, Thaddeus prince 197
Kotzebue, Augustus von 3–4, 339–40, 351
Krause (Kruze) K. F. dr (physician to Paul) 92
Krasnoe Selo 60
Kremlin (Moscow) 47, 234, 235, 236, 241

Index

Kremlin palace 238–9
Kronstadt 90
Küchelbecker, K. I. (first director of Pavlovsk) 153
Kuchuk Kainardji, treaty of 112
Kurakin, Alexander Borisovich, prince 33, 57, 59, 105, 110, 135, 138, 195, 201, 267
Kurakin, Alexis Borisovich, prince 201, 202, 219, 246, 249, 255, 260, 264, 267, 270, 280
Kurakins 213, 326
Kurakin brothers 239
Kusevich, Austrian general 306
Kushelev, G. G. colonel 200
Kutaisov, Ivan Pavlovich 174, 179, 203, 239, 264–6, 267, 269, 270, 331, 332, 338, 341, 343–4, 348
Kurland 199, 222, 331

labourers 181
Lafermière, François 58, 117, 176, 179
La Harpe, Frédéric Caesar 185, 205
La Harpe, Jean-François 59
Lambert, marquis de 307
land bank 245
landholders 238, 247, 253, 279
landlords (noble) 196, 251
landholding class 245
landed proprietors 255
Landgrafin of Hesse-Darmstadt 83, 84
Landgrave of Hesse-Darmstadt 83
landowners 181, 248–9, 251, 254
Langeron, Alexander Fedorovich (Andrault, comte de) general 332
langues 261, 272, 297
Latvia 222
La Vallette, Jean Parisot (grand master of the knights of Malta d. 1568) 262
La Valletta 259, 261, 271, 272
Lavater, Johann Kaspar 139–40
law 14, 166, 218, 220, 271
law code 219
League of Armed Neutrality (1708) 313
legitimacy 192, 206, 215, 220
legitimate authority 325
legitimate sovereign 220
Leibnitz, G. W. von 44
Leipzig 287
Leoben (peace of) 283, 285, 290

Leopold, archduke of Austria, German emperor 123, 128, 129–32, 141–2, 152, 199, 221
Lestocq, Armand 20, 21
Levant 290
Levesque, Pierre Charles 58
Levshin, Platon, priest and archbishop 46, 61–2, 85, 94, 102, 107, 111, 128, 236
liberal-constitutional principles 220
liberalizing age 322
liberators (conspirators as) 1
Lieven, Charlotte von, countess 2
Ligne, Charles Joseph prince de 138
Lindener, Fedor Ivanovich general 5, 162, 348
liquor monopolies 168
Lithuania 186, 222, 267
Litta family 132
Litta, Giulio count 259, 260, 261, 262, 273, 274, 275, 276, 280
Litta, Lorenzo, papal nuncio, archbishop of Thebes 237, 260, 263, 275
Little Russia 222, 257
Livorno 132
Lharidon de Penguilly, abbé 137
loans 248, 249, 250, 251, 252
loan premiums 255
Lobanov-Rostovskii, Andrei prince 340
local courts 150
local government 156, 221, 222–5, 355
local initiative 17
Locke, John 44
Lohde (castle) 186, 267
Loire chateaux 137
London 287, 311, 312, 313
Lopukhin, I. V. 196
Lopukhin, Pater Vasil'evich count 219, 270
Lopukhina, Anna Petrovna 266–7, 269–70
    see also Gagarina, Anna Petrovna; Lopukhina-Gagarina, Anna Petrovna
Lopukhina-Gagarina, Anna Petrovna 338
    see also Gagarina, Anna Petrovna Lopukhina, Anna Petrovna
Lopukhins 267
Louis XVI king of France 132, 136

Index

Louis XVIII king of France 258, 289, 308, 317
Louis of Hesse-Darmstadt 95
Low Countries 10, 115, 137
  see also Holland; Netherlands
loyalists (to Paul) 324
Lübeck 84
Lunéville 315
Lutheran 186, 223
luxury 212, 247
luxurious (style) 233
Lyons 132

Maasdam 137
Maine 137
Maisonnueve, Joseph Chevalier de 258–9
male primogeniture 167, 237
Malta, grand cross of 258, 262, 272
Malta (island of) 259, 272, 273, 274, 279
  seizure by Napoleon 271, 289
  Nelson refuses to relinquish 313–14
  Napoleon promises it to Paul 316
  see also knights of St John of Jerusalem, knights of Malta
Mamanov, A. M. (favourite of Catherine) 149
manual of arms 211
manufacturing 156, 168, 222
Mantua 130, 282
Marengo (battle of) 311, 314
Marie Antoinette queen of France 132, 133, 135–6
Marie de Medici 49
Mariia Fedorovna grand duchess, empress, dowager empress 48, 104, 150, 151, 157–8, 170, 172, 181, 190, 196, 203, 236, 237, 238, 241, 244, 257, 258, 259, 327, 340, 342, 343, 351
  and Paul's death 2–3
  importance for Russian history 95–6
  children with Paul 107–8
  and the young court's style 110–11
  and Joseph II 113–14, 118, 123–4
  crisis over western trip 115–16
  journals and trip correspondence 117–18
  in Vienna 119–22, 141
  in Venice 124, 125
  and Rome 126, 127
  and archduke Leopold 129, 131, 141, 142
  in Paris 132, 133, 134, 135, 136, 137
  at home in Montbeillard 139, 140
  return to St Petersburg 143, 144
  and life as grand duchess 148–9
  sees Gatchina as rival to Pavlovsk 153
  and Arkharov's fall 162
  and Paul's Crimean service 163–5
  and Paul's instruction on succession 166, 167
  and Nelidova 175, 176, 177, 178, 179–80
  approached by Catherine on succession 185
  and news of Catherine's stroke 188
  and the empress' party 201–2
  at the coronation 236, 237, 238, 241–2
  and the Bank of Assistance 245–6, 264
  supports émigrés 263
  and Paul's suspicions 265, 266, 326
  and rise of Lopukhins 267–9, 271
  and Paul's emotional instability 180, 329, 337
  see also Sophia Dorothea of Württemberg
Mariia Pavlovna grand duchess 107
'Marriage of Figaro' 133
masculine military principles 197
Masséna, André general and marshal of France 301
master of requests 224
materialism (new age values) 16
mercantile development 150
merchant community 254
merchants 155, 181, 250, 253, 256, 279
Mediterranean 10, 230, 289, 290, 300, 311
Melissino, Pierre Ivanovich general 200
Menshikov, Alexander Danilovich prince 19, 33
Mercy d'Argentau (Austrian diplomat) 133
Metternich (-Winneburg), Clemens Wenzel Lothar prince (Austrian statesman) 11, 320

Michael (archangel) 345
Michael palace 1, 270, 323, 324, 335, 340, 345, 346, 351
Michael Pavlovich grand duke 2, 107, 265
middle class 167
middle east 320
midwife 92
Mikhailovskii-Danilevskii, A. I. general 10
Milan 132, 259
militarism 17
military 168, 244, 279
military administration 227, 230, 355
military affairs 204, 217, 219, 222
military appointments 200
military code 211
military colonies 109
military discipline 271
military heritage 278
military intervention 285, 286
military orphanage 231
military performance 231
military reform 227–31, 233
military service 225
militarized (bureaucracy) 16, 17
Miliutin, D. M. colonel, count 10–11
Miloradovich, M. A. general 306
mining 168, 222
ministerial authority 221
ministerial government 146, 221
ministers 221
ministries 355
ministry for apanage 232
ministry of commerce 221
minorities (rights of) 222–3
Minsk 222
Minto, Gilbert Elliot first earl of 312
Mirovich, A. Ia. 74
Mitchell, Vice-Admiral Sir Andrew 310
Mittau 258, 289
mobilization (and change) 356
modern society 14, 250
modern world 277
modernity 271, 357
modernizing 14
modernizing world 356
Mogilev, archbishop of 127
Molière (Jean Baptiste Poquelin) 15
monarch 181, 182, 233, 325
monarchical activists 278

monarchical legitimacy 316
monarchies 311
monarchists 282
monarchy 14, 285, 315
Montbeillard 114, 139, 140, 176
Monetnaia kontora 248
monetary policy 248
money lenders 248
Le Moniteur universel 177
moral consciousness 277
moral disorder 182
moral failure 215
moral obligation (to overthrow a tyrant) 325
morality 142, 233
Morane, Pierre 9
Moreau, (French physician) 92
Morkov, Arkadii Ivanovich count 131, 186, 198–9
mortgage 251
mortgage schedule 255
Moscow 47, 74, 91, 113, 116, 197, 218, 221, 265, 288
  bubonic plague in 65, 66, 76, 77
  Paul popular in 83, 115, 235, 242–3, 266
  and offends nobility of 88
  Novikov press site in 195
  and Paul's coronation 233, 234
Montesquieu, Charles Louis de Secondat baron de la Brède et de 15, 17, 48, 64
Mount Vesuvius 127
Munich 141, 297
municipal authority 150, 221
Münnich (Minikh), Burkhard Khristofer von, general, count 40
Mussin-Pushkin, Valentine Platonovich general, field marshal 168, 330
Muttenthale 301

Naples 122, 126, 127, 128, 290, 292, 299, 308, 319
Napoleonic era 17
Naryshkin, Lev Alexandrovich 24, 26
Nathalia Alexievna grand duchess 79, 85, 86, 88, 89, 91–2, 99, 100, 103, 169, 203
  see also Wilhelmina of Hesse-Darmstadt
naval cadets 259

naval forces 259
navy 216
national uprising 324
Nassau-Siegen, Karl Heinrich Otto prince of 185
Neapolitan Bourbons 258
Necker, Jacques 136
Nelidov, Arkadii Ivanovich 267
Nelidova, Catherine Ivanovna 184, 200, 205, 236, 270, 281, 327, 329, 337–8
   affair with Paul 169–74
   and Mariia 174–6, 177, 178, 179–80
   Panin refuses to support 176–7
   and empress'party 201–2, 263–4, 265, 266, 267
   and the order of St George 237–8
   and coronation benifices 239
   influence on Paul ends 268–9
Neledinskii (-Meletskii), Iurii Alexandrovich 267
Nelson, Vice Admiral Horatio, viscount 308, 313, 314
Nepliuev, I. I. 33
Nerzhinsk 196
Netherlands 59, 137, 290, 291, 301, 303, 309
   see also Holland; Low Countries
neutral rights 272, 308, 313, 334
neutralist 279
neutralist policy 263
neutrality 282
Nevskii monastery 41, 193
new (liberal) political order 324, 349
New Russia 112
New-Skovoritska 153
Nice 285
Nicholas I, grand duke and emperor 16, 107, 167, 185, 200, 217, 236, 280, 324, 354, 355, 356
Nicolay, H. L. baron 58, 202, 246
Nile 300
'Ninette at Court' 136
nobility 233, 235, 242, 325
   Paul's animus toward 4, 5, 332
   and vision of 142
   in Catherine's reforms 150
   as governing caste 167
   and need for discipline 211, 225
   and rights under Paul 223, 224
   and peasant grants 241
   assistance bank for 245, 246, 247, 248, 250, 252, 254
   and the knights of Malta 276, 277
nobiliary privilege 271
noble 252
noble assemblies 223, 248
nobles 5, 223–4, 240, 248, 278
nobles' rights 4, 215, 220, 350
Nolcken, count (Swedish envoy) 20
Novgorod 193
Novi (battle of) 300
Novikov, N. I. 79, 195–6
Normandy 137
North Sea 10
northern alliance 168, 311, 313
northern system 111, 287, 316, 319
Novosil'tsev, Nikolai Nikolaevich 203, 330

oath of allegiance 167, 192, 214–15, 353
oberhofmeister (to Paul) 34, 44
Oberkirch, Henrietta Louise baroness 117, 132, 136, 137–9
Oberkirch memoirs 139
oberprocurator for the holy synod 223
obligation (moral) 233
obligatory service 167
Obolianinov, P. Kh. procuror-general and general 200, 219
obrok 240, 241, 250, 251, 252
   see also quit rent
obstetrical forceps 92
Odescalchi, Mgr. Antoine-Marie (papal secretary of state and nuncio to Florence) 274
officers 4, 181, 212, 231, 244, 279, 288, 323, 349, 350
officials 216
O'Hara, Anthony colonel 272–3
old regime 16
Old-Skovoritska 153
Olga Pavlovna grand duchess 107
open societies 355
operational code (Bank of Assistance) 255
oprichnina 278
opposition (to Paul) 6, 203, 243, 245, 325
Orange, prince of 294

Oranienbaum 39
order (in society) 14, 16, 168, 216, 220, 231, 318
Order of the Holy Ghost 134
Order of St Alexander Nevskii 237
Order of St Andrew 237
Order of St Anne 237
Order of St Catherine 237
Order of St George 237, 238
Order of St Vladimir 237, 238
Orenburg events 66–7
Orleans, duke of 133
Orlov (brothers) 38, 40
Orlov (faction) 72
Orlov, Alexis Grigorevich count 39, 41, 190, 192, 194
Orlov, Grigorii Grigorevich prince 24, 30, 40, 56, 73, 77, 78, 84, 86–7, 104, 116, 152
Orlovs 327, 354
orthodox 186
orthodoxy 121
Osten-Sacken, Baron Karl Ivanovich 57, 94, 105, 115, 132, 148, 179, 180
Ostermann, Ivan Andreevich count 198, 207, 239
Ottoman empire 112, 130, 208, 290, 315, 319
  see also the Porte; Turkey
Ottoman Turks 258
  see also Turks
Our Lady of Kazan (cathedral) 234
  see Kazan Cathedral
overseers 168, 241

pacifism 288, 308
pacifist 279
Paestum 127
Pahlen, Peter von der count, general 218, 270, 271, 338, 342, 343, 349, 350, 354
  leads *coup* against Paul 1, 323, 324, 334–5, 340–1, 351
  suffers Mariia's vengeance 2
  Paul suspicious 5
  dismissal and return 199, 331–2
  governor-general of St Petersburg 262
  hatred for Paul 332
  intermediary for Panin with Alexander 333
  and return of the internal exiles 341
  and confrontations with Paul 346–8
palace revolution 323, 334
Palermo 292
Panin, Ivan Vasil'evich 33
Panin, Nikita Ivanovich count 56, 70, 71, 72, 73–4, 83, 84, 89, 104, 105, 106, 114, 143, 144, 180, 189, 200, 218
  on Paul's legitimacy 27
  chosen as Paul's governor 33–4
  and regency for Paul (1762) 38
  educational programme 44–8, 57–60
  and Paul's health 53–4
  and Paul's 'Reflections...' 62–5
  'conspiracy' against Catherine 79
  and the Saldern affair 81, 82
  decline and dismissal 87–8
  his 'northern system' and Prussian affiliation 111, 112
  against European trip (1781) 115–16
  constitutional project 145–7
  death 148
  and Paul's 'instruction' 166, 167
  and rule of law 220
Panin, Nikita Petrovich count 2, 176–7, 271, 286, 315, 324, 327, 328, 331, 333–4, 335, 338, 340, 354
Panin, Peter Ivanovich, general, count 79, 109, 145
Panin party 12, 72, 86, 106, 114
Pantheon (Paris) 126, 127
papacy 317
papal bulls 223
papal communications 223
papal nuncio 260, 273, 274
  see also Litta, Lorenzo
papal states 115
paper money 216, 225, 226, 245, 253, 254, 255
  see also assignats
parade ground 228, 234
Paris 115, 132–6, 287, 289, 290, 300
Parker, Admiral Sir Hyde 314
parlement 136
parliamentary monarchy (English) 143

Index

Passek, Peter Bogdanovich captain later governor-general of White Russia 39, 193, 194, 327
passport system (internal) 156, 210
paternalism 355
Paul I grand duke and emperor:
  his murder 1, 351–3
  reactions to his death 3, 6, 13, 324, 325, 335–6, 346, 350
  temperament 3, 8, 9, 11, 15, 31–3, 51–5, 73, 103–6, 182, 232–3, 265, 322, 323, 330, 337–8, 344–5
  historiography on 6–15
  mental condition 7–8, 14, 328–30, 336–8
  health 9, 51, 53–5, 74–5, 76, 77, 175–6
  as a romantic 10
  as the people's defender 10, 168
  and the nobility, *see* nobility
  and reunification of eastern and western churches 10, 317
  as legislator 10, 12, 224
  as diplomat 10, 318–21
  opposition to aggression 10, 11, 168, 258, 318
  and Austria 10–11, 114–15, 122, 127, 129, 130–1, 140, 207, 282, 283–4, 291–3, 296–9, 300–8, 312; *see also* Austria, second coalition
  political philosophy 11–12, 14–15, 60–8, 69, 166–8, 220, 222–3, 271, 322
  and traditional values 17, 238, 271, 322
  and Catherine II 12, 17–18, 69–72, 77–80, 89, 107, 108–9, 130, 135–6, 150–1, 163–4, 165, 169, 178–9, 180, 184, 185–6, 193–5; *see also* Catherine II grand duchess and empress of Russia
  moral and philosophical environment 12, 28, 30, 44–60; *see also* Panin, Nikita Ivanovich count
  bureaucracy (militarized) 13
  place in Russian history 14, 16–17, 322, 355–7
  birth 19, 27–8, 29
  paternity 24–27
  and Peter the Great 27, 49, 98, 137–9; *see also* Peter I (the Great) emperor of Russia
  as heir (to Russian crown) 27–8, 39, 72
  and Empress Elizabeth 37
  and Catherine's *coup d'état* (1762) 39, 42–3, 73, 193–5
  and Pugachev 42, 80
  physical appearance 50–1
  sexual experience 55–7
  military interests 59–60, 109–10, 152, 158–60, 227–31
  and guards (after 1762) 71
  majority (age of) 72, 82–3
  public perceptions of 72, 88–9, 184, 189–90, 232–3, 242–3, 279–81
  inoculation 75–6
  and Saldern affair; *see* Saldern affair, Saldern, Casper von
  first marriage 83–95; *see also* Nathalia Alexievna
  and Potemkin 87, 107, 344; *see also* Potemkin, Grigorii Alexandrovich general, count, prince
  and Sophia Dorothea of Württemberg 95–6, 98, 99–103; *se also* Mariia Fedorovna grand duchess, empress, dowager empress
  and Berlin visit (1776) 96–8
  second marriage 104
  and Catherine's court 105–7, 109, 110, 111, 148, 149, 151, 152, 163–5, 180, 186–91; *see also* Catherine II grand duchess and empress
  on Alexander's birth 107–8
  and his European tour 112–142
  and Panin's constitutional project 145; *see also* Panin, Nikita Ivanovich count
  at Gatchina, *see* Gatchina
  compared with Catherine 157
  financial problems (as grand duke) 157–8
  and Nelidova 169–80; *see also* Nelidova, Catherine Ivanovna, Mariia Fedorovna grand duchess, empress, dowager empress
  on revolutions *see* revolution
  and *émigrés*, see *émigrés*
  in the succession, *see* succession

accession 192, 206, 243
  corrects 'injustices' 193–7
  and creates a new order 198–206,
    208–14
  and his foreign policy 207–208,
    282–321; see also second coalition,
    foreign policy (Russia)
  reorganization of government 206,
    216–9, 221–4, 243, 244–5, 252,
    280–1, 288, 322, 355
  minority rights and religious tolera-
    tion 222–3
  governing style 226–7, 244, 245,
    322
  military reforms 227–31
  coronation 233–243
  and Bank of Assistance for the
    Nobility, see Bank of Assistance for
    the Nobility
  economic initiatives 257
  and the knights of Malta, see knights
    of Malta, knights of St John of
    Jerusalem
  and the empress' party see empress'
    party (Mariia Fedorovna)
  conspiracy against 322–50; see also
    Alexander I grand duke and
    emperor, Bennigsen, Leo general,
    conspiracies, Kutaisov, Ivan
    Palvovich count, Mariia Fedorovna
    grand duchess, empress, dowager
    empress, Pahlen, Peter von der
    general and count, Panin, Nikita
    Petrovich count
  and Michael palace 345, 346
Pavlovsk 110, 148, 153, 155, 158, 170,
  265, 267, 344
pawnbrokers 248
peace 168, 215, 318
peasant uprisings 214–5, 244, 280, 288
  see also Pugachevshchina
peasants 155, 167, 168, 181, 196, 238,
  239–41, 247, 252, 257
peculation 217
permissiveness 211
Persia 150, 208, 283
Peter I (the Great) emperor of Russia
  19, 20, 154, 220, 327, 348
  in Paul's studies 49, 98
  as a model for Paul 62
  Paul's 'encounter' with his ghost
    137–9, 344
  and Paul's reforms 233, 237
  contrasted with Paul 356
Peter II emperor of Russia 75
Peter III (Charles Peter Ulrich of
  Holstein Gottorp, Peter Fedorovich)
  grand duke and emperor of
  Russia 13, 43, 44, 57, 74, 89, 145,
  167, 187, 190, 196, 197, 324
  heir and husband 20–2, 28
  and Paul's paternity 22–6
  and Catherine's pregnancies 30
  Pro-Prussian stance angers Elizabeth
    35
  and 1758 crisis 36
  removal as heir considered 37, 73
  accession and rift with Catherine
    37–8
  legislative programme and foreign
    policy 38–9
  Catherine's *coup* against 39–41
  'good tsar Peter' 42
  and Pugachev's revolt 80
  double funeral honours with
    Catherine 193–5
  compared with Paul 197–8, 244–5,
    347
  coup against Paul similar to
    1762 324
Peterburgskyia vedemosti 227
Peterhof 40
Peter–Paul fortress 193
Petrovskii palace 234, 235
Petrine heritage 19
Philip II of Spain 217
phthisis (consumption) 91
Piedmont 301, 305
Pius VI (pope) 126, 274, 275, 289
Pius VII (pope) 275, 316
plague (bubonic) 66, 76, 77
Pleshcheev, Sergei Ivanovich 179, 195,
  200, 267
Podolia 222
Poland 111, 115, 118, 130, 150, 197,
  246, 256, 259, 303
police 168, 196, 210, 212, 213, 354,
  355
police regulations 150
police spies 331
Polish priory (of knights of Malta) 226,
  258, 260, 261, 262, 289

political clubs 319
political economy 245
political reforms (review) 356
political stability 279
Pompeii 127
Poniatowski, Stanislaus, later Stanislaus Augustus kind of Poland 24, 26, 35, 110, 118, 197, 237
pope 127, 223, 274, 275, 276, 292, 298, 316, 317
  see also Pius VI; Pius VII
popular uprisings 308
  see also peasant uprisings; Pugachevshchina
porcelain 156
Poroshin, Simon Andreevich 45–6, 47, 48, 51–2, 55, 56
the Porte 283, 290
  see also Ottoman empire; Turkey
Potemkin, Grigorii Alexandrovich general, count, prince 72, 88, 112, 116, 131, 149, 163, 175, 229
  as Paul's great rival 87, 107, 344
  and Rostopchin 161
  and Bezborodko 199
'Potemkin's army' 237
Potocky, Ignaz 197
Potsdam 206
praetorian guard 278
Preobrazhenskii regiment 71, 73, 79–80, 209, 323, 349, 351
princes' (Italian and German) rights 315, 317
prescriptive rights 217
prices 279
priesthood 278
prikaz (military appointments) 200, 228
priorities (of knights of Malta) 272, 297
prisons (of Paris) 136
privileged classes 279, 280
procuror-general 201, 217, 218, 219, 246, 270
Protector of the knights of Malta 262, 276, 278
Provence, count of 133
proviant 227
provincial assembly 252, 255
provincial government (reorganization) 221, 248

provisioning crisis 296
Prussia 20, 122, 140, 141, 150, 180, 183, 303, 306, 319, 327, 334
  and the diplomatic revolution (1756) 35
  and Paul's first marriage 83–4
  compared with Russia 97
  as Russia's future 98
  and the Panin system 111–12
  Paul committed to 112, 121, 130
  limits to Paul's commitment to 198
  as channel to France 284, 286
  and the Repnin mission 284–5
  Paul's efforts to ally with (1796–7) 286–7
  holds aloof from coalition 290
  as Bonaparte's channel to Paul 311
  and Paul's new northern system 311–12, 313
  and war against England 314
Prussian court 198
Prussian drill 209, 214
Prussian ideals 142
Prussian manual of arms 17, 228
Prussian Silesia 141
prussianism 198, 228
prussianization (of army) 232
public order 142
Pudosta 153
Pufendorff 15
Pugachev, Emelion 42, 65, 214, 215
Pugachevshchina (Pugachev's revolt) 65–7, 80, 81
punishment code 231

quarrying (at Gatchina) 153
quit rent 240
  see also obrok

radical ideas 319
Radishchev, Alexander Nikolaevich 196
Ragsdale, Hugh 13, 14
Ransel, David 12, 145
'Rape of the Sabine Women' 154
rapprochement with France 316
Rastadt (congress) 287, 289, 291
rationalization (of government) 355
rationalizing mechanisms 147
Razumovskii, Alexis Grigorovich count, prince 20, 59, 73

Razumovskii, Andrei Kirilovich prince, ambassador to Vienna 81, 83, 84, 88, 89–91, 93, 102, 105, 127, 180, 284, 294, 295, 303, 304, 305
Rechtsstaat 64
recruitment 207, 208, 258, 282
reformer (Paul as) 14
regency 7, 333
regent 20, 167
Rehbinder, Maximilian Vladimirovich general 292, 300
Reiffenstein (German painter, Rome) 128
relief force (for Austria) 207
rent(s) 251, 255
repayment schedule (Bank of Assistance) 252
Repnin, N. V. prince 114, 195, 200, 284, 285
republic (of France) 260, 282, 285
republican government 301, 318
republicanism 319
republican regime 284
republicans 263
republican system 308
resignations (officers') 279, 326
resistance (to Paul's reforms) 213
Reuchlin, baron (Bavarian envoy) 297
reunification of eastern and western churches 317
Reval 84
revenues (state) 168
revisionist(s) (on Paul I) 11, 12–14, 15
revolution:
 of 1762 147, 192–3
 in France (1789) 150, 175, 180
 palace (reduce danger of) 166
 Paul's views of 181–2
 in Radishchev 196
 danger of in Russia 206, 214–16, 288
 and Paul's position on in France 285
 and 1801 *coup* as 324, 325
 Paul as cause for 326
 and Paul's overthrow to prevent 332
revolutionary government 260, 319
revolutionary ideas (spread of) 180
revolutionary ideology 319
revolutionary influence 282
revolutionary institutions 263
revolutionary principles 291

revolutionary republic (1825) 324
revolt 324
Rhine 10, 204, 285, 300, 301, 309
Rhine principalities 115
Ribas, Joseph admiral 331, 334
Richmond-on-Thames 330
Riga 331
right of rebellion 147
rights 150
Rimskii-Korsakov, A. M. general 300
 see also Korsakov, A. M. general
Rinaldi, (architect) 154
riots 215
Ripon, vice admiral (British) 310
ritual (and Paul) 235
Robertson, William (historian) 48
Robespierre, Maximilien 17
Rohan, Emmanuel de grand master of the knights of Malta (1775–97) 263
Rome 122, 126, 127, 128, 261, 289, 292, 306, 317
Roman Catholic Church 126, 317
Roman Catholic subjects (Russia) 260, 261
Roman catholicism 317
Roman republic 289
Romans (tyrannicides) 5, 325
Ropsha 40, 193
Rosenberg, Ursinius (Orsini) et, countess 124–5
Rosenberg, Andrei Grigorevich general (Russian) 296
Rostopchin, Fedor Vasil'evich count 218, 278, 307, 327, 338, 343
 character and career 161–2
 on Nelidova 173, 177
 on Paul 183
 with Paul on Catherine's last day 189, 190
 and Orlov's oath 192
 in Paul's government 200, 201, 270–1
 and the empress' party 203, 264
 and the pace of reform 207
 memo on foreign policy 315
 challenged by Panin 334
 and devotion to Paul 339
Rousseau, Jean Jacques 15, 152–3
ruble 225, 245
rule of law 220, 237

ruler 17, 181, 218, 325
ruler's authority 221
rules (regulations) 211, 354
ruling class(es) 142, 356
Rurik 350
Russia 10, 17, 19, 122, 142, 152, 245,
    260, 265, 271, 272, 278, 280, 281,
    303, 312, 315, 317, 322, 324, 328,
    334, 337
  as a developing society 14
  absolutism and the nineteenth century
    in 16, 355
  superior features of (in Kurakin cor-
    respondence) 59
  and Panin's 'northern system'
    111–12
  and *rapprochement* with Austria 113
  as asylum for Pius VI 126
  as a state too large to expand 130
  popularity of in Paris (1782) 133
  Panin's reform project for 145
  and importance of succession for 151
  Gatchina as a model for 157–8
  attacked by Sweden (1788) 165
  Paul's political prescriptions for 168
  and revolutionary subversion in 181
  and the revolutionary threat to 182,
    205–6, 215, 287–8, 319
  émigrés promote Alexander to
    save 185
  Radishchev on corruption in 196
  Poles in freed 197
  Prussia as a model for 198
  Alexander's hopes for on Paul's
    accession 204–5
  and tsar's authority in 217
  and governing in 220–1
  and centralization of government in
    222
  Paul and governing machinery in 224
  debt in (foreign and domestic) 225–6
  prussianized forces of 230
  Paul and the interests of 232–3, 283,
    292
  hereditary succession in 237
  and the Woot mission to 246
  increase of private debts in 253
  as field for exploitation 256
  and *émigrés* invited to 258
  and Malta 259
  as a European monarchy 261

émigré influence in 263
and the Vatican (over Paul's election
  as grand master) 275
as bastion against Jacobinism 276–7
and knights as instrument for reform
  of 278–9
and protecting Austria 284
seeking alliance with Prussia 286–7
as haven for refugees from revolution
  289
and reactions to French
  expansion 290
terms of support for Austria 293
deteriorating relations of with
  Austria 296–9
In Ancona crisis 306–7
and England 308–12, 316
and beginning *rapprochement* with
  France 314
and foreign policy of under Paul
  320–1
danger to from Paul 325
Paul as tyrant over 335–6
Paul's importance for 356–7
Russian fleet 259
Russian grand priory of the knights of
  Malta 261, 262, 272, 273, 274,
  275, 284, 320
Russian Orthodox Church 262
Russian Orthodox Priory 276
Russian prisoners of war 314, 315
Russo-papal relations 237
Russo-Prussian agreement 286
Russo-Turkish alliance 304
Russo-Turkish fleet 306
Russo-Turkish treaty (1799) 290

Sablukov, Nikolai Alexandrovich
  general 159, 209, 324, 338–9,
  343, 346, 348–9
sacred council (of knights of
  Malta) 262, 276
St Étienne (arms works) 132
St Gottard 301
St Julien, count (Austrian diplomat)
  299
St Peter's Basilica 126, 128
St Petersburg 33, 39, 294, 295,
  298
  and Paul's death 1–2, 354
  Paul's birth in 19

and conditions for health in 54
Razumovskii returns to 89
court returns to (for Nathalia's lying-
    in) 91
Joseph II invited to 113
Paul's supporters in (and correspond-
    ence with Kurakin) 135
rumours in on Paul and Mariia's
    return 144
place in Panin reform plan 146
Swedish threat to (1788) 165
Paul stays away from 186
and Paul's return to (on Catherine's
    stroke) 189
Radishchev permitted to return to
    196
Arkharov governor-general for 201
changed appearance of in Paul's reign
    208
new order in 210
governor-general of (in state council)
    218
spending on court in 226
ceremonial entrance of knights of
    Malta into 258, 262
Polish grand priory established in
    261, 289
different views of Paul in Moscow and
    266
reactions of knights in to fall of
    Malta 272
offered as new capital for knights of
    Malta 273–4
as congress site 303
Cobenzl isolated in and recalled from
    307
Bonaparte seeks contact with 311
English trading factory closed in 313
English fleet to attack 314
Pahlen as governor-general of 331
Michael palace as Paul's strong-point
    in 345
and visit of Gustave IV 346
Arakcheev and Lindener recalled to
    348
Saldern, Casper von 81, 82, 180
Saldern affair 81–3, 105
salons (of Paris) 136
salt 257
Saltykov, Nikolai Ivanovich count,
    general, marshal 72, 88, 145, 148,
    164, 200, 227, 267
Saltykov, Sergei Vasil'evich 24–6, 27,
    29, 56
Samborskii, Andrei Afanas'evich
    114–15, 155
Sardinia 303, 319, 329–30
Sardinian monarchy 302
Saul, Norman E. 13
savings 225
Savoy 285
Scandinavian monarchies 111
scepticism 16
Schlüsselburg fortress 71, 74, 195
Schönbrunn (Vienna) 120
school for administrators 224–5
    see also Iunker school
'science of physiognomy' 139–40
scrip (Bank) 249, 253, 254, 255
second coalition 10, 130, 258, 287,
    290, 291, 293, 299, 323, 328
second Russo-Turkish war 150, 198
les Secondats (Paul and Mariia) 113,
    164
secret committee (1801) 203, 354
security 14, 168, 181, 325
Ségur, Louis Philippe count 107, 151
self-indulgence (social threat) 182, 197
self-government (religious) 223
Semenovskii guards 39, 200, 209, 323,
    325, 343, 349, 351
senate 146–7, 201, 218–20, 224, 334
senators 219, 350
serfdom 196, 356
serfs 239, 240, 241, 247, 250, 253
Serra Capriola, Antoine Maresca-
    Donnorso duke (Neapolitan envoy)
    317
Seven Towers 164
service (obligatory) 233
serving officials 222
Shchernitsa (on Gatchina estate) 153
Sheremeteva, Anna Petrovna countess
    75
Shil'der, Nikolai Karlovich general 6–7
Shuvalov, Alexander Ivanovich 24, 36
Shuvalov, Ivan Ivanovich count 27, 36
Shuvalov, Ivan Ivanovich general (under
    Paul) 200
Shumigorskii, E. S. 7–8
Siberia 339
Sievers, Jakob Johann count 202

Skall (Austrian general) 306
Skariatin, Ia. F. 353
Skavronskii, Martin Karlovich count 32
smallpox 75–6
Smol'nyi institute 56, 170, 173, 177, 179, 202, 236, 267
social responsibility 216
social revolution 324
social value 355
society 197, 211, 212, 217
soldiers 4, 211, 235, 288
Solms, Viktor Frederick count (Prussian envoy) 84
Sophia (place) 189
Sophia Augusta Frederika of Anhalt-Zerbst 21
  see also Catherine II
Sophia Dorothea of Württemberg 83, 95–6, 98, 99–104
  see also Mariia Fedorovna grand duchess, empress, dowager empress
sovereign 220, 278
Spa 137
Spain 296, 305, 319
Spanish court 299
spies 217
Spiridov, admiral (Russian) 89
spontoon 5, 212
Sprengtporten, Georg-Magnus Russian general (emissary to Napoleon) 315
stability (as social value) 16, 182, 355
Stadholder 285
Stählin, Jakob von 22 n. 2, 44
state administration 17, 182, 244, 323
state council 146, 147, 166, 218, 220
state peasants 215, 240, 241
state's interests 168
state's power 211, 355
statutes 220
Stedingk, Curt von count 151, 194, 256, 275
Steinwehr, baron (Prussian officer in Russia) 162
Storch, Heinrich Friedrich 154
Strasburg 89
Stroganov, Paul Alexandrovich count 203
Stuttgart 140
subsidy 293, 317

subsistence 247
subversive doctrines 182, 319
subversion 277, 322, 355
succession 34, 231, 326, 355
  Peter's rule on 19, 220
  need for heir to stabilize 22
  Paul to replace grand duke Peter in 36, 37
  Paul to replace grand duke Peter in 36, 37
  Peter III to divorce and disinherit Paul 37
  Ivan VI as Peter's heir in 38
  and Paul's claims against Catherine 72–3
  and Saldern affair 81
  and Catherine's dissatisfaction with Paul 107, 143
  and Panin's reform plan 146, 147
  Paul and Ségur discuss 151–2
  in Paul's 'instruction' (1788) 166–7
  and Mariia's fears about 179–80
  émigrés to exclude Paul from 183
  Catherine to remove Paul from 184–6
  Paul allegedly destroys Catherine's decree on 190
  Paul's new law on 237
Suite of His Imperial Highness concerning the Affairs of the Quartermaster 228
Sully 154
Summer palace 39, 47, 345
sumptuary laws 211–2
surgeon 92
Sutton family 76
Suvorov, Alexander Vasil'evich prince, general, field marshal 230, 294, 295–6, 300, 301–3, 304, 305, 311, 312, 322
Svechin, Nikolai Sergeevich general 333, 340
Sweden 20, 34, 186, 259, 311, 312, 313, 318, 319, 334
Swedish politics 111
Swiss Alps 139
Switzerland 10, 185, 230, 290, 300, 301, 304, 311, 312, 322

Tacitus 15
tariffs 218, 257

tariff increases 226
tax 223, 254, 255
tax collection 216
tax increases 226
taxation 223
taxes 218, 245, 279
Talyzin, Fedor Ivanovich colonel (1801) 349
Tatarinov, I. M. 353
Teplov, G. N. 58
Teschen 141
Tessin Carl Gustav count 44
Texel 309
textiles 156
Thebes, archbishop of, see Litta, Lorenzo papal nuncio
Théâtre-français 136
thrift 245, 248
Thugut, Franz de Paula baron Austrian chancellor 284, 291–2, 293, 294, 295, 299, 300, 301, 302–3, 304, 305, 306, 312
Tiberius 185
totalitarian 16
Toulon 289
treasury 214, 225, 245, 255, 277
treasury income 255
Trieste 298
troops 285
Troppau 118
Troshchinskii, Dmitri Prokof'evich 206, 325, 349
Trubetskoi, N. N. prince 196
tsar 131, 157, 271, 306, 307, 313, 326, 327, 333, 349
  Leopold's view of Paul as future 129–30
  role in choosing high court officials 146
  a new model army once Paul becomes 159
  Prussian in style not politics (Paul) 198
  first parade appearance (Paul) 209
  required salute for 213
  and 'tyrannical inconsequence' 214
  and peasants 215
  and centralization of governing functions 217
  office requires magnificence 226
  ritual important for office of 233
  as head of Russian church 234
  and ceremonies before coronation 236
  rationalizes granting state peasants 240
  bond between gentry and 241
  coronation banquet a triumph for 243
  works with Woot 246
  knights' reward 262
  and infatuation with knights 278
  Paul after two years as 279
  intention to seek full alliance partnership 293
  Bavaria chooses to placate 297
  Bohemian priory and visit to 299
  and fighting at Zürich 305
  views on English treatment of Russian troops 310
  success of campaign for recognition of election 316
  authority over ecclesiastical matters 317
  justification for overthrow of a 325
  Pahlen and the 332, 347
  aroused against his (former) allies 334
  loyal servants of 339
  and arrest of imperial family 342
  and confrontation with conspirators 352
  and new retains aspects of the deceased 355
  see also Paul I grand duke and emperor
Tsarskoe Selo 47, 84, 153, 155
Turgenev, A. M. 196
Turin 132, 302
Turkey 283, 334
  see also Ottoman empire; the Porte
Turkish interests 289
Turks 130, 164, 165
Tuscany 128, 129
Tver gate 235
tyrant 3, 6, 13, 324, 325, 335, 346, 350
  see also Paul I grand duke and emperor
tyrannicides 1, 336
typhus 76

Ukraine 112, 239
uniforms 229–30

Ushakov, Fedor Fedorovich admiral 307
usury laws 250
usurers 155, 247, 250
utopian (Paul) 16

valuation (of properties) 251
value (of land) 250
Varela, peace of 151
Vasil'chikov, A. S. 77, 86–7
Vasiliev, A. I. 226, 246
Vatican 126, 275, 317
Velikii, Simon 57 n. 30
Venetian republic 144, 289
Venice 124–6, 140
Verigina, Nathalia Fedorovna, Mlle. 179
Versailles 134
Vertot, l'abbé 259
Viazzoli, Austrian consul-general 256–7, 335–6
vice-chancellor 201, 218, 267, 268, 270, 315, 327
Violier, Gabriel-François 176
Vienna 283, 286, 287, 290, 303, 304, 312
  Joseph II suggests visit to 114
  Paul and Mariia in 120, 121–2
  and Paul's knowledge of court in 131
  Paul and Mariia return to 140–1
  lack of influence on Paul 142
  rejected as channel to Directory 284
  reluctant for peace (1797) 291
  rejects Naples' plea for assistance 292
  advantage over Paul in alliance 293
  suggests Suvorov as commander 294
  and issue of Baron Hompesch 297–9
  difficulties with Suvorov 301–2
  Paul protests to 304
  breakdown of relations with Russia 305–7
  see also Austria
vocational training 156
Voltaire, François Marie Arouet de 48, 64, 348
Volynia 222
Vorontsov, Alexander Romanovich count 131, 196
Vorontsov, M. L. chancellor 34
Voronstov, Simon Romanovich count 131, 256, 310, 328, 330
Vorontsova, Elizabeth Romanovna 23, 35, 37, 40
Vyborg 222

Wachtparade 5, 227, 355
Waliszewski, Kasimir 8, 25
war aims (Russia and Austria) 290–3, 308
war college 200, 227
waterways 218
'well ordered police state' 12, 157
western Asia 283, 300, 316
westernization 247
westernizing 259
Westminster, treaty of 35
White Russia 193
Whitworth, Sir Charles (English minister in St Petersburg) 293, 308, 312, 330, 331, 334, 338
  bribes Kutaisov and Nelidova 174
  on quarrels over Nelidova 178–9
  on Paul and Prussia (1796) 198
  on Paul's new order 208, 210, 213, 214
  and financial issues 257
  discounts revolutionary danger (in Russia) 287–8
  reports Paul enthusiastic for 'the good cause' 291
  and Cobenzl 307
  recall requested 311
  connections with Panin and Zubovs 328
  considers Paul 'not in his senses' 328–9
Wickham, Thomas 312
Wiener Zeitung 121
Wilhelmina of Hesse-Darmstadt 84, 85, 90
  see also Nathalia Alexievna grand duchess
Williams, Sir Charles Hanbury 35
Winter palace 1, 47, 110, 150, 158, 165, 188, 189, 194, 209, 226, 345, 349, 351
women's rule 198
Woot, Robert 202, 226, 246, 249, 256, 264, 280
Wortman, Richard 14
Württemberg 83, 95, 263, 294, 304

York, duke of 309, 310
young court 114, 203

Zanta 289
Zherebtsova, Olga Alexandrovna 328, 341
Zubov brothers 349
Zubov, Nicholas Alexandrovich count 187, 188, 189, 323, 341, 353
Zubov, Platon Alexandrovich
  prince 87, 216, 229, 323, 328, 343
  insults Paul 149
  and failed Swedish negotiations 186, 187
  ignored as Catherine lay dying 189–90
  and Paul's treatment of 199
  considered Paul 'mad' 329
  entertained by Pahlen 331
  and Kutaisov's daughter 341
  and attack on Paul 350–2
  under Alexander I 354
Zubov, Valerian Alexandrovich, count 282–3, 323, 341, 354
Zubovs 338, 341, 343, 344, 350
Zubow, Valentin graf 9–10
Zubtsov, Aleksei Grigorevich 32
Zürich 139, 300, 301, 305, 310